SPORTS CINEMA
100 MOVIES

The Best of Hollywood's Athletic Heroes, Losers, Myths, and Misfits

Randy Williams

LIMELIGHT EDITIONS
LE
Books of the Performing Arts

Photograph Credits

Pages 363–367, images from *Rocky*; pages 373–378, images from *Raging Bull*; pages 344–348, images from *Champion*; pages 318–322, images from *Body and Soul*; pages 328–331, images from *The Set-Up*; pages 309–312, images from *Gentleman Jim*; pages 295–300, images from *Somebody Up There Likes Me*; pages 272–276, images from *The Harder They Fall*; pages 240–244, images from *When We Were Kings*; pages 223–226, images from *Here Comes Mr. Jordan*; pages 202–205, images from *Fat City*; pages 156–158, images from *The Great White Hope*; pages 140–142, images from *The Champ*; pages 137–139, images from *Battling Butler*; and pages 125–128, images from *City for Conquest*: courtesy of Steve Lott, Boxing Hall of Champions, Inc., New York, New York.

Pages 90–92, images from *Dogtown and Z-Boys*; pages 368–372, images from *Olympia*; and pages 227–233, images from *61**: courtesy of The Kobal Collection, New York, New York.

All other photographs are from the personal collection of the author.

Published in 2006 by Limelight Editions
512 Newark Pompton Turnpike
Pompton Plains, New Jersey 07444

www.limelighteditions.com

Book design by Mark Lerner

Printed in the United States of America

Library of Congress Cataloging-in-Publication Data is available upon request.
ISBN 0-87910-331-0

CONTENTS

ACKNOWLEDGMENTS

Film librarians: Ned Comstock at the USC Cinema-TV Library, Julie Graham at the UCLA Special Arts Collection Library, Barbara Hall at the Margaret Harrick Motion Picture Library, Randi Hokett at the USC Warner Bros. Archive, Caroline Sisneros at AFI, and Wayne Wilson, Bonita Carter, Shirley Ito, and Michael Salmon at the AAF library.

Family and friends who advised, debated, encouraged, and otherwise put up with me throughout the lengthy process, including among many others: Arina Mironova, Jeff Bettencourt, Travis Cranley, Mark Turner, Jim Vincent, Kerry Salzer, Roger Williams, Jim Botdorf, Monica Herdoiza, Laurie Selwitz, Geoff Nathanson, John Grogan, Danielle Sanchez, John Alexenko, Cobyann Berglund, Paul Fantazia, Mitchel Resnick, Cris Bacharach, Laurie Gonlag, Bob and Carole Daly. My parents, brothers, and sisters.

Past and present editors I've worked with through the years who have guided me with their journalistic passion, including Diane Robison, Gail Polevoi, Richard Stayton, Cao Jianjie, Mark Mravic, Bob Der, John Loesing, Leslie Yazel, Julie Wood, Sylvie Espagnac, Gianluca Gasparini, and Howard Burns. These are dedicated folks who've saved me (and many others) more times than I care to reveal in keeping my prose from veering out of bounds.

The countless screenwriters, directors, producers, actors, technicians, agents, and studio and guild administrators for sharing with me their recollections and candor about their participation in the featured films.

Appreciation to producers George Roy and Bud Greenspan as well as HBO Sports president Ross Greenburg for championing the sports documentary on television.

Mike Medavoy, a multifaceted movie authority whose love for film is infectious.

Frank Weimann and Lindsay Jurgensen at Literary Group International.

John Cerullo at Amadeus Press/Limelight Editions for sharing the passion along with his associates, Carol Flannery, Caroline Howell, and Gail Siragusa.

Jackie Raskin for keeping an eye on the bottom line.

Video rental outlets: Vidiots and Eddie Brandt's.

My sporting heroes: Lance Alworth, Abebe Bikila, Willie Mays, Jim Thorpe, and Jerry West.

My sports movie inspirations: Buster Keaton, James Cagney, Dennis Quaid, Jackie Gleason, Paul Newman, Jack Warden, Nick Nolte, Robert Rossen, and Ron Shelton.

Thank you all for making this possible.

INTRODUCTION

Since the development of motion pictures began in the late 19th century, interest in sports has grown immeasurably. In many parts of the world the attention given to sports is extraordinary. With millions attending sports events and year-long radio and television coverage around the clock supplemented by popular publications and video games, it all adds up to a multibillion-dollar industry.

This seemingly insatiable appetite for sports has also been a lightning rod for debate about whether the benefits outweigh the downside of athletics. Does the emphasis on winning (and its seductive cousins, fame and fortune) cloud judgment leading to drug use? Gambling? Bribery? Cheating? Or do its benefits, such as enhanced physical and mental fitness, increased self-discipline, greater opportunity for the underprivileged, and shared sense of success and kindred spirit, override the negatives? What are the driving forces behind the individuals?

By incorporating some of these issues with other themes, the best sports movies enhance what we see (and don't see) on the field of play.

Sports Cinema is a broad survey of movies centered on sports-oriented stories, characters, events, or backdrops. It is not an encyclopedia providing an entry for every sports movie ever made. It is a celebration of the best of the genre. This book is an in-depth companion guide to the class of the field.

Of the more than two thousand sports-themed movies that have been released, I hope the 100 films featured here will reflect the moviegoing audience's favorites. Comparing films, however, is an inexact science at best. Measuring comedies against dramas against documentaries against musicals is as difficult as is comparing films from different eras and different budgets, or the 1927 New York Yankees and the 1998 New York Yankees, or Sugar Ray Robinson and Sugar Ray Leonard. In the end the choices become the author's opinions. How could they be otherwise? How many times have you looked at the movie ratings in your local TV guide or the Academy's choice for an Oscar winner and disagreed with them?

Contrasting tastes are inevitable, and while I consider mine to be eclectic and truly representative of the best, *vive la différence!* I encourage you to compare and contrast your favorites with mine. Regardless of their rankings, the fact that these pictures make the list out of thousands of candidates makes them notable. Each stands alone. The very nature of sports demands a competitive way to assemble the best. And even though I've ranked them, the point to make is that if you're exploring the best of the genre, here is where you should start.

Just as the Los Angeles Lakers didn't win three consecutive NBA titles with Shaq and Kobe alone, the selections in this book are not based exclusively on star power and profit margins (on the whole, sports movies are not among the all-time box office leaders, but most have done well in relation to their generally modest budgets).

A fresh perspective on a well-worn subject, a larger look at life, technical innovations, pure entertainment value, verisimilitude, originality, revealing insight and perspectives via sporting characterizations, and historical importance cinematically were the key determining factors taken into account in the hundreds of hours I spent viewing these films. (I didn't know it at the time, but this book began for me over thirty years ago as a kid watching Burt Lancaster win (and lose) Olympic gold in *Jim Thorpe: All-American*.)

Obviously, as with any other genre, I also looked for engaging stories, distinguished performances, delivery of objectives, deft direction, enhancing music, and technical achievement.

Broadly stated, my definition of a sports movie is one with a sporting element that is significant to the progression of the picture via character, event, and/or story line. Accepting the standard dictionary definition of sport being "a competitive physical exercise," I would exclude a fine feature such as *Searching for Bobby Fischer*, calling chess a board game focusing on mental aspects. On the other side, I would also exclude the compelling film *Touching the Void*, considering mountain climbing more of a "man against mountain adventure" despite its rigorous physical demands.

I would also like to note that ancient sport is represented here as well. Ridley Scott's *Gladiator* vividly captures the mass spectacle of the time. Stanley Kubrick's *Spartacus* is another outstanding picture, yet its focus is far less on what happens inside the gladiatorial arena. With a story woven around a blood sport, following a general turned slave turned gladiator, as its title implies, *Gladiator* is a sword-and-sandal picture whose story advances more on the killing floor of the Colosseum.

Though not generally considered to be sports movies, as sports are not what drives the films, there are excellent pictures with memorable sports scenes most viewers are aware of. Some of these films, not covered in this book, include *City Lights*, *M*A*S*H*, *Diner*, *Ben-Hur*, *The Hurricane*, *The Big Lebowski*, *On the Waterfront*, *Forrest Gump*, *Stay Hungry*, and *The Quiet Man*, among others.

The inherent drama of sports has provided a powerful medium for many of cinema's leading performers. Buster Keaton, James Cagney, Katharine Hepburn, Humphrey Bogart, Paul Newman, Elizabeth Taylor, Robert Redford, Robert DeNiro, and Russell Crowe are just a few of Hollywood's top actors and actresses who have memorable sports-themed pictures on their esteemed credits.

Though the better ones achieve a high level of authenticity, the best sports movies don't pretend to be able to capture the real action we see in ballparks and on television every day. They do, however, capture the spectacle of sport with a wide range of emotions and issues. They do know that what's interesting is what you don't see: not the plays themselves, not the big game, but the drama between the plays. They do illuminate why sports matter so much. They do show the art and science of athletic movement. They do echo the leading social and cultural issues of the times in which they were made. They do offer revealing insight from the inside—-both inside the game and inside the minds of its gladiators. They do convey how sport is often a reflection of the human experience, with striving, struggling, the joy of achievement, and the despair of loss, both on an individual and a group level. They do present the lighter and darker sides of living.

From passion (*The Cup*) to cynicism (*North Dallas Forty*), from fantasy (*Field of*

Dreams) to culture clashes (*Mr. Baseball*) and racism (*The Jackie Robinson Story*), and from celebrating our need for heroes (*Knute Rockne: All-American*) to questioning it (*Cobb*), sports movies have covered a broad range of topics as an allegory of the human condition, an insightful window on society, and we are passionate about them.

Like brilliant artwork, outstanding movies are full of nuances in which new impressions are made with each viewing. The selections I've featured will constantly be reevaluated and the list amended as the next *Bull Durham, Hoop Dreams,* or *Chariots of Fire* debuts at a local art house, multiplex, or giant-screen theater.

In regard to the book's title, I realize not all the films featured here came from Hollywood or appeared on the silver screen; however, the vast majority were in fact produced and/or distributed through the studio system and shown theatrically. Foreign films, feature-length documentaries, and made-for-television movies were also considered. Extensive effort was made to locate copies of elusive titles, but only those actually viewed were eligible.

I would also like to acknowledge the work of Ken Burns, including his fine PBS miniseries, *Baseball;* Bud Greenspan and his *Olympiad* series; and Warren Miller, who after many decades of filmmaking continues to produce some of the greatest outdoor sports shots ever captured on celluloid.

This is a book by an enthusiast for casual moviegoers, sports fans, and film buffs. It is my hope that *Sports Cinema* will attract new enthusiasts and inspire similar explorations and a richer understanding of these films.

Comments, corrections, updates, questions, or suggestions can be forwarded to me at P.O. Box 16, Santa Monica, CA 90406, or via e-mail at sportscinema100@yahoo.com.

For more information visit our website at sportscinema100.com or amadeuspress.com.

—Randy Williams

SPECIAL RECOGNITION

No book about sports and film would be complete without paying tribute to the innovations and influence of NFL Films, a pioneer in sports and cinema since 1964. The artistic vision of founder Ed Sabol and his son, Steve, the company president, have not only shaped how we view games and highlights; their impact has been felt throughout Hollywood as well.

The winner of 80 Emmy Awards, NFL Films spawned the entire blooper industry (*Football Follies*) long before Dick Clark and Marv Albert brought in their talents. The legendary John Facenda set the standard for narrators. Today the company produces over 2,500 hours of programming for television annually, including the Discovery Channel, HBO, and MTV.

Hollywood filmmakers have sought their services from the beginning; NFL Films has been the technical advisor on just about every important football movie made over the last four decades. Their impact, however, goes beyond gridiron celluloid. Movie directors like Ron Howard (*Cinderella Man*) and Irvin Kershner (Star Wars' *The Empire Strikes Back*) have stated that NFL Films' use of montages, compelling close-ups, and slow-motion photography paired with live action and powerful music has made a significant impact on modern filmmaking.

"The storytelling…it's so clean, so concise…it's about emotions," says director David Anspaugh (*Hoosiers, Rudy, The Game of Their Lives*).

"What they do is capture the theatrical essence of telling a story," states Oscar-nominated film editor Don Zimmerman (*Heaven Can Wait, The Prince of Tides*).

And storytelling is Hollywood's stock in trade. Steve and Ed Sabol continue to set the standards.

SPORTS CINEMA 100 MOVIES

#100 MILLION DOLLAR LEGS

Screenwriters Nicholas Barrows, Henry Myers. **Story** Joe Mankiewicz. **Director** Edward Cline. **Producer** Herman Mankiewicz. **Cinematography** Arthur Todd. **Music** John Leipold. Paramount. 1932.

THE PLAYERS
Jack Oakie **Migg Tweeney**; W. C. Fields **The President**; Andy Clyde **The Major-Domo**; Lyda Roberti **Mata Machree**; Susan Fleming **Angela**; Ben Turpin **Mysterious man**; George Barbier **Mr. Baldwin**; Hugh Herbert **Secretary of the Treasury**; Bill Gilbert **Secretary of the Interior**; Vernon Dent **Secretary of Agriculture**; Sam Adams **Secretary of State**; Irving Bacon **Secretary of the Navy**; Teddy Hart **Secretary of War**; John Sinclair **Secretary of Labor**; Dickie Moore **Willie**; Ben Taggert **Ship's captain**; Hank Mann **Customs inspector**; Chick Collins **Jumper**; Syd Saylor **Starter at the Games**; Alan Bridge **Spy in cape**; Heinie Conklin **Spy in cape**; Eddie Dunn **Coachman**; Tyler Brooke **Olympics announcer**; Eddie Baker **Train official**; Hobart Bosworth **Olympics official starter**; Herbert Evans **Butler**; Billy Engle **Klopstokian athlete**; Charlie Hall **Klopstokian athlete**

THE GAME
"Klopstokia: A Far-Away Country. Chief Export: Goats and Nuts. Chief Import: Goats and Nuts. Chief Inhabitants: Goats and Nuts." So states the opening title of this silly satire of the Olympics.

Klopstokia is badly in need of money. Its President (W. C. Fields) is under attack from his cabinet. An American brush salesman, Migg Tweeney (Jack Oakie), in a mad dash to see his boss, Baldwin (George Barbier), literally runs into the President's daughter, Angela (Susan Fleming). They fall in love and he asks Angela to marry him. She says he must ask her father. The President has her suitor tossed to the guards but spares him when Angela convinces her father that Migg is a wizard and can help him with his financial problem. The President then tells Migg he can marry Angela if he can get him $8 million to save the country from bankruptcy. Noticing the President's strength, Migg suggests he enter his country into the upcoming Olympics in Los Angeles.

The cabinet meanwhile meets secretly to plot the removal of Klopstokia's President. They turn to Mata Machree (Lyda Roberti), the dancing siren no man can resist. For a hefty price she agrees to help the cabinet, and after she demonstrates her talents in a mesmerizing dance, they accept her demands.

Migg and Angela join the Klopstokian athletes on the boat headed for the Olympics in Los Angeles. Aboard the ship, Mata makes a move on some of the athletes, then on Migg, making Angela jealous. The President exercises on board.

Aboard a train on the next step of the long journey to Los Angeles, the cabinet chief is concerned that Mata is not doing her job. "You were going to lower the morale of the team; instead they fell in love with you and it went up," he accuses. She assures him that her plan is working. Before the end of the journey, she promises each of the smitten athletes individually that she'll rendezvous with them later that night.

Later she lures the teammates together and they fight one another over her. Mata's plan works as the Klopstokian athletes are now too exhausted to compete in the Olympics.

As the Games are in progress an angry Angela chases Mata all over the place, including off the diving board during competition. She eventually drags Mata into the locker room and forces her to tell the team that it has all been a conspiracy and that she is not in love with any of them. Migg then fires up the team and they head out to their respective events, producing fine results.

In weight lifting the main event comes down to a battle between the President and his chief political nemesis, the Treasury Secretary, announced as a "freelance entrant." Mata does her best to inspire the cabinet chief, and he comes through with an amazing lift of 700 pounds. Trying to put away the victory against the President, the Treasury Secretary asks Mata to give him a "double portion" of her dance. As she does, his feet begin to sink into the ground but with great effort he hoists 900 pounds, then collapses along with Mata to the ground. Lying there exhausted, he says,

TREASURY SECRETARY: I've done all I can do.

MATA: Me too. I done all I can do ... in public.

The President looks at the 1,000-pound weight and announces he can't go on. However, Migg steps on the President's foot, infuriating him. As Migg takes off in fear the President heaves the 1,000-pound weight far in the air, hurling it well ahead of the fleeing Migg, who trips over it. As a result, the President wins two medals—weight lifting and the shot put—in one motion, and Klopstokia wins the Olympics.

From the stands comes Migg's boss, Baldwin, who loves the Olympics and says he supports winners like the Klopstokian athletes, implying he'll help them out of their financial straits. When he is introduced to the President, they suddenly square off and Indian wrestle. The big Baldwin easily handles the exhausted President. Landing on his rear, the President tells a stunned Migg, "It's the climate; I've been drinking too much orange juice."

INSTANT REPLAY *Million Dollar Legs* is a wry, madcap spoof of the Olympics. It is also a silly satire of political power based on physical strength and of the strange irony involved in the use of amateur athletics as an avenue to monetary

Shown here as the President of Klopstokia, W. C. Fields was a renowned juggler.

gain. It is an endless procession of sight gags and verbal humor, and a poke at the spy game as well.

Released just before the actual 1932 Los Angeles Summer Olympics in July, *Million Dollar Legs* is a gem of wacky mayhem. Certainly a little thin on plot, it really hangs by a thread, but that thread is strong enough to weave together and hold a cornucopia of slapstick, witty dialogue, and indelible images in a surreal setting not unlike the Marx Brothers' *Duck Soup*.

Though the film was reportedly assembled as a vehicle for comedian Jack Oakie, W. C. Fields stole more than a few scenes, transposing his vaudeville gags onto the screen with great success. Director Cline filled his roster with comedic veterans from Mack Sennett's studios, including Ben Turpin, Andy Clyde, and Vern Dent.

"The woman no man can resist," Mata Machree (Lyda Roberti).

OUTSIDE THE LINES The film grew from Joe Mankiewicz's attendance at the 1928 Olympics in Amsterdam and was based on his short story "On Your Mark." … If juggling were an Olympic sport, W. C. Fields might have won a real gold medal, as he practiced daily in his youth and became proficient enough to travel the world working with the Ziegfeld Follies.… Actor Vernon Dent appeared in many Three Stooges shorts.… Actress Susan Fleming would go on to marry Harpo Marx, who starred with his brothers in the football comedy *Horse Feathers* (1932).… The 1939 film *Million Dollar Legs* was not a remake and starred Betty Grable.… Herman Mankiewicz, Joseph's brother, co-wrote baseball's *The Pride of St. Louis* (1952) and *The Pride of the Yankees* (1942), which earned him an Oscar nomination.… Herman also produced *Horse Feathers*.

ALL-STAR MOMENTS The speedy Presidential messenger, wearing a goat's head, outruns horses, cars, boats, and trains.

The cabinet members arrive at Mata Machree's mansion, where a sign says: "The woman that no man can resist. Not responsible for men left over 30 days." The cabinet members are rebuffed at the door and told, "Sorry. Madame is only resisted from two to four. Come back then."

As a love note slips out of Migg's (Oakie) hands into the river below, Angela (Fleming) calmly makes a perfect dive off the high bridge to retrieve it, foreshadowing a later use of her talents.

The parade of athletes at the Olympics' opening ceremonies finds the Klopstokian team entering on crutches and stretchers from fighting over Mata.

Angela's pursuit of Mata (Roberti) takes them up to the Olympic diving board in the middle of competition, where she proceeds to make a perfect dive and wins a medal.

The weight-lifting competition where Mata does her inspiring dance.

HOME COURT ADVANTAGE Available on VHS.

#99 ALL THE RIGHT MOVES

Screenwriter Michael Kane. **Director** Michael Chapman. **Producers** Stephen Deutsch, Phil Goldfarb, Gary Morton. **Cinematography** Jan de Bont. **Music** David Campbell. **Editing** David Garfield. **Art Direction** Mary Ann Biddle. Fox. 1983.

THE PLAYERS
Tom Cruise **Stef Djordjevic**; Craig T. Nelson **Coach Nickerson**; Lea Thompson **Lisa Litski**; Charles Cioffi **Pop Djordjevic**; Chris Penn **Brian**; Paul Carafotes **Salvucci**; Gary Graham **Greg Djordjevic**; Sandy Faison **Suzie**; James Baffico **Bosko**; Mel Winkler **Jess Covington**; George Betor **Tank**; Walter Briggs **Rifleman**; Leon Robinson **Shadow**; Jonas Miller **Mouse**; Donald Yanessa **Coach**; Debra Varnado **Charlotte**; Paige Lyn Price **Tracy**; Kyle Jackson **Sherman Williams**; Terry O'Quinn **Freeman Smith**; William Stibich **Kurowski**; Emma Chapman **Angela**; Donald Irwin **Principal**; Clayton Beaujon **Bar drunk**; Valerie Zabala **Gina**; Darlene Dudukovich **Civics teacher**; Victor Arnold **Bartender**; Dick Miller **Teacher in auditorium**; Bill Slivosky **Detective**; John Simkovic **Detective**

THE GAME High school senior Stef Djordjevic (Tom Cruise) is determined to use his football skills to gain a college scholarship and become an engineer as a way out of Ampipe, a dismal Pennsylvania steel town in economic decline.

Coach Nickerson (Craig T. Nelson) is equally eager for a better life and knows winning ball games is his ticket to a more lucrative coaching job in the college ranks.

They aren't the only ones pursuing big dreams. Stef's girlfriend, Lisa Litski (Lea Thompson), is a talented musician, and his teammate Brian Riley (Chris Penn) also hopes to win a football scholarship.

Stef and Coach Nickerson's common goals make them adversaries instead of teammates in their mutual quest, in no small part because of Stef's headstrong temperament, which rubs the coach the wrong way. This is exemplified in one scene when he talks back to the coach in a disagreement about how he's playing defense, to which the coach responds, "You do it my way or it's the highway, Djordjevic."

The tension between the two doesn't let up. As they go deeper into the season, both feel the pressure of their futures on the line with each passing day. Both are constantly aware of the looming presence of college scouts and recruiters, both in practice and at games, observing them from the sidelines.

Ultimately their futures come down to the big game against the Knights, a powerhouse team Coach Nickerson has never defeated. Late in the muddy, rainy game Stef intercepts a pass for the go-ahead score. A bit later, Stef makes a crucial error, getting called for pass interference by playing just the way Coach Nickerson told him not to in practice. His teammates' goal line stand prevents a score, so all the Bulldogs have to do is run out the clock. Unfortunately, a handoff is muffed and the Knights recover in the end zone for a game-winning score.

In the locker room Coach rips into Stef in front of his teammates. Stef fires back, saying they would have won the game if the coach had used better tactics by not handing off in the wet, muddy crucial final seconds: "If you would have had Rifleman [the QB] hold on to the ball then we'd have won the game. We didn't quit, you quit!"

Coach kicks Stef off the team.

Coach's disappointment in Stef is amplified when he spots him as part of a group of angry fans who trash the coach's house, blaming him for the school's loss. Stef was there, but only as a passenger; he simply needed a ride into town.

Later Stef goes to the bar and explains to Bosko (James Baffico), the lead instigator

Though constantly at odds, star defender Stef Djordjevic (Tom Cruise, left) and Coach Nickerson (Craig T. Nelson, right) share a desire to use football as a ticket to a better life out of depressed Ampipe.

in vandalizing Coach Nickerson's house, that he just wants to go to college and Coach Nickerson is basically blackballing him. He asks Bosko if he will explain to the coach what really happened that night. Bosko refuses and insults him, and they get into a fight. Lisa meets with Mrs. Nickerson to explain the situation she and Stef are in.

Sensing that he is destined to remain in dreary Ampipe, Stef slaves away alongside his brother in the steel mill. One afternoon as the workers file out at the end of another long shift, Coach Nickerson appears and apologizes to Stef. He then informs him that he got a job as a head coach at a college in California. Coach also wants Stef to play for him and offers the young man a full scholarship to play football and study engineering.

IN **PLAY** *All the Right Moves* was cinematographer Michael Chap-
m debut. Though he took minimal risks in his rookie
e ody of the pursuit of dreams, teenage values,

the clichés that plague many football films.
ero quarterback, since the lead plays defense
st about his ability to make a living from play-
his limited skills for a college education.
r intriguing twists. Stef isn't the only one who
ach and his girlfriend are just as driven. Director
Kane raise an interesting question through Lisa
provides full scholarships for athletes but practi-
ributions to society with other talents.
lanced performance, delivering his character's sensi-
ons with equal aplomb. Lea Thompson plays Cruise's

TOP: The Ampipe Bulldogs get ready for a pivotal game.

BOTTOM: Just like her boyfriend, Stef, Lisa Litski (Lea Thompson) has college dreams of her own.

similarly driven but pragmatic girlfriend with an unexpected sharpness, taking full advantage of the qualities not typically seen in the hero's love interest. Craig T. Nelson plays an obsessed high school coach with conviction and palpable volatility. Charles Cioffi as Stef's compassionate father and Chris Penn as the talented but unfortunate teammate draw memorable characterizations in limited screen time.

On the technical side, cinematographer Jan de Bont's atmospheric pictures along with David Garfield's rhythmic editing capture the dreary life in Ampipe well; moreover, their football scenes, smartly limited, are engrossing.

In the final analysis what captures the attention and best presents the story are the powerfully charged verbal exchanges between Cruise and Nelson. However, this strength is ultimately also a weakness. The repeated reliance on talking out conflict and motivation rather than dramatizing them detracts from the movie. The cumulative effect of everyone verbalizing their desire to get out of town saps some of the picture's energy as the audience prepares for what appears to be one mass exit from Drearysville.

Overall, *All the Right Moves* is distinguished from the other entertaining football films that treat similar small-town, blue-collar themes, like *Saturday's Hero* and *Varsity Blues,* with multiple character arcs, convincing performances, an authentic environment, and an able assist from a strong soundtrack.

OUTSIDE THE LINES
Actress Lea Thompson grew up dancing and won a scholarship to the Pennsylvania Ballet School followed by another to the San Francisco Ballet School.... Actor Leon Robinson (Shadow) attended Loyola College on a basketball scholarship after being a high school all-American out of New York.... Don Yanessa, one of Pennsylvania's leading coaches, also served as a technical advisor on this picture.... Cruise suffered a concussion shooting the football action.... Executive producer Gary Morton was Lucille Ball's husband.... Director Michael Chapman was nominated for an Oscar for his cinematography work on both *Raging Bull* (1980) and *The Fugitive* (1993).... The film's genesis came from a magazine article in *Geo.*... Editor David Garfield was the son of actor John Garfield, who starred in boxing's *Body and Soul* (1947).... The football sequences shot at night utilized an innovative lighting system that was also used for support at that year's Super Bowl coverage.... The filmmakers also used the mobile lighting system to simulate moonlight on the streets of Ampipe.

ALL-STAR MOMENTS
Coach Nickerson (Nelson) demonstrates his gung-ho approach when he takes an offensive lineman to task for a missed block, grabbing his face mask and jerking him around: "That was a third base slide. You block as good as a jelly doughnut. You want to play in college? Then play the way you've been taught!"

Assorted camera angles, reaction shots, and footage of the climactic game played in the rain and mud, including a slo-mo iso of Rifleman's muffed handoff and the team's ensuing defeat.

Each of the verbal exchanges between Coach and Stef (Cruise).

POST-GAME COMMENTS
Tom Cruise on what attracted him to his character:

What I like about Stef is that he has real goals. He's an individual who is very driven.... Stef is very sensitive to his surroundings—the mill, his father, and the unsatisfactory relationship they have with each other and the dying industry that has sapped his father's youth.[1]

Director Michael Chapman:

It's a football movie about how kids in a failing steel town in Pennsylvania need to get out and the only way, as is often the case, is through sports. Tom Cruise desperately wants to get out and make something of himself. He's a good but not brilliant student so he desperately needs to get a football scholarship.

I hope it is more than that. Unlike most sports movies the big game takes place halfway through the movie and they lose.

The movie goes on from there. I was very happy about that.[2]

Lea Thompson on her preparations for the picture, which included actually returning to high school in the Johnstown, Pennsylvania area where the movie takes place:

I had to take tests, do term papers, and what surprised me was that I could actually do it ... that my own high school experience wasn't that far away. I could remember all the math, the English, well, everything.

On a superficial level, the experience helped me with hair, make up and costume. It helped me decide on the "look" for Lisa. It also gave me a solid sense of her background: what it is like to grow up in a very ethnic steel town, where unemployment is high and just around the corner from nearly everyone. It helped me understand her roots, the kinds of prejudices that are prevalent, and the humor in her banter with the other girls.[3]

Director Michael Chapman on the authenticity of the football play, using a mix of local players and actors:

Because they were young and good football players, they really wanted to play. We sent two people to the hospital before lunch one day. One of them was Tom Cruise with a concussion. He was okay but we had to wrap for the day.[4]

Chapman, on how his cinematography skills helped him here as a director:

My years as a cameraman helped me decide where to put the camera. We made a kind of protective sled covered with mattresses, poking holes for the lens so we could get right into the line and players coming right at us. I wish I had some brilliant overall strategy but that's not how it's done. Most of the time it's bits and pieces done really well, figuring things out as you go, and we did that.[5]

HOME COURT ADVANTAGE Available on VHS and DVD.

#98 KNUTE ROCKNE: ALL-AMERICAN

Screenwriter Robert Bruckner. **Director** Lloyd Bacon. **Producers** Robert Fellows, Hall Wallis. **Cinematography** Tony Gaudio. **Editing** Ralph Dawson. **Music** Ray Heindorf. **Art Direction** Robert Haas. **Costume Designer** Milo Anderson. Warner Bros. 1940.

THE PLAYERS Pat O'Brien **Knute Rockne**; Gale Page **Bonnie Skiles Rockne**; Ronald Reagan **George Gipp**; Donald Crisp **Father John Callahan**; Albert Bassermann **Father Julius Nieuwland**; John Litel **Committee chairman**; Henry O'Neill **Doctor**; Owen Davis Jr. **Gus Dorias**; John Qualen **Lars Knutson Rockne**; Dorothy Tree **Martha Rockne**; Nick Lukats **Harry Stuhldreher, one of the Four Horsemen**; Kane Richmond **Elmer Layden, one of the Four Horsemen**; William Byrne **James "Jim" Crowley, one of the Four Horsemen**; Howard Jones **Himself**; Glenn "Pop" Warner **Himself**; Amos Alonzo Stagg **Himself**; William Spaulding **Himself**; Frank Mayo **Reporter**; William Marshall **Don Miller, one of the Four Horsemen**; Charles Trowbridge **Notre Dame professor**; Fredrik Vogeding **Elder**; Egon Brecher **Elder**; Rudolph Anders **Elder**; Charles Wilson **Gambler**; David Bruce **Player**; Lee Phelps **Army coach**; Bill Sheffield **Knute at 4**; Johnny Sheffield **Knute at 7**

THE GAME The son of Norwegian immigrants, young Knute grows up in the American Midwest fascinated by "the most wonderful game in the world"—football.

Years later, Rockne (Pat O'Brien) enrolls at Notre Dame. He plays football and excels in chemistry, so much so that Father Nieuwland (Albert Basserman) urges the young man to pursue science as a career, either as a chemist or as a teacher.

Now married (Gale Page), Rockne aims to make a living coaching football. Under the guidance of Father Callahan (Donald Crisp), Rockne proceeds to make a name for himself as the coach of the Fighting Irish. He spots the raw talent of George Gipp (Ronald Reagan) and makes some innovative contributions to the game, including the lateral shift on offense that was inspired by the choreography of some nightclub dancers, and opening up the game with the development of the forward pass (with his good friend and player Gus Dorias, played by Owen Davis Jr.) as an offensive weapon.

Rockne becomes one of the game's winningest coaches and wins a national championship. His success brings many lucrative offers to coach elsewhere, but he tells Father Callahan that Notre Dame is his home.

In one crucial game, Rockne, who has developed a case of phlebitis, defies doctor's orders to stay in bed, and with the aid of a wheelchair he visits the team at halftime when they're losing to Army. Coach Rockne inspires them with his "win one for the Gipper" speech (earlier, just before passing away at a young age, George had relayed some encouraging words to Coach Rockne from his deathbed).

Tragically, in 1931, Rockne's own career is cut short as he dies in a plane crash. His football innovations, "clean living," and building of well-rounded young men are his legacy.

INSTANT REPLAY *Knute Rockne: All–American* is a textbook example of a movie that reflects the period in which it was made. With the traces of the Great Depression still lingering, and a world at war, Hollywood's stock-in-trade myth-building, patriotic, escapist fare was exactly what audiences wanted. People were going to movies in record numbers. *Knute Rockne: All-American, Here Comes Mr. Jordan,* and *The Pride of the Yankees* were tailor-made for their day.

However, it is easy to see how someone distanced from the sports world would doubt this story's eligibility as full-length movie material. Many talented teachers, clergymen, and drill sergeants, among others, have instilled the principles of clean living and friendship in countless young men. Other pictures have shown how America has long been a bastion of hope and opportunity for immigrants to pursue their dreams, and how those immigrants have played a role in shaping our country's multiethnic social fabric.

The treatment given to Mr. Rockne's innovations could be seen as overly reverential. Additionally, there's not a whole lot of dramatic tension in the subject, in terms of internal conflicts and the pressures and complications of life. This is not to say that a subject has to be a social monster, as seen in *Cobb* and *Raging Bull*, to merit a big-screen presentation. Here is a loving husband and father, a well-liked teacher-turned-coach—but not a particularly distinctive character, especially for viewers disinclined toward gridiron games.

However, when viewed solely as an inspiring football docudrama of one of the sport's most innovative and successful coaches, *Knute Rockne: All-American* scores, largely due to a pair of career-making performances and one of the best makeup jobs of all time.

Pat O'Brien as Knute Rockne and Ronald Reagan as George Gipp were superb in their characterizations.

There was some trepidation when O'Brien won the role over his friend and frequent co-star, James Cagney, about whether he'd be able to capture the legendary football coach.

Thanks to his intense efforts to embody all of Rockne's mannerisms, including the staccato speech patterns, and with the help of amazing makeup work by Perc Westmore, Pat O'Brien gives the performance of a lifetime. With an empassioned fidelity of spirit O'Brien convincingly captures both the spirit and the distinguishing features of Knute Rockne.

As George Gipp, Ronald Reagan, with less than a dozen minutes of screen time, elicits strong emotional responses as he builds an almost father-son relationship with Coach Rockne before tragically succumbing to an early death.

His deathbed request and the subsequent "win-one-for-the-Gipper" speech by Knute are sports movie classics.

Lending able support is Donald Crisp. As he would do later in *National Velvet*, the veteran actor seems a natural as a father figure.

On the technical side, though the insertion of actual game action is not edited as well as it could have been, the realism of the picture is enhanced by the appearances of notable coaches like Amos Alonso Stagg, Pop Warner, Bill Spaulding, and Howard Jones when they join Rockne to defend their sport at a hearing.

Lloyd Bacon shows a steady hand directing his players using Robert Bruckner's script.

Brought to the screen by Jack Warner and Hal Wallis at a time when America demanded heroes, the picture is successful in the filmmakers' aims, imparting some inspiration through a story with a sufficient amount of real-life accuracy to ensure credibility.

As a cinematic tribute to a man who brought college football out of its own version of the "dead-ball" era with his offensive innovations as well as bringing eternal fame to a relatively small Catholic school in Indiana, it is easy to see how the inspirational

TOP: Success in football at Notre Dame begins in the trenches as Knute Rockne (Pat O'Brien, center) preaches to his players.

BOTTOM: George Gipp (Ronald Reagan, left) with coach Rockne (O'Brien).

tone of this picture would create a mystique so powerful that it would propel Rudy Ruettiger to make his own motion picture about Notre Dame football some 40 years later (*Rudy*).

Knute Rockne: All-American, Jim Thorpe: All-American, Everybody's All-American—Warner Bros. has done well with football-themed pictures with "all-American" in the title.

OUTSIDE THE LINES Football legend Jim Thorpe makes a cameo.... Lloyd Bacon directed the baseball pictures *Kill the Umpire* (1950) and *It Happens Every Spring* (1949).... There was lots of competition for the title role. Among the candidates were Robert Young, William Holden, James Cagney, and John Wayne.... It was the only picture besides *Rudy* with full access to the Notre Dame campus.... Nick Lukats, one of the last players to score a touchdown for Rockne, was an advisor who also portrayed Harry Stuhldreher, one of the "Four Horsemen.".... Bob Hope hosted a Hollywood star train trip to the Notre Dame campus for a special screening of the movie. On board were Ronald Reagan, Pat O'Brien, Jane Wyman, and Donald Crisp, among others.... Assistant director Jesse Hibbs was a tackle on the USC Trojans' first national championship football team in 1928.... Warner Bros. purchased a radio script from writer John Driscoll from the *Cavalcade of America* program to use select pages in the movie; however, it didn't include television rights because TV wasn't a major medium at the time. When the movie was eventually broadcast on TV the "win one for the Gipper" speech had to be cut due to rights issues. Later broadcasts restored them.... So popular was his performance that for the rest of his life, Pat O'Brien would often perform his Gipper speech at public functions.... Donald Crisp portrayed Elizabeth Taylor's father in *National Velvet* (1944).... He also appeared in the James Cagney boxing drama *City for Conquest* (1940).... Rockne, the Notre Dame football captain in 1913, coached the Fighting Irish from 1918 until his death in a plane crash in 1931.... The team won several national championships under his tutelage, and Rockne's winning percentage of .881 is among the very best.... Rockne was on his way to provide technical support in Los Angeles for a movie called *The Spirit of Notre Dame* when his plane crashed near Bazaar, Kansas.

ALL-STAR MOMENTS Notre Dame football practice. Young man walks over wearing a baseball glove. He caches a punt. He punts it back—far, far back. Impressed, Coach Rockne (O'Brien) calls out to him and asks if he's played football before. The young man is George Gipp (Reagan), who then joins the football team.

With Rockne standing at his deathbed, Gipp asks his coach, "Rock, someday when the team's up against it, the breaks are beating the boys, ask them to go in there with all they've got and win just one for the Gipper. I don't know where I'll be then, but I'll know about it and I'll be happy."

Someday comes, and against doctor's orders an ill Rockne is wheeled into the Fighting Irish locker room at halftime when they are down to Army. Rockne gives his Gipper speech, and Notre Dame comes back to edge Army 12—6.

HOME COURT ADVANTAGE Available on VHS.

#97 MR. BASEBALL

Screenwriters John Junkerman, Theo Pelletier, Gary Ross, Kevin Wade, Monte Merrick. **Director** Fred Schepisi. **Producers** John Kao, Jeff Silver, Doug Claybourne, Robert Newmeyer, Fred Schepisi. **Cinematography** Ian Baker. **Editing** Peter Honess. **Art Direction** Russell Smith. **Casting** Dianne Crittenden. **Music** Jerry Goldsmith. Universal. 1992.

THE PLAYERS Tom Selleck **Jack Elliot**; Ken Takakura **Uchiyama**; Aya Takanashi **Hiroko Uchiyama**; Toshi Shioya **Yoji Nishimura**; Dennis Haysbert **Max "Hammer" Dubois**; Kosuke Toyohara **Toshi Yamashita**; Toshizo Fujiwara **Ryoh Mukai**; Shoji Ohoki **Coach Hori**; Kenji Morinaga **Hiroshi Kurosawa**; Mak Takano **Shunji Igarashi**; Joh Nishimura **Tomophiko Ohmie**; Norihide Goto **Issei Itoi**; Kensuke Toita **Akito Yagi**; Naoki Fuji **Takuya Nishikawa**; Takanobu Hozumi **Hiroshi Nakamura**; Nicholas Cascone **Doc**; Shinsuke Aoki Nikawa **Dragons owner**; Rinzoh Suzuki Sato **Dragons executive**; Jun Hamamura **Hiroko's grandfather**; Mineko Yorozzuyo **Hiroko's grandmother**; Art LaFleur **Yankees manager**; Greg Goossen **Yankees coach**; Frank Thomas **Yankee rookie slugger**; Larry Pennell **Howie Gold**; Leon Lee **Lyle Massey**; Brad Lesley **Niven**; Tim McCarver **Himself**; Sean McDonough **Himself**; Hikari Takano **Commercial director**; Kinzoh Sakura **1st umpire**

THE GAME Jack Elliot (Tom Selleck) is an aging, power-hitting first baseman for the New York Yankees who is being shipped out to make room for a rising young slugger (Frank Thomas).

In denial about his recent production, Jack pleads his case for remaining in the team's starting lineup:

> **JACK:** I don't believe this. I'm a World Series MVP!
>
> **MANAGER:** That was four years ago, Jack.
>
> **COACH:** You hit .235 last season.
>
> **JACK:** Last season, I led this club in ninth-inning doubles for the month of August!

Elliot's pleas fall on deaf ears and the veteran is sent to play for the only team to make an offer for his services, the Chunichi Dragons in Japan. The team expects the American to power them past their rivals, the (Yomiuri) Tokyo Giants, and win the pennant.

Jack is the "ugly American" the moment he lands at the Tokyo airport—arrogant, rude, obnoxious, the pampered athlete insults teammates, threatens his translator, challenges the manager's authority, and generally has a very difficult time adjusting to Japanese customs. Despite all that, he starts out playing well, hitting superbly, and the local press showers him with praise, giving him the nickname "Mr. Baseball." He even begins a relationship that turns to romance with the team's pretty and feisty promotions manager, Hiroko (Aya Takenashi).

Teammate and fellow "gaijin" Max "Hammer" Dubois (Dennis Haysbert) does his best to give Jack the benefit of his years spent in Japanese baseball and to explain how America's pastime is different in the Land of the Rising Sun.

The Dragons' no-nonsense manager, Uchiyama (Ken Takakura), initially endures Elliot's overbearing, boorish, prima donna behavior. The league's home run record holder, Uchiyama knows a little something about hitting and tries to tell Jack he has a hole in his swing. Jack doesn't listen, but soon enough opposing pitchers find Jack's hole and he falls into a deep slump.

TOP: First base slugger Jack Elliott (Tom Selleck) reluctantly goes to Japan to revive his career.

MIDDLE: It doesn't take long for Elliott's frustrations to boil over.

BOTTOM: Jack ponders his future.

Unwilling to take advice, Jack quickly becomes more and more unproductive, until his frustration at the plate and in his foreign environment soon reaches his boiling point, lashing out at everyone around him. Ignoring coaches' signs in games, losing his temper, insulting teammates, disrespecting Hiroko, and starting brawls on the field, Elliot finds himself with nowhere to turn and only himself to blame.

Embarrassed and disgraced at the bench-clearing brawl, the team's owner uses the incident as an excuse to make the manager place Jack on indefinite suspension and let Uchiyama know that if he can't control his team and win the pennant his contract will not be renewed.

After an awkward surprise at a family dinner where Hiroko introduces her "boyfriend" Jack to her father, who turns out to be Uchiyama, the two men realize their baseball futures are on the line and co-dependent. The two characters, each reflecting colliding cultures and conflicting lifestyles, have more in common than either wants to admit, and can learn from one another.

Uchiyama informs Jack that ownership had initially wanted to bring over another player from America, but he had held out as the lone vote for Jack because he had seen something in viewing tapes that he thought could better help the team. Jack accepts Uchiyama's "my way or the highway" plan and the slugger's redemption process begins in earnest, developing a better physical condition as well as a more congenial attitude.

Jack apologizes to Hiroko for his behavior and surprises her at her office with flowers and champagne. At practice, speaking in weak but sincere Japanese, Jack promises to be a better teammate.

Elliot shows up at Coach Uchiyama's house, saying he has heard of an ancient Japanese tradition of "getting drunk and telling your boss off, and he can't hold it against you." The airing of personal grievances ends up with Jack telling Uchiyama he needs to change his attitude, lighten up, have more fun, and let the players enjoy their too-brief careers, because right now the players are so uptight "you couldn't get a greased BB up their butt." Finally Jack tells Uchiyama that he has a terrific daughter and should tell her so more often.

With Hammer and Jack instilling a freer, more aggressive spirit on the team, the Dragons proceed to loosen up and win more games as a result. Jack is hitting so well again that his agent, Doc (Nicholas Cascone), calls to say he might have a deal that would land Jack back in America playing for the Dodgers, and that he is flying over with a team executive to see Jack and seal the deal.

Hiroko hears the conversation and her coworker's words, "Foreigners leave," ring in her ears. Jack's success is a mixed bag for her, since she fears he'll go back to America without her. Despite Jack's offer to bring her along, Hiroko is upset, thinking he's not sincere—"Baseball and Jack always come before Hiroko and Jack.... I am not just a glove and bat that you can pack up and take along. I am a woman!"—and storms off.

With his agent and potential new employer in the stands, Jack proceeds to play a pivotal role in the Dragons' victory over the Giants to win the pennant. He does it not with power but with guile, driving in the winning run on a bunt.

Though in the end it is Hammer who appears to be going back to America as a Dodger, Jack finds his way back as well. In the final scene Jack is shown giving advice to a young rookie, as a smiling Hiroko looks on from the stands. They are together in America now, where Jack works as a coach for the Detroit Tigers.

Elliott's troubles in a foreign land are soothed by the charms of Hiroko (Aya Takanashi).

INSTANT REPLAY Though the basic story is a somewhat predictable fish-out-of-water culture clash, *Mr. Baseball,* like its star, Tom Selleck, is engaging.

Despite the dangers of having multiple writers (5), Australian director Fred Schepisi, somewhat a fish out of water himself on this type of film (*Russia House, A Cry in the Dark*), does a creditable job conveying in a humorous and thoughtful light some of the things each culture disrespects in the other's. There are plenty of sight gags, playing off Selleck's distinct height advantage with the Japanese, and even toilet humor, to vividly illustrate differing customs. Yes, plenty of the attempts at humor fall short, especially when they employ clichés, but in the end, though neither side fully accepts the other, there is a feeling that both are better off for the experience. This is a credit to the director's sensibilities, and to the cast.

The core Japanese cast give strong performances. Veteran Ken Takakura as the by-the-book, traditional groupthink, old school baseball manager is excellent. Toshi Shioya is well cast as the diplomatic translator. Aya Takanashi's formidable persona as the strong-willed Hiroko is a welcome respite from the docile, geisha-girl stereotypes seen too often in films, and her performance sets off the story's culture clash quite well.

On the American side, Dennis Haysbert's good buddy teammate is complementary to Selleck, whose physique, attitude, baseball skills, and acting ability combine to give us just enough of a sense of transformation from selfish, arrogant jock to a more humble and compassionate team player—a transition that is fun to watch.

But perhaps the game sequences, beautifully shot by cinematographer Ian Baker and seamlessly edited by Peter Honess, are the real all-stars in *Mr. Baseball.* Schepisi does a terrific job of getting the viewer into the action as well as the stands. Game scenes, precisely the trouble point in too many sports movies, have a genuine excitement and realism to them in *Mr. Baseball.*

OUTSIDE THE LINES Tom Selleck was a good volleyball and basketball player, attending USC on an athletic scholarship, and served as honorary captain for the U.S. men's Olympic volleyball team on several occasions.... Doug DeCinces and

Leon Lee, having played in Japan and in the majors, served as technical consultants. DeCinces played for the Angels and Orioles and Lee played for the Cardinals and was a batting coach for the Montreal Expos as well.... Reportedly the script was changed and the movie delayed after Matsushita purchased MCA Inc., which owned Universal, but even so the film certainly was no valentine to the Japanese.... The Chunichi Dragons are in the city of Nagoya.... Okazaki, Jingu, Kosaein, Yokohama, and the Tokyo Dome were other baseball stadiums used in the baseball sequences.... More than 100,000 citizens of Nagoya served as extras.... Selleck spent over a year training for his role, fielding and hitting with half a dozen major league squads including his hometown Detroit Tigers.... Actor Dennis Haysbert played a voodoo-worshipping ballplayer in *Major League* and also appeared in the sports-oriented drama *Love and Basketball*.... *Mr. Baseball* marked the 200th movie for the Japanese star Ken Takakura.... Actor Larry Pennell, who played a scout for the Los Angeles Dodgers, appeared opposite James Earl Jones in the ring in boxing's *The Great White Hope* (1970).... Brad Lesley, who pitched for the Reds and the Brewers as well as the Hankyu Braves, became a top broadcaster in Japan.... Producer Doug Claybourne was a first assistant director on *The Black Stallion* (1979).... The film's editor, Peter Honess, edited the British horse racing movie *Champions* (1984).

ALL-STAR MOMENTS   Gasping for breath after running wind sprints with his new team, Jack says, "[Athletes?] We're not athletes, we're baseball players."

Exemplifying linguistic differences and the idiosyncrasy of native expressions, Jack tells his translator as he heads out of the dugout with his team behind him, "It ain't over until the fat lady sings." Perplexed, his translator then turns around and tells the teammates what he said: "When the game is over a fat lady will sing to us."

In a nightmare Jack swings and misses over and over but can't understand why the umpire keeps letting him swing long after his third strike. He continues to flail miser-

Visiting Hiroko's grandparents, Jack is exposed to more Japanese culture.

ably at the ball and we finally hear the game announcer say, "Does the league have a rule on mercy killings?"

POST-GAME COMMENTS
The film's star, Tom Selleck, on his role:

> I've always wanted to play a major league ballplayer. And the character is one I liked very much. Jack is a player who had a genuine gift, and now he realizes it's slipping away from him. He's frightened, and so he becomes boastful. And he can be a real jerk. But he's a likable jerk.
>
> It's the classic fish-out-of-water story. Both Americans and Japanese love baseball, but they play it in very different ways. Naturally Jack thinks American baseball is better.[1]

Director Fred Schepisi, on Selleck's character and his romantic interest in the film:

> Jack goes to Japan thinking everyone's going to change for him, and of course it doesn't work that way. He doesn't learn Eastern spirituality or anything like that, but he does begin to look at Japan—and himself—in a different way. We poke fun at the Japanese way of life, and the Western way as well.
>
> The love story adds another dimension to the culture clash theme. [Hiroko is] trying to break out, even to be Westernized, in an attempt to become independent. So she understands what Jack's going through, and more than once she comes to his rescue.[2]

Schepisi on the differences between Japanese and American baseball:

> Japan has made the game its own, so much so that many Japanese have difficulty believing that it was actually invented in America. There's something about the game they really respond to deeply, the group dynamics and the self-sacrifice—like the samurai code of honor. The discipline of practice is admired as an end in itself—a thing to be mastered.
>
> Winning is great but losing is unacceptable, and if there's any doubt whether they can win, they'll play for a tie.[3]

Tom Selleck, on the two nations' baseball philosophies:

> The biggest difference between American and Japanese baseball is individuality vs. group. I don't say team because Americans take teamwork very seriously. But in Japan you play as a group, not as an individual in a group.[4]

TOP: A more relaxed Jack makes the Chunichi Dragons a contender.

BOTTOM: The education of a ballplayer continues. Team manager Uchiyama (Ken Takakura) is also the father of Jack's girlfriend, Hiroko.

HOME COURT ADVANTAGE
Available on VHS and DVD. Universal has released *Mr. Baseball* as a single. It is also paired with *Problem Child* on a two-disc DVD set. In the Triple Play set *Mr. Baseball* is included with *For the Love of the Game* and *Field of Dreams*.

#96 THE LOVE BUG

Screenwriters Don DaGradi, Bill Walsh. **Director** Robert Stevenson. **Producer** Bill Walsh. **Cinematography** Edward Colman. **Editing** Cotton Warburton. **Music** George Bruns. **Art Direction** John Mansbridge, Carroll Clark. **Supervisor Driving Sequences** Carey Loftin. **Special Effects** Peter Ellenshaw, Howard Jensen, Danny Lee, Eustace Lycett, Alan Maley, Robert Mattey. Disney. 1968.

THE PLAYERS Dean Jones **Jim Douglas**; Michelle Lee **Carole Bennett**; David Tomlinson **Peter Thorndyke**; Buddy Hackett **Tennessee Steinmetz**; Benson Fong **Mr. Wu**; Joe Flynn **Havershaw**; Andy Granatelli **Himself**; Joe Ross **Detective**; Barry Kelley **Police sergeant**; Iris Adrian **Carhop**; Gary Owens **TV host**; Chick Hearn **Race reporter**

THE GAME Unsuccessful and aging race car driver Jim Douglas (Dean Jones) is being told by friends and business associates to give up the sport. Even his portly, hippie, mechanic roommate, Tennessee Steinmetz (Buddy Hackett), suggests Jim should get out from behind the wheel.

Fate has other plans for Jim. Walking in the city he's distracted by an exotic car and the beautiful legs of a woman in the dealer's showroom. Going inside he meets Carole (Michele Lee) and then the fancy car dealership's owner, Peter Thorndyke (David Tomlinson). Thorndyke soon realizes Jim can't afford any of his fine vehicles and asks him to leave. At this time an oddly out-of-place Volkswagen beetle happens to roll out onto the showroom floor, bumping into Thorndyke, who physically assaults the small car. Jim is vocal about the dealer's disrespect for the vehicle.

Back at home, Jim is awoken by a cop who accuses him of stealing the VW, which is now inexplicably sitting in Jim's driveway. Jim confronts Peter, saying he's stooped pretty low to make a sale by setting him up as a thief. After things cool down, Jim, who is in need of transportation, works out a deal through Peter's assistant Carole to make monthly payments on the VW.

Taking a spin with Carole, Jim is dumbfounded by the car's amazing speed, power, and "mind of its own." He then explains away the small car's strange actions, attributing them to some physical defect that can be fixed: "They make 10,000 cars exactly the same way and for one or two of them to turn out very special ... I may be kidding myself but I think I could be making something out of that sad little bucket of bolts."

Riding in the VW with Jim down San Francisco's famous Lombard Street, Tennessee says he's giving the car a name, Herbie, after one of his uncles. A bit later Jim tells Carole he plans on racing "Herbie."

The veteran racer is pleasantly surprised when his little VW easily passes such muscle cars as Mustangs and Corvettes at the Jackrabbit Springs Raceway. Thorndyke, an avid race car driver himself, witnesses Herbie's phenomenal speed and quickly makes Jim an offer to get the VW back. Standing nearby, Carole suggests they make a wager since they're both entered in the same race the following week.

JIM AGREES: Racing. That's the name of the game. Put up or shut up. You got yourself a deal, Thorndyke.

THORNDYKE TO CAROLE: You keep an eye on your friend in the bug, my dear—I'm going to squash him.

Jim wins and Thorndyke becomes increasingly jealous. This pattern continues as the race season progresses. The more Jim succeeds, the more Thorndyke becomes obsessed with beating him and Herbie. Problems arise when Jim doesn't realize that Herbie's special talents are the major reason for his racing success. When Carole and Tennessee try to point out this seemingly obvious fact to Jim, his ego is bruised but his state of denial persists. To make matters worse, he wants to switch to a fancy Ferrari or something similar instead of staying with the VW, because "without a real car, I'm only half a man."

In order to afford his fancy European race car, Jim agrees to sell Herbie back to Thorndyke. Herbie's feelings are hurt and, knowing he's destined for the scrap heap when Thorndyke gets him back, he takes off by himself. In the fog of San Francisco he smashes into a Chinese store. The owner of the establishment, Mr. Wu (Benson Fong), turns out to be a racing enthusiast and wants to keep Herbie as payment for the damages. Jim, in no position to bargain, counters by saying he must drive Herbie in the El Dorado road race, and that if he wins Mr. Wu will get the prize money, as long as he sells the VW back to Jim. They agree.

Despite devious attempts by Thorndyke to sabotage Herbie, Jim goes on to win the race with the help of Carole and Tennessee, who ride along. Thorndyke's loss is apparently pretty costly. Seems he made a wager with Mr. Wu and now is reduced to working as a grease monkey at his former dealership, now known as "Imported European Motors, Another Tang Wu Enterprise."

Meanwhile Jim and Carole get married. As they prepare to drive off, Tennessee asks where they are going on their honeymoon. Climbing into the VW, Jim says, "We don't know, Herbie hasn't told us yet."

INSTANT REPLAY Smartly written with appeal for the whole family, it's easy to see why *The Love Bug* produced several sequels and a remake since its debut in 1968. It has been one of Disney's most popular franchises.

This innocent-looking VW will soon change the life of its new owner, Jim Douglas (Dean Jones, second from right), and Carole Bennett (Michelle Lee, right).

TOP: The scheming Peter Thorndyke (David Tomlinson) has had nothing but trouble since selling that VW to Jim Douglas.

BOTTOM: Herbie is capable of some unusual maneuvers, but the results speak for themselves.

What if, as Tennessee is convinced is the case, things have an inner life, a soul? Can a machine have an identity crisis and a deep-seated need for acceptance? If so, how does it affect the lives of humans that come into contact with it?

The filmmakers show a talent for camouflaging wide-ranging social themes under a humorous veneer of fantasy, funny stunts, and straight-up slapstick. By the end, *The Love Bug* magically elicits an emotional connection from the young, the old, and all those in between.

Producer Bill Walsh, who wrote the screenplays for *Mary Poppins* and *The Absent-Minded Professor,* presents a warm comedy with help from cowriter Don DaGradi. Veteran Disney director Robert Stevenson orchestrates Gordon Buford's original story with the right blend of pathos and merriment. He is helped by a fine cast and notable stunt work and special effects.

While admittedly the "star" in this film is an automobile, Herbie does get able support from Dean Jones, Michelle Lee, Buddy Hackett, and David Tomlinson on the front lines.

Jones's luckless good-guy racer is set off by the delightfully devilish veteran British performer Tomlinson as Thorndyke. Hackett's compassionate Zen hippie characterization reflects the times in a humorous vein and provides support for the belief that a car can have human attributes such as feelings. Lee works equally well in her scenes with Jones and Tomlinson. The actors bond to each other and their characters to give off a real feel to their experiences until we're insinuated into the fabric of their lives, outlandish as some of it may be.

The Love Bug is pure fun from start to finish, but it's also much more than that. It has a special quality that makes you leave wondering how such a hilarious film, which it is simply impossible to take seriously, can also be so affecting on a deep emotional level.

OUTSIDE THE LINES One of Dean Jones's first movie roles was in the boxing picture *Somebody Up There Likes Me* (1956).… Much of the stunt driving was done by Carey Loftin, who also doubled for Robert Mitchum in *Thunder Road* and for Lee Marvin in *Point Blank*.… Racing sequences were shot at tracks in California—Riverside, Monterey, and Willow Springs among others.… Benson Fong was a Hollywood restaurant owner (Ah Fong's).… Bill Walsh produced *The World's Greatest Athlete* (1973), which featured Jan Michael Vincent.

ALL-STAR MOMENTS In a well shot race, Thorndyke (Tomlinson) thinks he's got the victory until Herbie passes his Jaguar and squirts oil in his face on the way to taking the checkered flag.

Driven off the road in the woods, Thorndyke soon learns his new passenger is a bear and faints.

Carole (Lee) opens Herbie's glove box to see Thorndyke's face. As he yells, "Get me out of here!" she helps get him out, but Herbie's floor begins to split. While Tennessee welds it together the car splits into two, held together only by the axle.

HOME COURT ADVANTAGE Available on VHS and DVD. Disney released this original on DVD with three sequels.

#95 REMEMBER THE TITANS

Screenwriter Gregory Allen Howard. **Director** Boaz Yakin. **Producers** Jerry Bruckheimer, Chad Oman, Mike Stenson, Michael Flynn. **Cinematography** Philippe Rousselot. **Editing** Michael Tronick. **Music** Trevor Rabin. **Production Design** Deborah Evans. **Art Direction** Jonathan Short. **Costume Design** Judy Raskin. Disney. 2000.

THE PLAYERS Denzel Washington **Coach Herman Boone**; Will Patton **Coach Bill Yoast**; Wood Harris **Julius Campbell**; Ryan Hurst **Gerry Bertier**; Donald Faison **Petey Jones**; Craig Kirkwood **Jerry "Rev" Harris**; Ethan Suplee **Louie Lastik**; Kip Pardue **Ronnie "Sunshine" Bass**; Hayden Panettiere **Sheryl Yoast**; Nicole Ari Parker **Carol Boone**; Kate Bosworth **Emma Hoyt**; Earl Poitier **Blue Stanton**; Ryan Gosling **Alan Bosley**; Burgess Jenkins **Ray Budds**; Neal Ghant **Glascoe**; David Jefferson **Cook**; Preston Brant **Jerry Buck**; John Weatherly **Kirk Barker**; Greg Alan Williams **Coach Paul "Doc" Hines**; Brett Rice **Coach Tyrell**; Richard Fullerton **A. D. Watson**; J. Don Ferguson **Executive director**; Krysten Jones **Nicky Boone**; Afemo Omilami **Charles Campbell**; Andrew Masset **Colonel William Bass**; Tim Ware **Fred Bosley**; Tom Turbiville **Captain Hal**; Tom Nowicki **Coach Ed Henry**; Jim Grimshaw **Coach Taber**; David Dwyer **Coach Tolbert**; Bo Keister **Kip Tyler**; Rhubarb Jones **Radio announcer**; Bob Neal **Colorman**

THE GAME It is 1971 in Alexandria, Virginia, and federally mandated integration comes to T. C. Williams High School. Through a school board decision, highly successful and beloved white coach Bill Yoast (Will Patton) loses his top spot to Herman Boone (Denzel Washington), an accomplished black coach from North Carolina.

Yoast, concerned that some of his leading players may lose their chance at a college scholarship under the new coach, swallows his pride and stays on as defensive coordinator and assistant head coach as Boone assures him that "the best player will play. Color won't matter."

Despite threats from outraged white residents and resistance from white players led by team captain Gerry Bertier (Ryan Hurst), Coach Boone establishes his authority running a rigid, military-style operation.

Boone declares, "This is not a democracy. This is a dictatorship. I am the law."

But one of the effects of a grueling training camp where even Coach Yoast complains, "This isn't the Marines," is that the open hostility between the two coaches as well as between the black and white players evolves into grudging respect and loyalty.

This hard-won cohesion helps propel the Titans through the ups and downs of a tough season—off the field when the issue of race divides even family and friends, and on the field with talented, tough opponents.

Through all the adversity the Titans win the state championship and seem to become better people for the experiences they went through to get there.

INSTANT REPLAY In using the glory of an integrated football team's ultimate triumph as a symbolic victory over racism, *Remember the Titans* waters down the theme of bigotry. Then again, with toned-down violence and a noticeable absence of cussing, including the "N" word, producer Jerry Bruckheimer never aimed for this project to be a gridiron-based *Do the Right Thing, In the Heat of the Night, To Kill a Mockingbird,* or *Mississippi Burning*.

The mega-producer (*Armageddon, The Rock*) clearly aimed to reach the widest possible audience through a PG rating, but viewers could also read this approach as softpedaling the socially volatile issues in the movie, diminishing the story's integrity in the attempt to avoid ruffling the feathers of massive potential audience sectors.

TOP: Coach Herman Boone (Denzel Washington).

MIDDLE: At first, teammates Julius Campbell (Wood Harris, left) and Gerry Bertier (Ryan Hurst, right) don't see eye-to-eye.

BOTTOM: Player Petey Jones (Donald Faison, left) meets the new football coach (Washington, right).

While the picture's sugar-coated, politically correct presentation of early '70s race relations comes across as a bit light and manipulative, the film works overall on several levels.

Viscerally and emotionally the film is very atmospheric, with the photography and performances aided by a potent combination of Deborah Evans's production design and a smart selection of popular rock and R&B tunes from the day.

Taking a page from Oliver Stone's *Any Given Sunday,* Michael Tronick edits the game action sequences shot by Philippe Rousselot in a hyperkinetic style. The flash, speed, and intensity build in momentum toward the Titans' title march.

Basing the film on a true story, with a predictable victory in the climactic game inevitable, writer Gregory Allen Howard and director Boaz Yakin shine in depicting the journey toward that victory, and in the nuanced shadings of their lead characters.

Yakin astutely juggles the game action and complex player relationships while still giving full focus to the fireworks between Coach Boone (Denzel Washington) and Coach Yoast (Will Patton).

Enigmatic, perceptive, and hard-core, Denzel Washington's perfectionist Boone, wisely sketched by Howard, is not presented in fully heroic terms. While he's highly principled, knowing that taking Yoast's job isn't right, at the same time Boone won't hesitate to take an opportunity to advance his career.

It would, however, have been more fulfilling to see Boone's deeper emotional struggles.

Unquestionably at times his monologues are sermonizing, but Washington, like Humphrey Bogart in *The Harder They Fall,* excels at "speechmaking" and comes across in general very convincingly. One thing to note is that Washington had just come from another "based on a true story" exploration of social issues in *The Hurricane.*

Washington's opposite number, Will Patton, is very believable as the displaced but beloved coach who out of decency sacrifices his own pride and ambitions and accepts the loss of personal glory for the success of his players' growth and the program in general.

Unfortunately, the leads' performances are somewhat undermined by fellow cast members and shallow character arcs.

The bonding of white player Gerry Bertier (Ryan Hurst) and Julius Campbell (Wood Harris) happens so quickly that it feels forced and unreal. And the omnipresent Sheryl (Hayden Panettiere), the nine-year-old daughter of Coach Yoast, is disruptive and obnoxious. The youngster (Jonathan Lipnicki) in *Jerry Maguire* was humorous, but here we have an over-the-top characterization of a coach's daughter whose knowledge of stats, player psychology, and defensive schemes would make the New England Patriots' Super Bowl champion coach Bill Belichick envious.

In the end what you'll Remember (About) the Titans are the two coaches—Patton and Washington. Their commanding presence shows two actors at the top of their game.

OUTSIDE THE LINES Six years later Bruckheimer would take the historical sports/racial drama theme to the college hardwood with the film *Glory Road,* featuring Josh Lucas as Coach Don Haskins leading the first all-black starting five basketball team to an NCAA crown in 1966.... *Remember the Titans* was shot not in Virginia but various sites in Georgia.... The car accident that paralyzed Gerry Bertier in real life happened after the title game.... Bertier actually played in that game.... Two of the referees in the film, E. Y. Coley and B. Keith Harmon, who played the corrupt ref, are real-life officials in Atlanta.... Denzel Washington won the BET Award for Best Actor in this

LEFT: As coach Bill Yoast (Will Patton, left) looks on, Coach Boone emphasizes a point about his game plan.

ABOVE: "Sunshine," transfer quarterback Ronnie Bass (Kip Pardue).

role.... He also played NBA veteran guard Ray Allen's father in the Spike Lee basketball drama *He Got Game* (1998).... Gregory Allen Howard also wrote the story for boxing's *Ali* (2001) and shares credit for the college basketball picture *Glory Road* (2006).... Washington's first film role was in the made-for-TV drama *Wilma* (1977) about Olympic runner Wilma Rudolph.... It was also where he met his future wife, Pauletta.... Scott Dale also did stunts in golf's *The Legend of Bagger Vance* (2000).... Kip Pardue starred in the auto racing feature *Driven* (2001) with Sylvester Stallone.... Composer Trevor Rabin also created the music for basketball's *Coach Carter* (2005).... Kate Bosworth was a surfer in *Blue Crush* (2002).... Philippe Rousselot won an Oscar for his cinematography in *A River Runs Through It* (1992).... Wood Harris played in *Above the Rim* (1994).... Sports coordinator Michael Fisher also handled the football sequences for *Codebreakers* (2005) and the TV movies *Second String* (2002) and *Brian's Song* (2001), as well as the basketball action for *Even Money* (2005) and *Glory Road* (2006).... Jerry Bruckheimer produced the Tom Cruise auto racing drama *Days of Thunder* (1990).... Denzel Washington was an executive producer of the Oscar-nominated documentary *Hank Aaron: Chasing the Dream* (1995).

ALL-STAR MOMENTS After white players Gerry Bertier (Hurst) and Ray Budds (Burgess Jenkins) make demands to their new black coach about how he should select the team, Coach Boone (Washington) proceeds to let them know who's boss, calling them "Lewis and Martin" and making Gerry call him his "daddy."

The arrival of transfer quarterback Ronnie Bass (Will Pardue) in his dad's Corvette with long blond hair causes players to razz the hippie as a "fruitcake" until he stuns everyone with his throwing ability.

After black teammate Blue (Earl Poitier) gets under Gerry's skin, saying Ronnie's long hair reminds him of Gerry's mama, the momma jokes fly. Ronnie really loosens things up by planting a kiss on Gerry, who then has to be held back from hitting Ronnie.

After QB Ronnie lowbridges all-state defender Kip Tyler (Bo Keister), who is charging him, the opposing coach runs to the ref demanding a call for unnecessary roughness, to which the ref replies, "On the QB? You kiddin' me, coach?"

HOME COURT ADVANTAGE Available on VHS and DVD. In addition to releasing the film as a solo title, Disney has also offered *Remember the Titans* with *Pearl Harbor* in another two-disc DVD set.

#94 ON ANY SUNDAY

Screenwriter/Director Bruce Brown. **Executive Producer** Steve McQueen. **Cinematography** Nelson Tyler, Bob Collins, Don Shoemaker. **Editing** Don Shoemaker. **Music** Dominic Frontiere. Cinema V. 1971.

THE GAME Documentary filmmaker Bruce Brown explores the world of motorcycle racing using a format similar to his ode to surfing in *The Endless Summer*. To tie the diverse elements of the global sport together Brown takes an up close and personal look at some of its top practitioners like Mert Lawwill, Malcolm Smith, and the late actor Steve McQueen.

Nominated for an Academy Award for Best Documentary Feature, this film focuses on the athletic competition of motorcycling. It bears no relation to the motorcycle gang, biker films of the times such as *The Wild Angels*, *Scorpio Rising*, and *Hell's Angels on Wheels*.

Brown takes us through the different disciplines the dangerous sport offers at the highest level of competition and also examines the recreational enthusiasts who come from all walks of life.

INSTANT REPLAY Just as he did with *The Endless Summer*, Bruce Brown captures the participants' passion for their sport in a relaxed and engaging style.

On Any Sunday is visually stunning, and action is the key component. Using a dozen cameramen including himself, the director captures the excitement of a sport practiced worldwide as well as the nuances of the various disciplines. Brown is at the top of his game, blending time frames, locations, competitions, and dramatic content to create a thrilling poetry.

As in *The Endless Summer*, Brown uses two talented specialists, Mert Lawwill and Malcolm Smith, to put a human face to the many who crouch behind their handlebars and roar about at breakneck speeds. The late actor Steve McQueen holds his own, finishing in the top 10 in one race. It would have been nice to hear some of McQueen's comments about his love for the sport. The segments on those three individuals and their ups and downs are a strong unifying component of the film.

The picture features races both of speed and endurance. Profiled are ice racing, sidecar racing, drag racing, dirt track racing, hill racing, land speed racing, desert racing, and an English Trials competition where the object is to complete the course without letting your feet touch the ground no matter what you may encounter.

There is also an interesting look at the so-called "Olympics of motorbike racing," an event in Spain that combines all the assorted disciplines over a 6-day period.

Whether it's eating the dust of 1,000 competitors in the Mojave desert race or the thrills and spills of dirt track sprints, Brown conveys the participants' passion for the sport with his enthusiastic narration and beautiful photography and editing. He gives us an inside perspective on a risky and physically demanding sport that is at times violent and even deadly. Die-hard racers are willing to go on with a broken nose, broken leg, or, yes, even a broken back.

While there are professionals, like Mert Lawwill, who make a living at the sport, Brown is careful to feature the millions who are recreational enthusiasts.

One of the documentary's most indelible moments incorporates some of those everyday Joes in an aerial view of 1,000 racers lined up at a start line over a mile wide in a desert that resembles a massive tumbleweed convention.

Handling the difficult task of sustaining momentum without a real narrative line, Brown's ace photographers are seemingly everywhere—on helmets, fenders, handlebars, and in the air filling the screen with imaginative, captivating, and arresting shots, making the most of slow-motion and instant replay as well. As in his ode to surfing, it's Brown's pictures that are the true stars of *On Any Sunday.*

Certainly the camera results are enhanced by Don Shoemaker's dramatic editing, which gives the film a lyrical quality. Dominic Frontiere's musical score is a bit uneven, at times potent but sometimes intrusive in moments when we'd prefer the roar of the engines. The same goes for Brown's narration, which is informative, but sometimes letting the riveting footage speak for itself would be better.

Indeed, for sheer beauty, this vision of motorcycles on film has only been matched by the appearance of Ann-Margret in *C.C. and Company.*

OUTSIDE THE LINES Dominic Frontiere was the seventh husband of the former Georgia Rosenbloom, owner of the Los Angeles Rams NFL football team.... *On Any Sunday* was Bruce Brown's first movie since *The Endless Summer* (1966).... Steve McQueen was a producer on this film as well as his auto racing feature, *Le Mans* (1971).... Manufacturer Yamaha advanced several million dollars for the film's reissue in North America in 1974.... Frontiere also composed music for the cross-country auto racing movie *The Gumball Rally* (1976) as well as the football drama *Number One* (1969), starring Charlton Heston.

TOP: Bruce Brown also directed the classic surfing documentary 'The Endless Summer.'

MIDDLE: 'On Any Sunday' was nominated for a Best Documentary Oscar.

BOTTOM: An early version of a helmet-cam.

ALL STAR MOMENTS
Point-of-view camera shot putting the viewer in the driver's seat of a high-speed race.

Narrator's comment, "Professional motorbike racing is a violent world," accompanies footage of assorted brutal crashes.

Point-of-view and extreme close-up shots of both dirt track and mud racing.

Racing scenes of sidecar "monkeys" who maneuver close to the ground balancing the bike through turns.

Aerial shot of the 1,000 competitors lined up a mile wide at the start of the desert race.

Closing shots with the film's stars just "cowtrailing" over various terrain.

HOME COURT ADVANTAGE
Available on VHS and DVD. In addition to a standard release, Monterey Video released a three-disc version that also includes *On Any Sunday Revisited* and *On Any Sunday: Motocross, Malcolm, and More.*

#93 FRIDAY NIGHT LIGHTS

Screenwriters David Aaron Cohen, Peter Berg. **Director** Peter Berg. **Producers** Lee Berger, James Whitaker, John Cameron, Robert Graf, Sarah Aubrey, David Bernardi. **Cinematography** Tobias Schliessler. **Editing** Colby Parker Jr., David Rosenbloom. **Music** Explosions in the Sky, David Torn. **Production Design** Sharon Seymour. Universal. 2004.

THE PLAYERS
Billy Bob Thornton **Coach Gaines**; Derek Luke **Boobie Miles**; Jay Hernandez **Brian Chavez**; Lucas Black **Mike Winchell**; Garrett Hedlund **Don Billingsley**; Tim McGraw **Charles Billingsley**; Connie Britton **Sharon Gaines**; Lee Thompson Young **Chris Comer**; Lee Jackson **Ivory Christian**; Grover Coulson **L. V. Miles**; Connie Cooper **Mrs. Winchell**; Kasey Stevens **Flippy**; Ryanne Duzich **Melissa**; Amber Heard **Maria**; Morgan Farris **Jennifer Gaines**; Laine Kelly **Comer's girlfriend**; Gavin Grazer **Trapper**; Robert Flores **Reporter**; Turk Pipkin **Skip Baldwin**; Dr. Carey Windler **Dr. Rogers**; Tommy Kendrick **Odessa doctor**; Brad Leland **John Aubrey**; Lillian Langford **Nancy Aubrey**; Christian Kane **Brian**; Buddy Hale **Booster**; Ken Farmer **Booster**; Marco Perella **Booster**; Robert Weaver **Booster**; Wade Johnston **Coach Miller**; Barry Sykes **Permian play-by-play announcer**; Bob Thomas **Slammin' Sammy**; Gary Mack Griffin **Midland high school coach**; Katherine Willis **Booster's wife**; Angie Bolling **Booster's wife**; Roy Williams **Midland Lee asst. coach**

THE GAME *Friday Night Lights* chronicles the 1988 season of the Permian High School Panther football team in Odessa, Texas.

To all appearances, this west Texas oil town doesn't have a lot going for it. Its pride and joy is its high school football team, whose stadium is larger than many college stadiums and serves as a kind of religious shrine each Friday night in the fall. The Panthers' success or failure will determine the community's mood and self-image until the next season rolls around. The relentless pressure from boosters, parents, local media, the school's own storied gridiron history, and the football fanaticism throughout the state adds up to a heavy burden to lay on some 17-year-olds.

In his third season, Coach Gary Gaines (Billy Bob Thornton) is feeling the pressure to produce a state championship but remains levelheaded despite the oppressive expectations weighing on his team.

Some of the Panthers' best players are hoping to use their football skills as a way out of their hopeless hometown—not unlike Tom Cruise's character in *All the Right Moves*.

Top running back Boobie Miles (Derek Luke), living with his guardian uncle L.V. (Grover Coulson), has attracted the attention of some major colleges. He's more than confident that one day he'll be living the high life as a pro football star.

Quarterback Mike Winchell (Lucas Black), also fatherless, struggles with the emotional burden of looking after his ailing mother (Connie Cooper).

Don Billingsley (Garrett Hedlund) plays running back under the enormous pressure of his demanding father, Charles (Tim McGraw). Charles was one of the all-time great Texas high school football players and was a member of Odessa's championship team 20 years before. Stuck in a time warp, Charles is determined that his son will be a great player too, and berates him for every miscue. Don is having trouble living up to his dad's unreasonable standards.

As the season progresses, the coach does his best to help his squad handle the pressure of the community's relentless obsession with the Panthers' success.

Typical of what they face is when a booster pulls up to Coach Gaines and his family and urges, "Take us to state, Coach." When the coach responds, "Or what?" it's clear that anything less will not be good for his football career.

On the player side, Boobie Miles is so determined to excel that he tries to come back from a leg injury too fast against the advice of doctors, and ultimately ruins his promising football career.

Despite the loss of their star player, the Panthers fight and claw their way to the state championship game. Physically outmatched by a massive Dallas Carter squad, Permian proves to be a worthy opponent despite coming up short at the final whistle.

Although some of the key calls and the bounce of the ball didn't go their way, Coach Gaines is proud of his team's overall effort. Charles is also proud of his son Don's courageous play.

As graduating seniors like Don and Mike contemplate their life after Panther football, Coach Gaines begins preparing for next season, knowing the stakes of directing a football program in an obsessed community.

INSTANT REPLAY Working from the solid foundation laid down by his cousin's best-selling book (H.G. Bissinger's *Friday Night Lights: A Town, a Team and a Dream*), actor/director Peter Berg doesn't give us a traditional character study as much as illustrate the physical and emotional toll on the team through bits and pieces that the audience must assemble.

By presenting this world in a gritty documentary style, *Friday Night Lights* is more reminiscent of *Hoop Dreams* than it is of *Remember the Titans* or *Varsity Blues*. Its strong Texas flavor might remind viewers of *The Last Picture Show,* while the small, rural town that closely identifies with its high school sports team (though admittedly more rationally than in Berg's picture) has also been memorably treated in *Hoosiers.*

Berg's impressionistic adaptation scores high with its deeply atmospheric presen-

Coach Gaines (Billy Bob Thornton) addresses his team.

tation of the story, using Tobias Schliessler's shots of tired oil derricks, long, lonely stretches of road, dreary prairies, and multitudes of businesses closed on account of having "gone to the game" (though the latter is a bit overdone). He fills it out with a telling panorama of the various types of townsfolk in Odessa, whose often misplaced values are damaging their young men.

Berg's sociological survey, which uses his bleak sense of place as a strong background character, is lent able support by a few key performances.

Derek Luke, in taking on the formulaic injured star player, more than capably handles the tough chore of making his cocky, egotistical athlete sympathetic when the bottom falls out and his million-dollar NFL dreams are gone forever, forcing an illiterate young man to come back down to earth.

Permian star and tragic figure Boobie Miles (Derek Luke).

Grover Coulson as his guardian uncle is memorable as the supportive backbone of his nephew's dream. The scenes when they lie to the coach about the extent of Bobby's injury are very revealing, not only for the player but for the pressured coach whose fortunes are so closely tied to his superstar running back.

Singer Tim McGraw, a novice actor, does convincing work as the intense father still living in his high school glory 20 years later at the expense of his son. The misguided father tells his son, "You don't understand. This is the only thing you're ever going to have."

Jay Hernandez unfortunately is a bit of a wasted talent here. Seems he was better utilized in another Texas prairie—based sports movie, *The Rookie*.

Billy Bob Thornton doesn't embody what might be considered a stereotypical football coach—animated, burly, high-strung—but he does have his moments of high anxiety. His understated performance is an effective contrast to the chaos that surrounds him. It's the subtleties Thornton brings to the role—his expressive face as he calmly listens to the boosters who storm into his office espousing their half-baked theories on defensive schemes, or his eyes when he knows he's being lied to by Boobie and his uncle—that characterize this fine performance, demonstrating the artistry with which Thornton can move up and down the scale of emotional intensity.

Coach Gaines's obligatory halftime speeches are less Knute Rockne than Billy Graham, celebrating the life potential of these young men and deflecting the community's irrational priorities—though of course in their last 30 minutes together a victory would enhance the memories. It is consistent with the picture's overall perplexed theme that there's more to life than football, even when, for most, there isn't.

The big game is realistically conducted by veteran football second unit director Allan Graf. The frenetic pacing, edited by David Rosenbloom and Colby Parker Jr., feels like the sequences from an earlier Graf credit, Oliver Stone's *Any Given Sunday*. The use of the Houston Astrodome is a nice touch and another indication of the importance Texans bestow upon high school football.

The Dallas Carter coaches are portrayed in a shifty light during the negotiation, sideline, and halftime scenes, and on the whole the filmmakers go too far to paint the Dallas Carter squad as the black hats. The slow-motion iso shots of crunching tackles and devastating blocks alone make it easy to see the Dallas Carter squad as tough, nononsense physical giants.

Watching this depiction of young players who appear to engage in a brutal physical contest for the sheer reason of pleasing their oppressive adult community, one could say it's a high school football version of *Gladiator*. Any glory is fleeting, as there's no real joy when the triumph is in just surviving.

OUTSIDE THE LINES Peter Berg starred as a boxer in *The Great White Hype* (1996).... Billy Bob Thornton starred in the remake of *The Bad News Bears* (2005).... Second unit director Allan Graf was a lineman on the USC national champion football team in 1972.... Graf's sports coordinating credits include *Jerry Maguire* (1996) and *The Replacements* (2000).... Alan Pakula, a producer of the baseball drama *Fear Strikes Out* (1957), was set to direct this film but passed away before production began.... Jay Hernandez starred in the baseball drama *The Rookie* (2002).... Brian Grazer produced the female surfing feature *Blue Crush* (2002) as well as the boxing saga *Cinderella Man* (2005).... Roy Williams, who played for Permian in high school and is an assistant coach to Odessa's rival team here, is a wide receiver for the Detroit Lions.... Singer Tim McGraw's late father, Tug, pitched for the New York Mets and Philadelphia Phillies.

ALL-STAR MOMENTS L. V. Miles (Grover Coulson), guardian uncle to the team's star player, is in the stands with the scouts, who are duly impressed as they watch Boobie (Luke). Still, L. V. can't resist putting in a word for his nephew:

> He can spin left, he can spin right, don't make no difference. He can block, tackle, score the touchdown, snap the ball, hold the snap and kick the extra point. Boy will fill up the Gatorade cooler, walk the dog and paint your back porch. I'm telling you that boy can flat out play football.

Then Boobie throws on an option, and his uncle doesn't miss a beat: "And he can pass!"

Starkly contrasting shots of the barren geography (minus oil rigs) surrounding Permian High School and the near-professional quality of the school's football operation.

After cleaning out his locker and saying his goodbyes Boobie breaks down in the car with his uncle: "What the hell are we goin' to do?! I can't do nuthin' else but play football."

Chris Comer (Lee Thompson Young) fakes a reverse and returns a kick for a touchdown against Dallas Carter.

Calling his defenders in the crucial defensive situation, Coach Gaines (Thornton) explains what he wants executed:

> Okay, here's what we're going to do. We're going to do a Texas stunt. Now, Ivory, you and Steen, I want you to twist. Steen, you go first, Ivory, you come off his butt into the A gap. Lucas, I want you to shut the A gap too. Now let's shut these cocky sons-of-guns down. Let's go. Let's shut them down. Let's go.

As Mike (Black) throws his last pass to some kids out in the parking lot, intercut Coach Gaines dropping Mike's nameplate with those of the other seniors to make way for the new. Mike smiles a big smile, but Coach is already getting ready for next season.

HOME COURT ADVANTAGE Available on VHS and DVD. Universal has multiple releases, including a single as well as a two-disc set with *8 Mile*.

#92 LE MANS

Screenwriter Harry Kleiner. **Director** Lee Katzin. **Producers** Jack Reddish, Robert Relyea, Steve McQueen. **Cinematography** Rene Guissart, Robert Hauser. **Art Director** Nikita Knatz. **Editing** Don Ernst, John Woodcock. **Special Effects** Sass Bedig. National General. 1971.

THE PLAYERS Steve McQueen **Michael Delaney**; Siegfried Rauch **Erich Stahler**; Elga Andersen **Lisa Belgetti**; Ronald Hunt **David Townsend**; Jonathan Williams **Jonathan Burton**; Alfred Bell **Tommy Hopkins**; Jean Claude Bercq **Paul Jacques Dion**; Luc Merenda **Claude Aurac**; Fred Haltiner **Joann Ritter**; Chris Waite **Larry Wilson**; Louis Edlind **Mrs. Ritter**; Carlo Cecchi **Paolo Scandenza**; Angelo Infanti **Lugo Abratte**; Gino Cassani **Loretto Fuselli**; Michele Scalera **Vito Scaliso**; Richard Rudiger **Bruno Frohm**; Hal Hamilton **Chris Barnett**; Peter Parten **Peter Wiese**; Conrad Pringle **Tony Elkins**; Erich Glavitza **Josef Hauser**; Peter Huber **Max Kummel**

THE GAME Michael Delaney (Steve McQueen) is an aging but crafty driver for the Porsche team battling Ferrari rival Erich Stahler (Siegfried Rauch) in the hardest endurance race: the 24 Hours of Le Mans in France. Delaney is performing well until he's involved in a crash that puts him out of the race. Sidelined, Delaney talks with Lisa Belgetti (Elga Andersen), the widow of a driver killed in an accident in which Delaney was also involved the previous year. She says she has returned hoping to find answers. She asks Delaney what is so important about driving faster than anyone else.

Delaney answers: "A lot of people go through life doing things badly. Racing is important to men who do it well. Racing…it's life. Anything that happens before or after is just waiting."

Unexpectedly, the team manager then calls upon Delaney to switch with the driver of his other Porsche, so the veteran jumps back into the competition. As the race winds down to its final moments Delaney has worked his way back up to third place battling against Stahler, then finally overtakes his Ferrari rival to make it a Porsche 1, 2 finish as Larry Wilson (Chris Waite) takes the checkered flag.

INSTANT REPLAY *Le Mans* represents a passion of Steve McQueen, an avid and accomplished motorcycle and auto racer. While the story line is serviceable, outlining the characters' motivations and pressures, it is the absolutely brilliant photography, sound, and editing of the racing sequences that distinguish this picture.

McQueen's character, Michael Delaney, says it all when he explains, "A lot of people go through life doing things badly. Racing is important to men who do it well. Racing…it's life. Anything that happens before or after is just waiting." The race is the thing—and in this film, it is truly the main character.

From the early heart-pounding scenes of the race's start, the filmmakers succeed in their quest for authenticity, putting the viewer in the driver's seat of an inherently dramatic endurance race. We're never limited to process shots and rearview projections.

The picture's raw visceral power is complemented by McQueen's restrained approach, atypical for a Hollywood hero. He embodies the racer's single-mindedness with clarity: while he respects teammates and rivals, Delaney reserves all his emotional energy and focus for his work behind the wheel.

Well cast, sprinkled with real racers using actual race cars, and shot on the actual course incorporating enthusiastic spectators, *Le Mans* is highly atmospheric.

OUTSIDE THE LINES

The first 24-hour Le Mans race was held in 1923.... The nearly 8.5-mile circuit consists of roads used in everyday public transportation.... 16 cameras spread around the course were used to film the action, and 44 of the world's top racers participated.... Steve McQueen was a talented racer in his own right, finishing second in the 1970 Sebring 12-hour endurance race, and was right in the pack against legitimate professionals going 230 mph in his Porsche 917 in *Le Mans*.... The film's composer, Michael Legrand, also scored the music for *Brian's Song* (1971).... A half-dozen race cars worth $300,000 each were crashed intentionally to add to the movie's impact.... The Le Mans race draws 500,000 spectators annually.... Reportedly, John Sturges (*Bad Day at Black Rock, Gunfight at the OK Corral*) was set to direct the film. He directed McQueen in *The Great Escape*.... McQueen's film debut was in the boxing picture *Somebody Up There Likes Me* (1956).... McQueen starred as a rodeo cowboy in *Junior Bonner* (1971).... The actor also displayed his motorcycle skills in *On Any Sunday* (1971).

ALL-STAR MOMENTS

Flashback to Michael Delaney's crash.

Montage of moments leading to start of the race.

Assorted low-angle and point-of-view shots of the race.

The spectacular staging of a Ferrari crashing as it attempts to avoid another car.

The split-second buildup from a racer's point of view as Delaney crashes against a rail.

The tight battling for position among the lead cars intensifying as the race reaches its final stages.

POST-GAME COMMENTS

Steve McQueen:

> **People say that all racers are beckoning death, but it's not that way. I don't enjoy sheer speed over which you have no control. That frightens me. The**

TOP: Steve McQueen as racer Michael Delaney.

MIDDLE: Delaney shows the intense focus endurance racing demands.

BOTTOM: Delaney (McQueen, right), a perennial study in concentration.

RIGHT: An avid racer, McQueen did a lot of his own driving.

The 24 Hours of Le Mans is a hugely popular event in France.

challenge of racing is in the knowledge that your equipment is the best, that you are in command.[1]

This is the toughest picture I've ever made. We spent 5 months breaking our backs to get exactly what we wanted on film. I felt it was important to show truthfully what is probably one of the last honest competitive sports left in the world. There's no gambling or betting in motor racing, no dishonesty anywhere. The cars, the tracks, and the stopwatches separate the men from the boys and that's where it's at.[2]

A lot of people think actors can't do anything but get paid lots of money for performing. I had to beat the actor's image, to prove my capabilities in a sport that has always intrigued me. It's man against man, machine against machine when you're on that course. If I prove anything, I prove it as myself.[3]

You have to love what you're doing. All the fame or glory that can come your way either as an actor or racer means nothing if you don't believe in what you're doing. The racers I know aren't in it for the money. They race because it's something that's inside them. They know what they're doing. They're not courting death. They're courting being alive.[4]

HOME COURT ADVANTAGE Available on VHS and DVD.

#91 THE FRESHMAN

Screenwriters John Grey, Sam Taylor, Tim Whelan, Ted Wilde. **Director** Fred Newmeyer. **Producer** Harold Lloyd. **Cinematography** Henry Kohler, Walter Lundin. **Editing** Allen McNeil. **Art Direction** Liell Vedder. Pathe. 1925.

THE PLAYERS Harold Lloyd **Harold "Speedy" Lamb**; Jobyna Ralston **Peggy**; Brooks Benedict **College cad**; James Anderson **Chester Trask**; Hazel Keener **College belle**; Joe Harrington **Tailor**; Pat Harmon **College coach**; Charles Stevenson **Assistant coach**; Charles Farrell **Student (bell ringer)**; Gus Leonard **Waiter**; Oscar Smith **Dean's chauffeur**

THE GAME Harold Lamb (Harold Lloyd) is an eager, uncoordinated college freshman who longs to be a big man on campus. He practices relentlessly a quirky handshake jig and catch phrase used by the star of a film he studies over and over called *The College Hero*: "I'm just a regular fellow. Step right up and call me Speedy." His parents are not hopeful.

Harold begins the journey of his advanced education on a train, where he comes across a pretty young lady, Peggy (Jobyna Ralston). She is a shy and somewhat old-fashioned girl compared to the "flapper" types prevalent at the college they both attend, but Harold is instantly smitten with her.

He arrives at college as the film panel reads: "The opening of the Fall term at Tate University—a large football stadium with a college attached." As he gets off the train Harold is astonished to see his hero, Tate star Chet Trask (James Anderson), being greeted by a throng of friends and admirers getting off the same train.

Harold's attempt to emulate Chet's popularity goes awry from the start as he immediately falls prey to the campus prankster (Brooks Benedict) and as a result soon becomes the butt of jokes, loses his college savings, and is embarrassed in front of the entire student body.

The resilient Harold realizes that the key to his success is to become a member of the football team. He starts out by literally becoming the team's tackling dummy. Still, he thinks he's made an impression and believes he's made the team only to learn that he's merely a water boy.

At the Fall Frolic, the school's big annual dance, Harold suffers another setback in his quest for popularity as his poorly stitched suit comes apart at the seams on the dance floor. The campus cad makes a play for Peggy; Harold punches him, and the cad tells Harold everyone thinks of him as a loser. One student even does an imitation of Harold's handshake jig, and he is humiliated until Peggy tells him to grow up and just be himself.

Harold knows his best chance to prove himself is to get into the big game against rival Union State. As the game progresses, the bigger, stronger opponents cause one injury after another to Harold's teammates. At one point Harold thinks he's going in, but the coach has only called him over to give his jersey to another player.

When the injuries pile up Harold attempts to go in, but the coach sheepishly informs Harold that he's been just a water boy all along. Harold stands up for himself and demands to be given a chance to play and prove himself. He gets in but is flattened on the first play and is taken out on a stretcher. He comes to, though, hops off the stretcher, and heads back to the huddle only to get pummeled on the next play. Now

Harold "Speedy" Lamb (Harold Lloyd) on the lam.

seeing double, Harold manages to further embarrass himself by mistaking a derby the tailor has thrown onto the field for a football. He takes off running with it, causing the coach to begin pulling his hair out, at his wits' end with Harold's shenanigans.

Despite all the mishaps Harold perseveres, takes a fumble, shakes off tacklers left and right, and, though he's finally brought down at the goal line, it is determined that he has scored the winning touchdown.

Harold wins over his peers and wins the girl, Peggy. He has gone from the college zero to the college hero.

INSTANT REPLAY This is one of Harold Lloyd's best feature-length comedies and one of the most profitable films from the flapper and coonskin-coat era.

Lloyd's silly antics create mirth and merriment for the audience, and his witty title writers add to the laughs with their insightful comments poking fun at the many college films of the Roaring Twenties.

Losing his clothes at the dance, delivering a speech with a kitten crawling up his sweater, and serving as a human tackling dummy are just some of the predicaments Lloyd finds himself in that tickle the funny bone.

Speedy is lucky to have a tailor nearby (Joe Harrington).

Lloyd distinguishes himself from the Chaplin pathos and the mayhem of Mack Sennett's troops with his open, honest energy and the charm that lay in knowing he had an everyman quality. It's the fact that his character doesn't realize he's the campus joke that makes the audience and Peggy sympathize with him.

In the end Lloyd subtly questions the hero's achievement, presenting us with young imitators who look up to him after he's achieved the status he sought—and who look just as silly as he did at the beginning of the film with his corny handshake routine. He learns that an essential element of success is being true to oneself.

The Freshman is more of a character comedy spoofing college life as opposed to pure slapstick humor, and it is Harold Lloyd in fine form. The picture deals with the timeless school experiences of peer acceptance and growth of self-knowledge that still resonate today.

OUTSIDE THE LINES The football game was partially filmed during an actual game in Berkeley at halftime between Cal and Stanford.... *The Freshman* was second only to Charlie Chaplin's *The Gold Rush* (1925) as the most successful comedy feature movie of the silent era, grossing over $2.5 million on a budget of $300,000.... Over 20 years later director Preston Sturges used some of the football scenes in *The Sin of Harold Diddlebock* (1947).... Lloyd began his film career as an extra playing an American Indian in an Edison one-reeler in 1913.... In between his Hal Roach characters of Willie Work and Lonesome Luke, Lloyd worked with Mack Sennett.... Lloyd produced and starred in boxing's *The Milky Way* (1936).... Before beginning his Hollywood career, director Fred Newmeyer played professional baseball.... Among Newmeyer's directorial efforts was the football film *The Quarterback* (1926).... Lloyd re-released the film in 1953.

ALL-STAR MOMENTS An early panel graphic describing Harold's school: "The opening of the Fall term at Tate University—a large football stadium with a college attached."

Harold (Lloyd) as the human tackle dummy for the Tate football team.

Harold's suit falls apart at the big dance.

Harold's inept play when he finally gets into the big game before his winning score.

Harold's game-winning run as he shakes off tacklers left and right, just crossing the goal line for the victory.

#90 THE BLACK STALLION

Screenwriters Melissa Mathison, Jeanne Rosenberg, William Wittliff. (Novel by Walter Farley.) **Director** Carroll Ballard. **Producers** Francis Coppola, Fred Roos, Tom Sternberg. **Cinematography** Caleb Deschanel. **Editing** Robert Dalva. **Music** Carmine Coppola. **Art Direction** Aurelio Crugnola, Earl Preston. **Sound Supervisor** Alan Splet. **Horse Trainer** Glenn Randall. **Stunts** Jesse Wayne. United Artists. 1979.

THE PLAYERS Kelly Reno **Alec Ramsey**; Mickey Rooney **Henry Daley**; Cass-ole **The Black Stallion**; Teri Garr **Alec's mother**; Clarence Muse **Snoe**; Hoyt Axton **Alec's father**; Michael Higgins **Neville**; Ed McNamara **Jake**; John Burton **Jockey 1**; John Buchanan **Jockey 2**; Doghmi Larbi **The Arab**; Kristen Vigard **Becky**; Fausto Tozzi **Rescue captain**; John Karlson **Archaeologist**; Leopoldo Trieste **Priest**; Frank Cousins **African chieftain**; Don Hudson **Taurog**; Marne Maitland **Drake captain**; Tom Dahlgren **Veterinarian**

THE GAME A young boy, Alec Ramsey (Kelly Reno), is sailing aboard a ship off the North African coast with his father (Hoyt Axton) when tragedy strikes: the ship catches fire and sinks. Finding himself washed up on the shore of a deserted island, Alec comes across the ship's only other survivor, the big black horse he befriended aboard the vessel earlier. The horse is caught in some rocks by the rope tied around him, and Alec sets him free. As the days pass they form a bond and are finally rescued by some Italian fishermen.

Once Alec reaches home and is safe with his mother (Teri Garr), his horse, Black, takes off running through town and out into the country. Time passes and Alec thinks Black may be gone for good until he comes upon him in a barn owned by a former horse trainer, Henry Daley (Mickey Rooney). Henry recognizes Black's natural but untapped racing talent and begins training Alec as a jockey.

With the help of an influential horse racing broadcaster friend, Neville (Michael Higgins), Henry builds up Black's mysterious potential as a star horse, leading to a tension-filled, high-stakes match race where Black achieves a stunning victory.

INSTANT REPLAY Nature's beauty, as captured by the brilliant eye of cinematographer Caleb Deschanel, is the true star of *The Black Stallion*. From the movement and grace of the beautiful horse to the wonderful island vistas, this polished production is a vision of loveliness.

The lyrical montages of nature help fill out a rather simple film that, though well edited by Robert Dalva, runs a bit long. Despite that, *The Black Stallion*, based on Walter Farley's popular novel, is undeniably enjoyable family entertainment.

Director Carroll Ballard shows a talent for conveying the mythical aspects of the human-horse relationship while adroitly leaving room for the viewer's imagination. He is aided in that regard by the ever-capable Mickey Rooney, who seems to have his own stable of horse sensibilities when it comes to equine movies. His humor and humanity carry the day here, especially in the classic scene where he confides some insider jockey tips to the youngster. Rooney's Oscar-nominated effort as the wise old trainer is comparable to his great work in *National Velvet*, where he trained another kid, Elizabeth Taylor, to ride a racehorse.

Kelly Reno shows he can ride and gives a fine, understated performance as the freckle-faced survivor, a tough kid quietly determined to achieve his goal. Though she

doesn't have a lot to do, other than temporarily stand in the way of her son's dream, Teri Garr is appropriately sympathetic. The elderly horseman, Clarence Muse, brings some notable balance, offering his wisdom to the youngster.

But none of these fine performers can outshine Cass-ole. The horse portraying the wild stallion belongs in the same elite stable as equine stars Trigger and Silver.

The director orchestrated the project with a solid blend of terrific shots, just the right sound (earning Alan Splet an Oscar nomination) to match the camerawork, an emotional score by Carmine Coppola, long periods without dialogue to let the images speak for themselves, and top-level editing, both in the nature montages and in the climactic race, to present a vivid canvas of indelible scenes.

OUTSIDE THE LINES Rooney also starred in the boxing classic *Requiem for a Heavyweight* (1962)...11-year-old Kelly Reno, who grew up riding horses on a Colorado ranch, won out over more than 1,000 candidates in a nationwide search.... Walter Farley wrote the book while he was still in high school.... It would go on to sell over 20 million copies following its debut in 1941.... Glenn Randall first trained horses for movie work and personal appearances with Roy Rogers's Trigger.... Clarence Muse appeared in Disney's *The World's Greatest Athlete* (1973) and another horse racing feature, *Broadway Bill* (1934).... Cass-ole, a multi-titled Arabian show horse from Texas, was chosen for the lead after a lengthy search.... The Cinecitta studios in Rome were used for the shipwreck sequences.... Randall's horse training credits also include Silver for the *Lone Ranger* TV series and the chariot race in *Ben-Hur*.... A special mane was added to Cass-ole's existing mane to give it a wilder appearance.... Teri Garr appeared

TOP: Teri Garr is Alec's mother, Belle.

BOTTOM: Clarence Muse is Snoe.

RIGHT: Alec (Reno, left) and Henry Dailey (Mickey Rooney) grow close as they train the young boy's horse.

Alec's horse competes successfully against two champions.

in another horse racing film, *Let It Ride* (1989), with Richard Dreyfuss.... Three other horses were utilized as doubles.... Special swimming horses were used for the ocean scene.... The Woodbine and Ft. Erie race tracks in the Canadian province of Ontario were used for the training sessions and the race.... Ballard, a classmate of Francis Coppola at the UCLA Film School, was nominated for an Oscar with his 1967 documentary *Harvest*.... *The Black Stallion* was his feature debut.... Assistant director Doug Claybourne would produce *Mr. Baseball* (1992), featuring Tom Selleck.... Deschanel earned an Oscar nomination for his photography of *The Natural* (1984).... He also shot Neil Simon's *The Slugger's Wife* (1985).... Robert Dalva earned an Academy Award nomination for his editing work on this picture.... Actor-singer Hoyt Axton, who played Alec's father, later played the father of Shirley Muldowney, a female drag racing star, in *Heart Like a Wheel* (1983).... Jesse Wayne also did stunt work on *The Bad News Bears* (1976) and *The Love Bug* (1968).

ALL-STAR MOMENTS
Shot of the horse standing atop an island cliff overlooking the sea.

The start of the climactic race. The crowd is quiet with anticipation, and we see blood trickling from the Black Stallion's leg.

HOME COURT ADVANTAGE
Available on VHS and DVD. MGM has released this as a single and with *The Black Stallion Returns*. It is also included in a Family Classics Gift Set featuring *Chitty Chitty Bang Bang* and *Yours, Mine, and Ours*.

#89 Cool Runnings

Screenwriters Lynn Siefert, Michael Goldberg, Tommy Swerdlow. **Director** Jon Turteltaub. **Producer** Dawn Steel. **Cinematography** Phedon Papamichael. **Editing** Bruce Green. **Music** Nick Glennie-Smith, Hans Zimmer. **Costume Design** Grania Preston. Buena Vista. 1993.

THE PLAYERS Leon **Derice Bannock**; Doug E. Doug **Sanka Coffie**; Rawle Lewis **Junior Bevil**; Malik Yoba **Yul Brenner**; John Candy **Irv Blitzer**; Raymond Barry **Kurt Hemphill**; Peter Outerbridge **Josef Grool**; Paul Coeur **Roger**; Larry Gilman **Larry**; Charles Hyatt **Whitby Bevil Sr.**; Winston Stona **Coolidge**; Bertina Macauley **Joy Bannock**; Pauline Myrie **Momma Coffie**; Kristoffer Cooper **Winston**; Bill Dow **Registration official**; Jay Brazeau **Kroychzech**; Campbell Lane **Schindler**; Matthew Walker **German official**; Christopher Gaze **British official**; Jack Goth **Gremmer**; David Lovgren **Swiss captain**; Oliver Hunter **Joseph**; Fitz Weir **Uncle Ferte**; Michael London **Heckler**; Karyn Scott **Line dancer**; Craig Lehto **Bobsled starter**; John Morgan **Himself**; Al Trautwig **Himself**

THE GAME Jamaica's leading sprinter, Derice Bannock (Leon), sees his Olympic dreams "dashed" when he's accidentally tripped in the qualifying meet by competitor Junior Bevil (Rawle Lewis).

Derice pleads with Coolidge (Winston Stona), the Jamaican Olympic official, for a re-running of the race. Though he is denied, Derice is inspired when Coolidge tells him about an American coach living in Jamaica, Irv Blitzer (John Candy), who once tried to get Derice's sprinter father to switch sports and be part of an Olympic bobsled team.

Through charm, determination, and pleading Derice convinces Blitzer to coach him, his friend Sanka (Doug E. Doug), and two sprinters who also lost their chance at the Olympics, Junior Bevil and Yul Brenner (Malik Yoba), to try and qualify for the next Winter Olympics in the four-man bobsled.

The Jamaicans' lack of funds and unfamiliarity with the nuances of the sport notwithstanding, under Coach Blitzer they plow ahead with many ups and downs, often sliding on thin ice in their quest to succeed at the 1988 Calgary Olympics. In the freezing weather of Canada it's tough for these tropical troopers to be taken seriously.

They overcome ridicule from their world-class competitors, the media, and sport officials who also expose their coach's involvement in a cheating scandal from a previous Olympics. In the end their commitment, team spirit, and determination pays off as the four Jamaicans and Coach Blitzer leave Canada swelling with pride, their eighth-place performance having earned them the respect of their sledding peers.

INSTANT REPLAY A snowbound, comedic *Chariots of Fire*. A more urbane *The Gods Must Be Crazy*. Call it what you will, *Cool Runnings* is a well-executed story that succeeds in its aim—as an easygoing family entertainment that is inspiring to young and old alike.

As befits its Disney heritage, *Cool Runnings* takes an age-old sports movie formula of quarreling team members with an old, reluctant coach and places it within the context of a warm tropical island culture moved inside the cold, harsh environment of a Winter Olympics in Canada.

Director Jon Turteltaub keeps the story light, not preachy. Though the plot, *very* loosely based on a true story, is short on twists and surprises, Turteltaub keeps it interesting and prevents the characters from becoming too cartoonish on their road to

TOP: Primitive beginnings for the Jamaicans.

LEFT: Fundraising is coming along slowly.

respect, not an easy task in this comedy. Though it is hard to determine accurately, the characterizations are likely not very faithful to historical fact, but for most moviegoers the end result is a satisfactory feeling.

The engaging cast overcomes the script's hackneyed stock stereotypes, and the four sledders exude a good-natured energy. It is evident that each is more skilled at light situations than self-reflection, and the comedy scenes score distinctively higher than the more dramatic scenes. Doug E. Doug is particularly good in carrying the comedic torch throughout the feature as the outgoing, lovable Sanka.

John Candy gives one of the best performances of his career. Letting the four sledders deliver most of the slapstick comedy, Candy in his pivotal role as coach shows just the right warmth, passion, and genuine pathos, as when he reminds his driven sledder Derice, "If you're not enough without a gold medal, you're not enough with it."

The actual bobsledding scenes—both the humorous early training sessions in Jamaica and the exhilarating Olympic footage—are well done, conveying character and relationship as well as demonstrating the excitement, nerve, and skill involved in the sport. The point-of-view camera shots are ably executed and inspire an appreciation of the sport's ever-present danger.

Contributing mightily to the mix is an appealing array of reggae tunes whose light, sunny mood endures even through the frigid scenes of snowy Canada, which provide ample sources of humor.

Grania Preston's colorful costume design is another fine contribution to the picture.

It is not difficult to see why former Columbia studio chief Dawn Steel doggedly pursued this story as a pet project and endured many script and cast revisions. *Cool Runnings* is that rare movie that delivers to the whole family. It does so with just the right blend of comedy, feeling, and insight as we cheer for the underdog sledders and root for the successful redemption of the coach with a checkered past.

TOP: The learning curve is fraught with peril.

MIDDLE: A strange new world—and a cold one.

BOTTOM: The Jamaicans are proud of how far they've come.

You don't have to follow bobsledding to be drawn into this story, nor do the filmmakers seem to side with a particular nationality or become too sanctimonious with the typical sport movie life-lesson sermons. Sometimes winning doesn't mean coming in first place.

OUTSIDE THE LINES The picture was loosely based on the true story of a Jamaican bobsled team that competed in the 1988 Calgary Olympic Games.... John Candy died of a heart attack just a few months after this film's release.... Candy was a part owner of the Toronto Argonauts, a Canadian Football League franchise .... Candy also appeared in baseball's *Rookie of the Year* (1993).... In its early stages, *Cool Runnings* was to be called "Blue Maaga" and directed by Michael Ritchie, who receives a story credit here.... Ritchie has been involved as a writer, director, and producer in many sports films, including *Downhill Racer* (1969), *The Bad News Bears* (1976), and *Semi-Tough* (1978).... Susie Landau also produced the TV baseball drama *Tiger Town* (1983).... The film's sled, known as *Ragamuffin*, was presented to the Planet Hollywood restaurant in Chicago.... *Cool Runnings* is a Jamaican expression for "peaceful journey."...Actual footage of the real Jamaican bobsled team's accident was incorporated into the film.... Bruce Green also edited the baseball remake of *Angels in the Outfield* (1994).... George Carlin was also considered for the coach role.... Composer Hans Zimmer was nominated for the Best Score Academy Award for *Gladiator* (2000). He also created music for *Days of Thunder* (1990), *A League of Their Own* (1992), and *The Fan* (1996).... Zimmer won an Oscar for *The Lion King* (1994).... Michael Goldberg wrote the screenplay for the youth football feature *Little Giants* (1994).... Rexford Metz was also the cinematographer for Michael Mann's TV movie *The Jericho Mile* (1979), which starred Peter Strauss as a talented runner serving time for murder.

ALL-STAR MOMENTS Montage of the fledgling team's start practices with Coach Blitzer (Candy) telling them, "If you speed demons can't whip off an even 6 flat, you have a better chance of becoming a barbershop quartet." They produce an atrocious time of 14.3.

As coach explains the importance of being able to endure the cold weather we see Sanka (Doug) stick his frozen head out from inside an ice cream truck, breaking off a frozen dreadlock.

Coach's inspirational talk, including a prayer: "Our father who art in Calgary, bobsled be thy name. Thy kingdom come, gold medals won, on Earth as it is in turn 7."

HOME COURT ADVANTAGE Available on VHS and DVD. Disney has released this title as a solo DVD and in combination with *The Three Musketeers*.

#88 ROLLERBALL

Screenwriter William Harrison. **Director** Norman Jewison. **Producers** Norman Jewison, Hal Wallis, Patrick Palmer. **Cinematography** Douglas Slocombe. **Editing** Antony Gibbs. **Music** André Previn. **Production Design** John Box. **Art Direction** Robert Laing. **Costume Design** Julie Harris. United Artists. 1974.

THE PLAYERS
James Caan **Jonathan E.**; John Houseman **Bartholomew**; Maud Adams **Ella**; John Beck **Moonpie**; Moses Gunn **Cletus**; Pamela Hensley **Mackie**; Barbara Trentham **Daphne**; Shane Rimmer **Team executive**; Ralph Richardson **Librarian**; Angus MacInnes **Jonathan's guard #1**; Robert Ito **Oriental instructor**; Burnell Tucker **Jonathan's captain of guard**; Alfred Thomas **Team trainer**; Richard LeParmentier **Bartholomew's aide**; Burt Kwouk **Doctor**; Nancy Blair **Girl in library**; Loftus Burton **Reporter**; Abi Gouhad **Reporter**; Stephen Boyum **Biker**; Danny Wong **Biker**; Bob Leon **Biker**

THE GAME A future society has evolved to where the homogenization of corporate/government rule has left its citizens comfortably numb. The sport of Rollerball is a key outlet for man's aggressive nature and a popular diversion that vicariously satisfies people's hostile impulses. At the same time, with its capricious enforcement of nebulous and changeable rules, the sport demonstrates the futility of individual actions in a corrupt system. In the game as in life, the faceless state controls the flow of information and maintains the real power.

Complications arise when the sport's lone superstar, Jonathan E. (James Caan), refuses to retire and begins to question authority (represented by John Houseman as Bartholomew), while those in power fear that Jonathan's mass popularity will upset the status quo.

INSTANT REPLAY The strength of *Rollerball*, a sort of cerebral *Mad Max* meets *Kansas City Bomber* in *Westworld*, is its visual splendor. It is the action sequences on amazing sets that really sell the core of the story: the values of individuality in a corporate world run by faceless suits exploiting violence as part of their controlled society.

The original, imaginative, and simply brilliant design work of John Box, Julie Harris's costume designs, and Robert Laing's art direction are brought to life by Douglas Slocombe's fancy photography of a riveting game with a group of professional athletes and stuntmen who embrace it wholeheartedly, headed by jock actor James Caan.

The film's central theme of individual freedom and what happens when it is taken away may appear somewhat underdeveloped here. I believe this was a deliberate choice by writer William Harrison and director Norman Jewison, as the minimal backstory is what drives the lead character's search for meaning.

That is also why the dramatic scenes off the track at times seem prolonged and a bit dreary, because the filmmakers use visual metaphors rather than exposition to convey themes. The picture is a thinking rather than a feeling story. At the same time, several of those vignettes could have been better edited.

At times the game sequences become a bit repetitive, thus losing some of their shock value, but the performers are quite convincing in their intensity and vigor.

Caan epitomizes the sport's driven superstar. He is not only athletically skilled but shows a rare ability to question the trappings bestowed upon him.

John Houseman is well cast as the symbol of the all-controlling government/corporate entity that feels threatened by Caan's questioning of the system it controls.

Readily aiding the unrelenting dark atmosphere is the moody classical music. From the "Toccata and Fugue" that lowers as the film begins to the haunting soundtrack that closes the picture, the music stays with you long after the film is over, a credit to André Previn.

Despite tendencies toward heavy-handedness and self-importance, *Rollerball* endures as a provocative indictment not only of the rise of corporate power at the cost of personal freedoms, but also of our fascination with ritualized violence.

As Arnold Schwarzenegger would later do in *The Running Man*, Rollerball also pokes a dagger at the media conglomerates that package and promote organized violence perpetuating man's bloodlust for fun and profit. (Then again, if cable TV had been available back then, I'm sure the pay-per-view business for the gladiatorial activities at the Roman Colosseum would have flourished.)

Its sci-fi flavor puts *Rollerball* in the league of the few '70s message pictures that offer an interesting look at future societies—*Westworld, Zardoz, Soylent Green,* and *Logan's Run*. And of course, *Stars Wars* is a classic.

OUTSIDE THE LINES Based on William Harrison's original short story "Roller Ball Murders."...The game was real; when the film was made there were no blue screens or digital effects.... A German architect created the actual track....

Multi-Oscar-winning production designer John Box brought the concept to reality.... Box won a British Academy Award for Best Art Direction for his work here.... Skaters got up to speeds of 40 mph.... English roller hockey players, American roller derby players, stunt men, and motor bikers filled out the rosters.... The film was shot primarily in Munich, Germany. The Olympic basketball venue and the BMW building in that city were used extensively.... Director Norman Jewison said the concept for the rolling ball came from roulette tables.... Actor James Caan at the time was doing some rodeo riding.... Some of the technicians had also worked in the '72 Munich Olympics.... Asian students who were studying in Germany at the time were used as extras.... Some camera men were shooting while wearing roller skates and being pulled by motorcycles.... The ball used for filming was actually a fairly light aluminum ball, except for the close-ups, where a 10- to 12-pound steel ball was used.... The League of Nations building in Geneva was shot to represent the world library.... *Rollerball* was remade in 2002, starring Chris Klein and L. L. Cool J.

ALL-STAR MOMENTS
Opening scenes with dramatic music as players, game operators, refs, and even medical personnel prepare for the event.

Early game action sequences: Houston's Jonathan E. (Caan) fends off attackers; teammate Moonpie (John Beck) rolls down from the rail to throw a great block; opponents drag a teammate off the field. Rabid crowd (except for a shot of a woman sitting in a suite, who seems to be enjoying herself sewing) applauds Jonathan E.'s effort as he scores the first goal of the game.

Later in the same event after scoring an insurance goal assuring Houston's victory, Jonathan E. tells his teammate, "I love this game, Moonpie.... I love it," as adoring fans rush to the railing.

At a practice the game's superstar, Jonathan E., addresses players on what it takes to succeed, demonstrating some tricks of the trade, including the value of listening. Tuffy, a speedballer from Manila, is not paying attention and learns a painful lesson as he goes flying over Jonathan E on the track.

High and overhead shots of Tokyo players skating in unison and fans cheering in "unison."

In a wild game against Tokyo, Jonathan E. runs over a biker then past a defender to score a goal but holds his arm in pain. The crowd chants his name. It is 2—1 Houston in the 3rd period, and when a Tokyo biker runs over a Houston player on the ground he loses control and flies from the bike into the crowd. One fan from the frenzied Japanese crowd hurdles the barriers only to be roughed up by Houston players and falls to the gutter. Up in a private box we see a corporate "suit" laughing at it all.

Championship game. Dramatic buildup as Jonathan E. rolls to locker room and stares at his teammates, who look back at him silently. No "Gipper" speech. He then rolls on, putting on his helmet, and we see an iso shot of him rolling down the corridor to the track.

HOME COURT ADVANTAGE
Available on VHS and DVD.

TOP: In a violent game devised by all-powerful corporations to convey the futility of individuality, one player stands out, Jonathan E. (James Caan).

MIDDLE: The film's strength was its creation and presentation of a visually stunning game.

BOTTOM: Jonathan E. refuses to back down against the corporate powers, represented here by Bartholomew (John Houseman, left).

FACING PAGE: The work of 'Rollerball' production designer John Box earned him a British Academy Award for Best Art Direction.

#87 Hank Aaron: Chasing the Dream

Screenwriter/Director Mike Tollin. **Producers** Fred Golding, Tom McMahon, Brian Robbins, Vivian Schiller. **Cinematography** Chuck Cohen. **Music** Ed Smart. **Executive Producers** Denzel Washington, Pat Mitchell, Debra Chase, Jack Myers, David Houle. 1995.

THE PLAYERS Hank Aaron **Himself**; Dusty Baker **Himself**; Harry Belafonte **Himself**; Yogi Berra **Himself**; Barry Bonds **Himself**; Jimmy Carter **Himself**; Al Downing **Himself**; Ralph Garr **Himself**; Ken Griffey Jr. **Himself**; Milo Hamilton **Himself**; Jesse Jackson **Himself**; Maynard Jackson **Himself**; David Justice **Himself**; Mickey Mantle **Himself**; Eddie Mathews **Himself**; Willie Mays **Himself**; Willie McCovey **Himself**; Don Newcombe **Himself**; Frank Thomas **Himself**

ACTING CAST Dorian Harewood **Hank Aaron (voice-over)**; Bobby White Jr. **Hank Aaron I**; Glenn Griswold **Hank Aaron II**; David Crawford **Corneil**; Steve Coulter **Herbert Aaron Sr.**; Carol Mitchell-Leon **Estella Aaron**; Warren Young **Calvin Wardlaw**; Larry Thompson **Team owner**; Lenny Herb **Britt**; Brett Kinard **Cliff**; Bart Hansard **Scout**; Nicole Torre **Waitress**; Denny Wright **Rude reporter**

THE GAME The life of the all-time major league baseball home run king, Hank Aaron, is recounted in this Oscar-nominated documentary that utilizes live action footage, interviews, and dramatic re-creations.

The docudrama chronicles Aaron's rise to stardom. Beginning with his childhood games growing up in Alabama, the film takes us from his first professional stint with the Indianapolis Clowns through his rise in the major leagues and a very consistently productive career with the Braves franchise—including a world series title in '57, his historic home run that made him part of baseball lore, his final game, and his total of 755 homers that "gave the kids something to shoot for."

The film not only celebrates Aaron's achievements but also looks at the price he paid along the path to baseball immortality.

INSTANT REPLAY Filmmaker Tollin takes us deep into Aaron's world, using comments from his parents, siblings, wives, and kids as well as dramatizations of key moments in his career. He also presents the racial context of the times, addressing forced busing, the Klansmen, Martin Luther King, and the influence of Jackie Robinson.

Most strikingly, Tollin succeeds in conveying how what should have been a crowning moment in a legendary career was felt most of all as a relief. We feel for the new home run king when he says, "I'm just glad it's over."

Many of the game's greats marvel on camera at Aaron's milestones.

SANDY KOUFAX: "For me he was the toughest hitter to get out."

MICKEY MANTLE: "Hank was always just as good as Willie [Mays], Mickey, and the Duke [Snider], but he was stuck in Milwaukee."

MUHAMMAD ALI (speaking at a banquet with Aaron attending): "You are the greatest ballplayer of all time."

The result is a fitting tribute to one of the game's greatest performers.

OUTSIDE THE LINES In 1973 Milwaukee teen fan Sandy Tolan began a scrapbook on Hank Aaron. Tolan, who was white, also sent Aaron a letter encouraging him to overcome the racist threats he received, telling the slugger, "You're my hero. I believe in you." A quarter of a century later, Tolan met his teen idol, and out of that meeting came a book, *Me and Hank,* that used baseball as a prism to look at racism.... In 1994 a charity fund, the Chasing the Dream Foundation, was established to provide grants for kids with unique talents and limited financial resources.... Aaron turned his own dream into a 23-year career in major league baseball.... Aaron was named to the Hall of Fame in 1982.... Actor Dorian Harewood starred as Jesse Owens in a TV film about the Olympic star.... Teaming with partner Brian Robbins, Mike Tollin directed *Summer Catch* (2001) and produced HBO's sports agent series, *Arliss,* as well as the feature films *Dreamer* (2005), *Coach Carter* (2005), *Radio* (2003), *Hardball* (2001), and *Varsity Blues* (1999), and the documentaries *Hardwood Dreams* (1993), *Final Season* (1991), and *Hardwood Dreams: 10 Years Later* (2004).

ALL-STAR MOMENTS Just as Aaron connects with Al Downing's record-breaking pitch the film cuts to a dramatization of Aaron's youth to kick off the film.

Dramatization of northerners seeing blacks for the first time and reaching out to rub their skin. The black players say, without anger, "It don't come off."

Mets pitching great Tom Seaver telling the story of how Hank Aaron might have joined Willie Mays in the Giants outfield if the Braves hadn't offered just a few dollars more in negotiations.

Young Aaron being honored as a star minor leaguer in Jacksonville, Florida, when the money he is given is blown all over the field after the wind blows over the bag at home plate.

Aaron showing his hitting skills as a rookie, wearing #5 after being told he is too skinny to wear his coveted #44.

The 1957 World Series.

Hank's "performance" in a Wheaties commercial.

The climactic record-breaking 715th home run sequence.

The testimonials by the game's great players, young and old, marveling at what Aaron went through and what he accomplished.

HOME COURT ADVANTAGE Available on VHS.

TOP: The Hammer.

BOTTOM: Hank Aaron—then and now.

#86 VICTORY

Screenwriter Evan Jones, Yabo Yablonsky. **Director** John Huston. **Producer** Freddie Fields. **Cinematography** Gerry Fisher. **Editing** Roberto Silvi. **Production Design** Dennis Washington. **Music** Bill Conti. Paramount. 1981.

THE PLAYERS

Sylvester Stallone **Robert Hatch**; Michael Caine **Captain John Colby**; Max von Sydow **Major Karl von Steiner**; Daniel Massey **Colonel Waldron**; Tim Pigott-Smith **Rose**; Julian Curry **Sherlock**; Clive Morrison **The Forger**; Maurice Roeves **Pyrie**; Pelé **Corporal Luis Fernandez**; Bobby Moore **Terry Brady**; John Wark **Arthur**; Kevin O'Callaghan **Tony**; Co Prins **Pieter Van Beck**; Robin Turner **Schmidt**; Laurie Sivell **Dieter**; Arthur Brauss **Lutz**; Mike Summerbee **Sid**; Carole Laure **Renée**; Osvaldo Ardiles **Carlos Rey**; Kazimierz Deyna **Paul Wolchek**; Paul Van Himst **Michel Fileu**; Soren Lindsted **Erik**; Benoit Ferreux **Jean Paul**; Gary Waldhorn **Coach Mueller**; Hallvar Thoresen **Gunnar Hilsson**

THE GAME It is World War II, and Allied POWs are playing soccer in a Nazi camp. After observing them, a visiting German officer, Major Karl von Steiner (Max von Sydow), runs into a British officer, Captain John Colby (Michael Caine). As they talk, von Steiner, a former soccer player for the German national team, recognizes Colby, who was a player for his national team in England.

Von Steiner, who calls the war a regrettable mistake and prefers nations to "settle their differences on the pitch," comes up with the idea for a challenge soccer match, a "friendly" game to raise morale, between the prisoners and the local German army.

Both their superior officers, at first reluctant, take the idea and run with it—literally, in the case of the Allies. The Nazi propaganda machine sees a great opportunity and escalates this "local" game into a hyped-up confrontation of Allied all-stars drawn from multiple prisons against the mighty German national team at the hallowed Colombes Stadium in occupied France.

Colonel Waldron (Daniel Massey) sees the game as a chance to strike back at the Nazis by pulling off a mass escape at the stadium. However, to determine whether escape is even possible, Waldron asks American POW Robert Hatch (Sylvester Stallone) to sneak out of the camp, get to Paris, ask for the Resistance's help, check escape routes at the stadium, purposely get re-captured and return to camp for his report—all at the cost of the personal escape plans he's been making.

Hatch, who has made several futile attempts to bully his way onto Colby's squad as a goalie, is understandably reluctant ("This friggin' game is wrecking my life!") but agrees to do it.

After his recapture, Hatch lands in solitary confinement, and Waldron tells Colby that the only way to get him out before the match and assess his vital information is to appeal to von Steiner to release the American on the grounds that he is critical as the team's trainer.

Von Steiner denies the request, telling Colby he can get him another trainer. Colby, thinking fast, adds that Hatch is the team's goalie since their starter broke his arm. Von Steiner says if the German doctor he sends over verifies the prisoner's broken arm then he'll get Hatch released.

Back at the barracks, Colby is faced with the unpleasant task of telling Tony (Kevin O'Callaghan) not only that he won't be playing but also that they're going to have to break his arm!

With German guards all over stadium, the German marching band on the field,

Nazi radio announcers hyping the game, and the POW team warming up in their dressing room, members of the Resistance, dressed as road workers, climb down a nearby sewer and begin tunneling under the stadium toward the locker room.

The message is relayed to Hatch that the escape is on for halftime. In the stands, filled with local citizens, German guards, and Nazi officers, von Steiner's expectations of a "fair" game are quickly dashed when his superior officer informs him that with all that is at stake nothing could be left to chance, so the referees are under Nazi orders to ensure the German team doesn't lose to the prisoners. The honorable von Steiner is visibly disappointed but realizes his own precarious position and settles back uneasily to watch the tainted match.

The game begins and the Allies play well initially, but after some bad calls and non-calls by the refs, the Germans take a commanding 3-0 lead. Illegal, rough play by the Germans sends Allied star Luis Fernandez (Pelé) off the field with a broken rib while Hatch gets pummeled in the goal. Despite all that, the Allies manage to score a goal, making it 4-1 at half.

In the locker room, the Resistance breaks through and leads the Allies back down the sewer for their escape. As they climb down, however, some of the players really believe they can defeat the Germans and want to finish the game. Hatch can't believe what he is hearing, and a big argument ensues.

Amazingly, the players, including Hatch, return to the field, giving Waldron in the stands a near heart attack. The Allies quickly score a goal and the largely French crowd goes crazy. The crowd support spurs the team on even more; Hatch plays over his head making multiple saves, and even von Steiner perks up at the Allies' brilliant play. Eventually they draw to within one, down 4-3 with just a few minutes left. Luis gingerly returns to play and scores the tying goal on a spectacular bicycle kick. The Germans, however, on a dubious call are awarded a penalty kick that could win the game. Hatch makes a diving save, the Allied players celebrate, and the crazed fans storm past the guards onto the field. The fearless, jubilant fans slip jackets over the players and sneak them out of the stadium to freedom, lost among the crowd.

INSTANT REPLAY
"It's all madness." Silly? At times. Improbable? Perhaps. Ridiculous (Down 4-1 at half time with your star player injured and you blow

TOP: Major Karl von Steiner (Max von Sydow, left) and Captain John Colby (Michael Caine, right), former soccer players, talk about the sport.

BOTTOM: American prisoner Robert Hatch (Sylvester Stallone) escapes to secure help and information for a larger prisoner breakout planned for halftime of the match between the Allied prisoners and the Germans.

LEFT: The prisoners constantly have their backs to the wall.

off escaping to freedom to return for the completion of the game)? You decide. But, at the very least, this *Great Escape* meets *The Longest Yard* is beautifully shot.

The outstanding cinematography by Gerry Fisher and Roberto Silvi's editing, especially the difficult soccer sequences, carries the film. Bill Conti's score is dramatic and uplifting in the vein of his *Rocky* work.

The portrayal of Hatch—the stereotypical "ugly American," unskilled and uninformed about the game, smartly played by Stallone—as the one who cares far more about his freedom than about the game itself is used to demonstrate, albeit exaggeratedly, the significance that soccer holds for the rest of the world. The character of Karl von Steiner, rendered skillfully by Max von Sydow, stands for honor, a gentleman's agreement even between enemies.

Victory has several poignant scenes and important reminders of the real horrors of war sprinkled throughout its 117 minutes. These include the appearance in the POW camp of the more-than-half-starved prisoners who arrive from the East European death camps.

The movie is also quite comical in some of its more ludicrous moments, such as the pudgy POW Colby (Michael Caine) shouting, "Leave it, it's mine," to real-life soccer greats in chasing down a ball in the match, or Fernandez (Pelé) pleading with Hatch not to escape at halftime. Despite actors who couldn't play soccer and soccer players who couldn't act—and even if one can't overlook the fans running from the stadium wearing long hair and clothes from the late '70s—*Victory* works.

OUTSIDE THE LINES The last big game played at Paris's Colombes Stadium was the 1938 World Cup Final, won by Italy 4-2 over Hungary.... Inspiration for the film came from a 1962 Hungarian film by Zoltan Fabri, *Two Halftimes in Hell*.... After a series of defeats at the hands of malnourished players from Kiev in 1942, the Nazis brought in a Luftwaffe all-star team and threatened the Russian players with death if they dared to win, in what became known as "The Match of Death." Kiev won anyway, 5-3. Later the Gestapo would execute one player who was discovered to be a spy, and send his teammates to a concentration camp. A monument to those players stands outside Ukraine's main stadium in Kiev.... Stallone was also writing the script for *Rocky III* at the time of this film's production.... *Victory* was released abroad under

ABOVE: Colby (Caine, center) leads the halftime escape only to be convinced that the prisoners can win their match against the Nazis.

RIGHT: Luis Fernandez (Pelé) is instrumental in the prisoners' come-from-behind win.

John Huston (right) also directed the boxing drama 'Fat City.'

the title *Escape to Victory*.... Filming was interrupted by a SAG strike.... The Allied team included real-life soccer greats Bobby Moore (England), Osvaldo Ardiles (Argentina), Kazimierz Deyna (Poland), and Pelé (Brazil) among others.... The film was shot primarily in Hungary.... Reportedly pop star Elton John turned down a small role.... Stallone starred in a remake of Michael Caine's *Get Carter* (1971) in 2000.... Caine had worked with Huston previously in *The Man Who Would Be King* (1975).... Stallone, with zero soccer experience despite attending school in Switzerland, was tutored in his position by veteran British goalie Paul Cooper.... Pelé, who designed the film's plays, is soccer's all-time leading scorer with 1,279 goals in 1,363 games between 1956 and 1977, and is the only three-time World Cup winner.

ALL-STAR MOMENTS A defiant von Steiner (Max von Sydow) stands and applauds the Allies' play despite the glares from his Nazi superiors.

Hatch (Stallone) asks the Forger (Clive Morrison) when his fake ID papers will be ready. The Forger replies, "Well, you must realize this is my busy time. Everybody wants to escape in the good weather. Just be patient."

All of the montages of the game action.

As Colby (Caine) leads the POW players out of the hut wearing brand new red sweat suits, the other prisoners lying about shout insults and whistle derisively.

At the stadium a worried SS officer tells von Steiner, "This is madness; there's too many people together for security!" Von Steiner calmly replies, "It's all madness."

Assorted replays and angles of Fernandez's (Pelé) bicycle kick that scores the tying goal.

HOME COURT ADVANTAGE Available on VHS and DVD. Warner Bros. has released this title as a single DVD and a two-disc set with *American Flyers*.

#85 THE BINGO LONG TRAVELING ALL-STARS AND MOTOR KINGS

Screenwriters Hal Barwood, Matthew Robbins. **Director** John Badham. **Producer** Rob Cohen. **Cinematography** Bill Butler. **Editing** David Rawlins. **Music** William Goldstein. **Costume Design** Bernard Johnson. **Production Design** Lawrence Paull. Universal. 1976.

THE PLAYERS Billy Dee Williams **Bingo Long**; James Earl Jones **Leon Carter**; Richard Pryor **Charlie Snow**; Ted Ross **Sallison "Sallie" Potter, Owner Ebony Aces**; Mabel King **Bertha, Owner Charcoal Kings**; Rico Dawson **Willie Lee**; Sam Briston **Louis Keystone**; Jophery Brown **Champ Chambers**; Tony Burton **Isaac**; DeWayne Jessie **Rainbow (bat boy)**; Leon Wagner **Fat Sam**; Stan Shaw **Esquire Joe Callaway**; John McCurry **Walter Murchman**; Sam Laws **Henry Dunbar, Owner Elite Giants**; Alvin Childress **Horace, Owner Black Crackers**; Ken Foree **Honey (goon)**; Carl Gordon **Mack (goon)**; Ahna Capri **Prostitute**; Joel Fluellen **Mr. Holland**; Jester Hairston **Furry Taylor**; Sarina Grant **Pearline**; Steve Anderson **One-armed player**; Dero Austin **Midget catcher**; Lidia Kristen **Nurse**; Marcia McBroom **Violet**; Fred Covington **Auctioneer**; Emmett Ashford **Umpire**

THE GAME Baseball is deeply embedded as part of our national fabric, and its long history is rife with rags-to-riches stories. But in 1939, when this film is set, discrimination blocked the dreams of many black ballplayers. Though they occasionally played exhibition games in major league parks like Yankee Stadium, their opportunities were limited by segregation.

Playing in a Negro league, star pitcher Bingo Long (Billy Dee Williams) is fed up with the exploitative ways of Ebony Aces owner Sallie Potter (Ted Ross). When the frugal owner drops the seriously injured player Rainbow (DeWayne Jessie) from the team, leaving his teammate broke with no future, Bingo decides he's had enough and forms his own distinctive team, one with a little extra showmanship, an equivalent to basketball's Harlem Globetrotters.

Bingo names his all-star squad The Bingo Long Traveling All-Stars and Motor Kings because they barnstorm from town to town stuffed into two roadsters.

Naturally, this development doesn't sit well with the league's owners, as most have lost a key player, a major draw, to Bingo's unit and are having to operate on an even thinner margin as a result.

Potter gathers his fellow owners together and they devise ways to drive Bingo out of business. Their first action is to organize a boycott against the Motor Kings. This forces Bingo to play almost exclusively against amateur white teams like the House of David Jewish team.

Bingo does his best to keep the team afloat, using a clowning-around approach to appear nonthreatening to the largely rural, white spectators. But soon after Potter's goons attack Motor King teammate Charlie Snow (Richard Pryor), Leon Carter (James Earl Jones) quits. Bingo carries on without his star slugger.

With pressure on his pocketbook as well as from his fellow owners, led by Bertha (Mabel King), the lone female boss, Potter finally offers Bingo a deal. If the Motor Kings can beat his Negro all-star squad in a winner-take-all game, Bingo's team can officially join the league. If the Motor Kings lose, all the players must go back to their old teams, playing on half salary through the following season.

Confident of victory, Bingo agrees to the deal. He visits Leon, and though the slugger seems amenable, his return to the squad for the big game isn't promised. Bingo, ever the optimist, is confident his slugger will appear.

To hedge his bet, however, Potter has Leon kidnapped. During the big game Leon escapes and arrives in time to help the Motor Kings win. As they celebrate, the Motor Kings learn that one of their own, Esquire Joe Calloway (Stan Shaw), is headed to the Brooklyn Dodgers.

This happy event, the initial effort of breaking the color barrier, also foreshadows the end of the Negro Leagues, making the Motor Kings' victory somewhat pyrrhic.

INSTANT REPLAY Some of the sport's greatest players, like Cool Papa Bell and Josh Gibson, are little known to the general public because their feats were conducted on the other side of the tracks; thus, accurate records of their impressive careers are incomplete and have become obscured.

Though this picture is rooted in historical fact, its high-spirited look at a relatively underexposed aspect of black American history tends to downplay the serious enforced segregation these quality athletes had to endure. A more serious look at the same subject can be seen in *Soul of the Game* (1996).

Undoubtedly, *The Bingo Long Traveling All-Stars and Motor Kings* is friendly and entertaining. While some (including many veterans of the Negro leagues) felt it was short-sighted and irresponsible, the filmmakers deliberately chose a light, understated tone. They showed the teams' experiences and confrontations, and how the players chose to handle them, without trying to tell the audience what to think.

Indeed, the ways Bingo and his teammates elect to deal with the inequities they faced every day are part of the movie's charm. The script intelligently reflects some of those challenges, including having to deal with black club owners who operated just as the white owners of the majors did, exploiting their players financially.

John Badham's directorial film debut is an observant if formulaic effort with fairly predictable plot twists. Less frequent use of close-up framing would have provided a better sense of time and place. Badham's wise decision to allow his cast to improvise within his given framework was particularly effective in Richard Pryor's case. Pryor appears as a scheming ballplayer using various ethnic angles, from Cuban to American Indian, to break baseball's color barrier.

Badham also elicits one of the best performances of Billy Dee Williams's career. As Bingo Long, Williams's joyous exuberance and inexhaustible positivity (such as when he is put to the test of trying to keep his team together when they have to pick potatoes to keep going financially, and a couple of players quit) is infectious and stylish without being overly flamboyant.

Billy Dee's charm and grace match up well with his larger-than-life partner, James Earl Jones, as the Ruthian (or Gibsonian) Leon Carter; their camaraderie endures through the highs and lows of striving for success together.

One night, Leon explains lucidly to Bingo the slave/owner relationship in baseball. Leon's "be your own man" talk inspires Bingo. Jones delivers some of the film's hard truths straight up in his role of an exploited, very talented, and very frustrated ballplayer, not unlike what he did in *The Great White Hope* boxing drama.

The supporting cast is strong down the line. Mabel King as a bombastic team owner is particularly memorable, especially when she storms into the men's steam room to participate in the owners' latest scheme to bring down Bingo's team, or uses her power as an owner to get her players to sleep with her. Tony Burton gives a fine performance as one of these players; also notable is Joel Fluellen as the store owner who not only books Bingo's games but uses his own vaudeville experience to instruct the players on how to preen and strut down the rural main streets of small town USA to promote their local appearances.

The games themselves are well staged thanks to Badham's multi-camera coverage and fine athletic performances by both the actors and former pro players like Leon Wagner. Occasional special effects and smart use of slow motion, such as during Bingo's key strikeout pitch, are effective touches.

Lawrence Paull's production design and Bernard Johnson's costume work are captured magnificently by Bill Butler's photography. William Goldstein's rousing Dixieland-type music themes and Thelma Houston's performance of "Razzle Dazzle" are a fine complement.

The Bingo Long Traveling All-Stars and Motor Kings does a respectable job of juggling melodrama and farce. The film shows that it takes extraordinary athletic talent to perform the game overtly for laughs…yet the frustrations of the real ballplayers unable to ply their considerable skills in the majors must have been like the sadness behind a clown's tears.

OUTSIDE THE LINES Among the directorial candidates for this film was Steven Spielberg.... John Badham's next film would be *Saturday Night Fever* (1977).... Alvin Childress, one of the team owners in the picture, was Amos in the 1950s television series *Amos 'n' Andy*.... Ted Ross won a Tony award for his Broadway performance as the Cowardly Lion in *The Wiz*.... Leon Wagner was a major league all-star for the Los Angeles Angels.... Richard Pryor starred in the auto racing feature *Greased Lightning* (1977).... Jophery Brown, a former pitcher for the Cubs, was the film's stunt coordinator.... James Earl Jones was featured in the baseball films *Field of Dreams* (1989) and *The Sandlot* (1993).... Rico Dawson played infield for the Cardinals and the White Sox.... The film was based on William Brashler's novel.... In the book Bingo Long was a catcher based on the legendary Josh Gibson and Leon Carter was modeled after Satchel Paige, but during the casting the positions were switched overtly because Billy Dee had some pitching background.... Tony Burton was Apollo Creed's trainer in *Rocky* and worked on TV's boxing film *The Ray Mancini Story*.... Ball games were staged in two Georgia minor league parks, Macon's Luther Williams Field and Savannah's Grayson Stadium.... Billy Dee Williams starred as football great Gale Sayers in *Brian's Song* (1970).... James Earl Jones portrayed a champion boxer earning an Oscar nomination in *The Great White Hope* (1970) and prior to that won a Tony for the same role on Broadway.... Badham directed Kevin Costner in the cycling film *American Flyer* (1985).... Jones portrayed Malcolm X in *The Greatest* (1977), a film about Muhammad Ali.... Burton appeared in volleyball's *Side Out* (1986).... Stan Shaw starred as boxing great Joe Louis in TNT's *The Court Martial of Jackie Robinson* (1990).

ALL-STAR MOMENTS "What some people won't do": opening newsreel scene of a man eating razor blades, lying on bed of nails, and putting out a cigarette on his tongue.

When Bingo (Williams) shows up unexpectedly to talk about his idea with Leon (Jones), who is "entertaining" Pearline (Sarina Grant) in bed, she quickly covers herself up and runs to lock herself in the bathroom. "Oh, no!" she yells. "You didn't say nuttin' about no threesomes. I got a generous soul, but I ain't no Santa Claus."

The athleticism of the ballplayers when they perform for laughs.

The sequence where Bingo is making calls to recruit players across the country for his team. One is particularly timely as Isaac (Burton) is being forced to make love to Bertha, the team's plump lady owner (King), and is all too glad to get out.

The look of the House of David baseball team.

Bertha bursting into the men's steam room wearing a pink towel and hat over her oversized body, demanding to have her say to the other owners (all men) about keeping the league alive, reminding Potter that "we're starving in Chicago."

Charlie's (Pryor) suave pick-up moves with a lady at the Red Feather bar, which impress his shy teammate Esquire Joe (Shaw), but almost get him killed.

HOME COURT ADVANTAGE Available on VHS and DVD.

ABOVE: Bingo (Billy Dee Williams, right) asks Leon Carter (James Earl Jones) to resume playing for the All-Stars.

FACING PAGE: The Traveling All-Stars show their moves, dancing into the next town on their barnstorming tour.

#84 JUNIOR BONNER

Screenwriter Jeb Rosebrook. **Director** Sam Peckinpah. **Producer** Joe Wizan. **Cinematography** Lucien Ballard. **Editing** Robert Wolfe. **Music** Jerry Fielding. **Casting** Lynn Stalmaster. **Art Direction** Ted Haworth. Cinerama. 1972.

THE PLAYERS Steve McQueen **Junior Bonner**; Robert Preston **Ace Bonner**; Ida Lupino **Elvira Bonner**; Joe Don Baker **Curley Bonner**; Ben Johnson **Buck Roan**; Bill McKinney **Red Terwilige**; Mary Murphy **Ruth Bonner**; Barbara Leigh **Charmagne**; Sandra Deel **Nurse Arlis**; Don Barry **Homer Rutledge**; Charles Gray **Burt**; Matthew Peckinpah **Tim Bonner**; Sundown Spencer **Nick Bonner**; Dub Taylor **Del**

THE GAME A throwback individualist and rodeo star in the twilight of his career, Junior Bonner (Steve McQueen) is aching after his defeat by a tough bull named Sunshine. Still, he's happy to be returning to his hometown of Prescott, Arizona for the annual Frontier Days rodeo celebration, for the chance to see his parents and brother. Junior is also determined to get the bull's owner, Buck Roan (Ben Johnson), to give him another shot at riding Sunshine. If Junior hangs on for the minimum eight seconds, he'll have a chance at some good prize money. Perhaps just as importantly, the old cowboy will get a measure of redemption and regain some pride.

When Junior returns to Prescott, however, he finds that his parents, Ace (Robert Preston) and Elvira (Ida Lupino), have split up and his brother, Curley (Joe Don Baker), is getting rich selling off chunks of his father's land.

Ace has always been a dreamer, and his latest get-rich-quick scheme is ranching and gold digging in Australia. Curley is tired of Ace squandering money on losing propositions and refuses to front his father the money, keeping him on a tight allowance.

A poignant conversation between Ace and Elvira at an informal family reunion in a bar exemplifies their relationship:

ACE: By hook or crook I'm going to Australia.

ELVIRA: Well, you were always good at putting distance between us. I don't give a damn anymore. As far as I'm concerned you can go to hell or Australia. They're both the same to me.

A: Well, they're both down under. (They share a chuckle.)

E: Dreams. Sweet talk. That's all you are.

A: If you stay with me. I'll sweeten the dreams. (Elvira slaps him.)

A: Sure as hell I had that coming. But I'm leaving for good.

E: Well, then, all we have is today.

A: You've seen one rodeo, you've seen them all. (They walk off arm in arm.)

Rodeo day arrives. After the calf roping, bronco busting, and other events take place, Junior flashes back to his last disappointing ride of Sunshine. The moment is at hand. The announcer reminds the crowd that "bull riding is the most dangerous event in rodeo." Junior uses all his experience to become the first successful rider of Sunshine and wins nearly $1,000.

Old cowboy Ace Bonner (Robert Preston, left) reveals his plans to live in Australia to his son, rodeo veteran Junior (Steve McQueen, right).

After saying goodbye to his mother, Junior stops off and uses his winnings to buy his father a plane ticket to Australia so that Ace can pursue one more dream. Soon Junior is heading down the highway.

INSTANT REPLAY Steve McQueen as Junior Bonner personifies the dying old ways of the West. Stubbornly existing by the old code and gradually fading into the sunset, Sam Peckinpah's lead character is reminiscent of figures from the director's other Westerns like *Ride the High Country* and *The Ballad of Cable Hogue*. All are proud folks who'd rather die clinging to their beloved values of a bygone era, living by guts and their word, than align themselves with the greed, corruption, and impersonality of modern life with its relentless pursuit of the quick buck.

Ironically for a filmmaker with a penchant for heavy on-screen violence (*Straw Dogs, The Wild Bunch*), outside of a couple of flying fists and the physical danger inherent in rodeo, *Junior Bonner* is one of Peckinpah's gentlest pictures. This is a personal and insightful character study about the demise of the way of life of a rugged individualist ill at ease in the modern West. The movie's most symbolic moment is Junior watching the old family home being bulldozed for new development, under his business-driven brother's supervision.

The telling scene between the two brothers, Junior (McQueen) and Curley (Joe Don Baker), is a far-reaching moment that also symbolizes the battle between the lone individual and the faceless crowd. Curley has leveled the family land and put his father on an allowance, and is developing a trailer park with a rosy outlook for success. He tells Junior, "I'm working on my first million and you're still working on eight seconds."

Peckinpah's work is supported by a rich cast working off a spare but knowing script by Jeb Rosebrook. The leathery looks and drawl of Ben Johnson as a rodeo livestock supplier are the real deal. Joe Don Baker is convincing as a representative of the modern entrepreneurial spirit with no ties to the rodeo beloved by his father and brother. He's emblematic of a new generation of driven hustlers doing whatever it takes to be

Mr. and Mrs. Bonner (Preston and Ida Lupino).

a financial success. After all, he's not only leveled his father's land, he plans on selling his mother's home and putting her to work in one of his retail shops.

Speaking of mother, Ida Lupino (Elvira) is wonderfully matched with Robert Preston (Ace) as the estranged parents who love each other but realize they can no longer live together. The quiet pain she carries inside appears free of bitterness, though it seems she is the one who pays the price for her husband's irresponsibility.

The stellar Robert Preston (Ace) frankly steals the show as the still-rascally and genial raconteur who's too full of positive energy and fancy dreams to acknowledge he's past his prime. He contrasts well with McQueen as his son.

Steve McQueen's familiar low-key, steadfast solo-operator characterization is on display again here in a smart bit of casting. As the cowboy who's come to the realization that he can't go home again, yet uncertain of where clinging to his old ways will take him, McQueen is engaging; his performance comes across as almost effortless.

Lucien Ballard's fine photography and the exciting rodeo footage succeed in capturing the beauty and danger of the sport. A veteran Peckinpah cinematographer, Ballard also brilliantly presents the visual splendors of the American West's natural beauty—sparkling lakes, desert vegetation, farm fields—all against luminous sunrises and sunsets.

Junior Bonner is a well-observed examination of the values of the Old West, a favorite personal theme of Peckinpah. It is something also done well in *The Lusty Men* and *Seabiscuit*. In its rodeo action, the picture is comparable to Cliff Robertson's *J. W. Coop*.

An insightful study of the determined individual trying to swim upstream against the powerful current of changing times, this picture is also a telling family drama within a real slice of Americana. It is one of the acclaimed director's most underrated films

OUTSIDE THE LINES Director Peckinpah's son Matthew, appears in the film.... Steve McQueen's sporting resume includes the motorcycle documentary *On Any Sunday* (1971) and auto racing's *LeMans* (1971).... This was Robert Preston and Ida Lupino's first major film in years, as the former focused on theater and the actress wrote and directed.... Peckinpah and McQueen worked together again on *The Getaway* (1972).... One of McQueen's first feature films was boxing's *Somebody Up There Likes Me* (1956).... Ben Johnson appeared in the Muhammad Ali film *The Greatest* (1977) and won a Best Supporting Actor Oscar for *The Last Picture Show* (1971).... Joe Don Baker performed in baseball's *The Natural* (1984).... Joe Wizan and Michael Borofsky's other producing credits include the fight film *Split Decisions* (1988).... Production designer Edward Haworth applied those skills to *Mr. Baseball* (1992) and won an Academy Award for his art direction of *Sayonara* (1957).

ALL-STAR MOMENTS The bulldozer destroying his father's home as Junior (McQueen) barely saves his car from the same fate.

The assorted scenes from the Frontier Rodeo in Prescott, Arizona.

A barroom brawl is halted when the house band plays the national anthem and the combatants stop and salute.

Bullriding footage.

HOME COURT ADVANTAGE Available on VHS and DVD.

#83 BEND IT LIKE BECKHAM

Screenwriters Gurinder Chadha, Paul Mayeda Berges, Guljit Bindra. **Director** Gurinder Chadha. **Producers** Haneet Vaswani, Gurinder Chadha, Ulrich Felsberg, Russel Fischer, Simon Franks, Zygi Kamasa. **Cinematography** Jong Lin. **Editing** Justin Krish. **Music** Bally Sagoo, Melanie Chisholm, Craig Pruess. **Production Design** Nick Ellis. Fox. 2002.

THE PLAYERS Parminder Nagra **Jesminder "Jess" Bhamra**; Keira Knightley **Juliette "Jules" Paxton**; Jonathan Rhys-Meyers **Joe**; Anupam Kher **Mr. Bhamra**; Archie Panjabi **Pinky Bhamra**; Shaznay Lewis **Mel**; Frank Harper **Alan Paxton**; Juliet Stevenson **Paula Paxton**; Shaheen Khan **Mrs. Bhamra**; Ameeet Chana **Tony**; Pooja Shah **Meena**; Paven Virk **Bubbly**; Preeya Kalidas **Monica**; Trey Farley **Taz**; Saraj Chaudhry **Sonny**; Imran Ali **Gary**; Kulvinder Ghir **Teetu**; Harvey Virdi **Teetu's mother**; Ash Varrez **Teetu's father**; Adlyn Ross **Elderly aunt**; Shobu Kapoor **Polly**; Zorha Sehgal **Biji**; Ahsen Bhatti **Nairobi grandson**; Tanveer Ghani **Video man**; Nina Wadia **Wedding guest**; Gary Lineker **Himself**; Alan Hansen **Himself**; John Barnes **Himself**; John Motson **Himself (voice)**

THE GAME British teenager Jess Bhamra (Parminder Nagra) wants to pursue her soccer talents but is thwarted at every move by her strict Sikh Indian parents from East Africa (Anupam Kher, Shaheen Khan). Spotting her talents one day, fellow teen Jules Paxton (Keira Knightley) gets Jess a tryout on her club team. They become fast friends.

As her sister Pinky (Archie Panjabi) prepares for her big Indian wedding, Jess spends most of her time scheming and deceiving her parents so that she can continue to practice and play with hopes, planted by her new friend Jules, of perhaps playing professionally or at least earning a college scholarship.

Both girls fancy Joe, their coach (Jonathan Rhys-Meyers). During a road trip to a tournament in Hamburg, the girls have a falling-out when Jules sees Jess and Joe just as they are about to kiss. To make matters worse, Jess's parents find out about her soccer and demand that she give it up and become more of a traditional Sikh woman like her mother and her sister.

Despite her coach's appeal to her parents, it looks like Jess's playing days are over. But at Pinky's wedding, Jess's father, tired of seeing his daughter so unhappy, allows her to sneak out for the big game. Jess and Jules play well enough to earn scholarships. They also resume their friendship, while Jess and Joe leave open the possibility of romance when she returns to Britain.

INSTANT REPLAY Writer/director Gurinder Chadha takes the serious look at cultural assimilation seen in *East Is East,* and incorporates the Indian matrimonial rituals at the core of *Monsoon Wedding,* along with elements of *My Big Fat Greek Wedding* and *Billy Elliot,* into a humorous, uplifting stew that explores cultural and generational differences in a traditional Sikh family in modern London.

As she did in her previous film, *What's Cooking?,* Chadha shows an ability to portray multiculturalism with an affectionate and lighthearted touch.

Certainly one could say that the film is filled with stereotypes, but these caricatures undeniably help connect the story to a broader audience. In this regard, the writer/director is ably assisted by tremendous actors who find great fun in the stereotypes.

Anchoring the proceedings is Bollywood great, Anupam Kher. In his first English picture, Kher delivers some genuine warmth as a strict father with lost dreams, torn between cultural mandates and his daughter's atypical ambitions.

Jess (Parminder Nagra) admires her football hero, David Beckham.

A real find is Parminder Nagra. In her film debut here, she imbues Jess with a rebellious spirit, likability, and a physically exuberant determination. While she is a typical Brit teen, she's also under the roof of traditional Sikh parents and the influence of that culture. The engaging Nagra, in sneaking off to practice like Billy Elliot and his ballet lessons, is a joy to behold.

Keira Knightley shows a lot of spirit as Jess's leggy teammate. Both leads are burdened by overbearing mothers...who are terrific.

Shaheen Khan, playing Jess's mother, who sees kicking a ball as utterly incompatible with making a good chapatti, embodies the strict Sikh Indian parent from the old country.

Truly Madly Deeply's Juliet Stevenson is a scene-stealer as Jules's soccer-naïve mother and is greatly supported by the dependable Frank Harper as her spouse. Perplexed by her tomboyish daughter, Juliet delivers the definitive line, "There's a reason Sporty Spice is the only one without a feller."

Jonathan Rhys-Meyers is capable as the soccer coach and love interest of the two leads.

Speaking of soccer, the game sequences are edited reasonably well and somewhat evocative of Oliver Stone's *Any Given Sunday*. That is, they are tight, frenetic, loud and sometimes a bit of a mishmash, but include well-choreographed sequences that display the allure of the sport.

The opening dream sequence, where Jess is digitally inserted into the TV footage, is clumsily edited. Overall, though, Justin Krish's editing does elicit some laughs with its timeliness to reaction shots, and really shines in the juxtaposition shots between

Pinky's wedding and Jess's climactic game. The whole scenario is enhanced by Bally Sagoo's music.

With all the aforementioned influences the picture incorporates, *Bend It Like Beckham* undemandingly and affectionately offers a positive coming-of-age story of a young woman who rebels against her traditional cultural role. This Cinderella story with an ethnic twist is an entertaining quasi-social-documentary story about overcoming cultural and gender barriers as a young woman strives to reach her dreams.

OUTSIDE THE LINES

Many of the lead's teammates were professional soccer players.... Most of the wedding guests were writer/director Chadha's relatives.... The team playing Manchester United is the Belgian squad RSC Anderlecht.... Because soccer isn't as well known in the States, reportedly American marketing personnel suggested changing the title to "Move It Like Mia" in reference to former U.S. star Mia Hamm.... Anupam Kher has starred in more than 150 Bollywood films.... The professional team depicted in the film, the Women's United Soccer Association (WUSA), folded just weeks after the picture's American release.

TOP: Director and cowriter Gurinder Chadha.

BOTTOM: Jess with Joe, her coach (Jonathan Rhys-Meyers).

ALL-STAR MOMENTS

In a clothing store, shopping for bras, Jules's mother (Stevenson) grabs her daughter's breasts in making a point.

Jules's father (Harper) explaining the game of football to his wife using kitchen utensils and condiments.

Jess's father, slipping into the stands to watch his daughter play, one moment proud of her athletic talents, then ashamed when she gets tossed out for unsportsmanlike conduct.

Jules's mother embarrasses her daughter again when she yells at Jess in front of her sister and mother, accusing Jess of being a lesbian and berating her for wearing her shoes (lent by Jules for Pinky's wedding).

Jess's friend Tony (Ameet Chana) convinces Jess to leave her sister's wedding for the big game, and her father approves.

After the girls have gone to America to play soccer, Joe and Jess's father are playing cricket in the park across from Mr. Bhamra's house.

HOME COURT ADVANTAGE

Available on VHS and DVD. Fox has released this title in several DVD packages. It is part of two three-disc sets: one with *Divorce* and *The Banger Sisters,* and the other with *Drumline* and *Like Mike.* It also comes in two-disc sets with *Drumline* or *In America,* and as a single release.

#82 It Happens Every Spring

Screenwriter Valentine Davies (story with Shirley Smith). **Director** Lloyd Bacon. **Producer** William Perlberg. **Cinematography** Joseph MacDonald. **Editing** Bruce Pierce, Dorothy Spencer. **Music** Leigh Harline. **Musical Direction** Lionel Newman. Fox. 1949.

THE PLAYERS Ray Milland **Vernon Simpson**; Jean Peters **Deborah Greenleaf**; Paul Douglas **Monk Lanigan**; Ed Begley **Stone**; Ted de Corsia **Jimmy Dolan**; Ray Collins **Professor Greenleaf**; Jessie Landis **Mrs. Greenleaf**; Alan Hale Jr. **Schmidt**; Bill Murphy **Isbell**; Edward Keane **Bell**; William Green **Professor Forsythe**; Harry Chesire **Doctor**; John Butler **Fan**; Gene Evans **Mueller**; Al Eben **Parker**; Jane Van Duser **Ms. Mengalstein**; Ray Teal **Mac**; Mickey Simpson **Policeman**; Johnny Colkins **Boy**; Ruth Lee **Ms. Collins**; Debra Paget **Alice**

THE GAME Vernon Simpson (Ray Milland) is a chemistry teacher at a university and a diehard baseball fan. When a baseball from a kid's game smashes through his lab window, Vernon inadvertently discovers a strange occurrence: the now chemical-soaked baseball has become wood-repellent.

The next day Vernon tries out the formula by tossing pitches to some students who are dumbfounded when the ball curves away from their bats. His catcher, Schmidt (Alan Hale Jr.), yells out, "Wow! Did you see the hop on that ball? That's a regular dipsy doodle you got there, Professor. How'd you do it?" The professor replies that his pitch is "the result of a great deal of scientific research."

Vernon impresses Stone (Ed Begley), the owner of the St. Louis pro baseball club, during an impromptu tryout and is offered a contract. Management assigns the rookie to a veteran ballplayer, catcher Monk Lanigan (Paul Douglas), as a roommate because they think the scientist is a little crazy and will need someone to look out for him. Fearing a negative reaction by the school, Vernon calls himself "Kelly" to disguise his background. Vernon soon learns there's a massive hunt for him because his pretty coed girlfriend, Deborah Greenleaf (Jean Peters), the daughter of the university president, hasn't seen or heard from him in days. Vernon sends her a note asking her to trust him that things will work out and that he'll soon have enough money for them to get married.

Less trusting is Debbie's mother (Jessie Landis). When she runs into Vernon at a train station, she overhears the group of ballplayers he is standing with talking tough, mistakes them for gangsters, and now thinks her future son-in-law is mixed up with the mob.

Vernon has always dreamed of being a major league pitcher, and soon he is living his dream. His success draws unwanted attention from the press, who want to know more about this sudden star. Vernon tells them he learned to pitch in his free time in the military while based in southeast Asia.

Not sure what to believe—is her fiancé a pro pitcher, a gangster, or a scientist?—Debbie eventually trusts Vernon and begins enthusiastically supporting his baseball play.

Vernon has helped get his team to the championship game. Debbie, her mother, and friends are all in the stands rooting for him. The special formula that has helped make Vernon a pitching phenom (and that he passed off to his roommate as a hair tonic) is all gone; even the little bit he got by rubbing Lanigan's hair in the dugout between innings has worn off.

Now, in the late stages of a close game and holding onto a one-run lead, Vernon is pitching with the tying run on. Down to their last out, the opposition's big hitter smashes a line drive right up the middle. Vernon makes a desperate lunge and spears the ball barehanded. His team wins but Vernon's career is over; that last out fractured his hand and doctors say his pitching days are done.

At the train station Monk tries to ease Vernon's sadness by reminding him that he had the greatest single season a pitcher has ever had. Vernon is also concerned he won't be able to get his old job back.

MONK: [That] don't make no sense.

VERNON: A lot of things don't make sense, Monk. I was a chemistry teacher. I can tell you that now. And the sum of money I received for teaching science to youth of this state for an entire year was a little less than I got in a single afternoon for tossing a five-ounce sphere past a young man holding a wooden stick.

Arriving home Vernon is stunned when Debbie and her father are part of a group that has assembled to meet him. When he asks for his old job back, the president says no, but then adds that Vernon has been named the director of a new research laboratory, courtesy of Stone, who paid for it.

INSTANT REPLAY *It Happens Every Spring* is literally a screwball comedy.

The fact that it sustains amusing nonsense from a single wacky notion is a credit to writers Shirley Smith and Valentine Davies (*Miracle on 34th Street*) and director Lloyd Bacon, who show amazing skill in devising a myriad of variations on one joke. Bacon's pacing keeps the fragile plot going using the right touches of complications, romance, and business to throw a complete game.

Despite his suspect pitching form (though not bad for someone from baseball-less Wales), Ray Milland's subtle comedic timing and intelligence in his evolution from absentminded professor to mysterious baseball sensation is a delight to witness.

Jean Peters is nice to look at and adds some needed drama and romance, but the comedic trophy goes to Paul Douglas's Neanderthal catcher. Douglas's cynical veteran ballplayer has a natural feel.

The game sequences are edited well.

Scientist Vernon Simpson (Ray Milland) discovers a formula that will turn him into a star baseball pitcher.

The picture is helped through some crucial camera effects with the horsehide spheroid by Fred Sersen under Joe McDonald's supervision.

It Happens Every Spring is a pleasant bit of zaniness.

OUTSIDE THE LINES

Valentine Davies won an Academy Award for the original book *Miracle on 34th Street* (1947).... Davies also received an Oscar nomination for this story with Shirley Smith.... William Perlberg produced both those films.... He also produced boxing's *Golden Boy* (1939).... Perlberg's other baseball credit is *Rhubarb* (1951), which also starred Ray Milland.... Scenes were shot at Los Angeles's Wrigley Field and at USC.... Lloyd Bacon directed another baseball farce, *Kill the Umpire* (1950).... Paul Douglas played pro football and was a sportscaster at one time.... His football skills came into play when he starred in *The Guy Who Came Back* (1951).... He appeared in two other baseball features, *Rhubarb* and *Angels in the Outfield* (1951).... Lionel Newman composed the score for boxing's *The Great White Hope* (1970) and *The Harder They Fall* (1956).... Newman's other sporting credits include *Father Was a Fullback* (1949), *The Guy Who Came Back* (1951), *The Pride of St. Louis* (1952), *The Kid From Left Field* (1953), *The Racers* (1955), and *When the Legends Die* (1972).... Jean Peters was married to Howard Hughes.... Bacon directed *Knute Rockne: All-American* (1940) and *Indianapolis Speedway* (1939).... The director also performed as an actor in Charlie Chaplin's *Battling Charlie* (1915).... Alan Hale Jr. would gain fame as the Skipper on the *Gilligan's Island* TV series.

ALL-STAR MOMENTS

Vernon (Milland) first tries out his formula on some college students. His pitching is magical as the ball darts about unconventionally no matter where the batter swings.

Recurring gag where Vernon's baseball roommate Monk Lanigan (Douglas) performs a series of activities, like reading a newspaper, while pretending to listen to his wife, then occasionally walks over to the phone and says, "Yes, Mabel, I heard every word."

Humorous results on Monk's scalp after he applies Vernon's "hair tonic."

HOME COURT ADVANTAGE
Available on VHS.

#81 LOVE AND BASKETBALL

Screenwriter/Director Gina Prince-Bythewood. **Producers** Spike Lee, Jay Stern, Andrew Davis, Cynthia Guidry, Sam Kitt. **Cinematography** Reynaldo Villalobos. **Editing** Terilyn Shropshire. **Production Design** Jeffrey Howard. **Art Direction** Sue Chan. **Costume Design** Ruth Carter. New Line. 2000.

THE PLAYERS Omar Epps **Quincy McCall**; Sanaa Lathan **Monica Wright**; Alfre Woodard **Camille Wright**; Dennis Haysbert **Zeke McCall**; Debbi Morgan **Nona McCall**; Harry Lennix **Nathan Wright**; Kyla Pratt **Young Monica**; Glenndon Chatman **Young Quincy**; Christine Dunford **Coach Davis**; Erica Ringor **Sidra O'Neal**; Regina Hall **Lena Wright**; Jess Willard **Jamal**; Chris Warren Jr. **Kelvin**; Naykia Harris **Young Lena**; Tyra Banks **Kyra Kessler**; Colleen Matsuhara **UCLA coach**; Al Foster **Coach Hiserman**; Nathaniel Bellamy Jr. **High school ref #1**; Shar Jackson **Felicia**; Gabrielle Union **Shawnee**; James DuMont **Reporter**; April Griffin **Dorsey High player**; Boris Kodjoe **Jason**; Kara Brock **College girl #1**; Chick Hearn **Himself**; Stu Lantz **Himself**; Aichi Ali **College girl #2**; Charles O'Bannon **Reggie**; Robin Roberts **Herself**; Dick Vitale **Himself**; Jimmy Lennon Jr. **Sports announcer**; Terry Cummings **Himself**; Jesse Corti **Coach Parra**; Monica Calhoun **Kerry**

THE GAME Eleven-year-old Quincy McCall dreams of becoming a professional basketball player like his father, Zeke (Dennis Haysbert). When Monica Wright, a tomboy of the same age with similar aspirations, becomes his neighbor, it is the beginning of a long love-hate relationship.

Both grow up to star for their high school teams. Monica (Sanaa Lathan) has a rough edge about her that's not helped by her perception of her mother's lack of support (Alfre Woodard). Quincy (Omar Epps) is a big man on campus, popular with the ladies.

Their lifelong friendship blooms into romance as they both play for their college teams at USC.

Quincy's life becomes troubled after his father lies about his infidelities and his parents divorce. This leads to a breakup with Monica, and the two go their own ways. Quincy drops out of college to turn pro.

Several years pass, and both struggle in their professional careers. Monica, despite winning a championship in Barcelona, returns from Europe tired of the lonely grind in a foreign culture.

Upon returning to Los Angeles, Monica surprises Quincy by visiting him in the hospital where he's recovering from a leg injury. As they catch up Monica gets a surprise of her own: Quincy introduces Monica to his fiancée, Kyra (Tyra Banks).

Monica continues her deep soul-searching about what she wants out of life. Spurred by some inspiring words from her mother, Monica makes a final play for Quincy, her lifelong love.

INSTANT REPLAY A former college athlete, writer/director Gina Prince-Bythewood has all the right moves in this rare character study in which the female athlete measures up to the male athlete co-star, and then some.

Balancing the core demands of the story's sports action and romance, Bythewood's picture incorporates some refreshing angles. This is a sports story not only told from a woman's point of view but also centered in a well-to-do black community, showing that rich kids, regardless of ethnicity, have problems too.

In and around the romance, Bythewood goes deeper into the complex relationships of the respective families as well as exploring the struggles that aspiring female professional athletes face, especially in team sports.

TOP: Athletes. Lovers. Monica Wright (Sanaa Lathan) and Quincy McCall (Omar Epps).

MIDDLE: Quincy's parents (Debbi Morgan and Dennis Haysbert).

BOTTOM: Daughter and mother (Lathan and Alfre Woodard).

The writer/director is assisted by a capable cast. Sanaa Lathan comes across as very real in her multidimensional turn as lover, daughter, and hoopster. The chemistry between her and Omar Epps is believable throughout all their highs and lows. And, though Bythewood could have set up Monica's relationship with her mother (Alfre Woodard) more thoroughly, the scenes in which mother and daughter talk about "life choices" are some of the best in the film.

As a basketball player Lathan symbolizes the plight of female athletes in general, best evidenced by a terrific scene (in pre-WNBA days) showing her character's disenchantment, loneliness, and isolation when, unable to understand a word of her Spanish coach's pep talk, she goes on to win a hollow championship victory.

Omar Epps's Quincy, in contrast, *is* playing for glory and fame, and though the actor seems a bit old for the high school sequences, he scores off the hardcourt.

Epps convincingly presents the confident sports star whose world spins out of control with his parents' divorce. Dennis Haysbert is sharp as the flawed but loving athlete father who succumbs to the very temptations he warned his son about.

Debbi Morgan shows some range, going from bubbly trophy wife to heartbroken woman strengthened by her son's love. Alfre Woodard is her usual stellar self, giving a subtle yet complex performance as the sympathetic, pragmatic mother who simultaneously fears and admires her daughter's independent spirit and will.

Bythewood uses the metaphors of sport to give us a film that is more about the choices that we make than purely about love or basketball.

At the same time the filmmaker takes us where not many movies have ventured before. There has been an assortment of pictures involving women in relatively individual sports like figure skating, golf, tennis, and track, but here we get an insightful presentation of group dynamics among female athletes as well as the inequities they endure relative to their male counterparts. In Monica, we see not only the sacrifices and compromises women basketball players have had to make for the love of the game, but also how a female's aggressive drive is perceived by the public—and of course the huge differences in salary between the sexes in the same sport.

In the climactic scene, Bythewood cleverly avoids the last-second game-winning shot in the traditional sense. Instead she takes a symbolic page from her producer, Spike Lee. As Lee did with the father/son matchup in *He Got Game*, Bythewood keeps within Monica's personality and the parameters of the game of hearts that she and Quincy play.

Love and Basketball, while at times predictable and a bit overlong, incorporates some fine writing, including some fully realized characters given life by talented performers. It is one of the more insightful movies made about women in sports.

OUTSIDE THE LINES Both Lathan and Epps appeared in *The Wood*.... Production Designer Jeffrey Howard's credits include *Little Big League* (1994), *Talent for the Game* (1991), and *Major League* (1989).... Executive producer Spike Lee wrote and directed the basketball feature *He Got Game* (1998), starring Denzel Washington.... Lee is working on a boxing drama about Joe Louis/Max Schmeling with Budd Schulberg and Burt Sugar.... Lee also wrote a book about his well-known love of the NBA's New York Knicks: *Best Seat in the House: A Basketball Memoir*.... Alfre Woodard starred in the football drama *Radio* (2003) and the basketball feature *Blue Chips* (1994).... Reynaldo Villalobos also photographed the baseball comedy *Major League* (1989).... Two-time Oscar nominated costume designer Ruth Carter also worked on *Cobb* (1994) and

Monica (Lathan, center) would play professionally in Europe after succeeding in college ball.

The Great White Hype (1996)…. Dennis Haysbert starred in *Mr. Baseball* (1992) and *Major League* (1989)…. Among his first performances was in the TV movie *Grambling's White Tiger* (1981)…. Epps starred in the boxing drama *Against the Ropes* (2004), the *Major League* sequel and football's The Program (1993) with James Caan.

ALL-STAR MOMENTS Riding home in Quincy's car from a high school basketball game, much is revealed, especially after Monica (Sanaa Lathan) reads out loud a graphic letter a fellow student wanted her to give Quincy (Omar Epps). Quincy warns Monica about her "hot-ass temper," which he cites as a reason she's not being as highly recruited as she might be. She talks about the double standards in the sport between the sexes.

The couple's game of "strip" hoops in their college dorm room. "All's fair in love and basketball, baby."

Montages showing the different struggles of Quincy and Monica on the court.

Confrontation between Quincy and his dad, Zeke (Dennis Haysbert), in the young's man dorm room. He informs his dad that he's dropping out of school and turning pro.

Monica's experiences in Spain: professionally successful but ultimately empty.

Mother-daughter exchanges both in the kitchen and on the back patio where Mrs. Wright (Alfre Woodard) spurs her daughter to action with some kind words.

HOME COURT ADVANTAGE Available on VHS and DVD.

#80 GREGORY'S GIRL

Screenwriter Bill Forsyth. **Director** Bill Forsyth. **Producers** Davina Belling, Clive Parsons. **Cinematography** Michael Coulter. **Editing** John Gow. **Music** Colin Tully. **Art Direction** Adrienne Atkinson. Goldwyn. 1981.

THE PLAYERS John Gordon Sinclair **Gregory**; Dee Hepburn **Dorothy**; Jake D'Arcy **Phil Menzies**; Clare Grogan **Susan**; Robert Buchanan **Andy**; Alan Love **Eric**; Caroline Guthrie **Carol**; Carol McCartney **Margo**; Douglas Sannachan **Billy**; Allison Forster **Madeline**; Chic Murray **Headmaster**; Alex Norton **Alec**; John Bett **Alistair**; Dave Anderson **Gregory's father**; Billy Feeley **Mr. Anderson**; Maeve Watt **Miss Ford**; Graham Thompson **Charlie**; Muriel Romanes **Miss Welch**; Patrick Lewsley **Mr. Hall**; Ronald Girvin **Alan**; Pat Harkins **Kelvin**; Tony Whitmore **Gordon**; Billy Greenlees **Steve**; Denis Criman **Richard**; Christopher Higson **Man in penguin suit**

THE GAME Gangly teen Gregory (Gordon John Sinclair) and his classmates are beginning to discover girls and the world of romance in their small Scottish town. For Gregory, romance comes from a place he never would have expected.

As a forward on his school soccer team, Gregory is philosophical about their poor record, saying, "Football is entertainment. We give them a good laugh."

Gregory's not laughing when Coach Phil Menzies (Jake D'Arcy) informs him that he'll be looking at new players to replace Gregory as forward and that he had better learn to be a goalie.

Gregory's transfer is made easier when the one chosen to take his place is a well-developed girl named Dorothy (Dee Hepburn). Instantly smitten by his pretty new teammate, Gregory soon learns she's much more skilled at the game of soccer (and at handling the opposite sex) than he ever was.

Gregory's crush on Dorothy fills him with strange and powerful romantic feelings. In his confusion, he seeks advice from every quarter, the most practical of which comes from his 10-year-old sister, Madeline (Allison Forster).

Finally Gregory musters enough courage to ask Dorothy out. Nearly collapsing from joy when she accepts, Gregory excitedly prepares for the big event. In the meantime, after consultation with her friends, Dorothy apparently backs out. As he goes to meet her, Gregory is instead passed along from one girl to another in a scheme to match him up with Susan (Clare Grogan), who has had a secret crush on him for some time. His friends observe him with the different girls and are inspired to seek out the opposite sex themselves. Young and pleasantly mixed up, Gregory takes it all in stride and enjoys the evening.

With their quirky way of looking at things, Susan and Gregory hit it off and end the evening kissing. Adolescent infatuation takes a lovely turn for Gregory.

INSTANT REPLAY *Gregory's Girl* is a refreshing, realistic, and funny portrait of a timeless and universal rite of passage, shown through a Scottish filter.

Writer/director Bill Forsyth's take on a life phase filled with wonder, emotion, confusion, embarrassment, and sexual awakening has an innocent charm that is reminiscent of the '50s, and is peopled with quirky characters in clever situations.

Less graphic and more leisurely paced than equally entertaining American coming-of-age equivalents like *The Breakfast Club, Ferris Bueller's Day Off, Fast Times at Ridgemont*

Gregory (Gordon John Sinclair, second from left) and his classmates develop a newfound fascination with the opposite sex.

High, and *Grease, Gregory's Girl* is more in line with French director Francois Truffaut's *Small Change*.

With a script filled with insightful humor and well-observed truths about youthful infatuation, Forsyth overcomes the often static camerawork, bumpy editing, and uneven soundtrack to direct a modest and amiable story.

Along the way, the writer/director also manages to illustrate the difference between having a crush on someone and enjoying a real rapport. With the protagonist's lovesick situation resolved in one romantic summer night, Forsyth wonderfully exemplifies the topsy-turvy world of young love.

One of the popular notions examined here is the earlier maturation of girls compared to boys, and girls' innate sense of what they want in a romantic relationship. Forsyth amusingly uses the hero's 10-going-on-20 sister (Allison Forster) as a sort of love mentor to her older brother. The idea is further explored in the film's climax, when the girls conspire to set up a love match as they see it best working out.

In this ingenuous and naturalistic tale, the energetic young cast really hit their marks.

The aforementioned Forster is memorable as the worldly young sister whose performance is enhanced by another sophisticated 10-year-old, played by Denis Criman.

In a surprisingly small role, Dee Hepburn is rightly straightforward and somewhat enigmatic as the young man's object of desire. Her focus is less on romance than on improving her sports skills.

Much credit for the film's quirky humor goes to Gregory's classmates, Andy (Rob Buchanan) and Charlie (Graham Thompson). Andy scores some of the best lines while Charlie demonstrates a quiet version of raging hormones.

On the adult side, veteran comedian Chic Murray's piano-playing, pastry-loving, arrogant headmaster and the ambitious soccer coach Jake D'Arcy add some daft but deft texture to the story.

The picture, however, belongs to the character named in the title. Gordon John Sin-

TOP: Dorothy (Dee Hepburn) is the object of Gregory's interest.

MIDDLE: After a few awkward attempts to impress the girls at school, Gregory gets some advice on romance from his worldly 10-year-old sister, Madeline (Allison Forster).

BOTTOM: Dee is also the best player on an otherwise all-boys soccer team.

clair physically embodies the awkwardness of teen love. With the gangly limbs of a young colt, Sinclair takes in this new phase of his life with an engaging humor that is both self-deprecating and perceptive.

The lanky, likable teen symbolizes the uneasiness we all feel in our first crush. Sinclair is convincing as a lovesick adolescent who learns more about himself in the course of his initial foray into the world of romance.

While the performers never really went on to great success as thespians, as a whole they effectively provide a good-natured, warm, and at times melancholy trip down memory lane with an insightful look at the innocence of first love gone forever.

As he would later do in *Local Hero*, Forsyth shows an ability to incorporate local details into a very atmospheric and not overly sentimental story of universally resonant themes.

This perceptive social observation is a reminder that a talented filmmaker with a solid story can perform cinematic magic without all the bells and whistles of high-budget technology.

OUTSIDE THE LINES Much of the picture was re-dubbed to lessen the thick Scottish accents for the American market.... David Puttnam, who produced *Chariots of Fire*, produced director Forsyth's next picture, *Local Hero*, which starred Burt Lancaster.... Clare Grogan would gain notoriety leading the pop band Altered Images.... Bill Forsyth's screenplay won a British Academy Award over *Chariots of Fire*.... John Gordon Sinclair was nominated for Best Newcomer.... *Gregory's Girl* also had British Academy nominations for Best Director and Best Film.... A sequel, *Gregory's Two Girls*, came 18 years later.

ALL-STAR MOMENTS Young teen Gregory (Sinclair) arrives late for a home economics class to help out Steve (Billy Greenlees). Gregory tells Steve he's been "in love" since about "a half hour ago.... It feels great. I'm restless and I'm dizzy. It's wonderful. Bet I don't get any sleep tonight." Steve quips, "That sounds more like indigestion." When Gregory tells him it is someone on the football team, Steve replies, "Probably just a phase. Who is it? Andy?"

Smooth-talking youngster Richard (Climan) shows more nerve about women than Gregory as he asks to see Gregory's younger sister, Madeline. "Seducing children," Gregory scolds. "You're a freak. You're heading for big trouble." To which the kid calmly repeats his request to have Madeline (Forster) call him.

Playing goalie and his team down, Gregory pays less attention to the game than to his friend Andy (Buchanan), who is standing behind the goal talking about how it isn't natural for women to be playing the sport: "If women were meant to play football they'd have their tits somewhere else."

After another goal is scored against Gregory, an unhappy Dorothy (Hepburn) comes running up asking for the ball. Gregory cleans it off and hands it to her with a grin. Andy gets a good look at Dorothy and changes his tune: "We need more women on this team. More new blood."

HOME COURT ADVANTAGE Available on VHS and DVD.

#79 KINGPIN

Screenwriters Barry Fanaro, Mort Nathan. **Directors** Peter Farrelly and Bobby Farrelly. **Producers** Brad Krevoy, Steve Stabler, Brad Thomas, Steve Samples. **Cinematography** Mark Irwin. **Editing** Chris Greenbury. **Music** Freedy Johnston. MGM/UA. 1996.

THE PLAYERS
Woody Harrelson **Roy Munson**; Randy Quaid **Ishmael**; Vanessa Angel **Claudia**; Bill Murray **Ernie McCracken**; Chris Elliott **The Gambler**; William Jordan **Mr. Boorg**; Richard Tyson **Stiffy's owner**; Lin Shaye **Landlady**; Zen Gesner **Thomas**; Prudence Holmes **Mrs. Boorg**; Rob Moran **Stanley Osmanski**; Danny Green **Calvert Munson**; Will Rothhaar **Young Roy**; Jill Lytle **Odor Eater Babe**; Willie Beauchene **Bunion Boy**; Sayed Badreya **Fatima**; Linda Carola **Waitress**; Monica Shay **Floozy**; Danny Murphy **Beaver Valley bowling manager**; David Shackelford **Redneck stutterer**; Hank Brandt **Bowling priest**; Suzan Hughes **Waitress**; Michael Corrente **Scranton wino**; Herbie Flynn **Scranton wino**; Joe Krawlicky **Pennsylvania Hall of Fame bowler**; Googy Gress **Lancaster bowling manager**; Rose Smith-Lotenero **Amish babe**; Nancy Frey-Jarecki **Sarah Boorg**; Robby Thibeau **Lucas Boorg**; Helen Manfull **Grandma Boorg**; Mike Cerrone **Beaver Bowl hustler**; Mike Cavallo **Beaver Bowl hustler**; Rick Barker **Beaver Bowl hustler**; Roger Clemens **Skidmark**

THE GAME Taught the game by his father, young Iowa native Roy Munson (Woody Harrelson) sets out to make a name for himself in the sport of bowling. Everything is going well, but his bright future comes crashing down one night after he meets veteran bowler Ernie McCracken (Bill Murray).

When Ernie uses Roy to hustle some tough local players at a neighborhood alley, they realize Roy is a ringer and then and there end his career by mauling his hand in the ball return device.

For the next 17 years, Roy lives in a lost haze of booze, haunted by his landlady (Lin Shaye) and peddling bowling supplies to survive.

His life makes a sudden turn one day when he spots the bowling potential of Ishmael, an Amish man (Randy Quaid). Reluctant at first, Ishmael eventually becomes a student of the game under Roy's management with hopes of earning enough money to help save his family's farm. Their journey to bowling success is long and a bit twisted, and they endure their share of "gutter balls" on their way to success. With the help of their lady partner, Claudia (Vanessa Angel), the team is primed for the big time.

The climax comes when their paths cross with "Big Ern" again at a million-dollar tournament in Reno. Ernie calls Roy a loser, Ishmael takes a swing at him and misses, and his hand plows into a wall, forcing him to pull out of the tournament.

Ishmael then gets Roy fired up enough to qualify himself. The old talent returns as Roy makes it all the way to the finals against McCracken. Though Roy comes up short in their winner-take-all duel, he wins the girl, who made some cagey bets, and he makes good money doing endorsements. They share their good fortune with Ishmael, who returns to his Amish roots.

INSTANT REPLAY *Dumb and Dumber* takes a sporting turn here and becomes "A Gross and Grosser *Color of Money*." And what's wrong with that?

Disjointed as it is, this movie pulls out all the stops—there is no humor too low to mine and present. Sure, there are some comic whiffs, but the film still scores in typical lowbrow Farrelly style. Bobby and Peter, with co-writers Barry Fanaro and Mort Nathan, roll far from a perfect game here, but audiences know what to expect from

(Left to right) Roy Munson (Woody Harrelson), Claudia (Vanessa Angel), and Ishmael (Randy Quaid).

them by now. In this overlong film, hampered by awkward and lurching subplots, the filmmakers still score enough strikes with their sight gags, putdowns, and parodies to keep the belly laughs coming.

They are helped with some strong performances, particularly Woody Harrelson and Bill Murray.

Taking a page from Steve Martin's *Comedy Is Not Pretty*, Woody Harrelson gives a brave and poignant performance as bowling's version of *The Natural*. With a shaved head, paunch, and mangled hand, the actor playing Roy can't afford to be vain. What's more, Harrelson has the tough chore of bouncing quickly between wildly different moods, whether a scene calls for sympathy, slapstick, misery, or romance. It is a surprisingly affecting and funny turn as a young man seeing his once bright future gone bad.

Bill Murray plays the smarmy, slimy, sexist bowling champion Big Ern with a villainous glee that is tailor-made to his comedic talents. His outrageous comb-over and ridiculous outfits really add a lot to the characterization.

Vanessa Angel is more than voluptuous and makes the most of her bimbo role, showing spirit and backbone as well as comedic talent.

Randy Quaid, at times a bit hammy (but then I guess you have to be if you're going to stuff that physique into a bikini and perform at a strip club), provides an interesting contrast between his gawky physical dimensions and childlike personality.

In another of the film's decidedly unglamorous roles, Lin Shaye creates some indelible moments as Roy's exceedingly unattractive landlady.

With this talented group of players, the Farrelly brothers dared to take vulgar humor to new lows…or levels.

Juvenile, raunchy, goofy yet sentimental, *Kingpin* is a guilty pleasure. So what if it can't decide if it is a romance, sports flick, or buddy road movie? The picture is an amalgam, an amusing hybrid.

Go ahead, take yourself back to being a sophomore in a less politically correct time. Stoop to its level. You'll be bowled over by sheer silliness, laughing loud and laughing often.

OUTSIDE THE LINES The Farrelly Brothers also created *Fever Pitch* (2005), a baseball remake of the 1997 soccer film…. Lin Shaye is the sister of Bob Shaye, founder of New Line Cinema…. Jim Carrey was considered for the Bill Murray role…. Woody Harrelson took bowling lessons for weeks to prepare for the role but according to the filmmakers wasn't highly skilled despite being athletic…. Harrelson's sports movie credits include *Play it to the Bone* (1999), *White Men Can't Jump* (1992), and *Wildcats* (1986)…. The actor also wrote a basketball-themed play, *Two on Two*…. Michael Keaton and Chris Farley were also looking at the lead roles at one point in the film's development…. Baseball star Roger Clemens plays the jealous boyfriend, Skidmark…. Clemens also appeared in *Cobb* (1994)…. Bill Murray starred in *Caddyshack* (1980)…. Randy Quaid starred in the *Caddyshack* sequel and played a race car owner in *Days of Thunder* (1986) and a pro golfer in *Dead Solid Perfect* (1988)…. Professional golfers Brad Faxon and Billy Andrade make appearances as Roy's supporters back in his early days…. Pro bowlers Mark Roth, Brian Voss, Randy Pederson, and Justin Hromek also appear…. Sportscasters Chris Schenkel, Jon Dennis, and Chris Berman are part of the cast…. The band Blues Traveler appear in Amish clothes playing one of their tunes.

ALL-STAR MOMENTS Radio alarm goes on. Roy (Harrelson) awakens and can't get it to turn off so he smashes it with his hooked right hand. Going to scratch his head, he realizes he can't because the radio is still stuck on his hand. The radio continues to play despite having been smashed against the wall. Roy takes a swig of whiskey for breakfast.

Leaving his apartment, Roy talks to two neighbors as he heads to his car.

ROY: Hey, Herb, how's life?

HERB: Taking forever.

Herb is half-asleep with an oxygen hookup through his nose and a cigarette in his mouth. The other man talks to Roy.

MIKE: Roy, can you get sick drinkin' piss?

ROY: I think you can.

MIKE: Even if it's your own?

Just then Roy's landlady (Shaye) addresses Roy as "Captain Hook" and demands the rent money. Roy takes off.

Pulling up to a bowling alley, Roy has problems with his hook, pulling off his car mirror, then the door handle. Putting on his sport coat, he rips it with the hook. Eventually he puts on a fake hand with his state champion bowling ring.

After the unattractive landlady threatens to call the cops because Roy was in on a botched mugging attempt, he asks what he can do to make it up to her.

Cut to post-coital scene. Looking serene and satisfied, the ugly landlady lies in bed and smokes a cigarette; Roy, on the other hand, is hovering over the toilet throwing up.

Sitting in their buggies waiting for Roy, the Boorg family thinks he has bailed out

Roy throws strikes down the alley—and with the ladies.

Roy tries to win his first professional bowling championship in spite of Ernie McCracken's (Bill Murray) shenanigans.

because of the hard work. Instead Roy comes running up with what he thinks is a bucket of milk.

> ROY: Morning. I hope you don't mind, I got up a little early so I took the liberty of milking your cow for you. (He grins under his milk mustache.) Yeah, took her a while to warm up. She sure is a stubborn one...then, pow! all at once.

> (As Roy goes to drink from the bucket . . .)

> MR. BOORG: We don't have a cow. We have a bull.

Roy spits out what's in his mouth and excuses himself to go brush his teeth.

Helping the Amish build a barn, Roy accidentally nails his fake hand. Then, when the lunch bell rings, he drops his support of the roof and it collapses as he dashes to the food.

Ernie McCracken (Bill Murray) does a TV commercial for the United Fund. He is clearly enjoying this effort in support of fatherless families as he meets one pretty woman after another.

Roy returns to a bowling alley where he enjoyed success early in his career.

"Wow it's kind of intimidating to be in the presence of so many great athletes" (cut to pan shot of row of fat guys stuffing themselves, smoking, and drinking).

Climactic bowling match between Roy and Ernie.

HOME COURT ADVANTAGE Available on VHS and DVD.

#78 BLUE CHIPS

Screenwriter Ron Shelton. **Director** William Friedkin. **Producers** Michele Rappaport, Wolfgang Glattes. **Cinematography** Tom Priestley Jr. **Editing** Augie Hess, Robert Lambert, David Rosenbloom. **Music** Jeff Beck, Jed Lieber, Nile Rodgers. **Art Direction** Ed Verreaux. **Production Design** James Bissell. **Set Decoration** Thomas Roysden. Paramount. 1994.

THE PLAYERS Nick Nolte **Pete Bell**; Mary McDonnell **Jenny**; J. T. Walsh **Happy**; Ed O'Neill **Ed**; Alfre Woodard **Lavada McRae**; Bob Cousy **Vic**; Shaquille O'Neal **Neon Bodeaux**; Penny Hardaway **Butch McRae**; Matt Nover **Ricky**; Cylk Cozart **Slick**; Anthony C. Hall **Tony**; Kevin Benton **Jack**; Bill Cross **Freddie**; Marques Johnson **Mel**; Robert Wuhl **Marty**; Bobby Knight **Himself**; Rick Pitino **Himself**; George Raveling **Himself**; Larry Bird **Himself**; Sam Armato **College lecturer**; Jim Beaver **Ricky's father**; Todd Donoho **Himself**; Dick Vitale **Himself**; Frank Rossi **Charlie**; Jim Boeheim **Himself**; Dick Baker **Himself**; Marty Blake **Himself**; Lou Campinelli **Himself**; Jerry Tarkanian **Himself**; Eric Harmon **Referee**; Allan Malamud **Reporter**; Louis Gossett Jr. **Father Dawkins**

THE GAME Western University basketball coach Pete Bell (Nick Nolte) has enjoyed a very successful career, but with several concurrent mediocre seasons he's come under increasing pressure to reproduce his past glories, which include conference titles and national championships. To this point Coach Bell's program has been very clean; his players graduate and he hasn't had to pay off players to join his school.

After meeting with Marty (Robert Wuhl), a college hoops talent scout and marketing man, Coach Bell narrows his search down to three recruits who could turn his program around instantly and regain those heady days for the school. Neon Bodeaux (Shaquille O'Neal), an unknown giant from Louisiana; Ricky (Matt Nover), a farm boy from Indiana; and Butch McRae (Penny Hardaway), from the mean streets of Chicago, are his primary targets.

On the recruiting trip Coach Bell uses his contacts (Larry Bird, Slick, and Father Dawkins) to reach the talented young men and make his pitch. But Bell is competing with other top college coaches for these players, and after their tour of the campus, none commit. With no prospects signed up, Bell is at his wits' end.

Although it eats at him inside, Bell enlists the help of Happy (J. T. Walsh), the powerful alumni booster whom he detests. Happy makes the arrangements, and in the blink of an eye Bell has all three of his top prospects on his team. Neon is different, though—that is, he's not driven purely by money. He rejects a car he never requested and, with Bell's ex-wife's (Mary McDonnell) tutoring, gets the chance to see if college is for him. Ricky and Butch are financially taken care of and all three quickly turn the Dolphins' basketball fortunes around.

When Happy flaunts his influence in Bell's world, the coach tries to get rid of him, but Happy fights back. He reveals the story of how he already paid off one of Bell's best players, Tony (Anthony C. Hall), in a point shaving incident in a prior season. Happy threatens to make this public (it was hinted at previously by a news reporter Ed O'Neill).

In his first game with his star players, Coach Bell takes on the vaunted Indiana University team coached by Bobby Knight. Western wins, but Bell is so troubled by his conscience that in the post-game press conference he reveals the ugly truth, fingers Happy, and resigns, in effect ending his big-time coaching career.

INSTANT REPLAY *Blue Chips* boils down to an ethics and morality play. Through the protagonist, Coach Bell (Nolte), we are asked to consider what sacrifices and compromises an individual will make to reach his goal. Betraying his better instincts in order to save what he perceives at the time to be something of highest value to him, winning basketball at whatever price, Bell loses sight of himself. The young kids he's coaching become dollar signs in Bell's quest to add more championship banners to the school's fieldhouse rafters. He "became what [he] despised most."

In his fall from grace Bell learns some higher truths about who he is, a process that propels him to go forward sensing that personal redemption is around the corner—symbolized in his impromptu instruction of some kids he runs across playing basketball on a local playground.

Ron Shelton brings his usual authentic sporting dialogue, and William Friedkin's decision to shoot the basketball action in real game conditions, using real players and name coaches talking strategy in the heat of battle on the sidelines, is a smart one. The added touch of including Larry Bird, Bob Cousy, and recognizable college coaches on recruiting trips brings a very high caliber of verisimilitude.

Clearly the pivotal player of this picture is Nick Nolte. Nolte's passionate, even maniacal performance as the driven-to-win coach is riveting from the opening tirade to the closing playground scene. The actor's committed turn, drawing from a seemingly endless pool of energy, intensity, and drive, also embodies the internal demons that wrestle in his conscience about the cost of success.

Ironically, Nolte's character ends up the same way in this picture as the athlete he plays in *North Dallas Forty*: as a wide receiver for the North Dallas Bulls, fed up with all the big business, stifling rules, and politics, Nolte quits.

The rest of the cast rounds out a solid team; even the players, in roles admittedly not far from their own experiences, come off well. Shaquille O'Neal in particular is warm and engaging with a good sense of humor.

J. T. Walsh is devilishly good as the power behind the bench, the alumni string puller. Arrogant, manipulative, and at the same time pragmatic in his views about the existing system, Walsh plays it with some depth. Mary McDonnell has a tough role as

ABOVE: Competing coaches Pete Bell (Nick Nolte, right) and Bob Knight exchange greetings before their game.

RIGHT: Coach Bell is intense in all matters of the game.

the coach's ex-wife who delivers the obligatory preachy comments but comes across with a little bite and humor of her own. Alfre Woodard as the wary and determined mother staunchly pursuing a better life for her family via her son's basketball talents is convincing. So too is Ed O'Neill as the investigative reporter.

Though *The Program* with James Caan delivered a broader look at the college athletic business, the give and go of director Friedkin's frenetically real pacing and Shelton's insightful jock talk is attention-holding and scores for *Blue Chips*.

OUTSIDE THE LINES

Early in its development *Blue Chips* was at Fox studios, where Shelton created *White Men Can't Jump*.... Friedkin won an Oscar for directing *The French Connection*.... At the time the film came out Paramount's parent company also owned the New York Knicks.... Director Friedkin was a longtime Celtics fan and occasionally worked out with the team.... Bob Cousy authored several books, including *The Killer Instinct*, which explored the deception of amateur basketball recruiting.... Game action was shot at Frankfort High School in Frankfort, Indiana.... The majority of players appearing in the film trained at Loyola Marymount University in Los Angeles under the guidance of former Cal coach Pete Newell and Dallas Mavericks scout Dick Baker.... Some of the recruiting coaches appearing include Jerry Tarkanian, Lou Campanelli, and Jim Boeheim.... Nolte studied tapes of the late coach Jim Valvano and spent time with Bobby Knight to prepare for his role.... Louis Gossett Jr. starred in the boxing film *Diggstown*.... Director Friedkin's wife is veteran studio executive Sherry Lansing.... Early in his career Friedkin directed a TV special for David Wolper called *Pro Football: Mayhem on a Sunday Afternoon*.... For a period in the project's long development stage Al Pacino was committed to the role of Coach Bell.

ALL-STAR MOMENTS

Opening scene in which Coach Bell (Nolte) appears, leaves, and reappears several times in an intense pre-game locker room speech.

Bell goes nuts, getting into the ref's face during a game, taking the ball and kicking it high into the stands. He is subsequently ejected.

Recruiting coaches watching a small-town parade see Coach Bell grinning at them from behind the wheel, driving the prized recruit.

After Coach Bell reluctantly decides to use Happy's (Walsh) under-the-table recruiting services, the rich booster tells the coach, "Relax. We're gonna be on top again. I got a confession to make too. I screw a helluva lot better when we're winning, don't you?"

Reel feel to the game action, especially the game vs. Indiana and the alley-oop jam by Neon (O'Neal).

POST-GAME COMMENTS

Nick Nolte:

> Coaching is really a moment-by-moment decision-making process; there's no blueprint.... The key to coaching is being able to use your imagination. Read, react, create. You also have to prepare, do your homework, get the basics down. What separates the master craftsman from the average coach is his creativity. It's a thinking man's game.[1]

Director William Friedkin on the decision to use real players over actors:

TOP: Alfre Woodard plays Lavada McRae, a savvy mother of a prized basketball recruit.

MIDDLE: Local newspaper reporter Ed (Ed O'Neill) doggedly investigates illegal activities that he suspects have occurred within Coach Bell's basketball program.

BOTTOM: Coach Bell in action as his Western University Dolphins compete.

I wanted to look at the players in this film and know that these guys are really playing. . . I wanted there to be no doubt that you are watching great athletes in competition.[2]

Writer/executive producer Ron Shelton on the core of the story:

Pete Bell faces a pretty straightforward dilemma: "I've never cheated before and to keep my job I have to cheat. What do I do?" This is a story about a man who believes in rules, in laws, in civilization. The problem is he can't continue to do what he does well, which is teaching young men and coaching young men, without breaking the rules.... It becomes a question of what will he do to survive, to protect what he loves. It's about a guy who starts to accommodate his soul and wakes up one day to find out he has crossed the line.[3]

HOME COURT ADVANTAGE Available on VHS and DVD.

ABOVE: Key recruits to Coach Bell's team are Ricky (Matt Nover, left) and Neon (Shaquille O'Neal).

RIGHT: Neon demonstrates his talents.

#77 BIG WEDNESDAY

Screenwriters John Milius, Dennis Aaberg. **Director** John Milius. **Producers** Tamara Asseyev, Buzz Feitshans. **Cinematography** Bruce Surtees. **Editing** Carroll O'Meara, Robert Wolfe. **2nd Unit Director** Terry Leonard. **Composer** Basil Poledouris. **Producer Surf Sequences** Greg MacGillivray. **Water Photographers** Dan Merkel, George Greenough. **Still Photographer** Ron Grover. **Surf Photo Consultants** Roger Brown, Spyder Wills/Bud Browne. Warner Bros. 1978.

THE PLAYERS
Jan-Michael Vincent **Matt Johnson**; William Katt **Jack Barlow**; Gary Busey **Leroy Smith**; Sam Melville **Bear**; Lee Purcell **Peggy Gordon**; Patti D'Arbanville **Sally**; Barbara Hale **Mrs. Barlow**; Darrell Fetty **Waxer**; Reb Brown **Enforcer**; Robert Englund **Fly (Narrator)**; Fran Ryan **Lucy**; Joe Spinell **Psychologist**; Frank McRae **Sergeant**; Dennis Aaberg **Slick**; Gerry Lopez **Himself**; Michael Talbot **Hog**; Geoff Parks **Crusher**; Aesop Aquarian **Hippie**; Chris Woods **Lifeguard**; Jimmy Bracken **Kid surfer**; Kevin Schultz **Surfer**; Celia Kaye **Bear's bride**; Ian Cairns **Surfing double**; Jackie Dunn **Surfing double**; Bill Hamilton **Surfing double**; J. Riddle **Surfing double**; Peter Townend **Surfing double**

THE GAME *Big Wednesday* is a coming-of-age story covering a 12-year period in the lives of three lifelong friends who share a passion for surfing while growing up in southern California during the tumultuous '60s and early '70s.

The picture is divided into 4 parts, beginning with the summer of 1962 and concluding in the spring of 1974. Each part tackles a crucial period in the characters' lives, when the tides are high and their existence has come to a crossroads.

In 1962 Matt Johnson (Jan Michael Vincent), Jack Barlow (William Katt), and Leroy (Gary Busey) are teen surf gods at the local beach, an area known as "The Point" in Malibu. Their friendship, though deep, is constantly threatened because of personality differences that become more pronounced as their innocent summers give way to disillusionment on their obstacle-strewn road to becoming adults.

Matt is clearly the most talented surfer of the three; however, he takes on the responsibility of notoriety with reluctance, finds himself battling the demons of alcohol, and is dogged by the nagging notion that time has passed him by. Jack was "born old," always levelheaded and more mature than the others. Leroy is guided by his self-propelled image of being a wacky wildman gobbling up pain like candy.

But when we first see them in the summer of '62, the trio's only ambition is to ride the great wave so long predicted by Bear (Sam Melville), a former surfer who now makes surfboards.

At first, surfing, girls, and parties are their chief concerns. But their lifestyle changes during a road trip to seedy Tiajuana, Mexico. It begins as they sit by their car south of the border drinking beer, and Peggy Gordon (Lee Purcell) makes a stunning announcement that she is pregnant and Matt is the father. Later, as Leroy goes in search of female companionship, Matt, Peggy, Sally, and Jack enter a strip club that is filled with tough local characters and American servicemen on leave. Matt gets into a fight when someone insults Peggy, and the skirmish quickly escalates into a huge barroom brawl involving knives, bottles, and eventually guns. As they all scramble to leave before the cops arrest them, Matt realizes that it's a nasty world outside his beach community. Meeting back at Jack's car, which has been vandalized, the gang takes off, scurrying back to the friendly confines of home, with Leroy leaving his Mexican bride of a few hours standing in the middle of the road.

Stage 2. The West Swell. Fall 1965. Jack, now a lifeguard, gets his induction notice to join Uncle Sam's team in Vietnam. At the same time he has to kick a drunken Matt

Troubled surfing legend Matt Johnson (Jan-Michael Vincent) shares a lighter moment with Peggy Gordon (Lee Purcell).

off the beach as Johnson continues to fight facing the duties of being a husband and father. He is now barely recognizable to the locals as the onetime king of surfers.

Matt staggers off to Bear's surf shop, admitting he's a drunk, doesn't want to be a role model, and can't even surf with his friends anymore. Bear, now a prosperous businessman, tells Matt, "Growing up is hard, isn't it?"

After attending Bear's wedding, Matt, Leroy, and a few of their friends all go to the draft board for their induction together. Jack is already there dutifully standing in line and signs on. The others concoct various stories and props designed to get them declared ineligible. Matt fakes a leg injury. Waxer (Darrell Fetty) pretends to be gay, but that lands him in the Marines. Leroy tries for the insane route but ends up being taken away in an ambulance.

As the group gathers at Jack's house to wish him well in Vietnam, they watch the Watts race riots together on television. The endless innocent summers are gone.

Part 3. The North Swell. Winter 1968. Voice-over narration as we see huge waves roll in on a dark day: "Change wasn't in the beach, the rocks, or the waves; it was in the people. Some got married, some moved inland, some searched for a new spot. Some died."

After being the lone beach friend to attend the funeral of Waxer, who died serving his country, Matt is invited to a screening of a new surfing film, *Liquid Dreams*. With his wife and daughter, Matt watches with admiration as current surfing star Gerry Lopez masters the waves much to the delight of the young crowd. But when the picture flashes back to "pioneers like Matt Johnson," only his daughter seems pleased to see him on the screen. The youthful audience shouts for more of the current surfers. Matt is noticeably feeling old.

Later, showing up one day on the beach after returning safely from Vietnam, Jack goes surfing, where he and Matt catch up after three years. Jack learns that his old girlfriend Sally has gotten married and that Bear has fallen on hard times, while Leroy is off taking on bigger waves.

Not long afterward, Matt, Jack, and Leroy have a reunion of sorts at Waxer's gravesite, where they drink and reminisce under the moon, reflecting on friendship, death, and life passing by.

Part 4. The Great Swell. Spring 1974. "Big Wednesday," as waves are reaching epic proportions. Looking from the bluff by the crumbling archway, Matt descends the broken cement steps, surfboard under his arm, as he's done so many times before. He's met by Jack and Leroy. With a gathering crowd looking on, the trio walks toward the water, smiling at each other. Matt says, "Bear called it," as they paddle out on their boards to take on "the wave of a lifetime."

They have a great time surfing the giant waves, even getting the admiration of the young surfing star Gerry Lopez, who is also out there. The veterans hold their own until Matt gets swallowed up and flails against the rocks below, struggling against the powerful undertow. Jack and Leroy rescue him. Afterward, limping along the beach, he is stopped by a young surfer who has retrieved his board and wants to return it.

Matt considers his board for a second and then, in a moment signifying the passing of the torch to the next generation, tells the kid to keep it.

Walking back up the broken steps, Matts says, "Lopez, he's as good as they always said he was." There's a pause; then Leroy says, "So were we."

INSTANT REPLAY A bittersweet autobiographical film by writer/director John Milius, *Big Wednesday* is at times somewhat preachy and melodramatic, but often truly sharp. It blends nostalgia and reverence for the surfing world within the context of growing up in a period of much social upheaval. It is the kind of story that appeals to our own sentimental view of the past and journey into adulthood.

In this earnest study in the bonding of youth, the friends' relationship transcends time and distance. They share the carefree joys of freedom, living for riding the waves, then take the sometimes painful path to maturity in the shadows of Vietnam, and come to face their limitations and the added responsibilities of adulthood. Through it all, these friends, with their contrasting personalities, share a code that provides a unifying rationality to their lives.

The lead performers, William Katt, Gary Busey, and Jan Michael Vincent, are well cast (though it is a bit eerie how Busey's wildman character and Vincent's alcoholic character look like precursors to their real-life troubles). Despite a script that doesn't probe very deeply into their characters, they give some of the best performances of their careers. The female actors, as in other male-dominated Milius films such as *Magnum Force* and *Apocalypse Now*, are not given a lot to work with, though Lee Purcell's Peggy Gordon shows much poise and maturity in welcoming early motherhood.

Surfing takes on a mythic, epic dimension in this film, a sort of stylistic homage to John Ford's Western films. Indeed, the true star of *Big Wednesday* is the surf, which doubles as a metaphor of sorts, ebbing and flowing with the young men's lives. The surf photography of the giant waves dwarfs the cast literally and figuratively. The surfing sequences produced by Greg MacGillivray and shot by George Greenough and Dan Merkel are so vibrant and realistic that you feel the rush of water, the smell of salt air, and the wind at your back even sitting on the couch. Viewing the brilliant and innovative photography, you want to reach for a towel.

The cinematography of Bruce Surtees and still photography of Ron Grover contribute much to the stellar visual component of the film. Like *The Black Stallion*, this picture does well with extended periods of simple sensory pleasure that allow the viewer to soak in the beauty of nature's images.

Ultimately, while the plot and performances will move viewers who may never have picked up a board, it is the existential majesty and grandeur of the surf and nature herself that carry *Big Wednesday*.

OUTSIDE THE LINES

Celia Kaye, the Bear's wife, was director Milius's real-life wife.... The Tijuana, Mexico scenes were shot in El Paso, Texas.... Jan Michael Vincent played a sporting Tarzan-like character in Disney's *The World's Greatest Athlete* (1973).... Jeff Bridges reportedly was considered for one of the leads.... Jack Barlow's mother was Barbara Hale, who is William Katt's real-life mother.... Texas-born Busey learned to be a bull rider in his youth on an Oklahoma ranch.... Enhancing the picture's verisimilitude, the lead actors did a lot of their own surfing, though doubles were used for the more complex rides.... *Big Wednesday* airs annually during the summer months at outdoor cinema venues in Sydney, Australia.... Co-writer Dennis Aaberg appears in the film as one of the surfers who later becomes a drug dealer.... Gary Busey played a pitcher for the Chicago Cubs in *Rookie of the Year* (1993).... He also was one of the race car drivers in a cross country competition in *The Gumball Rally* (1976) .... Warner Bros.' original double location for Malibu was at La Libertad in El Salvador.... Sunset Beach in Hawaii served as the double location for Malibu as the "day like no other."...Milius recut a TV version called *Summer of Innocence*.

ALL-STAR MOMENTS

Jack's solitude as he rides one last wave before departing for Vietnam.

While a major housewrecker party rages all around her in her own home, Mrs. Barlow calmly sits in a side room reading *Catch 22*.

All of the surfing scenes, especially during the climactic "Big Wednesday" series of monster waves, including the underwater shots as Matt flounders helplessly in the fury of the currents and undertow.

HOME COURT ADVANTAGE

Available on VHS and DVD.

Though adulthood takes them on different paths, surfing will always remain a common bond. (Left to right) Johnson (Vincent), Jack Barlow (William Katt), and Leroy Smith (Gary Busey).

#76 EVERYBODY'S ALL-AMERICAN

Screenwriter Thomas Rickman. **Director** Taylor Hackford. **Producers** Laura Ziskin, Taylor Hackford, Ian Sander, Stuart Benjamin, Alan Blomquist. **Cinematography** Stephen Goldblatt. **Editing** Don Zimmerman. **Music** James Newton Howard. **Art Direction** George Jenson. **Casting** Nancy Klopper. Warner Bros. 1988.

THE PLAYERS Jessica Lange **Babs Rogers Grey**; Dennis Quaid **Gavin Grey**; Timothy Hutton **Donnie "Cake"**; John Goodman **Lawrence**; Carl Lumbly **Narvel Blue**; Ray Baker **Bolling Kiely**; Savannah Boucher **Darlene Kiely**; Patricia Clarkson **Leslie Stone**; Roy Stewart Sr. **Junie**; Pat Perkins **Willy Mae**; Kevin Brune **Roommate**; Joseph Meyer **Pep leader**; Wayne Knight **Fraternity pisser**; Aaron Neville **Man with a gun**; A. J. Duhe **Cleveland linebacker**; David Sheltraw **Georgia quarterback**; Shawn Burks **Georgia center**; Mike Fisher **Redskins quarterback**; Jeff Wickersham **Denver quarterback**; Chuck Hicks **Bigot**; Frank Deford **Café owner**; Lewis Erber Jr. **Broncos coach**

THE GAME In 1956 Gavin Grey (Dennis Quaid), the Grey Ghost, leads Louisiana University to a stunning Sugar Bowl victory. The all-American football player then marries his college sweetheart and Magnolia Queen, Babs (Jessica Lange). Life seems full of promise for the man who has it all...or is it just an illusion? Carried off on the shoulders of his teammates in a victory celebration, the hero gazes out over the adulatory crowd and feels an odd sense that his life has just peaked.

That nagging thought is explored over the next quarter-century of Gavin's life. In his small world of family and friends, Gavin leans heavily on former teammate, friend, and business partner Lawrence (John Goodman) as well as his intellectual nephew, Donnie "Cake" (Timothy Hutton).

As the glimmer of Gavin's golden years as a college football hero fades into a pro football career of comparative obscurity, Gavin resents having to live off his past heroics. Slowly degenerating into a pudgy, drunken story machine regaling jock-sniffing businessmen with tales of his glory days, he realizes his star has faded at the same time as his wife, through determination and self-discovery, is hitting her stride as a shrewd businesswoman.

Now a professor of history, Donnie has studied real heroes, and his lifelong admiration of Gavin gets knocked down a few notches as he witnesses over the years the Grey Ghost's all too real human faults and frailties.

Attending the 25-year reunion of his college's national championship team, Gavin is reminded that what came out of that time that had any real value was his love and marriage to Babs. For that, he states, "I'm the luckiest man that ever lived."

INSTANT REPLAY Producer/director Taylor Hackford and writer Tom Rickman take on an ambitious, sweeping saga covering four decades of American life. This tale of the beautiful Southern couple that embodies the American dream stretches from the mid 1950s to the early 1980s.

In essence, what this interesting Southern-flavored social history boils down to is a surprisingly insular story of what Prince Charming and Cinderella do when the glamour and adulation have faded.

Perhaps overstepping their boundaries by trying to pin a nationalistic angle on their "perfect couple" and by running a bit long, the filmmakers nevertheless have created a fine fable about the dangers of "having it all" early on, then having to

The legendary Gavin Grey (Dennis Quaid, left) catches his breath on the bench with friend and teammate Lawrence (John Goodman).

relive it every day for the rest of one's life until it all seems like a consuming fabrication.

"I've told those stories so many times, " the Grey Ghost complains to his wife, "that I've almost forgot it was me who had those things happen to him. It seems like somebody else."

Everybody's All-American is also a look at America's obsession with winning, heroes, and mythmaking, and the common human failing of building people up and watching their fall from grace with private glee, then discarding them for the next "hero."

The picture ultimately succeeds thanks to the hardworking performances of its two lead characters. Dennis Quaid embodies the decay of the glamour jock, rendering a sympathetic role with traces of tragedy that build as the story advances. Jessica Lange is equally successful in presenting a multidimensional character that is determined to weather the tough times and ultimately flourishes through self-discovery that reveals hidden talents. Their chemistry is believable.

Quaid, in particular, is remarkable in his physical transition from a graceful young jock to a man whose speech is slurred by alcohol and whose potbelly mirrors his expanding disillusionment. He shows us a man who enjoys the spotlight but also wants desperately to be accepted for who he is, not for his myth. Quaid has the picture's most telling moment when he's carried aloft by his teammates and instinctively knows the adulatory roar of the crowd will never be louder the rest of his life. The movie's focus on the role reversal of Lange emerging as the ultimate success is a pleasant twist to the old story of the fading of a star athlete's sports glory.

Most notable in the supporting cast is Ray Baker as the "jock-sniffing" businessman. He is simply superb as the pathetic hero-worshipper whom the star athlete cannot respect. John Goodman's good old boy is genuine, tragic, and memorable. Timothy Hutton, notable for his variable funky facial hair used to represent the passage of time and fashion, comes in and out of the leads' lives as essentially their sounding board. He ably conveys his disillusionment about the faded star persona of the uncle he once idolized.

Rickman's screenplay, based on Frank Deford's novel, remains entertaining despite the inherent dangers of losing focus in spreading itself out over such a long period of time and through a broad prism, trying to comment on many social issues at a time when the nation went through a multitude of drastic changes. Carl Lumbly shines in the subplot of the talented black ballplayer equal in talent to the Grey Ghost but never given the opportunity to develop because of his skin pigmentation.

The football sequences, generally speaking, have an authentic feel to them despite the difficulty that arises when intercutting game recreations with NFL Films footage.

Tracing the characters' lives over the decades is a complex operation, and Hackford gets some commendable assists from the set designers, makeup personnel, hairstylists and art directors. Here as in his other films—*The Idolmaker, La Bamba,* and most recently *Ray,* among others—Hackford is strong in the movie's soundtrack department. James Newton Howard's compositions contrast well with the rhythm and blues artists we hear from the '50s and '60s.

Like the Bruce Springsteen song that goes, "Glory days, they'll pass you by in the wink of a young girl's eye," Hackford presents an American tragedy that is purposely predictable and illustrates how quickly life goes by, including any fleeting moments in the sun. *Everybody's All-American* is at its best as the football star's legend fades into oblivion and the wife finds that her own success is just beginning.

TOP: An impromptu footrace between Gavin (Quaid, left) and Narvel Blue (Carl Lumbly).

BOTTOM: Magnolia Queen Babs Rogers (Jessica Lange) with future husband Gavin.

OUTSIDE THE LINES In Frank Deford's novel the college is located in North Carolina; reportedly Louisiana State University in Baton Rouge was chosen as the movie's backdrop due to better weather.... Inevitably, some felt the film's hero represented LSU's Heisman great Billy Cannon, who later had run-ins with the law, including a conviction on counterfeiting, and whose pro career never fulfilled lofty expectations.... Readers of the book thought the character was based on Charlie "Choo-Choo" Justice. In actuality it was a composite of many athletes the sportswriter had known.... Deford has a cameo as a café owner in the film.... Dennis Quaid, who didn't play on any collegiate athletic teams while studying drama at the University of Houston, is an avid golfer.... One of his drama classmates was Robert Wuhl (*Bull Durham, Arliss*).... Former New England Patriots safety Tim Fox fractured Quaid's collarbone tackling the star while filming a game sequence.... Director Taylor Hackford won an Academy Award for Best Live Action Short for *Teenage Father* (1978).... He was also one of the editors and producers of the Oscar-winning boxing documentary *When We Were Kings* (1996).... Reportedly Kevin Costner at one time was looking at the lead role, as was Tommy Lee Jones.... Some filming took place during halftime of actual LSU games.... The movie was also known as *When I Fall in Love*.... Tom Rickman was nominated for an Academy Award for Best Adapted Screenplay for *Coal Miner's Daughter* (1980).... He co-wrote roller derby's *Kansas City Bomber,* starring Raquel Welch (1972).... The film's Savannah Smith appeared in another football feature, *North Dallas Forty* (1979).... John Goodman played the baseball legend in *The Babe* (1992).... Goodman was offered a football scholarship at Southwest Missouri State University.... Makeup man Dick Smith won an Oscar for his work on *Amadeus* (1984).... Don Zimmerman's editing work includes sports movies, *The Scout* (1994), *Diggstown* (1992), *Rocky III* (1982), *Rocky IV* (1985), and *Heaven Can Wait* (1978).

ALL-STAR MOMENTS The game-winning play against Georgia when Gavin (Quaid) forces a turnover and Lawrence (Goodman) picks up the ball and rumbles down the field, then laterals back to Gavin, who scores a touchdown.

The cold, brutal reality of the grind of professional football is exemplified when Gavin gets nailed on a rainy, muddy field and is derisively told by unsympathetic

Gavin is joined by his wife, Babs, as he announces his retirement from professional football.

opponents, "Welcome to the big leagues, golden boy." Cut to the bleachers, where his wife, Babs (Lange), is told by one of the ladies sitting with her that they're all beauty queens from somewhere, but now they're just players' wives.

Gavin shows he is still wildly in love with his wife when he is asked to kiss the newly crowned beauty queen but instead kisses his wife passionately in front of the crowd, then takes her upstairs where everyone knows his intentions.

The snowy game sequence where Gavin tries a comeback but his fumble irritates the coach. Now he must watch from the sidelines as his replacement saves the day for his team. As teammates celebrate, Gavin stands grimly; knowing his pro career is over, he kicks his helmet, which rolls in the snow.

The embarrassment Gavin feels when he's announced at halftime of a game at his alma mater and realizes the young crowd's cheers aren't for him but for the home team coming back onto the field.

POST-GAME COMMENTS Taylor Hackford:

It's a story about how time erodes certain attitudes and changes circumstances...how the exalted can be diminished and how others can come to the fore. The story contains within it that "end of an era" when simple beauty could be celebrated without cynicism. We still need those icons but we don't feel comfortable about idolizing them with the same ease and trust.[1]

Jessica Lange:

I think what this story is about is the power and endurance of love, the fact that these two people have this kind of love for each other.[2]

Writer Tom Rickman:

The film is also a tragedy of an athlete's life, which has no second act. When everything depends on agility, youth, beauty, and strength, it's hard to build a life. When you spend a lifetime being acclaimed as a great player, you can come to expect the applause. And then, when your career is over, you pay the price of that early success, while those who haven't been given so much early on have a greater chance to grow.[3]

Dennis Quaid:

Football is a metaphor for what this film's really all about. You've been playing since high school. You go into college and the pros and your world is these guys in a locker room. Then all of a sudden one year it's over, and it's like you have to grow up. Now, how do you live your life after that? What kind of goals can you possibly set for yourself? It's bittersweet, is what it is.[4]

Director Hackford on the themes that drew him to the story:

I was particularly interested in that process of the noble athlete[s] who [are] blessed, like dancers, physically gifted from an early age, and are so much better than any of the rest of us. They have grace, elegance, they're just brilliant. There is something we find awe-inspiring about those with such physical gifts. When we are gawky teenagers they are flying higher and jumping further than anyone could possibly imagine. With that almost superhuman talent, we worship them. America in particular worships them. They become in their own way incredible celebrities, gods. There is this adulation that is paid to people who are blessed with that physical brilliance.

It was interesting for me to examine that. Gavin Grey is a rather humble guy. He feels a responsibility to the Grey Ghost. He is not a cheap sellout. But over the course of time is the tragedy that involves every one of these people and there is no avoiding it—and that is you get old. Physical brilliance diminishes.

At that point when the majority of us were living in their shadows, when we start to attain our moment of maturity [and] success, when we come into our own in our 30s, they have been eclipsed and have started their descent. Just as we begin climbing the heights they are descending. There is something incredibly tragic about that. I wanted to explore that ethos in America of our worship of heroes and [how] at the same time we're unprepared to seem them retired and broken down.[5]

Hackford on achieving verisimilitude with the football game sequences:

You have a major problem when dealing with sports in your films, Americans are experts. They look with a critical eye. When I did a dance movie I didn't feel everyone was an expert on ballet or tap dance, but in *Everybody's All-American* I really knew that there would be a lot of people looking at this—would the formations be correct? Would the play look credible? So what I did straight away was get a football coach, Lou Erber, who had been an offensive coordinator for the LA Rams and Buffalo Bills. He would actually put together a training camp and we hired many ex-pros and top college players. Cliff Branch, Tim Fox, Ray Chester. The point is we mixed these great players with the cast and didn't let the actors off the hook. Those are real hits in that movie.

Mike Papajohn deserves credit. He went to LSU, played football, and was also a pro baseball player. Dennis took a lot of hits but I had Mike double for him. Mike was a kamikaze because we had to show these were gladiators getting the crap kicked out of them.

Another thing I'm quite proud of was, I felt seamlessly, integrating real footage from NFL Films. They have great stuff but think about it from my side. If I put the real thing in, then have to cut to my own footage, I have an enormous challenge to get it right. I intercut the famous Bronco game and am proud of the intercut. Imagine us in LSU using fake snow.

We spent a month in training camp then shot all of the football sequences before shooting the drama elements of the picture. This was at a time before you had much digital technology. Those scenes of Dennis on the floor of Death Valley at LSU, which is a famous and wonderful stadium, was packed with fans as we shot at pre-game and halftime of actual Tiger games. We knew the audience would be experts so we had this precision logistical sequence to get all the game elements right.[6]

HOME COURT ADVANTAGE Available on VHS and DVD.

#75 PERSONAL BEST

Screenwriter/Director Robert Towne. **Executive Producer** David Geffen. **Cinematography** Michael Chapman, Caleb Deschanel. **Editing** Bud Smith, Jacqueline Cambas, Jere Huggins, Ned Humphreys, Walt Mulconery. **Music** Jill Fraser, Jack Nitsche, Craig Harris. **Production Design** Ron Hobbs. **Set Decoration** Rick Simpson. **Special Effects** Dale Newkirk. **Sound Editing** John Larsen. Warner Bros. 1982.

THE PLAYERS

Mariel Hemingway **Chris Cahill**; Scott Glenn **Terry Tingloff**; Patrice Donnelly **Tory Skinner**; Kenny Moore **Denny Stites**; Jim Moody **Roscoe Travis**; Kari Grosswilleer **Penny Brill**; Jodi Anderson **Nadia "Pooch" Anderson**; Maren Seidler **Tanya**; Martha Watson **Sheila**; Emily Dole **Maureen**; Pam Spencer **Jan**; Deby Laplante **Trish**; Mitzi McMillin **Laura**; Jane Frederick **Fern Wadkins**; Allan Feuerbach **Zenk**; Larry Pennell **Rick Cahill**; Jan Glotzer **Karen**; Charlie Jones **TV announcer**; Frank Shorter **TV announcer**; Chuck DeBus **Coach**; Robert Horn **Water polo coach**; Len Dawson **Football announcer**; Richard Martini **Meet manager**; Dr. Leroy Perry Jr. **Chiropractor**; Cindy Gilbert **Charlene Benveniste**; Jan Van Reenen **Yelovitch**; Luana Anders **Rita Cahill**; Linda Waltman **Debbie Floyd**; Marlene Harmon **Pam Burnside**

THE GAME At the U.S. Olympic track and field trials in Eugene, Oregon, athletes compete for the right to represent the United States in the 1976 Olympics in Montreal. Young hurdler Chris Cahill (Mariel Hemingway) loses her race but is later consoled by veteran pentathlete Tory Skinner (Patrice Donnelly), who qualified in her event.

Their friendship quickly turns into a love affair. Tory thinks Chris has the potential to make the next Olympic team if she commits to training. She asks her tough coach, Terry Tingloff (Scott Glenn), if he will coach Chris as well. He's suspicious of her motives and doesn't promise anything but does allow Chris to work out with the team. Chris's father (Larry Pennell) is not happy that Chris is training without any scholarship.

Tingloff is not initially impressed with Chris, but she changes his opinion of her with a win in the hurdle sprint at the 1978 World Student Games in Cali, Columbia. Coach offers her a full scholarship and convinces Chris to become a pentathlete like Tory.

This move creates a rivalry between the two girls and leads to their breakup. Chris suffers an injury during training and misses the Pan American Games, a big lead-up to the next Olympics. During rehabilitation she meets a water polo player, Dennis Stites (Kenny Moore), while swimming, then working in the weight room of the gym, and they begin dating.

Fully recovered, Chris now attempts to earn a spot on the 1980 American Olympic team. Sitting at a cafeteria with Coach Tingloff, Chris goes against his wishes and walks over to wish Tory well. During the pentathlon's five-event competition they both struggle to make the team. In the last event, the 800-meter run, Tory edges Chris for the win but they both make the Olympic team (unfortunately, the 1980 Olympics in Moscow would be boycotted by many nations, including the U.S.). The two girls remain friends.

INSTANT REPLAY *Personal Best* is a story of innocence and growing up that is beautifully and authentically presented against a backdrop of the rigors of training in women's pentathlon. It is about a young woman's coming of age, discovering who she is through her body.

Mariel Hemingway shows good form as emerging track star Chris Cahill.

The picture is a celebration of the athletic female form and how each physical and emotional hurdle Chris faces brings her a step closer to self-realization of her individual uniqueness, the fabric that comprises her distinct essence. *Personal Best* takes us through the agonies and ecstasies of female athletics and jock relationships, both among peers and with one's coach.

Mariel Hemingway gives a candid and natural performance, presenting youthful innocence and the purest of intentions. Physically, Hemingway's long legs and distinct facial features create the picture of athletic determination. She faces a daunting task of carrying on a romantic relationship with both a woman and a man as well as pulling off the multi-event challenges of portraying a pentathlete.

In her acting debut, track athlete Patrice Donnelly is surprisingly effective as Hemingway's lover and friend. She is appropriately and convincingly passionate, tough-minded, and reflective when the occasion calls for it. Together they make their relationship seem genuine.

Former world-class marathoner Kenny Moore is also making his screen debut in a relaxed, warm turn as Hemingway's philosophical boyfriend.

Veteran Scott Glenn as the tough but compassionate coach of the two ladies scores in this role by taking the screen's traditional craggy coach to another level. Appearing cold and calculating, Glenn is also willing to tolerate some abusive feedback if he thinks it will make the girls he coaches come out stronger. In subtle ways, the actor prepares the ground for the explosiveness that is sometimes called for in the role.

Glenn's speech about coaching women—"I could have been a man's coach. Do you really think that Chuck Noll has to worry that Franco Harris is going to cry if Terry Bradshaw won't talk to him? Jack Lambert can't play because Mel Blount hurt his feelings?"—is a nice matching bookend to Tom Hanks's "Are you crying? There's no crying in baseball!" in *A League of Their Own*.

TOP: (Left to right) Tory (Patrice Donnelly), Chris (Hemingway), and their coach, Terry (Scot Glenn).

MIDDLE: Shown here playing Chris's boyfriend, Kenny Moore was an Olympic runner.

BOTTOM: Filmmaker Robert Towne would write and direct another track-based feature, 'Without Limits,' featuring Billy Crudup as legendary runner Steve Prefontaine.

This is screenwriter Robert Towne's feature film directorial debut. It met with wrath from some critics, who dwelled on the lesbian aspect with comments like "undisguised voyeurism" and "the worst kind of exploitation and Peeping Tom fantasies." There is little analysis of why Chris and Tory have a sexual relationship, and Chris's later move to a heterosexual relationship has been seen as a convenient cop-out. However, Towne treats the lesbian sex scene with sensitivity and tact—not as pornography, but as two female athletes sharing a world of physical joy and pain. It is presented deliberately without depth or dimension, as a logical extension of an emerging young woman's body worship. The scene is filmed with a dignified sensuality and succeeds at the end in making the viewer feel closer to the two protagonists.

More important are the challenges presented on the fields of play and the bond between the two women as it is affected by competing against each other and by Hemingway's continuing self-discovery, including embarking on a heterosexual relationship.

Towne's appreciation of the female form in action is evident in his utilization of close-ups, iso shots, and the varying of camera speed, focus, and exposure simultaneously as the athletes compete in the same race. The filmmakers succeed in capturing the very real pained grimaces and strained body language of competitors really extending themselves.

Natural sounds such as the runners' breathing and footsteps contribute to the overall authenticity. Though the use of slow motion—and extended shots of feet in particular—can seem pretentious or simply boring, overall much credit goes to cinematographer Michael Chapman for his talents in presenting some riveting pictures. The editors literally sweat the details and do remarkable work.

Undoubtedly there are many who don't share in Towne's up close and personal celebration of physical perfection in the female form; nevertheless, *Personal Best* is notable for its sensitivity and passionate candor. Even though the main characters' individual backgrounds are inadequately addressed and dramatizing internal conflicts is always a difficult chore, Towne manages to capture the protagonists' intensity and determined approach, and to show that these qualities, so well documented in male athletes, also characterize the female sports world, where life is a competition, especially against oneself.

OUTSIDE THE LINES The genesis of the film came from Towne's chance encounter with pentathlete Jane Frederick in a UCLA weight room in 1976.... Mariel Hemingway trained with the Los Angeles Naturite Track Club in Los Angeles as well as with Olympic gold medal high jumper Dick Fosbury.... Music impresario David Geffen was executive producer.... The film was shot in Los Angeles, San Luis Obispo, and Hayward athletic field in Eugene, Oregon.... Mariel is the granddaughter of novelist Ernest Hemingway.... Costar Patrice Donnelly was a world-ranked pentathlete and member of the 1976 U.S. Olympic team.... Kenny Moore was a two-time Olympic marathoner who would co-write with Towne *Without Limits*.... Towne won an Oscar for his screenplay for *Chinatown* (1975).... Cinematographer Michael Chapman was nominated for an Academy Award for his *Raging Bull* (1980) photography.... This was Towne's feature film directorial debut.... Some within the track community took offense at the lesbian aspect of the film. Coach Paul Ward, who worked with women's field events as part of an Olympic development program, urged athletes to refuse to participate in the picture. Not many did, but one was Lorna Griffin, at the time the

American record holder in the discus.... No doubles were used; actors did their own athletics and athletes did their own acting, except that pentathlete Sharon Hatfield bore such a resemblance to Hemingway that the director used footage of her actual competition for some long-angle clips.... Donnelly, who did research for Towne on the script, also read for the role that went to Hemingway.... Originally set up at Warner Bros., the film was halted early in production due to a Screen Actors Guild strike.... Towne then took the project as an independent, finding financing through David Geffen.... An ensuing dispute between the director and executive producer caused another delay of several months.... The delays created scheduling conflicts; for example, some of the scenes were shot by cinematographer Caleb Deschanel (whose credits include *The Black Stallion*) since Chapman was previously committed to shooting Steve Martin's *Dead Men Don't Wear Plaid*.... During production came the news that the United States, along with many other countries, was boycotting the 1980 Moscow Olympics. Even though the story basically ends at the qualifying trials, the boycott had to be addressed in the script.... Sigourney Weaver was considered for the role of Tory Skinner.... Towne wrote the screenplay for the Tom Cruise auto racing film *Days of Thunder* (1986).... Editor Walt Mulroney's credits include *The Karate Kid* (1984).... Cinematographer Chapman directed the football film *All the Right Moves* (1983).... His photography credits include the animated movie *Space Jam* (1996).... Bud Smith won a British Academy Award for editing *Flashdance* (1983).... Smith also did cinematography work for the football feature *The Replacements* (2000).... Towne worked as an actor in Jack Nicholson's basketball film *Drive, He Said* (1971).

ALL-STAR MOMENTS The opening images of Chris Cahill in her hurdle race.

Coach kicking back sunning himself as his two girls struggle in their sandy beach hill run.

Chris sprinting past a male runner and her coach chiding the embarrassed man.

Slow-motion sequences of the final hurdle race when Tory and Chris compete head to head and the entire race sequence of the final event, the 800-meter run.

HOME COURT ADVANTAGE Available on VHS.

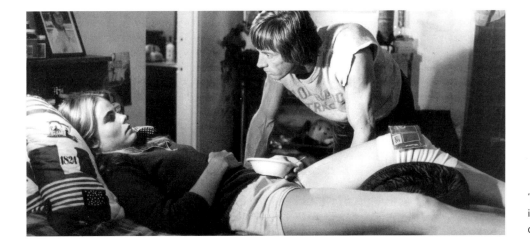

'Personal Best' is a study in athletic and romantic commitments.

#74 Dogtown and Z-Boys

Screenwriters Stacy Peralta, Craig Stecyk. **Director** Stacy Peralta. **Producers** Agi Orsi, Jay Wilson. **Cinematography** Peter Pilafian. **Editing** Paul Crowder. **Music Editing** Terry Wilson. Sony. 2001.

THE PLAYERS Sean Penn **Narrator**; Stacy Peralta **Himself (Zephyr skate team)**; Jeff Ho **Himself**; Tony Alva **Himself**; Henry Rollins **Himself**; Jay Adams **Himself**; Jeff Ament **Himself**; Bob Biniak **Himself**; Paul Constantineau **Himself**; Skip Engblom **Himself**; Tony Friedkin **Himself**; Glen Friedman **Himself**; Tony Hawk **Himself**; Shogo Kubo **Himself**; Joe Leahy **'50s voice announcer (narrator)**; Ian MacKaye **Himself**; Jim Muir **Himself**; Peggy Oki **Herself**; Nathan Pratt **Himself**; Wentzle Ruml **Himself**; Allen Sarlo **Himself**; Craig Stecyk **Himself**

THE GAME *Dogtown and Z-Boys* chronicles the lives of a unique skateboard team, the Zephyrs, within the social context of their 1970s Southern California environment.

Through these unconventionally fluid teens who surf in the morning and skateboard in the afternoon, we get a glimpse of the foundation of the extreme sports movement.

The origins of "going aerial," the style that would make superstars out of the group's Tony Alva and Jay Adams, are honed on the lips of empty swimming pools. Taking advantage of the extended drought in the area, the Zephyrs create their inventive flying maneuvers by sneaking into strangers' backyards, then move on to another, one step ahead of the police.

The Zephyr Skate Team (Z-Boys for short) take their swagger and disdain for tradition to the annual national championships in 1975 and steal the show with their radical, high-flying, surfer-influenced style.

In taking a sport that was going the way of the hula hoop and bringing its influence to sport, fashion, and music, the Z-Boys helped spawn a multimillion-dollar global industry. Events like snowboarding and aerials added to the Olympic program as well as entire competitions such as the X-Games can be traced back to the influence of the Lords of Dogtown, the Zephyrs.

INSTANT REPLAY *Dogtown and Z-Boys* is an entertaining blend of home movies, magazine stills, aerial maps, clippings, and interviews done with inventive editing and supported by terrific music from that era.

The filmmakers offer an engaging social history of a specific time and place, capturing well these "bad boy" (and lone girl) teens who came from lower middle-class roots to become pop stars simply by having a blast with their unique brand of improvisational purism.

Like the better documentaries, it succeeds in drawing in viewers unfamiliar with the subject; even those who've never ridden a skateboard feel a part of the action here. A lot of that credit belongs to film editor Paul Crowder, music editor Terry Wilson, and production designer Craig Stecyk.

While the story is compelling and culturally significant, there are many aspects of the film that prevent it from being a spectacular one.

As one of the original Zephyrs, director Stacy Peralta offers a penetrating insider view. He certainly gets his aging buddies at ease as they reflect on their glory days together, but as a documentary the film lacks balance.

The viewer really only experiences the sport through the Zephyrs' eyes. More viewpoints from rivals, promoters, family, neighbors, and friends would have helped, as would some more of the thoughtful introspection of the most gifted rider, Jay Adams, whose poor life choices resulted in jail time. Without a contrasting perspective, the self-mythologizing becomes burdensome.

Sean Penn's uninspired narration fails to match the hard-edged energy of Peralta's presentation, but at the same time we get the sense that the actor respects the material because of similar personal experiences in his youth.

The choice of partner Vans Shoes to finance the project creates a clubbiness that further weakens the balance we expect from a documentary.

Like Al Davis's Raiders, the Zephyrs saw themselves as outlaws, as a punk rock alternative to the conventional athlete; this was most evident in scenes from the national championships in 1975. In further illuminating the Zephyrs' uniqueness, Peralta's social anthropology brilliantly delineates how home-grown cultural aspects from the downtrodden side of their Santa Monica/Venice roots, such as gangs, graffiti art, hot rods, and surfing, all shaped their look and attitude.

In the end, *Dogtown and Z-Boys* doesn't go far enough to probe what drove and inspired these young daredevils. Lacking the objective style of a traditional documentary, the film still presents an appealing look at a universal theme within Peralta's unique subculture—energetic teens hungry for self-expression.

As they ride the asphalt waves with the improvisational skills of painters or jazz musicians, the Zephyrs' youthful exuberance as maestros on polyurethane wheels is a joy to watch.

OUTSIDE THE LINES The narrator, Sean Penn, also did some surfing and hanging out in the Dogtown area in his youth.... The *Dogtown* film was inspired by a 1999 Spin magazine article, "The Lords of Dogtown."...Extreme sports icon Tony

TOP: Improv is the name of the game.

BOTTOM: Peggy Oki.

LEFT: The field of play—an empty swimming pool, anybody's pool.

Champions take risks.

Hawk also appears in the film.... Stacy Peralta won Best Director for this documentary at the Sundance Film Festival.... Peralta also directed *Riding Giants* (2004), chronicling the origins and advancement of the surfing culture, which Penn also narrated.... Terry Wilson was the music editor for *Major League 3* (1998).... Peggy Oki was the only female member of the 12-person Zephyr team.... It was an East Coast surfer, Frank Gainsworthy, who developed the idea of putting polyurethane wheels on skateboards to allow more maneuverability, a cornerstone of the Z-Boys' success and a key to the sport's revival.... The film's soundtrack was nominated for a Grammy.... In its heyday the Pacific Ocean Park Pier, where the Zephyrs did much of their surfing, was known as the "Coney Island of the West."...Jeff Ho's surf shop with Skip Engblom and Craig Stecyk was the group's hangout and where a lot of the surfing influence in their style originated.... Tony Alva starred opposite Leif Garrett in *Skateboard* (1977).... The Z-boys' skating style was greatly influenced by Hawaiian surfer Larry Bertelman.

ALL-STAR MOMENTS
Early in the film we see a montage of the Z-Boys and hear the comment, "I was on summer vacation for 20 years."

The editing that intercuts between showing the surfing style the Z-Boys modeled themselves after, and their descriptions of how important style was and what they considered to be good or poor form. "Style was everything."

Clip of the director in his youth appearing on the original *Charlie's Angels* TV series then talking about skateboarding being his "ticket out" to a better life.

HOME COURT ADVANTAGE
Available on VHS and DVD. Several special edition DVDs but also various options paired with other titles. There are separate two-disc sets with *Lords of Dogtown* and *Riding Giants*.

#73 RUDY

Screenwriter Angelo Pizzo. **Director** David Anspaugh. **Producers** Lee Mayes, Robert Fried, Cary Woods, Angelo Pizzo. **Cinematography** Oliver Wood. **Editing** David Rosenbloom. **Music** Jerry Goldsmith. **Production Design** Robb Wilson King. TriStar. 1993.

THE PLAYERS
Sean Astin **Rudy Ruettiger**; Ned Beatty **Daniel**; Jon Favreau **D-Bob**; Greta Lind **Mary**; Scott Benjaminson **Frank**; Mary Ann Thebus **Betty**; Charles Dutton **Fortune**; Robert Prosky **Father Cavanaugh**; Lili Taylor **Sherry**; Christopher Reed **Pete**; Deborah Wittenberg **Young Sherry**; Christopher Erwin **7-year-old Mark**; Kevin Duda **9-year-old Bernie**; Robert Benirschke **11-year-old Mark**; Luke Massery **13-year-old Rudy**; Robert Steinmiller Jr. **13-year-old Pete**; Jake Armstrong **13-year-old Bernie**; John Duda **15-year-old Frank**; Joe Sikorra **17-year-old Johnny**; Gerry Becker **Father Ted**; Bob Swan **Father Zajak**; Leonard Kuberski **Classroom priest**; Father James Riehle **Locker room priest**; Robert Mohler **Johnny**; Todd Spicer **Boy in neighborhood**; Jason Miller **Ara Parseghian**; Jean Plumhoff **Fran**; Chelcie Ross **Dan Devine**; Spyridon Stratisos **Coach Gillespie**; John Beasley **Coach Warren**; Ron Dean **Coach Yonto**; Paul Bergan **Coach**; John Whitmer **Football trainer**; Vince Vaughn **Jamie O'Hara**

THE GAME Daniel "Rudy" Ruettiger (Sean Astin) grows up in an environment where he is constantly being told that success will elude him. He hears this from his teachers, friends, coaches, advisors, and especially his father (Ned Beatty).

The general consensus is that there's no way a short, stout kid with inadequate grades and athletic skills hailing from a large blue-collar family in a steel mill town will ever get into Notre Dame University, let alone make their hallowed football team. But those are precisely Rudy's goals, and he sets about achieving them.

Father Cavanaugh (Robert Prosky), appreciative of Rudy's drive, helps get him into nearby Holy Cross, where after much effort he gets the grades and manages to transfer to Notre Dame as a junior transfer.

To be close to his other goal, Rudy works as an aide to groundskeeper Fortune (Charles Dutton). Unable to afford even the dorm life, Rudy often sleeps in his boss's office down below the football stadium.

After tough tryouts Rudy manages to make the Fighting Irish football team, sort of, as a member of the brutal practice squad. Through his devotion and willingness to take a beating as a live tackling dummy day in and day out, Rudy slowly garners the players' and coaches' respect.

Coach Ara Parseghian (Jason Miller), impressed with Rudy's determination, promises the young man that he'll let him dress for one game before he graduates, enabling Rudy's name to be recorded as an official member of the team.

As the physical punishment is about to pay off, a new coach, Dan Devine (Chelcie Ross), takes over. Focused on establishing himself, Devine has little time for non-impact players, and it looks like Rudy's dream will elude him.

After a period of disillusionment where he gets encouragement from Fortune, Rudy stays the course. As the second season rolls along and the physical punishment he endures mounts, Rudy is rewarded. Through the leading players' support, the new coach finally yields, allowing Rudy to suit up in the last game.

Proud family and friends sit in the stands as Rudy leads the fighting Irish out of the tunnel and onto the field. Rudy finally enters the game with just seconds remaining and makes the most of it. He sacks the quarterback, and as the game ends Rudy is carried off the field by his jubilant teammates. A young man's exhaustive efforts to reach a dream have been fulfilled.

Father Cavanaugh (Robert Prosky) helps Rudy (Sean Astin) as he tries to gain entry into Notre Dame.

INSTANT REPLAY Part *Hoosiers*, and partly the sort of college football film popular in the '30s, '40s, and '50s, *Rudy* dances dangerously along the out-of-bounds markers with its sentimentality at times but ultimately is difficult not to like.

In contrast to their basketball gem, *Hoosiers*, Indiana filmmakers David Anspaugh and Angelo Pizzo put the emphasis here on personal striving. Thus the film avoids the overdone cinematic cliché of winning the big game and instead explores success as measured on a personal level.

Pizzo lays out a well-drawn story of the working class with fine characterizations that teammate Anspaugh unspools with really good pacing.

If *Rudy* offers few surprises, it also avoids superfluous subplots and the multiple pitfalls that threaten this type of picture, delivering in earnest and uplifting fashion.

Lacking the natural athletic gifts of Fighting Irish legend George Gipp, this pudgy, scrappy steelworker in his own way becomes a legend at Notre Dame, a kind of undersized Fifth Horseman. With a low-key, affecting performance, Sean Astin provides the right energy to the character throughout the ups and downs of the story and is a key reason for the success of the film's everyman appeal.

Astin is afforded some terrific cast mates, most notably Charles Dutton. Dutton's "tough love" groundskeeper, who keeps Rudy focused, is a dymanic performance, forceful yet melancholy. Veterans Robert Prosky and Ned Beatty expertly carry off their roles as Rudy's advisory priest and father respectively. Jon Favreau adds some humor as the bright, chubby, romance-hungry classmate.

Certainly aiding the performances and striking the right emotional chords is the brilliant music of Jerry Goldsmith, one of his better efforts in a long and distinguished career. Add in the Notre Dame fight songs and chants, the terrific pictures of the Notre Dame campus by cinematographer Oliver Wood, and the game action shot during halftime of a real game, and one gets a terrific sense of fall life in football-crazed South Bend.

Rudy is an engaging tribute to the power of the human spirit.

OUTSIDE THE LINES It was the first time in over 50 years that the University of Notre Dame gave filmmakers extensive access to the campus. The last time was *Knute Rockne: All-American*.... Most of the reenacted game scenes were shot at halftime of a Tennessee-Notre Dame game—a game that resulted in the Volunteers' biggest comeback in school history, coming back from 31-7 to win 35-34.... The crowd scenes of Rudy's final game were shot during halftime of an actual 1992 Boston College-Notre Dame game in which the real Rudy appears as one of the fans.... Ironically, the film's writer and director were graduates of rival Indiana University.... Actor Chelcie Ross, who played coach Dan Devine, also performed in Pizzo/Anspaugh's *Hoosiers* (1986).... Actor Jason Miller, who was nominated for an Oscar as Father Damien Karras in *The Exorcist*, wrote the play *That Championship Season*, for which he won a Tony award in 1973.... Jon Favreau's other sports movie appearances include *Wimbledon* (2004), *The Replacements* (2000), and the television film *Rocky Marciano* (1999), where he starred as the boxing champ.... Actor Charles Dutton directed *Against the Ropes* (2004), which featured Meg Ryan as a boxing manager.... Ned Beatty was featured in the Spike Lee basketball film *He Got Game* (1998).... Filmmakers David Anspaugh and Angelo Pizzo also teamed for the soccer drama *The Game of Their Lives* (2005).

TOP: Groundskeeper Fortune (Charles Dutton) gets Rudy a job maintaining the football field at Notre Dame.

BOTTOM: Astin (center) discusses a scene with writer Angelo Pizzo (left) and director David Anspaugh (right).

ALL-STAR MOMENTS Sitting in the break room at the steel mill, Pete (Christopher Reed) celebrates his friend Rudy's (Sean Astin) birthday by giving him a secondhand Notre Dame jacket. Telling Rudy, "My dad always said having dreams is what makes life tolerable," Pete lights a cigarette and stands the match in Rudy's cupcake as a candle. Rudy blows it out.

After failing to find a ticket to get in to see a Notre Dame game, Rudy, long after everyone has gone home, walks about in the empty stands, then picks up a program and sits high up in the stadium.

Teammates take sides as Rudy gets pummeled in practice. As a fight breaks out after Rudy makes a tackle, the coach reprimands the running back, telling him, "If you had 1/10 the heart of Ruettiger you'd have made all-American!"

Stadium shot when Rudy tells Fortune (Charles Dutton) he's quit the team. Fortune tears into him, saying, among other things, "You are so full of crap. You're five-foot-nothing. 100 [pounds] and nothing, and you've got hardly a speck of athletic ability, and you hung in with the best college football team in the land for two years."

POST-GAME COMMENTS Angelo Pizzo, the film's screenwriter, on *Rudy*:

> My goal and design in every film that I write is that it appeals to people that not only know nothing about the sport but don't even like sports. I've heard over and over again from people who hate football and never watch sports that they connect to *Rudy*.

Director David Anspaugh:

> By setting his goals, he discovers all sorts of wonderful things along the way. When he finally enters the game, anything else that happens is just icing on the cake. [2]

Former Notre Dame quarterback Joe Montana, describing the big moment for his teammate, the real Rudy:

The filmmakers of 'Rudy' also created 'Hoosiers.'

Guys just went crazy on the sideline. It was like we had won the national championship, that's how excited everybody was for Rudy.[3]

Actor Sean Astin on his title role:

As an actor, you look for characters who will help you show sides of yourself you don't often get to feel or portray. Rudy is a survivor, a go-getter. There is a tremendous integrity about his purpose and goals.[4]

Angelo Pizzo:

Sports are a metaphor. Unlike most sports movies, it's not about the state championship or a great athlete. It's really about the last guy on the bench. For a player with Rudy's ability to actually get on the field for 27 seconds is in some ways a more significant accomplishment than a gifted athlete throwing 3 touchdown passes in one game.[5]

HOME COURT ADVANTAGE Available on VHS and DVD. In addition to a standard release and a deluxe edition, Columbia TriStar has also paired *Rudy* in separate two-disc sets with *Big Fish, Radio,* and *Brian's Song.*

#72 ENTER THE DRAGON

Screenwriter Michael Allin. **Director** Robert Clouse. **Producers** Raymond Chow, Paul Heller, Fred Weintraub. **Cinematography** Gil Hubbs. **Editing** Kurt Hirschler, George Watters. **Music** Lalo Schifrin. **Costume Design** Louis Sheng. Warner Bros. 1973.

THE PLAYERS Bruce Lee **Lee**; John Saxon **Roper**; Jim Kelly **Williams**; Ahna Capri **Tania**; Kien Shih **Han**; Robert Wall **O'Harra**; Angela Mao Ying **Su Lin**; Betty Chung **Mei Ling**; Geoffrey Weeks **Braithwaite**; Peter Archer **Parsons**; Ho Lee Yan **Old Man**; Marlene Clark **Secretary**; Allan Kent **Golfer**; William Keller **Cop**; Mickey Caruso **Cop**; Bolo Yeung **Bolo**; Chuck Norris **Messenger**

THE GAME Lee (Bruce Lee), a Shaolin martial arts expert, is recruited by Mr. Braithwaite (Geoffrey Weeks), an Englishman representing an international intelligence agency, to gather evidence against Han (Kien Shih), a Shaolin renegade, powerful drug lord and slave owner.

Lee is motivated because Han's goons are responsible for his sister Su Lin's (Angela Mao) death, and because Han has broken the Shaolin code of honor. Lee accepts the invitation to a martial arts contest Han hosts on his island fortress in a remote area near Hong Kong. Only the best are invited. This includes two Americans, Roper (John Saxon) and Williams (Jim Kelly).

After a lavish welcoming party, Lee begins his spying and soon finds evidence against Han. Word gets back to Han about this breach in security. Humiliated, Han orders his guards to prove themselves in the martial arts tournament. They are all badly beaten. Lee also defeats O'Harra (Robert Wall), the man directly responsible for his sister's death. Bloodied and beaten, O'Harra then attacks Lee with a broken bottle. Lee kills him.

Han, a talented martial artist himself, beats Williams using his prosthetic metal hand after concluding that he was the one who spied and beat his guards.

Han then gives Roper a tour of his drug and slavery operation, hoping the American will work for him to expand his U.S. operation. Despite the clear threat in showing him the dead body of fellow American Williams, Roper refuses.

As Han orders the death of Lee and Roper, Lee radios to his British director for help and frees all the slaves, who help them overwhelm the remaining guards.

It comes down to a showdown between Lee and Han. Han now adds extended razor-edged fingers to his metal hand. The martial artists battle to the death. Eventually Han is impaled on a spear. Lee then rejoins Roper as Mr. Braithwaite's rescue operation lands on the island.

INSTANT REPLAY Jean-Claude Van Damme, Steven Seagal, Jet Li, Chuck Norris, Jackie Chan—several martial artists have enjoyed some success on the silver screen and even drawn in broader audiences, but none have the electrifying presence or achieved the legendary status of Bruce Lee.

In this first martial arts picture co-produced by a leading Hollywood studio, Bruce Lee displays the combination of skill, speed, grace, power, and energy that catapulted him to superstardom. Thanks to *Enter the Dragon*, over a quarter-century later Lee remains the definitive martial arts movie star—though mythmaking and cult status

TOP: Roper (John Saxon, left) in action against Bolo (Bolo Yeung).

BOTTOM: Tania (Ahna Capri) is part of a vision of loveliness.

due to his early death, not unlike James Dean and his early demise just before the release of *Rebel Without a Cause*, also play a role here.

Filmed after *Return of the Dragon* but released before it, *Enter the Dragon* takes the genre's usual simplistic plots built on revenge and incorporates a James Bond feel. Though the similarities to *Dr. No*—including the evil villain as a cat-loving, handless madman operating his dastardly empire from an island fortress—add depth to the story, *Enter the Dragon* remains essentially a showcase for the unique martial arts philosophy and physical talents of Bruce Lee.

From the opening scenes to the climactic battle, Lee uses his coolness and flat-out brilliant martial arts skills to educate and inspire about the power and balletic grace of his particular discipline of self-defense. It is one driven more by a philosophical and intellectual approach, "the art of fighting without fighting."

While the skeleton of a story serves mainly as a thread to hold together the fight sequences, Lee, though clearly a one-man army, is supported by some solid teammates in front of the camera and behind it.

In a difficult assignment, Robert Clouse directs the action with reasonably good pacing. He and his team create a very atmospheric environment, not only with brilliant sets and the vibrant costume design work of Louis Sheng, but also with highly evocative location shooting by Gill Hubbs. Hubbs's shots of the Hong Kong harbor area and the lavish party scenes are indelible.

Unquestionably it is the fight scenes, choreographed by and starring Bruce Lee, that make the film a classic.

Hollywood brought in Americans John Saxon and karate champion Jim Kelly. Saxon is a good contrast to the inwardly focused Lee. The veteran actor pulls off his role as a compulsive gambler, while Kelly performs well and scores the film's best lines. Ahna Capri is smooth, vivacious as the hostess Tania.

The foils include a well-cast, convincing group of villains. Peter Archer is the nasty New Zealander. Robert Wall as O'Harra is the man directly responsible for killing Lee's sister. Bolo Yeung is the enforcer. Kien Shih, as the king of the evil empire, puts a fine Oriental twist on his James Bondian heavy.

In the climactic battle, Shih is convincing as a desperate opponent in a fight to the death against Lee. It is well done on all fronts. Director Clouse's staging of that scene using a room full of mirrors is a nice homage to Orson Welles's *The Lady from Shanghai*.

The fight scenes, especially in the tournament and then against Han, are still impressive today. *Enter the Dragon* shows Bruce Lee at his best.

OUTSIDE THE LINES *Enter the Dragon* was the last film Bruce Lee completed before his death.... Jim Kelly was a U.S. karate champion.... Bruce Lee staged the fight scenes, which included the martial arts disciplines of karate, judo, hapkido, tae kwon do, and tai chi chuan.... Jackie Chan, though uncredited, helped supervise the stunts...and gets his neck broken as one of the guards trying to assault Lee.... This was really the first martial arts film by mainstream Hollywood, as Warner Bros. made a co-production deal with Hong Kong filmmaker Raymond Chow.... Hungarian-born actress Ahna Capri also appeared in baseball's *Bingo Long's Traveling All-Stars and Motor Kings* (1976).... In 1968 Chuck Norris became the Professional World Middleweight Karate Champion. He held the title undefeated until he retired in 1974.... One of Norris's students around that time was Steve McQueen, who encouraged Norris to get into acting.

Han (Kien Shih, left) feels the wrath of Lee (Bruce Lee).

ALL-STAR MOMENTS At a colorful Shaolin temple, Lee (Bruce Lee) does some impressive back flips over some students.

American martial artist Roper (Saxon) rides around a Hong Kong corner in a rickshaw, with rickshaws filled with his luggage following behind.

American contestant Williams (Kelly) is alone listening to music in his room when the hostess offers him a choice of girls for company. He chooses several.

Williams goes to meet Han (Shih) in his office. Han accuses Williams of spying. Williams drops Han's bodyguards, saying to his host, "Man, you come right out of a comic book." After Han slips off a glove to show the metal hand he fights with, however, Williams gets beaten to a pulp.

At the martial arts contest, O'Harra (Wall) tries to impress Lee by slugging through a thick board. Lee, shrugging it off, says, "Boards don't hit back." As they prepare to fight Lee flashes back to O'Harra's role in his sister's death. Lee proceeds to dismantle O'Harra in the contest even after O'Harra resorts to maneuvers well outside the rules of the sport.

Doing his spy work in the underground lair of the evil tournament promoter Han, Lee shows off his martial arts skills fending off many guards as well as his use of "numbchucks."

Climactic fight against Han.

HOME COURT ADVANTAGE Available on VHS and DVD. Several versions appear on DVD, including a 30th Anniversary Edition.

#71 TIN CUP

Screenwriters Ron Shelton, John Norville. **Director** Ron Shelton. **Producers** Gary Foster, David Lester. **Cinematography** Russell Boyd. **Editing** Kimberly Ray, Paul Seydor. **Music** William Ross. **Production Design** James Bissell. **Art Direction** Gae Buckley, Chris Burian-Mohr. Warner Bros. 1996.

THE PLAYERS Kevin Costner **Roy "Tin Cup" McAvoy**; Rene Russo **Dr. Molly Griswold**; Don Johnson **David Simms**; Cheech Marin **Romeo Posar**; Linda Hart **Doreen**; Dennis Burkley **Earl**; Rex Linn **Dewey**; Lou Myers **Clint**; Richard Lineback **Curt**; George Perez **Jose**; Mickey Jones **Turk**; Michael Milhoan **Boone**; Gary McCord **Himself/golf pro**; Craig Stadler **Himself/golf pro**; Peter Jacobsen **Himself/golf pro**; Jim Nantz **Himself/TV announcer**; Ken Venturi **Himself/TV announcer**; Ben Wright **Himself/TV announcer**; Frank Chirkanian **Himself/TV producer**; Lance Barrow **TV director**; Brian Hammons **TV announcer**; Mike Ritz **TV announcer**; Peter Kostis **TV field reporter**; Jimmy Roberts **TV reporter**; George Michael **TV host**; Kris Ancira **Golden Tassel dancer**; Sharyn McCreedy **Golden Tassel waitress**; Gregory Avellone **Fan behind ropes**; Kevin Wilson **Phil Mickelson's caddie**; Susan Cabral **Patient in exit room**; Steven Lewison **Simms's caddie**; Rob Harris **Simms's agent**; Allan Malamud **U.S. Open reporter**

THE GAME Roy McAvoy (Kevin Costner) is a talented but undisciplined golf pro living out of a trailer in a tiny Texas prairie town. He operates a driving range that has more armadillos than golfers.

Largely due to his inability to "play it safe" when the odds demand it, Roy has squandered his chance for stardom on the pro tour. He toils instead in obscurity at the range with his friend and caddy, Romeo (Cheech Marin).

One day a pretty female psychologist, Dr. Molly Griswold (Rene Russo), shows up at the range for a lesson. Roy is smitten. Molly however is dating Roy's rival, Dave Simms (Don Johnson). Dave is Roy's old college teammate who went on to success on the pro tour by steadily playing the percentages—just the opposite of Roy's style, as both players are aware.

Giving Molly lessons has rekindled Roy's love of the game. To impress her and win her heart, to knock his smarmy rival Dave down a few pegs, and to prove something to himself, Roy decides to not only qualify but win the U.S. Open, considered by many the most difficult tournament.

Success in the U.S. Open demands self-discipline and a smart strategy of patiently waiting for the few opportunities that present themselves and taking advantage of them when they arrive. These are precisely the areas lacking in Roy's game. It will take a lot of work to get his game under control, primarily in the mental and emotional aspects.

Molly agrees to be Roy's mental therapist, in a strictly professional capacity, to help him with his golf quest. They get off to a rocky start, though, as Roy suggests that perhaps he's "full of inner demons" and Molly retorts that he's "full of bullshit."

Out on the course, Romeo, who knows Roy's game better than anyone and understands what needs to be done to get it in shape for the U.S. Open, is constantly met with resistance in getting Roy to alter his old tendencies. But Molly and Romeo survive the highs and lows on the road to getting Roy ready, and he eventually qualifies for the grand slam event.

Romeo's strategy of getting Roy drunk the night before the first round of the U.S. Open (since he tends to play better with a hangover) backfires. Despite telling Romeo that he's learned his lesson and will play conservatively, "fairways and greens," Roy scores an 83. Meanwhile, his rival Simms takes the early lead with a 67.

On the next day, Roy storms back with a record 62. People are scratching their heads wondering who this range operator from Texas is and what he's doing atop the leaderboard.

In the third round, at a crucial juncture, Roy demonstrates that perhaps he hasn't learned his lesson. Roy goes against his caddy's suggestion of the proper club (backed up by the former champion and TV analyst Ken Venturi) and ends up with par when a more conservative approach might have yielded a birdie.

In the final round, Roy, with Romeo at his side and Molly in the gallery, is tied for the lead coming to the last hole in regulation. Simms, just one stroke back, plays the percentages and lays up on his shot from the 18th fairway ("Gutless wonder!" Roy mutters to his caddy). But Romeo suggests that Roy do the same, reminding him that birdie wins. However, Roy's old instincts take over; he wants the glory of getting in the record books and says an eagle will win with a record score.

Roy "Tin Cup" McAvoy (Kevin Costner) in action.

Ignoring Romeo's advice, Roy goes for it. At first it looks like the right idea, but the ball rolls off the green and into the water hazard. Despite reminders that he can still make par from the ball drop, Roy insists on hitting from the same spot, blaming "a gust of wind from the gods." His next shot finds the water, as do several more. Now the TV crew, Simms, and gallery are shaking their heads in disbelief at this bullheaded craziness. Doreen (Linda Hart), Roy's ex-girlfriend, is not surprised and tells Molly, standing next to her, "It's a miracle he lasted this long."

When Romeo informs Roy he has one ball left in the bag and if he misses he's disqualified, Molly breaks out giggling at the absurdity of it all but understands Roy and tells him just to "let it rip." Amazingly, the ball lands on the green and into the hole for a 12. The crowd yells, and Roy, feeling true to himself, holds his club triumphantly in the air. When Romeo says, "Well boss, we blew that one," Roy responds, "I didn't come here to play for no second, Romeo...and Simms will always be second."

When Roy laments having given away the U.S. Open, Molly makes light of the situation, reminding him that down the road people may not remember who won, but they'll always remember Roy's 12.

Later, back at his trailer, Molly points out that, while Roy has learned a little self-discipline, she's learned from him to take more risks—and that next year's U.S. Open beckons.

INSTANT REPLAY Undoubtedly, successful movies involving stick-oriented sports, outside of baseball, have been few and far between. I can't recall a tremendous field hockey, polo, or lacrosse feature, and while ice hockey has had some good representation (see *Slap Shot, Miracle*), there's a shortage of good golf films, despite the global popularity of the sport.

After *Pat and Mike* and *Caddyshack*, one is hard-pressed to fill out a foursome. While *Happy Gilmore* ("The price is wrong, bitch"), *The Caddy, Follow the Sun*, and *Dead Solid Perfect* (who can forget Hubert "Bad Hair" Wimberly?) have some entertaining elements, they do not make the cut.

Several productions from the 1930s, though not feature length and therefore not eligible for in-depth treatment here, are nevertheless worth mentioning. These are *The Golf Specialist,* with W. C. Fields; *Three Little Beers,* featuring The Three Stooges; and Bobby Jones's Vitaphone string of instructional shorts.

Tin Cup is a welcome third. Ron Shelton, a single handicapper himself, and former Stanford golfer John Norville, have written a smart script that pulls off the difficult

PGA veteran John Cook (center) adds some verisimilitude to the proceedings.

trick of staying true to the sport's fanatics (and they are) while providing a broad comedy that appeals to those who are inclined to think of a birdie as an obscene gesture.

One of the clever ways they achieve this is via Roy (Costner) and Molly's (Russo) patient-therapist relationship, which not only brings in the voice of a non-golfer (in Russo) but also offers an intelligent parody of the ways men and women verbally and emotionally play off each other.

This nutty romantic comedy is a modern version of the roles that once were written for the likes of Katharine Hepburn, Cary Grant, Jean Arthur, James Garner, Doris Day, and Rock Hudson. The banter between the sexes is timeless, full of wit, pathos, and an enchanting tension that is one of the writer/director's particular strengths.

Shelton overcomes the nearly impossible handicap of incorporating one of the least cinematic sports to tell a story about competing against ourselves, staying in control yet being willing to "go for it."

As his other sporting films suggest, Shelton knows from personal experience that while there's nobility in striving for perfection, in the end most lose, and that it's reaching for the unattainable through trial and error, through twists and traps, that makes for an interesting story. In his own way the loser really ends up a winner.

Tin Cup has many parallels to *Bull Durham,* which set standards that are tough to match. Essentially, once again Shelton uses the metaphors and rituals of sport to look at the intricacies of love and relationships in general.

One of the downsides of *Tin Cup* is that its pace, paralleling the sport, is leisurely. When the tempo becomes sluggish, the film feels self-indulgent. Some tighter editing would have prevented a few scenes from feeling drawn out and labored, rather like the pace of the armadillos that appear now and then.

At the same time, Shelton shows he has a real feel for the game, both in golf and in romance. His ability to draw out human flaws and idiosyncrasies via sports metaphors is unmatched. The former ballplayer does it by tweaking the traditional Rockyesque sports movie formula of all glory to the underdog via the big game.

McAvoy's (Costner) statement that "golf and sex are the only two things you don't need to be good at to enjoy" is representative of Shelton's skill in this picture at balancing the two.

Of course, Shelton gets plenty of help, beginning with a strong cast. Kevin Costner has done some of his best work under Shelton's relaxed yet watchful eye. As he did in *Bull Durham,* Costner shows a flair for the boyish underachieving dreamer that is both engaging and vulnerable...and a bit coarse. The actor shows real believability and depth here as an unfulfilled golf pro straddling the line between craziness and brilliance. It's in the sporting light romantic comedy that Costner shines. Just like Crash Davis, it's hard to think of anyone being better as Roy McAvoy.

Because of the inevitable comparisons to *Bull Durham,* Rene Russo had the difficult challenge of matching Susan Sarandon's command of the leading female role. Both are well-written characters, and Russo is engaging as the quirky, funny, and true prize coveted by the underdog as she eventually dumps her "horse's ass" boyfriend (Don Johnson) for McAvoy.

Though they may not achieve the same electricity as the romantic leads in *Bull Durham,* Costner and Russo work well together. In their initial "therapy" session, McAvoy declares love for Molly with such genuine innocence and earnestness that the therapist is in need of some professional help of her own. Russo's character is well drawn, full of the modern woman's fears, hopes, and goals. Russo is good at playing awkwardly adorable and a bit dizzy, kind of like Diane Keaton in *Annie Hall.* Russo's rare combination of beauty and skillful comedic timing puts her in the same league as Michelle Pfeiffer and Julia Roberts.

Her boyfriend, veteran golf pro David Simms—a superficial, calculating man whose successful public persona belies a nasty being—is played just right by Don Johnson. Shelton and Norville do a fine job of setting up the antagonism prickling just below the surface between Simms and McAvoy. Johnson looks like he's having a ball knowing he's just the kind of guy McAvoy reviles.

In support, Linda Hart is memorable in her few scenes as McAvoy's ex-girlfriend, but the most valuable player award goes to Cheech Marin as Romeo, McAvoy's caddy, confidant, and best friend. Marin proves he has some solid acting range, providing the story's balance and perspective as the mercurial McAvoy's voice of reason. Thumbing his nose at the golf hierarchy and mumbling pearls of wisdom while cleaning clubs at the dilapidated golf range, Marin's warmth, sincerity, and restrained yet gruff mugging is one of the best aspects of the picture. Intriguing char-

TOP: Cheech Marin stars as the wily, faithful caddy Romeo Posar.

BOTTOM: Costner watches pro Peter Jacobson's putting stroke.

acter interactions are typical of Shelton films, and McAvoy/Romeo's are at the core of *Tin Cup*.

Aiding the principal cast and lending much verisimilitude to the fine golf sequences are not only touring pros like Craig Stadler, Gary McCord, and Peter Jacobsen but also the CBS television crew that covers the PGA. The director stages the competition well, conveying a real sense of drama out on the links. As in *Bull Durham*, Shelton demonstrates an aesthetic appreciation of the sport.

James Bissell's production design on the first-rate courses lends even more credibility to the proceedings. Russell Boyd's photography captures the majestic surroundings of a major tournament. Overall the country, rock and roll, and Tex-Mex soundtrack is effective. Though William Ross's music at times feels overdone, tunes like "Crapped Out Again" and "Double Bogey Blues" really complement the bluesy, working-man feel of the picture.

It's practically a given that a Shelton film will find a way to be a contrarian look at the typical sports movie, and *Tin Cup* is no different in that regard. Certainly this picture shows the director's penchant for viewing the athletic life through also-rans and has-beens, and for celebrating the ambiguity in sports, romance, and life lessons in general. *Tin Cup* also artfully explores the nature of obsession, the drive to achieve rare success, and losing self-control. Now if we can only find a fourth player.

OUTSIDE THE LINES

OUTSIDE THE LINES PGA pro Gary McCord worked with Costner on his swing.... Russell Boyd was nominated for an Academy Award for his cinematography work on *Master and Commander: The Far Side of the World* (2003).... Ron Shelton was an infielder in the Baltimore Orioles minor league system for five years.... Rene Russo starred in the baseball comedy *Major League* (1989).... Kevin Costner has starred in three baseball features, *For the Love of the Game* (1999), *Field of Dreams* (1989), and *Bull Durham* (1988), and appeared in *Chasing Dreams* (1982).... Shelton's *Bull Durham* screenplay was nominated for an Oscar.... Don Johnson and Cheech Marin would pair up in the TV series *Nash Bridges*.... Production designer James Bissell's work appears in a TV movie about pitcher Satchel Paige, *Don't Look Back* (1981), and the basketball feature *Blue Chips* (1994).... Shelton is married to actress Lolita Davidovich, who starred in his boxing film *Play It to the Bone* (2000) and baseball's *Cobb* (1994).... She also performed in hockey's *Mystery, Alaska* (1999).... In addition to several Shelton films, Victoria Thomas also cast for Michael Mann's boxing epic *Ali* (2001).... The USGA, golf's governing body for the U.S. Open, assisted in *Tin Cup*'s production design.... Dennis Burkley appeared in Neil Simon's baseball picture *The Slugger's Wife* (1985).... Sound designer Kirk Francis has worked on five of Shelton's sporting films, including *Bull Durham*.... Actress Linda Hart is credited for the choreography in football's *Best of Times* (1986), for which Ron Shelton wrote the script and directed the football sequences.... Arnon Milchan was also executive producer of *Cobb*.... In addition to several of Shelton's films, the late sportswriter Allan Malamud also appeared in baseball's *Talent for the Game* (1991) and *Raging Bull* (1980).... *Tin Cup* was shot primarily in Texas and Arizona. ...Costner played a cyclist in *American Dreamers* (1985).... Australian native Boyd did the photography for Shelton's *Cobb* and *White Men Can't Jump* (1992), as well as horse racing's *Phar Lap* (1983).... Editor Paul Seydor has also worked with Shelton on *Cobb*, *White Men Can't Jump*, and *Play it to the Bone*.... His other sporting credits include *Major League II* (1994), and *The Program* (1993), which the film's co-editor Kimberly Ray also worked on.... Marin appeared in boxing's *The Great White Hype* (1996), co-written by Shelton.

ALL-STAR MOMENTS Opening sequence where the credits roll, Tex-Mex music plays, and we see more armadillos on the golf range than golfers.

Roy McAvoy (Costner) winning a golf match using a baseball bat and garden tools.

Exemplifying their differing golf philosophies, Roy abandons his caddy duties to make a play he feels David (Johnson) should.

> ROY: Thirteen years on the tour, you're still a pussy.

> DAVID: Thirteen years on the driving range. You still think this game is about your testosterone count.

Warming up on the driving range before the U.S. Open, a clearly nervous McAvoy shanks several balls dangerously close to fellow competitors.

McAvoy's club-breaking tirade causes his caddy (Marin) to storm off the course. Roy has to finish using one club. "I never miss with the 7 iron."

McAvoy's first encounter with Molly (Russo) at the driving range, where he espouses his philosophies about the sport and suggests that perhaps he's "chock full of inner demons." She smiles back, saying, "No, you're chock full of bullshit."

HOME COURT ADVANTAGE Available on VHS and DVD. Warner Bros. has released the title in various forms on DVD. The Kevin Costner Selection also includes *3000 Miles to Graceland* and *Robin Hood: Prince of Thieves*. It is also paired with *Joe Versus the Volcano*. *Tin Cup* is also offered as part of a multi-disc Romance Pack that includes *Dave*, *Forever Young*, *The American President*, *The Wedding Singer*, *Practical Magic*, *Message in a Bottle*, *My Big Fat Greek Wedding*, and *Alex and Emma*.

Golf pros and film actors pose with director Ron Shelton (6) on the set. 1. Peter Jacobson 2. Fred Couples 3. Gary McCord 4. Jerry Pate 5. Bruce Lietzke 6. Shelton 7. Kevin Costner 8. Don Johnson 9. Tommy Armour III 10. Corey Pavin 11. Cheech Marin.

#70 A LEAGUE OF THEIR OWN

Screenwriters Lowell Ganz, Babaloo Mandel. **Story** Kim Wilson, Kelly Candaele. **Director** Penny Marshall. **Producers** Elliott Abbott, Penny Marshall, Robert Greenhut, Ronne Clemmer, Bill Pace, Amy Lemisch, Joseph Hartwick. **Cinematography** Miroslav Ondricek. **Editing** Adam Bernardi, George Bowers. **Music** Hans Zimmer, Madonna. **Production Design** Bill Groom. **Art Direction** Tom Galvin. **Costume Design** Cynthia Flynt. Columbia. 1992.

THE PLAYERS
Tom Hanks **Jimmy Dugan**; Geena Davis **Dottie Hinson**; Lori Petty **Kit Keller**; Madonna **May Mordabito**; Rosie O'Donnell **Doris Murphy**; Megan Cavanaugh **Marla Hooch**; Tracy Reiner **Betty Horn**; Bitty Schram **Evelyn Gardner**; Ann Cusack **Shirley Baker**; Anne Ramsey **Helen Haley**; Freddie Simpson **Ellen Sue Gotlander**; Renee Coleman **Alice Gaspers**; Jon Lovitz **Ernie Capadino**; David Strathairn **Ira Lowenstein**; Garry Marshall **Walter Harvey**; Robin Knight **Beans Babbitt**; Pauline Brailsford **Miss Cuthbert**; Kelli Simpkins **Beverly Dixon**; Patti Pelton **Marbleann Wilkenson**; Neezer Tarleton **Neezer Dalton**; Connie Taylor **Connie Calhoun**; Eddie Jones **Dave Hooch**; Kathleen Marshall **Mumbles Brockman**; Sharon Szmidt **Vivian Ernst**; Bill Pullman **Bob Hinson**; Justin Scheller **Stilwell Gardner**; Rae Allen **Ma Keller**; David Lander **Radio sportscaster**; Lynn Cartwright **Older Dottie**; Joe Krowka **Heckler**; Tea Leoni **Racine player 1B**; Harry Shearer **Newsreel announcer**

THE GAME It is 1943 and baseball owner Garry Marshall is concerned that with all the men off fighting, the sport will have to be shut down for the duration of the war. However, with the help of his promotional guru Ira Lowenstein (David Strathairn) and scouts like Ernie Capadino (Jon Lovitz), a national talent search is made and a try-out in Chicago is conducted…for women players.

Sisters Dottie (Geena Davis) and Kit (Lori Petty) become the star pitcher and catcher for the Rockford Peaches. Coaching the team is Jimmy Dugan (Tom Hanks), a former slugger, now a drunken bum who'd rather be anywhere else. Their teammates include a tough third baseman, Doris Murphy (Rosie O'Donnell), speedster Mae Mordabito (Madonna) and slugger Marla Hooch (Megan Cavanaugh).

As they attend "charm school" and endure the long bus rides, the players get to know each other and coach Dugan sobers up enough to begin to care what happens. As the season reaches a critical phase, Dottie is sick of Kit's blaming her for her own frustration and asks to be transferred to another team—but instead it is Kit who finds herself transferred to Racine. The sibling rivalry intensifies as the sisters meet in the women's world series.

The series comes down to the decisive seventh game and Kit's team wins in a thriller.

INSTANT REPLAY Certainly *A League of Their Own* has its share of whiffs and, like a five-tool player that doesn't reach his potential, is disappointing in some areas where its approach is too soft. Overall, though, this queen of diamonds scores with an entertaining look at the pioneering women who bravely "traded their oven mitts for baseball mitts" during the tragedy of wartime.

The lighthearted look at the All-American Girls Professional Baseball League is more *Bad News Bears* than *Eight Men Out*, where Rosie the Riveter becomes "Belle Durham," because, as in Ron Shelton's classic, some of the picture's funniest moments occur off the field—in the locker rooms, at the nightclubs, and on the long bus rides.

Writers Lowell Ganz and Babaloo Mandel, despite creating some cliché sports movie team characters and predictable plot points, produce some sassy dialogue and capture well the prevailing social attitudes of the 1940s.

Most sports films written and/or directed by women, such as *Bend It Like Beckham,* *Blue Crush,* and *Wimbledon,* take a different viewpoint of athletic competition—one that gives more attention to social dynamics and relationships and is less driven by the imperative to Win! Win! Win!

Penny Marshall uses her baseball game sequences to show how sport, even for most of these women, was not all-encompassing. We see not only the women's relationships with each other, their manager, their owner, and the media but, more importantly, their confusion and internal struggles caused by suddenly finding themselves in transition. Now they have new roles, new opportunities that go against the images and principles fed to them all their lives about staying at home and caring for the family.

With the female group dynamic, feminist pioneer element, and historical presentation in a wartime context, Marshall admirably tries to cover a lot of ground. She's also a bit of a rascal at the helm, adept as a prankster here like she was with Tom Hanks in *Big.*

The director is surrounded by a solid team. Leading the way are Geena Davis and Hanks, both adroitly going against type. Coming from *Thelma and Louise,* where she played a neglected, naive, and spiteful wife, Davis is the pragmatic country girl who looks equally at home milking cows or spitting tobacco and helping her drunken manager run the team.

Hanks, normally seen as an affable sort, eats up this role as an overweight, blustery boor who manages, despite his vulgar ways—and with a little help from his players—to make the club a success.

Rosie O'Donnell is a real baseball card here as the talented, aggressive, tough bouncer turned ballplayer.

Madonna is a natural in a small, made-to-order role as the team's "easy girl," nicknamed "All the Way" Mae. She's also smart and a true team player. Her friendship with Doris (O'Donnell) and her commitment to helping a teammate learn to read (albeit from a dirty book) are highlights.

As good as he is as the conflicted baseball player in *Eight Men Out,* David Strathairn works well here too with a quiet dignity, this time on the management side. His boss, played by Penny's brother, Garry, is also solid as the candy bar magnate owner.

Stealing scenes as easily as Rickey Henderson pilfered bases is Jon Lovitz. Sadly presented as little more than an opening act, the comedian's deadpan delivery of some hilarious witticisms as the weary, crude baseball scout provides some needed edge to the proceedings.

A former dance hall hostess, "All the Way" Mae (Madonna) scores as a professional baseball player.

TOP: With helpless Rockford Peach Doris Murphy (Rosie O'Donnell, right) looking on, Kit Keller (Lori Petty) heads for home to score for the Racine Belles.

BOTTOM: A charm school instructor (Ellie Weingardt) is finding it a challenge to teach feminine grace to these professional ballplayers.

Behind the scenes, Marshall's roster includes Bill Groom and Cynthia Flynt, whose work in production and costume design delivers a rich period look. Of course the skimpy outfits—making the players look more like cheerleaders, prompted some of the film's zingers—"What do you think we are? Ballplayers or ballerinas?" and "You can't slide in that."

Marshall frames the picture with scenes of the women who gather years later at a reunion at the Hall of Fame. It serves as a fine tribute to the real ballplayers but would have better matched the whole story with some sharper editing.

A League of Their Own is solid, amiable entertainment. Still, one wonders whether a deeper probe into the social impact of the AAGPBL, at a time when most women's lives were directed by their husbands and fathers, might have made a good picture a terrific one, shedding more light on this amazing little pocket of both feminism and sports history.

OUTSIDE THE LINES The All-American Girls Professional Baseball League was started in 1943 by Chicago Cubs owner Phil Wrigley and lasted until 1954.... It included the Rockford (IL) Peaches, the Kenosha (WI) Comets, the South Bend (IN) Blue Sox, and the Racine (WI) Belles.... There were 15 players on a team plus a chaperone.... Racine beat Kenosha to win the league's first championship in a best-of-five series.... Players from the actual league are seen in the film's Hall of Fame scenes.... Debra Winger was in for the lead role but was replaced by Geena Davis late in the project.... Reportedly Brooke Shields, Demi Moore, Uma Thurman, and Ally Sheedy were tested for roles.... Tom Hanks's character was loosely baseball on slugger Jimmy Foxx.... The Hall of Famer briefly managed in the league.... Director Penny Marshall played secretary to sportswriter Oscar Madison (Jack Klugman) in the TV series *The Odd Couple*.... Her brother, Garry, produced the series.... Madonna cowrote the film's tune "This Used to be My Playground."...It was nominated for a Golden Globe award, as was Geena Davis for her performance.... At one stage David Anspaugh (*Rudy*, *Hoosiers*) was set to direct with James Belushi as coach.... Helen St. Aubin, the mother of the film's co-story-originator, Kelly Candaele, played in the league.... Her other son, Casey, was an infielder for the Montreal Expos and Houston Astros, and finished his career with the Cleveland Indians.... The film's "Harvey Park" was actually Wrigley Field.... St. John's baseball coach Joe Russo helped prep some of the actresses for their performances.... Geena Davis is a talented enough archer to have competed for a spot on the U.S. Olympic team.... Faye Dancer, the inspiration for the character played by Madonna, once stole over 100 bases in a season and has her gloves and spikes on display at the Baseball Hall of Fame.... Hanks directed an episode of the TV series version of this film.... Some of the names for the male groupies of the league were "locker room Leonards" and "clubhouse Clydes."...

While major league baseball became integrated in 1947, the women's league had no black players.... Lovitz reprised his baseball scouting role for the TV series version.... Actor David Strathairn also appeared in *Eight Men Out* (1988).... The screenwriting team of Lowell Ganz and Babaloo Mandel cowrote a baseball version of *Fever Pitch* (2005), a remake of the soccer-oriented 1997 film.

ALL-STAR MOMENTS The whole farm sequence from when Ernie (Lovitz), who has come to recruit Dottie (Davis) for a baseball team, asks Dottie and her sister Kit (Petty) if the milking process hurts the cows. Later he calls the roaming chickens "wild animals" and, as he walks to his car, says, "Ever hear of a leash?"

As Dottie and Kit arrive and walk onto the ball field Ernie says, "Hey, cowgirls, see the grass? Don't eat it."

Dottie and Kit don't hit it off with city girls Doris (O'Donnell) and Mae (Madonna), but the latter are impressed when Dottie makes a barehanded snag of a ball thrown hard at her by Doris.

Coach Jimmy Dugan (Hanks) staggers into the locker room, urinates, rips up one of the players' greeting cards, then staggers out, leaving the girls to make out the lineup.

After her error allowed the tying run to score, outfielder Evelyn (Bitty Schram) starts crying as coach Dugan reprimands her. "Are you crying?" Are you crying?" repeats Dugan. Evelyn shakes her head no. Dugan, exasperated, throws his arms out, saying, "There's no crying. There's no crying in baseball!"

Season-advancing montage that includes newspaper headlines about "trading oven mitts for baseball mitts."

In the dugout Mae asks Doris what would happen if her blouse came unbuttoned on the field and her breast popped out. Doris responds, "Think there are men in this country that ain't seen your bosoms?"

Coach Dugan offering one of the girls chewing tobacco, adding, "A lot of ballplayers use it." Dottie, sitting in the dugout, spits out tobacco like an old pro, and Dugan acknowledges her: "That sounded good."

POST-GAME COMMENTS Tom Hanks on his character:

> Besides money and alcohol, the only thing Jimmy relates to is good baseball, which he doesn't think he's ever going to see on this team. He's not going to take it seriously. He doesn't want to be there. He falls asleep in the dugout, but eventually he sees enough good playing that he gets involved. This is not the story of a ragtag team that's lousy then suddenly gets good. This is about a group of women who come out to play.[1]

Madonna on her preparations for the film:

> The hardest part was just really believing that I could play baseball so that every moment, even when I was standing on base, the body language would be natural. I'd have to go over and see Rosie, who's a great baseball player, and she'd coach me on everything. I'd even find myself watching baseball on television. Trying to learn how to make all those moments when I'm not actually playing, those in-between moments, look natural, too.[2]

Rod Dedeaux, former USC coach and one of the film's technical advisors, on Madonna's dedication to the sport:

> I really have a passion against faking baseball in pictures.... Nobody worked harder and was more dedicated than Madonna. In fact, it was a problem. She didn't feel she wanted to stop, even when her arm was tired or hurt. She felt as long as she could endure the pain, she wanted to play, and that was dangerous.[3]

HOME COURT ADVANTAGE Available on VHS and DVD.

TOP: Plucked from the family farm after her husband goes off to war, Dottie Hinson (Geena Davis) proves to be a talented player for the Rockford Peaches.

MIDDLE: Ira Lowenstein (David Strathairn, left), the league's promotional wizard, is a valuable asset to his boss, candy bar magnate Walter Harvey (Garry Marshall, right), the league's creator and owner.

BOTTOM: Sisters Dottie (Davis, left) and Kit (Petty, right) are fierce competitors.

#69 MAJOR LEAGUE

Screenwriter/Director David Ward. **Producers** Mark Rosenberg, Chris Chesser, Irby Smith, Julie Bergman, Joe Roth. **Cinematography** Reynaldo Villalobos. **Editing** Dennis Hill. **Music** Randy Newman, James Newton Howard. **Production Design** Jeffrey Howard. **Art Direction** John Reinhardt Jr. Paramount. 1989.

THE PLAYERS Tom Berenger **Jake Taylor**; Charlie Sheen **Rick Vaughn**; Corbin Bernsen **Roger Dorn**; Margaret Whitton **Rachel Phelps**; James Gammon **Lou Brown**; Rene Russo **Lynn Wells**; Wesley Snipes **Willie Mays Hayes**; Charles Cyphers **Charlie Donovan**; Chelcie Ross **Eddie Harris**; Dennis Haysbert **Pedro Cerrano**; Andy Romano **Pepper Leach**; Bob Uecker **Harry Doyle**; Steve Yeager **Duke Temple**; Peter Vuckovich **Haywood**; Stacy Carroll **Suzanne Dorn**; Skip Griparis **Monte, the colorman**; Michael Hart **Burton (Yankees player)**; Richard Pickren **Tom**; Kevin Crowley **Vic Bolito**; Mary Seibel **Thelma**; Bill Leff **Bobby James**; Mike Bacarella **Johnny Wynn**; Gary Houston **Ross Farmer**; Neil Flynn **Longshoreman**; Keith Uchima **Groundskeeper #1**; Kurt Uchima **Groundskeeper #2**; William Sinacore **Coleman**; Ward Ohrman **Arthur Holloway**; Marge Kotlisky **Claire Holloway**; Tony Mockus Jr. **Brent Bowden**; Deborah Wakeham **Janice Bowden**; Thomas Perdoff **Umpire #1**; Jeffrey Edwards **Umpire #2**

THE GAME After the owner of the Cleveland Indians dies, his widow, Rachel Phelps (Margaret Whitton), a former showgirl, concocts a scheme of fielding such an inept team that attendance will drop to abysmal levels, at which time she'll take the lures of Florida and relocate the franchise.

Team executive Charlie Donovan (Charles Cyphers) and manager Lou Brown (James Gammon) have their hands tied as they try to assemble a competitive team.

By opening day what they are able to come up with is a roster filled with has-beens and wannabes who don't scare any of their opponents. A speedster lacking in fundamentals, Willie Mays Hayes (Wesley Snipes) joins a group that includes a selfish prima donna third baseman (Corbin Bernsen), a recently released convict whose pitching arm is as out-of-control as his attitude (Charlie Sheen), a broken-down catcher who can barely walk (Tom Berenger), a voodoo-worshipping slugger (Dennis Haysbert), and an old rubber-armed pitcher (Chelcie Ross).

Unsurprisingly, they start out meeting Ms. Phelps's exceedingly low expectations, losing day after day. However, her plans backfire when the players find out about them and respond by coming together like never before. Despite her increasingly harsh attempts to destroy their camaraderie and stop them from winning, the Indians go on to win the decisive game against their dreaded Yankee rivals.

INSTANT REPLAY No fresh prospects here, and *Major League* certainly is not in a "league of its own" as a baseball classic. But like the Indians' manager, writer/director David Ward assembles some disparate elements from a wide roster of movies, and infuses some funny dialogue and sight gags into a group of performers who have a ball with the cartoon characterizations.

The rallying misfits are sort of an adult "Bad News Bears." The showgirl owner with devilish ways and the Yankees as the hated rivals hark back to Gwen Verdon in *Damn Yankees*. The aging catcher chasing romance, the Latino voodoo player, and the wild pitcher are at the core of *Bull Durham*. Still, while the plot isn't original, the engaging execution is the key stat here.

What Ward, a lifelong Indians fan, does particularly well are the details. Made at a time when the Indians actually were a laughingstock, Ward creates an energy that

Veteran catcher Jake Taylor (Tom Berenger) attempts to reunite with his old flame Lynn (Rene Russo).

really encapsulates what it's like for a city that comes together, swelling with civic pride, as their sports team climbs to the top. Randy Newman's "Burn On" is an interesting musical opener with a local flavor.

With the blue-collar workers in the streets, foreign groundskeepers, die-hard drum-banging fans in the cheap seats, and players coming around when they sense victory, *Major League* infuses the audience with enthusiasm as it employs the tried-and-true rags-to-riches formula.

Ward's solid pacing and comedic timing are greatly aided by the work of editor Dennis Hill, most notably when the team is being assembled in spring training and in their climactic victory.

Having a lot of fun playing a boy's game is a cast that is lively and so engaging one can't help but laugh along with all the nonsense. Taking Ward's knowing baseball lingo and quirky character outlines, just about all the major players get a chance to show their stuff here.

Both Tom Berenger and Charlie Sheen use their rough-edge personas to good effect. As the heart of the team, catcher Berenger handles well the difficult chore of carrying the romance, as well as his share of the comedic and tough-guy bits. Sheen's deadpan delivery as "Wild Thing" is some of his best work.

Margaret Whitton plays her flashy role for all it's worth, and in her film debut Rene Russo demonstrates the tools for bigger roles to come.

Lou Gammon, with his gravelly voice, throwback mustache, and likable gruffness, successfully embodies a veteran manager. Of course, former ballplayer Bob Uecker delivers with gusto many of the film's best lines while Wesley Snipes steals the physical comedy title.

Combining a losing scheme storyline used to good effect in Mel Brooks's *The Producers* and sophomoric slapstick found in *Police Academy* with a team version of the *Rocky* formula, David Ward doesn't deliver anything original, but by never taking itself seriously anyway and convincingly creating a rowdy, captivating, and knowing atmosphere peopled with zany characters, *Major League* is a fun and entertaining fantasy.

After inheriting the Cleveland Indians, new owner Rachel Phelps (Margaret Whitton) lays down the law. Players Willie Mays Hayes (Wesley Snipes, left) and Rick Vaughn (Charlie Sheen, right) pay attention.

OUTSIDE THE LINES Steve Yeager, the film's baseball advisor, was co-MVP of the 1981 World Series as his Dodgers beat the Yankees.... Only the exterior of Cleveland's Municipal Stadium was used.... Home game action took place in Milwaukee's County Stadium.... Many of the players at the scenes shot in Tucson, Arizona were members of the University of Arizona baseball team.... Pete Vuckovich, who played the Yankees' slugger Haywood, won the AL Cy Young award in 1982 pitching for the Brewers.... Charlie Sheen is an avid baseball fan; his favorite team is the Reds.... The actor paid more than $80K for the baseball that went between Bill Buckner's legs in the 1986 World Series.... Sheen also appeared in the baseball drama *Eight Men Out* (1988).... Actress Rene Russo also starred in golf's *Tin Cup* (1996).... Bob Uecker, whose batting average in his playing days as a catcher for the Braves, Phillies, and Cardinals hovered around .200, is a member of the Radio Hall of Fame, having broadcast Brewers games for over 30 years.... Reynaldo Villalobos was also the cinematographer for *Love and Basketball* (2000).... Wesley Snipes's sports movie credits include *Wildcats* (1986), *Streets of Gold* (1986), *White Men Can't Jump* (1992), *The Fan* (1996), *Futuresport* (1998), and *Undisputed* (2002).... Dennis Haysbert has appeared in *Grambling's White Tiger* (1981), *Mr. Baseball* (1992), and *Love and Basketball* (2000) as well as the *Major League* sequels.... Tom Berenger portrayed legendary college football coach Paul "Bear" Bryant in *The Junction Boys* (2002).... Composer James Newton Howard has earned credits on *Wildcats* (1986), *Everybody's All-American* (1988), *Diggstown* (1992), *Night and the City* (1992), and *Space Jam* (1996).... Writer/director David Ward won an Oscar for his screenplay of *The Sting* (1973).

ALL-STAR MOMENTS Lying in bed with a woman in a fleabag motel in Mexico, Jake (Berenger) is passed out wearing a huge sombrero when he gets a call from Donovan (Cyphers), the Indians' general manager, asking if he'd like to play in the majors. Berenger thinks it is a friend playing a prank and snaps back, "If you're going to pull this shit at least you can say you're from the Yankees. . . ."

The same thing happens to Donovan when he asks former coach Lou Brown (Gammon), now working in a tire store, if he wants to manage the Indians. Lou answers, "I'm not sure," and says Charlie will have to call back because he has "someone on the other line needing some whitewalls."

INDIANS EXECUTIVE LOOKING OVER A ROSTER SHEET: **I've never heard of half these guys. And the ones I do know are way past their prime.**

GENERAL MANAGER CHARLIE DONOVAN: **Most of these guys never had a prime.**

ANOTHER INDIANS EXECUTIVE: **This guy here is dead.**

NEW TEAM OWNER RACHEL PHELPS: **Cross him off, then.**

When Donovan tries to get pitcher Rick Vaughn (Sheen), Vaughn tells him he's not sure he can make the start date of spring training. He's in jail.

Willie Mays Hayes (Snipes) wakes up outdoors thinking he's been cut but impresses the coaches when he races in his pajamas past two players in a sprint. Manager yells out, impressed, "Get him a uniform!"

When Dorn comes over and points out that in his contract he doesn't have to do any calisthenics he doesn't think are necessary, Manager Brown takes the contract, throws it on the ground, urinates on it, zips up, then walks away.

TOP: Indians slugger Pedro Cerrano (Dennis Hasybert) believes voodoo helps his game.

BOTTOM: Manager Lou Brown (James Gammon) promises to remove an article of clothing from a replica of owner Phelps every time the Indians win a game. The team goes on to clinch the pennant.

Indians announcer Harry Doyle (Uecker) pours himself some whiskey as he informs his radio listeners of the new faces on the team. When he sticks his microphone out to hear the "roar of the crowd," the sparse opening-day crowd doesn't provide any. "Just a reminder, fans," he says, "about Die Hard Night coming up here at the stadium. Free admission to anyone who was actually alive the last time the Indians won a pennant."

We see Manager Brown standing naked in the locker room, complaining to team owner Rachel Phelps (Whitton) that he's tired of all the nickel-and-diming she's doing…and then we see Hayes starting a motorboat engine to get the whirlpool going again.

In a key game against New York, Doyle describes the new Yankee reliever coming to the mound: "The Duke leads the league in saves, strikeouts per inning, and hit batsmen. This guy threw at his own kind at a father/son game."

HOME COURT ADVANTAGE Available on VHS and DVD.

#68 FEAR STRIKES OUT

Screenwriters Ted Berkman, Raphael Blau. **Director** Robert Mulligan. **Producer** Alan Pakula. **Cinematography** Haskell Boggs. **Editing** Aaron Stell. **Music** Elmer Bernstein. **Costume Design** Edith Head. Paramount. 1957.

THE PLAYERS Anthony Perkins **Jimmy Piersall**; Karl Malden **John Piersall**; Norma Moore **Mary Piersall**; Adam Williams **Dr. Brown**; Perry Wilson **Mrs. John Piersall**; Peter Votrian **Young Jimmy**; Rand Harper **Radio announcer**; Brian Hutton **Bernie Sherwill**; Morgan Jones **Sandy Allen**; Gail Land **Alice**; Bart Burns **Joe Cronin**; Howard Price **Bill Tracy**; Dennis McMullen **Phil**; George Pembroke **Umpire**

THE GAME When he loses his blue-collar job over a dispute with his supervisor, John Piersall (Karl Malden) takes the opportunity to focus on honing the baseball skills of his only son (Anthony Perkins).

Skilled at the game himself, John never quite reached the high levels of the sport and is determined to see that his son makes the major leagues.

Despite winning the state championship as a star player for his high school, Jimmy can never quite do enough to earn the approval of his demanding father. For every word of praise he doles out, John follows it with a half-dozen more, criticizing every perceived nuance lacking in his son's game. Like a daily dose of poison, his father's relentless demands over the years are taking an emotional toll on the young man; still, Jimmy manages to impress some pro scouts and earn a contract.

Jimmy does well on the Red Sox's minor league team in Scranton, Pennsylvania, but his father doesn't let up; when Jimmy ranks third in the league in hitting, his father brings him down again by insisting that he should have been first.

Jimmy meets Mary (Norma Moore) and they fall in love. This romance relieves some of the pressure in his life and the two get married. They have a daughter and Jimmy moves up, playing well on the Red Sox's Louisville squad the next season.

It doesn't take long for John to suggest that his son looks to be a perennial minor leaguer—which just won't do. Just as Jimmy is brought to the point of exploding by his father's harrying, he is promoted to the major league team. Once there, he is stunned and confused when he learns management wants him to play shortstop, not the outfield position that his father has planned for him all these years.

Concerned more about the impression he's making on his father watching in the stands than anything else, Jimmy finally breaks under the pressure and goes berserk at a home game, much to the horror of fans and the genuine surprise of his father.

After much psychological treatment by Dr. Brown (Adam Williams), slowly father and son are reconciled. Jimmy eventually returns to playing professional baseball—this time not for his father, but for himself.

INSTANT REPLAY *Fear Strikes Out* is an intimate, intense, and involving portrait of the complexities of a psychological breakdown and recovery. Reminiscent of *The Three Faces of Eve* and *The Snake Pit* in that regard, this picture takes an unusual look at the sporting life.

Unlike other films that build sports figures into heroes of mythical proportions,

All his life Jimmy Piersall (Anthony Perkins, left) has been driven to be a pro ballplayer by his unrelenting father, John (Karl Malden, right).

Fear Strikes Out takes a decidedly dark look at the father-son relationship often associated with baseball.

Making his feature film debut here, veteran television director Robert Mulligan demonstrates his particular talent for father-son stories, suspense, and depicting the effects of mental stress. He would go on to direct *Blood Brothers*, *To Kill a Mockingbird*, and *Up the Down Staircase*.

Before this movie was made, Piersall's autobiography had already inspired a television movie starring Tab Hunter. One of the challenges the writers and director face with this type of story is that the latter part of the picture will inevitably seem less interesting simply because of the difficulty in dramatizing the slow, largely internal process of recovery from a breakdown. Fortunately for the filmmakers and the audience, here a brilliant young actor is able to pull it off.

It has often been stated that Anthony Perkins is among the worst silver screen performers between the lines of the diamond—and it's undeniable that he rivals William Bendix and Gary Cooper when it comes to lack of athletic talent. However, I'd like to offer that his awkwardness here is at least in part by clever design. His intense character shows the lifelong pressure of his father's expectations, so he's never really comfortable on the ball field. His weak form serves a dramatic purpose by suggesting that he's succeeded more on willpower than pure athleticism.

At the same time, I also feel the actor should have brought up his level of hitting and throwing form. Based on his editing of the baseball sequences, Mulligan seems to have felt the same.

It is abundantly clear that Anthony Perkins wasn't blessed as a 5-tool player, but you'd be hard-pressed to cast a better actor to go crazy at Fenway Park: "How was it? Was it good enough?! Did I show them?!"

TOP: Jimmy finds a little peace when he meets Mary (Norma Moore).

BOTTOM: The lifelong pressures take their toll on Jimmy (Perkins, right).

Here Perkins proves his talent for playing disturbed people. (A few years later he'd be immortalized with his performance in Alfred Hitchcock's *Psycho*.) His expressive, angular face alternates with apparent ease between the anguished look of a tortured soul on the verge of exploding and sly charm in romancing his future wife (Norma Moore). He also shows compassion and accuracy in the recovery phase when he defends his father, saying he wouldn't have made it as a ballplayer without him.

While the supporting cast is able, this really is about the pitching-catching battery of Karl Malden and Anthony Perkins.

Potentially a one-dimensional character as the oft-seen tyrannical father, Malden creates a fine portrait of a bitter old man trying to live his own failed dreams of a being a major league ballplayer through his son. Malden does it with a mixture of genuine love, uncompromising ambition for his only son, and ignorance of the emotional consequences he's creating.

Fear Strikes Out scores as both an absorbing psychological drama and a multitiered love story.

OUTSIDE THE LINES
Jimmy Piersall played 17 years in the major leagues.... The two-time all-star suffered from bipolar disorder.... Perkins was naturally left-handed and had to learn to throw right-handed.... He was trained by former Boston Brave Tommy Holmes.... Karl Malden won an Oscar for *A Streetcar Named Desire* (1954) and was nominated for *On the Waterfront* (1951).... Malden portrayed U.S. Olympic hockey coach Herb Brooks in the TV movie *Miracle on Ice* (1981).

ALL-STAR MOMENTS
The conversation between father (Karl Malden) and son (Anthony Perkins) after running through Jimmy's old school grounds. Standing under the bleachers, John demands to know his son's level of commitment to play in the majors starting with a minor league stint: "What have we been pouring our blood into? You want them to call you 'yella'? Well if that's what you want then you're no son of mine."

Night game. Crossing home plate after beating the throw to score, Jimmy loses it, running up the netting behind home plate and yelling to the crowd, "How was it? Was it good enough!?" He yells over to his dad, "Did I show them?!" After being restrained, he breaks lose and climbs the netting again. Eventually he is subdued and ends up in the hospital for the start of his long rehabilitation.

Well into his therapy, Jimmy opens up to his father: "All my life I've been splitting my gut to please you and I never could. No matter what I do, it's not enough. Dad, you're killing me." John is stunned, and Jimmy demands that he leave. Later, Jimmy tells the doctor (Adam Williams) that he wanted to kill his father. Slowly Jimmy resolves those demons and begins a new relationship with his dad.

HOME COURT ADVANTAGE
Available on VHS and DVD.

#67 16 Days of Glory

Director Bud Greenspan. **Producer** Nancy Beffa. **Cinematography** Robert Collins, Gil Hubbs, Michael Margulies. **Music** Lee Holdridge. **Editing** Andrew Squicciarini. **Narrator** David Perry. Cappy Productions. 1985.

THE GAME Veteran filmmaker Bud Greenspan documents the 1984 Summer Olympics in Los Angeles. From the pageantry of the opening ceremonies to the world-class competitions being played out at over a dozen venues, the movie gives a sense of the common bond among athletes: their years of dedication to a grueling training schedule, most for little or no monetary reward, earning instead the peer recognition that they are among the best in the world at a sport they love.

Featured competitors include British decathlete Daley Thompson, Norwegian marathoner Grete Waitz, American hurdler Edwin Moses, and German swimmer Michael Gross, as well as many other, lesser-known athletes.

INSTANT REPLAY Since he began filming the Olympics in 1952, Bud Greenspan has produced a wealth of beautiful stories and vivid pictures concerning the Games. Of his more than 150 Olympic-themed films, *16 Days of Glory* is his most artistic. Celebrating the few who are victorious but also the humanity of all the contestants, here as in his other films Greenspan typically chooses emotion over performance and mechanics.

With an army of technicians Greenspan shot over a million feet of film (which comes to about 200 hours) and took nine months to edit it down for a 2 1/2-hour theatrical release. The film, despite its occasional lapses of narration and music bordering on maudlin, succeeds because of the former reporter's ability to find the stories many Olympic broadcasters miss or choose not to feature.

Whether it's a female marathoner from Switzerland nearly collapsing just to finish or a Japanese judo legend dominating his field to earn a gold medal, Greenspan's strength is capturing the spirit of the Olympics via the efforts of the competing athletes, who demonstrate courage, strength, and commitment regardless of their country of origin, chosen sport, gender, race, and results.

OUTSIDE THE LINES The film was later reassembled into a multi-part television series.... Greenspan's Olympic-themed movies include *Wilma* (1977), the story of African-American sprinter Wilma Rudolph.... He also codirected *Endurance* (1998), a docudrama about Ethiopian distance runner Haile Gebrselassie.... Greenspan's spoken-word album, *Great Moments in Sport,* earned him a Gold Record.... Robert Primes was a cinematographer on the ski drama *Aspen Extreme* (1993).... Primes, with George Lucas, was also part of the photography team that shot the Rolling Stones documentary *Gimme Shelter*.... Greenspan has made several official films for the Olympics and earned an Olympic Order award from the International Olympic Committee.... His film on the Lillehammer Olympics airing on Disney earned him three Emmy awards.... First assistant director Art Levinson would go on to be a producer of the multi-Oscar winner *Breaking Away* (1979).... Gil Hubbs's cin-

TOP: Preeminent sports documentary writer/director Bud Greenspan (right) with American diving great Greg Louganis.

MIDDLE: Koji Gushiken of Japan defeats American Pete Vidmar by 25 thousandths of a point to become the all-around gymnastics champion.

BOTTOM: The most accomplished male athlete of the 1984 Los Angeles Olympic track competition, Carl Lewis.

ABOVE RIGHT: American hopeful Mary Decker (right) would soon have her Olympic dreams of success in the 3,000 meters dashed after getting tangled up with Zola Budd (center).

ematography credits include the documentary *This Is Elvis* (1981) and Bruce Lee's *Enter the Dragon* (1973) as well as the TV grappling film *The Wrestler* (1973).... Greenspan won a Peabody Award in 1997 for his body of television work.... His Olympic films have also appeared on the Showtime network, the Discovery Channel, ESPN, and PBS.... Greenspan has also authored many books on the subject of sports and the Olympics.... His *Olympiad Series* has been seen in more than 80 nations worldwide.... His work with ABC in creating features for their coverage of the 1980 Lake Placid Olympics earned Greenspan an Emmy.... Greenspan began as a sportscaster and became sports director at the New York radio station WMGM, the nation's largest at the time.

ALL-STAR MOMENTS
The opening ceremonies capacity crowd performing a card trick, creating a giant mosaic.

The camera coverage of the men's 400-meter hurdle final.

The reactions of the winner, Gaines (USA), and loser, Stockwell (Australia), when they touch the wall concluding the men's 100-meter swim race.

The fog-shrouded shots of the Olympic rowers.

The early stages of the women's marathon featuring Norway's Waitz and America's Samuelson, then a shot halfway through showing the size of Samuelson's lead in her gold medal run.

HOME COURT ADVANTAGE
Available on VHS.

#66 THE STRATTON STORY

Screenwriters Douglas Morrow, Guy Trosper. **Director** Sam Wood. **Cinematography** Harold Rosson. **Producer** Jack Cummings. **Editing** Ben Lewis. **Art Direction** Cedric Gibbons, Paul Groesse. **Set Decoration** Edwin Willis. **Costume Design** Helen Rose. **Music** Adolph Deutsch. **Special Effects** Arnold Gillespie, Warren Newcombe. MGM. 1949.

THE PLAYERS James Stewart **Monty Stratton**; June Allyson **Ethel Stratton**; Frank Morgan **Barney Wile**; Agnes Moorehead **Ma Stratton**; Robert Gist **Earnie**; Bill Williams **Eddie Dilson**; Bruce Cowling **Ted Lyons**; Cliff Clark **Josh Higgins**; Dean White **Luke Appling**; Gene Bearden **Himself**; Bill Dickey **Himself**; Jimmy Dykes **Himself**; Mervyn Shea **Himself**; Mary Lawrence **Dot**; Holmes Herbert **Doctor**; Pat Flaherty **Western manager**

THE GAME Pitching in a semi-pro game a few country miles from his Texas farm, Monty Stratton (James Stewart) catches the eye of former big leaguer Barney Wile (Frank Morgan). Wile, who let his own promising career decay through drink, convinces Monty he's got the tools to make it in the majors. Staying on as a farmhand through the winter, Wile teaches Monty all he knows in between chores. As spring arrives together they convince Monty's widowed, practical-minded mother (Agnes Moorehead) to let her son try out for the pros.

MA: [Is baseball] worth giving up the farm for?

BARNEY: If they take him on the least he'll get is $300 a month.

MA: Powerful lot of money for just throwing a ball.

Monty arranges for his cousin Earnie (Robert Gist) to manage the farm in his absence. He and Barney proceed to hitchhike to California, because the Chicago White Sox conduct their pre-season training in the golden state, and Barney knows the manager.

After some awkward moments at the practice field, manager Jimmy Dykes is impressed enough to have Monty work out and see if he can make the team before they break camp and head back to Chicago to open the regular season. On a break during tryouts, Monty is set up on a blind date by his teammate Eddie Dilson (Bill Williams). Monty meets and falls for a girl named Ethel (June Allyson). Leaving her house, a smitten Stratton walks down the sidewalk in a daze, forgetting the taxi they arrived in. Having admitted to Ethel he's never been in love, Monty is in a stupor. "Where do you think you're going?" demands the taxi driver. "Man, I sure don't know," Monty replies, and staggers back into the cab.

Impressive in his tryout, Monty is offered a contract, as is Barney: Monty to pitch and Barney to coach. In love and realizing his big league dreams, Monty is on top of the world. His first professional outing, however, brings him back to ground level. Monty is greeted rudely by the powerful New York Yankees, who knock him out of the box and to an early shower. Stratton is subsequently sent down to the minor leagues for some "seasoning."

Performing well, Stratton is soon recalled back to the big club, now as a married man. He and Ethel go to Chicago, where Stratton is a rookie sensation and they become proud parents of a son.

The newlyweds return to the family farm in Texas at the conclusion of the baseball

June Allyson as Monty's wife, Ethel.

season. There, however, the bright future suddenly turns dark and dismal when Monty, out hunting on his farm, trips and accidentally shoots himself in the leg.

At the hospital Ethel is told that her husband's leg must be amputated in order to save his life because of threatening gangrene. When Monty returns home he becomes sullen and bitter over the abrupt termination of his career.

Despite the best efforts of his wife, Monty continues to brood, losing interest in life, until he sees his young son trying to take his first steps. Snapping out of his self-pity, Monty resolves to learn to walk along with his boy and soon masters his artificial leg.

Soon Monty even begins to play catch with his wife, whose faith has helped her husband restore belief in himself. Tossing the ball with her on the farm one day, Monty loses his balance pitching off his prosthetic leg. As Ethel helps him up, she kisses him.

MONTY: That's the first time I've been kissed by a catcher.

ETHEL: Catchers don't do that?

MONTY: Not as a rule. Sort of slows up the game.

The competitive fires return, and to prove himself that he's overcome his handicap, Monty arranges to pitch in an all-star game. He pitches masterfully, even overcoming the opposition's resorting to bunting the ball. In the end Monty wins the game and the acclaim of the crowd in a triumph of personal courage.

INSTANT REPLAY
The Stratton Story is a rewarding, inspirational experience based on a true story of courage, dreams, determination and faith in human potential.

Heartwarming without being maudlin, the picture has a warm, real-life quality due in large part to the lead performers. Jimmy Stewart keeps the character on a believable plane in a difficult role that could easily fall into sappy sentimentality. The starring role is well suited to that awkward grace of his. Stewart's finely conceived interpretation is real and earnest, capturing self-pity, hopelessness, humor, and an indomitable spirit. It is an engaging and artful performance.

June Allyson is excellent as the supportive wife, with her heartfelt efforts to revive her husband's depressed spirits. Agnes Moorehead adds a strong, honest, homespun feel to her role as Monty's widowed mother.

The touching, balanced script by Douglas Morrow and Guy Trosper is in good hands with director Sam Wood. Wood, who also directed *The Pride of the Yankees*, for the most part keeps the baseball action in the background, maintaining Monty's internal struggles and family relationships at the forefront.

The baseball sequences are handled well and their authenticity enhanced by the appearance of real-life players, including Yankee great Bill Dickey. Producer Jack Cummings's attention to details, like using actual uniforms and filming the action in the stadiums where the pros play, contributed to the major league feel. Wood's pace is reflective of the difficult story, which the filmmakers handle with integrity and authenticity.

OUTSIDE THE LINES
Frank Morgan was the wizard in *The Wizard of Oz*.... Both Van Johnson and Gregory Peck were reportedly up for the lead role that went to James Stewart.... Johnson had to withdraw from consideration, as he was recovering

Yankee great Bill Dickey (center) plays a teammate of Monty's.

from a severe auto crash and was advised that the part would be too strenuous.... Sam Wood also directed *The Pride of the Yankees*.... The real Monty Stratton was an active pitcher into the '40s.... Screenwriter Douglas Morrow won an Academy Award for his story.... Morrow also wrote the adaptation for *Jim Thorpe: All-American*.... Wood directed the Marx Brothers in *A Day at the Races* and Stewart in the college football film *Navy, Blue, and Gold*.... June Allyson starred in a boxing film, *Right Cross,* in 1950.... She was married to the film's co-star, Dick Powell.... *Speed* was an auto racing film that featured Jimmy Stewart (1936).... Wood's early film credits include a football film, *One Minute to Play,* that featured gridiron legend Red Grange.... His directorial debut was a cross-country auto racing feature, *Double Speed,* in 1920.... Donna Reed was reportedly considered for the role that went to June Allyson.... Cast members Agnes Moorehead and Robert Gist were married to each other in the mid '50s.... The baseball sequences were filmed at Gilmore Field in Los Angeles, Wrigley Field in Chicago, and at American League stadiums in Chicago, Cleveland, Detroit, and Washington D.C. as well as Brookside Park in Pasadena, where the Chicago White Sox would conduct spring training.... Gene Bearden, the Indians' 20-game winner in 1948, appeared as himself.

ALL-STAR MOMENTS At the hospital after Monty has accidentally shot himself in the leg, his wife (Allyson) faces the grim reality.

> DOCTOR (HOLMES HERBERT): There's no alternative. It's his leg or his life.

> ETHEL: But his legs *are* his life.

Monty (Stewart) learns to walk on his artificial leg along with his son, who is taking his first steps as well.

Monty coming off the pitcher's mound with his artificial leg to make a key defensive play.

HOME COURT ADVANTAGE Available on VHS.

#65 DAMN YANKEES

Screenwriter George Abbott. (Novel by Douglass Wallop.) **Directors** George Abbott, Stanley Donen. **Producers** Abbott, Donen. **Music** Richard Adler, Jerry Ross. **Cinematography** Harold Lipstein. **Choreography** Bob Fosse, Pat Ferrier. **Musical Supervisor** Ray Heindorf. **Editing** Frank Bracht. **Production Design** William Eckart. **Art Direction** Stanley Fleischer. **Costume Design** Jean Eckart. Warner Bros. 1958.

THE PLAYERS
Tab Hunter **Joe Hardy**; Gwen Verdon **Lola**; Ray Walston **Mr. Applegate**; Robert Shafer **Joe Boyd**; Shannon Bolin **Meg Boyd**; Nathaniel Frey **Smokey**; Russ Brown **Benny Van Buren**; James Komack **Rocky**; Rae Allen **Gloria Thorpe**; Jean Stapleton **Sister Miller**; Albert Linville **Vernon**; Elizabeth Howell **Doris**; Bob Fosse **Mambo dancer**

THE GAME Devoted Washington Senators fan Joe Boyd (Robert Shafer) says aloud that he'd sell his soul to the devil to get a long ball hitter so his beloved Senators could beat the Yankees. Mr. Applegate (the devil, played by Ray Walston) hears Joe's declaration and offers to grant this devout Yankee hater the power to deliver Washington from the depths of the American League cellar.

When Joe hears this, he asks, "What about my wife? My job?"

Applegate answers, "This is a big operation; you can't let little things like that get in the way." Joe disappears and his seemingly psychic wife, despite her neighbor's concerns, feels he will return.

Old Joe Hardy is now transformed into young Joe Hardy (Tab Hunter). The devil has arranged for Joe to try out for the Senators. Impressively, he knocks the cover off the ball and soon helps the Senators work their way up the standings. Gloria Thorpe (Rae Allen), a female sportswriter, begins to investigate this mysterious Hardy who seems to have emerged onto the scene from nowhere. Meanwhile young Joe rents a room at Mrs. Hardy's house so he can keep an eye on the woman who's been his wife of many years.

The Senators are nearing the pennant, but it is all part of Applegate's scheme to raise Washingtonians' hopes and then bring them crashing down as the team fails in the end. And to keep young Joe distracted he employs Lola (Gwen Verdon), a 172-year-old witch and the devil's sexiest temptress, to mesmerize young Hardy.

> APPLEGATE: I've got thousands of Washington's fans drooling under the illusion that the Senators are going to win the pennant.

> LOLA: Chief, that's awfully good. When they lose there'll be suicides and heart attacks...just like the good old days!

The season comes down to the last game, and though Lola tries to use her charms to ensure that Joe misses the game, he makes it to the ballpark in time to make a brilliant play in center field. The devil doesn't give up easily, and as the ball flies deep into the outfield he turns young Joe back into old Joe. Nevertheless, old Joe makes the catch and the Senators win the pennant.

Old Joe makes a beeline for his home and wife, his soul safe now that the devil has reneged on the deal. Applegate pursues him: "Listen to me, you wife-loving louse. You sold me your soul. You can't run out on me like this. You thief. You crook. . . ." But it's too late even for the devil.

Lola (Gwen Verdon) and Joe Hardy (Tab Hunter).

INSTANT REPLAY The film musical comes straight from the hit Broadway play of the same name, based on the Faust legend and Douglass Wallop's novel *The Year the Yankees Lost the Pennant*. Most of the theater cast also performs in the movie, except for the male lead, Stephen Douglass. Tab Hunter, as the male lead here, is slightly out of his league trying to sing and dance with pros like Gwen Verdon, but does manage to draw empathy for his character. Verdon not only shines as a dancer but displays terrific comedic ability, playing off Walston's devilish wisecracks. Ray Walston is outstanding as Mr. Applegate; he has a good time, and it shows.

The music, a strong contribution by Adler and Ross, particularly in its variety, from the Latin "Who's Got the Pain?" to the down home "Shoeless Joe From Hannibal, Mo," provides the requisite diversity of pace that enhances the story line. Fosse's choreography is riveting, especially when the players are raising dust with a performance on the ball field.

Technically, the photography, costumes, lighting, makeup and set designs blend well to provide an eye- and ear-pleasing performance. Particular credit goes to Gordon Bau and his group for the makeup work of turning Verdon into a 172-year-old witch and back again, as well as art director Stanley Fleischer's vivid settings with creative help from William and Jean Eckart.

Perhaps not in the same league as *Singin' in the Rain*, with some demerits for its rather blunt ending, the film is nevertheless a faithful rendition of the hit Broadway musical. *Damn Yankees* is full of glossy imagery, appealing to the senses, and a hit to the funny bone. It may not measure up to its stage version, but "it's got heart."

OUTSIDE THE LINES The stage version ran for over 1,000 performances.... Producer/director George Abbott was nominated for an Academy Award for Best Orig-

inal Screenplay for *All Quiet on the Western Front* (1930).... Stanley Donen choreographed another baseball musical, *Take Me Out to the Ball Game* (1949).... Bob Fosse would win an Oscar for Best Director of *Cabaret* (1972).... He was married to Gwen Verdon.... Actress Jean Stapleton, known as Archie Bunker's wife, Edith, on TV's *All in the Family,* starred in a made-for-TV baseball movie, *Aunt Mary* (1979).... Outside the U.S. and Canada *Damn Yankees* was known as *What Lola Wants*.... The movie premiered in Denver, home of the New York Yankees Farm Club of the American Association.... The filmmakers shot footage of a series between the real Yankees and Senators for use in the film.... Walston won a Tony Award for his Broadway role as the devil in *Damn Yankees*.... Ray Heindorf was nominated for an Oscar for Best Scoring of a Motion Picture.... Location shooting included Wrigley Park in Los Angeles.

ALL-STAR MOMENTS
Mr. Applegate (the devil) introducing himself to Joe Boyd: "I'm quite a famous character. I'm handy with fire."

Lola looking forward to her boss, the devil, succeeding in his plan to let down all Washingtonians at the last possible second just as the coveted pennant is within their grasp: "Chief, that's awfully good. When they lose there'll be suicides and heart attacks...just like the good old days!"

Lola's song and dance in the Senator's locker room: "Whatever Lola Wants."

HOME COURT ADVANTAGE
Available on VHS and DVD.

TOP: Lola tucks in Mr. Applegate (Ray Walston).

BOTTOM: Hardy (Hunter, left) tries to explain himself to his coach and teammates.

RIGHT: Mr. Applegate is a bit frustrated at how things have progressed.

#64 City for Conquest

Screenwriter John Wexley. **Directors** Anatole Litvak, Jean Negulesco. **Producers** Anatole Litvak, William Cagney, Hal Wallis. **Cinematography** James Wong Howe, Sol Polito. **Editing** William Holmes. **Music** Max Steiner. **Art Direction** Robert Haas. Warner Bros. 1940.

THE PLAYERS

James Cagney **Danny Kenny**; Ann Sheridan **Peggy Nash**; Frank Craven **Old Timer**; Donald Crisp **Scotty MacPherson**; Frank McHugh **Mutt**; Arthur Kennedy **Eddie Kenny**; George Tobias **Pinky**; Jerome Cowan **Dutch**; Anthony Quinn **Murray Burns**; Elia Kazan **Googi Zucco**; Lee Patrick **Gladys**; Blanche Yurka **Mrs. Nash**; George Lloyd **Goldie**; Joyce Compton **Lilly**; Thurston Hall **Max Leonard**; Ben Welden **Cobb**; John Arledge **Vacuum salesman**; Ed Keane **Gaul**; Joseph Crehan **Doctor**; Selmer Jackson **Doctor**

THE GAME Childhood friends Danny Kenny (James Cagney), his brother, Eddie (Arthur Kennedy), and Peggy Nash (Ann Sheridan) take different paths to escape the slums of New York City's Lower East Side.

Initially Danny is content to be a truck driver, but he turns to his fistic talents and becomes a prizefighter in order to raise money to help his brother realize his dreams of writing a symphony for their native city. Meanwhile, Peggy, seduced by the bright light promises of suave dancer Murray Burns (Anthony Quinn), becomes his dance partner, and they build up a glowing reputation on the vaudeville circuit on their way to the big time.

Under the guidance of manager Scotty MacPherson (Donald Crisp), Danny experiences success in the ring. Determined to win Peggy back, Danny is convinced a championship victory will do the trick. He takes on Cannonball Wales (Joe Gray), but Wales's cheating manager, Cobb (Ben Welden), rubs his boxer's gloves with rosin, almost blinding Danny. Hearing the terrible beating on the radio, Peggy returns to Danny only to be sent away by Scotty.

Still nearly blind but feeling no self-pity, Danny, with the help of his manager, opens up a newsstand and uses the income to support his struggling brother's artistic goal. Eddie is just about to give up but his brother inspires him to fight on.

Soon Eddie's symphony is not only completed but opens in prestigious Carnegie Hall to thunderous approval. Before an appreciative crowd, a grateful Eddie takes a moment to dedicate the performance to his brother, Danny. After the concert, Peggy and Danny reconcile at his newsstand.

INSTANT REPLAY This urban folk tale is an ideal vehicle for James Cagney as the slugger from the slums of New York City's Lower East Side. The film succeeds primarily through his dramatic range. Leading a pack of hungry aspirants through the concrete jungles of Manhattan, Cagney's self-sacrificing, compassionate portrayal gives a real human feel to the struggles, heartaches, successes, and various paradoxes of life in the big city.

Director Anatole Litvak gives dimension to John Wexley's script, moving the picture along briskly for the most part and keeping the tension credible from scene to scene. Aiding the storytelling is Frank Craven as an ongoing commentator interpreting and philosophizing about the city spirit and values as well as the changes to the principals as time rolls on. It is straight out of Craven's duties in *Our Town* and works

JAMES CAGNEY and ANN SHERIDAN

WARNER BROS. "CITY FOR CONQUEST"

well in combination with Robert Haas's art direction and the pictures of James Wong Howe and Sol Polito. Together they give a real sense of the hustle and bustle of New York City and its distinctive elements, from the crowded dance halls to Stillman's gym, from the dirty docks to Broadway and penthouse parties.

Complementing the visuals is the powerful score of Max Steiner and Hugo Friedhofer's arrangements for symphony orchestra. Litvak's pacing takes a misstep, however, with a lingering scene of the full symphony performance, whose dramatic story value could have been made in a more concise manner, leaving viewers a little less restless.

The director does score well, though, with some realistic fight scenes sharply edited by William Holmes. Howe and Polito's splendid photography shows some actual heavy blows landing between the combatants in the ring. Cagney, a former boxer, carries himself well in the ring, but it's his characterization of the reluctant prizefighter, who participates only to finance his brother's musical dreams and win back his lady, that is memorable. Credible, appealing, engaging—too much cannot be said for the performance of James Cagney, who shoulders this story.

Cagney's support features leading lady Ann Sheridan, who is genuine as Peggy Nash, a driven girl with dreams of her own. Donald Crisp is solid as the sympathetic fight manager. Anthony Quinn is devilishly good as the selfish, arrogant dancer who plays to Peg's consuming ambitions of becoming a star. Lee Patrick's small role as Peg's supportive roommate adds a lot to the proceedings, as do newcomers Arthur Kennedy and Elia Kazan. Kennedy nails the characterization as Cagney's frustrated, sensitive composer brother. Passing through from the theater to the director's chair, Kazan is impressive as the charming gangster out to avenge the harm done to Danny, his childhood pal.

OUTSIDE THE LINES The film was based on Aben Kandel's novel.... This was Arthur Kennedy's feature debut.... He would also play a brother to another boxer, Kirk Douglas, in *Champion* (1949), earning an Oscar nomination.... The actor starred in the boxing drama *Knockout* (1941), which also featured Anthony Quinn.... Kennedy costarred as a rodeo star with Robert Mitchum in *The Lusty Men* (1952).... Also up for the role that eventually went to Anthony Quinn were George Raft and Cesar Romero.... Jean Negulesco assumed director duties after Litvak suffered an eye injury.... James Cagney was a former amateur boxer and longtime fight enthusiast.... The actor was trained by former welterweight pro Mushy Callahan as well as stunt man Harvey Parry.... This was also Elia Kazan's first screen role.... Kazan would win Best Director Academy Awards for *Gentleman's Agreement* (1947) and *On the Waterfront* (1954), and nominations for his directorial work on *East of Eden* (1955), *A Streetcar Named Desire* (1951), and *America, America* (1963).... Cagney owned trotting horses.... Reportedly Raoul Walsh was set to direct the film at one stage.... George Tobias would appear in another boxing film, *The Set-Up* (1949), as Robert Ryan's crooked manager.... Anthony Quinn starred as a veteran pugilist in *Requiem for a Heavyweight* (1962).... Cagney, Sheridan, and Tobias performed together in the comedy *Torrid Zone* (1940).... In casting *City for Conquest*, Ginger Rogers and Loretta Young were considered for the leading lady role, as was Barbara Stanwyck, who starred in the boxing drama *Golden Boy* (1939), featuring William Holden.... The film's editor, William Holmes, won an Academy Award for similar work in *Sergeant York* (1941).... Specially made four-ounce gloves, lighter than normal, were used by the actors to reduce fatigue.... Boxers Larry Williams, John Lester Johnson, Billy McGowan, Phil Bloom, and John Indrisano appear in the film.... Indrisano was also technical advisor for *The Set-Up*, *Right Cross* (1950), and *The Fighter* (1952), among other features.... Chinese-born cinematographer James Wong Howe was a former boxer and filmed boxing's *Body and Soul* (1947) in part by moving about the ring on roller skates.... Howe would win Academy Awards for his cinematography in *The Rose Tattoo* (1955) and *Hud* (1963).... Howe would shoot Robert Rossen's bullfighting picture, *The Brave Bulls* (1951).... Among his other credits, he directed *Go, Man, Go!* (1954), a basketball movie about the Harlem Globetrotters.... Donald Crisp starred in *Knute Rockne: All-American* (1940).... He also played Elizabeth Taylor's father in *National Velvet* (1944).... Crisp won an Oscar as the patriarch in another family drama, John Ford's *How Green Was My Valley* (1941).... Composer Max Steiner won Oscars for *Now, Voyager* (1942) and *Since You Went Away* (1944).... His music composition credits include *Casablanca* (1942) and *Gone With the Wind* (1939).... Ann Sheridan starred in *The Indianapolis Speedway* (1939) with Pat O'Brien, a remake of *The Crowd Roars* (1932), an auto racing movie starring James Cagney.... Among Sheridan's early credits is an appearance in *Casey at the Bat* (1927), featuring Wallace Beery.... Beery won an Academy Award for Best Actor as a boxer in *The Champ* (1931).... Cagney starred in other boxing movies, like *Winner Take All* (1932), and appeared in *Golden Gloves* (1940), which featured his sister, Jeanne.... Aussie-born actor George Lloyd appeared in the hockey film *Idol of the Crowds* (1937), starring John Wayne, and another boxing feature, *Golden Boy* (1939).... Robert Haas was also the art director for *Knute Rockne: All-American* (1940) as well as for Joe E. Brown's baseball comedy *Elmer the Great* (1933).

TOP: Danny Kenny (James Cagney) and his sweetheart, Peggy Nash (Ann Sheridan), both dream of a better life using their athletic skills (boxing and dancing).

BOTTOM: This is one of the more memorable performances by the great American actor James Cagney.

ALL-STAR MOMENTS Danny (Cagney) and Murray (Quinn) fight over Peg (Sheridan) in her dressing room. Danny's confused when she tells him to leave only to catch up to him outside, saying she feared he'd mess up Murray's face and they

JAMES CAGNEY and ANN SHERIDAN

WARNER BROS. "CITY FOR CONQUEST"

A man and a woman realize their childhood ambitions of escaping the East Side slums of New York to find success as adults.

would no longer be able to continue their dance tour, her dream. When they kiss and make up, a patrolling cop says, "What do you think this is, Lovers Lane?" As they walk down the sidewalk, the cop sees them kissing again and gives up.

Peg sees her own plight in her roommate Gladys's (Patrick) experience as they talk one night before bed. Driven by an overriding desire to burn a name for herself in the bright lights, Gladys ended up burning herself in lost love. Gladys tells Peg that her man didn't make a lot of money as a grease monkey but was "great on a thing called love." She says she'd crawl back to him on her hands and knees to Jersey City if he'd take her back. Peg doesn't want that to happen to her.

Fight action against Cannonball Wales (Joe Gray) and action in between rounds when Wales's manager, Cobb (Welden) starts rubbing rosin on Wales's gloves, saying, "If he can't see ya, he can't hit ya.'"

Danny blinded by the rosin in the middle of the ring as he tries to fend off his opponent.

HOME COURT ADVANTAGE Available on VHS.

#63 JIM THORPE: ALL-AMERICAN

Screenwriters Douglas Morrow, Vince Flaherty. **Director** Michael Curtiz. **Producer** Everett Freeman. **Cinematography** Ernest Haller. **Art Direction** Ed Carrere. **Music** Max Steiner. **Editing** Folmar Blangsted. Warner Bros. 1951.

THE PLAYERS Burt Lancaster **Jim Thorpe**; Charles Bickford **Glenn "Pop" Warner**; Phyllis Thaxter **Margaret Miller**; Steve Cochran **Peter Allendine**; Dick Wesson **Ed Guyac**; Jack Big Head **Little Boy**; Suni Warcloud **Wally Denny**; Al Mejia **Louis Tewanema**; Hubie Kerns **Tom Ashenbrunner**; Billy Gray **Jim Thorpe (as a child)**

THE GAME This biographical drama is about Jim Thorpe, a Sac and Fox Indian from Oklahoma, voted the greatest athlete of the first half of the 20th century.

Thorpe's athleticism is displayed early in defying his father, who drops him off at a white man's school in their horse and wagon only to return home and see that Jim has beaten him back, running 12 miles through the hills.

Jim's father tries to impress upon him the importance of a formal education. Though resenting the white man's ways, Jim fulfills his promise to his father, attending Carlisle Indian school in Pennsylvania. The government-run institution drew tribes from all over—Chippewa, Blackfoot, Shawnee, Sioux, and Cherokee. But the pent-up frustration from the confinement of classroom study is finally too much as one morning Jim bolts from his dorm room and takes off running for the sheer joy of it. Along the way he comes across some track athletes and takes them on, whipping them in his street clothes. The track coach, Pop Warner (Charles Bickford), checks his stopwatch, duly impressed, and induces Jim to join the track team.

Thorpe soon dominates all the events he attempts, from the sprints to the high jump and javelin. In one meet after another Thorpe and his lone teammate, Louis Tewanema (Al Mejia), take on entire track teams, whipping all comers.

Jim then meets and falls in love with coed Margaret Miller (Phyllis Thaxter). Thorpe, however, finds himself in a romantic competition for her affections with Carlisle's star football player, Peter Allendine (Steve Cochran). To impress her, Thorpe insists that Coach Warner, who also runs the football team, let him try out for the team.

Coach feels he's too valuable in track to risk injury on the football field, so Thorpe seethes under his leather helmet on the bench for most of the season. Finally, with injuries piling up, Pop is forced to let Thorpe play. Thorpe soon contributes to the team's success, then becomes a star in his own right, drawing national attention as a running back.

At a goodbye dance before one summer break, Jim gives Margaret a bracelet, telling her that they are of the same blood and he looks forward to seeing her next fall. When he returns to campus after working on a farm and also making money playing baseball, he is stunned to learn that Margaret isn't returning to Carlisle. Though the school relaxed admissions for her, she felt it wouldn't be right to continue there because she isn't a true Indian. Emotionally crushed, Thorpe throws himself into sports even more, becoming all-American in football.

One day Coach Warner tells Jim he doesn't look well and that he should report to the campus infirmary immediately. After some hesitation Jim reluctantly does as the

(Left to right) Carlisle's Wally Denny (Suni Warcloud), Peter Allendine (Steve Cochran), and coach Glenn "Pop" Warner (Charles Bickford).

coach says, only to find that the nurse on duty is Margaret. Pop leaves them, smiling to himself.

Margaret explains that she didn't contact him because he had told her earlier how much the right Indian background and heritage meant to him. Jim tells Margaret he still loves her, asks her to marry him (she accepts), and says he'll be happy working as a coach to provide for them when his playing days are over.

After a brutal football game against mighty Penn and its star all-American Ashenbrunner ends in a 13-13 tie, Thorpe is summoned to Coach Warner's office, where he is informed that the prized coaching job he sought has been given to someone else. Thorpe's first reaction is that he didn't get the position because of his heritage. As he turns to leave he sees a poster promoting the upcoming Olympic Games in Sweden and comes up with an idea. Jim tells Coach Warner he'll just have to work that much harder to get the coaching job he wants, so he aims to make a name for himself on the international stage.

With much training and press coverage, Thorpe succeeds with a dominating performance at the 1912 Stockholm Games, winning unprecedented gold in both the pentathlon and the decathlon. He returns home a hero. Jim marries Margaret and is told a coaching job is awaiting him in Virginia. Little does he know that events will soon unfold that will send his life spiraling downward and out of control.

After a hearing where he admits to having earned a few bucks playing baseball between sessions at Carlisle, and despite his pleas of ignorance and remorse as well as a noble defense presented by Coach Warner, Thorpe is banned from amateur competition and stripped of his Olympic medals.

Jim enters professional baseball to provide for his wife and baby boy. He doesn't get along, however, with Giants manager John McGraw, and soon quits, telling Margaret he's been offered work with a new professional football league in Ohio (at that time college football was THE game). As he did at Carlisle, Thorpe soon establishes himself as a star player.

One day, however, while Thorpe is on the road with the football team, his son's illness takes a turn for the worse and the young boy dies. Devastated, blaming himself, Thorpe becomes a changed man, no longer passionate about anything, including football. His descent into despair is rapid and fueled by alcohol, and eventually it ends his marriage. As Thorpe drifts aimlessly, his athletic skills erode until he can't even make an impression playing for small-town semi-pro football teams.

In Los Angeles, the once great champion bottoms out, wearing Indian gear to attract people to a local nightclub. He can't even hold that job, as the manager tells his aide, "We don't need that cigar store Indian. Give him $5 and let him blow."

The former Olympic champion is seemingly forgotten by everyone except Coach Warner. Heading in the opposite direction to even greater heights as a coach at Stanford University, Pop is in town to see some of his athletes compete in the 1932 Olympics in Los Angeles. He finds Jim and offers him an assistant coach position with him, but the proud Indian considers it charity and declines. The anger, disillusionment, and frustration Thorpe has bottled up is unleashed as he lashes out at his old mentor.

Coach tries to make him understand that one must stand up to life's hard knocks.

POP: Somewhere along the line you've gone completely haywire. Picked up the idea that the world owes you something. Well, it doesn't owe you a thing. So you've had some tough ones—you've been kicked around, they took your

Burt Lancaster (center) was an accomplished trapeze artist.

medals away—so what? All I can say is when the real battle started the great Jim Thorpe turned out to be a powder puff.

JIM: Thanks for the sermon but you're wasting your time.

POP: Yes. I guess I am at that.

Hesitantly Thorpe accepts Pop's earlier invitation to join him in the stands at the Los Angeles Coliseum for the opening ceremonies of the Olympics. They sit together, mostly in silence, until coach points out that the Vice President of the United States, Charles Curtis, who is in attendance and whose declaration officially opens the Games, is an American Indian as well. Coach then excuses himself to see his athletes.

Long after the ceremonies are completed, Thorpe sits alone. The empty stadium is silent except for the voices from his past speaking out in a flashback through his mind. This is the moment when he starts to come to terms with his life.

Earning a gold medal in two grueling multi-event competitions (pentathlon and decathlon) at the 1912 Stockholm Olympics, Jim Thorpe (Lancaster, kneeling) is honored by King Gustav V of Sweden.

Shortly afterward he comes across some kids playing sandlot football. The old pro gives them a few pointers on technique, then has an epiphany when the kids ask him to coach them for an upcoming game. Thorpe realizes his mission and becomes a youth football coach.

Shot in flashback, the film returns to the tribute dinner held in Thorpe's honor where Coach Warner concludes his remarks and shakes Thorpe's hand as they look up at an unveiling of a portrait of the great athlete.

INSTANT REPLAY Unusual for biographical films of famous figures made up to that period, *Jim Thorpe: All-American* spends a significant part of its story fully exploring the downward path of a sports hero.

Based on a book by Russell Birdwell and Thorpe, Doug Morrow's script (with an assist by the film's producer, Everett Freeman) tells the story in an unvarnished, earnest manner, with a detailed understanding of the title subject. Certainly this ran against the period's prevailing tendency of glorifying our idols. Faithfully depicting the life and times of Jim Thorpe, the movie pulls few punches, and even the end is sensibly devoid of any misleading sugar coating.

By intertwining the highs and lows of Thorpe's personal life with his famous sporting achievements presented in flashback, director Michael Curtiz skillfully offers up a tragic figure that is genuine and quite human. The filmmakers succeed in presenting the human frailties of a legendary sports figure who finds his rebellious way to success in the world of athletics, faces tragedy and thwarted ambitions in a shattering descent, and eventually finds bittersweet compromise. At once inspiring, tragic, pitiful, and insightful, *Jim Thorpe: All-American* is a compelling film of one of the great stories in American sports history.

The technical contributors, including cinematographer Ernest Haller, editor Folmar Blangsted, and art director Ed Carrere, help re-create historical sports events that give that aspect of the film an authentic and consistent look (though perhaps too consistent in one scene. If I'm not mistaken, when Thorpe steps to the victory stand to accept his gold medal in Stockholm at the 1912 Olympics, the stadium behind him looks like he is really at the Los Angeles Coliseum.)

No matter, as the real star of the film is...as you would expect, the star of the film. It was as though Burt Lancaster was born to play this role. Lancaster's effort, combining athleticism and acting ability to great effect, is an outstanding tour de force.

Charles Bickford as Coach Pop Warner, Thorpe's mentor, works with restraint, warmth and conviction. Bickford's kindliness and understanding in helping a young man find his way is natural and believable.

Phyllis Thaxter contributes as Jim's quietly compassionate wife and the victim of her husband's disappointments. Dick Wesson gives an energetic turn as one of Jim's closest friends.

Jim Thorpe performed Herculean feats on the field, but Burt Lancaster performs just as superbly on the screen.

"Pop" Warner pays tribute to the great Jim Thorpe.

OUTSIDE THE LINES Jim Thorpe, who was extensively used as a technical advisor for the film, died in 1953, two years after the movie's release.... Thorpe won gold medals in both the pentathlon and the decathlon at the 1912 Olympics in Stockholm.... At 17 Burt Lancaster joined a circus troupe as an acrobat.... Thorpe originally sold the rights to his story to MGM for $1,500.... At an early point in the film's long development producer Freeman considered Kirk Douglas for the lead.... It wasn't until 1982, 70 years after he earned them, that the International Olympic Committee returned the medals to Thorpe's family.... The film was shot primarily at Bacone Indian College in Muskogee, Oklahoma.... Curtiz, who won an Academy Award for Best Director of *Casablanca*, knew Thorpe well and was himself a member of the Hungarian national fencing team.... Doug Morrow won an Oscar for his screenplay about baseball player Monty Stratton, *The Stratton Story* (1948).... *Jim Thorpe: All-American* was released in the U.K. under the title *Man of Bronze*.... Lancaster's last major feature film role was in the baseball movie *Field of Dreams*.... Lancaster trained with a group of USC and UCLA football and track coaches and players for three months before filming began.... Al Mejia, who plays Carlisle's long-distance runner, Louis Tewanema, was in fact a sprinter at USC.... Jim Thorpe was a Sac and Fox Indian.... The man voted the greatest athlete of the first half-century appeared in several movies, including *King Kong* (1933) and *Captain Blood* (1935).

ALL-STAR MOMENTS In Thorpe's first collegiate track meet, the opposing coach wanders over to Pop Warner scratching his head and asks where his team is. Coach points to the two guys seated behind him and says, "Louis runs everything from the mile on up and Jim Thorpe does the rest."

An aging Thorpe sits alone in an empty stadium and voices from his past play in his head as Jim begins to come to terms with his life.

HOME COURT ADVANTAGE Available on VHS.

#62 THE ENDLESS SUMMER

Writer/Director/Producer/Photographer/Narrator Bruce Brown. **Photographers** Paul Allen, Bob Bagley, Paul Witzig. Cinema V. 1966.

THE GAME The surfing culture took a dive with the Annette and Frankie teen movies of the mid 1960s, such as *How to Stuff a Wild Bikini, Muscle Beach Party,* and *Beach Blanket Bingo,* featuring characters like Deadhead, Eric Von Zipper, Moondog, and Flex Martian. Following in their wake, filmmaker Brian Brown showcased a pair of accomplished young surfers from southern California, Mike Hynson and Robert August, and forged a definitive picture of the actual sport.

The Endless Summer is a global surfing safari in search of the perfect wave. This feature-length documentary is an exploration of the real world of surfing—its athletic skill, beauty, danger, and excitement.

Using a combination travelogue, home movie, and true-life adventure approach, Bruce Brown, who had been filming surfers since his naval days in Hawaii, illuminates surfdom's finer points through his narration and wondrous photography as we observe the surfers in action at locales all over the globe.

INSTANT REPLAY *The Endless Summer* is a unique venture in filmmaking. Its accomplishment is in presenting a subject that draws in even the most landlocked. There's no deep plot here. Two young men on a global journey to find the perfect wave provide an easy framework to build around.

Through brilliant photography, informative and easygoing narration, sharp editing, and mood music this imaginative documentary, light on technical tricks, conveys a genuine freedom and innocence in a beautiful ode to sun, sand, and surf.

Teetering atop the monstrous 40-foot waves at Hawaii's infamous Pipeline, you get a sense of the exhilaration of that moment of impending danger. Like watching a high wire act or a bullfighter, for that instant you're riveted in wonder at the real peril that exists even for the most skilled and graceful surfer. One false move and the challenger finds himself under an avalanche of turbulent water, not to mention the board, which becomes a flying lethal weapon. We also learn of other dangers, such as hidden rocks, brutal coral, poisonous fish, and of course sharks.

Unquestionably it is the photography that is the true star of the documentary. Brown's innovative camera work, such as the close-up shots of the surfers' ballet-like footwork, adds to that audience-participatory feel. His use of the telephoto and zoom in framing and pans combined with artful editing elucidates the intrinsic beauty of the sport's setting and the athletic skills of its participants.

Using the world as the backdrop, there's a sense of multiculturalism at play, whether the two protagonists are teaching Africans to surf or shooting the breeze with their Australian counterparts.

The varying aspects of the film are held together by the director's low-key but enthusiastic narration that contrasts nicely with the visual power and exotic locations presented on the screen. Some of his attempts at humor, flatter than the waves they encountered in Australia, are a minor irritant. There's also the annoying overuse of

Filmmaker Bruce Brown captured surfing as no one had done before, scoring points for the sport without using Annette Funicello.

words like "ultimate." At the same time Brown's narration doesn't turn us off with jargon but rather presents surfing terms when appropriate to provide the layperson with a better grasp of the subculture's world.

The music is a fine fit overall, ranging from twanging guitars (more Dick Dale than Beach Boys) to fuller orchestral arrangements that match the rise and fall of the waves. The Sandals deserve credit for their mood-setting theme.

Finding, filming, and riding the perfect wave off the coast of South Africa at Cape St. Francis is a delightful payoff and highlight to the participants' quest that took them over 35,000 miles on continents (Africa, Australia, North America), islands (Tahiti, Hawaii, New Zealand), and oceans (Atlantic, Indian, Pacific) on a nearly two-year project that used nine miles of film.

The Endless Summer is a documentary of buoyant brilliance featuring some of the most beautiful shots of the surfer's world ever captured on celluloid.

OUTSIDE THE LINES Filmmaker Bruce Brown tested his completed project in the most landlocked place he could come up with—Wichita, Kansas—where it proceeded to set box office records.... Still, he had skeptical film distributors who told him to prove it in New York.... The movie was shot on 16mm film with a Bolex camera that had to be wound up and could shoot for less than half a minute at a time.... Costar Robert August was just out of high school, where he was class president and an honor student.... Neither August nor costar Mike Hynson received any money for their roles.... The director was 26 at the time of filming.... Originally intending only to go to South Africa, Brown found it was much cheaper to fly around the world than straight back to California, hence the expansion of the movie.... The music group the Sandals created the soundtrack and refused to take any money for their efforts.... The band broke up in 1968 but reunited to create music for the sequel in 1994.... Brown's

From the shores of Hawaii to Western Africa to Tahiti and California, 'The Endless Summer' rode the best waves of the world.

son Dana would go on to write and edit his own surfing picture, *Step Into Liquid* (2003).... Mike Brown cobbled together money to rent a theater, blow the film up to 35mm, and advertise the movie.... From a $50,000 budget, *The Endless Summer* has gone on to earn over $25 million around the world.... Brown was dubbed by some film critics as the "Fellini of the Foam."...Surfing ocean waves originated over 3,000 years ago in Polynesia.... Some early surfboards weighed over 100 pounds.... Brown wasn't the first to make pure surf films; Bud Browne made *Hawaii Surfing Movie* and *Surf Down Under* in the 1950s, and Americans Greg Noll and John Severson and Australia's Bob Evans were other early pioneers. But Bruce Brown would take those early works to another level, beyond presentations to church groups, schools, and community centers.... This film was Brown's 6th movie about surfing.... Brown would also cover motorcycle racing with the 1971 documentary *On Any Sunday*.... In 2002 *The Endless Summer* was selected for preservation by the Library of Congress as part of the National Film Registry.

ALL-STAR MOMENTS Opening shots of sunrise and sunset.

Point-of-view camera shot atop a surfboard with Hawaii's Diamondhead in the background.

Teaching the locals of Ghana how to surf when they had never seen a surfboard before.

Pan shot of the tip of southern Africa. Cape Horn.

Sunset shot as the surfers tool in their truck down the isolated Indian Ocean coast of Africa on the way to the perfect wave.

The wild animals of Africa, such as the impalas and giraffes, and the surfers attempting to pet a wild zebra.

Finding and riding the perfect wave.

Camera work of the monster waves at Hawaii's Pipeline.

Closing shot of the surfers walking along the beach carrying their boards at sunset.

HOME COURT ADVANTAGE Available on VHS and DVD. Several single releases are available, as is a three-disc set that also includes *The Endless Summer 2* and *Endless Summer Revisited*.

#61 BATTLING BUTLER

Writers Al Boasberg, Ballard McDonald, Lex Neal, Charles Smith, Paul Gerard Smith. **Director** Buster Keaton. **Producer** Joseph Schenck. **Cinematographer** Bert Haines, Deveraux Jennings. MGM. 1926.

THE PLAYERS Buster Keaton **Alfred Butler**; Snitz Edwards **Martin the Valet**; Sally O'Neil **The Girl**; Francis McDonald **Alfred "Battling Butler"**; Mary O'Brien **Battling Butler's wife**; Tom Wilson **The Trainer**; Walter James **The Girl's father**; Budd Fine **The Girl's brother**

THE GAME Alfred Butler (Buster Keaton) is the pampered, unmotivated son of a wealthy man. He's so spoiled that his valet, Martin (Snitz Edwards), combs his hair for him and flicks the ashes off his cigarette.

Alfred's father fears his soft son will never amount to much if he doesn't learn to become more self-reliant. He suggests his son go on a camping trip, do some hunting and fishing. Alfred goes, but the idea of "roughing it" goes down the stream he sets camp at; with Martin dutifully serving him, he enjoys practically the same comforts as he does at home. Here, however he meets and falls for a girl (Sally O'Neil).

They meet in embarrassing circumstances when Alfred's feeble attempts at hunting end up with him nearly shooting her as she walks in the woods near her home. Later, Alfred's attempts at fishing turn out to be "all wet," but the girl saves him as she rows by in her boat after his sinks.

Having changed into formal wear, Alfred dines with the girl on a gourmet meal prepared by Martin. The girl's brother (Judd Fine) and father (Walter James) show up. They are not impressed by the comparatively diminutive Alfred and his fancy trappings. But Alfred is in love and wants to marry the girl.

The ever-doting Martin comes up with the idea of concocting a story that Alfred is actually the talented prizefighter Alfred "Battling Butler," who everyone reads about in the newspaper. The girl's relations now change their attitude about the little man. However, solving one problem begets another: Alfred now must convince them that he is a boxer without being discovered. When the real fighter with the same name wins his fight and earns a shot at the title with the Alabama Murderer, Martin tells Alfred he should confess his deception now before going though rigorous and painful training and perhaps a severe beating at the hands of a real boxer. Alfred says, "No, Martin, I'd rather be killed by the Alabama Murderer than have her know."

As a result of various circumstances and deceptions by Battling Butler's trainers, Alfred is led to believe he'll actually be fighting the feared boxer for the title. On the day of the fight he nervously changes into his boxing gear only to be told that the real Battling Butler is fighting his own fight. The trainer laughs at Alfred: "You didn't think we'd throw a championship just to get even with you?!"

Battling Butler destroys the Alabama Murderer to win the championship, but the fighting isn't over. The boxer Butler is still peeved at Alfred because he believes Alfred has been fooling around with his wife. (Not only is he mistaken, but in fact Alfred and his girl have just been married.) "I've been saving you for three weeks," barks the boxer to Alfred and starts pummeling the little man against the dressing room wall. Offering little resistance, Alfred endures the punishment until he sees his wife watching from the hallway. Suddenly Alfred becomes a fighting machine, raining a flurry of

blows that knocks out the new champ. In an animalistic rage, Alfred continues to pound on the boxer and has to be pulled off by trainers.

Not quite sure what got into him, Alfred walks to the door and hides his head in shame, telling his wife he's not the real Battling Butler: "I lied to you. I'm not even a fighter." She walks over and says, "I'm glad."

The movie ends with Alfred merrily walking arm-in-arm with his wife on a crowded city sidewalk, still wearing his boxing gloves and trunks with his top hat and walking stick.

INSTANT REPLAY Though not the timeless masterpiece that his film *The General* is, *Battling Butler* is classic Keaton. And classic Keaton is very, very entertaining. Oddly, the movie was adapted from a British musical comedy, but that background didn't prevent the actor from showing off his genius for physical comedy.

In the boxing sequences, Keaton draws belly laughs by getting caught in the ropes, mimicking his trainer's instructions while getting pummeled by a sparring partner, and taking punches while trying to fight back despite having one glove tied to the ropes.

The humor extends outside the ring as well, into the great outdoors with fishing and hunting.

Keaton's performing abilities were developed early when he participated as a child in his parents' vaudeville act. The youngster learned not to react to being knocked about, rolled down stairs, and tossed out windows. His experience of being a live prop served him well for the slapstick comedy of silent movies. *Battling Butler* reflects his mastery of the deadpan, maintaining composure in a sea of physical adversity. Behind

ABOVE: Boxing was immensely popular during the Roaring '20s.

RIGHT: Alfred Butler (Buster Keaton) rests while training for his big bout.

the so-called "Great Stone Face," Keaton executed some of the most amazing stunts and cleverest sight gags with the effortless ease of a fine athlete.

Sally O'Neil, typical of Keaton's leading ladies, doesn't have a lot to work with but is vibrant nonetheless.

Snitz Edwards brings subtle humor to the picture as the doting manservant.

Battling Butler is dominated by its star and director. Keaton's boxing scenes are comparable to Charlie Chaplin's in *City Lights*. Certainly Chaplin and Harold Lloyd were on the same high level as the superstars of the silent era, but it is Keaton's "grace under pressure" in facing physical adversity that distinguishes him. *Battling Butler* is a classic example.

Alfred with his girl (Sally O'Neil).

OUTSIDE THE LINES *Battling Butler* was among Keaton's most commercially successful films.... Keaton was one of the first filmmaking "hyphenates," excelling as actor, comedian, writer, director, and stuntman.... Joseph Frank "Buster" Keaton had a younger brother, Harry, and younger sister, Louise; both would appear in some of his movie shorts.... Sally O'Neil starred in the baseball movie *Slide, Kelly, Slide* (1927).... Hungarian-born Snitz Edwards also appeared with Keaton in *College* (1927).... The film's producer, Russian-born Joseph Schenck, would also produce *College*. He founded 20th Century with Daryl Zanuck in 1933 and led the merge with Fox two years later.... Lex Neal, one of the film's cowriters, also cowrote Harold Lloyd's college football film *The Freshman* (1925).

ALL-STAR MOMENTS The doting manservant Martin parting Alfred's hair and flicking his cigarette ashes for him in the opening scene.

Alfred and Martin heading out to rough it in the wild in a Rolls Royce-type vehicle.

The campsite is a huge, luxurious tent containing elaborate furnishings.

Out hunting, Alfred sees nothing to shoot, but the camera reveals all sorts of animals within range. When Alfred does shoot it's the wrong way, but it leads to his meeting the girl who will become his wife.

On the water in a one-man boat, Alfred is outsmarted by a duck he's trying to shoot that eventually causes him to sink.

In training for his fight Alfred makes an inauspicious debut, getting tangled and almost strangling in the ropes.

In the film's final scene, relieved to have come clean with his deception and discovered some physical prowess in himself, Alfred merrily walks down a crowded city sidewalk at night, still wearing his boxing shorts and gloves along with his top hat and walking stick.

HOME COURT ADVANTAGE Available on VHS and DVD. In addition to a standard DVD release from Image Entertainment, *Battling Butler* also makes up part of Kino's *Art of Buster Keaton,* a multi-disc set that includes *College, Go West, Sherlock Jr., Three Ages, Steamboat Bill Jr., Seven Chances, Saphead, Our Hospitality, Navigator,* and *The General.*

#60 THE CHAMP

Screenwriter Frances Marion. **Director/Producer** King Vidor. **Cinematography** Gordon Avil. **Editing** Hugh Wynn. **Art Direction** Cedric Gibbons. Fox. 1931.

THE PLAYERS Wallace Beery **Andy "Champ" Purcell**; Jackie Cooper **Dink Purcell**; Irene Rich **Linda Carleton**; Hale Hamilton **Tony Carleton**; Roscoe Ates **Sponge**; Edward Brophy **Tim**; Jesse Scott **Jonah**; Marcia Mae Jones **Mary Lou Carleton**; Frank Hagney **Manuel Corroga, Mexican champion**

THE GAME Former boxing champion Andy Purcell (Wallace Beery) is down and out and attempting a comeback, but continually sabotages himself with a drinking and gambling problem. His son, Dink (Jackie Cooper), idolizes his father and refers to Andy as "Champ." And despite being raised in an environment of pool halls, casinos, and cheap Tijuana hotels, Dink loves his dad.

In a bit of a role reversal, it is the young boy who tries to change his father's detrimental behavior. Dink's efforts to straighten out his dad fail, however, as Andy continues to backslide into drinking and gambling.

One day Andy wins a racehorse and gives him to Dink. Dink names him Little Champ, in honor of his dad. When they take Little Champ to the Tijuana racetrack, though he doesn't know it at the time, Dink meets his mother.

After losing custody of her son years ago when she and Andy divorced, Linda (Irene Rich) has since married an affluent gentleman, Tony Carleton (Hale Hamilton).

When Little Champ falls during a race and Andy finds himself deeper in debt, he accepts Tony's offer of $200 to allow Dink to meet his mother and spend some time with her.

Later on, finding Andy at a casino, Tony informs him that Dink would be better off living with his mother. Andy refuses and barely contains his temper when Tony resorts to threats of taking Dink from him.

That night, Andy's gambling losses not only leave him broke but he is forced to cover his debt by signing over ownership of Dink's horse. Andy promises his son he'll win the horse back, but in a desperate "double or nothing" gamble the Champ not only loses but gets arrested for instigating a drunken brawl.

Depressed after a sleepless night in jail, Andy realizes his son would be better off with his mother. Pretending he no longer wants his son around, Andy hopes Dink will be disillusioned. Instead, Dink tearfully pleads to stay. Finally, Andy hits him and Dink leaves, saying, "Okay, Champ, I'll go if you don't want me." Andy punishes himself by repeatedly slamming his fist against the jail cell wall.

Heading back to New York with his mother and her family, Dink decides to sneak off the train.

He returns to Andy, who has been bailed out of jail by Tony. Andy is inspired by his son's return and trains vigorously for a title bout. But Dink is worried about his father's age and physical condition, and even the doctor is concerned that Andy's heart may not be able to take the extreme physical exertion.

On fight night, Tony, realizing Dink's love for his father, assures Andy that he and Linda will not try to take Dink away again.

As the fight against the Mexican champ (Frank Hagney) progresses, Andy is pressed by his son and cornermen Tim (Edward Brophy) and Sponge (Roscoe Ates) to

Dink Purcell (Jackie Cooper) sits on his dad's lap (Wallace Beery).

quit. At one point Dink even tries to throw in the towel, but Andy is determined to win so he will be able to properly care for his son.

Andy takes a pounding but endures the punishment, winning by a knockout. As they walk from the ring, Andy proudly shows his son that he has bought back the horse he lost earlier, Little Champ.

The father and son's joy is soon shattered, however, as Andy dies of a heart attack lying on the training table. Despite his desperate and futile cries of "Champ!" Dink is eventually comforted by his mother, Linda, who has just arrived and carries her son away in her arms.

INSTANT REPLAY A sentimental story of a washed-up boxer inspired by the faith and support of an adoring son, *The Champ* is a simple yet compelling film.

It succeeds largely on the strength of its two lead characters. The physical contrast of the burly Beery and pipsqueak Cooper forms an interesting outer shell for two brilliantly performed characterizations, as the powerful father-son emotions could have easily been embarrassingly trite if handled by less talented performers.

Wallace Beery won an Academy Award for his impression of a drunken, worn-out pugilist. Beery juggles the right amounts of toughness and tenderness in a fine, understated way.

Jackie Cooper delivers with a terrific effort, handling scenes with the presence of a much older and more experienced thespian. Bringing much more scope and depth than might be expected for someone of his years, Cooper gives a superb performance capped by a genuinely heartfelt final scene when he loses his beloved "Champ" for good.

Certainly Frances Marion's Oscar-winning story and King Vidor's Oscar-nominated direction aided Beery and Cooper's work.

Nominated for best picture, *The Champ* would spawn many imitators in the underdog category.

OUTSIDE THE LINES The movie premiered at the Graumann's Chinese Theater in Hollywood. In attendance was Charles Curtis, Vice President of the United States.... Curtis also appeared in *Jim Thorpe: All-American*.... Jackie Cooper was nominated for an Academy Award in the title role of *Skippy* (1931).... In his mid teens Wallace Beery worked as part of a crew training elephants for the Ringling Bros. Circus.... Beery and Cooper would go on to star together in *The Bowery* (1933), *Treasure Island* (1934), and *O'Shaughnessy's Boy* (1935).... Beery shared his Best Actor Oscar for *The Champ* with *Dr. Jekyll and Mr. Hyde* star Frederic March. In actuality Beery got one less vote than March, but by the Academy's rules at the time, coming within two votes of the leader meant a tie.... Cooper would win an Emmy for his directing work on the TV series *M*A*S*H*.... Frances Marion altered her script for a 1953 movie called *The Clown*, starring Red Skelton as a fading comedian instead of a fading boxer.... *The Champ* was remade in 1979, featuring Jon Voight and Rick Schroeder.

ALL-STAR MOMENTS Sitting atop his dad's shoulders to watch their horse in a race, Dink in his excitement keeps yanking on his father's hair.

When Linda asks Dink what he's been told about her, Dink's says she's "a dame with a lot of jack." When she asks what he knows about his mother, Dink says, "She kicked the bucket before I was born." When Linda reveals that she is his mother and has remarried, Dink reasons that if she's "not married to the Champ anymore, I guess you're not my mother."

Jail scene where Andy smashes his fist against the wall, feeling guilty for striking his son to drive him away for his own good.

Happy reunion of father and son as they playfully spar and Andy ends up knocking the punching bag out the window.

Post-fight locker room, where Dink's cries of "I want the Champ!" are futile as Andy dies of a heart attack and the boy is carried out in the arms of his mother.

HOME COURT ADVANTAGE Available on VHS.

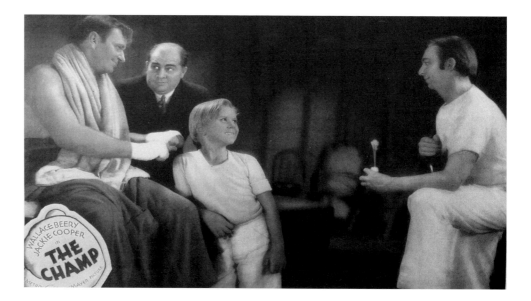

Beery (left) won a Best Actor Oscar as boxer Andy "Champ" Purcell.

#59 HE GOT GAME

Screenwriter/Director Spike Lee. **Producer** Jon Kilik. **Cinematography** Malik Hassan Sayeed. Editing Barry Alexander Brown. **Casting** Aisha Coley. **Music** Public Enemy, Aaron Copland. **Art Direction** David Stein. **Production Design** Wynn Thomas. **Set Decoration** Carolyn Cartwright. **Costume Design** Sandra Hernandez. **Special Effects** Randall Balsmeyer. **Technical Advisor** Earl Monroe. Buena Vista. 1998.

THE PLAYERS
Denzel Washington **Jake Shuttlesworth**; Ray Allen **Jesus Shuttlesworth**; Rosario Dawson **Lala Bonilla**; Zelda Harris **Mary Shuttlesworth**; Lonette McKee **Martha Shuttlesworth**; Hill Harper **Coleman "Booger" Sykes**; Milla Jovovich **Dakota Burns**; Jim Brown **Spivey**; Joseph Lyle Taylor **Crudup**; Ned Beatty **Warden Wyatt**; Bill Nunn **Uncle Bubba**; Michele Shay **Aunt Sally**; Roger Guenveur Smith **Big Time Willie**; Thomas Jefferson Byrd **Sweetness**; Arthur Nascarella **Coach Cincotta**; Rick Fox **Chick Deagan**; Al Palagonia **Dom Pagnotti**; John Turturro **Coach Billy Sunday**; Leonard Roberts **D'Andre Mackey**; Michael Jordan **Himself**; Reggie Miller **Himself**; Shaquille O'Neal **Himself**; John Thompson **Himself**; Dick Vitale **Himself**; Roy Williams **Himself**; Rick Pitino **Himself**; Nolan Richardson **Himself**; Charles Barkley **Himself**; Bill Walton **Himself**; Bobby Cremins **Himself**; Jim Boeheim **Himself**; John Chaney **Himself**; Robin Roberts **Herself**

THE GAME Jake Shuttlesworth (Denzel Washington), a former playground basketball legend, is serving time for the accidental slaying of his wife, Martha (Lonette McKee).

Meanwhile, their son, Jesus (Ray Allen), has been serving notice that he's grown into one of the best high school players in the country, playing for Lincoln High on Coney Island.

He Got Game is an ambitious movie that tells not one story but two. One concerns the very strained father-son relationship between Jake and Jesus, who bitterly holds his father responsible for his mother's death, and the other points up the corruption, betrayal, and use of young men as commodities in the high-stakes world of college athletics.

The picture opens with Jake being summoned to the warden's office. Warden Wyatt (Ned Beatty) lays out a deal to Jake: the governor, a former basketball player and alumni supporter of Big State college, will make his best efforts to reduce Jake's prison term if he can get his son, Jesus, the number one high school prospect in the country, to sign a letter of intent to attend Big State. Jake agrees to the deal, which is complicated by two things: there are only seven days left to declare college intentions, and Jesus has basically disowned his father.

With those strikes against him Jake takes on the mission. Under the watchful eyes of two parole officers, Spivey (Jim Brown) and Crudup (Joseph Lyle Taylor), Jake is given some money for street clothes and a tracking device affixed to his leg that requires a daily check-in.

Jesus meanwhile is constantly reminded that his choice of college will be "the most important decision of his life." His coach (Arthur Nascarella), Uncle Bubba (Bill Nunn), classmates, friends, and even his girlfriend, Lala Bonilla (Rosario Dawson), all want to have their say, but in reality, without much authoritative guidance Jesus is left alone to make that major choice.

Jake meets his daughter, Mary (Zelda Harris), outside her school. She's surprised but happy to see her father. She happily tells him she got a good grade in science, where they're studying "cells," to which her interned father says, "Me, too."

TOP: Being an avid sports fan has sharpened the keen eyes of director Spike Lee.

BOTTOM: The star (Denzel Washington, left) and director (Lee, right) discuss a scene.

Wary of the inevitable clash between her brother and father, Mary hesitates to invite Jake up to the apartment she lives in with Jesus. Jake promises to leave before his son returns home, but the happy father-daughter reunion is cut short when Jesus shows up. Their reunion is much less joyous and their conversation is awkward, Jesus telling his dad, "Time for you to get steppin', and I'd appreciate it if you don't ever walk through that door again." Jake says he'll speak with his son where he hangs out, down at the apartment complex basketball courts.

Jesus reports his father's visit to Uncle Bubba. Bubba says, "Man escaped like Shawshank" and suspects Jake "smells the money." Bubba takes the opportunity to express his vexation that, as Jesus's legal guardian, he hasn't been more involved in the college decision process. He adds that he's heard of deals of cash and cars and wonders where his cut is. Jesus is clearly disappointed and tells him, "When the real money comes in I'll take of everybody with interest."

Out on the basketball courts Jake catches up with Jesus and his cousin Booger (Hill Harper), who leaves so the father and son can talk. Jake tells his son he's proud of him and glad to see that all his hard work is paying off. He brings up the inevitable "most important decision of your life" topic, but Jesus is more interested in venting his anger on several subjects, including the name he was given, which, he tells his father, has caused him a lot of grief from his peers throughout his childhood. Jesus also wonders if his father ever even loved his mother. Jake says, "I loved her more than life itself," whereupon Jesus retorts, "You sure have a hell of a way of showing it."

Meanwhile, the hype surrounding Jesus builds, including a laudatory feature airing on ESPN and glowing comments from the Who's Who of the sport, such as Shaq, John Thompson, Rick Pitino, Reggie Miller, and Lute Olson.

Checking in back at the dumpy Surf Hotel, Jake strikes up a relationship with his "neighbor," a hooker named Dakota Burns (Milla Jovovich). Meanwhile, Jesus's girl Lala insists he meet with a "family friend" with ties to a big time agent, even though she knows that could jeopardize Jesus's college eligibility. "Big Time" Willie (Roger Guenveur Smith), a local hustler, gives Jesus a ride in his shiny red Mercedes and graphically lays out the various temptations facing a star athlete in the inner city.

Jesus succumbs to Lala's sexy persuasions and meets with an Italian sports agent, Dom Pagnotti (Al Palagonia), who mesmerizes the youngster, drawing him in with expensive watches and exotic cars. Still, Jesus isn't ready to jump straight to the pros and says that when he is, he's likely to go with a black agent. Dom breaks out the "green is the only color in business" routine, but it doesn't work.

We now have a series of flashbacks that fill in the backstory, including the death of Jesus's mother and scenes showing his love for her. At the same time we're given a glimpse of the early father-son relationship, with Jake driving his young son very hard in fundamental drills of the game, saying, "You got to work harder than the next man, it's the will of the man, not the skill of the man. Michael Jordan's lifting weights right now."

Back to current time: Jesus meets Jake at a Coney Island pier. There Jake tells his son the real story of how he got his name, which was not from the Bible but rather for Jake's basketball hero. Growing up in Philadelphia, Jake idolized player Earl Monroe, who was nicknamed Jesus because he was "the truth."

Then Jake, running out of time, lays it out, telling his son the real reason why he's out of prison, and asks where Big State is ranked on his list of college choices. Jesus says it's "in the top 10," and they part ways as Jesus leaves for a recruiting trip and Jake checks in with his parole officers.

At the Tech U. campus, star athlete Chick Deagan (Rick Fox) gives Jesus a tour he won't soon forget, including a hysterical pitch by basketball coach Billy Sunday (John Turturro), who prays, "Dear Lord, deliver Jesus to us," and culminating in the high schooler having sex with two buxom coeds.

While Jesus is away, Jake visits his wife's grave and expresses his deep feelings of loss.

Upon his return, Jesus is given an ultimatum by Lala, who says that she needs to know if he's going to take care of her financially. Their relationship abruptly ends when he doesn't commit, both having been unfaithful.

Jake is at the end of his rope. He meets Jesus at the familiar court, telling his son, "This is it. Judgment Day.… I ain't got no more time to beg your forgiveness or nothing like that so I'll make this real simple." He lays it out that they'll play a game of one-on-one to 11, father vs. son. If the father wins, the son signs the letter of intent to Big State; if the son wins he can do whatever he pleases. The stakes are clarified by Jesus and the game is on.

It's a helluva game, full of anger, trash talk, and years of pent-up emotion. Though Jake builds an early lead, he's no match for his son, who ultimately overwhelms him. Game over and the victorious Jesus is still full of venom, hurling insults—"Somebody call a stretcher," "Take your old ass back to Attica."

Jake says, "So you feel like a man now? Huh? Maybe you can stop hating me. Is that going to bring your mother back? Maybe we can start being father and son again now, huh?"

Jesus snaps, "You ain't my father."

As the parole officers come to collect Jake, he tells his son, "You look out for your-

The writer/director (right) talks with cast members Rosario Dawson (left) and Ray Allen (center).

self. You ain't got to worry about me anymore. But you get that hatred out of your heart, boy, or you gonna end up just another nigger like your father. It's your ball."

As the parole officers handcuff the elder Shuttlesworth he stares at his son, who flashes back to his mother calling his name from the apartment window above the courts: "Jesus!"

Decision day. Fellow students gather in the gym. Jesus is absent as his prepared statement is read by a school official. In attendance are Big Time Willie and Lala, who watch as the crowd cheers wildly when it is announced that Jesus will attend Big State and his sister will attend a nearby school. Jesus ends the statement blessing his father.

Back in prison Jake meets the warden, who tells him the governor has yet to inform him of Jake's prison status. Wyatt says technically Jake didn't get his son to sign but they do have time to wait.

The movie ends connecting father and son via a mystical basketball sequence in which Jake tosses the ball over the prison fence high in the sky and it comes down through the rafters of the empty gym at Big State where Jesus is practicing alone. Jesus drops the ball he was shooting with and grabs the one his father "sent." Jesus senses the connection with his father.

INSTANT REPLAY
The 1994 documentary *Hoop Dreams* was about two black youths trying to use basketball as a ticket out of the ghetto. Somewhere around the middle of the film, Spike Lee shows up at a Nike training camp for future collegians and makes this statement to the participants:

> You've got to realize that nobody cares about you. You're a black, you're a young male. All you're supposed to do is deal drugs and mug women. The only reason why you're here is so you can make their team win. And if the team wins those schools get a lot of money. This whole thing revolves around money.

You can add the line from *Jerry Maguire*—"Show me the money"—and you have another theme of Spike Lee's film.

This ambitious undertaking is a good representation of Lee's passion for the game. It's clear his deep involvement as a fan has served him well, especially with his insider's knowledge of basketball. The writer/director's enthusiasm for the sport is smartly tempered by his cynical view of what actually goes on off the court and behind closed doors. Lee's connections also yield solid verisimilitude with several cameos by top coaches and players of the game.

Essentially, *He Got Game* scores in its focus beyond the courts on the greed, pressures, and use of young men as commodities in the flesh-peddling world of big time sports. Lee uses Jesus's story to show how for most people, fame and glory turn out to be an unenviable burden, as one of the steep prices is not being sure who your friends are. *He Got Game* shows what it's like for the extremely few who might actually make it, while *Hoop Dreams* covers the other side of the dream, where most don't end up reaching their ultimate goal. The temptations on the way up are the same for both.

Lee's depiction of the business side of basketball makes it a fine complement to both *Blue Chips* and *Hoop Dreams*.

Rookie actor and NBA player Ray Allen, though not greatly stretched in the role of Jesus, is a pleasant surprise nonetheless. He embodies the dignity and poise needed to triumph over the pressurized circumstances surrounding "the biggest decision of his life."

He Got Game really benefits by the performance of Denzel Washington in its main story—that of the father-son relationship. The dynamic between Jake and Jesus is earnest and convincing. Washington really embodies the flawed man who made a tragic mistake that essentially ruined his life, including his relationship with his son. At the same time he's committed to making sure his son does the right thing. The actor excels in showing us Jake's internal struggle as he tries to connect with his estranged son.

The supporting cast is solid for the most part, especially Zelda Harris as daughter Mary. Her fine work is somewhat lost in that she isn't really to be found in the latter half of the film. Lee deserves credit for rolling the dice on casting basketball players in major roles, but both Allen and Rick Fox (Chick Deagan) pull it off convincingly. John Turturro is brilliant in a brief appearance as the over-the-top basketball coach Billy Sunday. Jim Brown brings a raw tension to his scenes as the hard-nosed parole officer, Spivey. Milla Jovovich is good in a very extraneous role as a prostitute who befriends Jake.

Some of the music and camera work actually detracts from the film. Certainly Chuck D and Public Enemy work well with the urban sport, but even though the opening montage is brilliantly assembled by Barry Alexander Brown, Aaron Copland's Americana background music doesn't match well overall with the assorted shots. Taken as a whole, however, the music not only adds dramatic impact but also heightens the themes of hopes and dreams by the film's end. Most of cinematographer Sayeed's shots are vivid, but there are times when his attempts to draw us closer by juggling the film speed and altering images serve more as a distraction. Finally, the sights and sounds of the mystical climax come across as a tad melodramatic.

Lee, savvy to the pitfalls of most sports movies, successfully avoids syrupy speeches about the "beauty of the game," and the few action sequences presented are well crafted. The filmmaker really scores with this picture by effectively combining the sys-

TOP: Unexpectedly back with his family, Jake faces an angry son, Jesus (Allen), as his daughter, Mary (Zelda Harris), observes.

BOTTOM: What's really at play—respect and understanding between father and son.

tematic greed and exploitation of big time sports with a volatile father-son relationship, creating a compelling story with a universal moral concern—the ability to truly forgive someone.

OUTSIDE THE LINES
Director Lee wrote a book documenting his love of the New York Knicks, called *Best Seat in the House: A Basketball Memoir*.... Ned Beatty played the father of the title character in the football film *Rudy* (1993).... Jim Brown, recognized as one of the greatest running backs in the history of the NFL, was also a standout lacrosse player at Syracuse University.... Actress Lonette McKee starred in *The First*, the Broadway play about baseball pioneer Jackie Robinson.... NBA Hall of Fame player Earl Monroe was a technical advisor on the film .... Denzel Washington won a Golden Globe award for his portrayal of boxer Ruben Carter in *The Hurricane* (1999).... One of Washington's first film appearances came in the story of the American Olympic legend Wilma Rudolph in *Wilma* (1977).... Washington also played a high school football coach in *Remember the Titans* (2000).... Spike Lee collaborated with NBA superstar Michael Jordan for a series of Nike shoe commercials resurrecting the Mars Blackmon character from his film *She's Got to Have It*.... Washington was executive producer on the baseball documentary *Hank Aaron: Chasing the Dream* (1995).... Lee was a producer for *Love and Basketball* (2000).

ALL-STAR MOMENTS
Billy Sunday's (Turturro) "Lord deliver us Jesus" pitch.

ESPN's mock "Jesus is the second coming" feature.

Big Time Willie's (Smith) talk with Jesus about inner-city temptations.

A shoe store clerk notices the tracking device on Jake's leg; Jake says it's for his arthritis, and the clerk says it must be going around.

The father-son, one-on-one game with the letter of intent on the line.

HOME COURT ADVANTAGE
Available on VHS and DVD. Disney has released this title singly and combined with *Good Morning, Vietnam* on DVD.

#58 BANG THE DRUM SLOWLY

Screenwriter Mark Harris. **Director** John Hancock. **Producer** Lois/Maurice Rosenfeld. **Cinematography** Richard Shore. **Editing** Richard Marks. **Music** Stephen Lawrence. **Production Design** Robert Gundlach. **Costume Design** Domingo Rodriguez. Paramount. 1973.

THE PLAYERS
Michael Moriarty **Henry Wiggen**; Robert DeNiro **Bruce Pearson**; Vincent Gardenia **Manager Dutch Schnell**; Phil Foster **Joe Jaros**; Ann Wedgeworth **Katie**; Heather MacRae **Holly**; Selma Diamond **Tootsie**; Tom Ligon **Piney Woods**; Tom Signorelli **Goose**; Andy Jarrell **Ugly**; Barbara Babcock **Team owner**; Maurice Rosenfeld **Team owner**; Marshall Efron **Bradley**; Danny Burks **Perry**; James Donahue **Canada**; Hector Elias **Dego**; Nicolas Surovy **Aleck Olson**; Hector Troy **George**; Tony Major **Jonah**; Barton Heyman **Red**; Ernesto Gonzalez **Dr. Chambers**; Alan Manson **Doc Loftus**; Jack Hollander **Tegwar player**; Lou Girolami **Tegwar player**; Arnold Kapnick **Detective**; Jean David **Dutch's wife**; Patrick McVey **Bruce's father**; Dorothy Neubert **Bruce's mother**

THE GAME
After a visit to the Mayo Clinic in Minnesota, major league ballplayer Bruce Pearson (Robert DeNiro) learns he has a terminal illness.

Riding home from the clinic with him is Henry Wiggen (Michael Moriarty). Wiggen is Bruce's New York Mammoth roommate and friend. Through Wiggen's voice-over, we learn that as a catcher Bruce had "a two-million-dollar promise but two cents on delivery. But the cruel joke is on him as he's dying."

A kind and considerate man, Henry dedicates himself to helping his less talented bumpkin batterymate through his last season. Henry becomes quite protective of Bruce's illness and does his best to keep it a secret for fear Pearson will be dismissed if the team finds out.

Upon learning that manager Dutch Schnell (Vincent Gardenia) is leaning toward dropping Bruce in favor of another catcher, Henry, in the middle of contract negotiations, surprises management by taking less money in exchange for a clause that ties him and Bruce together, thus assuring his friend won't go to the minors or get released outright since Henry is the Mammoths' franchise player.

As the season progresses teammates eventually learn of Bruce's ailment, but the knowledge brings the team closer together, and Bruce's play even improves noticeably. With the bickering and backstabbing gone, the new esprit des corps helps the Mammoths earn a playoff spot. Unfortunately, Bruce's illness takes a turn for the worse and he is physically incapable of playing in the post-season.

As Henry watches his friend board a plane home, Bruce tells him, "I'll be back in the spring and I'm going to be in shape then, you'll see." Henry humors his teammate but senses Bruce will never put on a uniform again. The Mammoths go on to win the World Series.

A month or so later we see Henry walking in a Georgia cemetery, the only teammate or official at Bruce's funeral. We hear Henry's thoughts on his late friend and how their friendship changed him: "He (Bruce) wasn't a bad fellow, no worse than most and probably better than some. And not a bad ballplayer neither when they gave him a chance, when they laid off him long enough. From here on in, I rag nobody."

INSTANT REPLAY
The ebb and flow of life set within the ebb and flow of a baseball season, *Bang the Drum Slowly* explores a subject that athletes in real life and sports-themed movies in general rarely do: death.

The New York Mammoths' star pitcher, Henry Wiggen (Michael Moriarity, left), with terminally ill catcher Bruce Pearson (Robert DeNiro).

In the course of doing so, the picture beautifully renders its core theme of courage and caring, of answering the call in grim times with dignity, grace, and compassion, as Henry Wiggens did for Bruce Pearson.

At the same time the film's most telling point is the players' superficial empathy for Bruce, evidenced by not even one joining Henry at their teammate's funeral.

Bang the Drum Slowly excels in its subtleties, making its points without depending on the histrionics of the final game or a maudlin deathbed scene. It addresses a wide range of humanity in a low-key way, from gold diggers to cold, bottom-line-driven management and the powder keg of a locker room filled with culturally biased players.

This story is applicable to any milieu; one doesn't have to like baseball to appreciate what is essentially a story of human relationships. However, it is precisely in the baseball where the few errors of the film occur. The editing and continuity with inserting taped footage into re-created action is generally quite poor. Additionally, Moriarty and DeNiro won't be mistaken for Greg Maddux and Mike Piazza. The sequence where a Pirates pitcher is followed on the next pitch by an Indians hurler in the same at bat is just one example of a little momentum lost. The rain delay scene, supposedly set at Yankee Stadium, clearly takes place elsewhere. A runner on base in one shot disappears in between frames. Though baseball is only the backdrop, the producers could have put a little more effort into the realism on the field.

Even though the filmmakers miss a few down on the diamond, they rally and score with terrific scenes off the playing field—in hotel rooms and lobbies, bars, and locker rooms.

Director John Hancock's pacing at times seems like episodic television, with convenient breaks for commercials, but overall his work emphasizes and rightly focuses on the powerful dialogue from the script by Mark Harris, who adapted it from his own novel.

Hancock's direction is generally unobtrusive and succeeds in maintaining credible melodrama even though the movie addresses difficult subject matter, made more challenging when we know from the opening scenes that the protagonist is terminally ill.

Unlike the Mammoths' inconsistent team chemistry, the cast enjoys a terrific chemistry, especially in the wordless rapport Moriarty and DeNiro share, or the game group dynamic Moriarty plays with Vincent Gardenia as Gardenia becomes obsessed with trying to discover Moriarty's "secret."

DeNiro gives a fine tragicomic performance as an earnest, unworldly athlete, conveying well the terminally ill young man's inner struggle against inevitable and understandable self-pity.

Michael Moriarty's sensitive role with a powerful underlying strength is best summed up in the line he delivers holding his dying friend and trying to find a rational meaning in the tragic circumstances: "Everybody knows everybody is dying. That's why people are as good as they are."

The thoroughly likable, touching, and even funny presentation succeeds because it's a tale full of genuine dignity and compassion, and Michael Moriarty embodies those elements in his fine delivery. Though it happens at the airport and not on the diamond, Moriarty's wet-eyed goodbye to his dying teammate refutes Tom Hanks's famed line from *A League of Their Own*; sometimes there *is* crying in baseball.

Providing much of the humor is Vincent Gardenia as the weary team manager fixated on trying to find out his star pitcher's motive for helping a marginal ballplayer.

Music is also a key player in this project. Stephen Lawrence's score is smartly spare. The filmmakers also use music quite effectively within a scene with a performance by one of the characters. Passing the time during a rain delay, Piney Woods (Tom Ligon), the back-up catcher, plays guitar and sings *The Streets of Laredo* in the Mammoths' locker room. The reaction shots of Bruce Pearson, listening to this tune symbolic of the brevity of human life, say a lot more than words ever could about the tragedy of the young man's fate.

That scene is representative of the film as a whole in its reflection not only of how precious life is individually, but also of the importance of treating one's fellow man with respect. People shouldn't have to know they are dying in order to treat each other better.

Bang the Drum Slowly is less a game and more a measurement of character.

OUTSIDE THE LINES *Bang the Drum Slowly* was originally produced on television as part of the U.S. Steel Hour in 1956.... Paul Newman played the role of Henry Wiggen with Albert Salmi as Bruce Pearson and George Peppard as Piney Woods.... Vincent Gardenia received an Oscar nomination for his supporting work as the manager.... This was Danny Aiello's first major film.... Michael Moriarty starred in the hockey film *The Deadliest Season* (1977).... Vincent Gardenia starred in the TV series version of the cycling movie *Breaking Away* (1980—81).... Mark Harris wrote a series of baseball novels beginning in the 1950s: *The Southpaw, A Ticket for a Seamstitch*,

TOP: Katie (Ann Wedgeworth) and Bruce.

BOTTOM: Bruce gets rid of his mementos.

and *It Looked Like Forever*…. Robert DeNiro won an Oscar for his portrayal of boxer Jake LaMotta in *Raging Bull* (1980)…. DeNiro's other baseball film credit is *The Fan* (1996)…. John Hancock was nominated for an Academy Award for his short film, *Sticky My Fingers, Fleet My Feet* (1971), about touch football…. Gardenia was a bartender in *The Hustler* (1961) and a detective in *Heaven Can Wait* (1978)…. Reportedly Michael Moriarty's grandfather, George, not only played major league ball but later became an umpire for over a quarter-century…. CCNY coach Del Bethel was a consultant on the film…. DeNiro spent time in Georgia to get the accent right.

ALL-STAR MOMENTS The opening scene of the 2 teammates jogging around the ball field.

Various attempts by manager Dutch (Gardenia) to find out "what the hell is going on!?"

As the two men fish, Henry (Moriarty) realizes he'll never be able to fully share his friend's burden.

Sitting up in his bed, a scared Bruce (DeNiro) says, "Everybody'd be nice to you if they knew you were dying." Henry replies, "Everybody knows everybody is dying. That's why people are as good as they are."

POST-GAME COMMENTS Robert DeNiro on his preparations for the lead role:

> We would practice pitching every day. Michael Moriarty would practice pitching and I'd practice throwing and catching. When I wasn't shooting I'd watch the television to look at the catchers. Any game there was, I would watch. Just by observing the catcher's stance I learned a lot of things. I'd note what they were doing and I'd pick off the ones automatically that I could do or could relate to. Then I would think about which scenes in the script I could use [them] in.[1]

DeNiro on capturing the character's accent:

> I traveled to Georgia to get the correct inflection of words. I talked with the mayor of a small Georgia town that Pearson might have lived in. I looked around at clothing stores and at the manner of dress of the people—and I learned how to chew tobacco.[2]

HOME COURT ADVANTAGE Available on VHS and DVD.

#57 THE BAD NEWS BEARS

Writer Bill Lancaster. **Director** Michael Ritchie. **Producer** Stanley Jaffe. **Cinematography** John Alonzo. **Music** Jerry Fielding. **Editing** Richard Harris. **Production Design** Polly Platt. Paramount. 1976.

THE PLAYERS Walter Matthau **Coach Morris Buttermaker**; Tatum O'Neal **Amanda Whurlizter**; Vic Morrow **Coach Roy Turner**; Ben Piazza **Councilman Whitewood**; Chris Barnes **Tanner Boyle**; Jackie Earle Haley **Kelly Leak**; Gary Lee Cavagnaro **Engelberg**; Joyce van Patten **Ms. Cleveland**; Alfred Lutter **Ogilvie**; Erin Blunt **Ahmad Abdul Rahim**; David Pollock **Rudi Stein**; Quinn Smith **Timmy Lupus**; David Stambaugh **Toby Whitewood**; Brandon Cruz **Joey Turner**; Scott Firestone **Regi Tower**; George Gonzalez **Miguel Agilar**; Jaime Escobedo **Jose Agilar**; Brett Marx **Jimmy Feldman**; Shari Summers **Mrs. Turner**; Maurice Marks **Announcer**; Joe Brooks **Umpire**; Bill Sorrells **Mr. Tower**; George Wyner **White Sox manager**; Charles Matthau **Athletic**; David Lazarus **Yankee**

THE GAME City Councilman Whitewood (Ben Piazza) hires a drunken former minor league pitcher-turned-pool-cleaner, Morris Buttermaker (Walter Matthau), to coach a team of multiracial misfits (including the city official's son) on a Little League squad located in southern California.

Almost immediately Morris is overwhelmed by this ragtag group of foul-mouthed and largely untalented kids. After seeing the team blasted by more organized and skilled players, Whitewood leads a move by the parents to disband the team and save their children from potential psychic scars (and themselves from further embarrassment).

Coach Buttermaker doesn't give up as easily and corrals two ringers, first a smart and talented girl pitcher, Amanda Whurlitzer (Tatum O'Neal), and later a tough-talking, power-hitting delinquent named Kelly Leak (Jackie Earl Haley).

Slowly but surely these two stars lead the otherwise hapless Bears out of the cellar and into contention. Ultimately, they qualify to take on the Yankees for the league title. But success has come at a price, as the teammates who initially welcomed Kelly's great skills now resent him for "hogging" all the play, even though he's only following the coach's instructions.

They clear the air before the championship game—or at least the coach thinks so—but at one point they're down and "playing like dead fish." Coach Buttermaker can't figure it out. After the Yankees' zealous coach, Roy Turner (Vic Morrow), strikes his son (Brandon Cruz) for disobeying his pitching instructions, the Bears start to come alive. Even though they fall short, their group effort is felt by everyone and there's a sense of team pride. The Bears promise the champion Yankees "they'll be back."

INSTANT REPLAY America's obsession with winning—not unique, but often characterized by a distinct fervor beyond all logical sense of proportion—takes a pounding here where it all starts, youth sports.

No director was better qualified for this special aspect of social observation than Michael Ritchie. Ritchie has often explored the excesses, absurdities, and rituals of competition in American culture, whether in beauty contests (*Smile*), politics (*The Candidate*), or the Olympics (*Downhill Racer*).

In *The Bad News Bears* director Ritchie is aided by Bill Lancaster's humorous, insightful, and more than a bit salty script that uses a melting pot of smart-ass kids to

A former professional pitcher turned pool cleaner, Morris Buttermaker (Walter Matthau) returns to the game to coach a gang of misfits.

express grown-up viewpoints and address concerns such as the value of the joy of playing without concern for the final score. Ritchie brings the script to life without being overly sentimental. *The Bad News Bears* smartly and lightheartedly shows how adults impart their values to children, and how children learn from each other and then turn around to teach their elders.

There are elements of excess, like the constant cussing that outdoes sailor talk and Coach Buttermaker's handing out beers to the kids. Elsewhere, laughs abound and points are made without going over the top. The most telling sequence uses a minimum of words: when the opposing coach strikes his son on the pitcher's mound, the ensuing silence on the field and in the stands speaks volumes.

The cast is brilliant as a whole, with almost every member playing a strategically important role. Walter Matthau's lovable grouch is reminiscent of Wallace Beery in *The Champ* and, from his own library, sportswriter Oscar Madison in *The Odd Couple*. Tatum O'Neal is simply smart as the sassy young girl far ahead of her teammates on the maturity ladder. Jackie Earl Haley shows some spunk as the young punk more interested in girls and motorbikes than sports. All of the other kids are smartly woven into the story (particularly memorable is shortstop Tanner Boyle, played by Chris Barnes). But Joyce Van Patten's Ms. Cleveland is underwritten, as we are left wanting to see more of her. Vic Morrow nails the serious coach role. The film's success practically created the kid sports film flurry that followed.

Despite some excess crudities passing for cuteness, the makers of *The Bad News Bears* score with their sharp, satirical observation of the destructive side of competition shown through the prism of that hallowed American institution known as Little League baseball.

OUTSIDE THE LINES The film's screenwriter was actor Burt Lancaster's son.... Tatum O'Neal had won an Oscar for her performance in *Paper Moon,* costarring with her father, Ryan, three years earlier.... Jackie Earl Haley would star in the cycling feature *Breaking Away* (1979).... The success of *The Bad News Bears* produced several sequels.... O'Neal's preparation for the film included playing Frisbee with her father and being tutored in pitching by Pat Harrison, a USC assistant baseball coach.... Walter Matthau was the original slob sportswriter Oscar Madison in Neil Simon's 1965 Broadway production of *The Odd Couple,* then reprised that role with Jack Lemmon in the film version a few years later.... He won the Best Supporting Actor Academy Award in 1966 for his work in *The Fortune Cookie*.... Michael Ritchie was involved in a wide range of sports-themed films as a writer and director, including *Downhill Racer* (1966), *Semi-Tough* (1977), *Wildcats* (1986), *Diggstown* (1992), *Cool Runnings* (1993), *The Scout* (1994), and *Big Shot: Confessions of a Campus Bookie* (2002).

ALL-STAR MOMENTS Throwing a fit, then a baseball that breaks the window of the coach's car, Engelberg (Gary Lee Cavagnaro) is taking nothing from Coach Buttermaker (Matthau).

> **COACH: Guys, somebody's going to pay for this windshield. And I think, Engelberg, it's going to be your father.**
>
> **ENGELBERG: Bullshit!**

As the kids do his job of cleaning a pool at a home high atop a hill, Coach Buttermaker arrives with the team's uniforms. Engelberg asks if he can go swimming, but Coach says, "No. Don't jump in, Engelberg, you'll flood the valley."

Buttermaker lies in a lounge chair and one of the kids fixes him a perfect martini as the others sit around and listen to their coach describe in detail the time he struck out Ted Williams.

After an argument with Coach Buttermaker the camera follows Amanda (O'Neal) out of the dugout. The camera moves around to her face, which is streaked with tears shining in the sun, then cuts back to the dugout, where the coach is swigging a beer and shedding tears as well.

After a big opponent spikes Amanda, sliding feet high into home plate, little Tanner (Barnes) runs over to the culprit, saying, "Hey, that's not allowed!" and proceeds to flatten the big kid with a kick to his privates. A bench-clearing brawl ensues.

HOME COURT ADVANTAGE Available on VHS and DVD. Paramount offers this picture three ways on DVD: As a solo title; combined with the remake, starring Billy Bob Thornton; Triple Play version with the original and *Bad News Bears in Breaking Training* and *Bad News Bears in Japan.*

TOP: Coach Buttermaker with his star pitcher, Amanda Whurlitzer (Tatum O'Neal).

MIDDLE: Vic Morrow is Coach Turner and Joyce Van Patten is Cleveland, the league administrator.

BOTTOM: The old pro returns to the mound again, albeit a little closer to home plate.

#56 THE GREAT WHITE HOPE

Screenwriter Howard Sackler. **Director** Martin Ritt. **Producer** Lawrence Turman. **Cinematography** Burnett Guffey. **Editing** William Reynolds. **Music** Lionel Newman. **Production Design** John DeCuir. **Art Direction** Jack Smith. **Costume Design** Irene Sharaff. Fox. 1970.

THE PLAYERS
James Earl Jones **Jack Jefferson**; Jane Alexander **Eleanor**; Lou Gilbert **Goldie**; Joel Fluellen **Tick**; Chester Morris **Pop Weaver**; Robert Webber **Dixon**; Marlene Warfield **Clara**; RG Armstrong **Cap'n Dean**; Hal Holbrook **Cameron**; Beah Richards **Mama Tiny**; Moses Gunn **Scipio**; Lloyd Gough **Smitty**; George Eberling **Fred**; Larry Pennell **Brady**; Roy Glenn Sr. **Pastor**; Marcel Dalio **French promoter**; Rudy Acosta **El Jefe**; Virginia Capers **Sister Pearl**; Scatman Crothers **Barker**; Basil Dignam **English official**; Manuel Padilla **Paco**; Karl Alberty **Hans**; Rockne Tarkington **Rudy**; Bill Walker **Deacon**; Oscar Beregi **Ragosy**; Jim Beattie **The Kid**

THE GAME It is 1913, and despite the concerted efforts of prejudiced white fight promoters (Chester Morris and George Ebeling) and former champion Frank Brady (Larry Pennell) to keep the heavyweight title from staying with African-American Jack Jefferson (James Earl Jones), the black boxer is simply too good and thoroughly whips Brady.

Jefferson's joy is short-lived, though; his real fight begins outside the ring, where the black population feels he has turned from them and whites see him as a threat. Matters are exacerbated by Jefferson's living openly with a white woman, Eleanor (Jane Alexander), whom he met on a boat back from Australia where he won the championship before the Brady fight.

Fearing that Jefferson's power as a symbol may lead to revolts, the government prepares a shady legal campaign to neutralize him.

After being arrested by federal agent Dixon (Robert Webber) for violating the Mann Act by transporting Eleanor across state lines for the purpose of illicit sexual relations, Jack gets out on bail and concocts a plan to avoid the harassment.

Though his mother's house is under surveillance, Jefferson manages to escape from there to Canada by pretending to be a baseball player for the black Detroit Blue Jays team heading north to play a game in Montreal.

However, controversy follows Jack, and after Canadian authorities revoke his boxing license, Jack and Eleanor go to Europe. But back in the States the boxing powers and federal agent Dixon devise a plan to help each other. If they can find a great white hope and victory is assured over Jefferson, then the government can avoid what they feel is an inevitable uprising and the racist boxing powers can get the title belt returned to a white boxer. Word gets out that if Jack were to come back and be defeated the government would be open to reducing his sentence.

Meanwhile, pressures are mounting as Jack becomes more and more on edge and Eleanor is frustrated at their increasing emotional distance. With war on the horizon and money scarce, Jack and Eleanor go to Jaurez, Mexico. Now living in squalor, Jack's pent-up frustrations explode, and he demands that Eleanor leave him. He rebuffs her at every turn until she finally responds, "You win, Daddy," and runs off down the street. Around that time federal agent Dixon arrives with the Juarez police chief. Dixon demands that Jefferson fight and lose to the white challenger in Havana or face extradition by the Mexican authorities, resulting in a long jail term in America.

Just as Jack turns them down, even at gunpoint, two locals enter carrying Eleanor's lifeless body. In her despair she has committed suicide, throwing herself down a well and breaking her neck. A shaken and enraged Jefferson now agrees to the fight conditions.

With the bout refereed by Brady, a capacity crowd under the hot Cuban sun watches Jack get thrashed by the challenger. Despite bravely enduring a beating, Jack eventually gets knocked out.

The jubilant fans parade their new white champ around the ring, then past a beaten Jack. Jefferson and his trainer, Tick (Joel Fluellen), and manager, Goldie (Lou Gilbert), walk down a quiet hallway as the screaming crowd noise fades away.

Jane Alexander as Eleanor and James Earl Jones as Jack bring their Tony-winning stage performances to the silver screen.

INSTANT REPLAY A compelling drama whose power comes not from boxing but from the strong acting outside the ropes, *The Great White Hope* features James Earl Jones in top form.

Replicating his stage characterization, Jones gives us the full range physically, psychologically, and emotionally of the first black heavyweight boxing champion.

Intelligent with an intense and commanding presence, Jones embodies and delivers all the triumphs, frustrations, and turmoil of Jack Jefferson, a thinly veiled stand-in for real-life champ Jack Johnson.

Jane Alexander also comes from the stage version as the charming, wary, and ultimately tragic figure of Jack's white lover, Eleanor.

The leads are well supported by fellow *Hope* stage performers Marlene Warfield, Lou Gilbert, and George Ebeling as Jack's estranged wife, his manager, and one of his opponent's managers respectively.

Other players in this superior cast are Chester Morris as bigoted promoter Pop Weaver, R. G. Armstrong as the ex-boxer who supports the plan hatched by Dixon the federal agent (Robert Webber), and Joel Fluellen as Jack's longtime trainer and friend.

Their movements are well orchestrated by director Martin Ritt. Ritt, whose ease with social awareness themes is evidenced by his work in *Sounder* and *Hud,* among others, is also a good choice to choreograph so many stage performers here since he started out as a Broadway actor.

Working from Pulitzer Prize winner Howard Sackler's screenplay, Ritt's pacing and William Reynolds's editing move the film along well, with the exception of a noticeable slowdown in the European and Mexican exile scenes.

The director is given excellent production values to work with here. Producer Lawrence Turman provides a strong visual background for the story. The filmmakers' choices of Spain as the location for the European and Mexican scenes and Globe, Arizona as 1913 Reno are authentically dressed up by the brilliant production design efforts of John DeCuir and enhanced through Irene Sharaff's authentic costume work. The vivid imagery is caught on celluloid by the imaginative skills of cinematographer Burnett Guffey.

This intense, emotional, compelling, and tragic character study about a larger-than-life figure is the product of a wide range of film artists at their best.

OUTSIDE THE LINES Loosely based on the life of heavyweight champion Jack Johnson, the film is derived from the Pulitzer Prize-winning Broadway play written by Howard Sackler.... The play also starred James Earl Jones and Jane Alexander.... Three other cast members from the play were in the picture: Lou Goldie, Marlene Warfield, and George Ebeling.... Jones and Alexander won Tony awards for their stage

performances and were nominated for Academy Awards in the film version.... This was Alexander's film debut.... Jones's sports movie credits include *Field of Dreams* (1989); *The Sandlot* (1993) and *Sandlot 2* (2005), *Best of the Best* (1989); *The Greatest* (1977); and *Bingo Long's Traveling All-Stars and Motor Kings* (1976).... Former junior welterweight champ Mushy Callahan helped train Jones for the boxing role.... Production designer John DeCuir and art director Jack Martin Smith shared with others an Oscar for Art Direction on *Hello, Dolly!* (1969).... Producer Lawrence Turman was nominated for a Best Picture Oscar for *The Graduate* (1967).... Cinematographer Burnett Guffey also shot the boxing pictures *Kid Galahad* (1962) and *The Harder They Fall* (1956).... He won an Oscar for shooting *Bonnie and Clyde* (1967).... Actor Victor McLaglen, who won an Academy Award for his role in *The Informer* (1935), was a solid boxer before becoming a thespian.... He actually fought Jack Johnson in an exhibition bout long before he fought John Wayne in *The Quiet Man*, in which he was nominated for an Oscar.... Ritt, one of the Hollywood blackball victims of the 1950s, ironically would direct other victims in a comedic twist on those events in *The Front* (1976), which starred Woody Allen.... Ritt also acted, portraying a baseball manager in *The Slugger's Wife* (1985).

ALL-STAR MOMENTS In front of the press, Jack Jefferson's (Jones) former lover Clara (Marleen Warfield) storms in and accuses him of adultery with Eleanor (Alexander). Jack says she's only back because her lover is in jail and she wants part of his big upcoming payday: "I'm from the jungle like you, baby, and I hear the drums." She is escorted out kicking and screaming as Jack's manager, Goldie (Gilbert), pleads with the press to keep a lid on the incident.

When Eleanor drowns herself after arguing bitterly with her lover in Mexico, a despondent Jack reluctantly accepts government officials' deal: in a fixed fight in Cuba, he will lose his title to a white contender in exchange for his freedom.

Climactic fight action against The Kid (Jim Beattie).

HOME COURT ADVANTAGE Available on VHS and DVD.

top: Money and success attract admirers—new and old.

middle: Eleanor and Jack's relationship ends in tragedy.

bottom: Jack (Jones, right) displays his undeniable boxing talents.

right: A hard road to glory.

#55 Blood and Sand

Screenwriter Jo Swerling. (Novel by Vicente Ibanez.) **Director** Rouben Mamoulian. **Producer** Darryl Zanuck. **Associate Producer** Robert Kane. **Cinematography** Ernest Palmer, Ray Rennahan. **Editing** Robert Bischoff. **Art Direction** Richard Day, Joseph Wright. **Music** Alfred Newman. **Set Decoration** Thomas Little. **Costume Design** Travis Banton. **Technical Advisor** Budd Boetticher. **Technicolor Director** Natalie Kalmus. Fox. 1941.

THE PLAYERS
Tyrone Power **Juan Gallardo**; Linda Darnell **Carmen Espinosa**; Rita Hayworth **Dona Sol des Muire**; Alla Nazimova **Señora Gallardo**; Anthony Quinn **Manola de Palma**; J. Carroll Naish **Garabato**; John Carradine **Nacional**; Laird Cregar **Natalio Curro**; Lynn Bari **Encarnación**; Vicente Gomez **Guitarist**; Monty Banks **Antonio Lopez**; George Reeves **Captain Pierre Lauren**; Pedro de Cordoba **Don José Alvarez**; Fortunio Bonanova **Pedro Espinosa**; Victor Kilian **Priest**; Adrian Morris **La Pulga**; Charles Stevens **Pablo Gomez**; Rex Downing **Juan as a child**; Ann Todd **Carmen as a child**; Cora Collins **Encarnación as a child**; Russell Hicks **Marquis**; Maurice Cass **Reader on the train**; John Wallace **Francisco**; Jacqueline Dalya **Gachi**; Thornton Edwards **Doctor**

THE GAME
Juan Gallardo (Tyrone Power) dreams of becoming a famous matador like his father, who was killed in the bullring. Despite years of struggle, growing up in poverty, and against his mother's (Alla Nazimova) pleas, Juan slowly builds himself into one of Spain's leading matadors with the help of his friends Manola (Anthony Quinn), Nacional (John Carradine), and an old broken-down matador who now works as his servant, Garabato (J. Carroll Naish), among others.

Juan marries his childhood sweetheart, Carmen (Linda Darnell). Success and fame seem to be his until he falls under the spell of a wealthy, worldly temptress, Dona Sol (Rita Hayworth). She is struck by his grace and bravado watching him perform one afternoon at the plaza de toros. Juan soon becomes so infatuated that he begins to neglect all that is close to him, including his wife, family, and friends. He engages in a torrid love affair with Dona Sol, and his skills in the ring become very sloppy. Manola is now touted by esteemed critic Curro (Laird Cregar) as being more skilled than his friend, Juan, who has lost his edge.

It takes the death in the bullring of his friend Nacional, and the humiliation of Dona Sol tiring of him and taking up with Manola, to turn Juan's head back around. The devoted Carmen tells her husband she was "waiting for the sickness [adultery] to pass." He reunites with his wife, promising her he'll retire after one more major bullfight.

In that fight, Curro joins the capacity crowd in booing Gallardo lustily; however, those boos soon turn to cheers as they all recognize that Juan's artistry in the ring has returned. Juan's triumph is short-lived. As he turns to acknowledge the cheers of the fickle crowd he is fatally gored by a Muira bull, the same breed that killed his father. He dies, telling Carmen she was his only love.

Outside the fighting continues as we hear the roar of the rabid crowd. Manola too has done well. Dona Sol and the fans cheer him as he basks in the applause, standing near the blood in the sand where Juan was fatally gored just moments before.

INSTANT REPLAY
Director Mamoulian and producer Zanuck present the wonderfully striking contrasts of the world of bullfighting. While the lavish altars, marble interiors, jewelry, and fancy costumes may appear a bit extravagant at times, overall this pageantry provides a colorful contrast to the dark dealings of death in the

Wealthy temptress Dona Sol des Muire (Rita Hayworth) with famous bullfighter Juan Gallardo (Tyrone Power).

bullring—the horrific type of "death in the afternoon" that Ernest Hemingway vividly lays out in his famous book of that title.

From the brilliant moon shots to the colorful costumes, it is easy to see how the director was influenced by the great painters such as Goya and El Greco. This is a key element that sets the film apart from the 1922 original featuring Rudolf Valentino. Ernest Palmer and Ray Rennahan won Oscars for their vibrant cinematography with this picture.

Though his pace is sometimes a bit static, Mamuolian rewards patience with fine character development, thanks in no small part to a brilliant cast. Power's conception of Gallardo mirrors the description in Ibanez's novel. He is convincing as the uneducated but gallant matador who redeems himself, but just in time to meet death in the afternoon. Linda Darnell gives an empathetic feel to her role as the loyal, betrayed wife.

Radiant Rita Hayworth as the heartless seductress contrasts nicely with Darnell, playing the part with a devilish fervor. Anthony Quinn and J. Carrol Naish are solid while Laird Cregar carves out a large persona as the bullfight critic. Though he carries on well, especially in his comments about the dark side of the sport, John Carradine comes across as a bit of strange casting, mostly from a physical standpoint. Alla Nazimova gives an impassioned turn as Power's mother and the widow of a matador, a sad figure with a touch of clairvoyance about her son's fate. Still, she understands that bullfighting is Juan's life and he cannot leave it.

Jo Swerling's script finely incorporates the riches of character and narrative contained in the novel. Alfred Newman's foreboding music enhances the scenes expertly, as does the guitar work of Vicente Gomez. The staging of the bullfighting under Delgado and Budd Boetticher is a difficult assignment well done, especially considering the film industry's animal cruelty regulations limiting what could be shown. The director handles those fight sequences by shrewdly using symbolism and cutaways like hearing the roar of the crowd knowing a bull has been killed as we see Juan and Carmen in the small chapel inside the arena. Mamoulian demonstrates well the fickleness of human nature—friends and family turning on each other and fans running from failure but always looking to identify with success.

The filmmakers present a "moving painting" worthy of the best Spanish artists, bringing alive a powerful novel of love and danger, pride and death, friendship and romance.

OUTSIDE THE LINES Ray Rennahan competed against himself for the Best Color Cinematography Oscar.... He won the Academy Award for his work on this film but was also nominated for *Louisiana Purchase*, working with Harry Hallenberger.... Many of the backgrounds on the Fox lot were fashioned after famous Goya and El Greco paintings .... Ernest Palmer and Rennahan also shot the horse racing film *Kentucky* (1938), which won an Oscar for Walter Brennan as Best Supporting Actor.... Rennahan also won an Oscar for *Gone with the Wind* (1939).... Darryl Zanuck had made a remake of Douglas Fairbanks Sr.'s *The Mark of Zorro*, directed by Rouben Mamoulian and starring Tyrone Power and Linda Darnell. The remake was a success, so he went looking for another silent film to remake and chose *Blood and Sand*.... The 1922 original starred Rudolph Valentino.... Footage of the great matador Armillitas was spliced into the film for some of the bullfight scenes.... Budd Boetticher, a former Ohio State football player turned professional matador down in Mexico, was a technical advisor.... Boetticher directed the bullfighting film *The Bullfighter and the Lady* (1951), for which he earned an Oscar nomination for his story.... That film was produced by John Wayne and starred Robert Stack.... Sharon Stone played the Rita Hayworth role in a remake in 1989 opposite Chris Rydell.... Hayworth's father, Eduardo Cansino, was a famous Spanish dancer, and her mother, Volga Hayworth, was a Broadway showgirl.... Real matadors take two hours to get into their uniforms.... Some of the world-class matadors wear costumes of silk and gold embroidery worth over $20,000.... Most of the location shooting was in and around Mexico City.... Mexico-born Anthony Quinn won Oscars for Best Supporting Actor in *Viva Zapata!* (1952) and *Lust for Life* (1956).... Jane Russell, Carole Landis, and Dorothy Lamour were also reportedly considered for the Hayworth role.... It's said that Landis refused to dye her hair for the part.... *Blood and Sand* received Oscar nominations for Best Art Direction and Interior Decoration in addition to its color cinematography win.... The film's producer, Fox Studios, under Darryl Zanuck, licensed the use of paintings by renowned Spanish bullfight artist Carlos Llopis in their marketing posters and other promotional materials.... According to studio records, Fox considered a remake in 1957 starring Sophia Loren as Dona Sol but didn't pursue it due to legal rights hurdles.... The film's trailer was among the first that used Technicolor.... Mamoulian also directed the boxing drama *Golden Boy* (1939) with William Holden.... Hayworth was a famous pinup girl of WWII.... Linda Darnell performed in the football drama *The Guy Who Came Back* (1951) and boxing's *The Great John L.* (1945).... Former prizefighter Quinn used his pugilistic knowledge as an actor in several boxing features, including the Harold Lloyd boxing comedy *The Milky Way* (1936), James Cagney's fight film *City for Conquest* (1940), and *Knockout* (1941), then starred as a boxer in *Requiem for a Heavyweight* (1962).... He would also appear in another bullfighting film, *The Brave Bulls* (1951).... J. Carrol Naish had a role in Joe E. Brown's baseball comedy *Elmer the Great* (1933) and worked for Mamoulian in *Golden Boy*.... Boetticher produced a documentary on famed matador Carlos Arruza, but the subject and some film crew members were killed in a car crash.... Actor George Reeves would go on to fame in television as Superman.... Movie mogul Darryl Zanuck, known for producing such films as *The Longest Day* (1962), *All About Eve* (1950), and *The Grapes of Wrath* (1940), also brought to the screen the football musical comedy *Pigskin Parade* (1936), which featured the singing film debut of teen Judy Garland.... Russian-born screenwriter Jo Swerling, who co-wrote *It's a Wonderful Life* (1946), shared an Academy Award nomination for the screenplay The Pride of the Yankees (1942).

It doesn't take long for the matador to fall under the pretty siren's spell.

ALL-STAR MOMENTS Mother Gallardo (Nazimova), scrubbing floors for a living, answers her young son Juan's (Power) statement that he's dedicating himself to become a matador: "That's what your father said, too. And here I am. You are your father, come back to plague me again. He died once and I died a thousand times, every time he went into the ring, and now you. You want me to die a thousand times more?"

The young and cocky emerging matador Juan is full of himself. As he returns home by train there's a huge crowd gathered with a band on the platform. Juan thinks it's for him, but it isn't; the only person waiting for him is his mother.

As seductress Dona Sol (Hayworth) takes her seat at the arena, friends ask journalist Curro (Cregar) who she is. He points to the bullring, then to her, and says, "If this is death in the afternoon, she is death in the evening."

Bullfighting scenes that also show the bloodthirsty faces of the fans.

ABOVE: Gallardo with his lifelong love, Carmen Espinosa (Linda Darnell, right), and his mistress (Hayworth).

RIGHT: The fickle beauty now engages two matadors as Manola de Palma (Anthony Quinn, right) enters the scene.

Juan's wife, Carmen (Darnell), comes to Dona Sol's house, and when Dona Sol asks, "Is there anything I can offer you?" Carmen calmly replies, "Yes. My husband."

The final scene. As Manola (Quinn) waves to the crowd throwing hats and flowers into the ring to acknowledge his bullfighting efforts, the camera pans to a nearby spot: a pool of blood in the sand where only moments ago Gallardo was fatally gored.

POST-GAME COMMENTS
Director Rouben Mamoulian, on experimenting with Technicolor filming, explaining how he actually painted rather than merely photographed his scenes, aiming for color at all times to harmonize with mood and action:

> I used regular spray guns, too. By tinting the clothes of our players just before the cameras roll, we get an oil texture that kills the flatness and resembles a painting.[1]

Mamoulian on incorporating Spain's great artists into his picture:

> Since the setting is Spain, we turned to the old Spanish masters and the modern artists for both composition and color. We went to Murillo for his browns in our early scenes with Linda Darnell. In the marketplaces we used the style and coloring of Sorolla, the great master of light who painted some of the best market scenes in the history of art. Goya is another whom we patterned after.[2]

HOME COURT ADVANTAGE
Available on VHS.

#54 GRAND PRIX

Screenwriter Robert Aurthur. **Director** John Frankenheimer. **Producer** Edward Lewis. **Cinematography** Lionel Lindon. **Editing** Frederic Steinkamp, Stu Linder, Henry Berman, Frank Santillo. **Music** Maurice Jarre. **Production Design** Richard Sylbert. **Sound** Frank Milton, Roy Charman, Gordon Daniel. MGM. 1966.

THE PLAYERS James Garner **Pete Aron**; Eva Marie Saint **Louise Frederickson**; Yves Montand **Jean-Pierre Sarti**; Toshiro Mifune **Izo Yamura**; Brian Bedford **Scott Stoddard**; Jessica Walter **Pat Stoddard**; Antonio Sabato **Nino Barlini**; Francoise Hardy **Lisa**; Adolfo Celi **Agostini Manetta**; Claude Dauphin **Hugo Simon**; Enzo Fiermonte **Guido**; Genevieve Page **Monique Delvaux-Sarti**; Jack Watson **Jeff Jordan**; Don O'Brien **Wallace Bennett**; Phil Hill **Tim Randolph**; Graham Hill **Bob Turner**; Bernard Cahier **Journalist**; Albert Remy **Doctor**; Alan Fordney **Sportscaster**; Anthony Marsh **Sportscaster**; Tommy Franklin **Sportscaster**

THE GAME Racing on the streets of Monte Carlo, British Grand Prix driver Scott Stoddard (Brian Bedford) is leading the race. He is holding off the challenge of Jean-Pierre Sarti (Yves Montand) when he gets involved in a serious accident with his American teammate Pete Aron (James Garner). Stoddard hits a wall and is seriously injured, while Aron ends up in the harbor and swims out relatively unscathed. It appears Stoddard may never walk again, let alone race.

Aron is subsequently fired. He then goes to rivals at Ferrari but is told by the owner: "There are fewer than 30 men qualified to drive Formula One. A mere half-dozen to win. At this moment I'm inclined to think you are not one of them."

As Stoddard recuperates in a hospital his wife, Pat (Jessica Walter), is conspicuously absent, fed up with the whole racing scene and her husband's obsession both with the sport and with the haunting memory of his late brother, a former racing champion.

Meanwhile, veteran French driver and former world champion Sarti, estranged from his wife (Genevieve Page), falls for Louise Frederickson (Eva Marie Saint), an American woman on a business assignment to the racing circuit. Sarti is considering retiring and going away with her after the season.

Aron, getting chummy with Stoddard's wife, finds a ride for a team with a Japanese owner, Izo Yamura (Toshiro Mifune). As Pete's return is victorious with a win in Germany, Stoddard has vowed to return to racing and win back his wife. He works valiantly to rehabilitate his broken-down body and spirits.

Amazingly, the Brit wins in his first comeback effort and semi-reconciles with his wife. "I haven't changed much," he says to Pat. "I really can't promise you anything."

"That's all right," answers Pat. "That's the problem, really, people promise each other too much."

The key race in Monza, Italy finds the driver standings very tight. Wily but weary Sarti, now almost constantly with his American lady, takes the pole position, but his car stalls and he must start from the back. Later in the race, he suffers a fiery and fatal crash. Up front, Pete and Scott have been battling amongst the leaders and Pete takes the checkered flag. With Scott's 2nd-place finish also comes a second chance with his wife. Pete's victory earns him the overall championship but ultimately feels empty.

INSTANT REPLAY Motoring enthusiast John Frankenheimer set out to create the ultimate auto racing film. Though the narrative spine at times receives a yellow flag for its predictable romantic elements, and the film could have benefited from a prologue to better explain the sport to non-fans, those weaknesses are linked to the film's greatest strength: the overwhelming spectacle of the racing sequences.

By opening with an extended racing scene and setting the atmosphere before laying out the characters, Frankenheimer is also laying out his priorities: an emphasis on the technical. The story is fictional but the varied courses throughout Europe and some of its racers are quite real.

The filmmakers effectively put the audience in the driver's seat to feel the thrills and dangers of high-speed racing.

The *Grand Prix* cast gives convincing performances that keep us concerned about the personal dramas of the men and women involved in the racing circuit. Yves Montaud is quite real as the fatalistic but still competitive veteran driver who seems to know where his future lies. Eva Marie Saint as Montaud's lover conveys brilliantly the anguished outsider who, in the end, suffers the indignity of being displaced by Montaud's estranged wife (poignantly played by Genevieve Page in a brief appearance) in

the grim ambulance ride. Antonio Sabato embodies the brash young driver full of overtly carefree optimism and bravado.

Jesscia Walter is quite credible as the woman seemingly attracted to men living on the edge but unable to understand them. Brian Bedford has the Brit with the stiff upper lip in all his trials and tribulations on and off the track down pat. Toshiro Mifune is effective as the Japanese industrialist intent on owning a winning team.

ABOVE: The perils of the sport.

FACING PAGE: The thrill of Grand Prix racing begins anew.

Perhaps the most complete performance by a cast member is given by James Garner. More than James Cagney, Robert Taylor, Clark Gable, or any other star to that point, Garner knowingly captures the quietly confident racer driven to win at a high price. It is his real talent behind the wheel that sets him apart. Garner is effective as the conflicted man attracted, like a bullfighter, to the occupational hazards of a sport where he risks death at every turn, yet finding in the end that the elite skill, glamour, and roar of the crowd don't add up to personal fulfillment.

Undoubtedly *Grand Prix* achieves its main purpose: to be as true to the look and feel of Grand Prix as possible. The filmmakers' use of actual racecourses and real drivers is a good move toward verisimilitude. Credit for that aspect goes to production designer Richard Sylbert, who seamlessly made the actual European tracks and surrounding sights an exciting part of the stunning visual presentation.

Lionel Lindon's cinematography is brilliant. His cameramen, Jean Georges Fontenelle, Yann LeMasson, and John Stephens, are everywhere, including inside the racing machines, even using cameras mounted on the cars just inches off the ground, operated by remote control. Saul Bass creates memorable montage work. Teaming with the sharp and innovative pictures are the Oscar-winning sound and sound effects captured and mixed by Frank Milton, Roy Charman, and Gordon Daniel.

The Academy Award-winning editing team of Frederic Steinkamp, Henry Berman, Stu Linder, and Frank Santillo clearly does superb work in effectively sorting out what are literally miles of footage. Wisely, Frankenheimer varies his shot length, selection, and presentation (slow motion, split screen, superimposed images) to maintain the tension and excitement throughout the extensive racing sequences. Maurice Jarre's music is a fine complement to the vibrant visuals.

All the technical elements are enhanced by a relatively new theater technology in vogue at the time. "Cinerama" really heightens the audience participation with its sweeping widescreen imagery and multidirectional sound.

Unfortunately, writer Robert Aurthur and the director refrain from a deeper exploration of the psyche of these valiant thrill-seekers and the reasons behind their obsession with the sport. Though he hints at them through the characters played by Garner and Montaud in particular, in the end Frankenheimer keeps this breed's deepest guiding forces a mystery. The chief character here is the race car.

Grand Prix remains the standard bearer in capturing the sights and sounds of auto racing. Only Steve McQueen's *Le Mans* challenges this picture in conveying the sheer sensation of speed and the danger of the sport.

OUTSIDE THE LINES Carroll Shelby's racing car company was a consultant on the film, providing racing equipment.... Eva Marie Saint won the Best Supporting Actress Academy Award starring opposite Marlon Brando in *On the Waterfront* (1954).... Stu Linder also edited the baseball feature *The Natural* (1984).... French composer Maurice Jarre won Oscars for his work with David Lean on *Doctor Zhivago* (1962), *Lawrence of Arabia* (1964), and *A Passage to India* (1984).... Jessica Walter

played the wife of Charlton Heston's grizzled NFL quarterback in *Number One* (1969).... Steinkamp edited another auto racing film, *Bobby Deerfield* (1977).... Production designer Richard Sylbert won Academy Awards for his work on *Dick Tracy* (1990) and *Who's Afraid of Virginia Woolf?* (1966).... John Frankenheimer, a frequent collaborator with Burt Lancaster, had discussions with the actor about starring in this film. . . . Lionel Lindon's cinematography work won him an Oscar for *Around the World in 80 Days* (1956).... The 40-plus hours of film footage were edited down to about 50 minutes on screen.... Goodyear used their blimps with animated electric signs to promote the film across the country.... Rock Hudson was considering this picture as a coproduction and leading role.... Frank Milton's sound credits include the Elvis Presley racing film *Speedway* (1968).... Milton won Oscars for *Ben-Hur* (1959) and *How the West Was Won* (1963).

ALL-STAR MOMENTS The riveting opening racing scene and spectacular crash in the Monte Carlo harbor.

The perspective of British racer Scott Stoddard (Bedford) in telling his wife (Walter) he wants her back: "You know one of the most beautiful things about a car? If it isn't working properly you can strip the skin off, expose the inside, find out exactly what the trouble is, pull out the faulty part, and replace it with a new one. If we can only do that with people."

The point-of-view angles of the various races, including the high bank shots at Monza.

The fiery crash of Sarti (Montaud) over an embankment.

Louise's (Saint) hysterical scene after her lover's crash: with his blood on her hands she cries out to the spectators, "Is this what you want?! Is this what you came for?!"

Post-race scene: after all the cheering and celebration are done, newly crowned champion Pete Aron (Garner) is alone in more ways than one, standing on an empty raceway.

HOME COURT ADVANTAGE Available on VHS.

ABOVE: A skilled driver in his own right, actor James Garner (Pete Aron) did a lot of his own racing.

RIGHT: The filmmakers took racing on celluloid to a new level and were rewarded with Academy Awards for sound and editing.

#53 CINDERELLA MAN

Screenwriters Cliff Hollingsworth, Akiva Goldsman. **Director** Ron Howard. **Producers** Brian Grazer, Todd Hallowell, Ron Howard, Penny Marshall. **Cinematography** Salvatore Totino. **Editing** Daniel Hanley, Mike Hill. **Music** Thomas Newman. **Production Design** Wynn Thomas. **Art Direction** Peter Grundy, Dan Yarhi. **Costume Design** Daniel Orlandi. Universal Pictures. 2005.

THE PLAYERS Russell Crowe **Jim Braddock**; Renee Zellweger **Mae Braddock**; Paul Giamatti **Joe Gould**; Craig Bierko **Max Baer**; Paddy Considine **Mike Wilson**; Bruce McGill **Jimmy Johnston**; David Huband **Ford Bond**; Connor Price **Jay Braddock**; Ariel Waller **Rosemarie Braddock**; Patrick Louis **Howard Braddock**; Rosemarie DeWitt **Sara**; Linda Kash **Lucille Gold**; Nicholas Campbell **Sporty Lewis**; Gene Pyrz **Jake**; Chuck Shamata **Father Rorick**; Ron Canada **Joe Jeanette**; Alicia Johnston **Alice**; Troy Amos-Ross **John Henry Lewis**; Mark Simmons **Art Lasky**; Art Binkowski **Corn Griffin**; David Litzinger **Abe Feldman**; Matthew Taylor **Primo Carnera**; Rance Howard **Announcer Al Fazin**; Fulvio Cecere **Ref McAvoy**; Clint Howard **Ref**; Gerry Ellison **Ref**; Bill Mackie **Ref**; Ray Marsh **Ref**; Fernand Chretien **Ref**; Dave Dunbar **Ref**; Ken James **Ancil Hoffman**; Rufus Crawford **Lewis's coach**; Angelo Dundee **Angelo the cornerman**

THE GAME It's the late 1920s and life is good for prizefighter James Braddock (Russell Crowe). He lives in a nice single-family home in New Jersey with his devoted wife, Mae (Renee Zellweger), and their three children. Under the watchful eye of his trainer/manager, Joe Gould (Paul Giamatti), Braddock's toughness and talent help garner consistent victories that bode well for his boxing career and a shot at the title.

Unfortunately, just a few years later, Braddock, like millions of other Americans, finds himself struggling just to keep his family alive during the Great Depression. Having lost their home, the Braddocks are now cramped into a dingy apartment. Matters aren't helped when James breaks his hand in a lowly club fight and gets his boxing license revoked by fight promoter Jimmy Johnston (Bruce McGill).

Braddock's struggles deepen as he seeks dock work or whatever he can get. At one point he finds himself begging from former boxing associates for enough money just to pay a utility bill to keep his family from freezing.

Slowly his fortunes turn around, and it is in the ring that Braddock finds opportunity once again. With the help of Joe Gould, Braddock gets a second chance and makes the most of it. Overcoming high odds by defeating several top-ranked opponents, Braddock eventually finds himself getting a title shot against the dangerous Max Baer (Craig Bierko). Responsible for the deaths of two boxers, Baer is an imposing figure.

In a match pitting Bear's physical superiority against the challenger's ring savvy, fight finesse, and will, both give and take tremendous punishment. In the end Braddock not only goes the distance but ends the battle in style, still taking the fight to the champ in the 15th round, despite Baer's awesome ability to score a win with just one punch.

The new heavyweight champion of the world's faith and belief in himself has paid off.

INSTANT REPLAY This riches-to-rags-to-riches saga takes a different tack than many movies involving boxing. Some of the most memorable performances in fight pictures have involved deeply conflicted boxers full of inner demons using the ring as a metaphor for fighting their way out of what's troubling them emotionally and psychologically. Classic examples include *Body and Soul*, *Champion*, and *Raging Bull*.

Cinderella Man is a dissimilar story in that the featured fighter is an introspective,

ABOVE: Jim Braddock (Russell Crowe) and wife Mae (Renee Zellweger).

RIGHT: Braddock trains hard to provide for his family.

levelheaded, and uncomplicated family man. He's not chasing broads, fighting mental opponents, soaking up the limelight and booze, or flashing an arrogant attitude. He is more of an Everyman who happens to have a higher public profile because he's a boxer. This is a story about a working man struggling to overcome the same adversities and horrific challenges that faced countless breadwinners in a time period where most were living life on the ragged edge.

Cinderella Man's plot lines, characterizations, and settings incorporate elements of *Rocky, Seabiscuit,* and *It's a Wonderful Life*. It is also a picture that easily could have been made in the late 1930s as a forerunner to the theme of the beloved, humble sports star found at the core of *Knute Rockne: All-American* and *The Pride of the Yankees*.

Despite the film not being in fighting trim at 2½ hours, director Ron Howard assembles an engrossing heroic fable with a knowing touch in the vein of *Apollo 13*, his other historical story with a predictable ending. Here Howard couldn't have employed a better hero than that Oscar-winning *Gladiator*, Russell Crowe.

In *Cinderella Man* Crowe once again shows complete mastery of his craft. From the expressive eyes, lopsided grin, and Joisey accent to his compassion and of course his boxing skills, the man from down under embodies Irish-American James Braddock with the effortlessness of the brilliant acting chameleon he is. The truth is, the real Braddock wasn't an overly compelling or multidimensional man, but you'd never know it as Crowe, master of the small details, brings out little traces of humor, low-key confidence, and embedded toughness.

Crowe delivers with a conviction that isn't matched by the very talented Renee Zellweger, who comes across better as the supportive young woman in *Jerry Maguire*. Admittedly, her role as the loving wife who supports her husband, and at the same time is against his profession, is a tough and thankless one. Perhaps this is largely a case of yet another otherwise capable actress unable to hold her own with the riveting Crowe.

Matching up better is Paul Giamatti as Braddock's fleshy, feisty, and clever manager/ trainer, Joe Gould. Fresh from a terrific turn in *Sideways*, Giamatti's animated energy and contagious humor complement Crowe's more low-key delivery.

Where the filmmakers falter a bit is in the characterization of heavyweight champion Max Baer. While it's true that Baer was ultimately responsible for the deaths of two boxers, the heavy guilt he lived with thereafter meant he was never really the same fighter again, a fact this film ignores.

Craig Bierko is outstanding with what he's given, playing the womanizing, popular clown aspect of Baer to perfection. His imposing physical presence adds to the drama.

Whether it was the pressure to reduce risks that comes with a huge budget, or a choice of dramatic expedience over historical fact, the filmmakers don't seem to have faith in the audience's ability to distinguish the good guy from the bad guy, even though they must be aware that the best movies color each with a fair amount of gray.

Here they take no chances, painting the bad guy, Baer, as something of a sadist. It would have been more compelling to show a conflicted Baer torn between putting forth his best effort to knock out the previously unknockout-able Braddock, and his guilty conscience and concern that he might kill someone again.

What Ron Howard does excel in is details and atmosphere. His technical crew here provides us with an amazingly authentic representation of a dark period in world history, the Great Depression.

The writers' historical research is well implemented by Wynn Thomas's production design, including the evocative costume and set design work of Daniel Orlandi and Michael's Madden's crew respectively. The music by Thomas Newman adds to the atmosphere, and capturing it all with a sepia-tinged verisimilitude is the photography of Salvatore Totino and the editing duo of Mike Hill and Dan Hanley.

The fight scenes, capably handled by Nick Powell and Steve Lucescu, are presented in line with the story's themes. Howard's use of handheld cameras and flashback technique helps tie in the boxing sequences as they relate to the overall story.

Through an amazing sports comeback story within a compelling historical backdrop, Ron Howard gives us a stirring drama full of genuine pathos symbolized by the warmth and humanity of Russell Crowe's performance as James Braddock.

TOP: Zellweger played Tom Cruise's special lady in 'Jerry Maguire.'

BOTTOM: The proud father shares a light moment with his children.

OUTSIDE THE LINES Crowe won an Oscar for his performance in *Gladiator* (2000).... The actor starred in the hockey picture *Mystery, Alaska* (1999) .... The boxer Max Baer appeared in several movies, including *The Harder They Fall* (1956), and costarred with Myrna Loy in *The Prizefighter and the Lady* (1933).... All the film's bouts were shot in Toronto at the Maple Leaf Garden, made to look like New York's Madison Square Garden as well as Madison Square Garden Bowl in Long Island City.... Producer Penny Marshall directed *A League of Their Own* (1992).... Renee Zellweger costarred in *Jerry Maguire* (1996).... Crowe trained with Muhammad Ali's longtime trainer, Angelo Dundee.... Crowe suffered a shoulder injuryduring training, delaying production .... Professional boxers Art Binkowski, John Henry Lewis, and Mark Simmons were cast as Crowe's opponents.... Salvatore Totino, the film's cinematographer, devised what he called a "tirecam" to better capture the feel of being inside the ring and seeing the punches coming at you. It was essentially two tires pressed together with a camera inside, supported by a bridle, covered with foam, and hanging from a bungee contraption, and the actors would actually punch it.... Totino also shot Oliver Stone's *Any Given Sunday* (1999).... At various stages in the film's development reportedly Billy Bob Thornton was to direct and Ben Affleck to star as Braddock.... Wynn Thomas was also the production designer for Spike Lee's *He Got Game* (1998).

TOP: Braddock with his longtime manager, Joe Gould (Paul Giamatti).

BOTTOM: The Cinderella Man at his best.

RIGHT: Director Ron Howard goes over fight scenes with his star.

ALL-STAR MOMENTS After forcing his son (Connor Price) to return some meat he stole from a butcher, James Braddock (Crowe) softly but sternly lectures his boy, "No matter what happens, we don't steal, not ever." Father then allays his son's fears that he might be sent away to live with relatives.

Braddock offers his hungry daughter (Ariel Waller) his slim piece of meat for breakfast, telling her he dreamt he was full from a big meal.

With his back against the wall, the ever-proud Braddock is forced to beg for change from his former boxing associates to get enough money to pay an energy bill to keep his family form freezing.

Fearing her husband may be fatally struck in the title bout against Max Baer (Bierko), Mae (Zellweger) goes to church to pray and light a candle, only to find the whole community also praying for her beloved husband.

POST-GAME COMMENTS Angelo Dundee, Muhammad Ali's trainer for over 20 years, on how he prepared Russell Crowe for his boxing role:

> Russell Crowe is an athlete. He hikes, bikes, swims, kayaking. He is also a yoga guy. Lots of stretching. His commitment to authenticity went down to minute details. He knew boxers back then didn't have cut physiques chiseled from weight training, so we emphasized cardio and countless hours of sparring. I put him through calisthenics that I used to put Muhammad through—belly exercises, leg exercises, bicycling on the flat of your back.

> He picked up everything. Russell didn't know how to hit a light bag. It is a technique. You hit it with the side of your hands, not your fists. If you see the movie, you'll see how fluid he was with it. He became very good. We set him up in proper stance, which was pretty easy because in 1935 the boxing stance was fairly simple. It was straight ahead, keep your hands up. Russell handled the training very well, didn't burn the candle at both ends. I told him, "Leave it here" when he comes to the gym. He listened and I think the effort pays off.[1]

HOME COURT ADVANTAGE Available on DVD.

#52 COBB

Screenwriter/Director Ron Shelton. **Producer** David Lester. **Cinematography** Russell Boyd. **Editing** Kimberly Ray, Paul Seydor. **Music** Elliot Goldenthal. **Production Design** Armin Ganz, Scott Ritenour. **Art Direction** Charles Butcher, Troy Sizemore. Warner Bros. 1994.

THE PLAYERS Tommy Lee Jones **Ty Cobb**; Robert Wuhl **Al Stump**; Lolita Davidovitch **Ramona**; Ned Bellamy **Ray**; Scott Burkholder **Jimmy**; Allan Malamud **Mud**; Bill Caplan **Bill**; Jeff Fellenzer **Sportswriter**; Doug Krikorian **Sportswriter**; Gavin Smith **Bartender**; Lou Myers **Willie**; William Utay **Jameson**; Kenneth Campbell **Professor Cobb**; Rhoda Griffis **Ty's mother**; Tyler Logan Cobb **Young Ty**; Rev. Gary Morris **Baptist minister**; Harry Herthum **Gambler**; Jay Chevalier **Gambler**; Roger Clemens **Opposing pitcher**; George Rafferty **Teammate**; Jay Tibbs **Teammate**; Rodney Max **Umpire**; Gary Talbert **Opposing catcher**; Fred Lewis **Philly fan**; David Hodges **Philly fan**; Joy Michiel **Last Chance Hotel clerk**; Michael Hrushowy **Harrah's Club manager**; Eloy Casados **Louis Prima**; Stepehen Mendillo **Mickey Cochrane**; Ernie Harwell **Hall of Fame MC**; Tom Todoroff **Hall of Fame announcer**; Janice Certain **Cobb's daughter**; Bradley Whitford **Process server**; Bill Wittman **Newsreel narrator**

THE GAME Retired baseball legend Ty Cobb (Tommy Lee Jones) is in ill health. Feeling misunderstood and widely despised, the holder of over 40 hitting and base running records wants to set the record straight, the way he sees it. He chooses nationally renowned sportswriter Al Stump (Robert Wuhl) to co-write his official biography before he passes away.

Stump, feeling honored as he gets the news while sitting among his peers that he's been handpicked by the baseball great himself, soon realizes that the public perception of Cobb as a nasty, bigoted, abusive man is correct.

From their initial meeting at Cobb's Lake Tahoe mansion to their subsequent road trip that takes them to Reno, the Baseball Hall of Fame in New York, and then to the retired star's hometown of Royston, Georgia, Stump realizes he doesn't have much control of the situation. "The Georgia Peach" prefers to whitewash his monstrous behavior and focus on sharing his knowledge and insights into the game—and reveals his deal with the publisher that gives him final editorial control.

Torn between writing the dark truth (incorporating the youthful trauma of Cobb's mother's involvement in the killing of his father) and simply focusing on the legend's athletic brilliance, Stump decides to write both versions. The sportswriter ends up submitting the sanitized version presented by Cobb.

INSTANT REPLAY This cynical, disturbing reflection on our hero system is darkly powerful. Using storytelling methods more like *Citizen Kane* than *Bull Durham*, writer/director Ron Shelton presents a protagonist much more like Jake LaMotta in *Raging Bull* than Crash Davis.

Like the classic Orson Welles picture, Shelton opens *Cobb* with a laudatory newsreel of the main character. The film also uses a journalist on a journey to probe the internal makeup of the central figure. Like in *Citizen Kane,* a key incident is played several times to help illustrate Cobb's psychosocial makeup. The murder of his father by his mother and her secret lover is the film's "rosebud."

Shelton uses a clever approach by focusing on the final years of the long-retired baseball great. This is no *Pride of the Yankees* or *The Stratton Story;* in fact, the director purposely reduces the baseball elements. This helps and hinders the picture. Outside

TOP: Tommy Lee Jones as Detroit Tigers star Ty Cobb.

BOTTOM: The former ballplayer is driven by demons.

of the opening newsreel, a flashback sequence, the newsreel played again at the award dinner, and clips at the closing credits, there's little baseball action at all.

The film's detractors felt a brief newsreel highlighting his athletic accomplishments was not enough to convey to the average viewer in the mid 1990s why Ty Cobb is considered one of baseball's greatest players and why we'd value his insights in a book about how to play the game.

Cobb is much more than a profile of a man's statistical excellence. Not really as much a biography as a dark character study, the film aims to illustrate the dangers of creating false gods in any walk of life. By focusing on the man and not the sport, this picture effectively crosses over to represent the very human flaws of any high-achieving public figure. *Cobb* exemplifies how our idols almost never measure up despite our culture's almost desperate need for heroes.

By blurring the lines of the title character's genius and humanity, myth and fact, Shelton purposely refrains from giving cut-and-dried answers to explain what made Cobb tick. The movie illustrates how far Americans will go—overlooking morally repulsive behavior, resisting any questioning of the greatness of a designated hero, and romanticizing and reshaping the past—all to appease our consuming need for flawless stars.

Essentially a two-character road drama (a format used to good effect in Al Pacino's *Scent of a Woman*), *Cobb,* though unpleasant, is as engrossing as it is unflinching. Well cast, the film features Robert Wuhl as the starry-eyed sportswriter Al Stump and Tommy Lee Jones as the lonely, bigoted, and angry Ty Cobb.

In a role tailor-made for his talents, Jones gives one of his best performances: vibrant, maniacally energetic, and repulsively mesmerizing. Though he does repeat certain characteristics from recent efforts in *The Client, Blown Away,* and *Natural Born Killers,* nevertheless Jones conveys brilliantly the inner torment of a man haunted by his father's death, his mother's infidelity, and his sense that his own place in history may be overshadowed by his boorish behavior and cruel actions. The conflicted man's in-your-face, crazy-like-a-fox essence comes at you, spikes high, and carries the film as a complex paradox.

Robert Wuhl is terrific as the adulating sportswriter who endures the old man's threats and tirades as the price of learning about the nature of greatness while going through his own personal turmoil and in the end compromising his own principles. As the face of the audience, Wuhl's docile persona is set up just right for Jones's intense character to play off of as the harried biographer asks his questions and interprets Cobb's responses.

In support, Lolita Davidovitch is engaging as the atypical, somewhat naïve casino cigarette girl who endures Cobb's rage, innocently coming between the two men. Bradley Whitford is noteworthy as the process server who suffers through a rare Stump rage (much to Cobb's amusement). Lou Myers is fine as Cobb's tortured black house servant, Willie, particularly on the icy drive through snowy Lake Tahoe, where he turns the tables and pulls a gun on his boss (also to Cobb's amusement).

Like Scorsese's Oscar-winning boxing drama *Raging Bull,* Shelton's *Cobb* illustrates graphically that more often than we know, greatness has nothing to do with goodness. The reality gap between the media's portrayal and the public's perception of the celebrity's actual personality is a key theme of *Cobb.*

The sportswriter's decision to "publish a lie and put the truth in the closet" is reminiscent of the final scene in the boxing drama *Champion* (1949). After Michael

Cobb and sportswriter Al Stump (Robert Wuhl).

"Midge" Kelly (Kirk Douglas) claws his way to the boxing title, betraying his family and associates along the way, he suddenly dies of a brain seizure after a bout. Facing the media for a comment, his alienated brother, Connie (Arthur Kennedy), is pressed for a statement. His initial reaction is to reveal how much of a monster his brother had become, but he ends up preserving the public's perception of Midge, saying, "He was a champion. He went out like a champion. He was a credit to the fight game. To the very end."

Like *Champion* and *Raging Bull*, *Cobb* succeeds in presenting an unredeemable character in stark, chilling fashion. At the same time Shelton raises the question that perhaps this human degradation isn't all the result of personal demons. In fact, the filmmaker allows that in some ways perhaps the old man was right after all—"people are no damn good."

How much is the public to blame for making individuals who excel in a small endeavor into gods and heroes (like Cobb, who is given special treatment wherever he goes simply because he owns some baseball records)? In a country with an insatiable, unhealthy desire for celebrity worship, are we not partially to blame for the road to glory being littered with corpses? In our rush to annoint a superstar do we in fact give license to building human monsters, to putting a spin on their misdeeds so as to clean up and preserve their mythology in the annals of time? As the voice of the audience, Stump confesses in the film's final scenes, "I needed him [Cobb] to be a hero. It is my weakness."

Though *Cobb* runs too long, with Stump's gape-mouthed reactions to the retired ballplayer's outlandish behavior becoming redundant and excessive, still Shelton skillfully compresses multiple events and plot points as part of a bold directorial vision as the sportswriter wrestles with his conscience.

The writer/director delivers a rare picture that captures the dark side of the Amer-

ican dream. By focusing on the nature of celebrity itself and not the sports action that made the title character a public figure, he provides a penetrating, downbeat drama that reaches across the American social strata and is applicable to any endeavor that feels the need to designate fellow humans as heroes of mythic proportions.

Shelton succeeds in his brave aim, best summed up by Davidovitch's cigarette girl, Ramona, who comments to Stump that "greatness is overrated."

OUTSIDE THE LINES

Ron Shelton played for several seasons in the Baltimore Orioles minor league system as an infielder.... Part of Shelton's research came from Al Stump's three-part article in *True* magazine: "Ty Cobb's Wild Ten-Month Fight to Live."...Robert Wuhl was a vendor at the Astrodome while attending the University of Houston.... One of his classmates in drama was Dennis Quaid.... The Cal-Neva Lodge in Tahoe served for the nightclub scenes in Reno.... Tommy Lee Jones won an Academy Award for Best Supporting Actor in *The Fugitive* (1993).... Jones is a talented polo player.... Cinematographer Russell Boyd also shot *Tin Cup* (1996), *White Men Can't Jump* (1992) and horse racing's *Phar Lap* (1983) and won an Oscar for his cinematography of *Master and Commander: The Far Side of the World* (2003).... Jones broke his ankle just before rehearsals practicing sliding at his Texas ranch; scenes scheduled for Tiger Stadium were scrapped and the baseball action moved south.... Robert Wuhl created and starred in *Arliss,* a TV series about a sports agent, for HBO.... Singer Jimmy Buffett appears as "the armless guy."...Makeup artist Ve Neill won Academy Awards for her work on *Ed Wood* (1994), *Mrs. Doubtfire* (1993), and *Beetlejuice* (1988).... The Baseball Hall of Fame interiors were shot at a synagogue in Los Angeles.... Ironically, the longtime home of the Negro League Birmingham Black Barons, Rickwood Field in Alabama, was used for the baseball scenes.... Film editor Kimberly Ray's credits include *The Program* (1993), *Major League II* (1994), and *White Men Can't Jump*.... The film's composer, Elliot Goldenthal, won an Academy Award for the music score on *Frida* (2002).... Victoria Thomas also cast for *Ali* (2001), *White Men Can't Jump* (1992), *Play It to the Bone* (2000), and *Tin Cup* (1996).... Lawrence "Crash" Davis, the man whose name was pulled at random from an encyclopedia for Costner's character name in *Bull Durham,* plays ballplayer Sam Crawford here.... Wuhl starred in the made-for-TV boxing drama *Percy and Thunder,* starring James Earl Jones (1993), and in the basketball feature *Blue Chips* (1994).... Detroit Tigers veteran announcer Ernie Harwell also appeared in a made-for-TV baseball drama, *Aunt Mary* (1979), starring Jean Stapleton.

ALL-STAR MOMENTS

Initial gathering of sportswriters at a lounge arguing about the best boxer pound for pound, the best male singer, and the best baseball player of all time.

Outside Cobb's mansion enjoying his pipe and watching the snow fall, Stump's (Wuhl) peaceful walk is abruptly halted when he sees the dead deer he thought Cobb (Jones) had missed when the old man fired his gun at it several days earlier from an upstairs window.

Cobb and Stump's treacherous drive down the mountains through a snowstorm to Reno includes a funny argument between Willie (Myers) and Cobb when Al asks who the best ballplayer of all time is. The racist Ty goes nuts when Willie sings the praises of the top black ballplayers like Willie Mays, Cool Papa Bell, and Satchel Paige, who could "throw a pork chop past a wolf."

Scene portraying Cobb's playing days when he sharpens his cleats, takes on hecklers, and faces an imposing pitcher (Clemens), ducking a knockdown pitch then roping a double. Cobb then proceeds to steal third and home and start a bench-clearing brawl.

Ty's progression from pleasant anticipation to rage when he reads what Stump has written about him: ". . . pathetic, paranoid, and lost in the past!…What is this shit?!" He wakes Stump up and waves the papers at him, then proceeds to lecture the writer that legends are not pathetic.

As Al pours himself a drink, he threatens that if Ty dies before the book is done, he'll write it his way. After Cobb says he won't die before then, Al says he'll write slow. The gravely ill old ballplayer responds, "I'll die slow."

Sequence where Cobb forces Ramona to have sex only to reveal that he is basically impotent. He pays her handsomely to lie and tell others that sex with him was the best she ever had.

After Cobb dies, Al returns to the lounge to see his fellow sportswriters doing what they always do—sitting around arguing—but when they ask him if the rumors about Cobb being a misanthrope are true, Stump lies, telling them, "The truth is…a prince and a great man has fallen." The sportswriters are pleased to hear that. They toast to the memory of that great ballplayer, Ty Cobb.

POST-GAME COMMENTS Writer/director Ron Shelton on the origins of his film interest in "The Georgia Peach":

> *My Life in Baseball* by Ty Cobb with Al Stump was the first hardback I ever bought with money I earned from mowing lawns. When I read the book, I thought it was great, but I had a vague notion that there was more to the story. Then around 1980 I saw an article written by Al Stump. It told about a Cobb that wasn't in his book.
>
> The first book was about a great hitter and daring base runner. It was a baseball book. The second story was about a reckless, incorrigible man who was refusing to die quietly. And I thought about the writer who had written both versions of a truth.[1]

Shelton on Cobb's character:

> Cobb was among the first sports superstars, the first sports millionaires. He fought for players' rights. He supported several old ballplayers who went broke and he did it anonymously. Yet most of his rages were public and defied any sense of public relations. His whole life he didn't care what people thought about him. Yet facing death, he seemed to care too much.
>
> There is something unknowable about Cobb, something about him that won't let anyone get too close—no second baseman, no teammate, no wife, no member of his own family. And yet there's something compelling about him.[2]

Shelton on audience reticence to watching heavy lead characters, comparing this aspect of his film with *Raging Bull*:

> I made a movie about a monster, Ty Cobb. Audiences have a hard time with those, where you say, "Lookit, we're not going to make a fake monster, we're

going to give you a real monster." Audiences have a tough time watching movies about dark souls who don't apologize at the end of the third act.[3]

Costar Robert Wuhl relates a story as to why the film didn't connect as well as it might have in America:

> I was playing in a golf tournament with Sean Connery, who comes up to me and says, "You were in that movie, *Cobb*. I'll you why it didn't do well, because it told the truth about what it takes to be great in society and not giving a shit. And Americans don't want to see that."[4]

Shelton on the same topic:

> The last line of the movie Al Stump (Wuhl) says, in effect, "It wasn't about him (Cobb), it was about me, because I wanted him to be something he was not. It's not about his weaknesses, it's about my weaknesses." That asks the audience to walk out of the theater re-examining their own lives and priorities. I was hoping it would also be exalting in a certain way because there are also things about Cobb we could learn from in the best sense. Our society has not changed.

> People don't want to recognize that. With all the intrusive TV cameras and Access Hollywood shows and tabloids, we [see] that many of our rock and roll, sports, political, music, and film heroes are debauchers, perverts. That is the truth. We don't have to name names and yet we all act as if Cobb was from another [planet]. Heck no! If people can entertain us we forgive everything. That is not a very pleasant message.[5]

HOME COURT ADVANTAGE Available on VHS and DVD.

#51 PAT AND MIKE

Writers Ruth Gordon, Garson Kanin. **Director** George Cukor. **Producer** Lawrence Weingarten. **Cinematography** William Daniels. **Editing** George Boemler. **Music** David Raskin. **Art Direction** Cedric Gibbons, Urie McCleary. **Special Effects** Warren Newcombe. MGM. 1952.

THE PLAYERS
Spencer Tracy **Mike Conovan**; Katharine Hepburn **Pat Pemberton**; William Ching **Collier Ward**; Aldo Ray **David Hucko**; Sammy White **Barney Grau**; George Mathews **Spec Cauley**; Jim Backus **Charles Barry**; Charles Buchinksi **Hank Taslins**; Frank Richards **Sam Garsell**; Chuck Connors **Patrol officer**; Loring Smith **Mr. Beminger**; Phyllis Povah **Mrs. Beminger**; Joseph Bernard **Gibby**; Owen McGiveney **Harry MacWade**; Lou Lubin **Waiter**; Carl Switzer **Bus boy**; William Self **Pat's caddy**; Tom Harmon **Sportscaster (uncredited)**; Babe Didrikson Zaharias **Herself**; Alice Marble **Herself**; Don Budge **Himself**; Betty Hicks **Herself**; Helen Dettweiler **Herself**; Frank Parker **Himself**; Beverly Hanson **Herself**; Gussie Moran **Herself**

THE GAME Pat Pemberton (Katharine Hepburn), a college physical education instructor, is engaged to a school administrator, Collier Ward (William Ching). Though she loves him, Pat has an inferiority complex that is largely imposed by her stuffy, domineering beau. Their relationship is exemplified early in a golf match. In a mixed foursome playing with a wealthy older couple, Pat is instructed by Collier to look good in a losing effort because his real intent is to elicit money from the pair for their college coffers. Politely biting her tongue as Mrs. Beminger (Phyllis Povah) goes on and on advising Pat how she can improve her game, Pat almost makes it through the day. Walking off the final green, she finally loses her temper as the older lady continues to give unsolicited advice. In a fit Pat forces Mrs. Beminger to sit down and take notice of how good she really is. She proceeds to knock a row of balls with rhythmic precision, then tosses the club and stalks off.

Local golf pro Charles Barry (Jim Backus), having seen Pat's brilliant display, offers to mold her natural talent and have her compete against the best. She enters a golf tournament to test her physical prowess but also to prove to Collier and herself that she is a "somebody."

At the tournament her skills catch the eye of sports promoter Mike Conovan (Spencer Tracy). Conovan unsuccessfully tries to convince Pat to throw the tournament, as there's more money to be made gambling in the sport. Pat creates a sensation by having the golf championship in her grasp until she gets flustered by Collier's presence during the final holes. It seems every time her fiancé shows up Pat "gets frazzled," losing her self-confidence.

Collier would rather his lady gave up the athletic life to be his nice, quiet housewife. Pat is not ready to put away the sporting gear, and makes a deal with the likable but somewhat unscrupulous Conovan.

The sports promoter, seeing her champion potential and lucrative possibilities, makes Pat his top client, handling her with the same loving care as his favorite racehorse, Little Nell. In addition to horse racing, the street-smart Conovan is also involved in boxing, managing heavyweight hopeful David Hucko (Aldo Ray). Those two sports lend themselves to shady characters, and to this point Mike has primarily made his living fixing sports events. Now, with his new client already becoming a rising star in both golf and tennis, Mike tries to go legit before Pat uncovers his schemes.

Under Conovan's stern yet compassionate guidance, Pat, now in top form, barnstorms across the country making a name for herself on the professional tennis circuit.

TOP: 'Pat and Mike' was the seventh onscreen pairing of one of Hollywood's great romantic comedy duos, Spencer Tracy and Katharine Hepburn.

BOTTOM: Hepburn demonstrated good form as a golfer.

However, in an important match that she is winning, Collier appears and again Pat melts down, losing the match in embarrassing fashion.

Mike thinks her problems are a result of his rigorous training regimen and apologizes, but Pat reveals that it is Collier's presence that disables her.

As she gains notice in the sports pages, Mike's gambling underworld partners appear to remind him that they prefer to stay with their illegitimate ways. Forced to make a stand that he's gone straight with Pat, Mike gets into a rumble with the tough guys (one is Charles Buchinski, later known as Charles Bronson). Pat joins the fray, saving Mike (much to his embarrassment), and tells him that she'll go whichever way he decides.

After the fracas, Pat is having a restless night and is awoken by Mike's sneezing as he makes his nightly bed check on his client. Collier shows up, accuses them of having an affair, and storms out, saying he might be better off without her.

The mutual attraction that was there at the beginning has clearly blossomed beyond professional boundaries as Pat and Mike realize they're in love. In the end Mike has given Pat the confidence she needed to succeed in the battle within herself. She proves she's "cured," sinking a tough putt with Collier staring her down from the gallery.

The "long shot" relationship of the natural athlete and her street-smart manager has become like Pat's tee shots: "right down the middle," or, as Conovan says, "five-o, five-o"—something that was never possible with Collier.

INSTANT REPLAY Like the elements of a good mixed doubles tennis match, *Pat and Mike* has solid contributions by two men and two women. Making the most of the comedic potentialities of the Oscar-nominated script by Ruth Gordon and Garson Kanin, Spencer Tracy and Katharine Hepburn do a terrific job with a wonderful chemistry that is displayed most of all in their verbal volleying. This match is well conducted by the steady chair umpiring of director George Cukor, who keeps the forceful presence of Tracy and Hepburn's impetuous retorts in an engaging rally.

The director also presents the sports scenes with good rhythm, such as having the cameras "strolling" along with the golfers and their galleries, or putting you on the court during the baseline rallies on the indoor tennis circuit.

The supporting cast includes Aldo Ray's boxing palooka, who is solid, but it is really the two stars' graceful teamwork that makes *Pat and Mike* work. Hepburn, showing off previously little-known athleticism (and shapely legs from her Broadway stage days), is believable as a talented golfer and tennis player, especially when you consider that the actress was 44 when filming the role. Tracy and his Runyonesque sporting pals catch that world well, even down to their knowing vocabulary, enhanced by the appearance of several star athletes.

Mid-century American values are evident here; the romance, for example, is all implied. (The intimate side of the leads' relationship is represented by Tracy shaking Hepburn's hand, saying, "Okay, kid, you got a deal.") On the other hand, the movie was somewhat ahead of its time with its strong feminist message of self-reliance, looking beyond traditional roles and showing women as more independent-minded than convention admitted.

OUTSIDE THE LINES Kanin came up with the idea for the film as he watched his friend Hepburn playing tennis against the great Bill Tilden.... The 44-

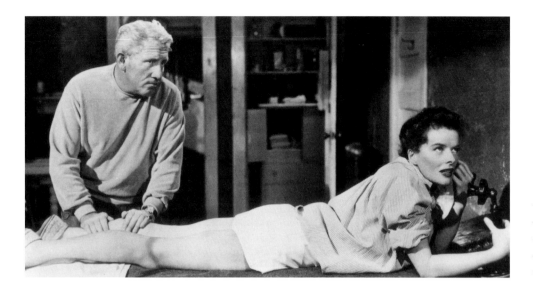

"Not much meat on her but what's there is cherce"—Mike Conovan (Tracy) describing his client athlete Pat Pemberton (Hepburn).

year-old Hepburn did all the sports scenes herself.... Kanin and Gordon's screenplay was nominated for an Oscar.... The husband-and-wife writing team also wrote the screenplay for the Cukor/Hepburn/Tracy film *Adam's Rib*.... Gordon won an Academy Award as Best Supporting Actress in *Rosemary's Baby* (1968).... Patrol officer Chuck Connors played professional baseball for the Dodgers and Cubs and professional basketball for the Celtics.... Many top golf and tennis stars appeared as themselves in the film, including Don Budge, Gussie Moran, Beverly Hanson, Betty Hicks, Alice Marble, Frank Parker, Helen Dettweiler, and the legendary Babe Didrikson Zaharias.... Aldo Ray made his acting debut as a cynical football player in *Saturday's Hero* (1931).... The uncredited golf announcer was football great Tom Harmon.... Host to major PGA events, the Riviera Country Club in Pacific Palisades was used for the golf tournament scenes.... Jim Backus, who would go on to TV immortality as Thurston Howell III on *Gilligans's Island,* made his film debut in the football film that starred his old friend, Victor Mature, in *Easy Living* (1949).

ALL-STAR MOMENTS Pat (Hepburn) pushes the arrogant, unbelieving old lady (Povah) down in a chair, telling her to "watch this," and proceeds to hit a series of golf balls perfectly one after the other.

Winding down his pitch to become her manager, Mike (Tracy) tells Pat, "I don't think you have ever been properly handled." Pat replies, "That's right, not even by myself."

In a nightmare sequence Pat has a meltdown in the middle of her tennis match, imagining that she's playing with a tiny racket, the net is raised to the roof whenever she hits, her opponent has a giant racket, and all the while her fiancé's image is everywhere, laughing at her misfortune.

HOME COURT ADVANTAGE Available on VHS and DVD. In addition to a DVD solo release, Warner Bros. has incorporated this title as part of *Tracy & Hepburn: The Signature Collection,* a set that also includes *Adam's Rib, Woman of the Year,* and *The Spencer Tracy Legacy: A Tribute to Katherine Hepburn.*

#50 WHITE MEN CAN'T JUMP

Screenwriter/Director Ron Shelton. **Producers** David Lester, Don Miller, Michele Rappaport. **Cinematography** Russell Boyd. **Music** Bennie Wallace. **Editing** Paul Seydor. **Casting** Victoria Thomas. **Production Design** Dennis Washington. **Art Direction** Roger Fortune. **Set Decoration** Robert Benton. Fox. 1992.

THE PLAYERS Wesley Snipes **Sidney Deane**; Woody Harrelson **Billy Hoyle**; Rosie Perez **Gloria Clemente**; Tyra Ferrell **Rhonda Deane**; Cylk Cozart **Robert**; Kadeem Hardison **Junior**; Ernest Harden Jr. **George**; John Marshall Jones **Walter**; Marques Johnson **Raymond**; David Roberson **T. J.**; Kevin Benton **Zeke**; Nigel Miguel **Dwight "The Flight" McGhee**; Duane Martin **Willie Lewis**; Eloy Hendricks **Tony Stucci**; Frank Rossi **Frank Stucci**; Freeman Williams **Duck Johnson**; Louis Price **Eddie "The King" Faroo**; Bill Henderson **The Venice Beach Boys**; Sonny Craver **The Venice Beach Boys**; Jon Hendricks **The Venice Beach Boys**; Alex Trebek **Himself**; Reggie Leon **Reggie**; Sarah Stavrou **Etiwanda**; Reynaldo Rey **Tad**; Lanei Chapman **Lanei**; Irene Nettles **Real estate agent**; Torri Whitehead **Tanya**; Lisa McDowell **Alisa**; Dion Vines **The Bank**; Allan Malamud **Rocket scientist**

THE GAME Basketball hustlers Billy Hoyle (Woody Harrelson) and Sidney Deane (Wesley Snipes) meet at the Venice Beach public basketball courts and decide to join forces in a sort of floating con game on unsuspecting players throughout the playgrounds of Los Angeles.

Off the court Sidney is getting pressure from his wife (Tyra Ferrell) to get a better job so they can move with their young child to a safer neighborhood. Woody's girlfriend, Gloria Clemente (Rosie Perez), has been saving with Billy and building up a nest egg for their future together. Gloria is also obsessed with winning on the TV show *Jeopardy* and spends all her time studying.

The partnership, shaky as any pairing of two hustlers would be, is paying off. Sidney helps set up the scams, and despite Billy being on the run from two loan sharks trying to collect on a debt from his college playing days, they are doing well…until Sidney conspires with their opponents in a high-stakes match-up and secretly shares the winnings for throwing the game.

Billy sheepishly informs Gloria he's blown their savings. Gloria doesn't take the loss lightly and meets with Sidney's wife, Rhonda. Meanwhile in the other room Billy angrily expresses his disappointment in Sidney: "Hey, man, I trusted you. There are rules to hustling. There are ethics involved."

Appearing just as Billy is ready to assault Sidney, the two women force their men to band together again and enter a sponsored two-on-two competition for $5,000. Despite tough competition Billy and Sidney win it all. The joy is short-lived, however, as Billy loses his winnings in an ego-protecting wager with Sidney that he can dunk the ball (therein lies the title).

Unsurprisingly, Gloria is more than upset that Billy has lost the money again.

She is also frustrated that *Jeopardy* isn't going to call her, since she knows she can win: "I am overwhelmed with more useless goddamn information than any human being on this fucking planet!"

She walks out on Billy, but he wins her back by helping her achieve her dream when Sidney uses some of his contacts to get her on *Jeopardy*. Gloria offers Billy a significant portion of her winnings to get good clothes for a job interview for a regular life. Meanwhile Sidney's home has been robbed and his wife, her patience at an end, insists that they move right away.

Two of the big time hustlers, Eddie "The King" Faroo (Louis Price) and Duck Johnson (Freeman Williams), are back in town and Sidney sees victory over them as a way out of the poor neighborhood for his family. Billy, a compulsive gambler, is torn between Gloria and his need to prove himself—complicated by the desire to help Sidney, who helped Gloria.

Billy tries to compromise by telling Gloria he "guarantees" victory, something he's never done before. Gloria isn't buying and is clearly let down. Leaving him with a kiss, she skates away.

Sure enough, Billy and Sidney win on an alley-oop slam by Billy, but the victory is hollow as they return to find Gloria gone, this time for good.

Sidney tries to console Billy, saying it might be for the best, but as they walk into the sunset at Venice Beach they start trash talking and sure enough that leads to a game of one-on-one.

INSTANT REPLAY
White Men Can't Jump scores with the entertaining inside moves of a pair of ebony and ivory playground hoops hustlers who don't want to grow up despite the pressures to do so by the women who love them.

It is a smart and humorous look at friendship, loyalty, and multiculturalism using the street game subculture as the backdrop.

White Men Can't Jump excels at presenting the improvisational grace of the artists that play the game, but that's only part of the entertaining package. The speed with which they play, though impressive, can't keep up with the pace of the nonstop trash talk: "Oh, man, shut your anorexic-malnutrition-tapeworm-having-overdose-Dick-Gregory-Bahama-diet-drinkin' ass up."

Writer/director Ron Shelton succeeds in delivering all the posturing, rituals, poetry, streetside democracy, and theater this colorful stage offers with a light touch. The prejudice and antagonism between whites and blacks is humorously presented so that we don't feel preached to, and the characters' relationships suggest that under-

Former UCLA standout Marques Johnson (as Raymond, second from left) is part of a duo duped by Billy Hoyle (Woody Harrelson, right) and Sidney Deane (Wesley Snipes, left).

TOP: Writer/director Ron Shelton (right) played the game well enough to earn a college scholarship.

MIDDLE: Billy with his girlfriend, Gloria (Rosie Perez), who dreams of being a contestant on 'Jeopardy.'

BOTTOM: 'White Men Can't Jump' is as much about the language of the street game as the style of play itself. Both are pretty coarse.

standing between different races is often more easily achieved than understanding between the sexes. As in most of his films, Shelton presents women characters who are stronger and more intelligent than their male counterparts, in this case a couple of Peter Pans trying to make a living at a kids' game on the playgrounds.

It is off the court that the film suffers from a little "garbage time" with its somewhat mechanical subplot of two goofy hoods trying to chase down Harrelson for debts. There's sufficient, genuine tension without this, in Woody and Wesley's double crosses and corresponding favors.

In an interesting twist, Shelton presents a clever look at the competitive nature of women with Rosie Perez's game show obsession.

Overall the actors give wonderful characterizations. The director elicits some fine performances from Snipes and Harrelson in particular. The duo's chemistry is the key to the picture. Well suited and quite believable in their roles, this odd couple works very well together. Their delivery of Shelton's dead-on salty street talk is some of the best patter in recent cinema history.

Ms. Perez offers one of the better female turns since Shelton's *Bull Durham* brought us Susan Sarandon as Annie Savoy. Perez's frenzied and tenacious pursuit of a game show appearance on *Jeopardy* is comical and her relationship with Woody has an easy ring of truth to it.

Still, everything in *White Men Can't Jump* comes back to the playground "action" and its wagering, dissing, and style of play. Snipes and Harrelson hold their own as believable street ballers (though they won't be mistaken for Curly Neal and Pete Maravich). Shelton smartly uses former professionals in the mix, including Marques Johnson and Freeman Williams.

On the technical team, Russell Boyd's cinematography is as beautiful as Shelton's dialogue is comically foul. Well choreographed and edited, the games are appealing for the non-sports fan as well, providing a vivid sense of the Los Angeles playground atmosphere.

Ron Shelton's talent for blending insightful verbal expression, humor, romance, and friendships along the fringes of sport is a distinctive approach that scores again for the former ballplayer in *White Men Can't Jump*.

OUTSIDE THE LINES Wesley Snipes and Woody Harrelson made their film debuts together in the Goldie Hawn football film *Wildcats* (1986).... Lost in translation: in Spain *White Men Can't Jump* became known as *White Men Don't Know How To Stick It In*.... Reportedly Twin Peaks' David Duchovny was also up for the Harrelson role.... Lafayette Park in Los Angeles and Venice Beach were the film's primary locations.... Freeman Williams was drafted by the Boston Celtics in 1978.... Woody costarred in Shelton's boxing film, *Play It to the Bone* (2000).... Cylk Cozart has appeared in the sports films *Heaven Is a Playground* (1991), *Soul of the Game* (1996), as well as in Shelton's *Blue Chips* and *Play It to the Bone*.... UCLA theater major and 5-time NBA all-star Marques Johnson also appeared in basketball's *Cornbread, Earl and Me* (1975).... Johnson's character here, "Raymond," was loosely based on a 7-foot center of the Detroit Pistons, Reggie Harding, who died of a gunshot wound.... Ron Shelton earned a Masters in Fine Arts at Arizona.... In addition to working on *Tin Cup* and *Cobb*, Australian cinematographer Russell Boyd shot the horse racing saga *Phar Lap*.... Shelton cowrote two of the songs on the film's soundtrack: "If I Lose" and "Gloria."

ALL-STAR MOMENTS
Early scene of Billy (Harrelson) looking up through the hoop at the sky dissolving into some game action with Sidney (Snipes) backing up his trash talk with solid play.

Raymond (Marques Johnson) excuses himself to go to his car to get the stake money but instead gets a gun, tries to rob a store, and ends up selling his gun to the store owner. After he loses Ray realizes been swindled and announces he's going to get his gun and come back and "shoot everybody." Sidney, Wesley, Gloria and the crowd scramble out.

Billy taunting Flight and Willie in the middle of their game from the sidelines with gems like "I got an idea, let's stop right now and just gather up these bricks and let's build a shelter for the homeless so maybe your mother has a place to live."

After two misses in an expensive wager that Billy can't dunk Sidney goes over to pump up Billy's air Nikes and says, "Billy, listen to me. White men can't jump." Billy proceeds to fail on his last try.

Gloria's *Jeopardy* appearance, including facing off against a rocket scientist, played by the late sportswriter Alan Malamud.

The choreography, editing, and play in the climactic game where Billy wins with a dunk.

POST-GAME COMMENTS
Ron Shelton on the nature of street ball:

Pickup ball is relatively cheap therapy. In basketball you scream and yell and curse and threaten fights and get all over somebody's ancestry—real or imagined—and after a few minutes you get bored and get on with the game. It seems to me that's a very civilized ritual. 1

Ron Shelton:

The playground game is pretty raggedy, but it's full of élan and showmanship and wonderful physical moves. Guys argue 5 minutes for every 2 minutes of playing. You can be the greatest player in the world, but if you come to a new playground you have to earn your way. You have to prove it on the court all over again. 2

Wesley Snipes on his character, Sidney Deane:

Sidney is a good-hearted guy, but the basketball court is his stage. This is his place to be king of the mountain. When you don't have things given to you, you have to learn to get what you need, and you use whatever talents you have to get it. 3

Woody Harrelson on playing the game as a teen growing up in Lebanon, Ohio:

At first I played in a white section of town, but hardly anyone would show for pick-up games, so I found a court in the black section of town, Pleasant Square. It was probably odd for them to see this one white kid down there, but after a while, I became very comfortable. So it's ironic that now I'm the only white guy in the film.4

Actress Rosie Perez on Shelton's prominent women characters:

Ron's women are strong, they're powerful, they're very sexy, and they confuse men to the hilt. I think the total unpredictability of women entices Ron, and it reflects in his writing, especially in his dialogue between men and women. 5

HOME COURT ADVANTAGE
Available on VHS and DVD.

#49 WITHOUT LIMITS

Screenwriters Robert Towne, Kenny Moore. **Director** Robert Towne. **Producers** Tom Cruise, Paula Wagner, Jonathan Sanger. **Cinematography** Conrad Hall. **Editing** Robert Lambert, Claire Simpson. **Music** Randy Miller. **Production Design** William Creber. **Art Direction** William Durell. **Casting** Richard Pagano. Warner Bros. 1998.

THE PLAYERS Billy Crudup **Steve Prefontaine**; Donald Sutherland **Bill Bowerman**; Monica Potter **Mary Marckx**; Jeremy Sisto **Frank Shorter**; Matthew Lillard **Roscoe Devine**; Billy Burke **Kenny Moore**; Dean Norris **Bill Dellinger**; Adam Setliff **Mac Wilkins**; Nicholas Oleson **Russ Francis**; Gabriel Olds **Don Kardong**; William Mapother **Bob Peters**; Judith Ivey **Barbara Bowerman**; Frank Shorter **Fred Long**; Charlie Jones **TV announcer**; William Friedkin **TV director**; Pat Porter **Lasse Viren**; Steve Ave **Mohammed Gammoudi**; Tom Ansberry **Emiel Puttemans**; Ashley Thompson **Ian Stewart**

THE GAME Cocky, charismatic distance runner Steve Prefontaine (Billy Crudup) takes his natural talents to the University of Oregon, known for its strong running program. There he trains under legendary coach Bill Bowerman (Donald Sutherland) and romances fellow student Mary Marckx (Monica Potter).

"Pre," as he quickly becomes known to fans and associates, is a stylish front-runner who often clashes with Coach Bowerman on matters of style, technique, and strategy. Despite the coach's fact-laden sermons about the wasted energy of always running in the lead, Pre stubbornly keeps to his ways. Winning isn't everything to Pre; how you run is what matters.

What Coach Bowerman calls a craft to be learned with various strategies to employ, Pre simply calls art. Getting by on instinct, Pre breaks various American records and enjoys great success that leads him to representing the U.S. in the 5,000-meter run at the 1972 Munich Olympics. Pre's gallant efforts against the world's best runners fall short, however, as, adhering to his natural front-running style, he finishes out of the medal competition.

Devastated, Pre takes a long time to recover from the emotional letdown. When he commits to return to the next Olympics despite a lucrative offer to turn professional, Pre is focused and reinvigorated by the challenge. He begins working out under his old coach's tutelage and rebuilding his natural gift of being able to endure more pain than any of the competition—thriving on it, like the cheers of his supportive throng, as a life force.

Tragedy strikes one night in 1975 when Pre is killed in a car accident at age 24, a year before the Montreal Olympics and well before he reached his prime. Like a shooting star, Steve Prefontaine was a beautiful sight to behold in his all-too-brief but brilliant career on the track.

INSTANT REPLAY *Without Limits* is a biographical drama that at its core is about the relationship between two successful, stubborn men engaged in a running philosophical debate on whose approach is best. Track happens to be the medium.

The following exchange as Coach Bowerman tries to explain why Pre's insistence on front running cost him a race exemplifies their divergent theories.

PRE: "What else do you call laying back for 2½ miles and then stealing a race in the last 200 yards?"

COACH: "Winning!"

PRE: "Well, I don't want to do that."

COACH: "You don't want to win?"

PRE: "I don't want to win unless I know I've done my best and the only way I know to do that is to run out front and flat out until I have nothing left. Winning any other way is chickenshit!"

No stranger to track cinema (*Personal Best* was his directorial debut), Towne co-wrote this feature with Steve Prefontaine's Olympic teammate Kenny Moore. Their knowledge and experience with the backdrop of athletics is clearly evident. The filmmakers not only present the race sequences with verisimilitude, they smartly place the film's emphasis on Pre's head rather than his feet. The movie is more interested in the psychological and emotional makeup of the world-class runner than his stride.

Without Limits was preceded by Steve James's *Prefontaine*, which, using a quasi-documentary style, doesn't have as compelling a narrative as Towne's version, but it does include a fine lead performance by Jared Leto. James's film effectively explored many of the same points as *Without Limits* and was done on a much smaller budget; however, the coach-athlete relationship wasn't as well drawn.

TOP: Billy Crudup is Steve Prefontaine.

bottom: Pre charms coed Mary Marckx (Monica Potter).

It is precisely the performances of the coach and athlete that distinguish *Without Limits*. Coming from the Broadway stage, Billy Crudup earns raves for his rendition of the trailblazing American runner. Dramatizing charisma is not easy, but Crudup conveys aspects of his character's personality that were highly visible, and a complex inside that wasn't, with equal aplomb. He plays the character smartly not as a legend but as a struggling human being. Physically, with his intense eyes, moppy hair, piston legs, and wonderful mimicry of Prefontaine's running style, Crudup embodies the track star.

Donald Sutherland is equally compelling as the proud coach Bill Bowerman. His interpretation is subtler than Lee Emory's intense portrait in *Prefontaine*. Sutherland speaks volumes with a simple facial expression or gesture, his wry authoritarian presence embodying wisdom without words.

The chemistry between Crudup and Sutherland is heartfelt and real. Their clash of wills is at times intense, but you can sense the mutual respect that exists all along. Their athletic May-December relationship represents a fine metaphor for various stages of life and attitude that goes beyond the track. Each changed the other's life.

Director Towne presents a difficult sport with a good pace, keeping close to the factual details in the context of a real day-to-day living feel. The fine character development as the picture steadily builds results in a genuine belief in the conflict and consequences of the players.

Robert Towne's technical team plays a major role in capturing the essence of the story. The production design, art direction, and costume team of William Creber, William Durell, and Grania Preston present a very atmospheric sense of time and place. Conrad Hall's detailed and brilliant photography, especially the off-road training, jostling of the running pack on the track, and the racing scenes overall, is dramatic and suspenseful even if one knows the outcome.

The editing work of Robert Lambert and Claire Simpson—incorporating slow motion, multitiered natural sound, and stirring music, and seamlessly weaving in film

Writer-director Robert Towne bravely attempts to dissect greatness, exploring the opposing viewpoints of athlete and coach (Donald Sutherland as Bill Bowerman, right).

from the actual race, shot for the 1973 Olympic documentary *Visions of Eight*—results in some of the best running sequences on film.

Towne smartly hints at the complex forces that drove Prefontaine without pushing a convenient upbeat, tidy ending on us. It is an earnest look at the power of belief. Prefontaine called running his art, and *Without Limits* is artfully done.

OUTSIDE THE LINES Tom Cruise, producer of *Without Limits*, considered starring in the picture as well.... CBS aired a documentary about Prefontaine in 1995 called *Fire on the Track*.... That show's producer, John Lutz, would sign with Disney to make *Prefontaine*, starring Jared Leto.... Not wanting to cause confusion among moviegoers after the release of that version, Warner Bros. went through several names for its feature—such as "Pre" and "The Front Runner"—before settling on *Without Limits*.... Writer Kenny Moore appeared in *Personal Best* as Mariel Hemingway's runner boyfriend.... Moore was a two-time Olympian.... Conrad Hall also shot John Huston's boxing drama *Fat City* (1972).... Robert Lampert edited David Wolper's 1973 Olympic documentary, *Visions of Eight*.... *Jerry Maguire* and *Bull Durham* are among music supervisor Danny Bramson's credits.... At one point Steve Prefontaine held seven American records between 2,000 and 10,000 meters.... The Olympic sequence was shot at Citrus College in Glendora, California.... The bulk of the running sequences were shot in and around Hayward Field in Eugene, Oregon.... Coach Bill Bowerman developed the first Nike shoe with the aid of a waffle iron.... Accomplished runners who participated in the film include Jeff Atkinson, Pat Porter and Tom Ansberry.... Prefontaine's efforts for athlete rights against the AAU led others to take the baton and eventually gain significant freedoms to compete.... Editor Claire Simpson won an Oscar for *Platoon*.... Crudup trained for the role with former Olympic hurdler Patrice Donnelly, who starred in *Personal Best*.... *Blue Chips* director William Friedkin appears as a TV sports director.

ALL-STAR MOMENTS The race sequences that focus on the natural sounds of the runners breathing and footsteps, with the camera inside the pack capturing the jostling.

Coach Bowerman's (Sutherland) eulogy delivered at the track where Pre (Crudup) gained his fame.

HOME COURT ADVANTAGE Available on VHS and DVD.

#48 THE COLOR OF MONEY

Screenwriter Richard Price. **Director** Martin Scorsese. **Producers** Irving Axelrod, Barbara De Fina. **Cinematography** Michael Ballhaus. **Editing** Thelma Schoonmaker. **Music** Gary Chang, Eric Clapton, Robbie Robertson. **Production Design** Boris Leven. Buena Vista. 1986.

THE PLAYERS
Paul Newman **Eddie Felson**; Tom Cruise **Vincent Lauria**; Mary E. Mastrantonio **Carmen**; Helen Shaver **Janelle**; John Turturro **Julian**; Bill Cobbs **Orvis**; Robert Agins **Earl**; Alvin Anastasia **Kennedy**; Elizabeth Bracco **Diane**; Vito D'Ambrosino **Lou**; Keith McCready **Grady Seasons**; Grady Matthews **Dad**; Steve Mizerak **Dale**; Jerry Piller **Tom**; Forest Whitaker **Amos**; Bruce Young **Mosella**; Joe Guastaferro **Chuck the bartender**; Chrtistina Sigel **Waitress**

THE GAME Having gone on to success as a liquor salesman, the now middle-aged pool hustler Eddie Felson (Paul Newman) has money but is still unfulfilled. One day his spirit is awakened when sees a younger version of himself in Vincent Lauria (Tom Cruise), a brash and raw but talented pool player.

It takes all his guile and manipulative skills, but Eddie finally convinces Vince—and, not insignificantly the young man's cynical, ambitious girlfriend, Carmen (Mary Elizabeth Mastrantonio)—to join him on the road to learn the finer points of pool hustling for big money on the way to a major tournament in Atlantic City.

The road to riches, however, is filled with potholes. The exuberant, impatient Vince fails to learn his lessons early on in how to set up an opponent by convincingly throwing a few games, evidenced by this exchange:

VINCE: Don't worry, I'm not going to lose often.

EDDIE: Yes, you will. That's what I'm gonna teach ya. Sometimes if you lose, you win.

At the same time Eddie is in a power play of sorts with Carmen, whom Vince depends on heavily for emotional support. Eddie explains to Carmen how together they can make Vince a champ: "We got a racehorse here. A thoroughbred. You make him feel good. I teach him how to run. You understand? We're business people."

"Pool excellence is not about excellent pool," Eddie tells his young student, "it's about being a student of human moves." Felson adds, "You gotta have balls and you gotta have brains. You got too much of one and not enough of the other." Slowly Vince sees the benefits of the hustle and becomes fairly proficient at it.

Somewhat jealous of Vince's success, Eddie begins drinking and sloppily falls victim to another hustler himself (Amos, played by Forest Whitaker). Felson then ends the student-mentor relationship and the money-hungry Carmen eagerly takes over the role of manager for Vince. Eddie, determined to demonstrate that he still has the talent, begins steadily training for a good showing himself at the Atlantic City tournament.

In the end the old man has taught his protégé all too well. Thinking he legitimately beat Vince in a showdown deep into the prestigious tournament, Eddie is dumbfounded and angered when he realizes he's been hustled by the same young man he taught how to hustle. After a heated conversation, Eddie pleads for Vince to give him his "best game" in a private match. Reluctantly, Vince agrees, because he knows Eddie will spend his twilight years coming after him until he defeats Vince at his best.

INSTANT REPLAY This morality play featuring the redemption of hustler Eddie Felson is brilliantly presented by director Martin Scorsese, who ably shows how the game of pool is an ideal activity for the exploration of one of the director's favorite themes: the corruption of innocence.

Like director Robert Rossen in *The Hustler*, Scorsese, a veteran of grit, provides a realistic atmosphere of slimy losers and hard-edged veterans on society's outside. He is aided by real players like Steve Mizerak as well as raw-looking characters like music star Iggy Pop.

Unlike the 1961 hit, however, this film takes a comparatively glitzy approach, punching up everything for dramatic effect. Beginning with the pictures of cinematographer Michael Ballhaus, Scorsese provides a wide array of elaborate shots, such as slow motion, superimpositions, and dissolves, to tell the story.

A puff of chalk from a break, Newman's face reflected in a ball—the variety of lighting, shots, and rhythms produces a visual splendor that helps magnify a rather small table sport that essentially is locked into one repeating physical action: leaning over the velvet playing field and performing a single basic motion.

Aiding the photographer's work is the laser editing of Thelma Schoonmaker (*Raging Bull*). She keeps the pace rolling, though the story does lag a bit in the final third frame, largely because the pool scenes become too plentiful and somewhat repetitive despite the cinematographer's magnificent efforts under Scorsese. One unforgettable shot is the cathedral-like overhead look at the dozens of pool tables in the climactic tournament.

The movie is also greatly enhanced by a terrific blend of music. From Robbie Robertson's original score to Eric Clapton's contribution and the timely use of Warren Zevon's "Werewolves of London," *The Color of Money* is enhanced by a fine array of mood-setting jazz, blues, and rock and roll.

In front of the camera, Paul Newman gives an Oscar-winning performance as Eddie Felson. Near perfect, Newman commands without overstating in a very natural performance.

Paul Newman would win his first Academy Award with this performance.

Ironically, nearly a quarter-century after filming *The Hustler,* Newman finds himself playing shades of characters from the earlier picture: he's now the man he came to despise, played originally by George C. Scott, while at the same time his smooth, urbane game is more reminiscent of Jackie Gleason's Minnesota Fats.

Some of the film's comedy comes from Newman's rather humorous insistence about the discipline of corruption. By the end Newman has certainly learned the lessons of "character."

Newman's dominant charisma presents a tough challenge for those sharing screen time here, but Tom Cruise rises to the occasion with energy and flair. His character may not be as compelling as that of young Eddie in *The Hustler,* simply because Vince doesn't have the same hunger that young Eddie did. The knowledge that his family isn't destitute and therefore Vince doesn't really *need* to win takes away what was at the riveting core of the drama in *The Hustler.*

Mary Elizabeth Mastrantonio is terrific in an unusual role. Though a bit underutilized, the actress is convincing as a tough-seeming young woman who shares a cunning, manipulative trait with Eddie and knows she holds the strings of Vince's emotions. Ambitious yet uncertain, she excels as part of this trio of characters driven by self-interest.

The actors are supported by sharp dialogue from the tight and starkly honest script by Richard Price.

Although *The Color of Money* utilizes that age-old formula of the student aspiring to defeat the teacher, Scorsese goes beyond the sport and across the generations to present a well-crafted exploration of the nature of character, deception, selfishness, corruption, redemption, and generally ambiguous relationships.

This vibrant, flashy look at the path and collision of colorful balls plays out well as a metaphor of sorts for the clashing of the three lead characters.

OUTSIDE THE LINES Most of the film was shot on location in Chicago.... The film's editor, Thelma Schoonmaker, won an Oscar for her work on boxing's *Raging Bull* (1980).... Costume designer Richard Bruno also worked on the football fantasy *Heaven Can Wait* (1978).... He won a British Academy Award for his work on *Goodfellas* (1990).... Mary Elizabeth Mastrantonio was nominated here for an Oscar for Best Supporting Actress.... Richard Price was likewise nominated for his screenplay and Boris Leven and Karen O'Hara for art direction and set decoration.... Tom Cruise was coached in pool by the reigning world champion at the time, Michael Sigel, who was the picture's technical advisor.... Murreys, the pool table manufacturing company, shipped over three dozen tables, each weighing over 1,000 pounds, from California to Illinois for the production.... Paul Newman ran the family's sporting goods business in Cleveland for a time before going to college.... John Turturro portrayed sportscaster Howard Cosell in *Monday Night Mayhem,* a TNT film.... Turturro made his feature film debut in Scorsese's *Raging Bull* (1980).... With the exception of a single shot (Tom's shot of having to jump two balls to sink another), Cruise and Newman performed all their own pool shots.... Former pool champions appearing the film include Steve Mizerak, Jimmy Mataya, and Louis Louis.... The voice-over at the film's introduction explaining the 9-ball game is Martin Scorsese.... The director's dad, Charles, appears in the film.... Ballhaus also shot golf's *The Legend of Bagger Vance* (2000).

Three for the road: (left to right) Tom Cruise, Mary Elizabeth Mastrantonio, and Paul Newman.

ALL-STAR MOMENTS Eddie (Newman), despite having material success, can't hide his pleasure in gambling: "Money won is twice as nice as money earned."

As part of a hustle, Eddie puts his arm around Vince's (Cruise) girlfriend, Carmen (Mastrantonio), and the jealous Vince gleefully plays his part, yelling over to Eddie, "Hey, Gramps. Put your teeth back in, get your hands off your daughter and pay attention. You just might learn something today."

Close-up of chalk flying off the cue ball as the stick makes contact.

A tight 360° shot of Eddie's face, then another shot of Eddie's image reflecting off a ball during play in an important match.

The overhead tilt shot of the tournament poolroom, featuring a multitude of pool tables, creating an almost cathedral-like feel.

POST-GAME COMMENTS Paul Newman:

> *The Color of Money* is about rediscovering what makes you happy. Felson has been compromising all his life and has become the very thing he hated. In the final analysis, that's what he liberates himself from.[1]

Martin Scorsese on the connections to *The Hustler*:

> We wanted this movie to stand on its own. The movie's only link to *The Hustler* is the character Felson. He's no longer a pool player. He's now on the outside of the game looking in and with a whole new perspective. 2

Tom Cruise:

> My character undergoes an interesting transformation. When you first meet him, he's pure and his game is not manipulative. As the film progresses, Felson educates Vincent in the true way of life—"Money won is better than money earned, and sometimes it pays to dump off." I think the beauty of the piece is that he (Felson) currupts this young "thoroughbred's" mind while truly believing he is doing Vincent a favor.

> In *The Color of Money* we're talking about good and evil with a whole different frame of morals. That's what Scorsese does with his movies. He takes you inside his characters and introduces you to different moralities. In the end, he doesn't try to clean it all up and justify everything. But within the framework there is a resolution.[3]

HOME COURT ADVANTAGE Available on VHS and DVD.

#47 THE ROOKIE

Screenwriter Mike Rich. **Director** John Lee Hancock. **Producers** Gordon Gray, Mark Ciardi, Mark Johnson, Phil Steuer. **Cinematography** John Schwartzman. **Editing** Eric Beason. **Music** Carter Burwell. **Production Design** Bruce Finlayson. **Art Director** Kevin Constant. **Technical Advisors/Consultants** Mark Ellis, Steve Canter, Jim Gott, Jim Morris. Disney. 2002.

THE PLAYERS Dennis Quaid **Jimmy Morris**; Rachel Griffiths **Lorri**; Jay Hernandez **Joaquin "Wack" Campos**; Angus Jones **Hunter**; Brian Cox **Jim Sr.**; Beth Grant **Jimmy's mother**; Rick Gonzalez **Rudy Bonilla**; Chad Lindberg **Joe David West**; Angelo Spizzirri **Joel de la Garza**; Royce Applegate **Henry**; Russell Richardson **Brooks**; David Blackwell **Cal**; Raynor Scheine **Frank**; Blue Deckert **Baseball scout Dave Peterson**; Daniel Kamin **Durham manager Mac**; Rebecca Spicher **Jessica**; Ray Rivera **Janitor**; Marco Sanchez **Sanchez**; Cynthia Dorn **Esther**; Robert Logan **Steve Dearborn**; Cory Harris **Cory Jones**; Seth Spiker **Tryout catcher**; Beau Holden **Orlando heckler**; Brandon Smith **Orlando manager**; Richard Dillard **Devil Rays manager**; James Fletcher **Devil Rays pitching coach**

THE GAME

After an injury-plagued appearance in the minor leagues in his 20s, onetime pitching phenom Jimmy Morris (Dennis Quaid) is now teaching high school science, coaching the school's baseball team, and living with his wife, Lorri (Rachel Griffiths), and three kids outside Big Lake, Texas.

One day after playing catch at high school practice Jimmy discovers that his once-painful arm injury has gone away and he's throwing harder than ever. His players are awestruck when he throws heat at them in batting practice. During a pep talk after a blowout loss, Jimmy addresses his players and talks about dreams, effort, and potential. The teens turn around and make a proposition to their coach. If the Owls make the playoffs, then their coach has to try out for a major league team. Thinking it's an easy promise to make his underperforming team play better, Jimmy, believing he's too old to make a pro squad, agrees to the deal.

Sure enough the Owls make the playoffs and Jimmy's off to attend a Tampa Bay Devil Rays tryout. A veteran scout, Dave Peterson (Blue Deckert), recognizes Jimmy, assumes he's bringing a kid or a young friend to the tryout, and tries unsuccessfully to hide his surprise when Jimmy tells him he's there to try out himself.

After a long wait, with his young son Hunter (Angus Jones) watching through the fence, Jimmy gets set on the mound and proceeds to throw some serious fastballs that have the scouts double-checking their radar guns.

Jimmy tells his wife he doesn't know how he's able to throw harder and faster than he did 15 years ago, but the team has an interest in him. After some debate, Lorri feels it's best for their son and Jimmy that he take their offer and give it his best effort.

Down in the Tampa Bay minor league system in Orlando, then in Durham, North Carolina, Jimmy battles for weeks the old man jokes, teammate resentment, family debt, and missing his wife and kids. On the verge of quitting his comeback attempt, he sees a TV report about his story and is rejuvenated watching some Little Leaguers playing nearby.

Not long afterward, Bulls coach Mac (Daniel Kamin) informs Jimmy that both he and Brooks (Russell Richardson) are being called up to the big team. Not only has Jimmy made it to the majors, but his debut is in front of fellow Texans. He and Brooks join the Devil Rays, who are playing the Texas Rangers in Arlington outside Dallas.

As the Rangers build up a lead, Morris is called on and with family and friends in

attendance gets a big strikeout to end an inning. Jimmy celebrates his promotion and his status as the oldest rookie in 30 years with family and friends.

The real-life Morris would go on to pitch in the majors for two seasons.

INSTANT REPLAY When it comes to pictures with a sports motif, Dennis Quaid is no rookie. Some of the actor's more notable turns include *Everybody's All-American, Any Given Sunday,* and *Breaking Away.*

Freshman director John Lee Hancock wisely partners up with Quaid, a fellow Texan, whose performance deserves most of the credit for a very compelling film.

Quaid's highly professional delivery of the conflicted family man with a second chance at his dream is the picture's best feature. Using a two-generational plot line, *The Rookie* is a compelling drama of fathers and sons. Even though he's nearly 10 years older than the real-life character he portrays, Quaid brings added dimensions to the archetype of the all-American sports star with a real sense of determination, vacillating hopefulness, and a quiet joy about his good fortune.

Given an authentic sense of place through Hancock's direction, Rich's regional dialogue, and cinematographer John Schwartzman's austere and distinctive shots of the Lone Star state's landscape, *The Rookie* is a Texas-flavored blend of baseball fantasies like *Field of Dreams* and *The Natural* while remaining reasonably faithful to the facts of a true story celebrating the unlikely success of a high school science teacher turned professional pitcher.

Interestingly, this G-rated film is geared more to adults than children. Though it is slowly paced at times and runs a bit long, *The Rookie* is successful in addressing several themes, including midlife concerns meeting up with faded dreams and unusual opportunities.

Again, it's Quaid's emotionally reserved turn that distinguishes this picture. In his chillingly real sense of sadness and isolation on the road to success, his very believ-

TOP: Jim Morris (Dennis Quaid, right) science teacher and baseball coach for the Big Lake (Texas) High School Owls.

MIDDLE: The Owls celebrate a moment of victory.

BOTTOM: The Morris family: (left to right) Jim (Quaid), daughter Jessica (Rebecca Spicher), wife Lorri (Rachel Griffiths), and son Hunter (Angus Jones).

RIGHT: Having guided his team to the district championship, Coach Morris must now fulfill a promise he made to his players and try out for the major leagues.

able pitching battles on the mound, and his palpable struggles with major life decisions, the actor shines, making athletic accomplishment and the emotional high and lows of family life fuel emotions and sentiments that are honestly earned.

Part *It's a Wonderful Life* (small-town ties), part *Frequency* (father-son connection), and part *Rookie of the Year* (pitching phenom), *The Rookie* delivers with emotional clarity and an inspiring sense of possibility.

OUTSIDE THE LINES The film was shot in and around Austin, Texas.... Beth Grant appeared in the TV series *Coach*.... John Bissell's music credits include golf's *The Legend of Bagger Vance* (2000).... Producer Mark Johnson won an Oscar for *Rain Man* (1988), and his credits include *The Natural* (1984).... Editor Eric Beason worked on another baseball film, *For the Love of the Game* (1999).... Costume designer Bruce Finlayson also worked on *Mr. Baseball* (1992).... *The Rookie* was screened at the White House by President Goerge W. Bush, a former owner of the Texas Rangers club.... Quaid trained for the role with former Los Angeles Dodgers pitcher Jim Gott.... The real Jim Morris makes a cameo as a minor league umpire in the film.... Carter Burwell composed the music for the hockey film *Mystery, Alaska* (1999), starring Russell Crowe.... Former collegiate football players Mark Ellis and Rob Miller have coordinated sports sequences in various capacities for numerous films, including *Any Given Sunday* (1999), *Radio* (2003), *The Junction Boys* (2002), *Mr. 3000* (2004), *Coach Carter* (2005), *The Longest Yard* (2005), *Four Minutes* (2005), *Invincible* (2006), and *Benchwarmers* (2006).... Assisting Ellis with this project was former major league pitcher Thomas Landrum.... Brian Cox played a soccer coach in *A Shot at Glory* opposite Robert Duvall.... Coproducer Mark Ciardi pitched for the Milwaukee Brewers.

TOP: Having to choose between a steady job in education and the chance to pitch professionally and possibly reach the majors is not an easy decision for the breadwinning family man.

MIDDLE: Jim is determined to make the most of his last chance to achieve his dream of pitching in the majors.

BOTTOM: Jim shares a moment with his estranged father (Brian Cox, left).

ALL-STAR MOMENTS As Jimmy (Quaid) rides his bike into town he passes a movie theater. On the marquee it says: *Bang the Drum Slowly*. The Robert DeNiro baseball movie was directed by another director of the same name, John Hancock.

Jimmy shows disappointment when the traffic speed detector shows that his pitch clocked at only 76 mph, but as he walks by a flickering light shows it really to be 96 mph. He never sees it.

Montage of Jimmy's high school players finally getting a piece of his fastball during batting practice.

As he changes his kid's diapers, Jimmy is called to the mound to try out. He subsequently stuns the scouts, who can't believe their radar guns indicating he's throwing 98 mph; neither can Jimmy.

POST-GAME COMMENTS Dennis Quaid on the film's theme:

> This is a story about a guy who you'd think would have given up on his dreams, but never did. The dream might have been dormant for a long time, but he never stopped wanting to do this one thing. That's something everyone can relate to.[1]

Producer Mark Johnson:

> What I appreciated about this story was that it was not just a baseball story, but really a classic American story about redemption, about a second chance,

TOP: The real Jim Morris (left) with Quaid.

BOTTOM: The director (left) confers with his star.

RIGHT: Director John Lee Hancock, like his star, Dennis Quaid, felt strongly about making their home state (Texas) an important part of the story.

about following your dream. There's something unfulfilled in Jim's life—a dream that he was never able to attain, that's always been just beyond his grasp. And finally, in middle age, he's given the push to go chase that dream one more time.[2]

Director John Lee Hancock on the particular challenges of making sports movies:

One thing I didn't realize was how tough sports movies are to shoot. They are very hard. Whenever you're doing sports action stuff it's kind of like doing tile mosaics and a tiny little piece doesn't seem to mean much until you take a few steps back and look at the whole thing. It takes 8 to 12 setups just to capture a double play depending on how detailed you want to get. So you've got a shot to line up of a foot going into a bag with dust flying. It's boring, let's face it. But you have to stay very focused. We had 51 setups because we didn't have a huge budget where we could shoot forever and ever. We had to fly.[3]

HOME COURT ADVANTAGE Available on VHS and DVD.

#46 SOUL OF THE GAME

Screenwriter David Himmelstein. **Director** Kevin Rodney Sullivan. **Producers** Mike Medavoy, Bob Papazian, Gary Hoffman, Kevin Kelly Brown. **Cinematography** Sandi Sissel. **Editing** Victor Du Bois. **Music** Lee Holdridge. **Casting** Reuben Cannon, David Giella. **Production Design** Chester Kaczenski. **Costume Design** Luke Reichle. **Art Direction** Marc Dabe. HBO. 1996.

THE PLAYERS Delroy Lindo **Satchel Paige**; Mykelti Williamson **Josh Gibson**; Edward Hermann **Branch Rickey**; Blair Underwood **Jackie Robinson**; Salli Richardson **Lahoma**; Gina Ravera **Grace**; R. Lee Ermey **Wilkie**; Obba Babatunde **Cum Posey**; Cylk Cozart **Zo Perry**; J. D. Hall **Gus Greenlee**; Jerry Hardin **Happy Chandler**; Brent Jennings **Frank Duncan**; Richard Riehle **Pete Harmon**; Armand Asselin **Rip**; Joey Banks **Link Rudolph**; Paul Bates **Orderly**; Bruce Beatty **Reporter**; Guy Boyd **Clark Griffith**; Stacye Branche **Ella Fitzgerald**; Gregg Burge **Bill Robinson**; Ed Cambridge **Bellhop**; Edwin Morrow **Young Willie Mays**; Isaiah Washington **Adult Willie Mays**; Oscar Williams **Grays manager**; Holiday Freeman **Secretary Lillian**; Mimi Cozzens **Jane Rickey**; Daniel Estrin **Paper boy**; Jesse Goins **Reporter John Givens**; Lou Richards **Radio announcer**; David Johnson **Roy Campanella**; Edith Fields **Nurse**; Terrence Riggins **Orderly**

THE GAME It is early 1945 and World War II is coming to an end. The moderate Happy Chandler (Jerry Hardin) has replaced Kenesaw Mountain Landis as the commissioner of baseball and the wheels are in motion to break the color barrier in the major leagues.

Soul of the Game is the story of how that came about, told through a character study of the leading candidates: Satchel Paige, Josh Gibson, and Jackie Robinson.

Brooklyn Dodger executive Branch Rickey (Edward Hermann), driven partly by a desire to get his name in the history books, partly by the economics of winning, and partly by a wish to redress racial injustice, sets out to find the best candidate to be the first black ballplayer in the majors.

Mr. Rickey uses his scouts to compose a profile of each man under the cover of wanting to create a Negro League expansion team, the Brown Dodgers.

The seasoned baseball executive knows that talent alone won't be enough. The player he needs is a man whose integrity, personal discipline, character, and reputation are impeccable. He needs someone strong enough *not* to fight back, because this player will face more scrutiny, criticism, and outright hostility on and off the field than anyone who's ever played the game.

Satchel Paige (Delroy Lindo) and Josh Gibson (Mykelti Williamson) are the league superstars. Gibson, a power-hitting catcher, has hit more home runs than Babe Ruth. Paige, a wily pitcher and engaging personality (and not surprisingly a fan favorite), cheats Father Time with his productivity well past the age when others are slowing down.

Both Satchel and Josh are very proud men. Each is certain he will be the one the major leagues select first.

As the season progresses and we follow Paige, Gibson, and Robinson on and off the field, Rickey picks up on some character flaws, particularly with the two veterans. Paige seems more interested in entertaining fans a few innings at a time than throwing hard for a complete game to help his club win. Gibson unfortunately has mental ailments that, along with deep frustrations, contribute to embarrassing public outbursts that are not helped by substance abuse.

Robinson eventually meets with Rickey in the Dodger offices and is told to keep their talks a secret, especially from Paige and Gibson. Rickey's ultimate decision, however, is

Delroy Lindo plays legendary pitcher Satchel Paige.

hastened when he learns of an impending announcement by the mayor of New York City. Fiorello LaGuardia (Al Rossi) reveals that he intends to impose economic sanctions on major league baseball if they don't integrate by the start of the 1946 season.

Alarmed at the news, Rickey, seeing his glory as a pioneer fade before his eyes, immediately signs Robinson before the mayor goes public with his plan: a heavy blow to the enormous pride of Paige and Gibson.

Paige would eventually make the majors, beginning with the Cleveland Indians in 1948 (becoming Rookie of the Year at the age of 42). The luckless Gibson would die of a tumor at age 36, only a few months before Robinson's Dodger debut.

Jackie Robinson flourished in the majors and would be elected to the baseball hall of fame in 1962. Both Paige and Gibson would later make the same honor based on their Negro League play.

INSTANT REPLAY The heart and soul of this made-for-cable movie is the seamless melding of actors and characters. Reuben Cannon and David Giella's casting eyes are impeccable all down the line. In physical appearance, age, and persona, these performers truly brought the historical figures to life. The completely convincing transformations of the leads is comparable to the Emmy-winning casting of another historical baseball drama, *61**.

In keeping with his self-promoting character, Delroy Lindo is particularly entertaining as wily showman pitcher Satchel Paige. Lindo's performance doesn't miss a detail. From the storytelling to the loosey-goosey pitching form and the knowing smile and swagger, Lindo nails it on and off the field. What is most interesting is what we see behind the showboating public persona. The veteran stage and screen actor embodies one of the most colorful personalities ever to play the game.

In Jackie Robinson, Blair Underwood takes on a very different personality. Using a page from his role as attorney Jonathan Rollins on the *LA Law* television series, Underwood captures well the pragmatic and businesslike persona of his character, who does his best to keep the enormous pressures inside.

Edward Hermann's erudite pontificating is suitable for the role of Branch Rickey. His performance also provides us with a fresh look that leaves it unclear precisely what drove this man to lead the break in the baseball color barrier. In this picture he doesn't receive sainthood just because he's the lone white character in baseball moving toward ending racial segregation in the sport. Instead, what propels the story is his insistence that his scouts look deeply at the candidates' characters, knowing they already have the physical tools.

Veteran character actor F. Lee Ermey is noticeably underutilized as the innovative owner of the Kansas City Monarchs, and steals every scene he's in.

Accurately conveying the styles of the times, the producers provide a colorful and realistic environment for director Kevin Sullivan's look at an underexposed aspect of American history.

Sandi Sissel's photography draws out well the old Negro League ballparks like Rickwood Field in Huntington, Alabama, and Luke Reichle's costume design helps create an overall nostalgic feel to the picture. Cheter Kaczenski's production design with Marc Dabe's art direction lends much authenticity.

The baseball action sequences are fine if limited. The performances on the diamond further the story by drawing out, in another way, the personalities of the three ballplayers.

However, it is a non-baseball scene that is perhaps the most telling about the near-impossible environment facing anyone hoping to break down the color barriers at a time when segregation was still deeply rooted in this nation.

Driving along a country road with his lady, Lahoma (Salli Richardson), and Jackie, Satchel pulls over to a small fruit stand. Lahoma strikes up a conversation with a young, innocent-looking girl (Erika Flores), and even offers to fix her hair like the movie stars she reads about. The girl is pleased with all the attention Lahoma gives her, but when Lahoma asks to use the restroom, the girl calmly and without malice says, "Daddy don't let niggers inside the house." Lahoma glares back at her as she heads back to the car. The little girl waves and says goodbye, unaware that anything's wrong. Driving away, Satchel isn't surprised.

Though the definitive baseball film of this era is yet to be made, David Himmelstein has written an entertaining drama. *Soul of the Game* covers a lot of ground.

OUTSIDE THE LINES Satchel Paige was the subject of a TV movie starring Louis Gossett Jr., *Don't Look Back* (1981).... Edward Hermann portrayed Yankee great Lou Gehrig in *A Love Affair: The Eleanor and Lou Gehrig Story* (1979).... Joey Banks, son of Cubs great Ernie Banks, helped train some of the actors.... F. Lee Ermey played legendary track coach Bill Bowerman in *Prefontaine* (1997).... *Soul of the Game* was also known as *Baseball in Black and White* and *Field of Honor*.... Mykelti Williamson made his film debut in Bruce Lee's martial arts picture *Enter the Dragon* (1973).... David Himmelstein was one of the screenwriters for the baseball drama *Talent for the Game* (1991).... Delroy Lindo was one of the voices for the Ken Burns miniseries *Baseball* (1994).

ALL-STAR MOMENTS Playing in a winter league game south of the border, Satchel (Lindo) embarrasses the hitter. This triggers a bench-clearing brawl that is out of control until the umpire fires a pistol shot into the air.

Satch's calculated meeting with Branch Rickey (Hermann) as he pretends to work on his fishing technique in the locker room.

HOME COURT ADVANTAGE Available on VHS and DVD.

#45 JERRY MAGUIRE

Screenwriter/Director Cameron Crowe. **Producers** James Brooks, Laurence Mark, Richard Sakai, Bruce Pustin, Cameron Crowe, John Scholfield. **Cinematography** Janusz Kaminski. **Editing** Joe Hutshing, David Moritz. **Music** Nancy Wilson. **Production Design** Stephen Lineweaver. **Art Direction** Virginia Randolph, Clayton Hartley. Columbia TriStar. 1996.

THE PLAYERS Tom Cruise **Jerry Maguire**; Cuba Gooding Jr. **Rod Tidwell**; Renee Zellweger **Dorothy Boyd**; Kelly Preston **Avery Bishop**; Bonnie Hunt **Laurel Boyd**; Jerry O'Connell **Frank Cushman**; Jay Mohr **Bob Sugar**; Regina King **Marcee Tidwell**; Jonathan Lipnicki **Ray Boyd**; Todd Louiso **Chad the nanny**; Mark Pellington **Bill Dooler**; Jeremy Suarez **Tyson Tidwell**; Jared Jussim **Dicky Fox**; Ben Smith **Keith Cushman**; Ingrid Beer **Anne-Louise**; Jann Wenner **Scully**; Nada Despotovich **Wendy**; Alexandra Wentworth **Bobbi Fallon**; Aries Spears **Tee Pee**; Kelly Coffield **Jan**; Alice Crowe **Alice**; Glenn Frey **Dennis Wilburn**; Donal Logue **Rick**; Jerry Cantrell **Jesus of CopyMat**; Beau Bridges **Matt Cushman**; Eric Stoltz **Ethan Valhere**; Tom Gallop **Ben**; Beaumont Bacon **Cleo**; Lisa Amsterdam **Patricia Logan**; Russell Lunday **Doctor**; Leslie Upson **Flight attendant**; Roy Firestone **Himself**; Troy Aikman **Himself**; Tim McDonald **Himself**

THE GAME Tired of how impersonal his business has become, sports agent Jerry Maguire (Tom Cruise) does some soul-searching to come up with a better way to handle clients.

His mission statement focuses on fewer clients and more personal attention. He impulsively distributes his manifesto, "Things We Think and Do Not Say," around the office of his employer, Sports Management International. Overtly he is lauded by fellow agents but at lunch the next week he is fired by his colleague Bob Sugar (Jay Mohr): "You should see yourself. You said fewer clients. You put it all down on paper. Jesus Christ! What about me? You know what I went through knowing I was going to have to fire my mentor?"

Back at the office Jerry frantically makes calls telling his clients what has happened. After demanding that Jerry "show me the money!" wide receiver Rod Tidwell (Cuba Gooding Jr.) retains Maguire as his agent. He's the only one of Jerry's 72 clients who remains with him.

At the end of the day, when Jerry states his case to the large room filled with agents and assistants, no one is willing to go with Jerry and his new operating style except for a woman from accounting who was inspired by his mission statement, Dorothy Boyd (Renee Zellweger).

Dorothy's sister, Laurel (Bonnie Hunt), is concerned about her leaving a large, steady company for a very uncertain future with an agent going solo. "You're a single mother," she points out; "you've given up the right to be frivolous."

There are plenty of challenges ahead as Jerry operates on his own, competing with everyone for clients but now without corporate muscle. Just as he's on the verge of signing a top NFL draft pick, Frank Cushman (Jerry O'Connell), his nemesis Bob Sugar steals him away. On top of that he breaks up with his fiancée, Avery Bishop (Kelly Preston), herself a driven dealmaker.

Through his struggles and Rod's influence, Jerry changes, becoming more personable and committed to relationships both with his clients and in his personal life.

What starts out as a working relationship between Jerry and Dorothy turns romantic. Jerry also gets along well with Dorothy's young son, Ray (Jonathan Lipnicki).

Despite the trepidation of her sister, a regular of a divorced women's group,

FACING PAGE: Cuba Gooding Jr. won an Academy Award for Best Supporting Actor as NFL receiver Rod Tidwell.

Dorothy tells Laurel she loves Jerry "for the man he wants to be and for the man he almost is."

Dorothy and Jerry marry. Jerry's close relationship with his biggest client, Rod Tidwell, having endured some turbulent times, now becomes a source of envy for Bob Sugar.

INSTANT REPLAY More than in any of the other movies he's written (*Fast Times at Ridgemont High, Say Anything, Singles*) Cameron Crowe's esteemed film influences are in full view here.

Taking a page from his mentor James Brooks, a producer on this project, Crowe weaves comedy, drama, and romance in a way that is reminiscent of Brooks's *Terms of Endearment*, particularly in its incisive dialogue, keeping the viewer off-balance, and a simply engaging story. Thematically Crowe's take on big business here bears a resemblance to *The Apartment*, by one of his heroes, Billy Wilder.

Influences aside, Crowe delivers a smart, comprehensive script filled with telling details, subtleties, multilayered characters, and some dynamic relationships.

It is those relationships, against the backdrop of the greed, glamour, and selfishness of pro football and big time sports in general, exploring loyalty, interracial friendship, the meaning of success, and love, that are the essence of the story.

Tom Cruise does some of his best acting here. Yes, the actor has portrayed elements of this character before as the slick young man who fights through a crisis—in

What began as a working relationship turns into a romantic one between Jerry Maguire (Tom Cruise) and Dorothy Boyd (Renee Zellweger).

Cocktail, Top Gun, and *Rain Man,* among others—but with the wide array of demons and insecurities Crowe has laid out for him here, Cruise's journey to redemption has never been played out with more openness and range.

Dorothy Boyd, his love interest, is played by Renee Zellweger. With her round face and warm eyes, Zellweger gives a fine turn as the vulnerable single mother at times desperate but deep down convinced she has made the right decision. Jonathan Lipnicki is comical and suggests a real connection with Jerry.

Leading a women's divorce group, protecting her sister, and delivering zinger after zinger, Bonnie Hunt is a standout, so much so that you are left wanting more. Jared Jussim is convincing as the wise old man who occasionally appears on the screen dispensing pearls of wisdom from his life experiences.

In an Oscar-winning performance, Cuba Gooding Jr. nails the role of his career. He embodies the modern athlete, complete with a cocky strut, sizable ego, and unquenchable thirst for money (the glory of the game?—well, that's there too, just down the list).

But the twist here is that his persona is completely different on the home front and his deep family values influence and help change his emotionally lost agent, Jerry Maguire. With Regina King's fine work as Rod's wife, Marcee, the Tidwells convey not only the love and joy of marriage but also the highs and lows and shared ideals (including a fair amount of greed).

The best relationship, the one between Jerry and Rod, is also one of the curiosities of the picture thematically. While Rod learns about drive and ambition from Jerry and Jerry learns about loyalty and the joys of family from Rod, in the end it seems the audience is getting a mixed signal. All the high ideals espoused while pointing a finger at characters like Bob Sugar (Jay Mohr) seem only half true in the end, because it feels what is celebrated more than the marriage of Jerry and Dorothy is the new multimillion-dollar contract Jerry has garnered for Rod. Jerry's spiritual redemption therefore seems a bit shallow. But then, as Michael Douglas's Gordon Gekko character from *Wall Street* said, "Greed is good." Certainly Marcee drives both her husband and Jerry hard for the money, so in a way that is also part of the package the Tidwells impart to Jerry.

The assorted pop tunes of the soundtrack by Crowe's wife Nancy, from the rock band Heart, also help convey the story's emotions, particularly Tom Petty's "Free Fallin." That is one of the picture's true successes—putting in play the wide range of human emotion.

Through the use of recognizable athletes, agents, and broadcasters, the filmmakers enhance the verisimilitude of that world but wisely concentrate their story off the field.

With the keen observational skills of the journalist he once was, Cameron Crowe delivers a smart social commentary wrapped up as a romantic comedy against a gridiron backdrop.

OUTSIDE THE LINES Cuba Gooding Jr. won an Oscar for Best Supporting Actor.... *Jerry Maguire* was also nominated for four other Academy Awards, including Best Picture, Best Actor (Cruise), and Best Editing .... Writer/director Cameron Crowe's research included spending time with agents like Leigh Steinberg.... Renee Zellweger costarred opposite Russell Crowe in the boxing drama *Cinderella Man* (2005).... To enhance the realism several recognizable figures from pro football made appearances, including Al Michaels, Troy Aikman, Herman Moore, Drew Bledsoe, Frank Gifford, and Warren Moon, among others.... Tom Cruise's sports-motif picture credits include *All the Right Moves* (1983), *The Color of Money* (1986), and *Days of Thunder* (1990). . . .Crowe had tried to get director Billy Wilder for the mentor Dicky Fox role.... Cinematographer Janusz Kaminski has won two Oscars for his work on *Schindler's List* (1993) and *Saving Private Ryan* (1998).... He also photographed the football picture *Little Giants* (1994).... At one point Mira Sorvino and Courtney Love were considered for the role of Dorothy Boyd.... The "show me the money" line came from Cardinals safety Tim McDonald.... Actress Bonnie Hunt is an avid Chicago Cubs fan and performed in a Chicago stage production of *Bright Lights Night Baseball*.... Cuba Gooding Jr. is a talented hockey player.... Arizona State University's Sun Devil Stadium was the setting for the football sequences.... Reportedly the title role was conceived with Tom Hanks in mind.... Comedian Jay Mohr has hosted sports shows on ESPN and Fox Sports.... Former Laker cheerleader Paula Abdul helped Gooding Jr. choreograph his touchdown celebration.

ALL-STAR MOMENTS Copy clerk Jesus of CopyMat (Jerry Cantrell) runs copies of Jerry Maguire's (Cruise) new manifesto, then tells him, "That's how you become great, man, hang your balls out there."

At the airport, Dorothy (Zellweger) looks for her son, Ray (Lipnicki), who is standing in a tray in the carousel bag waving to passengers. As she walks with Jerry the kid comes between them, grabs both their hands, and wants to swing.

In a phone conversation Rod (Gooding) tests Jerry's commitment, demanding that he repeat, "Show me the money!" Jerry yells it repeatedly, finishing up with, "I love black people! Show me the money!" "Congratulations," Rod says finally, "you're still my agent."

Jerry inadvertently learns how a potential huge deal is negated when his ex-associate Bob Sugar (Mohr) thinks he's talking to his client when it is Jerry on the other line learning that he's been dropped and his client has gone over to Bob for representation.

When Jerry ends the relationship with his girlfriend, Avery (Preston), she feigns hurt but then turns around and knocks him to the ground, saying, "I won't let you hurt me, Jerry. I'm too strong for you. Loser."

Cut to image of Jerry's mentor saying "Roll with the punches. Tomorrow's another day."

Jerry's cell phone rings. It's Rod Tidwell, and little Ray picks up the phone. The kid chuckles because Rod is rambling on about himself thinking it is Jerry he's speaking to. Cut to Rod in the bathtub with his son. Ray tells Rod he talks too much, then hangs up on him.

At practice Rod makes a brilliant catch, then runs into the goalpost. Jerry watches from the sidelines while making arrangements for Rod's contract negotiations with Arizona cardinal owner, Dennis Wilburn (Glenn Frey).

Alone in the kitchen cleaning up after the marriage of Dorothy and Jerry, Laurel (Hunt), Dorothy's sister, toasts Jerry, then tells him, "You fuck this up, I will kill you." As she walks out Jerry swallows hard and says, "I'm glad we had this talk."

HOME COURT ADVANTAGE Available on VHS and DVD.

#44 FAT CITY

Writer Leonard Gardner. **Director** John Huston. **Producer** Ray Stark. **Cinematography** Conrad Hall. **Editing** Walter Thompson. **Music** Marvin Hamlisch, Kris Kristofferson. **Production Design** Richard Sylbert. **Set Decoration** Morris Hoffman. Columbia. 1972.

THE PLAYERS Stacy Keach **Tully**; Jeff Bridges **Ernie**; Susan Tyrrell **Oma**; Candy Clark **Faye**; Nicholas Colasanto **Ruben**; Art Aragon **Babe**; Curtis Cokes **Earl**; Sixto Rodriguez **Lucero**; Billy Walker **Wes**; Wayne Mahan **Buford**; Ruben Navarro **Fuentes**

THE GAME Stagnating in between retirement and his youthful prime, alcoholic boxer Tully (Stacy Keach) gets by as a farm laborer in a small California town. With the encouragement of fellow drunk Oma (Susan Tyrrell), the woman he lives with while her lover is in jail, Tully attempts a comeback. Oma has her own problems, feeling outcast and discriminated against for having a black boyfriend.

In a gym Tully meets Ernie (Jeff Bridges), is impressed with his athleticism, and encourages the young fighter to get together with his old trainer, Ruben (Nicholas Colasanto). Ernie begins to show promise, and despite some setbacks the kid doesn't get discouraged.

Tully, in a constant fight with his internal demons, asks Ruben to help him get into shape for a comeback. Tully wins in his initial return to the ring but then complains about his share of the winnings to Ruben: "All my sweat and blood for a lousy $100!?"

Tully shows up at Oma's but her man Earl (Curtis Cokes) has returned from jail and she doesn't want to see Tully again.

Sitting in a coffee shop, Tully tells Ernie, "Before you can get rollin', your life makes a beeline for the drain."

INSTANT REPLAY More of a slice of life than a traditionally structured cinematic tale, *Fat City* is a downbeat parable centering on two men, short on intelligence, ambition, and/or opportunity, who are slowly worn down by their bleak, rudderless existence in a small town wasteland.

Depicting a world of bitter barflies, drifters, and migrant laborers, *Fat City* is an uncompromising but compassionate look at how these contrasting men view the sport of boxing as their way out of this grim, dead-end environment.

One (Stacy Keach) is a prematurely aging, battle-scarred former contender fighting his own internal demons and never completely committed to his prizefighting comeback. The other (Jeff Bridges) is young, inexperienced, yet hopeful and energetic but nevertheless naively headed for disillusionment.

Raw in its presentation, this metaphor for the American dream of a second chance is more about the constant sparring demanded by life itself, and the futility (Keach) and the power (Bridges) of hope.

Done with spare but potent dialogue, it is Keach's remark at the film's end— "Before you can get rolling, your life makes a beeline for the drain"—that encapsulates his perspective.

The picture takes a different look at boxing, one without the assorted racketeers and double-crossing managers so prevalent in the boxing pictures of the '40s and '50s. It is a stark and atmospheric presentation of the underside of the undercard of small-time boxing. A pair of victims futilely try to punch their way out to a better existence.

Director John Huston, a former boxer himself, captures and sustains the bleak small-town, small-time boxing milieu of Leonard Gardner's novel and subsequent script.

Huston's screen presentation succeeds in making the audience feel they are there despite editor Walter Thompson's sometimes jarring work. The characters in their spare dialogue waste no words saying what's on their minds. The picture's overall texture gives the impression that its protagonists are quite real because you observe and hear them in real time. There's no rush to fill the scenes with wall-to-wall dialogue. You feel you're sitting there with them at the coffee shop, comfortable in the silence.

Conrad Hall's cinematography helps create that real-life feel. The photographer's quiet, almost fly-on-the wall camerawork is particularly engaging outside the ring and inside the dumpy hotels and rundown cafés, or out in the farm fields and orchards of onions and walnuts.

Huston uses his own small-time boxing experiences in presenting the fight action—and even more so the fringes of the fight game—to give both the sports fan and non-fans an insider's view of the gang of characters that fill this world of nickel-and-dime boxing. The fighters reusing the blood- and sweat-soaked trunks of a fellow boxer who's just emerged from the ring, and the Mexican fighter (Sixto Rodriguez) who buses in for the bout and goes to battle despite pissing blood, then grabs the next bus out a loser with a few more dollars than he arrived with, are unforgettable snippets.

The players naturally contribute a lot to the film. Stacy Keach's ambivalence and Jeff Bridges' youthful optimism work well in their contrasting use of boxing as their way out. Keach presents a fine turn here as a boxer dulled by the physical pounding but sharp enough to sense that deep down he knows he's a loser.

On those days of clarity Keach is aware that his dreams are unrealistic and his optimism is self-deceiving, so he returns to his self-defeating patterns. Reminiscent of Marlon Brando's Terry Malloy ("I coulda been a contender") from *On the Waterfront*, this is one of Keach's finest performances in a career that has a lot of fine performances.

Jeff Bridges is well cast as the good natured, simpleminded young man following the doomed path of Keach, though his role is abridged from the character in the novel. Bridges and Candy Clark share an excellent chemistry in a relationship full of poignancy. Nicholas Colasanto embodies the optimistic and compassionate small time trainer/manager/father/mother who genuinely cares for "his boys."

Susan Tyrrell is the emotionally beaten down, alcoholic semi-lover of Keach and girlfriend to a jailed black man (played with warmth and dignity by ex-boxer Curtis Cokes). In this author's opinion, though she has some interesting social observations and her failed marriages help explain some of her behavior, Oma comes across as boorish, self-pitying, and one-dimensional, in a portrayal that becomes stale and repetitive very quickly. On the other hand, supporters of Tyrrell's performance may say that she bravely represents the bottom of the barrel, an isolated, liquor-filled world of depression where she will remain and where others like Tully are headed.

One of John Huston's better films, *Fat City* is a piece of Americana whose bald look, gritty atmosphere, focus on losers, and simple truths put it in the same rank as *The Asphalt Jungle* and *The Treasure of the Sierra Madre*.

OUTSIDE THE LINES Curtis Cokes was a former welterweight champion and is a member of the Boxing Hall of Fame.... Reportedly Huston initially wanted

ABOVE: Susan Tyrrell earned an Oscar nomination as Oma.

BELOW: "Before you can get rollin', your life makes a beeline for the drain."

Marlon Brando for the role of Tully.... Technical advisor Al Silvani coached Paul Newman for boxing's *Somebody Up There Likes Me* (1956).... Susan Tyrrell was nominated for an Oscar for her role.... *Fat City* was re-released in 1987.... Art Aragon was a former professional boxer.... Jeff Bridges starred as a stock car racer in *The Last American Hero* (1973).... He also played millionaire Charles Howard in horse racing's *Seabiscuit* (2003).... "Fat city" is a gambling term for doing well, the good life.... The film was shot in Stockton, California.... Colasanto appeared in *Raging Bull* (1980).... Conrad Hall also shot *Without Limits* (1998).... Fight trainer José Torres was world light heavyweight champion beginning in 1965, when he beat Willie Pastrano.... Torres also wrote biographies of Muhammad Ali (*Sting Like a Bee*) and Mike Tyson (*Fire and Fear*).

ALL-STAR MOMENTS

Ernie (Bridges) enters the ring for his first bout and is introduced as "Irish" Ernie Munger. He tells Ruben (Colasanto) he's not Irish. Ruben tells him he set it up that way so they'd read about him and know that he's white.

In the locker room right after his bout Ernie is told to quickly take off his sweaty, bloody trunks and give them to another fighter, Wes (Billy Walker), whose fight is next.

Ernie trying on a new boxing robe that makes him look like Elvis in Vegas. Ernie barely gets his fancy robe off when he's knocked out in the first few seconds of the first round.

Tully (Keach) toils in the fields listening with quiet amusement as fellow laborers pass the time talking about their relationships with women and why they didn't work out.

POST-GAME COMMENTS Stacy Keach on the sport of boxing:

> One thing I learned in training for *Fat City* with José Torres (a former world light heavyweight champion and Olympic medalist) was there's probably no form of work that's harder than training to box. If you don't think it's tough just shadow box for two minutes.[1]

Keach on why the "sweet science" is such a popular movie subject:

> It is the most basic, primitive form of one-on-one competition that we have. Two guys get in a ring and try to knock each other out. That's pretty basic. I think that's appealing to our nature. There's nothing else like it. You have no accoutrements, no weapons; it's your fists, basically.[2]

Keach on his own fistic abilities:

> That's one thing I couldn't do, I could never take a punch. I had a glass jaw. In fact during *Fat City* we were filming the fight sequences and after we'd completed the choreographed routine Huston came forward and said, "All right, boys, that's fine, now just go out there and box." We did and Sixto Rodriguez [a former professional fighter playing Keach's opponent, "Lucero," who had 87 pro fights as a light heavyweight] tells me, "Hit me, man, just hit me as hard as you want to anywhere," and I did and his right hand just came out of nowhere and clocked me and knocked me out. And that's the shot they used in the movie.[3]

Costar Jeff Bridges on how the role came about for him and why the picture has endured:

> My brother (Beau) was originally up for the role, but he was too old. He recommended me. It's a long story but involves John Huston interviewing me at the Prado in Spain and being food-poisoned. As far as why it's become a classic, John Huston would be the main answer. He was a terrifically gifted man. [It was] a tale so well written by Leonard Gardner. Conrad Hall's photography was brilliant and quite revolutionary at the time. Stacy Keach and Susan Tyrrell gave wonderful performances as did Candy Clark.[4]

Boxing historian Bert Sugar on the insight the film presented about the sport:

> *Fat City* shows the underbelly of both society and boxing. These were the hardscrabble kids where the only way they could make it in life was through boxing. Nothing glamorous about that movie. Once you tear away the veneer of the championship fights, that's what boxing is all about.[5]

HOME COURT ADVANTAGE Available on VHS and DVD.

#43 THE PRIDE OF THE YANKEES

Screenwriters Jo Swerling, Herman Mankiewicz. **Director** Sam Wood. **Producer** Samuel Goldwyn. **Cinematography** Rudolph Mate. **Editing** Daniel Mandell. **Music** Leigh Harline. **Production Design** William Menzies. **Art Direction** Perry Ferguson, McClure Capps. RKO. 1942.

THE PLAYERS Gary Cooper **Lou Gehrig**; Teresa Wright **Eleanor Gehrig**; Walter Brennan **Sam Blake**; Dan Duryea **Hank Hannerman**; Babe Ruth **Himself**; Elsa Janssen **Mom Gehrig**; Ludwig Stossel **Pop Gehrig**; Virginia Gilmore **Myra**; Bill Dickey **Himself**; Ernie Adams **Miller Huggins**; Pierre Watkin **Mr. Twitchell**; Harry Harvey **Joe McCarthy**; Addison Richards **Coach**; Robert Meusel **Himself**; Makr Koening **Himself**; Bill Stern **Himself**; Hardie Albright **Van Tuyl**; Edward Fielding **Clinic doctor**; George Lessey **Mayor of New Rochelle**; Vaughan Glaser **Doctor in Gehrig's house**; Douglas Croft **Young Gehrig**; Rip Russell **Laddie**; Frank Faylen **Third base coach**; George McDonald **Wally Pip**; Gene Collins **Billy**; David Holt **Billy at 17**; David Manley **Mayor of NYC, Fiorella La Guardia**; Max Willenz **Colletti**; Jimmy Valentine **Sasha**; Anita Bolster **Sasha's mother**; Robert Winkler **Murphy**; Bill Chaney **Newsboy**; Janet Chapman **Tessie**; Edgar Barrier **Hospital doctor**

THE GAME Lou Gehrig (Gary Cooper), the only child of poor German immigrants, grows up in New York dreaming of becoming a ballplayer. That is a not a career choice shared by his mother (Elsa Janssen), who prefers that her son become an engineer "like your Uncle Otto."

Years later when he enrolls at Columbia University where his mother works as a cook, Lou's athletic talents are spotted by sportswriter Sam Blake (Walter Brennan). When Blake approaches Lou about playing professional baseball, Lou reluctantly declines, saying that his mother wants him to be an engineer. But after Mrs. Gehrig falls ill and there is concern about financing proper medical care for her, Lou covertly signs with the New York Yankees to cover his mother's health bills. Lou and his father (Ludwig Stossell) cook up a story that Lou is going to Harvard when in fact he's playing ball for the Yankees' minor league team in Hartford.

Through dedication and hard work Lou improves his skills and makes the big squad. Once he's back in New York, his mother, now recovered, is upset with her son's ruse but eventually accepts his decision.

On a road trip in Chicago now as the Yankees' first baseman, Lou meets, woos, and marries Eleanor Twitchell (Teresa Wright). Mrs. Gehrig, no longer her son's "best girl," is noticeably jealous at first but learns to accept the change in their lives.

Year after year Lou steadily contributes to the Yankees' success. Because of his strength and durability Gehrig is dubbed "The Iron Horse." Happily married and one of the game's true stars, Lou seemingly has it all. But shortly after being honored for playing in his 2,000th straight game, the Iron Horse feels a strange weakness in his body.

Upon finishing some medical exams, Lou asks the doctor for a straight answer: "Go ahead Doc, I'm a man that likes to know his batting average." The doctor informs Lou that his playing days are over.

LOU: Is it three strikes, doc?

DOCTOR: You want it straight?

LOU: Sure I do. Straight.

FACING PAGE: Eleanor (Teresa Wright) with her "Tanglefoot," Lou Gehrig (Gary Cooper).

DOCTOR: It's three strikes.

LOU: Doc, I've learned one thing. All the arguing in the world can't change the decision of the umpire.

Before he learns how much time he has, they are informed that Mrs. Gehrig is coming to the office.

Lou asks that no one tells his wife that his illness (amyotrophic lateral sclerosis, a nerve disease) is fatal, but Eleanor guesses the truth. Still, she summons the courage to maintain a pretense that her husband will recover.

Their hero's career over, thousands jam Yankee Stadium for a special tribute to the fallen Iron Horse.

Standing with former teammates, Gehrig delivers a humble speech expressing appreciation for family, friends, the press, and fellow ballplayers. The great ballplayer ends by saying, "People all say that I've had a bad break. But today, today I consider myself the luckiest man on the face of the earth."

INSTANT REPLAY Lou Gehrig was everybody's all-American. Yes, Gary Cooper is not much of a ballplayer, nor does he greatly resemble the Iron Horse, but the actor handles the difficult assignment with great aplomb.

Translating a quiet hero in cinematic terms is never easy, yet producer Sam Gold-

wyn signed the right player for the role. Gary Cooper excels at portraying just such a protagonist, as evidenced by his brilliant turns in *Sergeant York* and *High Noon*.

Despite the aforementioned handicaps, Cooper delivers a very convincing characterization showing the legendary ballplayer's innate human qualities that made the Yankee slugger so beloved. The "luckiest man" farewell speech was as moving a moment as there's been on celluloid.

Director Sam Wood deserves a lot of the credit here, deftly balancing drama, sentiment, and humor. Wood seems to have the touch for juggling these elements, not only here but in two other classic sports-themed films, *A Day at the Races* and *The Stratton Story*.

The Pride of the Yankees, though, is really a love story doubleheader. There is the public's love for Gehrig but also the love between Lou and Eleanor (which would be the subject of a movie 36 years later in *A Love Affair: The Eleanor and Lou Gehrig Story*).

In this picture, Cooper and Teresa Wright make a fine pair, conveying a romantic chemistry that is warm and sincere. Wright comes across as genuine and expressive both in handling a domineering mother-in-law and in coping with a terminally ill husband. Their romance, by the way, is enhanced by the use of Irving Berlin's classic "Always" as the couple's love song.

The film's supporting cast fill out their positions with varying degrees of success. Elsa Janssen and Ludwig Stossel convincingly embody Lou's hardworking German-American parents.

Walter Brennan as Sam Blake illustrates the deep bond sportswriters and athletes sometimes developed back then—something that is rarely seen in today's sports world. At times, it is over the top here. Dan Duryea provides some welcome contrast as the cynical sportswriter Hank Hannerman.

Portraying oneself on the screen is much more difficult than it looks. Here Babe

Ruth is at home and at ease, perhaps because the legendary slugger was a natural ham. (Years later baseball great Jackie Robinson would pull off the much more difficult challenge of carrying an entire picture, portraying himself in *The Jackie Robinson Story*.)

Nevertheless, one of the shortcomings of *The Pride of the Yankees* is a lack of depth in exploring Gehrig's relationship with teammate and fellow superstar Babe Ruth.

Overall *The Pride of the Yankees,* with its sterling lead performances, is one of motion pictures' quintessential biographies, a faithful chronicle that is both personal and far reaching at the same time.

Coming on the eve of the United States' entry into World War II, the picture's themes of triumph and tragedy really struck a chord with the public, as the symbolism of the American dream had never been more eloquently presented.

'The Pride of the Yankees' would earn 11 Academy Award nominations, including Best Picture.

OUTSIDE THE LINES Many Yankee greats appear as themselves in the picture, including Babe Ruth, Bill Dickey, Mark Koenig, and Bob Meusel.... Sam Wood also directed *The Stratton Story* (1949) and the Marx Brothers in *A Day at the Races* (1937).... Russian-born writer Jo Swerling wrote *Blood and Sand* (1941), a bullfighting remake of the silent picture that starred Rudolph Valentino.... Gary Cooper wasn't left-handed, so the film had to be reversed, requiring players and coaches to wear reversed numbers and run from home to third.... *Pride of the Yankees* cowriter Herman Mankiewicz was nominated with Swerling for an Oscar.... Mankiewicz also wrote *The Pride of St. Louis* (1952), featuring Dan Dailey as pitcher Dizzy Dean.... He wrote *Citizen Kane* with Orson Welles and produced the W. C. Fields Olympic comedy *Million Dollar Legs* (1932).... Walter Brennan won an Oscar for Best Supporting Actor as a horse breeder in *Kentucky* (1939).... Part of Gehrig's "farewell" speech was included on the top-selling record *I Can Hear It Now,* which was an audible history of the years 1932—1945 that also included Churchill, Hitler, Roosevelt, and Stalin.... Babe Ruth wasn't the only Yankee legend to be featured in Hollywood films. Lou Gehrig starred in the 1938 Western *Rawhide,* playing one of several ranchers being coerced by shady characters.... Gehrig's record for 2,130 consecutive games was broken by Cal Ripken in 1995.... Following his death, amyotrophic lateral sclerosis became more popularly known as "Lou Gehrig's disease."...Reportedly Spencer Tracy was one of the early considerations for the Gehrig role, as was Cary Grant.... The same year she was nominated for a Leading Actress Oscar as Mrs. Gehrig, Theresa Wright won an Oscar for her role in *Mrs. Miniver* in the Best Supporting Actress category.... In 1978 a made-for-TV movie about Gehrig was made, entitled *A Love Affair: The Eleanor and Lou Gehrig Story,* featuring Edward Hermann as Gehrig.... *The Pride of the Yankees* was nominated for 11 Academy Awards.... Dan Mandell won an Oscar for Best Editing.

ALL-STAR MOMENTS Sequences around and including Lou Gehrig (Cooper) and his "luckiest man on the face of the earth" speech.

HOME COURT ADVANTAGE Available on VHS and DVD. Interestingly, HBO released a colorized version. This title is also available as part of a four-disc gift set that also includes *Bull Durham, The Jackie Robinson Story,* and *Eight Men Out.*

#42 PHAR LAP

Screenwriter David Williamson. **Director** Simon Wincer. **Producer** John Sexton. **Cinematography** Russell Boyd. **Editing** Tony Paterson. **Music** Bruce Rowland. **Production Design** Lawrence Eastwood. Fox. 1983.

THE PLAYERS
Tom Burlinson **Tommy Woodcock**; Martin Vaughan **Harry Telford**; Ron Liebman **Dave Davis**; Celia De Burgh **Vi Telford**; Gia Carides **Emma**; Judy Morris **Bea Davis**; Richard Morgan **Cashy Martin**; Vincent Ball **Lachlan McKinnon**; Redmond Phillips **Sir Samuel Horden**; James Steele **Jim Pike**; Brian Granrott **Reporter**; Roger Newcombe **James Crofton**; Robert Grubb **William Nielsen**; Peter Whitford **Bert Wolfe**; Alan Wylie **Randwick reporter**; John Stanton **Eric Connolly**; Alan Wilson **Jockey in steam room**; Ross O'Donovan **Strapper**; Ashley Grenville **Strapper**; Pat Thomson **Edith**; Les Foxcroft **Brazier man**; Warwick Moss **McReady**; Henry Duvall **Mr. Ping**; Steve Bannister **Young Cappy Telford**; Richard Terrill **Older Cappy Telford**; Justin Ridley **Newsboy**; Kelvyn Worth **Newsboy**; Simon Wells **Newsboy**; Anthony Hawkins **Guy Raymond**; John Russell **Race commentator**; Len Kaserman **Baron Long**; Tommy Woodcock **Trainer**; Brian Adams **Mike Vincente**; Paul Riley **Billy Elliott**; Maggie Millar **May Holmes**

THE GAME 1928. Sydney, Australia. Despite the animal's lack of pedigree, quirky trainer Harry Telford (Martin Vaughan) purchases Phar Lap on instinct and extensive research into the horse's family history. Even his wife, Vi (Celia DeBurgh), complains to him: "He's a bit skinny, isn't he, Harry?"

The Australian trainer's American financier/promoter, Dave Davis (Ron Liebman), is equally disappointed on first appearances. "This is not a horse, Harry. It's a cross between a sheepdog and a kangaroo." Harry feels that Phar Lap's deep bloodlines reveal a champ in the making. When Dave tells him to sell the horse, Harry says he'll lease him from Dave only because he can't afford to buy him but strongly believes in the horse's potential. They agree that Harry will pay for his upkeep and give Dave 1/3 of his winnings over the next three years.

Soon Harry becomes a laughingstock among his fellow trainers as they watch him futilely try to get the horse in racing form. On the track his horse isn't making matters any brighter. Phar Lap finishes dead last in his first effort and not much better in subsequent races. One day, however, stable boy Tommy Woodcock's (Tom Burlinson) diligence and caring for the horse pays off and Phar Lap's racing heritage begins to show. Soon Phar Lap is not only winning but dominating the Australian horse racing world, much to the surprise of Dave, who's quick to take financial advantage of the turn of events.

With the first big payoff, Harry's wife wants them to get out of debt, invest in property, and leave the training business. Vi reminds her husband that he called training "a rotten life, up at 3:30 A.M. and dead tired by late afternoon." Harry indignantly snaps back: "What do you expect me to do, woman?! Sneak off back to the bush just when I get my chance?" Harry apologizes for his outburst but reveals to her that he's proved his point: "I know more about bloodlines and training than any other bastard in this country. By the time I'm finished they'll all know it."

Phar Lap's unprecedented success has also caused consternation among the bluebloods who run the racing industry. They give the horse extraordinary weight handicaps but still the phenom bucks the oddsmakers. Despite all the success, Dave presents Harry with financial figures that show he'll be bankrupt within six months, since he's over-extended himself by enlarging his training business that won't produce another Phar Lap in the near future. Dave offers a plan to have Phar Lap scratch one of the two major races after inflating the odds and making wagers across the country. Harry's too proud for that and is determined to win both the Melbourne Cup and the Caulfield Cup. "Any trainer worth his salt dreams of winning both races," insists the stubborn trainer.

Later, however, swallowing his pride and bowing to Dave's demands, Harry discreetly pulls the horse from one of the races. Not long afterward, death threats and suspicious reporters come to dominate his life. A reporter informs him, "Someone's put £50,000 on Amonus to win the Caulfield and Phar Lap to win the Melbourne. Odds 30 to 1." He reminds Harry, "If Amonus wins the Caulfield the only way some bookies can save their necks is to stop Phar Lap from winning the Melbourne."

Tom Burlinson stars as Tommy Woodcock, the stable boy who befriends the legendary racehorse, Phar Lap.

After a disturbing phone call threatens to "turn Phar Lap into dog meat if he isn't pulled from the Cup," Dave, rather than calling the police, who he fears will find out about his wagering deal, takes matters into his own hands and hires private security to guard Harry, his family, Phar Lap and the jockey around the clock. Despite being shot at, Tommy and Phar Lap manage to make it to the big race.

Phar Lap wins the Cup in typical runaway fashion. His winning ways continue in Australia despite the increasingly unfair handicap of weights that the jockeys say are threatening the horse's health. Despite Harry's apprehensions, Dave makes a very lucrative deal to race Phar Lap in Mexico and California. Harry's too committed to his many other young horses to make the journey and convinces Dave that Tommy can train Phar Lap abroad.

March, 1932. Caliente, Mexico. Despite some foot problems that slow down his training, Phar Lap wins with a strategy Tommy uses against Dave's orders, deepening the rift between the two on the subject of handling the horse. Dave's troubles are magnified when he's given a foreboding message from a gambling insider: "If something's good, that's okay; but if something's too good, it upsets the whole system."

Two weeks later while sleeping in a stable in northern California, Phar Lap becomes very ill. A doctor is summoned and initially suspects the horse ate some wet alfalfa but goes for some more help. Despite Tommy's best effort to keep the horse moving, Phar Lap falls to the ground, lets out a painful groan, and dies. An extensive autopsy fails to provide a definitive cause of death but it's implied that many feel foul play was present.

The news shocks the world. A reporter pushes a distraught Harry for a response: "Why do you think there's been this incredible reaction to Phar Lap's death? After all, he was just a horse." Harry retorts, "He wasn't *just* a horse! He was the best."

INSTANT REPLAY Appropriately developed by respectful Aussie filmmakers, this true story is presented with pride, dignity, and restraint.

With its underdog story and stirring music, this picture has been called "a four-legged Rocky." Finally, its strong boy-horse relationship and brilliant photography make this project reminiscent of *The Black Stallion*. Good company to be in.

Simon Wincer's somewhat conservative direction is enhanced by the extremely talented cinematographer Russell Boyd. Boyd's credits to that point included *Gallipoli*, *The Year of Living Dangerously*, *Picnic at Hanging Rock*, and *Tender Mercies*.

Boyd's old-time, photograph-like earth tones give a real sense of place and time, certainly enhancing the storytelling.

The racing sequences are handled with an authentic feel, though it might have been

an interesting test to see if a reduction in slow-motion usage would have increased the tension and excitement. Certainly if the technical capabilities had been available at that time to capture the races like Gary Ross did in *Seabiscuit*, it would have made a very good picture even better.

Boyd's camera work is complemented by the wealth of period details presented by production designer Lawrence Eastwood's crew. Together their efforts really deliver the mood and trappings of Australia in the 1930s in terms of dress, cars, and overall atmosphere.

Bruce Rowland's music, reminiscent of *Chariots of Fire,* generally complements the visual proceedings.

The smart writing of David Williamson avoids predictable characterizations. He is aided in that effort by a strong cast, especially the leading men, Tom Burlinson, Martin Vaughan, and Ron Liebman.

Certainly Vaughan's impressive turn as the stubborn, determined, unorthodox trainer pitted against a supremely talented but somewhat undisciplined horse on the road to becoming a champion is riveting entertainment. Vaughan's internal strength in fighting off the skeptics and commitment to what he believes in is stirring.

Add Tom Burlinson's heartfelt dedication and compassion for the welfare of the freakishly talented racehorse and you have a troika that is very hard not to root for.

Ron Liebman is excellent as Phar Lap's Jewish American owner. Sometimes pragmatic, sometimes funny, sometimes selfish but deep down a compassionate softie, Liebman's character shows some real backbone in his fight against the prejudiced racing elite (brilliantly caricatured by Vincent Ball).

A note should be made here as to the talents of Towering Inferno, a magnificent horse that convincingly played the legendary Phar Lap.

Phar Lap succeeds in its warm and simple presentation of how this magnificent horse (he won 37 of 51 starts) lifted the spirits of a nation mired in the Depression, and of the tragedy of its mysterious death.

OUTSIDE THE LINES The film is based on the book by Michael Wilkinson.... Over three dozen horses were brought in to use in race sequences. They were

TOP: It would be a stable boy (Burlinson as Woodcock) who would exert the greatest influence in developing Phar Lap into a champion.

BOTTOM: Phar Lap's owners, Dave and Bea Davis (Ron Liebman and Judy Morris), are jubilant as their horse, whom everyone considered a loser, wins his first race.

RIGHT: Trainer Harry Telford (Martin Vaughan, left) informs owner Dave Davis (Liebman, center) that the great Phar Lap has sustained injuries that may prevent him from ever racing again. Tommy Woodcock looks on.

rated in ability from 1 to 36 and jockeys were instructed by director Wincer to race them like a real race.... The real Tommy Woodcock appears in the film as a veteran trainer.... With its reddish-brown appearance the gelding Phar Lap was known as "The Red Terror."...Dying before his appearance at the Tanforan track in the San Francisco Bay Area, Phar Lap was within $50,000 of becoming the greatest money winner of all time.... The film's producer, John Sexton, first heard of the story from his father, who'd been part of the crowd that witnessed the 1930 Melbourne Cup.... The picture's release came at a time of the death of another great racehorse, Swale.... At the time the film was Australia's most expensive production at $5.5 million.... To promote the film in the U.K., a special race was staged and broadcast by the BBC.... Phar Lap was stuffed and mounted and placed on display at the Museum of Natural History in Melbourne.

ALL-STAR MOMENTS Montage of Harry (Vaughan) riding Phar Lap hard up and down the steep sand dunes.

Harry interrupts Dave's (Liebman) cricket game at a posh club to ask for entry fee money to race his horse. Dave agrees but sets some conditions, one of which is that the horse must be entered under Harry's name so as to not embarrass Dave with the wealthy folks he's aspiring to socialize with. And if the horse doesn't race well Harry must agree to sell him. Harry replies, "Race well? He's gotta win. I owe more than 300 quid and can't pay me rent."

After suffering many setbacks, Phar Lap finally wins, proving Harry's faith. Tommy (Burlinson) runs back to the stables to tell Harry he's got to come out and accept the victory sash. Harry breaks down, telling Tommy he can't.

Harry's wife (De Burgh) goes over the books and announces their desperate financial straits. Harry admits that his influence on Phar Lap is less than others imagine and proclaims his faith that the horse, competing without him in North America, will win some money to save their home:

> He'll win at Caliente. And he'll win everywhere else he races. For years I've
> kidded myself that I made that horse. Truth is he would've been a champion
> no matter who trained him. I've got 20 colts out there with bloodlines as good
> or better than his. I've trained them all exactly the same. Every one's a dud.
> He's a freak.

Going against the owner's orders ("I'll kill you, Woodcock!"), Tommy orchestrates a brilliant strategy that leads to Phar Lap's final victory despite an injured foot at Caliente.

POST-GAME COMMENTS Writer David Williamson:

> After my earlier refusals to listen I realized it's not just the story of a racehorse
> who went on to become the fastest horse in the world. The way a diverse group
> of characters' destinies are linked to this horse, the interplay between the
> characters, the intrigue, the attempts on the horse's life...it's a really unique
> story, and a very important part of Australia's rich and colorful history.[1]

HOME COURT ADVANTAGE Available on VHS.

#41 THE LONELINESS OF THE LONG-DISTANCE RUNNER

Screenwriter Alan Sillitoe. **Director/Producer** Tony Richardson. **Cinematography** Walter Lassally. **Music** John Addison. **Editing** Antony Gibbs. **Production Design** Ralph Brinton. **Costume Design** Sophie Harris. British Lion Film. 1962.

THE PLAYERS
Tom Courtenay **Colin Smith**; Michael Redgrave **Reformatory governor**; Avis Bunnage **Mrs. Smith**; Dervis Ward **Detective**; James Bolam **Mike**; Topsy Jane **Audrey**; Alec McCowen **Brown**; Joe Robinson **Roach**; Phillip Martin **Stacey**; Raymond Dyer **Gordon**; James Cairncross **Mr. Jones**; Peter Madden **Mr. Smith**; Peter Duguid **Doctor**; James Fox **Public school runner**; Julia Foster **Gladys**; John Bull **Ronalds**; Robert Percival **Tory politician**

THE GAME A rebellious young man at odds with himself tries to escape his dreary environment by running. Colin Smith (Tom Courtenay), a social misfit, angry at the societal systems he's confronted with, runs toward a cloudy future while trying to leave behind a haunting past.

When Colin is sent to reform school for a burglary, his athletic ability is soon noticed by the school's governor (Michael Redgrave). The governor tries to harness Colin's natural running abilities to win a coveted cross-country race in the name of school pride, but in fact it's for the governor's personal glory. While the schoolmaster tries to convince his young protégé that developing his talents could be his ticket to a better life, perhaps even the Olympics someday, Colin seems a bit wary.

Meanwhile through a series of flashbacks we learn about Colin's past: the agonizing death of his father lying in bed, and his mother (Avis Bunnage) quickly taking a lover (Raymond Dyer) and frivolously spending the meager but much-needed insurance money. With no authoritative figure around, Colin becomes a hoodlum. He steals cars, breaks into slot machines, and is told by his girlfriend, Audrey (Topsy Jane), that he's headed for a life of crime ending up in prison.

Back at the Bruxton Towers reformatory Colin gets into a fight with a fellow delinquent, Stacey (Phillip Martin), who is jealous of Colin's running prowess. Colin fears punishment, but the governor wants to win the cup so badly that instead he puts Colin on an expanded training schedule. Surprised, Colin says he'll do his best.

Despite warnings from his staff, the governor allows Colin to take a training run outside the school grounds without supervision. The ensuing workout gives the young man a sense of freedom, if only for a short period. Colin's run is intercut with assorted flashbacks designed to reveal the sources of the youngster's behavioral problems, which are largely centered around his family life.

For Colin running is his "therapy," his way of dealing with the repressive world he finds himself in and the restless spirit that channels his anger and frustration. It is the haunting memories from those flashbacks during his runs, and at the same time the governor's abnormal obsession with winning a running race through Colin, that provoke him to strike back at the restraining forces those two elements represent to him.

When his partner in crime, Mike (James Bolam), ends up at the same reformatory, Colin tells him that he feels he's being turned into a "bloody racehorse" by the governor's desire to use Colin to win prestige for his school.

With the participants line up for race day, the governor points out Colin to the pub-

Troubled young man Colin Smith (Tom Courtenay, right) enters reform school, where the authorities try to take advantage of his running prowess.

lic school's chief, then tells Colin, "We're counting on you." With much fanfare, school bands playing and students lining the route, the five-mile cross-country race begins. As Colin struggles up a hill he flashes back to various comments and images of the governor, his mother, and his girlfriend. Slowly, he moves to the front of the field. He hears the voice of the governor say, "It's my ambition to see Colin win that cup for the school." He then hears the voice of Audrey wondering why Colin always seems to be running away from things. Colin now takes the lead.

The anxious governor sees the first runners coming into view through his binoculars and is naturally quite pleased to see Colin running well in first place. As the race announcer bellows out that "no one has a chance of catching Colin now," Colin hears the voice of the governor in his head again: "The sooner we have your cooperation, the sooner you'll be out of here—always remember who has the whip hand."

About 35 yards from the finish, with the crowd cheering him on and the governor all ready to accept the cup, Colin, with thoughts of his dying father, the cup, and the wasted insurance money in his head, stops running and gasps for breath.

Soon the second place runner, one from the public school (James Fox), passes Colin, who wipes his brow and smirks, feeling he's won twice. He proved to himself he could have won the race and managed to make a statement to the system he feels has boxed him in. It's a temporary victory, as he's soon back in shop class in the reformatory, but for Colin it was worth it.

INSTANT REPLAY Director Tony Richardson captures the bitterness and resentment that was indicative of the working class and specifically the "angry young men" of Britain in the 1950s and '60s. The director uses imaginative and technically daring methods to communicate the barren, bleak hopelessness of the alienated youth.

TOP: Michael Redgrave is the Reformatory Governor.

MIDDLE: Colin, the angry young rebel at the Reformatory (far right).

BOTTOM: Fleeting romance.

The use of sound in the open landscape (that is, no sound at all except the wind and splashing mud) along with the stark black and white photography of Walter Lassally really provides a sense of the loneliness of a long distance runner. Richardson's use of flashback, though generally effective, is overdone.

Alan Sillitoe's script, a biting social commentary based on his own short story, is appropriately spare, as is Tom Courtenay's (as Colin Smith) embodiment of the rebel without a cause. His character is pretty much the same at the picture's conclusion as he was at its start.

Colin is fairly devoid of hope and therefore has little ambition. Like the film itself overall, its lead character is relentlessly grim and downbeat. Colin's rebellion is without any outward hope or glory; rather, it is a brief personal statement left for individuals to interpret on their own.

Both Courtenay and Michael Redgrave physically and dramatically personify the massive gap between their two generations and classes. Courtenay's hollowed face, unpolished accent, boyish haircut, impish physique, and combination of a rough, brooding outer persona and deep sensitivity wonderfully contrast with Redgrave's aloof, patrician schoolmaster with a slightly pompous tone.

Like Richard Harris in *This Sporting Life*, Paul Newman in *Somebody Up There Likes Me*, William Gates and Arthur Agee in *Hoop Dreams*, Marlon Brando in *On the Waterfront*, and Ray Allen in *He Got Game*, Tom Courtenay's character has the double-edged opportunity to transcend his disadvantaged socioeconomic status through his physical talents. Not everyone is a winner.

OUTSIDE THE LINES The film was also known as *Rebel With a Cause*.... Tony Richardson would win an Academy Award for Best Director the next year for *Tom Jones*.... This marked Tom Courtenay's movie debut and won him a British Academy Award as Most Promising Newcomer to Leading Film Roles.

ALL-STAR MOMENTS Colin's sense of freedom is on display as he's allowed to run unsupervised outside the school.

As the detective questions Colin at the suspect's doorstep, money from the burglary begins to seep out of the drainpipe next to the door as a result of the rain. Colin takes off running with the detective in hot pursuit.

Climactic scene in which Colin deliberately stops short of the finish line, knowing he could have won.

HOME COURT ADVANTAGE Available on VHS and DVD.

#40 National Velvet

Screenwriters Helen Deutsch, Theodore Reeves. **Director** Clarence Brown. **Producer** Pandro Berman. **Cinematography** Leonard Smith. **Editng** Robert Kern. **Music** Herbert Stothart. **Art Direction** Cedric Gibbons, Urie McCleary. **Set Decoration** Edwin Willis, Mildred Griffiths. MGM. 1944.

THE PLAYERS Mickey Rooney **Mike Taylor**; Elizabeth Taylor **Velvet Brown**; Anne Revere **Mrs. Brown**; Donald Crisp **Mr. Brown**; Angela Lansbury **Edwina Brown**; Jackie Jenkins **Donald Brown**; Juanita Quigley **Malvolia Brown**; Reginald Owen **Farmer Ede**; Eugene Loring **Mr. Taski**; Wally Cassell **Jockey**; Billy Bevan **Constable**; Terry Kilburn **Ted**; Norma Varden **Miss Sims**; Alec Craig **Tim**; William Austin **Reporter**; Aubrey Mather **Entry official**; Arthur Shields **Mr. Hallam**; Frank Benson **Englishman**; Dennis Hoey **Mr. Greenford**; Frederic Worlock **Stewart**; Matthew Boulton **Entry Clerk**; Harry Allen **Van driver**; Colin Campbell **Cockney**; Alec Harford **Valet**; Donald Curtis **American**; Arthur Treacher **Man with umbrella**

THE GAME Mike Taylor (Mickey Rooney), a young drifter, befriends preteen schoolgirl Velvet Brown (Elizabeth Taylor) as they admire a beautiful but undisciplined horse galloping through the English countryside. The horse's owner, farmer Ede (Reginald Owen), calls him Pirate, and Velvet calls him "the Pie" for short. She has a way with horses, and as the Pie takes off, she is able to prevent him from running away, stopping him in his tracks.

As it turns out, Mike's deceased father used to coach Velvet's mother (Anne Revere), a former champion swimmer. Despite Mr. Brown's (Donald Crisp) skepticism about this young man's character, the Browns take Mike in, and he helps out with their family butcher business.

Velvet learns that Mike is a former jockey who's been afraid of riding ever since he was involved in a racing accident that caused the death of a fellow jockey.

As farmer Ede decides to raffle off the unruly Pie, Velvet wins the horse and reveals her dream of running him in the Grand National, one of England's biggest races. Velvet's mother gives her daughter the prize money she earned for swimming the English Channel so that Velvet can pay the Grand National entry fees, telling her, "There's a time for everything."

Mike trains the Pie and Velvet tirelessly, even overcoming a life-threatening illness to the horse. Mike hires a jockey for the race but Velvet is not convinced the rider has his heart in the race and refuses to let him ride.

While Velvet is asleep Mike can't resist and takes the Pie out for a run. He returns to find Velvet asleep in a jockey suit. She awakens and convinces Mike that "they won't know if you cut my hair. Pie will take care of me." Mike can see nothing will stop Velvet from her dream and goes along with the scheme.

Sure enough Velvet and the Pie run a brilliant race and win. Velvet faints and upon examination the doctor realizes the winning jockey is a girl and therefore disqualified. Undaunted, Velvet and the Pie have proved themselves champions and return home heroes.

Through his experience with Velvet and the Pie and the entire Brown family, Mike, rejuvenated and full of hope for his own future, ventures out on his own. Velvet is sad, but her mother reminds her that "there's a time for everything." The young girl catches up to Mike, who's whistling as he walks down the road, and they say their goodbyes.

TOP: Velvet Brown (Elizabeth Taylor) and Mike Taylor (Mickey Rooney).

BOTTOM: Anne Revere, who won an Oscar in this role as Elizabeth Taylor's mother, would soon play John Garfield's mother in the boxing drama 'Body and Soul.'

INSTANT REPLAY Producer Pandro Berman utilizes available resources to turn in a fine all-round production under the steady hand of director Clarence Brown. With the rich photography of Leonard Smith, production design led by the masterful Cedric Gibbons, and music by Herbert Stothart, *National Velvet* combines all the best attributes of entertainment.

The fine script by Helen Deutsch and Theodore Reeves, adapted from Enid Bagnold's novel, provides the nucleus of a deeply probing family drama.

The dialogue, particularly between Mrs. Brown and her daughter Velvet and between Mr. Brown and Mike, is sharp and sincere. It is that very real, honest quality that is the cornerstone of the film's success.

Anne Revere's matter-of-fact demeanor, her compassion and philosophical bent, rightfully earned her an Oscar as Best Supporting Actress. Elizabeth Taylor becomes a full-fledged star here with a completely natural performance. Mickey Rooney, more usually known for his ebullient persona, is brilliant in his restraint, allowing Taylor to shine.

Donald Crisp as Mr. Brown distinguishes himself as the pragmatic father who supports his wife and young daughter's unique qualities despite not really understanding their deep passions.

Director Clarence Brown effectively builds the suspense of the very realistic climactic race sequence and wisely concludes the film with a look to the future.

One shouldn't overlook the performance of the four-legged cast member, as the uncredited Pie shows range, beginning with a flighty attitude then overcoming a potentially fatal illness and ultimately showing the drive of a champion racer.

Eloquently delivered in all aspects, *National Velvet* could have easily been pretentious and maudlin. Instead it's two hours of visual splendor and endearing characterizations, an inspiring and skillfully assembled drama.

OUTSIDE THE LINES One of Mickey Rooney's first roles was in the baseball drama *Death on the Diamond* (1934) and an auto racing film, *High Speed* (1932) (as Mickey Maguire), but the actor's film reel is full of horse sagas: *Down the Stretch* (1936), *Thoroughbreds Don't Cry* (1937), *Stablemates* (1938), *The Black Stallion* (1979), *Lighting: The White Stallion* (1986), and a TV movie, *Bluegrass* (1988).... He earned a nomination for Best Supporting Actor in *The Black Stallion*.... Rooney also played Anthony Quinn's trainer in the boxing film *Requiem for a Heavyweight* (1962)...Anne Revere, who won an Oscar for Best Supporting Actress as Elizabeth Taylor's mother, also performed in the boxing movie *Body and Soul* (1947), starring John Garfield.... *National Velvet* was adapted from Enid Bagnold's novel, which also made the London stage.... Clarence Brown produced and directed baseball's *Angels in the Outfield* (1951).... Actress Angela Lansbury appeared in a 1984 television movie, *The First Olympics: Athens 1986*.... Pandro Berman, who would produce films like *Gunga Din, Top Hat,* and *The Hunchback of Notre Dame*, also assembled a football film, *The Big Game* (1936).... Shirley Temple and Katharine Hepburn were among the candidates for *National Velvet* as the film rights to the novel floated between Paramount and MGM studios for several years. Apparently, finding an actress who could handle a horse proved to be quite challenging.... Robert Kern won an Academy Award for his editing of this film.... Kern edited a wide range of sports movies: boxing's *The Prizefighter and the Lady* (1933), football's *Navy, Blue, and Gold* (1937), and baseball's *Angels in the Outfield* (1951).... *National Velvet* was made into a television series.... *National Velvet* was revisited in *International Velvet* (1978), starring Tatum O'Neal.

After production was complete, Ms. Taylor was allowed to keep the horse that starred with her.

ALL-STAR MOMENTS When asked by Mike if she's ever just taken hours to think, Velvet says, "All the time about horses. All day and every night." When Velvet asks Mike if he really likes horses, she is stunned when he answers, "I hate them." She doesn't believe him because he knows too much about them, but then Mike adds, "That's when you really hate something, when you know too much about it."

After Mike explains to Velvet the difficulty of her dream, her mother tells her daughter:

> Everyone should have a chance at a breathtaking piece of folly once in her life.
> I was only 20 when they said a woman couldn't swim the English Channel.
> You're 12 and want your horse to win the Grand National. Your dream has come
> early, but remember, Velvet, it will have to last you all the rest of your life.

Then she gives Velvet the money for the Grand National entry fee.

Making his way through the crowd to find a viewing spot to watch the race, the short-statured Mike has a difficult time.

The photography and editing of the big race.

HOME COURT ADVANTAGE Available on VHS and DVD. MGM originally released it, then Warner Bros., which also followed with two others—one combining it with *Black Beauty* and the other an Elizabeth Taylor Signature Collection that also includes *Butterfield 8, Cat on a Hot Tin Roof,* and *Father of the Bride.*

#39 CADDYSHACK

Screenwriters Brian Doyle-Murray, Harold Ramis, Douglas Kenney, David Thomas. **Director** Harold Ramis. **Producer** Jon Peters, Douglas Kenney. **Cinematography** Stevan Larner. **Editing** William Carruth, David Bretherton. **Production Design** Stan Jolley. **Music** Kenny Loggins, Johnny Mandel. Warner Bros. 1980.

THE PLAYERS Chevy Chase **Ty Webb**; Rodney Dangerfield **Al Czervik**; Ted Knight **Judge Smails**; Michael O'Keefe **Danny Noonan**; Bill Murray **Carl Spackler**; Sarah Holcomb **Maggie O'Hooligan**; Scott Colomby **Tony D'Annunzio**; Cindy Morgan **Lacey Underall**; Dan Resin **Dr. Beeper**; Henry Wilcoxon **Bishop**; Elaine Aiken **Mrs. Noonan**; Albert Salmi **Mr. Noonan**; Ann Ryerson **Grace**; Brian Doyle-Murray **Lou Loomis**; Hamilton Mitchell **Motormouth**; Peter Berkrot **Angie D'Annunzio**; John Barmon Jr. **Spaulding Smalls**; Lois Kibbee **Mrs. Smalls**; Brian McConnachie **Scott**; Tony Santini **Gatsby**; Ann Crilly **Suki**; Cordis Heard **Wally**; Scott Sudden **Richard Richards**; Jackie Davis **Smoke**; Thomas Carlin **Sandy MacReedy**; Minerva Scelza **Joey D'Annunzio**; Kenneth Burritt **Mr. Havercamp**; Rebecca Burritt **Mrs. Havercamp**; Bobbie Kosstrin **Noble Noyes**; Scott Jackson **Chuck Schick**; Anna Upstrom **Blonde bombshell**; Tony Gulliver **Old caddy Ray**; Judy Arman **Beeper's girlfriend**

THE GAME Young caddy Danny Noonan (Michael O'Keefe) seeks to earn the annual scholarship given out by Bushwood Country Club president Judge Smails (Ted Knight). While his parents would like to see him go to college, Danny isn't sure he wants to.

Danny needs to sway the tightly wound judge but ends up wooing the old man's pretty niece, Lacey Underall (Cindy Morgan). This doesn't help his scholarship chances.

Though the judge eventually awards Danny the scholarship, he threatens to revoke it if Danny's team beats him in a match play event where the young man has replaced the injured Al Czervik (Rodney Dangerfield). Despite the threat, Danny sinks the winning putt.

INSTANT REPLAY *Caddyshack* is like the 1960s British music supergroup Cream. Both only need the barest of threads as a base for their great improv skills, and you enjoy wherever they take you.

The plot, about social classes and a young man trying to identify with the right adult model, quickly gets lost in the high grass here as all eyes soon turn to the roving comedic talents of Chevy Chase, Ted Knight, Bill Murray, and Rodney Dangerfield. Their shots are all over the place but they do not disappoint.

Under Harold Ramis's loose directorial reins, Chase delivers a solid deadpan performance as the wealthy, half suave, half bumbling, spaced-out, antiestablishment member of the country club. His blind golf-playing musings are terrific, both ludicrous and enlightening at the same time.

Ted Knight's pompous, mean-spirited, self-absorbed judge and country club president is played to perfection as the guy you love to hate—and the guy the others play off of to hilarious effect.

Give Bill Murray "something for the effort" here in his role as the demented groundskeeper. Persisting in an Elmer Fudd-type hunt for the gopher making a mess of the course, developing grass one can play on and then smoke after a round, and wiping out a flower bed in becoming the "Cinderella story," Murray's Carl Spackler was largely improvised and clearly expanded from an originally small role.

Murray's performance exemplifies why the work of these four leads pretty much pushed the title story about coming-of-age caddies to the background.

In his first major film, Rodney Dangerfield is amusingly vulgar as the loud, newly rich real estate developer with a disrespect and irreverence for the establishment. The character refreshingly illustrates that class has nothing to do with money. His oil to Knight's water produces some the film's most humorous moments.

Whether it's the country club dinner, yacht party, or golf tournament, the raunchy comedian works any gathering here like a Vegas showroom. Though Dangerfield has repeated this characterization in subsequent features, he's at the top of his game in *Caddyshack*. A blue-collar bull in a white, elitist china shop, Dangerfield matches up well against shop owner Ted Knight.

Technically, the photography is merely workmanlike, though Dangerfield's ultra-loud attire would still show color if the film had been shot in black and white. The gopher sounds more like the dolphin in the old TV series *Flipper* but serves as an amusing adversary to the Bushwood Country Club and Murray in particular. The music, from John Mandel's score to Kenny Loggins' tunes, is recorded at deafening levels.

From an idea by Brian Doyle Murray, who plays caddy boss Lou Loomis, *Caddyshack* is based on the real-life youth experiences of the Murrays and executed by the makers of *Animal House*, Doug Kenney and Harold Ramis. The two films certainly share a penchant for sophomoric humor and antiestablishment sentiments. Both have permeated pop culture and become cult classics, indicating that sometimes there is a place for doo-doo in the swimming pool and being on "double-secret" probation. Anyone care for a Baby Ruth bar?

OUTSIDE THE LINES Jon Peters also produced the boxing comedy *The Main Event* (1979) and the wrestling picture *VisionQuest* (1985), as well as the TV movie *Finish Line* (1989), a true story about a demanding track coach and his runner son.... *Caddyshack* was Harold Ramis's directorial debut.... The film was shot primarily in the Florida area at the Rolling Hills Club in Ft. Lauderdale and the Boca Raton Hotel and Country Club.... The film was inspired by writer Brian Doyle-Murray's own experiences when he and his brother, Bill, caddied in their youth at the Indian Hill Golf Club in Winnetka, Illinois.... Over 20 years later the movie would spawn a television series, *The Sweet Spot*, starring Bill Murray and four of his brothers.... The gopher and tunnel system were designed by John Dykstra, whose special effects work includes *Star Wars*.... In 2001 Caddyshack restaurants began operating in Florida and South Carolina.... While several writers were involved in the final script, much of the movie was improvised, including

TOP: "It's in the hole!"

LEFT: (Left to right) Ty Webb (Chevy Chase), Carl Spackler (Bill Murray), Al Czervik (Rodney Dangerfield), Judge Smails (Ted Knight).

Murray's "Cinderella story" scene.... The movie's enduring appeal was a factor in a somewhat embarrassing moment for wrestler-turned-governor of Minnesota Jesse Ventura: upon meeting the Dalai Lama, Ventura asked him if he had ever seen *Caddyshack*. The Holy Man had not.... At various stages of casting Mickey Rourke was lining up to be Danny Noonan and Don Rickles nearly got the Dangerfield role.... Michael O'Keefe worked with pros from the Winged Foot CC in New York on his swing.... Bill Murray, at various times, has had an ownership stake in several minor league baseball clubs, including the St. Paul Saints.... Murray starred with Woody Harrelson and Randy Quaid in the bowling comedy *Kingpin* (1996) as well as the animated basketball feature *Space Jam* (1996).... Michael O'Keefe starred in baseball's *The Slugger's Wife* (1985).... Brian Doyle-Murray appeared regularly on the TV series *Good Sports*.... Doyle-Murray was also a cast member of the TV movie *Babe Ruth* (1991).... Rodney Dangerfield hadn't played golf before making this film.... He also wrote most of his own lines.... Albert Salmi starred with Paul Newman in the 1956 live telecast of *Bang the Drum Slowly* on the U.S. Steel Hour as the doomed ballplayer Bruce Pearson, a role Robert DeNiro would play in a 1973 feature version.... Jon Peters was a producer of Michael Mann's boxing film, *Ali* (2001).... David Bretherton won an Oscar for his editing work on *Cabaret* (1972).

ALL-STAR MOMENTS Carl's (Murray) fantasy scene: "This crowd has gone deadly silent, a Cinderella story outta nowhere. Former greenskeeper and now about to become the Master champion...it's in the hole...it's in the hole!"

Carl's Dalai Lama story: "And so I say, 'Hey, Lama. Hey, how 'bout a little somethin', you know, for the effort, you know?' And he says to me, 'Oh, there won't be any money, but when you die, on your deathbed, you will receive total consciousness.' So I got that goin' for me. Which is nice."

At a fancy dinner Al Czervik (Dangerfield) says, "Oh, this is your wife, huh? A lovely lady. Hey, baby, you must've been something before electricity. . . .You're a lot of woman, you know that? Yeah, wanna make $14 the hard way?"

Judge Smails (Knight): "I've sentenced boys younger than you to the gas chamber. Didn't want to do it. I felt I owed it to them."

The bishop (Henry Wilcoxon) thanks the Almighty as he proceeds to play the best round of his life with Carl caddying for him in a howling thunderstorm. But as he lifts his club toward the heavens he's struck dead by lightning.

Czervik races his yacht out of control, smashing smaller boats throughout the harbor.

After the judge kicks his errant ball to improve his lie he gets hit in the groin by Czervik's shot coming up the fairway behind him. Al says, "I should've yelled, 'two!'"

The Jaws-spoof chaos that ensues when a candy bar lying at the bottom of the pool is mistaken for a turd. Later as Carl cleans the pool he takes a bite out of it, causing the Judge's wife to faint.

As the Judge's wife attempts to christen their new boat the champagne bottle doesn't break, but the nose of the boat does and falls off into the water.

HOME COURT ADVANTAGE Available on VHS and DVD. Warner Bros. has released numerous DVD versions: as a single release, multiple anniversary editions, and combined with other titles like *Blazing Saddles*. There's also a Chevy Chase Collection with *Funny Farm* and *Spies Like Us*.

#38 HERE COMES MR. JORDAN

Screenwriters Sidney Buchman, Seton Miller. (Play by Harry Segall.) **Director** Alexander Hall. **Producer** Everett Riskin. **Cinematography** Joseph Walker. **Editing** Viola Lawrence. **Music** Frederick Hollander. **Art Direction** Lionel Banks. **Costumes** Edith Head. Columbia. 1941.

THE PLAYERS Robert Montgomery **Joe Pendleton/Bruce Farnsworth/Ralph Murdoch**; Evelyn Keyes **Bette Logan**; Claude Rains **Mr. Jordan**; Rita Johnson **Julia Farnsworth**; Edward Horton **Messenger 7013**; James Gleason **Max "Pop" Corkle**; John Emery **Tony Abbott**; Donald MacBride **Inspector Williams**; Don Costello **Lefty**; Halliwell Hobbes **Sisk**; Benny Rubin **Bugsy**; Joseph Crehan **Doctor**; Tom Hanlon **Announcer**; Lloyd Bridges **Pilot**; William Newell **Handler**; Abe Roth **Referee**; Joe Hickey **Gilbert**; Billy Dawson **Johnny**; Warren Ashe **Charlie**; Bert Young **Taxi driver**; John Rogers **Escort**

THE GAME Putting his nervous trainer, Max Corkle (James Gleason), at ease, leading prizefighter Joe Pendleton (Robert Montgomery) tells him he can handle piloting his own plane back to New York. After all, he is known as "The Flying Pug." Joe adds that nothing can go wrong as long as he brings his beloved saxophone with him.

Playing a few tunes on his musical instrument, Joe is paying little attention to flying, and his plane crashes. The deceased boxer's spirit is escorted by heavenly Messenger 7013 (Edward Horton) up to meet Mr. Jordan (Claude Rains), who is supervising newly arrived souls. Mr. Jordan is horrified to learn that the new, over-eager escort grabbed Joe a bit early and he's not actually due to arrive for another 50 years. Returning to earth, they learn that Joe's body has been cremated, so Mr. Jordan scours the world for a suitable corporeal overcoat that's "in the pink" for Pendleton to live in.

Joe hasn't come across anything that's suitable for him when they arrive at a rich industrialist's mansion, where millionaire Bruce Farnsworth is just about to be murdered by his scheming wife Julia (Rita Johnson) and her lover, Mr. Farnsworth's secretary, Tony Abbott (John Emery).

Joe is all set to refuse this body too until he sees Bette Logan (Evelyn Keyes), who has arrived at the estate to ask the tycoon for help in clearing her father's name, claiming Mr. Farnsworth's business dealings led to her father being wrongly imprisoned. Joe reluctantly agrees to take over the body only temporarily to help Bette. Jordan informs Joe that although others will see him as Farnsworth, he'll still have his own personality.

Naturally Julia and Tony are stunned when Joe (as Bruce), whom they believed they'd murdered, enters the room. Joe is a little nervous at first but gathers himself when Sisk (Halliwell Hobbes), a butler, gives him a saxophone to play. Joe then orders Tony to help get Bette's father out of jail.

Bette is naturally grateful but confused as to who Joe really is. When Jordan returns to help Joe find a more permanent body, Joe, sensing that Bette likes him in Bruce's body, decides to get the industrialist's body in shape to box. The messenger reminds Joe that he's destined to be the next world champion boxer regardless of what body he's in. Joe insists on building up Bruce Farnsworth's body so he can romance Bette too.

When Joe calls for his old trainer Max, Corkle just about flips out when Pendleton tells him the whole story of what happened to him. After Joe convinces him by playing the saxophone, Corkle realizes it is Joe and faints. Max then agrees to make a deal for a fight against "K.O." Murdoch and get Joe in shape.

'Here Comes Mr. Jordan' earned seven Oscar nominations, including Best Actor (Robert Montgomery).

As Julia and Tony continue to plot Joe's death, the Messenger returns to insist that Joe must leave Mr. Farnsworth's body. Joe then desperately tries to convince Bette they have a future together and begs her not to forget him. Perhaps someday, he says, if a man approaches her, maybe even a boxer, she'll recognize that quality by looking at his eyes and give him a chance.

Jordan explains that Joe as Farnsworth wasn't meant to be, but adds that if his love for Bette was meant to be, it will happen. Farnsworth is soon shot by Tony. Joe and Jordan go searching for another body.

Upon learning of Mr. Farnsworth's disappearance, Max suspects foul play and investigators are brought in. Jordan and Joe return to the Farnsworth mansion to pick up his saxophone. Arriving at the same time, Bette, Max, Julia, Tony, and others are being questioned by inspector Williams (Donald MacBride). Max is telling crazy stories about Joe being Bruce Farnsworth. Julia claims her husband was insane. When Max accuses Julia and Tony of murdering her husband, the inspector demands he provide proof. Joe and Jordan look on helplessly since he's now invisible. Max turns on the radio to listen to the Murdoch-Gilbert fight. Jordan then explains that Murdoch was shot by gamblers at ringside because he wouldn't throw the fight. He's dead unless Joe takes over his body.

Joe becomes Murdoch, pulling himself off the canvas to defeat Gilbert and become world champion, his destiny. The fight announcer is naturally stunned: "He's up at the count of nine. Murdoch is up, full of fight. One minute lying there like a dead man. Now on his feet like a dynamo. It's amazing!" When Max hears that Murdoch took a saxophone from his corner, he realizes it is Joe.

Rushing to the locker room, Max is greeted by Joe, who fires Murdoch's dishonest managers and later tells Max that Bruce's body is hidden in the mansion basement. Max informs the police, who then arrest Julia and Tony.

Jordan arrives to inform Joe that all things work out and that Murdoch is now his destiny. Joe balks and wants a different body, feeling it was Murdoch, not him, who won the title. But Jordan transplants Joe's soul permanently into Murdoch, erasing all connection to Joe Pendleton. "From now on he's "K. O." Murdoch. No more memory of Joseph Pendleton. Everything will be all right."

Emerging from the shower, the new champ completely confuses Max when he offers him a job as his manager. After getting dressed Murdoch runs into Bette out in the hallway. She's there looking for Max. They talk until the lights go out. He comforts her, and when the lights come back on, she recognizes that look Joe told her about in this stranger's eyes and accepts his invitation out.

As they walk out, Jordan looks on with a smile and salutes them: "So long, champ."

INSTANT REPLAY Originating from Harry Segall's play *Heaven Can Wait,* the Oscar-winning scripters for *Here Comes Mr. Jordan,* Seton Miller and Sidney Buchman, provide some brilliant twists and turns in their clever adaptation, laying a solid foundation for Alexander Hall to direct from.

Hall, in an Oscar-nominated effort, keeps the story hopping, brushing some serious tones into this comical fantasy rather than reducing it to a slapstick farce. It's a tough job made easier by the fine screenplay, Joseph Walker's cinematography, and a talented cast.

In an Oscar-nominated lead performance, Robert Montgomery uses his experience in the fantastic and simply strange (*The Earl of Chicago, Rage in Heaven, Night Must Fall*)

and goes in a different direction, showing some good comedic timing in an engaging characterization.

Over and above the metaphysical journey elements of *Outward Bound* and the humorous vein of the supernatural *Topper* (featuring Cary Grant) both present in this picture, Montgomery gives this inventive twist on the afterlife a very human base. His character's understandable bewilderment at suddenly becoming a lost soul is believable in one of the more unbelievable movies out there.

Claude Rains's subtle, wise, and compassionate performance is delivered with the right level of restraint, patiently explaining the heavenly mysteries to Montgomery without pulling a holier-than-thou attitude.

James Gleason's Oscar-nominated performance as the perplexed boxing manager is colorfully handled, providing some memorable scenes. Edward Horton's bumbling but far from humble rookie escort brings some fine celestial mirth to the proceedings as well.

Evelyn Keyes plays the unusual romantic lead with charm and grace, somehow knowing who her man is regardless of which body he's using.

Producer Everett Riskin's experience in producing romantic and screwball comedies like *Holiday* with Katherine Hepburn, *The Awful Truth* with Cary Grant, and *Theodora Goes Wild* with Irene Dunne pays off in this charming romantic fantasy about the strange operations of the hereafter. *Here Comes Mr. Jordan* is smart, funny, different, and enjoyable.

OUTSIDE THE LINES The film was remade as *Heaven Can Wait,* starring Warren Beatty as a football player, in 1978.... Some characters returned in a 1947 sequel, *Down to Earth,* that featured Rita Hayworth.... The title *Down to Earth* was used for a second remake of *Here Comes Mr. Jordan* in 2001, starring Chris Rock.... Robert Montgomery's actress daughter Elizabeth was best known as the star of the long-running TV series *Bewitched....* Harry Segall won an Oscar for Best Writing, Original Story.... Immediately following the film Montgomery enlisted in the navy.... Sidney Buchman wrote the college football film *Saturday's Hero* (1951).... His career was stalled that same year as he refused to name names to the House Un-American Activities Committee and was blacklisted until the early '60s when he went to work in Europe.... Seton Miller cowrote the James Cagney auto racing picture *The Crowd Roars* (1932) as well as boxing's *Kid Galahad* (1937).... James Gleason starred in the college football film *The Big Game* (1936).... Joseph Walker was the cinematographer for the horse racing feature *Broadway Bill* (1934).... Reportedly the original was purchased as a vehicle for Cary Grant, who joined Gleason, Rains and Keyes in a 1942 radio theater broadcast of the film.

ALL-STAR MOMENTS As Joe and Bette sweet-talk each other, the heavenly messenger (Horton) stands by and mutters, "How long does this drivel go on?"

Joe tries to explain to Max that he is now millionaire industrialist Bruce Farnsworth. He's only successful in convincing his old trainer after he reveals some inside info that only Joe could know and then plays the saxophone.

HOME COURT ADVANTAGE Available on VHS.

Screenwriter Hank Steinberg. **Director** Billy Crystal. **Producers** Robert Colesberry, Billy Crystal, Ross Greenburg. **Cinematography** Haskell Wexler. **Editing** Michael Jablow. **Casting** Mali Finn. **Visual Effects Supervisor** Mitchell Drain. **Production Design** Rusty Smith. **Music** Marc Shaiman. **Technical Advisor** Paul Gallo. HBO. 2001.

THE PLAYERS Barry Pepper **Roger Maris**; Thomas Jane **Mickey Mantle**; Richard Masur **Milt Kahn**; Jennifer Crystal Foley **Pat Maris (1961)**; Donald Moffat **Ford Frick**; Bruce McGill **Ralph Houk**; Chris Bauer **Bob Cerv**; Peter Jacobson **Artie Green**; Chris McDonald **Mel Allen**; Joe Grifasi **Phil Rizzuto**; Renee Taylor **Claire Ruth**; Anthony Michael Hall **Whitey Ford**; Pat Crowley **Pat Maris (1998)**; Bob Gunton **Dan Topping**; Bobby Hosea **Elston Howard**; Seymour Cassell **Sam Simon**; Todd Bacile **Heckling fan**; Michael Nouri **Joe DiMaggio**.

THE GAME   "This is a fantastic story, fellas. Two great Yankees playing in the 'House That Ruth Built,' both going for his record. It's great for baseball," states sportswriter Milt Kahn (Richard Masur) to a group of his peers in *61**.

In the 1961 season teammates Roger Maris and Mickey Mantle battle each other for the hallowed single-season home run record of 60 set by Babe Ruth in 1927: two titans in Yankee uniforms looking to eclipse the mark of another legend who wore pinstripes. Mantle has come up through the Yankee organization and, despite being saddled with the impossible expectation that he will be the next Joe DiMaggio (much to the disdain of Joltin' Joe), is a Yankee hero. Maris, on the other hand, is a newcomer, an outsider to the fanatic Bronx fans, having joined the team the season before last through a trade with the Kansas City Athletics.

For some reason these two sluggers seem to bring out the best in each other. In the previous season, Mantle edged Maris out for the American League Home Run title (40-39) but Maris won the AL Most Valuable Player honor. As the spring of '61 turns into a hot summer, the M&M Boys are slamming homers at a sizzling pace. Ruth's record has withstood all challenges for over three decades, but this two-man slugfest is going at such a phenomenal rate that the Bambino's mark is in real danger. The Yankee teammates' home run derby duel garners national attention. Playing in the media capital, with its many competing local newspapers, magnifies the spotlight on them even more.

Against the backdrop of Mantle and Maris's pursuit of Ruth's record, *61** is really about celebrity and how two opposite personalities handled it and each other.

Both Mantle and Maris are small-town country boys. Mickey comes from a mining family in Oklahoma while Roger hails from North Dakota.

Mantle (Thomas Jane), with his matinee-idol looks, ready quips, and shrewd country grin, finesses the press corps and becomes a media darling, brushing over his character flaws. His private life is driven by his firm belief that because many men in his family died before reaching middle age, he is going to live like there is no tomorrow. (In real life, this assumption drove his destructive behavior, fueling a self-fulfilling prophecy.) Mantle's world is dominated by extramarital sex, booze, and painkillers.

Roger Maris (Barry Pepper) is introverted, blunt, private, and non-colorful—in short, ill suited for the fast pace and glitter of New York. A hardworking, dedicated family man, Maris refuses to change his modest, somewhat stoic personality to appease his critics. As a result, with his sweet swing propelling him to baseball immortality, Maris's mood turns sour as the pressures of the press and fans' expectations began weighing heavily on his shoulders. Unwilling and unable to play the media game, Maris is cut no slack by a predatory media.

The sports fans of New York can be shameless, as Mantle himself learned when he first came up and didn't meet their unreal expectations of him. The press fertilizes the seeds of the fans' dislike of Maris by luring the inarticulate slugger and twisting his locker room quotes into misleading banner headlines that paint him as a villain and imply that his home run chase with Mantle is a personal war.

In one telling scene Maris is jumped on by the press in the locker room after a game. They come at him from all angles, questioning his focus and team spirit and asking him why a poll says 80% of the fans prefer Mickey over him.

> MARIS: I don't know. Maybe I'm not a New York kind of guy. I'm just some dumb
> redneck from North Dakota.

> SAM (REPORTER): Is that how you think fans think of you?

> MARIS: Shit, I don't know how they see me.

As Maris turns away to seek the solitude of the trainers' room he storms past his manager, Ralph Houk (Bruce McGill), pleading for some help. When Houk turns to writer Kahn to ask what was going on, Kahn explains, "Those [reporters] are a bunch of wild dogs," and walks off, disgusted at the attack by his fellow sportswriters.

The next day's headlines read "80% Pick Mick. Maris Sulks." Accompanying photos make Maris look bitter.

As the race heats up even more, the fans go from ambivalence to open antagonism, subjecting Roger to unwarranted boos, cruel heckling, and even death threats. There are scenes where Maris gets the shakes from reading a death threat, chain smokes, gets a strange rash, and begins losing his hair in clumps, all due to stress. Now everything Maris says or does is twisted by the media to portray the outsider as an ungrateful Yankee to the Bronx faithful. Even the one writer (Kahn) who more or less supported him begins to turn after Maris stands him up on an exclusive interview.

The fans, who once booed Mantle for not being the baseball deity they had expected, now began to cheer the Mick and turn on Maris. This is best exemplified in one particular game at Yankee Stadium when Maris is loudly booed after hitting a home run at his own home field, followed by a standing ovation for Mantle merely walking to the plate.

In the press box two reporters are aware of the strange moment.

> ARTY: Can you believe this? They're booing him in his own ballpark!

> MILT: Yeah. I wonder why, Arty [referring to Arty's multiple nasty columns on
> Maris].

Teammates see what is going on and are ashamed of their fans, who are on their feet and cheering so loud for Mickey, who is merely standing at the plate, that the umpire has to call time out.

> ARTY: I've never seen him get a hand like this before.

> MILT: He's never been the underdog before.

One TV reporter says the two players are feuding like Ruth and Gehrig once did, and

Barry Pepper as Roger Maris (left) and Thomas Jane as Mickey Mantle (right).

are not on speaking terms. Watching a TV reporter talking about their "battles," Mantle turns to Roger and asks, "Are we feuding?"

ROGER: Yeah I guess so, it's on TV.

MICK: Fuck you, then.

ROGER: Up yours.

They laugh it off.

As different as they are, these two competitors and teammates become friends, using their opposing lifestyles to help pull each other through the season, sharing the loneliness of long-distance swingers.

Mantle is a carousing, somewhat reckless person but also kind and straightforward, an aspect of his persona that leads to a strong bond with Maris. Maris works hard at reeling in Mick's wild living. He achieves some limited success by having Mick move into the Queens apartment he shares with teammate Bob Cerv (Chris Bauer) and laying down some tight ground rules. On the flip side Mick attempts to help Roger with his media troubles by explaining some of his own hard lessons learned from his early days, but Maris stubbornly will not change.

Reaching the late innings of the season, Mantle, hobbled by a hip injury and an addiction to the high life, becomes a spectator, finishing with 54 home runs in 153 games. He'll root for his roommate from a hospital bed. Roger is now all alone in facing the unprecedented media blitz.

Maris now becomes even more sullen and recalcitrant toward the press and fans as he chases not only the record but the ghost of the Babe and its defenders.

Babe Ruth's widow (Renee Taylor) and Commissioner Ford Frick (Donald Moffat), a former ghostwriter for Ruth, aren't very good at concealing their wishes that Ruth's record not be broken. Sitting in the stands during a game with Roger's wife, Pat (Jen-

TOP: Before he'd even allow the actor to hold a bat, former Boston Red Sox star Reggie Smith had Jane swing a samurai sword while balancing on a piece of wood. Recalls Jane, "Reggie could tell by the sound that the blade made in the air whether or not my swing was in line."

MIDDLE: Barry Pepper was nominated for an Emmy for playing Roger Maris.

BOTTOM: '61" won a well-deserved Emmy for Outstanding Casting (Mali Finn).

nifer Crystal Foley), and a Yankee PR official, Mrs. Ruth candidly tells them that the Babe loved his record and wouldn't have been at all happy to see it broken.

At his wits' end, Maris, comforted by his wife who accompanies him during the final games, steels himself for one last push. But even on the eve of his record-breaking performance, Roger, who can't understand why the fans only have room for one hero, tells Pat, "I want to do it. It may not count to everybody else, but I'll know. I'm going to hit that home run."

He does but the historic shot rings somewhat hollow. Commissioner Frick uses his authority to come up with a demeaning asterisk to be affixed to Maris's HR number 61 in the record book, since Maris had eight more games to play than Ruth did. (The asterisk was removed 30 years later by Commissioner Fay Vincent. Unfortunately, it was too late for Roger, who had died of cancer six years previously.)

The new home run king (*) upon visiting Mickey in the hospital sums it up when he tells his pal, "Greatest season of my life but wouldn't want to do it again."

INSTANT REPLAY *61** has been in the making since the day an eight-year-old walked into Yankee Stadium with his father and witnessed Mickey Mantle hit a tremendous home run. Many years later, that child, grown up and acting in a movie *City Slickers*, told his friends when riding horses at a dude ranch that the best day in his life was the first time his father took him to Yankee Stadium and he saw Mickey Mantle hit a home run.

Billy Crystal earns his directoral pinstripes by using the right blend of insider knowledge, talent, respect, and dedication in bringing this chapter of baseball history to the small screen. "This film is certainly no valentine to Mickey," states Crystal. "We showed all his faults that he'd overcome later in his life. I wouldn't have done it if I couldn't have told it this way. Otherwise the story wouldn't have the dynamics it does."[1]

The director was also the executive producer, and he put together a team that gave the film the bigger-budget look of a theatrical release. The sound and vision duo of Haskell Wexler and Robert Grieve, particularly with the baseball scenes, gives us wonderful pictures on the field of play. (Grieve's group won an Emmy for sound editing.) Wexler's cinematography combined with brilliant art direction from Denise Hudson and the production design of Rusty Smith converted Detroit's Tiger Stadium into the Yankee Stadium of 1961. From the old flannel uniforms to the monuments in the outfield to veteran Yankee public address announcer Bob Sheppard calling out the lineup, viewers are provided a sense of sitting inside the House That Ruth Built.

Musically, perhaps the best enhancement is the poignant Lyle Lovett tune, "Nobody Knows Me," that helped convey Maris's loneliness in the big city.

Steinberg's evocative teleplay provides an insightful look at the human frailties behind the intense glare of the spotlight. His script uses two reporters, Maris supporter Milt Kahn (Richard Masur) and pro-Mantle Artie Green (Peter Jacobsen), to propel the story forward, giving us the facts along the way.

While *61** features a solid supporting cast, undoubtedly Crystal's pivotal players are the lead performers. A major virtue of *61** is the physical resemblance of the two lead actors to their characters as well as their skill in capturing the sluggers' distinct personas. (Mali Finn won an Emmy for casting.)

Thomas Jane embodies the immense charisma of The Mick down to the Oklahoma drawl, playing Mantle with the right balance of affability, vulnerability, and courage to make it clear why the Yankee hero was so idolized.

If the M&M Boys were chasing the ghost of Babe Ruth, Barry Pepper is eerily plausible as the ghost of Roger Maris. With his buzz cut and moody expressions, his swing and his blunt talk, the Canadian-born actor is practically a clone of Maris. The understated seriousness in Pepper's portrayal really brings Roger's well-documented brittle psyche to the surface.

Pepper's role as Maris also has interesting parallels to his role as Pvt. Jackson in Steven Spielberg's World War II drama *Saving Private Ryan*, the film in which Crystal first noticed his resemblance to the Yankee slugger.

Both Maris and Jackson are characters of quiet, introspective, and focused intensity. Both are provocative and tragic characters, men of quiet dignity utilizing their special skills in extremely stressful situations, winning then ultimately losing. (Pepper was nominated for an Emmy as Maris.)

Jane and Pepper are potent, handling with ease the intertwining aspects of rivalry and camaraderie that the M&M Boys shared. Both characters are flawed heroes facing their own demons, and the filmmakers ably convey their battles to come to terms with them.

Bracketing the film with TV coverage of St. Louis Cardinal Mark McGwire's breaking of Roger's record in 1998 (since broken by San Francisco Giant Barry Bonds in 2001) also brings to mind how players of this era, like McGwire, Sosa, Jeter, and Bonds, would have reacted if they had found themselves in Maris's position when there were no ground rules for handling the media blitz. There was no precedent for Maris.

Though the press and to a lesser extent the fans are presented as the chief villains, the stubborn Maris did not help his own cause, more or less ignoring the advice from his friend Mantle about playing the media game.

With such an insider's perspective, a fan's love of the game, and a team of pinstriped consultants (Yogi Berra, Whitey Ford, the Maris and Mantle families), it's no surprise that Crystal delivers this saga right, scoring high on verisimilitude. He takes minimal creative license despite most of the audience knowing the outcome and provides a humanized peek at fame.

OUTSIDE THE LINES Billy Crystal played baseball while attending Marshall University.... Actors Thomas Jane and Barry Pepper, who hadn't played organized baseball, learned to hit at a baseball academy run by former Boston Red Sox all-star Reggie Smith.... In 1991 baseball commissioner Fay Vincent removed the asterisk and the record was Maris's alone.... Roger Maris died of cancer in 1985.... Actor Bruce McGill, who plays Yankees manager Ralph Houk, also portrayed flamboyant golfer Walter Hagen in Robert Redford's *The Legend of Bagger Vance* (2000) and a boxing promoter in *Cinderella Man* (2005).... Actor Richard Masur (sportswriter Milt Kahn) appeared in Ron Shelton's *Play It to the Bone* as a boxing promoter.... Crystal's comedic skills first came to the media's attention via his impressions of sports icons Howard Cosell and Muhammad Ali.... Crystal's daughter, Jennifer Crystal Foley, played Maris's wife, Pat.... Crystal directed and starred in *Forget Paris*, a romantic comedy about a professional basketball referee.... Crystal became good friends with his idol Mantle after both appeared on the *Dinah Shore Show* in 1977.... When Mantle died in 1995, Crystal cowrote the eulogy with sportscaster Bob Costas.... Former Los Angeles Dodgers pitcher Tom Candiotti portrayed Baltimore Orioles knuckleballer Hoyt Wilhelm.... More than 1,200 experienced ballplayers in Detroit and Los Angeles tried out to play

The film's director, Billy Crystal (right), took a considerable risk on Thomas Jane, as the actor had never played organized baseball.

the approximately 50 roles as teammates, coaches, and opponents.... Crystal is part owner of the Arizona Diamondbacks.... Mantle and Maris starred as themselves in a youth baseball movie *Safe at Home* in 1962.

ALL-STAR MOMENTS Mantle addressing the press: "That's just great, one guy's got me all washed up, the other's got me beatin' Ruth's record. You guys should get together and make up your minds and tell me how I am so I know how to play."

Mark McGwire hitting a long fly ball that dissolves into a time warp of Roger Maris catching a fly ball in Yankee Stadium, taking us back to the 1961 season.

Telling Mantle that he hit home runs the last few times he ate them, Maris dishes up an ugly, greasy, gray scrambled egg concoction. When teammate and roommate Bob Cerv inquires how he likes them, Mantle says, "They're shit but I'm in a bit of a slump so I'll try anything." Cut to a montage of a Mantle and Maris home run binge followed by a shot of Cerv now trying the eggs.

POST-GAME COMMENTS Billy Crystal on his empathy for Roger Maris and what he went through in what should have been the slugger's finest hour:

> Maris was an honest, hardworking family man who didn't have a lot to say in the media frenzy that was New York, so the press turned on him and Roger became surly and moody. That's how he was depicted and the pressure drove him crazy. The tragedy of Roger Maris was that he couldn't enjoy his march into history.[2]

Actor Thomas Jane, who portrayed Mickey Mantle, on his lack of experience in the sport and how a former all-star trained him for the role:

I didn't have any baseball background. Reggie Smith helped me with every aspect of the game. Plain and simple, Reggie taught me how to play the game.

We didn't have very much time. Reggie did what he had to do. He had me swinging a samurai sword balancing on a two-by-four before I was even allowed to hold a bat. Reggie could tell by the sound that the blade made in the air whether or not my swing was in line.

Some of my favorite times were playing catch with Reggie Smith. The dew was still on the grass. I'd show up in the morning and I wouldn't go home until late in the afternoon when the sun was going down.

It was a great time, a great way to feel your way into the game. Spending all day on the ball field with a great master like Reggie Smith—it was the time of my life.[3]

Jane, on what he learned after studying everything he could about his character:

Mickey Mantle was one of the greatest natural athletes of all time.

It seemed like he never had to work at it. He could play a double header hung over and still knock 'em out of the park. He could play with one arm. He hit the famous one-armed home run. He was one of the fastest guys ever to play the game before he blew his knee out.

To see so much talent tied up into one man and at the same time so much self-destruction—it was a great character. I just fell in love with the man.[4]

Ross Greenburg, executive producer and president of HBO Sports.

The best films get some kind of reaction out of you. When you shed a tear, you know you've seen a good film. We felt we did that with 61*.[5]

Crystal on how much *61** meant to him:

This has come to be the most personal thing I've ever been associated with. I don't think I've loved anything the way I loved doing this movie.[6]

HOME COURT ADVANTAGE Available on VHS and DVD. HBO released it individually, with *Do You Believe in Miracles? The Story of the 1980 U.S. Hockey Team*, and with *Babe Ruth*.

#36 MIRACLE

Screenwriter Eric Guggenheim. **Director** Gavin O'Connor. **Producers** Mark Ciardi, Gordon Gray, Justis Greene, Ross Greenburg. **Cinematography** Daniel Stoloff. **Editing** John Gilroy. **Music** Mark Isham. **Production Designer** John Willett. **Costume Designer** Tom Bronson. Disney. 2004.

THE PLAYERS
Kurt Russell **Herb Brooks**; Patricia Clarkson **Patty Brooks**; Noah Emmerich **Craig Patrick**; Sean McCann **Walter Bush**; Kenneth Welsh **Doc Nagobads**; Eddie Cahill **Jim Craig**; Patrick Demsey **Mike Eruzione**; Michael Mantenuto **Jack O'Callahan**; Nathan West **Rob McClanahan**; Kenneth Mitchell **Ralph Cox**; Eric Peter-Kaiser **Mark Johnson**; Bobby Hanson **David Silk**; Joseph Cure **Mike Ramsey**; Billy Schneider **Buzz Schneider**; Nate Miller **John Harrington**; Chris Koch **Mark Pavelich**; Kris Wilson **Phil Verchota**; Steve Kovalcik **Dave Christian**; Sam Skoryna **Steve Janaszak**; Pete Duffy **Bob Suter**; Nick Postle **Bill Baker**; Casey Burnette **Ken Morrow**; Scott Johnson **Steve Christoff**; Trevor Alto **Neal Broten**; Robbie MacGregor **Eric Strobel**; Joe Hemsworth **Mark Wells**; Adam Knight **Tim Harrer**; Sarah Anne Hepher **Kelly Brooks**; Evan Smith **Danny Brooks**; Bill Mondy **Lou Nanne**; Tom Butler **Bob Allen**; Don Davis **Bob Fleming**; Malcolm Stewart **Donald Craig**

THE GAME Heading into the 1980s, America was, according to President Carter, having a "crisis of confidence." Our national psyche was at a low ebb: the hostage crisis in Iran, long gas lines, high interest rates and unemployment...and a heated political battle with the Soviet Union would result in a boycott of the Summer Olympics. Our nation was looking for hope and inspiration. It would come from an unlikely source.

Miracle is the story of the 1980 U.S. ice hockey team and its amazing defeat of the greatest team ever, the Soviet Union, on their way to an unforgettable gold medal. It is the process of how they were brought together and worked through their differences to become champions largely thanks to the drive and dedication of an unconventional and uncompromising coach, Herb Brooks (Kurt Russell).

Brooks, who won three NCAA championships as coach at the University of Minnesota, has a personal heartache from his own playing career. He was the last person cut from the 1960 U.S. hockey team, the last team to defeat the Soviets in the Olympics for the gold medal.

Addressing national hockey federation executives as they strategize for their Olympic program, Brooks stuns them when he explains that the only way to defeat the hockey powers of the Eastern Bloc is to change the traditional American training methods and playing style.

Brooks tells them he'd install a hybrid of Canadian and Soviet methods emphasizing the highest level of team speed, conditioning, and most of all, team chemistry.

Coach stresses the importance of the latter: "All-star teams fail because they rely solely on the individual's talent. The Soviets win because they take that talent and use it inside a system that's designed for the betterment of the team. My goal is to beat them at their own game."

Soon Brooks receives a call that he's got he job.

With the help of assistant coach Craig Patrick (Noah Emmerich), Coach Brooks conducts tryouts and assembles a team primarily from the hockey hotbeds of Boston and Minnesota and without input from the hockey federation. This is going to be his team, win or lose.

The unspoken rivalry, conflicting styles, and regional pride of the players creates an immediate challenge for Brooks.

The following months of training are arduous, full of conflict and disappointing exhibition play. However, by force of will and his acceptance of the players' wrath, Coach Brooks slowly brings the team together. The values he talked about in his job interview are showing up, no small feat when teaching young men a new style of play under enormous time pressures and a skeptical management.

Even after a crushing loss to the Soviets in an exhibition game just a few days before the Olympics, Coach Brooks calmly tells the press, "I think we're going to be all right." After lighting a fire under his goalie, Jim Craig (Eddie Cahill), and getting key player Jack O'Callahan (Michael Mantenuto) back from injury, Brooks's team jells as a unit.

They open Olympic competition in Lake Placid, New York with a satisfactory tie against powerful Sweden, then demolish the second best team in the world, the Czechs, 7-3. Wins follow over Norway, Romania, and West Germany.

Now comes the pivotal game against the squad that embarrassed them only a few days ago, the Soviet Union.

As the players get ready to head to the ice, Coach Brooks addresses his squad in the locker room:

> Great moments are born from great opportunity. And that's what you have here tonight, boys. That's what you earned here tonight. One game. If we played them 10 times they might win 9. But not this game. Not tonight. Tonight we skate with them. Tonight we stay with them. And we shut them down because we can!
>
> Tonight we are the greatest hockey team in the world. You were born to be hockey players, every one of you.
>
> You were meant to be here tonight. This is your time. Their time is done. It's over. I'm sick and tired of hearing about what a great hockey team the Soviets have. Screw 'em. This is your time. Now go out and take it.

Inspired by the coach's impassioned declaration, the American squad, barely averaging 21 years of age, takes the game to the mighty Soviets, many of whom have played together for 15 years!

It's a tough physical battle, with the Soviets holding a 3-2 edge heading into the final period. The Americans hang tough and with goals by Mark Johnson (Eric Kaiser) and Mike Eruzione (Patrick Demsey) take the lead 4-3 with 10 minutes left.

The final 10 minutes feel like an eternity, especially for goalie Jim Craig, but his brilliant play supported by still energetic teammates holds off the world's greatest team to earn an upset victory for the ages.

The momentum from the historic win carries over into the Americans' gold medal match to defeat Finland for the Olympic title.

This group of unheralded young men, forged under a brilliant and dedicated coach, lifts the spirits of an entire nation with their inspiring team effort.

INSTANT REPLAY *Miracle,* while a true team sports Cinderella story, is really about a man's dream achieved by molding the talents of young men for one specific goal.

The filmmakers explore an original coach, one with a philosophical bent to his ideas, strategies, and methods.

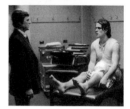

TOP: Told at every turn that his band of collegiate players has no chance against the mighty Soviet team, tough and visionary coach Herb Brooks (Kurt Russell) leads his underdog squad to a historic gold medal run.

MIDDLE: From college to the Olympics, new national teammates Mike Eruzione (Patrick Demsey, left) and Rob McClanahan (Nathan West, right).

BOTTOM: Coach Brooks (Russell) tests the toughness of Jack O'Callahan (Michael Mantenuto, right).

Seemingly writers Eric Guggenheim and Mike Rich, along with director Gavin O'Connor, have given little backstory to flesh out those players. I feel this was done intentionally to serve two purposes: it helps convey coach Brooks's "no 'I' in 'team' " philosophy and of course results in putting the story's focus on the coach himself. The team players remain just that.

As this is a story about Herb Brooks, the picture really lives or dies based on the performance of that lead character. And Kurt Russell, whose career has spanned over four decades, delivers some of his finest work here.

From the physical mimicry of the paunch, bad hair, steady gum-chewing, lefty writing, and clipped Minnesota accent to the stone-wall face behind which lies a reservoir of intensity, drive, creativity, and also a certain self-induced loneliness, Russell gives a complete characterization, full of nuances and intricacies, of a complex man.

While Russell nailed the persona of a coach in a performance that exceeds even Pat O'Brien's terrific turn as Knute Rockne, where the former minor league baseball player takes sports cinema to a new level is in the exploration of the mental side of coaching.

Like the great coaches, including Bill Parcells, Scotty Bowman, and Red Auerbach, Russell expertly demonstrates Brooks's gifts as a master psychologist, able to use any number of mind manipulations to wring the best out of his players' talents.

The writers provide some terrific material that show this psychology at work with just one coaching gem after another:

> "I'm not looking for the best players, Craig, I'm looking for the right ones."

> "When you pull on that jersey you represent yourself and your teammates. And the name on the front [USA] is a helluva lot more important than the name on the back."

> "You want to make this team? You better play at a better level that's gonna force me to keep you here."

TOP: Jack O'Callahan (Mantenuto, left), Buzz Schneider (Billy Schneider, center) and Mark Pavelich (Chris Koch, right) chase down the puck.

RIGHT: "Do you believe in miracles?" ...."Yes!"

But Russell not only convincingly expresses Coach Brooks's alternating tough love and compassionate motivational powers with his stirring speeches and acidic wit; the actor also gets inside the man with his ability to express so much without words, such as in the telling scene where, at his moment of greatest professional joy, he escapes to the bowels of the arena for a moment of private exultation after the win over the Soviets.

While Russell shows a complete internalization of his character, the few other professionals in the cast perform capably. Noah Emmerich is convincing as assistant coach Craig Patrick, the good cop loyal to Coach Brooks yet understanding of his sometimes difficult treatment of the players. Patricia Clarkson as the ignored wife manages to inject her usual intelligence and the subtle expressiveness she's displayed in limited roles before, including the football saga *Everybody's All-American*.

In the story's ties to the sociopolitical world stage, *Miracle* resembles *Seabiscuit*. Both are about a dramatic underdog victory that rejuvenates a nation at a down time when it really needed it. It's not a stretch to compare the mighty Soviet hockey team to War Admiral, but in the end, while it's difficult to measure, most records and accounts indicate that Seabiscuit actually had a greater impact on the country, if only because horse racing in the late 1930s had a much broader appeal than hockey did in 1980—and high interest rates and gas lines pale in comparison with the sheer economic disaster of the Great Depression. Still, both were undeniably truly inspirational sport events.

The re-creation of the hockey event gave the filmmakers their greatest technical challenge, especially since it's such a well-chronicled story with most knowing the outcome. This is where director O'Connor knew that having hockey players who could act was a better choice than teaching actors to play hockey.

Starting with the exceedingly difficult task of creating over 100 plays, securing equipment from that era, and getting the modern players to look natural with the dated gear, much credit for the verisimilitude goes to sports wranglers Mark Ellis and his partner, Rob Miller.

Together with the foundation laid down by Ellis and Miller, O'Connor's director of photography Daniel Stoloff and editor John Gilroy accomplish the near impossible, not only building suspense in a game whose results are already well known but achieving such veracity that viewers feel they're out on the ice as eyewitnesses to the speed, physicality, and power of the sport.

Add in the fairly seamless and energetic re-broadcast work of Al Michaels, who called the original game, and the result is one of the more believable and satisfying "climactic big game" formula finishes on record.

If the devil is in the details, producers Mark Ciardi and Gordon Gray have created one helluva movie, not only in O'Connor's realistic staging of the game with his savvy use of real players, but most of all in the real and truthful embodiment by Kurt Russell of an unconventional yet masterful coach.

OUTSIDE THE LINES Herb Brooks was the last player cut from the 1960 gold-medal-winning U.S. Olympic hockey team.... Bill Ranford (Edmonton Oilers) was a stand-in for the Craig Patrick goalie role.... The more than 100 intricate plays were devised by director O'Connor, cinematographer Danny Stoloff, Mark Ellis and Rob Miller of Reel Sports Solutions, who also played a lead role in casting the players and running the training camp in Vancouver.... They supervised the North American tryouts,

TOP: Coach Brooks with wife Patti (Patricia Clarkson).

BOTTOM: Goalie Jim Craig (Eddie Cahill), the heart of America's stunning victory.

where 4,000 applicants vied for 21 player roles.... An additional 1,500 hockey players applied for the 65 slots to fill the Soviet and European slots in Vancouver.... At one point Michael Douglas was interested in the Brooks role.... Coach Brooks led the University of Minnesota to three NCAA titles.... Billy Schneider portrays his father, Buzz, a key player on the U.S. team.... Mayhem Pictures' Mark Ciardi and Gordon Gray also produced baseball's *The Rookie* (2002) and football's *Invincible* (2006).... Actor Kurt Russell's son, Wyatt, is a promising goalie playing in the Vancouver area.... Game action was filmed at the Agridome adjacent to the old arena where the Vancouver Canucks used to play .... Producer Ciardi was a former major league pitcher for the Milwaukee Brewers.... Russell spent several months learning to write left-handed to portray Brooks more accurately.... NHL veteran Ryan Walter served as a technical advisor.... Several former NHL players were cast for critical roles as part of the Soviet team: Mike MacWilliam (NY Rangers), Sasha Lakovic (NJ Devils), Todd Harkins (NY Islanders).... Randy Heath (NY Rangers) played for the Swedish team.... Attorney Roger Watts, a Vladislav Tretiak expert, put his law practice on hold for several months to play the esteemed Soviet goalie.... Russell's baseball skills took him to AA level in the Angels farm system until a shoulder injury ended his baseball career.... Cameraman Scotty Waugh captured some of the game action by skating along with the players on the ice using a "pogo cam."...Sound designer Rob Nokes was able to provide the distinct noise differences not only between the different types of ice but also between the different blades used by Americans, Soviets, and Europeans.... The same subject was covered in a 1981 made-for-TV movie, *Miracle on Ice*.... It starred Karl Malden as Coach Brooks.... The U.S. team defeated Finland 4-3 in the gold medal game to complete the "miracle."

ALL-STAR MOMENTS In a pre-Olympic tune-up game against Norway, Coach Brooks (Russell) expresses his displeasure with his team's performance: "You guys don't want to work during the game? No problem. We'll work now." And as the fans file out Brooks has then run line drills time after time, telling them, "Think you can win on talent alone? Gentleman, you don't have enough talent to win on talent alone."

Later he adds, "Each and every one of you, when you pull on that jersey you represent yourself and your teammates. And the name on the front is a helluva lot more important than the one on the back! Get that through your head." And orders them to run more drills.

In between periods in the Olympic game against Sweden a disappointed Coach Brooks addresses his team in the locker room: "This is unbelievable. You guys are playing like this is some kind of throwaway game in Rochester." He calls one of his players a quitter, which riles up the team as intended, and they manage a crucial tie.

In his pre-game talk before the game against the Soviets, Coach Brooks addresses his players: "...Tonight *we* are the greatest hockey team in the world.... You were meant to be here tonight. This is your time. It's over. I'm sick and tired of hearing about what a great hockey team the Soviets have. Screw 'em. This is *your* time. Now go out and take it." Coach walks out. U.S. goes on to win 4-3.

POST-GAME COMMENTS Director Gavin O'Connor on his decision to cast talented hockey players who had the potential to be taught acting rather than the other way around:

I guess ignorance is bliss. People thought I was nuts but that was my easiest decision. My feeling is, "Can I get actors to play at the level that I needed them to play, which was Olympic caliber—which is impossible—or do I get kids who can play the sport at that level, have a physical resemblance to the players, are from the same region as the players with the local dialect, can shoot righty or lefty like the real player, and then teach them how to *not* act?"[1]

Coproducer Gordon Gray on the team's impact beyond the sports pages:

It is important to understand the political and social environment in our nation a quarter-century ago. The Iran hostage crisis, the gas lines, President Carter's "crisis of confidence" speech and the Russians in Afghanistan. We were down on ourselves and looking for a spark. In many ways it was a genesis of a rebirth of our nation to start feeling good about ourselves.[2]

Coproducer Mark Ciardi on the game sequences:

It is a monumental task in recreating the game and breaking down the plays like they unfolded in the game. How much do you want to show? One of the critical factors is making the audience feel like they're inside the action. We used a unique camera that was hand held, braced on mounts, as the operator skates around getting inside the action. It's never been filmed like this before, getting that drama out on the ice.[3]

Hockey coordinator Mark Ellis talks about his challenges to capture plays exactly as people remember them on national television on that unforgettable day the U.S. beat Russia:

You've got a guy going 35 miles per hour—as fast as he can—in between two or three cameras on ice, trying to make sure he gets a pass coming from more than 30 yards away that lands right on his stick, controls the puck, and then puts the puck in just the right place in the goal—and make sure the goalie misses it with his glove by a hair. And get it all done in three takes. It's one of the toughest things I've ever done. If we didn't get those goals right, we might as well have packed it up and gone home. We had to make it real: we had to make it feel for the audience like it felt when it happened 24 years ago.[4]

Rob Miller, Ellis's partner, points out there were a lot of details off the ice as well they had to get right:

Miracle was a historical project that everyone knows, making it even more important to be accurate and detailed as possible. We broke down the action of what really happened just like a coach does. And we drew up playbooks from that. Compiling all the stats from all the participants. Even the players' shooting tendencies, what the players were doing before they made the Olympic team and 20 years after the games.[5]

HOME COURT ADVANTAGE Available on VHS and DVD.

#35 WHEN WE WERE KINGS

Director Leon Gast. **Producers** Leon Gast, David Sonnenberg, Taylor Hackford. **Coproducers** Keith Robinson, Vikram Jayanti. **Cinematography** Albert Maysles, Kevin Keating, Paul Goldsmoth, Rod Young, Maryse Alberti. **Editing** Leon Gast, Taylor Hackford, Jeff Levy-Hinte, Keith Robinson. Gramercy. 1996.

THE GAME Emerging from over two decades of legal and financial hurdles, filmmaker Leon Gast's documentary centers on the 1974 heavyweight title fight between imposing champion George Foreman and Muhammad Ali, who at 32 has lost 3½ years of his prime in forced retirement for his refusal to be drafted by the American military to fight in Vietnam.

When We Were Kings ultimately is the story of Muhammad Ali's greatest performance, inside and out of the ring.

Forced to give up his crown, Ali seeks a then-record three-time heavyweight title. To do this Ali has to go through the younger, bigger, and stronger current champion who dispatched formidable foes Ken Norton and Joe Frazier much more savagely than Ali did when he fought them.

At the film's core is the story of how a former great champion works his underdog image to his advantage, garnering the popular support of the local citizenry.

In this case the locals are the oppressed populace of Zaire, an African police state run by President Mobutu Sese Seko. Promoter Don King gets the dictator to put up the millions for the event.

Gast captures the whole experience, which includes highlights from a music festival that featured performances by B. B. King and James Brown, but mostly his camera focuses on Ali and his training and mingling with the people of Kinshasha. George Foreman really isn't featured prior to the fight outside of news conferences. However, a sequence showing him pounding the heavy bag is a good illustration of why journalists feared Ali could be in mortal danger.

The filmmakers present the fight and intercut the action in the ring with interviews of respected eyewitness journalists George Plimpton and Norman Mailer. Their observations about the real fear they saw in Ali and the fighter's unorthodox "rope a dope" strategy, along with Spike Lee's insightful comments about the overall impact of Ali who would defy the odds and go on to win the bout, really enhance the images we see.

INSTANT REPLAY *When We Were Kings* was conceived as a celebration of black pride: two black boxers in a heavyweight title fight promoted by a black entrepreneur, in conjunction with a music festival comprised of black performers from both Africa and America, financed by a black head of state from a black African nation.

Though an injury sustained by the reigning champion, George Foreman, delayed the title bout by several weeks, it was Muhammad Ali's sheer charisma that changed the direction of the documentary from an Afrocentric Woodstock (B. B. King and James Brown were the headliners) to a vibrant, electrifying monument to Ali's global appeal.

Delayed for 22 years because of legal and financial issues, *When We Were Kings* unintentionally creates a time capsule that proves Ali was a mesmerizing, born leader whose reach extended far beyond fight fans.

Muhammad Ali's physical grace and commitment to his social conscience, his disarming way with words and childlike playfulness drew hordes of non-boxing fans to his sport like no one has done before or since. Ali undoubtedly is one of the most important sociopolitical figures of his era, and this film exemplifies the reconnection of black America to Africa through the fighter's undeniable people-power.

Filmmaker Gast, with the help of producer Taylor Hackford, illustrates Ali's impact with insightful interviews from prominent writers Norman Mailer and George Plimpton as well as filmmaker Spike Lee.

Gast also demonstrates Ali's standard methodology of denigrating his opponent. Turning his real fear of Foreman into a popular cause, Ali won the hearts and souls of the citizens of Zaire, who rallied behind his David to bring down Foreman, the mighty Goliath. Entering the ring to the crowd's "Ali Bomaye!" the underdog fights the smartest and bravest bout of his life.

It must be noted that Foreman doesn't help his cause by arriving with his German shepherd, the very type of dog used by the Belgians to police the people of the Congo. The champ is also reticent to mingle with the locals, preferring to isolate himself in his living quarters while Ali does road work alongside the everyday people and spends time getting to know the Zairians up close and personal.

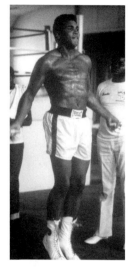

Muhammad Ali reaching peak fitness for the "Rumble in the Jungle."

Gast presents George Foreman as a dour champion with a sullen demeanor and bad attitude but at the same time an indomitable fighting machine whose proven power is underscored by the commentary of the sports media that are present, including Howard Cosell, who feels Ali may not survive the fight.

The flip side of Foreman's noticeable absence from the film is that it in effect creates a looming silence. It is almost as if this unseen mighty behemoth represents the shadow of death.

Ironically, *When We Were Kings* essentially has become a moment frozen in time, whereas the two warriors depicted in that moment have changed quite a bit since then. The haughty, thuggish slugger George Foreman would go on to become a plump, jovial, and wealthy TV pitchman. As for Muhammad Ali, we get a sense of his role as an African American leader in all his athletic glory compared to his current physical difficulties and the effects of Parkinson's disease.

The film is an excursion into history that would be largely forgotten now if it had been released in the '70s. Instead, it has become a valued and vivid document with the perspective that the distance of time affords.

Hired originally to cover the music festival, Gast deserves a lot of credit for his improvisational skills in focusing on the fighters. The fascinating development of how Africa took Ali to its heart ensures a highly memorable story.

Gast and Hackford create an exhilarating portrait of a unique man, but this paean to Muhammad Ali would have been more interesting if Foreman had come across as more than a mere adversary, especially given that he has undergone one of the most amazing transformations of a public persona in modern times.

Additionally, while we see Ali speaking with pride about the "blackness" of the whole event—from the airline pilots who flew him there to the music festival performers, to the fans that filled the stadium—we don't hear his views on the fact that this African-American celebration that filled the boxer's bank account was financed by a murderous despot.

Another small flaw in a fine documentary is the lack of time given to Spike Lee's insightful comments. The filmmaker's points seem cut off, yet his reflections are key in reaching across that generation gap for those who are too young to remember Ali in his prime.

When We Were Kings is so much more than a fight film and a benchmark in black history. It is also a symbol of the fleeting nature of athletic greatness, a moving record of a tremendous athlete, devout Muslim, and assertive role model whose agile mouth was often quicker than his stinging jabs but who would become muted by the ravages of Parkinson's disease. Still the film remains the definitive account of a point in time that propelled a brash, charismatic man into a legend that reached far beyond the sporting fields.

OUTSIDE THE LINES *When We Were Kings* was nominated for an Academy Award for Best Feature Documentary.... Ali stayed in a villa alongside the Congo river in a complex where visiting diplomats would stay.... The fight took place at 4:00 A.M. local time to accommodate pay TV theaters back in America.... Foreman was 40—0 with 37 knockouts before being beaten by Ali.... Some of the music clients of the film's producer David Sonnenberg include The Spin Doctors, Joan Osborne, Meat Loaf, and The Fugees.... This was Don King's first major promotion.... The music performers at this festival in Zaire included the Crusaders, Bill Withers, B. B. King, James Brown, and the Spinners.... The film won a documentary prize at the Sundance Film Festival.... Nearly 300,000 feet of film sat in Gast's apartment for a dozen years waiting for financing to complete the processing.... After the fight, Gast went to secure funding for the film's completion, but the company that backed him turned out to be essentially a one-man operation; that man, former Finance Minister of Liberia Stephen Talbot, would die in a plane crash.... Motion Picture Academy rules at the time allowed only two people to receive the documentary feature award, so when it went to Gast and Sonnenberg, Taylor Hackford filed for a rule change, feeling he had provided significant new material and had final cut.... The mortal fear Foreman inspired (and the media fueled) was so prevalent around the fight that Ali's doctors had a plane standing by at the Kinshasha airport ready to fly the fighter to a hospital in Madrid should that prove necessary.... Gast, who had made films about the Grateful Dead and Latin music, recalled approaching the promoters about directing the music festival and learning that David Wolper, Roman Polanski, and Motown's Barry Gordy had also put in bids to direct the movie.... Hackford won an Oscar for Best Live Action Short Subject for *Teenage Father* (1978).... He would direct the football saga *Everybody's All-American* (1988).... Thomas Hauser's book was the basis for the Oscar-winning film *Missing* (1982).... George Plimpton has written books about professional hockey, golf, and football.... Norman Mailer's *The Executioner's Song,* a TV movie he adapted from his book, won an Emmy for Tommy Lee Jones (1982).... Taylor Hackford was nominated for a Best Director Oscar for *Ray* (2005).

ALL-STAR MOMENTS Intercut statements of Howard Cosell saying that Ali isn't the same man he was 10 years ago, then Ali saying he spoke with Mrs. Cosell and she told him Howard isn't the same man he was 2 years ago.

Ali sitting outside explaining to a man and a woman how his winning punch against Sonny Liston was faster than a blink of an eye, joking that everyone at ringside missed it because they all blinked at the same time.

Classic Ali spewing words of disparagement about his opponent as he works out in the ring using the popular local chant "Ali, Bomaye!"

FACING PAGE: With his immense charm, Ali easily succeeded in garnering local support.

Muhammad Ali—-the champion once again.

As local natives play music and a witch doctor dances, writer George Plimpton talks about soothsayers and a witch doctor saying a woman with trembling hands "got to" Foreman.

The moments inside the ring before the opening bell and the ensuing action, followed by Mailer's description of what Ali was really thinking.

Plimpton recalls telling Mailer at ringside about Ali's "rope a dope" strategy as it unfolded; then the film cuts to the mysterious woman the witch doctor mentioned doing a dance over the image of the fight action.

Montage of Ali mingling with the local citizens, signing autographs, posing for pictures, and shaking hands.

Repeated shot of Ali during some roadwork takes on the camera, talking trash. The film freezes as Ali throws a punch and we can hear him say, "Sucker, you ain't got nothing."

POST-GAME COMMENTS Producer/editor Taylor Hackford on athletic greatness:

> Ali was 32 in Zaire. He should never have won that fight. Foreman was 25 and had annihilated Joe Frazier and Ken Norton. Foreman had dispensed with ease two great boxers who had taken Ali to the limit. In that instance it should've been someone who was over the hill as a physical specimen. Yet through his brain and his heart, only the greats like Ali, who paid the price for what he believed in, could come back in that fight, take the punishment, until he turned it around and delivered it out and beat a man who should have beat Ali to a pulp. That is heroism beyond belief, through mental discipline and huge, huge courage that represents that you can't ever count anyone out. If in fact your mental determination and courage is big enough you can overcome any odds. It is still about the tragedy of age but also the triumph of will and character, which is what I think is inherent in any great, great athlete.[1]

HOME COURT ADVANTAGE Available on DVD. DVD releases from both Polygram and Universal.

#34 A DAY AT THE RACES

Screenwriters Robert Pirosh, George Seaton, George Oppenheimer. **Director** Sam Wood. **Producers** Max Siegel, Sam Wood. **Cinematography** Joseph Ruttenberg. **Music** Walter Jurmann, Bronislau Kaper. **Editing** Frank Hull. **Art Direction** Cedric Gibbons. MGM. 1937.

THE PLAYERS Groucho Marx **Dr. Hugo Hackenbush**; Chico Marx **Tony**; Harpo Marx **Stuffy**; Allan Jones **Gil Stewart**; Maureen O'Sullivan **Judy Standish**; Margaret Dumont **Emily Upjohn**; Leonard Ceeley **Whitmore**; Douglass Dumbrille **Morgan**; Esther Muir **Flo Marlowe**; Sig Ruman **Dr. Leopold Steinberg**; Robert Middlemass **Sheriff**; Vivien Fay **Dancer**

THE GAME Judy Standish (Maureen O'Sullivan) is the owner of the Standish Sanitarium. Her business is in financial peril and on the brink of bankruptcy. She confides her problem to fiancé Gil Stewart (Allen Jones). Gil informs her that he has just purchased a racehorse, Hi Hat, with the last of their money. Judy's upset because Gil is gambling away their future on a long shot.

Waiting in the wings to steal the sanitarium at a bargain are the villainous Mr. Morgan (Douglas Dumbrille) and his conspirator, Whitmore (Leonard Creeley). Morgan, owner of the local racetrack and hotel, aims to convert Judy's business into a casino.

The one person who could keep the sanitarium afloat is wealthy resident hypochondriac Emily Upjohn (Margaret Dumont). Dissatisfied with the medical service, she threatens to leave the sanitarium, saying, "I'm going to someone who understands me. I'm going to Dr. Hackenbush .... Why, I didn't know there was a thing the matter with me until I met him!" Tony (Chico Marx), a good friend of Judy's, wires Dr. Hackenbush (Groucho Marx). The horse doctor leaves his veterinary practice to come run the sanitarium. This buys Judy some time.

Despite Dr. Hackenbush's romantic sway with Emily, the financial survival of Judy's sanitarium comes down to Gil's horse winning the big race. Hi Hat and his jockey, Stuffy (Harpo Marx), overcome Morgan's efforts to prevent them from entering the race and barely make the starting gate.

Though Stuffy doesn't win with Hi Hat, it is discovered that Hi Hat and Morgan's horse, Small Wonder, were switched when they were upset in one of the jumps. Morgan's jockey actually rode Hi Hat to victory!

The earnings from the win help save the sanitarium.

INSTANT REPLAY *A Day at the Races* was the Marx Brothers' follow-up to their brilliant *A Night at the Opera*.

Like the best of the Three Stooges shorts, the Marx Brothers shine brightest in high society, surrounded by formal, stuffy characters.

Here the comedy troupe employs its success formula of fresh and original zany gags bridged by musical interludes. While Chico's piano talents and Harpo's harp skills are on full display, the extended musical numbers by Allan Jones and Ivie Anderson and the Crinoline Choir really work against the tempo of the madcap situations and outrageous routines that show the trio at the top of their comedic game. During that era it was not unusual for studios to incorporate lavish musical productions to help distract moviegoers from the economic woes of the Great Depression. Overall, however,

the musical scenes really do a disservice to the rhythm of the comedy. Fortunately, the vaudevillian comedy routines like the medical exam, the "tootsie-frootsie" ice cream/code book, and the wallpapering of people are enough to overcome the uninspired, overlong musical numbers that drag down the pace.

One musical interlude does stand out if only for the great energy presented by the black artists performing in it, led by Harpo as a sort of Pied Piper. It must be remembered that it was very difficult for African-Americans to get regular work in mainstream cinema then, and these performers are terrific.

Outside of the musical numbers, director Sam Wood integrates the romantic subplot well and moves smoothly between the sanitarium and the racetrack.

The horse racing sequences are capably presented and provide some of the film's most memorable scenes, including the Marx Brothers evading the police as they succeed in delaying the race by diverting patrons looking for parking spots onto the track.

All things considered, *A Day at the Races* succeeds because the eccentric and masterful mirthmaking in it represents some of the Marx Brothers' best work.

OUTSIDE THE LINES Legendary producer Irving Thalberg died, at age 37, before this production was completed.... His brother-in-law, Lawrence Weingarten, took over producing the project (both uncredited).... Weingarten also produced the sports comedy *Pat and Mike* (1952), featuring Kathryn Hepburn and Spencer Tracy.... The film's choreographer, David Gould, was nominated for an Oscar for Best Dance Direction.... At one stage the film was known as *Peace and Quiet*.... Over the many months and numerous script drafts, the material was tested on live audiences in a series of over 100 stage performances throughout the country.... The Marx Brothers did the same for *A Night at the Opera*, which was also directed by Sam Wood.... The film's horse racing scenes were shot at the Santa Anita racetrack.... Screenwriter Robert Pirosh won an Oscar for his script for *Battleground* (1949).... Actress Margaret

ABOVE: Groucho Marx (center) as Dr. Hugo Z. Hackenbush, a horse doctor who becomes head of the Standish sanitarium.

RIGHT: When Tony (Chico Marx, second from left) accuses her of being part of a frame-up, Flo (Esther Muir) says, "I've never been so humiliated in all my life." Dr. Hackenbush adds, "Well, it's early yet."

Dumont was also an opera singer.... Besides appearing in many Marx Brothers stage and film productions, Dumont was also featured in movies with Abbott and Costello and Laurel and Hardy.... Sam Wood also directed the baseball features *The Pride of the Yankees* (1942) and *The Stratton Story* (1949).... The director's other sporting feature credits include *The Huddle* (1932), *Navy Blue and Gold* (1937), *Stablemates* (1938), and the silent films *Excuse My Dust* (1920) and *One Minute to Play* (1926), which featured Red Grange.... Actor Douglas Dumbrille appeared in other horse racing films, including *Broadway Bill* (1934) and *Kentucky* (1938).... The Marx Brothers' real names were Leonard (Chico), Julius (Groucho), and Adolph Arthur (Harpo).... Reportedly due to many real-life doctors named Quackenbush threatening to sue, the studio, despite Groucho's resistance, changed his character's name to Hackenbush.... One of Maureen O'Sullivan's daughters is actress Mia Farrow.... O'Sullivan starred as Jane in several Tarzan movies featuring swimming great Johnny Weissmuller in the title role.... Another uncredited producer of this film, George Oppenheimer, also cowrote the boxing movie *The Crowd Roars* (1938), which starred Maureen O'Sullivan and was remade nine years later featuring Mickey Rooney in the title role as "Killer McCoy."

ALL-STAR MOMENTS Dr. Hackenbush (Groucho) taking a pulse: "Either he's dead or my watch has stopped."

Dr. Hackenbush describes his education.

DR. HACKENBUSH: Oh well, uh, to begin with I took four years at Vassar.

MRS. UPJOHN (DUMONT): Vassar? But that's a girls' college.

DR. HACKENBUSH: I found that out the third year.

Romantically positioned in a private room, seductress Flo Marlowe (Esther Muir) tells Dr. Hackenbush to "Hold me closer," to which the doctor replies, "If I was any closer I'd be in back of you."

Tony (Chico) takes the doctor for all his money with phony advice at the betting window and so the doctor ends up selling "tootsie-frootsie" ice cream, looking for another sucker.

MRS. UPJOHN: Dr. Hackenbush tells me I'm the only case in history. I have high blood pressure on my right side and low blood pressure on my left side.

DR. STEINBERG (RUMAN): There is no such thing. She looks as healthy as any woman I have ever met.

DR. HACKENBUSH: You don't look like as though you ever met a healthy woman.

As Stuffy reaches over for something to drink and grabs a bottle, Dr. Hackenbush yells to him: "Hey, don't drink that poison. That's $4 an ounce!"

Stuffy (Harpo) picks up the piano playing from Tony, who runs off being chased by the cops. When his vigorous playing helps cause the instrument to collapse, Stuffy grabs the string section inside the piano and uprights it, playing a terrific harp with the orchestra backing.

Tony creates chaos when he directs racing fans to park their cars all over the track, making it difficult for the jockeys to hold back their anxious horses.

Dr. Hackenbush declares, "Emily, I have a confession to make. I really am a horse doctor. Marry me and I'll never look at another horse."

Stuffy racing the horse Hi Hat. The horse balks at the first jump but then flies over with ease once Stuffy shows him a photo of enemy Morgan (Dumbrille).

Low-angle, tight horse racing action.

POST-GAME COMMENTS Chico Marx on the sociological "science" of comedy:

> Our theater test of laughs before making a picture gives us one advantage. We know just about how long each such tested laugh will be and so can space our gags so laughs won't interrupt them. Without such tests players require time to learn the technique. Maureen O'Sullivan, our leading lady, took several days to "catch on" to the system.[1]

Maureen O'Sullivan recalls that education:

> Playing *A Day at the Races* was my first introduction to farce comedy. And I discovered that it required a technique all its own. Above all else it demanded a spacing in the dialogue speeches so that the words were not covered up by laughs.[2]

HOME COURT ADVANTAGE Available on VHS and DVD. Warner Bros. has released several versions on DVD, including a two-disc set combined with *A Night at the Opera* and a multi-disc collection that includes *At the Circus, Big Store, A Day at the Races, Go West, A Night at the Opera, A Night in Casablanca,* and *Room Service.*

#33 GLADIATOR

Screenwriters David Franzoni, John Logan, William Nicholson. **Director** Ridley Scott. **Producers** Laurie MacDonald, Walter Parkes, Douglas Wick, David Franzoni, Branko Lustig, Terry Needham. **Cinematography** John Mathieson. **Editing** Pietro Scalia. **Music** Hans Zimmer, Klaus Badelt, Lisa Gerrard. **Production Design** Arthur Max. **Art Direction** Peter Russell, John King, David Allday, Keith Pain, Ben Fernandez. **Set Decoration** Sonja Klaus, Jille Azis, Crispian Sallis, Elli Griff. **Costume Design** Janty Yates. **Special Effects** John Nelson. **Stunt Coordinator** Phil Neilson. Dreamworks. 2000.

THE PLAYERS Russell Crowe **Maximus**; Joaquin Phoenix **Commodus**; Connie Nielsen **Lucilla**; Oliver Reed **Proximo**; Richard Harris **Marcus Aurelius**; Derek Jacobi **Gracchus**; Djimon Hounsou **Juba**; David Schofield **Falco**; John Shrapnel **Gaius**; Tomas Arana **Quintus**; Ralph Moeller **Hagen**; David Hemmings **Cassius**; Tommy Flanagan **Cicero**; Sven-Ole Thorsen **Tiger**; Omid Djalili **Slave trader**; Nicholas McGaughey **Praetorian officer**; Chris Kell **Scribe**; Tony Curran **Assassin**; Mark Lewis **Assassin**; John Quinn **Valerius**; Alun Raglan **Praetorian guard**; David Bailie **Engineer**; Chick Allen **German leader**; David Nicholls **Giant man**; Al Ashton **Rome trainer**; Billy Dowd **Narrator**; Ray Calleja **Lucius's attendant**; Gianina Facio **Maximus's wife**; Giorgio Cantarini **Maximus's son**

THE GAME Guiding powerful armies to victory, general Maximus (Russell Crowe) earns the eternal gratitude of his emperor, Marcus Aurelius (Richard Harris).

The closeness shared by these two combined with Maximus's desire for a Roman return to higher virtues puts him in mortal conflict with the emperor's jealous and corrupt son, Commodus (Joaquin Phoenix).

Driven to emotional extremes by his father's favoritism, Commodus kills his father, ascends the throne, and orders the execution of Maximus and his famliy.

Maximus barely escapes but is forced into slavery. Slave owner Proximo (Oliver Reed) soon recognizes Maximus's talents and trains him to be part of a group of gladiators. With the help of fellow slaves like Juba (Djimon Hounsou), Maximus turns his rage into a vengeful quest to return to Rome to assassinate the new emperor, Commodus, who killed his wife and son.

Knowing the power of the will of the people, Maximus earns their admiration by becoming one of Rome's leading gladiators, thus gaining the opportunity to earn his revenge, even at the ultimate price.

INSTANT REPLAY Reviving a bygone genre with a verisimilitude that is nothing short of exceptional, Ridley Scott, with literally a cast (and crew) of thousands, brilliantly delivers a mix of old-fashioned storytelling and cutting-edge technology, rendering ancient Rome in all its glory and depravity.

From the opening battle, which recalls *Saving Private Ryan* in its unflinching depiction of the bloody chaos of war, *Gladiator* engulfs the viewer immediately and doesn't reopen the time capsule until the closing credits.

The picture incorporates time frames, key characters, and plot points from 1964's *The Fall of the Roman Empire,* and its editing style, symbolism, cinematography, pageantry, and sweeping historical presentation show the influence of pictures like *Spartacus, The Robe, Demetrius and the Gladiators, Barabbas, Quo Vadis?,* and *Ben-Hur.* But what *Gladiator* does exceptionally well is use technology to enliven the sword-and-sandals bloodsport to unprecedented levels that match the demands of an audience used to the digital exploits of films like *The Matrix.*

Laying the foundation is Arthur Max's production design team of set designers and

art directors, the elaborate costume work of Janty Yates, and the extensive computer enhancement efforts of John Nelson and Robin Shenfield's team at Mill Film among others. John Mathieson's cinematography, Pierto Scalia's editing, and the music of Hans Zimmer take it from there, giving us a second-century Rome that's never looked so real.

Phil Nielsen's army of stuntmen, as well as a group of animal trainers and armorers, all play an important role in lending overall authenticity to a complex project.

On paper the gang of accomplished writers box themselves in a bit with their terrific setup. The plot progresses with such logical inevitability that the plot twists—even the intrigue of scheming Roman senators—seem to lack urgency and suspense.

Of course, it's the people that are at the core of the story, and here the writers' sharp characterizations (and smart reduction of the genre's tendency to "speechify" their dialogue) come to life with strong and memorable performances from a complex and talented cast.

As a slave on a mission to avenge his family's murder at the hands of an evil ruler, Maximus becomes the rooting interest, a hero who's lost everything except his pride and will to survive.

Following up on his best actor nomination in *The Insider* (1999), Russell Crowe delivers his finest performance to date, anchoring the epic with a commanding presence reminiscent of Kirk Douglas in *Spartacus*.

Spartacus and *Gladiator* share other similarities, but a key difference is that Crowe's mission is more of a solo payback within the gladiatorial arena whereas Douglas leads a campaign against injustice along a broad sweep of territory with his army.

Crowe ably combines physical authority with melancholy, a sort of dead-inside, raw force full of hurt and rage. All through the (overlong) picture, the principled general-turned-gladiator's intense convictions remain dynamic and consistent.

Providing an excellent contrast both physically and emotionally is Joaquin Phoenix. His ruthless intensity, deep neurosis, and insatiable need to be loved as the overmatched leader Commodus are played to grand dramatic effect. It's a slightly different approach than Christopher Plummer's gleefully lunatic characterization in *The Fall of the Roman Empire*. Both are quite effective.

Oliver Reed, who passed away during production, steals more than a few scenes as the enterprising gladiator promoter using Maximus to return to the big leagues in Rome. Reed shrewdly shows the political machinations and intrigue of his position, not unlike Peter Ustinov's Lentulus Batiatus in *Spartacus*. It is a terrific performance for Reed to be remembered by.

As portrayed by Connie Nielsen, Lucilla, the politically savvy and regally beautiful daughter of Aurelius and sister of Commodus, earns an insightful tribute from her father: "If only you had been born a man, what a Caesar you would have made."

This is the ever-capable Richard Harris, in the role played by Alec Guinness in *The Fall of the Roman Empire* (which also twists history by having the emperor murdered and not killed by a plague). Harris is thoroughly convincing as the dignified leader realizing in the twilight of his life that while he's succeeded in building an empire, his family life has suffered from the demands of his position, leaving him sadly conflicted.

In a small but significant role, Djimon Hounsou provides some needed friendship with his philosophical and spiritually centered presence as Maximus's fellow slave, Juba.

I, Claudius veteran Derek Jacobi is well cast as the influential Roman Gracchus.

Certainly inspired by a variety of movies, *Gladiator* as a Shakespearean revenge

Maximus (Russell Crowe) gets ready for battle.

tragedy marshals those influences to take viewers on a high-tech adventure of the grandeur and gore of ancient Rome.

From the opening frames and Maximus's words—"On my signal, unleash hell"—Ridley Scott vividly presents the dark side of one of history's greatest empires.

OUTSIDE THE LINES
Nominated for a dozen Academy Awards, *Gladiator* won Best Sound, Best Effects, Best Costume Design, and Best Picture.... Russell Crowe also won an Oscar for this role.... The gory gladiator spectacles were partially designed to harden Roman citizens to the sight of blood so they could better endure the hardships of war.... Actor Oliver Reed passed away during production.... The film was shot primarily in Malta, Morocco, England, and Italy.... Crowe portrayed boxing champion James Braddock in *Cinderella Man* (2005).... Richard Harris was nominated for an Academy Award and a British Academy Award for his role in *This Sporting Life* (1963).... His rugby role also earned him the award for Best Male Performer at Cannes.... 2,000 extras were joined by over 30,000 computer-generated spectators to fill out the arena crowds.... Crowe starred in the hockey film *Mystery, Alaska* (1999).... Cowriter John Logan also cowrote the screenplay for Oliver Stone's football drama *Any Given Sunday*.... The real Commodus, an avid supporter of the gladiatorial games, was strangled to death by an athlete, Narcissus. . . .Ridley Scott directed the sailing saga *White Squall* (1996).

ALL-STAR MOMENTS
As General Maximus (Russell Crowe) stands with his officers, out of the mist comes a messenger galloping toward them on a white horse. He arrives beheaded and with an arrow through his torso. Cut to the enemy holding the messenger's head, leading his men on to a fight. Cut back to Maximus's officer Quintus (Tomas Arana), who says, "People should know when they are conquered."

Graphic battle that ensues, including catapults sending flaming arrows into the sky and General Maximus, knocked off his horse, fighting with his sword.

Wide shot of Rome with its massive buildings and Colosseum during the parade for the new emperor.

After a fight to the death in the Roman arena, the general-turned-slave/gladiator Maximus turns to the royal box and the stunned, silent crowd and asks them, "Are you not entertained? Is this not why you are here?" He throws down his weapon and spits, while a roar of appreciation builds in the bloodthirsty crowd.

Maximus leads a group of gladiators pitted against well-armed soldiers with chariots. Impressed, Emperor Commodus (Joaquin Phoenix) goes down to the arena floor to meet him. When the fighter takes off his helmet, the emperor is stunned to see that it is Maximus, who he thought was dead. The gladiator threatens the emperor: "Father to a murdered son, husband to a murdered wife…I will have my vengeance in this life or the next." The emperor is speechless. With the crowd behind their favorite gladiator, yelling, "Live, live!" the emperor is in a no-win situation. Reluctantly he gives the "thumbs up" sign to the crowd. Maximus lives to see another day.

Maximus's fight takes on a new dimension. He defeats tigers in the arena. Again the emperor is perplexed.

> EMPEROR: What am I going to do with you? You simply won't die. Are we so different, you and I? You take life when you have to, as I do.
>
> MAXIMUS: I have only one more life to take. Then it is done.

HOME COURT ADVANTAGE Available on VHS and DVD. Universal has released this title as part of a seven-disc Best Pictures Ultimate Collection that also includes *All Quiet on the Western Front, Deer Hunter, Lost Weekend, Out of Africa, The Sting,* and *American Beauty*. Dreamworks has released several versions, including one teamed with *The Last Castle*.

TOP: Envious of Maximus's popularity with the people and his own father (Richard Harris as Marcus Aurelius), the new emperor, Commodus (Joaquin Phoenix), is determined to make his own mark.

MIDDLE: Commodus's beautiful sister, Lucilla (Connie Nielsen).

BOTTOM: The killing floor that is the Colosseum.

RIGHT: In the Colosseum, Maximus (Crowe, right) faces deadly opponents of varying types.

#32 MILLION DOLLAR BABY

Screenwriter Paul Haggis. **Director** Clint Eastwood. **Producers** Al Ruddy, Tom Rosenberg, Paul Haggis, Clint Eastwood, Gary Lucchesi, Robert Lorenz. **Cinematography** Thomas Stern. **Editing** Joel Cox. **Music** Clint Eastwood. **Production Design** Harry Bumstead. **Art Direction** Jack Taylor Jr. Warner Bros. 2004.

THE PLAYERS Clint Eastwood **Frankie Dunn**; Hilary Swank **Maggie Fitzgerald**; Morgan Freeman **Eddie "Scrap Iron" Dupris**; Jay Baruchel **Danger Barch**; Mike Colter **Big Willie Little**; Lucia Rijker **Billie "The Blue Bear"**; Brian O'Byrne **Father Horvak**; Margo Martindale **Earline Fitzgerald**; Riki Lindhome **Mardell Fitzgerald**; Dean Familton **Ref #1**; Bruce Forman **Guitarist**; Naveen **Pakistani**; Morgan Eastwood **Young girl in truck**; Dave Powledge **Counterman at diner**; V. J. Foster **Ref #3**; Don Familton **Ring announcer**; Lo Ming **Rehab doctor**; Susan Krebs **Rehab nurse**; Sunshine Parkman **Rehab nurse #2**; Kim Danneberg **Rehab nurse #3**; Jamison Yang **Paramedic**; Erica Grant **Nurse**; Mark Chait **J. D. Fitzgerald**; Michael Peña **Omar**; Dr. Louis Moret **Ref #2**; Jon Schurle II **Ref #4**; Marty Sammon **Ref #5**; Steven Porter **Ref #6**; Ray Corona **Ref #7**; Jim Cantafio **Ring doctor #1**; Marco Rodriguez **Second at Vegas fight**; Tom McCleister **Lawyer**; Ned Eisenberg **Sally Mendoza**; Bruce MacVittie **Mickey Mack**; Mark Thompson **Radio commentator**; Benito Martinez **Billie's manager**

THE GAME Talented old school boxing trainer/manager Frankie Dunn (Clint Eastwood) operates a ramshackle gym, The Hit Pit, in Los Angeles with former contender Eddie "Scrap Iron" Dupris (Morgan Freeman). A career man in the fight game, Dunn has little to show for his efforts, and just when it looks like one of his pupils is on the brink of stardom, the contender (Mike Colter) leaves Frankie for a higher-profile manager. Dunn's overly cautious attitude (his motto is "always protect yourself") has cost him personally and professionally.

Enter Maggie Fitzgerald (Hilary Swank). A dirt-poor yet ambitious and energetic woman of 31, she arrives with the single-minded goal of becoming a boxing champion, more to earn respect than fame. When she asks Frankie to train her, it is no surprise that the conservative old man has no interest in "the latest freak show out there"—women's boxing.

With the help of Scrap, who sees determination and raw talent in her, along with her own respectful yet unrelenting persistence in seeking out Frankie's wealth of knowledge, Maggie eventually gets Dunn to show her the ropes.

This unlikely partnership that begins as a temporary arrangement grows into something much deeper and more profound, so that Maggie and Frankie seem less like coach and athlete than surrogate father and daughter. But just as they appear to be within reach of an improbable championship after her string of victories, a tragic event takes place in the ring that changes their lives forever.

INSTANT REPLAY Clint Eastwood, in directing his 25th film, has skillfully combined the fairy-tale elements of *Rocky*, certain noir aspects of *The Set-Up*, and the naked reality of John Huston's *Fat City*. This unconventional three-person character study of compassion, dignity, and the ironic twists of dreams is life-and-death real.

Beginning with Paul Haggis's tight and crafty script, the picture captures well the details of the unforgiving fight game. Adapted from veteran boxing man Jerry Boyd's collection of short stories, *Rope Burns: Stories From the Corner* (as F. X. Toole), the script skirts the edges of clichés and heavy-handed metaphors. Seemingly leading us into the familiar *Karate Kid* arena, Haggis instead puts a clever twist on the formulaic blueprint and produces something much more penetrating and powerful.

TOP: Frankie Dunn (Clint Eastwood) and his latest boxing project, Maggie Fitzgerald (Hilary Swank).

BOTTOM: Morgan Freeman won a Best Supporting Actor Oscar as Eddie "Scrap Iron" Dupris.

The writer and director are provided with an authentic boxing world by the production design work of the venerable Henry Bumstead (Academy Awards for *The Sting* and *To Kill a Mockingbird*) and the cinematography of Tom Stern. In particular, Bumstead's dark gym and Stern's grayish long shadows instill a gritty visual base that suits the story well. The result is a kind of noir film, like *Champion* or *The Harder They Fall*, out of time. Between the characters and the gym you feel like you're in a 1950s boxing picture.

Eastwood, besides providing the film's original music with appropriate understatement, also steps from behind the camera to give one of his more affecting performances (that wasn't Dirty Harry crying in church). In his palpable paternal feelings for Maggie, which create an emotional rejuvenation in a character estranged from his own daughter, and his amusing and cantankerous banter with Scrap, Eastwood can say a lot with a verbal economy worthy of his trademark lean directing style.

Morgan Freeman, in a variation on a role he owns (see *The Shawshank Redemption*, *Driving Miss Daisy*, *Bruce Almighty*, and *Unforgiven*), provides a much-needed character of compassion and experience as a catalyst for the film's advancement. Though Freeman's narration is sometimes watered down with corny aphorisms, in lesser hands this anchoring role might have fallen flat and insincere.

The chemistry between Freeman's Scrap and Eastwood's Frankie is like an old married couple or, in sports cinema terms, like crusty Burgess Meredith's Mickey from *Rocky* and Tommy Lee Jones's cantankerous *Cobb* going at each other. Their conversation using worn socks as an allegory for a tough life shows two old acting pros at their underplaying best.

This picture, though, belongs to Hilary Swank. At times inspiring, heartbreaking, and engaging with her unbridled enthusiasm, courteous manner, and focus, Swank's Maggie Fitzgerald is her best role since she won her first Oscar in *Boys Don't Cry*, evidenced by her second Best Actress Oscar here.

Swank also succeeds in her physical transformation, attaining the look of a boxer. The traditional training montages are treated with refreshing easy-paced lessons that focus more on the science of the "sweet science" as both Scrap and Frankie impart their wisdom. The fight scenes are not exceptionally noteworthy other than the filmmakers' smart use of story to back up Maggie's power-punching quick KOs as she rises up the ranks, allowing them to keep the fight scenes brief. Nevertheless, Swank impressively does all her own work in the ring.

The better movies often succeed by demanding that the viewer pause for reflection, ponder and consider new perspectives long after the lights go back on. In that vein, *Million Dollar Baby* illustrates life's fragility and what we take for granted without being blatantly manipulative, staying true to its well-drawn characters.

Million Dollar Baby is a crowning achievement that has brought another legend named Oscar back to boxing.

OUTSIDE THE LINES *Million Dollar Baby* won four Academy Awards, including Best Picture, Best Director, Best Actress, and Best Supporting Actor…. Al Ruddy created the story for *The Longest Yard*, which he produced…. Hector Roca, trainer for fight champions like Arturo Gatti, Buddy McGirt, and Iran Barkley, trained Hilary Swank at venerable Gleason's Gym in Brooklyn…. Joel Cox won an Oscar for his editing work on *Unforgiven* (1992)…. Four-time boxing champion Lucia Rijker appears as Swank's opponent Billie "The Blue Bear" in the movie…. Al Ruddy won an

Oscar for producing *The Godfather*.... Margo Martindale, playing Swank's mother, made her feature debut in the auto racing drama *Days of Thunder* (1990).... Henry Bumstead was the art director for hockey's *Slap Shot* (1977).

ALL-STAR MOMENTS As Scrap (Freeman) turns down the lights to close the gym for the evening, he hears someone punching a bag. Seeing that it is Maggie (Swank), he comes over to give her some tips.

Later, we hear his voice-over: "If there's magic in boxing, it's the magic of fighting battles beyond endurance, beyond cracked ribs, ruptured kidneys, and detached retinas. It's the magic of risking everything for a dream that nobody sees but you."

Exchange between Scrap and Frankie (Eastwood), who's in his office reading a book in Gaelic, about leading contender Willie (Colter) leaving Frankie for a more prominent manager. Scrap argues that Willie was ready for a title shot long ago and challenges Frankie's philosophy of carefully bringing along a contender because he feels he really has just one shot. Scrap exclaims, "You just protected yourself out of a championship fight. How do you say that in Gaelic?"

Frankie finally relents and offers to train Maggie, at least temporarily. Maggie summarizes her environment:

> ... my brother's in prison, my sister cheats on welfare by pretending one of her babies is still alive, my daddy's dead and my momma weighs 312 pounds. If I was thinking straight I'd go back home, find a used trailer, buy a deep fryer and some Oreos. Problem is this is the only thing I ever felt good doin'. If I'm too old for this then I got nuthin'. That enough truth to suit you?

Perplexed after Scrap's explanation about the holes in his socks, Frankie asks if Scrap would buy some new ones if he gave him the money. "Well," says Scrap, "I'd be tempted but I couldn't say for sure. It might find its way to the track."

After being set up to be occupied dealing with an overflowing toilet, Scrap comes out of the bathroom to see mean-spirited boxer Shawrelle (Anthony Mackie) pummel-

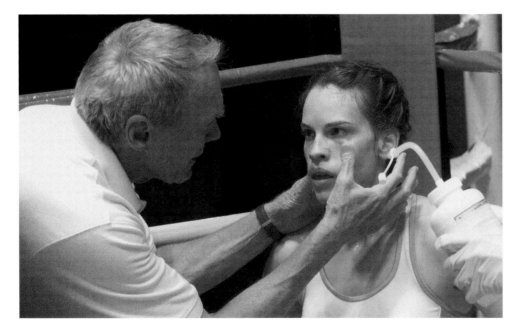

TOP: The fateful bout against the "Blue Bear" (Lucia Rijker).

BOTTOM: Maggie works on the fundamentals.

RIGHT: Frankie tends to Maggie between rounds.

ing a defenseless, mentally challenged kid, Danger Barch (Jay Baruchel). Scrap storms into the ring and pummels Shawrelle after tending to a bloodied Danger.

With her lawyer present, Maggie's mother tries to get her daughter to sign over control of her assets "to protect your money": "It will take care of your family the way your daddy would have wanted you to." The injured Maggie can't write, so her mother puts the pen in her mouth. Maggie is deeply disappointed in her:

> Mama, you take Mardell and J. D. and get home before I tell your lawyer there
>   that you're so worried about your welfare that you never signed those house
>   papers like you were supposed to. So any time I feel like it I can sell that house
>   from under your fat, lazy hillbilly ass. And if you ever come back that is exactly
>   what I will do.

Mother and kids storm out of the room.

As Frankie loads some lethal materials into his gym bag, Scrap tries to lighten the turmoil within Frankie and his guilt over Maggie's incapacitated physical condition.

> SCRAP: You made her the best fighter she could be.

> FRANKIE: ...and I killed her.

> SCRAP: Don't say that. Maggie walked through that door with nothing but guts.
>   No chance in the world of being what she needed to be. A year and a half later
>   she's fighting for the championship of the world. You did that. People die every
>   day, Frankie. Mopping floors. Washing dishes. And you know what their last
>   thought was? "I never got my shot." Because of you Maggie got her shot. If
>   she dies today, you know what her last thought will be? "I think I did all
>   right."...I know I could rest with that.

POST-GAME COMMENTS Screenwriter/producer Paul Haggis on "voices"
calling during the writing process:

> I wrote the[Scrap] role for Morgan Freeman. I wrote the Frankie role for either
>   Clint Eastwood or Paul Newman. I don't usually write with an actor in mind.
>   Strangely, in this case I did. I was hearing their voices when I was writing. The
>   characters always talk to you when you write. But usually they are voices that
>   aren't identifiable. I was worried about that. I was worried about *Shawshank*. I
>   didn't have a choice, the characters were telling me which way to go. 1

Producer Al Ruddy on the roots of the project:

> Anjelica (Huston) calls and asks me to read this story, "Million Dollar Baby."
>   And she adds, "If you don't cry, don't call me back."[2]

The cagey producer with a keen sense for story read it, cried and called her back the next day. They agreed Anjelica would direct and he would produce. (Huston had to drop out later for a Julia Roberts project she was working on.) The multi-year journey to production began.

(Note: John Huston, Angelica's father, directed the acclaimed boxing drama *Fat City* in 1972.)

Paul Haggis on the difficulties in getting the picture made:

They all passed. It is easy to understand. You look at that script. I describe it in tone as *Leaving Las Vegas*, only depressing. It fools you, though. It has punch.

It's about a girl boxer. Oh come on! Who wants to see a movie about a girl boxer? Nobody does. There wasn't one element where you said, "Oh, I have to see it." The element was Clint. That's the only reason they considered the project. If I was doing this movie no studio would have done this. Look at the story. It's not going to happen. That's why we'd have had to do it independent.

It didn't fit into any slot. It didn't fit into a sports movie. Wasn't a traditional drama because of the boxing. It certainly had the feel of pulp, of being noirish. That just dated it. It just didn't fit neatly into any one category or genre comfortably. It needed someone who really believed in it. And Clint, when he read it, really believed in it.[3]

Al Ruddy, on sports movie formulas and clichés, why they work and the twists his boxing film took:

When you do something involving sports you know what the structure is. It's a framework in which generally you know what the ground rules are. Things are cliché because they're often repeated truths. It depends on how you want to play it. So we all try to be inventive. Getting enough twists and turns. That's why they'll always do sports, I don't care what it is, *Downhill Racer*, *This Sporting Life*....

It is an arena in which we examine the human condition. The athlete against all odds, how he deals with triumph and failure. It's a pretty raw crucible in which to play human emotions.[4]

HOME COURT ADVANTAGE Available on VHS and DVD. Warner Bros. has released several versions, including one combined with *Unforgiven*.

Clint Eastwood earned an Oscar for his directorial efforts.

#31 HORSE FEATHERS

Screenwriters Bert Kalmar, S. J. Perelman, Will Johnstone, Harry Ruby. **Director** Norman McLeod. **Producer** Herman Mankiewicz. **Cinematography** Ray June. **Music** Harry Ruby. Paramount. 1932.

THE PLAYERS Groucho Marx **Professor Quincy Adams Wagstaff**; Chico Marx **Barovelli**; Harpo Marx **Pinky**; Zeppo Marx **Frank Wagstaff**; Thelma Todd **Connie Bailey**; David Landau **Jennings**; Nat Pendleton **MacHardie**; James Pierce **Mullen**; Robert Greig **Biology professor**; Reginald Barlow **Retiring Huxley president**; Florine McKinney **Peggy Carrington**; EH Calvert **Professor in Wagstaff's office**; Edward Le Saint **Professor in Wagstaff's office**; Frank Rice **Doorman at speakeasy**; Arthur Sheekman **Man at typewriter**

THE GAME Professor Quincy Adams Wagstaff (Groucho Marx) takes over as president of Huxley College to help his son Frank (Zeppo Marx) graduate after attending the school for a dozen years.

After the faculty and student body join Professor Wagstaff in an impromptu song and dance that arises from his inaugural speech, Frank is admonished by his father for taking 12 years to graduate, and in that time span dating only one "college widow," whereas he himself dated three "college widows" while attending three different colleges in 12 years.

Frank informs his father that the school has had a new college president each year since 1888, which is also the last time Huxley won a football game. He tells his dad that they can defeat rival Darwin by securing the services of two great football players that hang out at a nearby speakeasy.

Before the Huxley president can get there, Jennings (David Landau), a representative of opposing Darwin College, has already made a deal with the two stars, Mullens (James Pierce) and MacHardie (Nat Pendleton).

After finally managing to get into the speakeasy, Professor Wagstaff somehow mistakes iceman and bootlegger Barovelli (Chico Marx) and mute dogcatcher Pinky (Harpo Marx) for footballers, first signing them up for the game, then enrolling them as students.

Jennings asks his ward, "college widow" Connie Bailey, to get Huxley's football plays from one of its players, Frank, with whom she is "very good" friends.

Frank shows up at her place, but soon thereafter so does Professor Wagstaff, who hopes to convince the shapely young lady to give up his son so he can graduate (offering himself as a replacement). Pinky and Barovelli also show up delivering ice; then Jennings reappears and tosses them all out.

After football practice, when he learns that Pinky and Barovelli are clearly not ballplayers, Professor Wagstaff asks them to go and kidnap Mullens and MacHardie from the Darwin squad.

Jennings asks Connie to get the Huxley plays from Professor Wagstaff, but her efforts turn out all wet when she and the college president go rowing, he exposes her romantic cover, and she falls in the lake.

Meanwhile Pinky and Barovelli's attempts to kidnap the two football stars fail and the game begins with Mullens and MacHardie playing for Darwin and helping them build a 12-0 lead over Huxley.

Together Professor Wagstaff, Barovelli, Pinky, and Frank arrive in time to employ a bag of tricks heretofore unseen on the football field (and not seen since) to help give Huxley a comeback victory. In the end, Barovelli, Pinky, and Professor Wagstaff all marry Connie.

INSTANT REPLAY *Horse Feathers* is the fourth film starring the Marx Brothers. Their previous efforts included *Cocoanuts, Animal Crackers,* and *Monkey Business.* Like its predecessors, *Horse Feathers* is full of wit and originality within a sea of slapstick mayhem.

Perhaps more than the others, this picture provides an opportunity to draw upon the brothers' singular comic specialties and meld them into a festival of laughs. Credit for this should also go to director Norman McCleod, who supervised the boys in *Monkey Business,* allowing them the freedom to play out their distinctive style well honed from years in vaudeville and theater. Led by Groucho's endless insults and quirky flirtations, *Horse Feathers* incorporates Chico's butchering of the language and mischievous dealings, Harpo's pantomime skills and comical literal translations, and Zeppo's straight man persona to produce an indelible team performance in a team sport picture.

One of Hollywood's favorite comic targets at the time was the university, and the Marx Brothers attack it with gusto here. They are aided by witty dialogue from the writing team of Bill Johnstone, Bert Kalmar, S. J. Perelman, and Harry Ruby. The supporting performers lend able assistance. Thelma Todd is well cast as the charming, attractive foil.

The musical numbers, while typically serving as a buffer from the burlesque, are also comical. As we see the musical talents of Groucho, Chico, and Harpo on the guitar, piano, and harp respectively and Zeppo singing, the lyrics by Harry Ruby and Bert Kalmar, such as those in "I'm Against It," as well as the dancing professors, are funny in their own right.

The jokes and sight gags come fast and often. The real name of the game is not football but nonsense, and the Marx Brothers play it uniquely well.

OUTSIDE THE LINES S. J. Perelman won an Oscar for Best Adapted Screenplay for *Around the World in 80 Days* (1956).... Writer/songwriter Harry Ruby

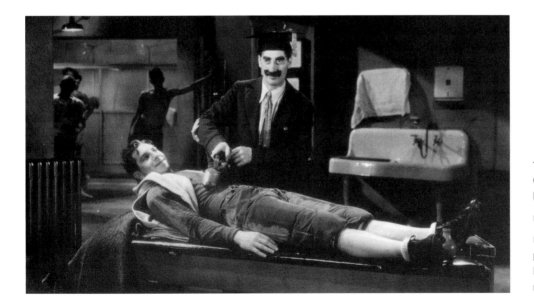

TOP: Professor Wagstaff (Groucho Marx, left) and Barovelli (Chico Marx).

BOTTOM: "Swordfish."

LEFT: Zeppo Marx (on table) portrays the player/son of Professor Wagstaff (Groucho, right).

appeared as himself in baseball's *Angels in the Outfield* (1951).... Thelma Todd performed in the boxing comedy *Palooka* (1934).... Nat Pendleton was an American Olympic gold medal wrestler in the 1920 Summer Games in Antwerp, Belgium.... He also appeared in the boxing drama *The Crowd Roars* (1938), featuring Robert Taylor, as well as football's *The Spirit of Notre Dame* (1931) and *College Coach* (1933).... *Horse Feathers* producer Herman Mankiewicz cowrote the Oscar winning screenplay *Citizen Kane* (1941) and baseball's *The Pride of the Yankees* (1942).... He also wrote the biopic of pitcher Dizzy Dean in *The Pride of St. Louis* (1952).

ALL-STAR MOMENTS
Pinky (Harpo) mocking the cop as he's being issued a ticket for blocking traffic, then taking off after a dog only to end up locking the police officer in his dog truck.

The new Huxley president Professor Wagstaff (Groucho) talks with two professors standing in his office:

WAGSTAFF: Have we got a stadium?

PROFESSORS: Yes.

WAGSTAFF: Have we got a college?

PROFESSORS: Yes.

WAGSTAFF: Well, we can't support both. Tomorrow we start tearing down the college.

PROFESSORS: But where will the students sleep?

WAGSTAFF: Where they always sleep. In the classroom.

Connie's (Todd) unsuccessful efforts to romance the Huxley football plays from Professor Wagstaff while rowing out on a lake.

Barovelli (Chico) and Professor Wagstaff's repartee in ascertaining the password for entry to the speakeasy followed by Pinky's inventive and lucky gambling within the joint.

The football game:

—Professor Wagstaff running onto the field in uniform and morning coat to make an illegal tackle.

—Pinky's end run while eating a hot dog.

—Frank's (Zeppo) long run aided by Pinky's timely distribution of banana peels against the defense.

—The Pinky-led long touchdown "run" using a horse-drawn garbage-bin-turned-chariot for the winning score.

The final scene when Barovelli, Pinky, and Professor Wagstaff all marry the College Widow.

HOME COURT ADVANTAGE
Available on VHS and DVD. Universal first released *Horse Feathers* as a solo title, then later as part of a six-disc Silver Screen Collection including *Animal Crackers, Cocoanuts, Duck Soup,* and *Monkey Business.* Image Entertainment released a three-disc set with *Duck Soup* and *Animal Crackers.*

#30 DOWNHILL RACER

Screenwriter James Salter. **Director** Michael Ritchie. **Producer** Richard Gregson. **Cinematography** Brian Probyn. **Editing** Nick Archer. **Music** Kenyon Hopkins. **Art Direction** Ian Whittaker. **Costume Design** Cynthia May. Paramount. 1969.

THE PLAYERS Robert Redford **David Chappellet**; Gene Hackman **Eugene Claire**; Camilla Sparv **Carole Stahl**; Karl Michael Vogler **Machet**; James McMullan **Creech**; Christian Doermer **Brumm**; Dabney Coleman **Mayo**; Kenneth Kirk **D. K. Bryan**; Jerry Dexter **Ron Engel**; Walter Stroud **David's father**; Rip McManus **Bruce Devore**; Carole Carle **Lena**; Joe Jay Jalbert **Tommy**; Tom Kirk **Stiles**; Robert Brendlin **Announcer**; Noam Pitlik **Television announcer**; Alexander Stampfer **Skier #16**; Walter Gnika **Austrian journalist**; Werner Heyking **Helgerson**; Robin Hutton-Potts **Gabriel**; Oren Stevens **Kinsmith**; Kathleen Crowley **Journalist**; Heini Schuler **Meier**; Peter Rohr **Boyriven**; Arnold Alpiger **Hinsch**; Eddie Waldburger **Haas**; Marco Walli **Istel**; Rudi Gertsch **Selznick**

THE GAME David Chappellet (Robert Redford), an aloof, self-absorbed young man from a small town, is hell-bent on achieving success as a skier at the world-class level. He has the looks and talent that may combine to win him fame and fortune.

Arriving in Europe at the sport's most glamorous venues, Chappellet immediately clashes with Eugene Claire (Gene Hackman), the United States national ski team coach. Chappellet's selfish displays, such as refusing to race because he feels he should have gotten a better starting number in the draw, don't win him any points with Claire.

Nevertheless, Chappellet's talent and looks soon draw media attention as well as a pretty woman whom he begins dating (Camilla Sparv as Carole Stahl).

Between seasons he makes a quick visit to his tiny Colorado hometown to inform his father of his progress.

Mr. Chappellet (Walter Stroud) asks David what his neighbors have been asking him: "What's he do it for?"

DAVID: Well, I'll be famous. I'll be champion.

FATHER (unimpressed): World's full of them.

David, speechless and suddenly feeling empty, has no answer as he reaches for a box of crackers.

As the seasons pass and the time comes for the Olympic Games, the awkward relationship between the coach and his distant but talented skier boils over when Dave challenges a leading teammate, Creech (James McMullan), to a race despite practice being officially over. When Creech is injured in the race, he loses his chance to compete in the Olympics.

Now with the Olympics upon them, and with everything they've both worked for on the line, coach and skier warily put their differences aside, at least temporarily, to focus on the challenge at hand: winning against the greatest competitors the sport has to offer.

After putting up a terrific time and holding off the best skiers from Switzerland and France, Chappellet wins the gold medal but soon realizes the win is hollow. Before the victory celebration is over, Chappellet has the empty feeling that perhaps the effort and sacrifice weren't worth it.

INSTANT REPLAY As he would do in *The Candidate, Smile,* and *The Bad News Bears,* in *Downhill Racer* director Michael Ritchie probes one of his favorite topics: competition and what price success?

These films explore the dark truth that many stars are simply not as charismatic off the field of play as they are on it. They also address the enormous pressure American society in particular puts on athletes to win, and the effects of that pressure on the athletes.

Here, adapting James Salter's lean script in a fictionalized, quasi-documentary style, Ritchie provides a dramatic study of driven people who sacrifice a great deal for success only to experience fleeting fulfillment.

Robert Redford is an abominable snowman, cold to the entire team concept and to the wisdom of his coach, yet when left to his own devices, he sets the slopes ablaze with his natural talents.

He is convincing as a sullen, relentless athlete driven to the point that not even the disapproval of his father (Walter Stroud in a brief but telling appearance) nor the charms of a pretty woman (Camilla Sparv) can keep him from his deeply coveted objective: skiing the fastest.

Gene Hackman is on target in a difficult role as the hardworking coach impressing upon his unimpressionable star the values of sportsmanship, moral fiber, and an appreciation for the sponsors that essentially fund his goal of Olympic gold.

The sights and sounds of *Downhill Racer* are nothing short of magnificent, all the more impressive since the film was produced with a relatively small budget.

Brian Probyn's stunning cinematography not only captures the beauty of the sport's magnificent venues and surroundings set in the Alps, but with the help of pro skiers like Joe Jay Jalbert skiing down the mountains following the performers with his own camera, one really gets a sense of the exhilaration and danger of the sport.

Much credit goes to Eldon Ruberg and Kevin Sutton, who capture the natural sounds of the wind and skis hurtling over the snow.

In another sound realm, Kenyon Hopkins's music is an affecting accompaniment to the proceedings.

Mixing it all with a knowing hand is editor Rich Harris.

Producer Richard Gregson and art directors Nick Archer and Ian Whittaker provide a very authentic backdrop for the story, with snippets from the actual Olympic world that give the production a documentary feel.

Overall, Michael Ritchie's winning feature debut scores in providing a real sense of the beauty and danger of skiing and, via the telling performance of Robert Redford (all the more impressive given the inarticulateness of his character), the price that is sometimes paid for an all-consuming effort to achieve world-class athletic glory.

OUTSIDE THE LINES Shot on location in Europe, some of the sites include the Jungfrau region of Switzerland and Kitzbuhel, Austria.... At one point in its development the project was being considered by director Roman Polanski.... Documentary footage was filmed of the 1968 Olympics in Grenoble, France.... The film's premiere was held in Reno, Nevada.

ALL-STAR MOMENTS Opening frames with assorted shots of the whole racing scene, from the mountains to the fans to the broadcasters to the racers' concentration anticipating the next competitor.

First racer flying down the hill followed by alternating resumption of racing and freeze frames through opening credits.

Natural sounds and point-of-view camera work as David (Redford) makes his first run.

Montage of Carole (Sparv) and David on a leisurely ski run.

As snow falls and fog rolls in, a skier begins his run but soon wipes out.

Conversation between Coach Claire (Hackman) and David after David, disobeying a directive from the coach, challenges teammate Creech (McMullan) to an impromptu race in which Creech is injured.

> **DAVID:** What's there to understand? I'm here to ski fast and I ski fast. That's all there is to it.
>
> **COACH:** That's it, huh? Yeah, you ski fast. You race, but you're reckless. You rack up a lot. No consistency. That's what Creech has.
>
> **DAVID:** It doesn't win a medal.
>
> **COACH:** It counts for a lot. It comes from a certain consideration for a sport. A desire to learn. Something you never had. You never had any real education, did you?...All you ever had was your skis. And that's not enough.

FACING PAGE: David Chappellet (Robert Redford) has the talent and daring to be a world-class competitor.

TOP: The intensity of Olympic competition.

BOTTOM: Chappellet (Redford) on his gold medal run.

David's winning run, followed by his empty response to a reporter's question.

REPORTER: What are you going to do now?

DAVID: Slow down, I guess. I don't know.

Carole Stahl (Camilla Sparv) with David.

POST-GAME COMMENTS Robert Redford on what attracted him to do a ski picture:

There is cruelty to sport—all sport—that had never been shown on film. I felt the harsh drama of the ski circuit was the ideal subject for a film. The kind of honest, hard-hitting film I was interested in making.

I wanted to try to get beneath the glamour and show racing as it really is, clouded by pressures and politics. Some elemental things had to be spelled out for the ordinary moviegoer, so my guess is that knowledgeable skiers will find a few technical quibbles. We determined, though, that the overall view would be accurate. We were not out to show the pretty, pretty Alps, what racers called "the pedestrians'" world. Racing is a serious subject and we were serious about it.

We try to go beneath and inside the sport to find out what the mystique is.[1]

Gene Hackman as Coach Claire:

My role in the film is to bring the recognition of these pressures to Robert Redford as a winning member of the U.S. ski team in the story. I think the character is a very realistic one, since any competitive skier understands the temptations and intrigue which go hand in hand with success in the sport. Through my portrayal of the coach, the audience is made to understand them too.[2]

Redford on the film's core theme:

The real reason I wanted to make the film is to point out what I call the "success syndrome" of American athletes. I felt a true story of the ski world offered a fresh and exciting approach to such a viewpoint. There's a tremendous stress in athletics to have our athletes win all the time. I feel this distorts the value of a sport.[3]

HOME COURT ADVANTAGE Available on VHS.

#29 COLLEGE

Screenplay Bryan Foy, Carl Harbaugh. **Director** James Horne, Buster Keaton (uncredited). **Producer** Joe Schenck. **Cinematography** Bert Haines, Devereaux Jennings. **Editing** Sherman Kell. United Artists. 1927.

THE PLAYERS Buster Keaton **Ronald**; Anne Cornwall **Mary Haines**; Harold Goodwin **Jeff**; Snitz Edwards **The Dean**; Florence Turner **Ronald's mother**; Flora Bramley **Mary's friend**; Sam Crawford **Baseball coach**; Carl Harbaugh **Rowing coach**

THE GAME Class valedictorian Ronald (Buster Keaton) delivers a speech at his high school graduation painting the virtues of academics over athletics. It is not well received by the jock-admiring student body. Only his mother (Florence Turner) supports him.

After his address, the school's most popular girl, Mary Haines (Anne Cornwall), the gal Ronald is in love with, lays it out, telling him she's not going to pay him any attention unless he proves himself as an athlete. She then takes off with the brawny jock Jeff Brown (Harold Goodwin).

The following semester Ronald enrolls at Clayton College, where Mary is also a student, and works as a soda clerk to support himself. That job doesn't work out, though, and neither does his position as a "colored" waiter where he tries to avoid embarrassment when one day Jeff and Mary come to dine.

Ronald decides to give athletics a go, but his efforts to make the school baseball team are disastrous. Mary witnesses his valiant but failed attempts in track and field. Ronald's focus on sports has caused his grades to drop, and he's admonished by the dean (Snitz Edwards). The frustrated student explains that his academic work has suffered in his quest to win Mary's heart through athletics, and the empathetic dean arranges for Ronald to become the coxswain on the school's rowing team, where he ingeniously helps the team to a major victory.

When the team gets back to the locker room, Ronald receives a call from Mary. In a jealous rage, Jeff has kidnapped her in her own room. Showing great athleticism dashing through the crowded campus, Ronald valiantly pole vaults into Mary's second-floor living quarters and saves her as Jeff scurries out a window. Unfortunately, the Dean immediately arrives on the scene and, finding them together in Mary's room, expels them both instantly.

Undaunted, Ronald takes Mary down the fire escape and to a chapel to be married. They raise a family and grow old together until the day they die.

INSTANT REPLAY Perhaps no other Keaton film showed the comedian's physical grace more than *College*, reportedly Keaton's personal favorite among his own pictures. Unfortunately, it came in between two of his greatest films, *The General* (1927) and *Steamboat Bill Jr.* (1928), and its comparatively inferior narrative spine is exposed as a result. Additionally, it was linked to Harold Lloyd's earlier film, *The Freshman* (1925), which had a similar story line (though it seems clear that Keaton had more athletic talent). It takes a superb athlete to comically portray a bad one, and Keaton's unique style of physical comedy is on full display here.

While his supporting cast is serviceable, it is Buster's athletic misadventures that

The academically oriented Dean (Snitz Edwards) tells new student Ronald (Buster Keaton, right), "A boy like you can make this athlete-infested college a seat of learning once more."

carry the film. Even off the playing fields, his routine as a "colored" waiter is memorable and shameful at the same time. His soda clerk scenes are humorous. The brief montage at the end that shows Ronald and Mary as not living so happily ever after seems a bit out of place and is certainly a break from the cliché romantic endings. It is in fact an interesting revelation, at the same time humorous and sad. Keaton conveys what happens in real life after the conventional marriages that happily conclude romantic formula movies.

Keaton's scenes of physical dexterity in baseball, athletics, and rowing are indelible. Whether he's letting balls get by him playing defense in baseball, trying to mimic the different track athletes in events like hurdling or tossing the hammer, or falling through the rowboat, the laughs are loud and sustained. Interestingly, we see his real athleticism when he runs across campus to save Mary. Keaton did all his own work except the vaulting into the second-floor room.

Like Charlie Chaplin and Harold Lloyd, Keaton knew most people are entertained by another person's embarrassments and predicaments. Keaton draws an everyman character full of pathos, who garners empathy through his ridiculousness. In *College*, Keaton gives an education as a man on top of his game in terms of physical humor.

OUTSIDE THE LINES Snitz Edwards also starred with Buster in his boxing picture *Battling Butler* (1926).... Actor/writer Carl Harbaugh also appeared in Errol Flynn's boxing movie, *Gentleman Jim* (1942).... The crew boat headed up by Keaton is called "Damfino," which was also the name of the boat in his short *The Boat* (1921).... Keaton was 32 at the time of this film and was in great shape, but collegiate athlete Lee Barnes, from USC, did the pole vault scene as Keaton's double. This was a rare occurrence, as Buster enjoyed the challenges of physical humor in his films, but in this case Keaton couldn't afford the time it would take to train to do this one stunt.... Barnes won the Olympic gold medal in pole vaulting at the 1924 Games in Amsterdam as a 17-year-old from Hollywood High School.... *College* was one of Keaton's more profitable pictures.... Keaton's favorite sport, both as a spectator and a participant, was baseball.... The film's baseball scenes were shot at Bovard Athletic Field, part of the University of Southern California campus.... Director James Horne would also direct many Laurel and Hardy comedies.... Russian-born producer Joe Schenck also produced *Battling Butler*.... 67 years later actor Sam Crawford returned to the screen to appear in the basketball drama *Blue Chips* (1994).

ALL-STAR MOMENTS Ronald's valedictorian speech, delivered in an ill-fitting suit to a pro sports crowd, on the curse of athletics: "Future generations depend upon brains and not upon jumping the discus or hurdling the javelin. What have Ty Ruth or Babe Dempsey done for science?"

Pranksters confront Ronald, wrap him up in a blanket, and toss him into the air, where he sees a fat lady getting dressed on the second floor and she throws an umbrella at him. Ronald pulls at the building facade and the fat lady comes tumbling down. The pranksters scatter and Ronald emerges from under her oversized robe.

All sporting efforts by Ronald—baseball, track, rowing.

Ronald's skill in running through the crowd to save Mary, who is kidnapped in her own room across the campus.

HOME COURT ADVANTAGE Available on VHS and DVD. *College* has been released as a solo title by Kino and Genius Entertainment. It has also been released with *The Milky Way* and *The General*, separately with *Lil' Abner*, and in the sets Buster Keaton: The Great Stone Face of Comedy *and The Art of Buster Keaton*, an 11-disc set from Kino.

Ronald (Keaton, left) has a lot to learn about rowing.

#28 THE NATURAL

Screenwriters Roger Towne, Phil Dusenberry. **Director** Barry Levinson. **Producers** Philip Breen, Roger Towne, Mark Johnson, Robert Colesberry. **Cinematography** Caleb Deschanel. **Editing** Stu Linder. **Music** Randy Newman. **Production Design** Mel Bourne, Angelo Graham. TriStar. 1984.

THE PLAYERS

Robert Redford **Roy Hobbs**; Robert Duvall **Max Mercy**; Glenn Close **Iris Gaines**; Wilford Brimley **Pop Fisher**; Kim Basinger **Memo Paris**; Barbara Hershey **Harriet Bird**; Robert Prosky **The Judge**; Richard Farnsworth **Red Blow**; Joe Don Baker **The Whammer**; John Finnegan **Sam Simpson**; Alan Fudge **Ed Hobbs**; Paul Sullivan Jr. **Young Roy**; Rachel Hall **Young Iris**; Robert Rich III **Ted Hobbs**; Michael Madsen **Bump Bailey**; Jon Van Ness **John Olsen**; Mickey Treanor **Doc Dizzy**; George Wilkosz **Bobby Savoy**; Anthony Ferrara **Coach Wilson**; Philip Mankowski **Hank Benz**; Danny Aiello III **Emil LaJong**; Joe Castellano **Allie Stubbs**; Eddie Cipot **Gabby Laslow**; Ken Grassano **Al Fowler**; Robert Kalaf **Cal Baker**; Barry Kivel **Pat McGee**; Steven Kronovet **Tommy Hinkle**; James Meyer **Dutch Schultz**; Michael Starr **Boone**; Sam Green **Murphy**; Darren McGavin **Gus Sands**; Peter Poth **Dr. Knobb**; Elizabeth Klein **Nurse**; Joe Strand **Umpire final game**

THE GAME Young Roy Hobbs (Paul Sullivan) is devastated by the death of his father, who taught him to play baseball. One night during a thunderstorm, the young boy, still dreaming of becoming a ballplayer, carves a bat from a tree struck by lightning and calls it "Wonderboy."

Now a young man, Roy Hobbs (Robert Redford) tells his girlfriend, Iris Gaines (Glenn Close), that he's leaving for a major league baseball tryout and will come back for her.

Even on his train journey Hobbs demonstrates why he is going to be a star. During a stopover in a field near a carnival, Hobbs impresses a leading sportswriter, Max Mercy (Robert Duvall), when he strikes out a Ruthian slugger called The Whammer (Joe Don Baker) on just three pitches.

Back on the train he meets a beautiful woman, Harried Bird (Barbara Hershey). She asks Roy what he wants to achieve.

Roy wants people to one day say, "There goes Roy Hobbs, the best there ever was."

He asks if she'll come see him play. Harriet says she will, then quickly vanishes.

In Chicago, Roy gets a surprise call at his hotel room. It is Harriet. She invites him to her hotel room, where she shoots him.

Sixteen years later, unknown ballplayer Roy Hobbs reappears and signs to play for the New York Knights. He confounds the team manager (Wilford Brimley), but eventually Roy's hitting helps turn the team's fortunes around. The team begins to lose again, however, when Roy meets a gambler's mistress, Memo Paris (Kim Basinger), and his ability to produce on the field diminishes.

Roy's playing turns around when he meets Iris again and is inspired to return to his stellar play. The team's return to success is complicated however by a contractual deal between Pop Fisher, the team manager, and the team owner, the Judge (Robert Prosky). Seems early on when Pop had some financial difficulties he had to sell 10% of his share of the team to the Judge. There was a clause in the contract that if the Knights won Pop could buy his shares back and the Judge must go. If the Knights lose, Pop is out: a winner-take-all deal.

The Judge offers a bribe to Roy, who rejects it.

At a party the gambler's seductress serves something to Roy that is poisonous.

In the hospital Roy learns he could die from complications of the old bullet wound, because his stomach won't have time to heal if he returns to baseball too soon.

The Whammer, a Ruthian figure played by Joe Don Baker, is about to see why Roy Hobbs is The Natural.

Defying doctor's orders and inspired when he sees Iris in the stands with a young boy (their son), Roy leads the Knights to victory.

INSTANT REPLAY Just as a screenplay is a basic blueprint to which other film craftsmen add their talents to produce a multidimensional creation, a book source often changes along the way to suit the visual and commercial needs that film-making demands.

While Bernard Malamud's novel was a darker look at heroes, screenwriter Roger Towne and director Barry Levinson chose to lighten the heavy themes of Malamud's work.

So seen in the context of a fairy tale with a more upbeat ending, *The Natural* succeeds on many fronts. If one is inclined to look at the darker side of our sporting gods, one of the better examples is Ron Shelton's *Cobb*, about baseball great Ty Cobb.

While *The Natural* runs a bit long, is overly sentimental, and overreaches especially with the almost comic-book feel of Hobbs's light-crashing home run, the picture is for the most part quite engaging.

In this Arthurian fable where Roy Hobbs appropriately plays for the Knights and uses his bat like the sword of Excalibur, *The Natural* is about second chances, which even the very gifted sometimes need.

One of the foremost aspects of the film's appeal is its visual splendor. From the attention to detail and texture of the story to the simply beautiful photography, we are swept up into a time machine and deposited in 1930s America.

Caleb Deschanel's camera work is absolutely brilliant. As he did in *The Black Stallion*, Deschanel ably conveys many of the story's themes through visual expression rather than dialogue. His ability to express varying emotional states through his lens and lighting, from dark passages to sun-drenched silhouettes, is a highlight of the film.

The cinematographer is expertly aided by authentic art direction. The production design team of Mel Bourne, Angelo Graham, Gloria Gresham, Bernie Pollack, John Sweeney, and Bruce Weintraub pays close attention to detail, from trains to carnival uniforms, from the hats of the day to city streets.

As for the baseball sequences themselves, outside the aforementioned light-smashing home run, the game action assembled by director Levinson, an avid Baltimore Orioles fan, offers a fairly realistic depiction of the times. The baseball scene outside the ballpark where Hobbs strikes out The Whammer in an open field is a classic image.

Working with editor Stu Linder, who won an Oscar for his work in the racing drama *Grand Prix*, Levinson takes slow-motion shots of baseball to another level here (though overdoing it a bit at times).

Matching the mythmaking combination of the production design and Deschanel's pictures are the tunes of composer Randy Newman. Newman's score contributes much to the emotional scope of the picture, and the stirring combination of music and slow-motion photography has since been emulated by many documentaries.

As for the players, Robert Redford, 46 at the time of the production, certainly had a formidable task and ultimately delivers mixed results. His character seems little changed by his journey. Though he embodies an older ballplayer with a fine grace, Redford comes across at various stages as distant, studied, self-absorbed, one-dimensional, and taciturn for a man living his dream. While one would expect his character to be guarded based on his experiences, Redford's demeanor makes it difficult for the audience to get behind the protagonist. There's precious little natural emotion we can latch onto.

Two veterans who fill out the roster terrifically are the gruff Wilford Brimley and subtle Richard Farnsworth as Redford's baseball coaches.

In the same sense off the field, Glenn Close and Kim Basinger ably play opposites: Close as the classic good girl with a noble persona and Basinger as the devilish platinum blonde.

In his brief appearance as a legendary slugger, Joe Don Baker hams it up quite convincingly, as does Robert Duvall, who adds some spice to the picture as a cagey sportswriter. Darren McGavin brings a memorable element to the story as the nasty gambler.

The Natural is a more upbeat version of the popular novel, a prettier package that shows less of the hero's inner struggle. At the same time there's much more to the "Wonderboy" bat than meets the ball.

Despite the film's inevitable swings and misses in taking on a difficult and dark subject, director Levinson has engagingly and attentively fashioned the symbolism of success in baseball into a beautifully stylized feel-good fairy tale about temptations, self-discovery, and second chances.

Robert Redford stars as Roy Hobbs, a gifted baseball player who overcomes misfortune to excel in the sport.

The mysterious Harriet Byrd (Barbara Hershey) causes Roy's dream of baseball stardom to be pushed back 16 years.

OUTSIDE THE LINES The film finale differs from Bernard Malamud's 1952 novel in that in the picture Hobbs hits a home run but in the book he strikes out.… Actor Richard Farnsworth was a stuntman for many decades, doubling for the likes of Gary Cooper, Henry Fonda, and Roy Rogers.… Glenn Close received an Oscar nomination for her role in this film.… The actress is a three-time Tony winner.… *The Natural* was also nominated for three other Academy Awards, including Best Original Score, Best Cinematography, and Best Art Direction-Set Decoration.… Over this project's long development period various actors were up for the role of Hobbs, including Nick Nolte, Michael

Douglas, and Jon Voight.... Redford, who was 46 at the time the picture was in production, earned a baseball scholarship to the University of Colorado but dropped out of school.... The film's screenwriter and producer, Roger Towne, is the brother of writer/director Robert Towne (*Personal Best, Without Limits*).... Caleb Deschanel, who was nominated for an Oscar here, was also the cinematographer for *The Black Stallion* (1979).... The picture was filmed partly in Buffalo's War Memorial stadium, which was built in the 1930s and was home to the minor league AA Bisons team.... All High Stadium, built in 1929 in Buffalo, served as Wrigley Field.... Robert Duvall's sports movie credits include *Kicking and Screaming* (2005), *A Shot at Glory* (2000), *Days of Thunder* (1990), *The Terry Fox Story* (1983), and *The Greatest* (1977).... Redford's character wore #9 because the actor's childhood hero was slugger Ted Williams.... .Barbara Hershey also starred in *Hoosiers* (1986).... Former major league Rookie of the Year Joe Charboneau of the Cleveland Indians appears in the film.... The film's shooting scene with Barbara Hershey was based on a real-life incident in 1949 when Eddie Waitkus, an all-star first baseman for the Philadelphia Phillies, was shot in the chest by a deranged 19-year-old typist, Ruth Steinhagen, from a Chicago insurance company.... Waitkus recovered from his chest wound and Ruth was committed to a state mental institute.... It took Hobbs 16 years to return to baseball, but after several operations Waitkus returned within a year and was a key factor in the team's 1950 pennant-winning effort.... Redford, who produced the golf feature *The Legend of Bagger Vance* (2000), starred in *Little Fauss and Big Halsy* (1970) as well as *Downhill Racer* (1969).... In his next sports film, which is about Jackie Robinson, Redford is scheduled to portray Dodgers executive Branch Rickey.... The film's batboy, George Wilkosz, was found working at his parents' produce stand in Buffalo; *The Natural* is his only movie appearance.... The film's editor, Stu Linder, won an Oscar for his work on *Grand Prix* (1966).

Glenn Close is Roy's lady, Iris.

ALL-STAR MOMENTS
After watching Roy (Redford) knock off pins with his accurate throwing at a carnival, Sam (Finnegan) challenges The Whammer (Baker).

> SAM: I got $10 here that says he strikes out Whamballs here out on three pitched balls.

> WHAMMER: Well, you old boozer, your brain must be full of mush. This shitkicker couldn't strike me out with 100 pitches.

After two pitches and two strikes we see a slo-mo tight shot as Roy releases the ball then Whammer swings and misses with the ball slamming into the catcher's glove for strike three.

To prove his hitting skills Roy steps into the batter's box during practice. He crushes the first two pitches. The embarrassed pitcher then says, "Try this one, Grandpa." With teammates and the batboy watching, Roy proceeds to hammer that and continues his impressive hitting display. Roy then winks at the batboy. His disbelieving coach, Pop (Brimley), questions the legality of Roy's bat and orders him to go "shag some flies."

HOME COURT ADVANTAGE
Available on VHS on DVD.

#27 THE HARDER THEY FALL

Screenwriter Philip Yordan. **Director** Mark Robson. **Producer** Philip Yordan. **Cinematography** Burnett Guffey. **Editing** Jerome Thoms. **Art Direction** William Flannery. Columbia. 1956.

THE PLAYERS
Humphrey Bogart **Eddie Willis**; Rod Steiger **Nick Benko**; Jan Sterling **Beth Willis**; Mike Lane **Toro Moreno**; Max Baer **Buddy Brannen**; Jersey Joe Walcott **George**; Harold Stone **Art Leavitt**; Edward Andrews **Jim Weyerhause**; Carlos Montalban **Luis Agrandi**; Nehemiah Persoff **Leo**; Felice Orlandi **Vince Fawcett**; Herbie Faye **Max**; Rusty Lane **Danny McKeogh**; Jack Albertson **Pop**; Val Avery **Frank**; Tommy Herman **Tommy**; Vinnie De Carlo **Joey**; Pat Comiskey **Gus Dundee**; Matt Murphy **Sailor Rigazzo**; Marian Carr **Alice**; Abel Fernandez **Chief Firebird**; Joe Greb **Ex-fighter**; Lewis Smith **Brannen's manager**; Everett Glass **Minister**; William Roerick **Lawyer**; Lillian Culver **Mrs. Harding**; Pat Dane **Shirley**; Tina Carver **Mrs. Benko**; Jack Daly **Reporter**; Richard Norris **Reporter**; Stafford Repp **Reporter**; Mark Scott **Reporter**; Mort Mills **Reporter**; Michael Granger **Doctor**; Paul Frees **Priest**

THE GAME Despite the battle put up by his conscience and his wife (Jan Sterling), unemployed sportswriter Eddie Willis (Humphrey Bogart) takes the money and joins slick fight racketeer Nick Benko (Rod Steiger) in transforming a weak-jawed, untalented physical giant of a boxer named Toro Moreno (Mike Lane) into a title contender through smoke and mirrors, namely fixed fights and Willis's myth-building press corps work.

Despite the pleas of sportswriters like Art Leavitt (Harold Stone) and seeing the sport's deadly toll on pros like aging pugilist Gus Dundee (Pat Comiskey), Willis continues the charade, building up the overmatched Moreno working toward the grand title payday.

By the time Toro reaches the "height" of his career, everyone except Moreno knows his fights have been fixed. On the eve of the title fight against Buddy Brannen (Max Baer), who refuses to carry Moreno and instead aims for a severe beating, it takes just one punch from Moreno's sympathetic trainer (Jersey Joe Wolcott) to bring the big man down to earth. At the same time, Willis has learned that Benko plans to withhold all the earnings Moreno has made, and his conscience reasserts itself. As he ushers Moreno to safety, escorting him to a plane that will take him back home to South America, Willis ends up giving the big man all his own earnings.

Back in his financial hole but with a cleaner conscience, Willis ignores Benko's continuing threats and proceeds to write a riveting exposé of the corruption in the fight game.

INSTANT REPLAY *The Harder They Fall* is main event material. The picture, with its realistic social conscience, pulls few punches in looking at the human cost of the fight game. The twist here is that we see through the eyes of a journalist.

Using a powerful left-right combination that incorporates elements of the 1950s exposés *Blackboard Jungle* and *On the Waterfront* as well as an unrelenting look at the dark side of boxing seen in the late 1940s (and in director Mark Robson's other boxing classic, *Champion*, and Robert Wise's *The Set-Up*), Robson masterfully presents a noirish picture that explores not only the exploitation of boxers but also the power of publicity and mythmaking in this country.

Philip Yordan's script, based on the Budd Schulberg novel, while at times a bit heavy-handed with self-righteous monologues, overall provides a smart, hard-hitting, and realistic look at the underside of the fight game of the '50s.

Robson uses Yordan's template and fashions a gritty yet compassionate indictment of the "sweet science." Helping the director achieve this on the technical side is Burnett Guffey's harsh black and white cinematography with William Flannery's authentic art direction and the compelling score of composer Hugo Friedhofer, all concisely edited by Jerome Thoms.

The real emotional punch, however, comes from the performances of the entire cast, led by two heavyweights.

In a brilliant bit of casting, *The Harder They Fall* provides a rare glimpse of two very talented performers whose contrasting approaches to their craft provide a great fight within a fight.

Humphrey Bogart, in a fitting final performance, yet again expertly gives us that complex person—cynical, disillusioned, whose integrity and honesty go toe-to-toe with his assorted weaknesses and vices (the whole range of which register on his face). This is a study of an old master at work.

While the actual fight sequences vary in verisimilitude, the sparks really fly outside the ring in the scenes between Bogart and Rod Steiger. Neither is about to have any scene stolen and their intensity is quite compelling.

Steiger, from the relatively new school of method acting whereby one embodies the

(Left to right) Toro Moreno (Mike Lane), Eddie Willis (Humphrey Bogart), Beth Willis (Jan Sterling). This would be Humphrey Bogart's last movie.

traits and problems of the character and thus becomes him, wastes no time taking complete advantage of his character's aggressiveness, which helps give the picture its raw power and hard edge. Curiously, though, despite the successes he seizes, Steiger's Benko continues to operate from a sort of frenzied desperation that undermines his menacing persona by the film's end.

SPORTS CINEMA

The supporting cast, from the pros to the rookies, contributes ably to the project.

In his debut performance, Mike Lane as Toro Moreno handles surprisingly well the tough dual chore of presenting his boxer character as simultaneously sympathetic and comic. Jan Sterling is steady, though her character is a bit underwritten, as Bogey's understanding wife, who verbalizes his conscience. Harold Stone's fine rendering of the compassionate, perceptive sportswriter Art Leavitt is never more evident than in his interview with down-and-out boxer Joe Greb.

Adding to the authenticity are former heavyweight champion Jersey Joe Wolcott as the sympathetic trainer and Max Baer as a cocky opponent of Moreno.

The Harder They Fall is a darkly compelling story whose uncompromising tone is a terrific legacy for two of the silver screen's most memorable performers, Rod Steiger and Humphrey Bogart, a pair of gifted thespian heavyweights.

OUTSIDE THE LINES
This was Bogart's last film, as he would soon die from cancer.... The story was loosely based on mammoth Italian boxer Primo Carnera, and the screenplay was adapted from Budd Schulberg's novel.... Schulberg won an Oscar for his screenplay for *On the Waterfront* (1954).... Burnett Guffey was nominated for an Academy Award for his cinematography.... Guffey also shot *The Great White Hope* (1970).... Former heavyweight champion Max Baer costarred with Myrna Loy in *The Prizefighter and the Lady* (1933).... Primo Carnera appeared as himself in that film.... In 1951 Jersey Joe Walcott at 37 became the oldest heavyweight champion.... In 1994 George Foreman broke his record, winning the crown at age 44.... Making his film debut here, Mike Lane was a professional wrestler known as "Tarzan Mike."...Jan Sterling was married to Paul Douglas, who starred in the baseball features *It Happens Every Spring* (1949) and *Angels in the Outfield* (1951).... Former boxer John Indrisano was a technical advisor.... Among his many boxing films credits are *The Set-Up* (1949), *Somebody Up There Likes Me* (1956), and *Right Cross* (1950).... Mark Robson also directed *Champion* (1949), starring Kirk Douglas.

ALL-STAR MOMENTS
Fans suspect Gus Dundee (Pat Comiskey) is taking a dive in his lackluster fight against Toro Moreno (Mike Lane). When he goes down in the third fans boo and throw debris in the ring. When he leaves on a stretcher an elderly lady yells out, "You're yellow, Gus!"

In fact, Gus was seriously injured in a previous fight against Buddy Brannen (Max Baer), and his bout with Moreno has brought the damage to the fore. As Gus lies in the hospital bed, promoter Nick Benko demands that his press agent, Eddie Willis (Humphrey Bogart) use some of his writing magic to satisfy the doubts of the press.

NICK: Eddie, listen, you gotta do something because it's going to look lousy for us if the press plays up the angle that Gus was finished after the Brannen fight. You gotta make up a story, something for the morning papers.

EDDIE: You mean something like, "Gus was a formidable opponent but when he climbed into the ring with the Wild Man of the Andes (Moreno), he was gambling with his life."

NICK: That's wonderful.

EDDIE: And you want to put the New York Boxing Commission on notice of that.

NICK: Great. That's exactly right.

EDDIE: It sure is great. How can you be worrying about the press when Gus is lying in there with a tube in his head?

As the press take photos of Gus being wheeled by in the hospital staff, Nick pours on the charm. Eddie is disgusted.

Sportswriter Art Leavitt (Harold Stone) interviewing down-and-out ex-boxer Joe Greb "standing outside Barney's Beanery from Skid Row in Los Angeles."

Toro, who is convinced he is responsible for killing Gus with his boxing prowess, is told the truth when Eddie enters his hotel room.

EDDIE: ...let me tell you something. You couldn't kill somebody unless you had a gun.

TORO: What do you mean?!

EDDIE: Just what I said. You can't punch. You're a fake. You never hurt anyone.

TORO: I punch. They go boom. Twenty-six men.

EDDIE: Every one was a fix or a pushover.

TORO: I don't believe you.

EDDIE: I don't care what you believe. It's the truth. You're not even a 10th-rate fighter. You're what they call a bum.

TORO: I'm no bum. I train hard and I fight hard. I do not know my own strength.

EDDIE: Read all those lies I write about you. Nick Benko paid me to make up those fairy tales so people would think you couldn't be hurt.

TORO: No one could hurt The Toro.

EDDIE: Oh, any saloon fighter could wipe up the floor with you.

TORO: Go away, Eddie, go away.

Eddie calls in old cornerman George (Jersey Joe Walcott). Eddie says the only way to convince Toro is to get hit by "this old broken-down war horse." Reluctantly, George complies. After decking him with one punch. George helps Toro up. Eddie pronounces, "...you don't punch hard enough to bust an egg.... You better go home before you get yourself badly hurt. . . ."

At Nick's hotel room Eddie picks up his share, but when he asks for Toro's so he can bring it to him, Leo (Nehemiah Persoff) explains that Toro doesn't get his cut until after expenses. It turns out to be less than $50 for a million-dollar gate!

Eddie escorts Toro to the airport to get him back to his native Argentina. Eddie's share was $26,000, and he gives it all to Toro. Back at his apartment, Benko threatens him but Eddie stands his ground: "You gonna have your muscle men work me over? I can still write from a hospital bed.... A man that gives away $26,000 you can't talk to. I want to tell you one more thing. I wouldn't give 26 cents for your future."

HOME COURT ADVANTAGE Available on DVD.

#26 EIGHT MEN OUT

Screenwriter/Director John Sayles. **Producers** Barbara Boyle, Jerry Offsay, Sarah Pillsbury, Midge Sanford. **Cinematography** Robert Richardson. **Editing** John Tintori. **Music** Mason Daring. **Production Design** Nora Chavooshian. **Art Direction** Dan Bishop. **Costume Design** Cynthia Flynt, Brenda Whitney. Orion. 1988.

THE PLAYERS
John Cusack **Buck Weaver**; John Mahoney **Kid Gleason**; Jace Alexander **Dickie Kerr**; Gordon Clapp **Ray Schalk**; Michael Rooker **Chick Gandil**; Don Harvey **Swede Risberg**; Bill Irwin **Eddie Collins**; D. B. Sweeney **Shoeless Joe Jackson**; David Strathairn **Eddie Cicotte**; Michael Lerner **Arnold Rothstein**; Perry Lang **Fred McMullin**; James Read **Claude "Lefty" Williams**; Jim Desmond **Smitty**; John Sayles **Ring Lardner**; Studs Terkel **Hugh Fullerton**; Richard Edson **Billy Maharg**; Christopher Lloyd **Bill Burns**; Michael Mantell **Abe Attell**; Kevin Tighe **Sports Sullivan**; Eliot Asinof **Heydler**; Clyde Bassett **Ban Johnson**; Clifton James **Charles Comiskey**; John Craig **Rothstein's attorney**; Michael Laskin **Austrian**; Randle Mell **Ahearn**; Robert Motz **D.A.**; Bill Raymond **Ben Short**; Barbara Garrick **Helen Weaver**; Wendy Makkena **Kate Jackson**; Maggie Renzi **Rose Cicotte**; Nancy Travis **Lyria Williams**; Brad Garrett **Pee Wee**; Tay Strathairn **Bucky**; Jesse Vincent **Scooter**; John Anderson **Judge Kenesaw Mountain Landis**

THE GAME Clearly one of the dominant teams in the league, the Chicago White Sox of 1919 are so rich in talent that they can practically field their own all-star team.

Pitcher Eddie Cicotte (David Strathairn) and Claude "Lefty" Williams (James Reed) have a terrific catcher, Ray Schalk (Gordon Clapp), to throw to and great support in the field and at bat with gifted teammates like Buck Weaver (John Cusack), Eddie Collins (Bill Irwin), Hap Felsch (Charlie Sheen), and the great Shoeless Joe Jackson (D. B. Sweeney).

Despite all the skill on display, with the exception of Collins, the White Sox players are grossly underpaid by a notoriously cheap owner, Charles Comiskey (Clifton James). This has never been more evident than when the players' joy at winning the pennant literally turns sour because their owner shows his appreciation by supplying them with flat champagne as their bonus—and when Comiskey denies his always-dependable pitcher Cicotte a bonus he's earned.

Unfortunately, the players don't have a lot of recourse. In an era of no free agency the reserve clause basically keeps the players beholden to Comiskey for their baseball livelihood. Soon, however, the financial dispute between labor and management will take on nasty dimensions.

Figuring more money could be made illegally than from salaries and winning bonuses, word gets out to the gambling underground that several of the White Sox players would be willing to fix their World Series games against the Cincinnati Reds if the price was right.

In meeting with first baseman Chick Gandil (Michael Rooker), gambler Sport Sullivan (Kevin Tighe) has a hard time believing that six or seven of the game's greatest ballplayers would be willing to accept a payoff.

Chick tells him, "You never played for Charles Comiskey."

As Chick approaches various teammates, some readily agree while others are more conflicted, not only reluctant to taint the game they love and their fans' trust but concerned about their family responsibilities. One thing is for sure: they are all motivated to get back at baseball's Scrooge, Charles Comiskey.

The World Series begins but as the White Sox lose the first game, making the gamblers happy, Gandil's dirty coalition of teammates, never very cohesive, begins to

Writer/director John Sayles's version of the 1919 Chicago White Sox.

unravel from a crisis of conscience, not helped by the suspicions of their purist manager Kid Gleason (John Mahoney) and the observant eyes of reporters Ring Lardner (John Sayles) and Hugh Fullerton (Studs Terkel).

After the White Sox lose the Series in eight games, newspaper headlines are filled with allegations of a fix. Owner Comiskey offers a reward of $10,000 for evidence and an investigation ensues.

At this time Comiskey and the other owners welcome a new baseball commissioner who is given absolute power to restore some of the lost integrity of the game.

The new commissioner, Judge Kenesaw Mountain Landis (John Anderson), scribbles notes while attending the trial of the eight White Sox players suspected of participating in the fix. Eventually the grand jury finds the players not guilty.

The players' relief is only temporary, because soon afterward the iron-fisted new commissioner lowers the boom, reading a powerful statement he's prepared before a gathered press corps:

Regardless of the verdict of juries, no player who throws a ball game, no player who undertakes or promises to throw a game, no player who sits in conference with a bunch of crooked players and gamblers where the ways and means of throwing a ball game were discussed and does not promptly tell his club about it, will ever play professional baseball again.

Thus ends the professional careers of eight players of the 1919 Chicago White Sox.

INSTANT REPLAY *Eight Men Out* uses one of sports' greatest scandals as a socioeconomic and political representation of a period of American history at an end of its innocence. The year 1919 was a powder keg that would explode into the Roaring '20s.

As Robert Redford and Alan Pakula do in *Quiz Show* and *All the President's Men*, writer/director John Sayles provides an interesting examination of a scandal that shook the public's faith in a national institution.

Eight Men Out is a fascinating picture that earns high marks for being very atmospheric, incorporating realistic and dramatic baseball game sequences. It does have shortcomings, however, and almost all can be traced back to the scope of the subject matter. With enough information here to fill a miniseries, let alone a two-hour feature, even the most rudimentary factual elements compete with character development of a massive ensemble cast, making the story hard to grasp for those uninitiated to the event going into the theater.

Sayles gives the viewer a clue, though, by using the familiar universal themes of power, ignorance, greed, corruption, and temptation that go back to the days of the Roman Senate, and by making money the star.

Though "lefty" Sayles's sympathies lie with the exploited ballplayers, he doesn't condone their actions as did author Eliot Asinoff in the book on which the film is based.

Those ballplayers, despite having to compete for precious screen time in their own competition of "Who's on first?" are uniformly terrific.

Michael Rooker and Don Harvey are quite convincing in their efforts to get the key players to participate in their scheme, making their subsequent desperation when the plan unravels all the more effective.

Two actors in relatively small roles, D. B. Sweeney as Shoeless Joe Jackson and Charlie Sheen as Hap Felsch, markedly enhance the game sequences with their very real baseball skills.

John Cusack is solid as the story's conscience, the deeply conflicted third baseman Buck Weaver. He is the muddied idealist, in on the scheming but taking no money, determined to give his very best and live up to the trust invested by his many fans.

David Strathairn is simply wonderful as the weary, exploited pitcher in the autumn of his career sadly knowing he's doing the wrong thing but seeing no alternative.

As manager Kid Gleason, John Mahoney gives a passionate turn, refusing to believe the dark side has gotten the better of his players.

The gamblers, too, are well cast. Michael Lerner is particularly noteworthy as the big-time gambler Arnold Rothstein, endlessly seeking revenge for the scars of his youth, when he was ridiculed for his lack of athleticism.

Time permitting, Sayles shows he can draw fine three-dimensional portraits, giving shades of gray to both good and bad guys like Weaver and Rothstein.

Though Sayles himself as sports writer Ring Lardner and Studs Terkel as High Fullerton deliver some of the best lines as a sort of Greek chorus to the proceedings, it might have been more interesting if they had played up their Woodward and Bernstein role more.

Veteran Clifton James physically embodies the greedy owner Charles Comiskey, who lives the good life at his players' expense and has the girth to prove it.

The outstanding production design efforts of Nora Chavooshian and the costume work by Cynthia Flynt and Brenda Whitney provide a fine canvas for the perfomers' efforts in spite of a tight budget.

It's all put on celluloid by the capable artistry of cinematographer Robert Richardson.

Sayles should also be credited for making the games convincingly dramatic despite many knowing the outcome. In this aspect the filmmaker is well supported by the editing of John Tintori and the technical advisory work of former White Sox player Ken Berry.

TOP: John Cusack as Sox player George "Buck" Weaver.

BOTTOM: (Left to right) Bill Burns (Christopher Lloyd), Billy Maharg (Richard Edson), and Smitty (Jim Desmond).

Among the press covering the trial are Ring Lardner (John Sayles, center) and Hugh Fullerton (Studs Terkel, right).

Writer/director John Sayles, despite time constraints, effectively uses the national pastime to illustrate the state of our nation and where it was headed at the end of an era.

OUTSIDE THE LINES The film was based on Eliot Asinof's book.... The author appears in the film as National League President John Heydler.... He also played for the Philadelphia Phillies in their farm system for a few years.... Former White Sox outfielder Ken Berry was an advisor.... The filmmakers used Bush Stadium in Indianapolis to represent Comiskey Park as well as Redland Field.... Bush Stadium was at one time home to the Montreal Expos' farm team, the Indianapolis Indians.... D. B. Sweeney, who trained with the Minnesota Twins' minor league team in Kenosha to learn to hit left-handed, played a hockey player-turned-figure-skater in *The Cutting Edge* (1992).... His other sports-themed credits include *Going to the Mat* (2004), *Hard Ball* (2001), and *Heaven is a Playground* (1991).... The actor also was one of the narrators for the Fox Sports Net series *Beyond the Glory*.... The judge who orders Weaver (John Cusack) to sit down after his outburst is actually the actor's father.... Reportedly Babe Ruth called Shoeless Joe Jackson the greatest natural hitter he ever saw.... Jackson earned his nickname by taking off new spikes in the middle of a game that had given him blisters and proceeding to hit well barefoot.... Over the years of this project's long development, among the actors approached for various roles were Kurt Russell, Emilio Estevez, Stacy Keach, Dennis Quaid, Ed Harris, Jeff Daniels, and Kevin Bacon.... Actor Strathairn attended the Ringling Bros. Clown College and subsequently worked as a clown for several months in a traveling circus early in his career.... He also played a promotion man in baseball's *A League of Their Own* (1992).... Charlie Sheen starred in the baseball comedy *Major League* (1989) and its sequel.... Christopher Lloyd starred in the baseball remake *Angels in the Outfield* (1994).

ALL-STAR MOMENTS Camera work and editing between the catcher, Ray Schalk (Clapp), calling signals and the pitcher, Eddie Cicotte (Strathairn), and subsequent game action early in the picture with shots of authentic equipment of the times. Later the team owner Charles Comiskey (James) tells the press, "Fifty years of baseball—he's still got the best knuckleball I've ever seen."

Later, in Comiskey's office, Eddie demands his bonus: "You said if I won 30 games this year, there'd be a $10k bonus." The owner points outs he's only won 29. Eddie says it wasn't his fault; he missed five starts be being benched when he was good to go. Comiskey said they had to rest his arm for the World Series. Eddie is not convinced but leaves without his bonus.

After the Sox's Ray turns a single into a double, the players and fans watch a plane circle above. It drops a dummy wearing a White Sox uniform, which lands near the Sox dugout. As the players stand over it, Kid, the Sox manager (Mahoney), sarcastically looks at Lefty (James Read), whom Kid suspects of not giving his all, and says, "Ask if it can pitch."

Small-time hoods Bill (Christopher Lloyd) and Billy (Richard Edson) approach Abe (Michael Mantell) for the players' cut of the take. They are told "it's all out on bets" and that they have the players under control because they can't go screaming to the cops. Abe tosses them a much smaller amount to divide among the bribed ballplayers. It's now Bill and Billy's problem to make a deal that will shortchange the players either way. "Come on, Bill, it stinks in here," Abe says. "Tell them bums to make it look good tomorrow." Just down the hallway Comiskey is fuming at what is going on.

TOP: Pitcher Eddie Cicotte (David Strathairn).

BOTTOM: Talented outfielder Shoeless Joe Jackson (D. B. Sweeney) surrounded by reporters.

Entertaining pitching sequence of Dickie Kerr (Jace Alexander) throwing and hitting to help the White Sox win the game.

Pissed about the whole thing and determined to pitch a great game, Eddie does a turnabout much to the chagrin of the gamblers, who thought they had him in their pocket. The White Sox win the game on Eddie's brilliant pitching performance.

Buck Weaver's (Cusack) appeal to the judge that he's being lumped in with the others even though he "didn't take a dime" and that the prosecution isn't even asking the right questions as tough new commissioner Judge Kenesaw Mountain Landis (Anderson) looks on.

When the verdict is read, "not guilty on all charges," the sportswriters whisper to each other:

RING LARDNER (Sayles): That was a bigger fix than the Series.

HUGH FULLERTON (Terkel): Gamblers 8, baseball nothing.

Years later at a ballpark in Hoboken, New Jersey, some kids in the stands are impressed with the play of a left-handed hitting outfielder and ask, "Who is that guy?" One fan insists it is Joe Jackson even though he's listed under another name. Buck Weaver is sitting near them and says, "I saw him play.... those players are all gone now." We see Joe rip the ball for a triple.

HOME COURT ADVANTAGE Available on VHS and DVD. Originally released by MGM, the studio has also included it in a 4-disc "Grand Slam" set with *Bull Durham*, *The Jackie Robinson Story*, and *The Pride of the Yankees*.

#25 NIGHT AND THE CITY

Screenwriter Jo Eisinger. (Novel by Gerald Kersh.) **Director** Jules Dassin. **Producer** Sam Engel. **Cinematography** Max Greene. **Editing** Nick DeMaggio, Sidney Stone. **Music** Franz Waxman. **Art Direction** CP Norman. Fox. 1950.

THE PLAYERS Richard Widmark **Harry Fabian**; Gene Tierney **Mary Bristol**; Googie Withers **Helen Nosseross**; Francis Sullivan **Phil Nosseross**; Herbert Lom **Kristo**; Stanislaus Zbyszko **Gregorius**; Mike Mazurki **Strangler**; Hugh Marlowe **Adam Dunne**; Ken Richmond **Nikolas**; Charles Farrell **Beer**; James Hayter **Figler**; Eliot Makeham **Pinkney**; Edward Chapman **Hoskins**; Maureen Delaney **Anna O'Leary**; Betty Shale **Mrs. Pinkney**; Thomas Gallagher **Bagrag**; Russell Westwood **Yosh**; Ada Reeve **Molly**

THE GAME Harry Fabian (Richard Widmark) works for the rotund Phil Nosseross (Francis Sullivan) as a glib tout for the Silver Fox night club on the dark side of London, cajoling unsuspecting people looking for a good time to check out the titillating shows. He is a man driven to "be somebody" and is full of wild schemes geared towards making himself "big time." His girlfriend , Mary Bristol (Gene Tierney), is the only one patient enough to listen—and even she just wants him to return her love and get a decent job.

One night Harry goes to a sports arena to hustle some more suckers to go the club, but he's spotted as a barker. As he's being tossed out Fabian overhears the famous Greco-Roman wrestler Gregorius (Zbyszko) complain that he's disgusted with all this fake wrestling. His son, Kristo (Herbert Lom), the area's kingpin wrestling promoter, pleads with his father to stay, to no avail. Fabian ingratiates himself with Gregorius and his friend Nikolas (Ken Richmond), passing himself off as an up-and-coming promoter who will return Greco-Roman wrestling to a top commercial draw, and makes a deal with them over drinks. Hearing that his father has lent himself to Fabian, Kristo threatens to kill Harry if he misuses his father's name.

Sensing his chance, Fabian asks his boss to lend him the wrestling promotion money but is turned down. He then appeals to his boss's wife, Helen (Googie Withers), with whom he's had an affair. Helen agrees to get him the money, but only if he can make arrangements for her to get a nightclub license and strike out on her own so she can dump her domineering and repulsive husband once and for all.

Ever resourceful when he smells an opportunity, Fabian succeeds in securing the proper papers for Helen. She leaves her husband, who now suspects that Harry has had a fling with his wife. Nosseross goes to powerful promoter Kristo and works out a deal to wreck Fabian. To play it out Mr. Nosseross tells Harry that he will finance his wrestling match, but only if The Strangler (Mike Mazurki) is Gregorius's opponent. Harry knows this won't go over well with his only ace, Gregorius, since The Strangler represents all of the new trends in the sport that the old wrestler hates. Meeting at a gym, The Strangler insults Gregorius and a huge battle ensues that Harry is helpless to stop. During the fight, the old man suffers a stroke.

Kristo arrives in time to see his father, Gregorius, die. Fabian, knowing he's the fall guy, takes off running for his life. Helen and his old boss refuse to help him and Harry has no alternative but to run through the dark streets of the poor side of London, haunted by the knowledge that anyone he comes across could be a hired gun out to kill him.

"I just want to be somebody"—shady schemer Harry Fabian (Richard Widmark, right) is overmatched at every turn.

He winds up at the door of an old lady, Anna O'Leary (Maureen Delaney), whom he's dealt with in the past. He pours his soul out to her, revealing his fears—but his remorse is insincere. As he's so often done in the past, he's trying to sweet-talk his friend into supporting his crazy ways. Somehow Harry's guardian angel, his only true love, Mary, finds him, but it's too late: Kristo's henchman have also found him. Though he escapes their clutches, he finally runs into The Strangler, who kills him and tosses his corpse into the Thames.

INSTANT REPLAY Jules Dassin's London is not a pretty place. The director takes us on an uncompromising, dark journey through a part of the city no tourists see by choice. With the help of producer Sam Engle and a vivid and literate screenplay by Jo Eisinger, Dassin presents London's ugly underbelly in a fine adaptation of the bestselling novel. Max Greene's photography, C. P. Norman's art direction, and Franz Waxman's music combine to fill the screen with a grim, moody realism against the very real back streets of London.

Night and the City reminds one of another of Dassin's films, *The Naked City,* as in both the city is a major element of the picture as opposed to being a mere backdrop to the action. The authentic environment does a lot to establish the bleak feel and unrelenting intensity that pours forth from the opening scenes.

The film is full of vicious, unscrupulous people living dangerous lives on the edge of disaster. As in most film noir pictures, nobody is really a saint. Richard Widmark's Harry Fabian is the embodiment of this sinister, cannibalistic world. Widmark is convincing and memorable in this character study of a crooked, hysterical, sniveling hustler/dreamer bent on doing whatever it takes to make a name for himself. The American actor is brilliantly devilish as the film practically revels in his deep pockets

Stanislaus Zbyszko (as Gregorius, second from left), a three-time world wrestling champion, was 73 at the time of filming.

filled not with gold but with deceptions and lies. From neglecting the only woman who loves him to having an affair with his boss's wife, Widmark tosses loyalty and sentiment down the gutter, sacrificing everything to his overriding drive to be a player.

Gene Tierney makes do with a limited opportunity as the patient heroine. As the nightclub owners, Francis Sullivan and Googie Withers exemplify conniving and moral bankruptcy. Withers is spot on as the selfish, scheming, two-timing wife who grows to abhor her corpulent husband who starves for her affection. Sullivan too is smart and oily. Stanislaus Zbyszko as the wrestling traditionalist is a pleasant surprise; outside of Tierney, he provides the only real sympathetic character in the film. His battle with Mike Mazurki is riveting, especially when the grossly outweighed Widmark tries to break it up. Herbert Lom imbues the influential promoter with a cold, sinister danger.

Dassin's efforts to create a morbidly interesting film of unremitting suspense and ever-rising menace seem contrived at times. Overall, however, *Night and the City* is a relentlessly dark dramatization of Gerald Kersh's novel.

OUTSIDE THE LINES
Stanislaus Zbyszko was a three-time world heavyweight wrestling champion and was 73 at the time of filming.... This would be the last film Dassin would work on for a major American studio, as he was blackballed after being identified as a Communist by director Ed Dmytryk at a House Un-American Activities Committee meeting.... He directed films in France and Greece before being allowed to work in Hollywood again in the mid '60s.... This film was remade with Robert DeNiro in 1992 featuring New York City.... Austrian-born former professional wrestler Mike Mazurki performed in the boxing film *Gentleman Jim* (1942).... Actress Gene Tierney was a candidate for the lead role that went to Elizabeth Taylor in *National Velvet* (1944).

ALL-STAR MOMENTS
Opening scenes as a frantic Harry Fabian (Widmark), running from trouble, hides out at his girlfriend's place and shamelessly asks Mary (Tierney) for money on a racing scam: "[Just] 300 pounds for a life of ease.... I just want to be somebody."

The fight between Gregorius (Zbyszko) and The Strangler (Mazurki).

The close-up shots of the desperate look on Harry's face as he runs through the dangerous streets of London.

POST-GAME COMMENTS
Director Jules Dassin on why he made London an integral foreground instead of merely a background in *Night and the City* (as he did with New York City in *Naked City*):

> I look at cities as if they were actors, and let them tell me something about themselves.[1]

The 70-night production incorporated London landmarks like Victoria Station, Marble Arch, King's Hall, and London Bridge.

HOME COURT ADVANTAGE
Available on DVD.

#24 FIELD OF DREAMS

Screenwriter/Director Phil Alden Robinson. **Producers** Lawrence Gordon, Charles Gordon. **Cinematography** John Lindley. **Editing** Ian Crafford. **Music** James Horner. **Production Design** Dennis Gassner. **Art Direction** Leslie McDonald. **Costume Design** Linda Bass. Universal. 1989.

THE PLAYERS Kevin Costner **Ray Kinsella**; Amy Madigan **Annie Kinsella**; Gaby Hoffman **Karin Kinsella**; Ray Liotta **Shoeless Joe Jackson**; Timothy Busfield **Mark**; James Earl Jones **Terence Mann**; Burt Lancaster **Dr. Archie "Moonlight" Graham**; Frank Whaley **Archie Graham**; Dwier Brown **John Kinsella**; James Andelin **Feed store farmer**; Steve Eastin **Eddie Cicotte**; Mary Anne Kean **Feed store lady**; Fern Parsons **Annie's mother**; Kelly Coffield **Dee, Mark's wife**; Michael Milhoan **Buck Weaver**; Charles Hoyes **Swede Risberg**; Art LaFleur **Chick Gandil**; Lee Garlington **Beulah, angry PTA lady**; Mike Nussbaum **Principal**; Larry Brandenburg **PTA heckler**; Mary Gershon **PTA heckler**; Robert Kurcz **PTA heckler**; Don Ross **Boston butcher**; Geoffrey Nauffts **Boston pump jockey**; Beatrice Fredman **Boston Yenta**; Anne Seymour **Chisholm newspaper publisher**; George Biasi **Bar patron**; Joseph Ryan **Bar patron**; Howard Sherf **Bar patron**; Brian Frankish **Umpire**

THE GAME Ray Kinsella (Kevin Costner), a former Berkeley radical turned Iowa corn farmer, begins a life-altering journey in his mid 30s after hearing a strange voice saying, as he walks among his rows of corn, "If you build it, he will come."

An intelligent, thoughtful man, Ray soon questions his sanity, then his life path. More than anything Ray is petrified of becoming like his late father, who he believes led a dreary existence by giving up a potential career in baseball for a humdrum job and a family.

The voice soon convinces Ray to take a risky leap of faith by plowing under some of his cornfield and building a beautiful ball field where his father's hero, Shoeless Joe Jackson, a star player from the infamous Chicago White Sox who fixed the 1919 World Series, can return to play.

Supported by his wife (Amy Madigan), Ray proceeds to risk bankruptcy and do something "radical" with his life. Despite the dire warnings from his concerned brother-in-law (Timothy Busfield), and with the help of cryptic messages that bring powerful figures into his life (James Earl Jones as activist writer Terence Mann and Burt Lancaster as Doc Graham), Ray continues to go forward not really knowing what this quest means.

On the verge of financial ruin, Ray comes to face to face with his dead father in the form of the young talented ballplayer he once was. Father and son enjoy a catch that symbolizes the healing of wounds unspoken.

It is via this shared father-son love of baseball that Ray is able to save the farm, which becomes a popular tourist attraction.

INSTANT REPLAY The slogan of the Amazing Mets of 1969 was, "Ya' Gotta Believe." They went on to an improbable World Series win.

Field of Dreams—hardball heaven or hokum? Diamonds are forever or cornier than Orville Redenbacher's chief product? There is no real middle ground in a fantasy like this. It's a test of one man's faith in using the national pastime to come to terms with his late father by bringing together a disparate group of men with ties to the grand old game.

All the bases are filled with sentimentality, and for the faithful followers, *Field of*

TOP: Kevin Costner as Ray Kinsella.

BOTTOM: Terence Mann (James Earl Jones)

Dreams scores with a magic not seen since Frank Capra tested Jimmy Stewart in *It's a Wonderful Life*.

It is a fable of loss and redemption, using the soul of the game to explore the bonds between father and son. The film is a poetic reminder of how sports in general impact male relationships—friends, family, and strangers alike.

Directing from his own script adapted from W. P. Kinsella's novel *Shoeless Joe*, Phil Alden Robinson builds a nostalgic, old-fashioned mystery about an individual who doesn't really know what he's seeking until he finds it.

In sketching his characterizations, Robinson integrates traditional values of the heartland with the counterculture influences we see in Kinsella, his wife, and Mann, '60s activists.

The key to it all is the performances, because any misstep among them could cause the fragile sentimentality at the foundation of this story to tumble over into an overdone mess of mushy melodrama.

At the center is Kevin Costner, who wisely plays it low-key with a subdued sense of childlike wonder. It's no small task pulling off being a former radical student in a Gary Cooper or Jimmy Stewart style, always dancing along the edges of appearing ridiculous. Questions of plausibility lurk in the bullpen always ready to take over. Costner handles that constant threat with a convincing everyman performance.

Amy Madigan lends a lot as his extraordinarily understanding, smart wife, delivered with supportive spunk.

James Earl Jones's curmudgeonly Terence Mann replaces the novel's J. D. Salinger. Despite his regal presence, it is a bit of a wasted performance from an excellent actor. Jones's "Why baseball? People will most definitely come" speech falls a bit flat.

At the same time the reappearance of the team from the afterlife would have had a deeper impact and added to the dream fulfillment theme if they had learned something from their celestial journey and included some black ball players as part of their Iowa corn field homestand.

As the key figure from that ghostly squad, Ray Liotta does a lot with very little. Appropriately a bit mysterious, often couched in shadows and fog, and awe-inspiring as the great Shoeless Joe Jackson, Liotta convincingly plays with the natural detachment his character calls for. But here too an opportunity is missed in that an elaboration on some of Joe's errors in judgment would have enhanced the honest feel of the picture.

In perhaps one of the best written and performed minor roles in sports cinema history, Robinson serves up wonderful material that Burt Lancaster hits out of the park—er, cornfield. It serves as an appropriate memorial to a great actor in his last major film appearance.

Based on a real person who actually had a one-game career in the major leagues, Lancaster's Doc Graham is thoroughly believable as a man fully satisfied with the life he has led and the choices he has made.

Robinson's dig at a celebrity-obsessed culture also puts sports in perspective via Lancaster's characterization as a man who knows he made the right decision in dedicating himself where he was needed most, as a small-town doctor, foregoing the glorious but less fulfilling career as a baseball player.

"If I'd only gotten to be a doctor for five minutes, that would be a tragedy," says Graham.

While this fantasy is capably shot by John Lindley and enhanced by James Horner's music, the magic really comes from the performers themselves. It is their convincing work, without a backstop full of special effects, that is at the heart of *Field of Dreams*.

"Ya' Gotta Believe."

Dr. Archie "Moonlight" Graham (Burt Lancaster, left) with Ray holding his daughter (Gaby Hoffman).

OUTSIDE THE LINES The picture is based on the Canadian writer W. P. Kinsella's novel *Shoeless Joe*.... Former White Sox/Orioles infielder Don Buford was also a consultant.... Writer/director Phil Alden Robinson wrote the role of Mann specifically for James Earl Jones after seeing him perform in *Fences* on Broadway.... During production there was a major drought and the crew had to spend thousands for extra water for the cornfields. Since the ballpark grass had naturally gone brown, they painted it green.... The film was nominated for three Academy Awards: Best Picture, Best Adapted Screenplay, and Best Original Score.... Burt Lancaster's character was based on a real Archibald "Moonlight" Graham.... After a solid minor league stint with the Charlotte Hornets of the North Carolina League, Graham's major league career lasted less than one game, coming in as a late-inning replacement in the outfield for the New York Giants on June 29, 1905. Though Graham didn't hit or have a fielding opportunity, the Giants did beat Brooklyn and went on to win the World Series that year, defeating the Philadelphia Athletics 4 games to 1.... Graham left to pursue his goal of becoming a doctor.... Thousands visit the field in Dyersville, Iowa (about 25 miles west of Dubuque and just over 200 from Chicago) where the film was shot, including many Japanese tourists, as the film was very popular in Japan.... Costner had starred in another baseball picture less than a year before, *Bull Durham*.... Costner also starred in the baseball drama *For the Love of the Game* (1999).... Though he appeared in *Chasing Dreams* (1982) briefly as a medical student, Costner was not central to the baseball story.

ALL-STAR MOMENTS Mann (Jones) sitting at the cornfield bleacher gives Ray (Costner) the "People will come, Ray.... People will most definitely come" soliloquy as Mark (Busfield) warns Ray of impending financial disaster if he proceeds: "You build a baseball field in the middle of nowhere and you sit here and stare at nothing...."

Having gone with his "vision," Ray asks Shoeless Joe Jackson (Liotta), "Hey Dad? Want to have a catch?" Joe replies, "I'd like that." As they play catch we see many, many cars lined up to come to the field.

HOME COURT ADVANTAGE Available on VHS and DVD. Universal has released this title in several DVD versions: combined with *For the Love of the Game*; Baseball Triple Play: *Field of Dreams*, *Mr. Baseball*, and *For the Love of the Game*; combined with *October Sky*; as a multi-disc anniversary edition.

#23 SEABISCUIT

Screenwriter/Director Gary Ross. **Producers** Kathleen Kennedy, Frank Marshall, Gary Ross, Jane Sindell. **Cinematography** John Schwartzman. **Editing** William Goldenberg. **Music** Randy Newman. **Production Design** Jeannine Oppewall. **Costume Design** Judianna Makovsky. **Wrangler** Rusty Hendrickson. **Technical Consultant** Laura Hillenbrand. Universal. 2003.

THE PLAYERS
Tobey Maguire **Red Pollard**; Jeff Bridges **Charles Howard**; Chris Cooper **Tom Smith**; Elizabeth Banks **Marcela Howard**; William Macy **Tick Tock McGlaughlin**; Gary Stevens **George Woolf**; Valerie Mahaffey **Annie Howard**; Michael O'Neill **Mr. Pollard**; Annie Corley **Mrs. Pollard**; Michael Angarano **Young Red Pollard**; Eddie Jones **Samuel Riddle**; Ed Lauter **Charles Strub**; Kingston DuCoeur **Sam**; Chris McCarron **Charley Kurtsinger**; Dyllan Christopher **Frankie Howard**; Royce Applegate **Dutch Doogan**; Sam Bottoms **Mr. Blodget**; Michael Ensign **Steamer owner**; Shay Duffin **Sunny Fitzsimmons**; Robin Bissell **Horace Halsteder**; Paige King **Tick Tock's gal**; Pat Skipper **Seabiscuit's vet**; Gianni Russo **Alberto Gianini**; Clif Alvey **Angry trainer**; Dan Daily **Saratoga trainer**; Michael Silver **Baltimore doctor**; Matt Miller **Pimlico starter**; Gary Ross **Pimlico track announcer**; David McCullough **Narrator**

THE GAME Emerging from the depths of the Great Depression, an unlikely racehorse would buck the odds and amass a string of victories that would elevate the nation's spirits and make them forget their woes for a while.

Sixty-five years later Seabiscuit inspires anew.

This true-life drama, based on Laura Hillenbrand's best-selling book, *Seabiscuit* is the story of how three very different men, misfits from diverse backgrounds, would come together in almost pre-ordained fashion, changing each other's lives in their mutual quest to build a smallish, obstinate horse into a champion.

In the character sketches that comprise the first act of the film, we learn about each man's journey, and the horse's as well.

Charles Howard (Jeff Bridges) is a self-made millionaire and natural-born promoter. He came out west as a bicycle repairman but saw an opportunity in a new-fangled mode of transportation, the automobile, and led the growth of that industry in California with his superior sales abilities. Despite his success, Howard has suffered a personal tragedy that left him looking for meaning. His young son Frankie (Dyllan Christopher), died in a car accident and his marriage failed.

Tom Smith (Chris Cooper) is an old-fashioned horse whisperer. A folksy, taciturn man of the dying Old West, Smith has an almost telepathic ability to understand horses. But the old cowboy's way of life is fading with the sunset as the West he knew becomes more and more commercialized.

Jockey Red Pollard (Tobey Maguire) is a talented, literate rider (though considered big for a jockey). Red suffers from the emotional trauma of being abandoned by his parents at a young age and is blind in one eye.

Even the horse, Seabiscuit, has struggled despite coming from an esteemed bloodline. The young horse fails to improve as he grows. Legendary trainer Sonny Fitzsimmons (Shay Duffin) wonders upon seeing him if Seabiscuit is "a race horse or a lead pony?" When hard work doesn't take care of what the trainer at first believed to be laziness, the owner and trainers just make Seabiscuit a training partner to faster horses, forcing him to lose head-to-head duels. This train-to-lose method doesn't help matters, and Seabiscuit grows up increasingly obstinate and angry, running in claiming races and mostly losing.

Despite being described by a veteran horse promoter (Ed Lauter) as a "crackpot who lives in the bushes," Tom Smith is hired by Charles Howard to help him find and train a racehorse.

A few months later, standing at the track rail in the pre-dawn mist of an early morning workout, Smith is struck by one horse as they stare at each other. Howard buys that horse, Seabiscuit, at the bargain basement price of $2,000.

Soon afterward as Howard, his second wife, Marcela (Elizabeth Banks), and Smith stand at the stable watching their new purchase throw a fit, owner and trainer talk.

HOWARD: What exactly is it you like?

SMITH: He's got spirit.

HOWARD: Can he be ridden?

SMITH: Oh, sure... (*Seabiscuit rears up*) eventually.

Later, through a chance encounter and an incident at some stables, Smith sees Red Pollard and notices that the oversized jockey has a fiery temperament similar to that of his undersized horse. Red builds a rapport with Seabiscuit, calling him "Pops." Together the three men begin the long road of tearing down the bad habits the horse has been taught and re-educating Seabiscuit into a winner.

After many disappointments and frustrations their efforts pay off in a big way as Seabiscuit begins winning on a more-than-regular basis. As the victories pile up, Howard, ever the showman, proposes a match race against the comparatively monstrous War Admiral, the reigning Triple Crown winner.

Believing Seabiscuit isn't in his horse's class, War Admiral's East Coast—based owner, Samuel Riddle (Eddie Jones), repeatedly rejects the challenge. Showing a little of that old-money East Coast snobbery, Jones responds with comments like, "You wouldn't put Jack Dempsey in the ring with a middleweight."

Pressing on, Howard then takes his populist little-guy campaign to the public with a whistle-stop tour designed to draw in the press and make Seabiscuit the people's underdog champ. Typical of his big-city, little-town train station speeches is the following: "Our horse is too small, our jockey is too big, our trainer is too old, and I'm too dumb to know the difference! You'd think they'd want to race us instead of running away."

The ploy eventually works as Riddle yields to the public pressure. He agrees to a match race between Seabiscuit and War Admiral, albeit largely on his terms, including racing on War Admiral's "home track," Pimlico in Baltimore.

Unfortunately, Red seriously injures his leg, but rather than cancel the race, he insists that his friend George "The Iceman" Woolf (Gary Stevens) ride Seabiscuit.

With Red giving him special handling tips from his hospital bed and keen strategy from Smith, Woolf wins the race in impressive fashion.

Soon thereafter, however, Seabiscuit seriously injures his leg in a race. Both he and Red go through a long rehabilitation together. Red dreams of the day he can avenge the narrow loss they had at the fabled Santa Anita Handicap race.

With a homemade brace and knowing that any mishap could prevent him from ever walking again, Red perseveres, winning the coveted race and fulfilling his dream.

INSTANT REPLAY There have been a lot of negative comments about *Seabiscuit* being slow out of the gate, and the horse not appearing until ¾ of an hour

TOP: The owner and his horse meet the press.

BOTTOM: Actor Jeff Bridges, who grew up going to the races with his grandfather, is an avid horseman, riding often at his ranch in Montana.

into the movie. While the title refers to the equine star, the film is undeniably about people and their journey. That is one of the keys to the film's success—it centers less on the races and more on the interactions of the main characters.

Author Laura Hillenbrand explains in a press release that she and the film's writer/director Gary Ross share a love of horse racing, and Seabiscuit is a compelling horse, but that the focus of the story is on the human angle.

Lots of people say, "I've never been to a horse race," or "I don't like horses," but they say they liked the story. I think that's because of the people in it—and that was always my focus, these three men. That's why the cover of the book doesn't have the horse's head on it. I made a very deliberate decision to focus on the faces of the people so that you know this is a human story.[1]

"It wouldn't be the biggest-selling book in America if it was just about horse racing," notes Ross.

Nearly all of the film's few shortcomings, however, can be traced to the massive challenge of retaining the scope and spectacle of the 400-page bestseller and adapting it into a compelling and entertaining 2½-hour movie. There is such a wealth of material that the project could easily have been a television miniseries.

In being true to the book, the film has to use a lot of exposition, perhaps at the expense of some character depth and intriguing subplots. For example, Elizabeth Banks's role as Charles Howard's second wife is somewhat underwritten. The real Marcela was intelligent, quite cultured, outgoing and adventurous. It's a lot to explore for someone with much influence on a lead character.

Additionally, one of the core appeals of the sport is conspicuous in its relative absence from the film, and that is gambling. A humorous angle would have brought some needed lightness (in addition to that supplied by the zany radio announcer energetically played by William Macy) to offset the dramatic tone.

An effective tool overall, David McCullough's narration is certainly informative, but the danger is that this Ken Burns—type approach can at times feel like a history lesson from a National Geographic program. One notable example is that so many scenes are devoted to the horse developing a fast start, but at the beginning of the historic match race with War Admiral, the film covers that all-important start with the stills of people listening on the radio. Could those stills have had the same impact after we actually saw the start ourselves?

Those observations notwithstanding, writer/director Gary Ross does an excellent job of putting the audience in that social context of tough times where a quartet of underdogs could provide some badly needed inspiration. Much credit for that should go to production designer Jeannine Oppewall and costume designer Judianna Makovsky, both of whom earned Oscar nominations here and for similar work in Ross's *Pleasantville*. Their design details enliven this story of 1930s America. John Schwartzman's Oscar-nominated cinematography and Randy Newman's old-fashioned and often bittersweet music complete the sharp technical presentation.

Ross's masterful orchestration of all the elements makes this the most successful sports movie in establishing a 20th-century period piece setting since *The Natural*.

In putting words to the pictures, Ross's script is populist storytelling at its best. Old-fashioned, earnest, thoughtful, Ross's text meets the tricky demands of creating composite characters and fictionalizing elements without losing the virtues of the story.

"Sometimes when the little guy doesn't know he's the little guy, he can do big things."…"The future is the finish line."…"Sometimes all somebody needs is a second

TOP: (Left to right) Jockey Red Pollard (Tobey Maguire), trainer Tom Smith (Chris Cooper), and the owner of Seabiscuit, Charles Howard (Jeff Bridges).

MIDDLE: Red courageously prepares to race again despite a severe leg injury.

BOTTOM: Maguire gets some instruction from director Gary Ross.

FACING PAGE: The filmmakers went to great lengths to create horse racing verisimilitude.

chance" —while the simple dialogue is part of the film's charm and helps convey the themes and times, such phrases threaten to soften a story that's already very emotional. But the terrific actors prevent that from happening.

As Seabiscuit's owner, Charles Howard, Jeff Bridges is wonderful, delivering the cheerful homilies in Will Rogers fashion with a folksy charm. His character is also not unlike his title role of the automobile visionary in *Tucker: A Man and His Dream* (1988).

Chris Cooper's taciturn westerner recalls the classic Western work of another Cooper (Gary): a kind, quiet, observant characterization, delivered effortlessly.

In moving from spiderwebs to thoroughbreds, Tobey Maguire raises his thespian stock through a convincing portrayal of the hard-luck jockey's resiliency.

William Macy brings comic relief as the high-voltage, Walter Winchell-esque radio announcer, Tick Tock McLaughlin. His role is reminiscent of a similar character in another horse racing film, *The Black Stallion*.

In his screen debut, Hall of Fame jockey Gary Stevens presents some genuine acting ability in a charismatic and authentic turn as George "The Iceman" Woolf. Michael Angarano's vulnerable performance as young Red Pollard is memorable. Eddie Jones is fine representing the film's "villain," the owner of War Admiral.

Several horses played various aspects of Seabiscuit, from racing to training to kicking about. Lead wrangler Rusty Hendrickson took his horse sense far and wide to find the right type of horses to fulfill the various story demands of the legendary Seabiscuit.

While the film excels in the interaction between the main characters, Gary Ross's presentation of the racing sequences make them perhaps the best ever caught on celluloid.

Ever the salesman, Howard drums up popular support for Seabiscuit.

Nostrils flaring, eyes wide, hair bouncing in the wind with the bobbing of their powerful necks, hooves pounding—one of the most exciting sights in all of sport is a pack of thoroughbreds thundering down the track at 40 mph with colorful jockeys sitting atop them trying to concentrate and steer over 1,000 pounds of heart and muscle first across the finish line above the roar of the crowd.

Months and months of planning and practice, race design by Hall of Fame jockey Chris McCarron, Oscar-nominated sound design, brilliant photography from unique camera mounts, riveting editing—Ross's enormous efforts pay off handsomely to capture the sound and fury that is thoroughbred racing in all its aesthetics, splendor, and danger. This verisimilitude immeasurably enhances the story line and demonstrates the pure entertainment value of racing.

Across the board, horse racing movies have produced very few winners. Of the genre's 200-plus films, most have ended up in the also-ran category.

A sports and social history, *Seabiscuit* joins a precious few (including *National Velvet, Phar Lap, A Day at the Races,* and *The Black Stallion*) in the winners circle.

OUTSIDE THE LINES

Seabiscuit was nominated for seven Academy Awards.... The film was based on Laura Hillenbrand's best-selling book.... Director of photography John Schwartzman also shot the baseball film *The Rookie* (2002), in which *Seabiscuit* cast member Royce Applegate appeared.... Ross is the owner, along with producers Kathleen Kennedy, Frank Marshall, and Steven Spielberg, of a thoroughbred named Atswhatimtalknbout.... The film's executive producer, Roger Birnbaum, also produced the remake of *Angels in the Outfield* (1994) and basketball's *Celtic Pride* (1996).... William Goldenberg was part of director Michael Mann's editing team for the boxing drama *Ali* (2001).... Seabiscuit was named 1938 Horse of the Year.... Chris Cooper raised cattle with his father for over 20 years.... The Fairplex in Pomona, California doubled as Tijuana's Agua Caliente racetrack.... Shirley Temple starred in a fictionalized rendition called *The Story of Seabiscuit* (1949).... Hall of Fame jockey Gary Stevens and his horses have earned over $200 million.... Their 4,700 victories include eight Triple Crown races.... Gary Ross cowrote two baseball comedies: *Mr. Baseball* (1992) and *Little Big League* (1994).... Another Hall of Fame jockey, Chris McCarron, in addition to riding "War Admiral" as Charles Kurtsinger in the climactic race, was also the film's chief race designer, working with other jockeys, wranglers, and the technical crew to choreograph the action sequences.... Jeff Bridges is an avid horse rider with a ranch in Montana.... Executive producer Gary Barber also supervised both sequels to the baseball comedy *Major League*.... War Admiral was played by one of his own descendants, a gelding named Verboom.... The match race (Pimlico) was shot at Keeneland in Lexington, Kentucky.... Many of the shots from the races were captured by rigging cameras to a Hummer vehicle as it drove alongside the horses around the track.... In 1972, Bridges played a boxer opposite Stacy Keach in John Huston's *Fat City*.... A year later he'd star in the auto racing picture *The Last American Hero*.... Ed Lauter, who also appeared in *The Last American Hero*, starred as a vindictive prison guard in football's *The Longest Yard* (1974).... The actor would later appear in another sports-prison drama, *The Jericho Mile* (1979).... Ross was nominated for Best Screenplay Oscars for *Big* (1988) and *Dave* (1993).... Frank Marshall produced the IMAX film *Olympic Glory* (1999) about the Nagano Winter Games.... Michael O'Neill appeared in the golf feature *The Legend of Bagger Vance* (2000), in which Judianna Makovsky was also the costume designer.... More than 40 horses were utilized in the film, with 10 portraying Seabiscuit at various stages.... Kathleen

A race for the ages. Seabiscuit en route to victory over War Admiral.

Kennedy was the executive producer of *Schindler's List* (1993), which won an Academy Award for Best Picture.... Andrew Neskoromny was also the art director for hockey's *Mystery, Alaska* (1999).... Gary Ross's father, Arthur, co-wrote *The Creature from the Black Lagoon* (1954).... Annie Corley played a coach in the basketball comedy *Juwanna Man* (2002).... William Macy made several appearances in the ABC television series *Sports Night* (2002) as Sam Donovan, a ratings expert.... Many scenes were shot with Maguire sitting atop an Equicizer, a mechanical workout machine that safely simulated horse racing and also made it easier to capture mid-race chatter.... An estimated 40 million Americans listened to the match race between Seabiscuit and War Admiral.

ALL-STAR MOMENTS Young Red Pollard (Angarano) being abandoned by his parents at a dirt horse-racing track and told to use his "gift" of racing horses.

One of Red's (Maguire) early races where he's exposed to a belligerent jockey who physically attacks him during the race and then gets reprimanded by his boss: "A nose!? You lose a race by a nose you better fall off trying!"

Assorted angles of all the race sequences.

The Tijuana nightclub where the women carry the jockeys and race each other down the hallway.

Charles Howard (Bridges) emerges from the dark through the bushes in his fancy suit to meet Tom Smith (Cooper).

Begging for a ride, Red offers to hot-walk a horse and mutters to him the whole time, calling the horse "an old gluepot."

A confident jockey comes away shaken with his shirt torn after Smith warns him that Seabiscuit is unruly.

One morning when Tom appears at the stables, he sees Red sitting atop a pile of beer.

TOM: Where's the horse?

RED: Signing autographs.

The match race.

POST-GAME COMMENTS   Actor Jeff Bridges on the skills of a jockey:

Before you really get into it, most people kind of think you're really just a passenger merely sitting on this animal. But so much goes into the physicality like the legs and hands, (both) have to be very strong.

Then there's the whole chess game of the event, how are you going to make your move? The races are very short but you have to make your strategy. Communicating adjustment strategies on the fly to your horse based on what is actually happening during the course of the race. The psychological game just like in boxing or other sports. How can you intimidate your competition? It's all part of it. Another thing is a talented jockey's understanding of his horse, taking advantage of its personality.[2]

Writer/director Gary Ross on the danger of the sport:

Horse racing may have the highest mortality rate of any sport. If you have an accident in a car, the vehicle is designed to protect you. If you fall off a half-ton horse going 40 mph, well.... the odds are not good.[3]

Author Laura Hillenbrand on the extent of Seabiscuit's popularity:

You could compare him to Tiger Woods and Michael Jordan but really he greatly exceeded that. Seabiscuit was meaningful in a way they are not. Muhammad Ali had a broad appeal but I don't think he had the kind of appeal that penetrated every household in the country. Ali was a huge star but he was not in the most popular sport and I don't think you find a lot of women who were into boxing like they were into horse racing. I was doing an interview on *Good Morning America* and Dr. Nancy Sniderman said her mother recalled that one could walk down any street in America during the '30s and there'd be no one on the street but you could hear in every open window, the radio playing Seabiscuit's races. It was that big. Everyone was into it.[4]

Ross adds:

He was bigger than Joe DiMaggio. In fact in 1938, he [Seabiscuit] got more press coverage than Roosevelt and Hitler. Seabiscuit was a folk hero to people because they felt broken just the way he had been broken. It wasn't that he was such a great racehorse; there've been better racehorses. It really was that Seabiscuit overcame such personal odds and had lost so much and struggled greatly and then came back. That was right at a time (the Great Depression) when the country wanted to come back, so he became unbelievably famous.[5]

HOME COURT ADVANTAGE   Available on VHS and DVD. Universal has released several versions, including a three-disc DVD with *A Beautiful Mind*.

#22 SOMEBODY UP THERE LIKES ME

Screenwriter Ernest Lehman. **Director** Robert Wise. **Producer** Charles Schnee. **Cinematography** Joseph Ruttenberg. **Editing** Albert Akst. **Art Direction** Cedric Gibbons, Malcolm Brown. **Set Decoration, Production Design** Keogh Gleason, Edwin Willis. **Music** Bronislau Kaper. **Technical Advisor** John Indrisano. MGM. 1956.

THE PLAYERS
Paul Newman **Rocky Graziano (Rocco Barbella)**; Pier Angeli **Norma Graziano**; Harold Stone **Nick Barbella**; Eileen Heckart **Mrs. Barbella**; Everett Sloane **Irving Cohen**; Joseph Buloff **Benny**; Sal Mineo **Romolo**; Judson Pratt **Johnny Hyland**; Robert Loggia **Frankie Peppo**; Clancy Cooper **Captain Lancheck**; John Eldredge **Warden Niles**; Theodore Newton **Commissioner Eagan**; Mart Crowley **Lou Stillman**; Court Shepard **Tony Zale**; Russ Conway **Captain Grifton**; Ray Walker **Ring announcer**; Billy Nelson **Commissioner**; Arch Johnson **Heldon**; Steve McQueen **Fidel**; Charles Green **Curtis Hightower**; Michael Dante **Shorty**; Donna Jo Gribble **Yolanda Barbella**; Jan Gillum **Young Yolanda**; Terry Rangno **Young Rocky**; Frank Campanella **Detective**; Robert Easton **Corporal Quinbury**; Dean Jones **Private**; Harry Wismer **Himself**; Sam Taub **Radio announcer**

THE GAME Growing up in the dismal slums of New York's Lower East Side, Rocky Barbella's destiny seems set. In one of the opening scenes of the picture, as they watch the young hoodlum escape from their grasp and take off down the dark street after throwing a brick through a storefront window, one cop turns to the other and says in a thick Irish accent, "There goes another little greaseball on his way. Ten years from now, the death house at Sing Sing."

The cop's prediction is well on the way to coming true. Now a teenager, Rocky (Paul Newman) has developed an uncontrollable and rebellious nature, an unregenerate attitude, and a growing list of petty crimes. Raised by an exasperated mother (Eileen Heckart) with a broken spirit and a father (Harold Stone) who drowns his troubles and failures in drink, Rocky leads a gang (that includes Sal Mineo and Steve McQueen) through street fights and robberies that soon land him in reform school, then prison on Riker's Island for assaulting authorities. It is there that he meets a shady boxing hustler, Frankie Peppo (Robert Loggia), who is impressed with Rocky's raw punching power and offers to help him get some quick money in the fight business when they get out. Rocky declines Peppo's offer, saying, "The only club fighter I ever knew [his father, Nick] is a bigger bum than I am." Frankie tells Rocky where to contact him should he change his mind.

Having completed his sentence, Rocky is handed his release papers by the warden, but his freedom doesn't last long. Outside the prison gates Rocky is met by two government officials who inform him that he's "volunteering" for the Army. It is January 1942 and America has entered World War II.

Despite his claims to the warden that he's a changed man, it doesn't take long for Rocky to revert to his rebellious ways in the military. He threatens a corporal, then punches a captain and immediately goes AWOL.

He shows up at hoodlum pal Romolo's (Sal Mineo) to hide and rest and to think of a way to earn quick money to bribe the captain he's just floored. Recalling the offer by his former fellow inmate Frankie Peppo, Rocky shows up at the gym that Peppo supposedly operates from. Gym owner Lou Stillman (Mart Crowley), however, informs Rocky that Frankie is currently operating out of Sing Sing prison. Just then fight manager Irving Cohen (Everett Sloane) leans over the ring ropes to tell Lou that he's in immediate need of a sparring partner. Desperate, Rocky asks for the job. When asked his name, Rocky looks at a wine bottle a trainer is holding, sees the label, and

Rocky Graziano (Paul Newman) channels his anger, frustrations, and energy into pursuing success in the ring.

answers, "Rocky, Rocky Graziano." "Like the Italian wine?" Cohen asks. "Yeah," says Rocky.

Once in the ring Rocky is impressive, quickly earning money as a club fighter. However, he's eventually caught and, facing a military court, is dishonorably discharged and sentenced to a year of hard labor in Leavenworth prison.

Inside he catches the attention of physical instructor Johnny Hyland (Judson Pratt), who convinces Rocky to "make that hate work for you inside the ring making a living." After intense training and committed to a pugilistic career that will serve as his road to salvation, Rocky, now a free man, rapidly ascends the fighting ranks, building on triumph after triumph under the guidance of Irving Cohen. At the same time Rocky is introduced to his sister's friend Norma (Pier Angeli) and an awkward romance begins.

Despite Norma's deep aversion to Rocky's bloody profession, the two fall in love and get married. Soon they become parents of a baby daughter. This domestic bliss helps Rocky shed the rebellious nature that was his worst enemy. Rocky eventually earns a title shot against champion Tony Zale (Court Shepard).

Listening to the fight on the radio with Rocky's mother, Ida, Norma weeps as her husband loses the bout. Ida tells her daughter-in-law that the good and the bad come as a package.

Frankie Peppo emerges from prison and threatens to expose Rocky's criminal past to Norma if Graziano doesn't throw his next fight. Despite pressures from the boxing commission and district attorney's office to name those connected with fixing matches, Rocky remains tight-lipped and his New York boxing license is revoked; the rematch with Zale is off. To make matters worse, word has gotten out (Peppo claims it wasn't him) and newspaper headlines inform Norma of Rocky's dishonorable discharge and prison stint.

Norma stands by her man and soon Irving brings the news that a Zale rematch is set in Chicago. Training in the Windy City, Rocky is on edge, perceiving slights from everyone, and in a moment of confused panic flies back to New York.

In his old neighborhood Rocky talks with sweet shop owner Benny (Joesph Buloff), who is glad to see Rocky because most of the old gang, he says, have ended up crippled, in prison, or dead. Walking down the street he runs into Romolo, and in him he recognizes the direction his life would have taken had it not been for the support of Johnny Hyland and Norma. He suggests that his friend "turn over a new leaf" but sees the futility of his words and runs off after giving Romolo a wad of cash. Later, he comes across the same shop window he broke as a kid; a symbol of how far he's come, this time the window features a poster of himself endorsing razor blades.

Rocky shows up at his parents' old apartment. In a cathartic, emotional conversation that eventually brings tears to his father's eyes, Mr. Barbella tells his son, "Be a champ, like I never was." Rocky returns to Chicago even more determined to win.

Up against defending champion Zale, "the finest piece of steel ever to come out of Gary, Indiana," Graziano has his hands full and takes a pounding early. He tells Irving between rounds, "That guys hits hard." Irving retorts, "Well, hit him back, it's legal."

Despite facing the continuing barrage from the champ, Rocky begins to score some shots of his own. In separate scenes we see Rocky's family and friends listening intently to the radio broadcast of the fight. Rocky comes on in the later rounds scoring heavily and taking control, eventually winning the match and becoming the new champion.

Riding along in a convertible with his wife in a victory parade, Rocky tells Norma, "You know I've been lucky.... Somebody up there likes me." Mrs. Graziano answers, "Somebody down here, too."

Rocky with his wife, Norma (Pier Angeli).

INSTANT REPLAY This story of a man's redemption through love is dominated by a career-setting showcase performance by Paul Newman. Outstanding efforts in front of the camera and behind it rightfully earned the film three Academy Award nominations (though amazingly Newman wasn't nominated). *Somebody Up There Likes Me* won two Oscars for cinematography and art direction/set design.

Under the skillful direction of Robert Wise and the production supervision of Charles Schnee, the movie, based on Rocky Graziano's biography written with Rowland Barber, really begins in earnest on the page with a profound screenplay by the talented Ernest Lehman (screenwriter for *The Sound of Music, West Side Story, North by Northwest*). The script, loaded with sharp socioeconomic observations, is projected superbly on the screen with Jospeh Ruttenberg's cinematography and Gibbons and Brown's art direction. Both the settings of the East Side slum life and the dramatic fighting sequences are excellent and very realistic. The fine editing work of Albert Akst earned him an Oscar nomination.

There are similarities and striking differences to other sports movies of that era. *Somebody Up There Likes Me* at times has the tough, dark, edgy, real-life feel of *On the Waterfront*, yet also contains elements of the Jimmy Stewart baseball film *The Stratton Story*, a movie about a man's redemption through his wife's love. This film also presents a flip side to two other boxing movies that focus on the corrupt, unsavory aspects of the sport; *The Harder They Fall*, with Humphrey Bogart and Rod Steiger, and

As 'Champion' did for Kirk Douglas, a boxing drama made Paul Newman a star.

Robert Wise's *The Set-Up*, featuring Robert Ryan, both of which are much less optimistic.

What distinguishes *Somebody Up There Likes Me* more than anything is Newman's masterful ability to create a sympathetic hero out of a juvenile delinquent, dishonorably discharged serviceman, and ex-con, even while at times he brings the audience to the edge of hating this misguided, foolish hoodlum.

Newman's efforts are supported by the brilliant performances of a large cast. Pier Angeli performs with a beautiful sensitivity as Rocky's wife, providing the love that will take Graziano down a better path and bring the audience to support Rocky's rise from the slums. Sal Mineo succeeds in the difficult challenge of trying to embody the symbol of what Rocky might have become. Eileen Heckart gives a solid performance as Rocky's bewildered mother nearly falling into the abyss of hopelessness. Rocky's father, played by Harold Stone (who also has a key role in another boxing film, *The Harder They Fall*), flirts with being over the top but overall maintains well the tragic figure of lost dreams who almost drinks himself into oblivion. In a fine film debut, Robert Loggia is convincing as boxing hustler Frankie Peppo. Veteran Everett Sloane is a joy to watch as Rocky's manager, the sometimes exasperated, often humorous Irving Cohen.

Musically the varying moods of the movie are skillfully underscored by Bronislau Kaper's arrangements, and Perry Como's title song performance aptly bookends the film.

The filmmakers wisely make a point of keeping the actual fight scenes to a minimum. As a result, when the climactic bout comes, the viewers are on the edge of their seats in anticipation. The verisimilitude of the boxing scenes is a credit to technical advisor John Indrisano (who did a similarly fine job for director Wise earlier in *The Set-Up*) and amateur boxer Courtland Shepard, a look-alike and fight-alike Tony Zale. The director's pacing and Ruttenberg's camera work all contribute to the riveting authenticity of a prizefight.

At times brutal, grim, and tough, and at other times funny, heartwarming, and exciting, *Somebody Up There Likes Me* remains one of the more accomplished films in movie history.

OUTSIDE THE LINES *Somebody Up There Likes Me* was based on Rocky Graziano's biography written with Rowland Barber.... Producer Charles Schnee, a Yale law school graduate, also was a screenwriter, winning an Academy Award for his script for *The Bad and the Beautiful* (1950).... Schnee also wrote the screenplays for the John Sturges boxing film *Right Cross* (1950) and the football film *Easy Living* (1949), featuring Victor Mature.... Paul Newman attended Kenyon College on an athletic scholarship before studying at the drama school at Yale.... After being nominated six times for Best Actor Newman won with his seventh nomination, reprising his role as Fast Eddie Felson in *The Color of Money*.... *Somebody Up There Likes Me* marked actor Robert Loggia's film debut.... Loggia would star in other films involving boxing—*Triumph of the Spirit* (1989) and *Gladiator* (1992)—as well as football's *Necessary Roughness* (1991).... Russian-born photojournalist turned cinematographer Joseph Ruttenberg also shot the Marx Brothers comedy *A Day at the Races* (1937).... A veteran of stage, screen, and television, Eileen Heckart won an Academy Award for Best Supporting Actress in *Butterflies Are Free*.... Newman starred in the live TV version of the baseball drama *Bang the Drum Slowly* (1956).... Ernest Lehman (*The Sound of*

Music, West Side Story, and *North by Northwest*) also wrote the football terrorist movie *Black Sunday* (1977).... Robert Wise had previously directed another boxing film, *The Set-Up* (1949).... Wise won double Oscars as director/producer for *West Side Story* (1961) and *The Sound of Music* (1965).... Wise was the editor of *Citizen Kane* (1941).... Wise twice partnered with producer/director Mark Robson (*Champion, The Harder They Fall*) in a production company.... This film was Newman's third movie after *The Silver Chalice* (1954) and *The Rack* (1956) were poorly received.... Over his unparalleled career Irish architect Cedric Gibbons would win a dozen Academy Awards as an art director.... Gibbons was nominated for an Oscar for his work on *National Velvet* (1944).... Rocky Graziano was the world middleweight boxing champion in 1947—48 and was inducted into the Boxing Hall of Fame in 1991.... The lead role in *Somebody Up There Likes Me* was originally intended for James Dean before he died in an auto accident.

ALL-STAR MOMENTS The first appearance of Paul Newman as Rocky running through the dark streets of the slums away from the cops with a picturesque bridge looming in the background.

In "applying" for a job as a sparring partner while trying to distance himself from his past, Rocky, when asked his name, looks over at a trainer holding a bottle of wine, reads the label and answers, "Rocky...Rocky Graziano."

MANAGER (Sloane): Like the Italian wine.

ROCKY: Yeah.

When the manager sends him to the locker room to get workout clothes he adds, "Make sure you get a cup [jock]," to which Rocky responds, "Oh, that's okay, Mr. Cohen, I don't need no cup, I'll drink out of the bottle."

Inside a theater watching a movie with Rocky, during a love scene Norma (Angeli) reaches out for Rocky's hand. Rocky thinks she wants some popcorn so he turns her palm over and pours some onto it.

Montage of Rocky returning home after a fight; each time his daughter is a little older, and each time he's a little more banged up. Finally Rocky comes home covered with bandages and bruises, and his ghastly appearance frightens Norma, but the daughter laughs and says, "Mommy, it's only Daddy."

Fight scene in the rematch as the camera uses the boxers' point of view. Close-up punching sequences intercut with separate shots of Rocky's family and friends listening to the radio broadcast and end with a tight shot of the press's flash cameras and official ringing the bell to end the round.

POST-GAME COMMENTS Actor Robert Loggia (Frankie Peppo) on how Paul Newman got the lead role as Rocky Graziano:

I liked what Paul did that actually got him the Graziano part. In *Silver Chalice* they said, "He's a good-looking guy but looks like a girl in that toga with Pier Angeli." His career over and done with. James Dean was supposed to do Ernest Hemingway's *The Battler (Playwrights '56)*, a punch-drunk fighter in skid row. Dean died in the accident so an instant replacement was needed because it was all set and Paul got the role. Being a punch drunk they put all this makeup on him so he's no longer the pretty boy and was quite convincing as a punch-drunk boxer. That is how he got *Somebody Up There Likes Me*.[1]

Robert Wise on his lead actor's preparations:

I was familiar with Paul's stage work and after meeting him he just seemed right. He and I would spend a lot of time with Rocky (Graziano) in his old neighborhood, where we'd meet his friends and [see] the places he hung out. Rocky provided us with a lot of stills from that era and we also got a tape from a magazine interview Rocky did. That was quite helpful as it enabled Paul to study it and capture the cadence of Rocky's speech. I felt Paul did a brilliant characterization in a wonderful performance.[2]

Robert Loggia on shooting a scene that was adversely affected by the weather:

We were supposed to be in the heat of summer. We were shirtless building a road as a pick and shovel [prison] gang. It's supposed to be 110° in the shade. In true Hollywood fashion—this always happen—it was the coldest day you can imagine. There was ice on the ground. So pouring water over us to show the sweat was actually freezing to our body. Rocky (Newman) asks for a drink of water but the sadistic guard throws it in Rocky's face. As a result Paul hits him with a jab and a hook but the guard leans the wrong way and Paul splits his cheek from his eyebrow to his jawline. It [was] so cold his skin had split. In cold weather your skin has no give to it. The blood just poured out.[3]

Wise on the preliminary casting of champion boxer Tony Zale as himself:

Zale had fought Rocky three times and was still in great shape. He was working with youth groups in Chicago. Someone told me Tony could portray himself pretty good so we brought him in. During some rehearsals I had an assistant come to me saying I should see what [was] going on with Newman and Zale in the ring. Paul was athletic but had never boxed. Newman was shying away not from being afraid but rather believing if he accidentally landed a blow Zale might have a reflex action, reverting to his boxing instincts without thinking. I went to the set, saw this, and realized we had a problem. Fortunately we found an amateur boxer that looked very much like Zale (Court Shepard).[4]

HOME COURT ADVANTAGE Available on VHS.

#21 HEAVEN CAN WAIT

Screenwriters Elaine May, Warren Beatty. (Based on a play by Harry Segall.) **Producer** Warren Beatty. **Directors** Warren Beatty, Buck Henry. **Cinematography** William Fraker. **Editing** Robert Jones, Don Zimmerman. **Music** Dave Grusin. **Production Design** Paul Sylbert, Edwin O'Donovan. **Executive Producer** Howard Koch Jr., Charles Maguire. Paramount. 1978.

THE PLAYERS
Warren Beatty **Joe Pendleton/Leo Farnsworth/Tom Jarrett**; Julie Christie **Betty Logan**; James Mason **Mr. Jordan**; Jack Warden **Max Corkle**; Charles Grodin **Tony Abbott**; Dyan Cannon **Julia Farnsworth**; Buck Henry **The Escort**; Joseph Maher **Sisk**; Vincent Gardenia **Lt. Krim**; Hamilton Camp **Bentley**; Arthur Malet **Everett**; Dolph Sweet **Head coach**; RG Armstrong **General manager**; Ed Peck **Trainer**; Deacon Jones **Gorman**; Roger Bowen **Newspaper reporter**; John Randolph **Former team owner**; Curt Cowdy **Football announcer**; Al DeRogatis **Football announcer**; Brynat Gumbel **Sportscaster**; Dick Enberg **Sports reporter**

THE GAME Though it has the same title as a 1943 Ernst Lubitsch film, *Heaven Can Wait* is actually a remake of the 1941 film *Here Comes Mr. Jordan*.

Robert Montgomery stars as a boxer in the original, and in the remake Warren Beatty plays a pro football quarterback for the Los Angeles Rams.

Joe Pendleton (Beatty) finds himself in heaven prematurely as a rookie mistake by a celestial messenger (Buck Henry) who pulled him out of a traffic accident before he was quite dead. Joe learns that they cannot correct the mistake quickly, and a "higher authority," Mr. Jordan (James Mason), personally takes over the case after it is learned that Joe's body has been cremated.

Joe, in the prime of his life and within reach of his goal of leading his team to victory in the Super Bowl, is understandably miffed (in any event, Joe has got to be the only person ever to raise hell about going to heaven). Mr. Jordan offers him a few alternative bodies back in the mortal realm, including a high-wire walker and a race-car driver, but Joe dismisses one for being too short and therefore unable to see over the line and the other because his teammates won't understand German. Exhausted from their search after rejecting so many candidates, Mr. Jordan tells Joe to widen his horizons.

They arrive at billionaire industrialist Leo Farnsworth's mansion. Joe is unimpressed and despite seeing Leo's scheming, adulterous wife (Dyan Cannon) and his executive secretary, Tony Abbott (Charles Grodin), plotting Leo's murder, Joe is ready to leave and seek another candidate until he casts his eyes on a passionate environmentalist teacher from Britain who appears on the scene.

Betty Logan (Julie Christie) has come armed with a petition to halt construction of an oil refinery that could destroy her little community of Paglesham in England. It's love at first sight for Joe—a love so deep that Betty will be able to see it in another man's eyes when Joe is forced to change bodies again at the end.

Joe arranges to take temporary possession of Leo's body to help her out. At this point the film really goes down two interwoven paths. One is the journey toward the Super Bowl with Joe, despite his new body and newfound wealth, leading his team as quarterback. The other is directed by his feelings for Betty.

To those ends Joe hires his beloved coach, Max Corkle (Jack Warden), to get the body of the industrialist in shape to play football. He also buys the Los Angeles Rams football team.

In his new guise and effort directed squarely at winning Betty's heart, Joe as Leo Farnsworth proceeds to confound everyone with his radical "personality and character change." To the stunned press on hand, Joe/Leo proceeds to befuddle his larcenous, greedy board of directors by addressing openly and honestly charges that his conglomerate is decimating the porpoise population with their tuna fleets; poisoning the atmosphere with their plastics and chemicals; and uprooting long-established communities and ecosystems to build refineries.

Just as it looks as if everything's going to work out, the relentless Mrs. Farnsworth and Tony Abbott succeed in killing Leo Farnsworth and Joe is forced to find another body.

Nothing can prevent Joe from achieving his Super Bowl dream, and in the end he assumes the identity (thus losing the memory of himself) of former teammate Tom Jarrett and goes on to win not only the big game but also the love of Ms. Logan, who, as destiny would have it, is able to make the connection in the dark tunnel outside the victorious locker room.

INSTANT REPLAY It is exceedingly rare for a remake to be better than its original, but *Heaven Can Wait* is such a film. Nominated for nine Academy Awards and winning an Oscar for Best Art Direction, the picture is a warm, funny romantic comedy.

Following the blueprint of *Here Comes Mr. Jordan*, the remake is faithful to the original story yet more contemporary in tone. The filmmakers, for example, incorporate references to environmental and energy concerns, which were particularly hot buttons at the time—"green" policies over corporate greed.

From the leads to the whole supporting cast, the performances are excellent. War-

TOP: 'Heaven Can Wait' earned nine Oscar nominations.

RIGHT: The understandably perplexed trainer of the Los Angeles Rams, Max Corkle (Jack Warden, center), doesn't know what to think when wealthy, middle-aged industrialist Leo Farnsworth (Warren Beatty, left) asks to help get him in shape to play quarterback for his football team—while at the same time talking to another person he can't see or hear (Mr. Jordan, played by James Mason, right).

ren Beatty is genuinely charming throughout his various incarnations. Cannon and Grodin shine as the bungling schemers, James Mason is classy and charming just as Claude Rains was in the same role in the original. Joseph Maher is the embodiment of the gentlemanly butler and Jack Warden is outstanding as the perplexed coach.

Real-life sports announcers (Curt Cowdy, Al DeRogatis, Dick Enberg, and Bryant Gumbel) and actual NFL players (Deacon Jones, Les Josephson, Charlie Cowan) bring a sense of verisimilitude to all the football action. Detracting slightly from that authentic feel is the use of Beatty's voice, twice, for another player in the huddle who is telling Joe/Leo to calm down and not get so excited.

The script and direction are strong, providing an entertaining mix of visual and verbal humor along with a romance that grows nicely as the film progresses. Credit to Buck Henry and Elaine May for their creative efforts yielding a wealth of visual and verbal comedy. Accompanying the vivid pictures of William Fraker is the light, mellow score that garnered composer Dave Grusin an Oscar nomination.

Heaven Can Wait offers contemporary yet old-fashioned escapism. A pleasant fantasy that brings forward what the best films of Hollywood from the 1930s and '40s did so well, a feel-good sentimentality and optimism mixed with lighthearted comedy.

TOP: The schemers: the industrialist's wife, Julia (Dyan Cannon), and his assistant, Tony Abbott (Charles Grodin).

MIDDLE: Julie Christie in a familiar role as Beatty's love interest, Betty Logan.

BOTTOM: Reportedly, in the initial stages of the project, producer Beatty wanted to stick to the same sport used in the original film 'Here Comes Mr. Jordan'—boxing—and wanted Muhammad Ali to star.

OUTSIDE THE LINES

Beatty is the only filmmaker in history to receive Oscar nominations in the categories of acting, writing, producing, and directing for a single film twice (*Heaven Can Wait*, 1978; *Reds*, 1981) He won an Academy Award for directing *Reds*. . . .Beatty is the brother of actress Shirley MacLaine. . . .Codirectors Buck Henry and Warren Beatty both made their film directing debuts with *Heaven Can Wait*. . . .Beatty excelled as a football player in high school, turning down 10 college football scholarships in order to study theater at Northwestern, where he graduated in 1959. . . .A former prizefighter, Jack Warden played both ways as a semi-pro football player in New Jersey.... Warden won an Emmy for his portrayal of legendary NFL coach George Halas in *Brian's Song*. . . .Edwin O'Donovan's work on *Heaven Can Wait* won him an Oscar for Art Direction, sharing it with the film's production designer, Paul Sylbert, and set designer, George Gaines.

ALL-STAR MOMENTS

With Joe/Leo (Beatty) using household servants to catch his football passes and leading them in calisthenics and jogging around the ornate garden grounds, a befuddled trainer Max (Warden) pleads with Joe/Leo: "Joe, you don't understand. You're playing football with a bunch of butlers! We're [the Rams] in the Super Bowl, this isn't going to work."

High atop the Los Angeles Coliseum watching the Rams practice, the former owner (John Randolph) mutters to his assistant (Richard O'Brien), "The son of a bitch got my team."

ASSISTANT: What kind of pressure did he use?

FORMER OWNER: Well I asked for $67 million and he [Joe/Leo] said "okay."

ASSISTANT: Ruthless bastard.

HOME COURT ADVANTAGE
Available on VHS and DVD.

#20 HOOSIERS

Screenwriter Angelo Pizzo. **Director** David Anspaugh. **Producers** John Daly, Carter De Haven, Derek Gibson, Angelo Pizzo. **Cinematography** Fred Murphy. **Editing** Carroll O'Meara. **Music** Jerry Goldsmith. Orion. 1986.

THE PLAYERS Gene Hackman **Coach Norman Dale**; Barbara Hershey **Myra Fleener**; Dennis Hopper **Wilbur "Shooter" Flatch**; Sheb Wooley **Cletus**; Fern Persons **Opal Fleener**; Chelcie Ross **George**; Robert Swan **Rollin**; Michael O'Guinne **Rooster**; Wil Dewit **Reverend Doty**; John Thompson **Sheriff Finley**; Michael Sassone **Preacher Purl**; Gloria Dorson **Millie**; Mike Dalzell **Mayor Carl**; Calvert Welker **Junior**; Eric Gilliom **J. June**; Brad Boyle **Whit**; Steve Hollar **Rade**; Robert Boyle **Referee, Oolitic**; Mike Dalzell **Carl**; Brad Long **Buddy Walker**; David Neidorf **Everett Flatch**; Sam Smiley **Referee, Cedar Knob**; Ralph Shively **Doc Buggins**; Tom McConnell **Coach, Cedar Knob**; Dennis Farkas **Player, Cedar Knob**; Rich Komenich **Reporter**; Ray Crowe **Coach, State**; Ray Craft **Official, Finals**; Maris Valainis **Jimmy Chitwood**; Tom Carnegie **PA announcer, Finals**; Scott Summers **Strap Purl**; Larua Robling **Hickory cheerleader**; Libbey Schenck **Hickory cheerleader**; Nancy Harris **Hickory cheerleader**; Kent Poole **Merle**

THE GAME He was once a formidable college basketball coach, but a dark incident finds Norman Dale (Gene Hackman) arriving in the small Indiana town of Hickory to start his new job teaching and coaching the high school basketball team, an opportunity provided by the school's principal, Cletus (Sheb Wooley), an old friend.

From the start, Coach Dale's "my way or the highway" approach offends not only several key returning players but also the local residents who are used to having input.

Dale's troubles are advanced when the team's best player, Jimmy Chitwood (Maris Valainis), refuses to play for the new coach because of his devotion to the enduring memory of Norman's predecessor.

A teacher, Myra Fleener (Barbara Hershey), who is also acting principal as Cletus becomes quite ill, is very protective of Jimmy. She is therefore wary of Coach Dale as he tries to forge a relationship with her. She tells him that a man his age comes to a place like this only if he's running from something or has no place to go. Coach doesn't make any demands and lets Jimmy know he's free to do what he wants with his talents.

Meanwhile another key player, Buddy Walker (Brad Long), gets out of line at the first practice and is told to leave. Unsurprisingly Hickory's first few games are horrendous losses.

One supportive resident of Hickory, Wilbur "Shooter" Flatch (Dennis Hopper), is very knowledgeable about both the game in general and Coach Dale's approach. The problem is that he is the town drunk. This is especially embarrassing for his son, Everett (David Niedorf), a player on the team. Dale offers Shooter the opportunity to be his unpaid assistant coach if he can lay off the bottle.

Shooter is tested when Coach Dale gets ejected a couple of times as the season progresses. After a shaky start he proves his strategic talents.

Myra finds out that Coach Dale struck a player while coaching at Ithaca. At the same time she appreciates him staying away from Jimmy and trying to help Wilbur. They become friendlier.

Meanwhile the town's anger at Coach Dale's methods and the team's lackluster performance leads to a town hall vote on his ouster. He not only survives the vote, but Jimmy announces he'll play for Coach Dale.

The team jells through Coach Dale's insistence on fundamentals and they go on a winning streak. Unfortunately Wilbur has fallen off the wagon and shows up at a game drunk. He is sent to the hospital, where Coach Dale visits him and says, "A couple months in here and you'll be as dry as the Sahara." He tells Shooter he is still a big part of the team.

Under Coach Dale's strict regimen of fundamentals, Hickory's winning ways lead them through some tight games in the sectional and regional playoffs, then on to the state championship. Under the bright lights of Indianapolis's Butler University Fieldhouse, the small school wins the title.

INSTANT REPLAY   *Hoosiers* is an enjoyable slice of 1950s small-town midwestern Americana. It succeeds on many levels but it all starts with the filmmakers.

Screenwriter Angelo Pizzo and director David Anspaugh, both Indiana natives, have devised a homespun tale that beautifully captures time and place via a keen eye for detail.

From the dialogue of the men gathered at the barber shop to the pictures of the farms with neighbors pitching in to harvest corn, and their living and dying with their high school team's performance from week to week, *Hoosiers* provides an authentic landscape for its characters and simply conveys what the indoor game means to the locals during the isolation of the winter season. With its packed crowds even for pep rallies, the town shutting down as they caravan for a road game, and town hall meetings to conduct business about a basketball coach's performance, the picture is rich in detail and texture. (The 2004 football film *Friday Night Lights* takes a similar tack.)

Pizzo and Anspaugh receive vital support from the music of Jerry Goldsmith and Fred Murphy's photography. As Martin Scorsese does with the pool hall in Atlantic City in *The Color of Money*, Anspaugh uses light and angles to give his gyms a sort of ecclesiastical feel, a representation of how integral basketball is to the residents of Hickory and the sport to Indiana in general. The shots of the farms, the old school gym,

Indiana plays a central role in 'Hoosiers.' It is the home state of its filmmakers, writer Angelo Pizzo and director David Anspaugh.

TOP: Myra Fleener (Barbara Hershey) and Norman Dale (Gene Hackman).

MIDDLE: The troubled "Shooter" (Dennis Hopper, center).

BOTTOM: The newly crowned champs.

and the main street shops add to a sense of rural community roots, while Goldsmith's Oscar-nominated score provides both an energetic feel to the game action and at the same time a pastoral sense for the country setting.

The production design by David and Janis Lubin, David Nichols, and Brendan Smith, and Jane Anderson's costume work, all enhance the picture's verisimilitude.

Of course, filling out those costumes is where *Hoosiers* reaches another level.

In perhaps one of his best performances, and there have been quite a few, Gene Hackman embodies the picture's themes of redemption as a skilled coach with a dark past, teaching the players (and the citizens of Hickory) to respect his authority as coach and to give outsiders a chance.

The veteran actor manages a difficult mix of compassion, suppressed anger, intense desire to win, and a strength of character with an everyman feel, a complexity that adds up to being quite human.

In a role that earned him an Academy Award nomination, Dennis Hopper also earns some measure of redemption as a former star player who blew the big game and turned into the town drunk. He's given a second chance by conveying his knowledge of the game to the school's current crop of players, including his son.

Hopper's "Shooter" brings a welcome blend of humor and empathy, and a crazy-like-a-fox dimension to the story. His melancholy portrayal of a man constantly fighting his demons delivers some keen insights on and off the court, and leaving his character arc unresolved by the film's end enhances the story.

Barbara Hershey, in a more perfunctory role, embodies those who don't see the fleeting glory of sport but must operate in a world that is sports-mad. Her romantic relationship with Hackman falls a bit flat primarily due to editing choices; important set-up scenes between the two were eliminated, reportedly in order to meet a studio mandate to keep the picture within a certain running time. (This is also the reason why we suddenly and inexplicably see a player return to the Hickory team after being kicked off in the first meeting with the new coach.)

Regarding the basketball action, only one cast member representing the players was actually an actor (David Niedorf as Everett). The filmmakers astutely use the game itself to advance the story as opposed to lots of dialogue from non-actors.

Carroll O'Meara's editing overall provides a good pacing of the games. It must be remembered that 1950s high school basketball was a very different game than the high-flying NBA we're used to watching today. No fancy dribbling between fancy shoes leading to an alley-oop pass for an "in yo' face" slam dunk. Set shots were the norm of the day and were done without a lot of histrionics.

Hoosiers runs the gamut of sports movie clichés—redemption, misfits, underdog team, winning the big game—but it's all to the good in this splendidly detailed canvas of a specific place and time, with very human characterizations of not only the leads but the myriad townspeople. The picture delivers a genuine feel, as if the filmmakers had gone back in time and made a home movie of their roots.

OUTSIDE THE LINES Classmates at Indiana University, director David Anspaugh and writer/producer Angelo Pizzo teamed for the football drama *Rudy* (1993) and soccer's *Game of Their Lives* (2005).... *Hoosiers* was inspired by the real-life 1954 Milan, Indiana championship team.... David Niedorf (Everett), who played Shooter's son, was the only actor on the team before filming began.... He also appeared in *Bull Durham* (1988) and now is reportedly a professional poker player....

Maris Valainis had no acting background when he beat out several hundred applicants for the role of Jimmy Chitwood.... He got the acting bug, moved to Hollywood, and struggled for several years, getting by on his real athletic talent, golfing, where he managed some courses as a local pro.... The Chitwood character was partially based on Bobby Plump, who led Milan to the state title in 1954, making the game-winning shot and winning the Trester and Mr. Basketball Awards.... Plump turned down full rides to Indiana University, Purdue, and Michigan State to attend Butler University.... Harry Dean Stanton was also circling the role of Shooter.... Dennis Hopper was nominated for an Academy Award.... As was Jerry Goldsmith for his musical score.... Because the term "hoosier" wasn't well known abroad the picture appeared overseas as *Best Shot*.... Gene Hackman grew up just over 50 miles from where the picture was shot.... He appeared in a golf picture, *Banning* (1967), and played a football coach in *The Replacements* (2000) and a ski coach to Olympian Robert Redford in *Downhill Racer* (1969).... Actress Barbara Hershey appeared with Redford in baseball's *The Natural* (1984).... At one point Jack Nicholson expressed interest in the role of Coach Dale.... The championship game was played at Butler University's Hinkle Fieldhouse, which has long hosted the state finals.

ALL-STAR MOMENTS Sequence where Dale (Hackman) informs George (Chelcie Ross) that he's the new coach. As George walks away he mutters he'll have Dale's ass hung up if he screws up the team. Dale calmly looks past the threat, asking George to leave the basketball behind on his way out.

Dale then introduces himself to his new team. "Let's see the hand I've been dealt here."

One player, Buddy Walker (Long), ignores the new coach and talks to another teammate while the new coach addresses the team. Dale tells him to leave and return only when he gets some respect. A teammate joins him. The new coach is left with just four players and a short equipment manager.

After purposely getting himself kicked out of a tight game on the road, Dale leaves the fortunes of the team to assistant coach Wilbur (Hopper). It's a test for Wilbur (the father of Hickory player Everett, played by Neidorf), who is trying to stay sober. In setting up the game-winning shot, he tells his players, "Run the picket fence and don't get caught watching the paint dry." Hickory goes on to win 60—58.

In a pre-game talk before the game against Linton, Dale tells his players not to focus on the score and that if they play to the best of their abilities he'll consider them winners either way. Hickory wins in a "barn burner."

Arriving for the state championships in Indianapolis, Dale helps soothe his small-town players' nerves by having them use a tape measure and realize that the court and basket dimensions are the same as back home.

POST-GAME COMMENTS Writer/producer Angelo Pizzo recalling the nucleus of how the film idea came about in a conversation with directing partner David Anspaugh:

> We were talking about basketball, which isn't unusual. Everybody in Indiana talks about basketball. But then the conversation drifted into what it must have been like to be a hometown hero in the postwar era, before Elvis and the

Beatles, when the only TV set in town was in the window of the general store and the interstate highway was a two-lane blacktop. And then of course the real David and Goliath story, a modern-day folk myth, the 1954 Milan High School Championship. We decided there was a movie there somewhere. We imagined being the ones to make it.[1]

Gene Hackman on how the role was a personal voyage back in time for him:

To the youngsters in the cast, it's a "period" picture. To me, the cars, the clothes, the hairstyles, everything is just about the way it was the day I left Danville. I simply stepped back into my own past.[2]

(Hackman was raised only 60 miles from the Richmond, Indiana location in Danville, Illinois.)

Barbara Hershey on her character:

She's fiercely proud of Hickory, but determined to help its brightest youngsters get away to a better life. She despises the hero worship of high school sports but is attracted, despite herself, to the new coach. Up 'til then, one suspects, her luck with men has been pretty awful.[3]

Writer/producer Angelo Pizzo on what his film is about:

Redemption. About individuals succeeding through the help of each other.[4]

Pizzo, a Bloomington, Indiana native, on why he felt the film's writer had to be a Hoosier:

The sociocultural dynamic between town and school works (differently) in every kind of big college town. I thought the relationship between basketball and the state was a key one. For a movie like *Hoosiers* I felt the place was important, so important—if not more important than any of the characters—that I wanted to find an Indiana writer. A writer not even from Illinois. Not even from Ohio. But from Indiana. I put the search out to all agents: "Wanted: writer from Indiana." I read a lot of stuff but nothing quite worked for me.[5]

HOME COURT ADVANTAGE Available on VHS and DVD. Initial version released by Artisan, but MGM has since released two versions, the latest a "Collector's Edition."

#19 GENTLEMAN JIM

Screenwriters Vincent Lawrence, Horace McCoy. **Director** Raoul Walsh. **Producer** Robert Buckner. **Cinematography** Sidney Hickox. **Editing** Jack Killifer. **Music** Heinz Roemheld. **Art Direction** Ted Smith. **Costume Design** Milo Anderson. Warner Bros. 1942.

THE PLAYERS Errol Flynn **James J. Corbett**; Alexis Smith **Victoria Ware**; Alan Hale **Pat Corbett**; Jack Carson **Walter Lowrie**; John Loder **Clinton DeWitt**; William Frawley **Billy Delaney**; Ward Bond **John L. Sullivan**; Minor Watson **Buck Ware**; Dorothy Vaughan **Ma Corbett**; Arthur Shields **Father Burke**; Rhys Williams **Harry Watson**; Madeleine LeBeau **Anna Held**; Wallis Clark **Judge Geary**; James Flavin **George Corbett**; Pat Flaherty **Harry Corbett**; Marilyn Phillips **Mary Corbett**; Henry O'Hara **Colis Huntington**; Frank Mayo **Governor Stanford**; Harry Crocker **Charles Crocker**; Carl Harbaugh **Smith**; Fred Kelsey **Sutro**; Sammy Stein **Joe Choynski**; Mike Mazurki **Jake Kilrain**; Edwin Stanley **President McInnes**

THE GAME Jim Corbett (Errol Flynn) is a brash, dashing, opportunistic bank clerk in late 19th-century San Francisco. When a beautiful woman, Victoria Ware (Alexis Smith), arrives to withdraw some money for her wealthy father back at the exclusive Olympic Club, Corbett seizes his chance by pretending he's a senior executive and offers to help her carry the heavy silver dollars back for her.

Once inside the hallowed halls of the private club to which he has coveted membership, Corbett makes the most of it. Coming from a large, blue-collar, brawling Irish family, Corbett holds his own in an impromptu boxing match against an esteemed coach. Judge Geary (Wallis Clark) is impressed and convinces Victoria to sponsor Corbett for club membership. She is simultaneously repelled by and attracted to Jim's arrogance.

Using an innovative style of boxing based on quickness and finesse with the great footwork of a dancer, Corbett makes a meteoric rise to the height of the sport.

Soon the young Irishman finds himself in a title bout against the long-reigning popular champion, John L. Sullivan (Ward Bond). The world championship is to be held in New Orleans.

The problem is, Sullivan demands that Corbett make a side bet of $10,000 to guarantee his showing up. Seeing this as an opportunity to pound some humility into the cocky Corbett, Victoria secretly puts up the money and relishes viewing the beating from her ringside seat.

Unfortunately for Ms. Ware, Corbett provides a fight of sheer artistry: slipping and sliding the powerful punches of the much bigger Sullivan, wearing him down, and scoring consistently in the process.

When Corbett wins with a knockout in the 21st round, Victoria finds herself cheering Jim's bravura performance. Realizing that Corbett is thoughtful and backs up his brash boasts, she falls for him completely.

At a party where the new and former champions exchange words of mutual respect and admiration, Corbett and Victoria exchange insults then kisses as he tells her, "You're going to make a marvelous Corbett."

INSTANT REPLAY *Gentleman Jim* is a lively and entertaining fictionalized biography of the father of modern boxing. Starting from Jim Corbett's autobiography, *The Roar of the Crowd*, writers Vincent Lawrence and Horace McCoy provide action king Raoul Walsh a colorful template from which to direct.

Though it's quite atmospheric in representing not only the opulence of the times but also the poor side of 1890s San Francisco, *Gentleman Jim* is one of the premiere pictures that focuses more on actual boxing than the themes of corruption, comebacks, and psychological portraits common in other fine pugilistic performances.

Producer Robert Buckner and Warner Bros. go all out to show not only the amazing popularity of the sport but also a time when boxing was in a key transitional period. While there's plenty of comedy and romance, this remains a fight fan's film, thanks to the brilliantly staged fights and terrific backdrops like the huge waterfront barge, and the contrasting boxing styles, body types, and personalities of the two key combatants, Jim Corbett and John L. Sullivan.

Sullivan was the embodiment of the "old school" fighters—burly, enormously strong men who used their massive muscles to club each other with powerful blows until one couldn't answer the bell.

Unable to compete in that way largely because of his comparatively slight physical stature, Corbett introduced a whole new style based on fancy footwork, quick, cumulative jabbing, endurance, and ring savvy emphasizing brain over brawn.

To that end actors Ward Bond and Errol Flynn are ideally suited to symbolize those contrasts. In one of his best supporting roles in a long career, Bond is outstanding as the somewhat tragic hero John L. Sullivan, whose reign at the top has come to an end. He is a proud and popular brawler realizing that time has caught up to him in a young man's game. The final scene he shares wth Flynn, where the old and new champions exchange sincere compliments and best wishes, is a classic.

Like his role in *The Adventures of Robin Hood*, this character fits Errol Flynn like a glove, in this case a pair of boxing gloves.

Already bearing a physical resemblance to the title character, Flynn worked very

Bank clerk Jim Corbett (Errol Flynn) makes a career change after meeting Victoria Ware (Alexis Smith).

diligently with Corbett expert Ed Cochrane and trained heavily with fighter Mushy Callahan to emulate Corbett's style. The actor's detailed preparations to slip into Corbett's skin pay off tremendously.

Flynn is simply dynamic as a charismatic, manipulative, good-natured rascal (let's just say it wasn't a stretch). With his sincerity and physical grace, Flynn gives us one of the greatest performances of his career and reportedly his favorite.

Besides Ward Bond, Flynn's terrific turn is aided by a talented supporting cast. Alexis Smith not only provides a pretty face but is convincing in the ongoing banter and verbal parrying with Flynn. It's entertaining to see this woman, obviously in love but determined not to express it, find ways to humble the object of her affections.

The Flynn-Smith matchup is reminiscent of the engaging chemistry Flynn shares with Olivia de Havilland in such Warner Bros. pictures as the aforementioned *Hood*, *Captain Blood*, and 1941's *They Died With Their Boots On*, also directed by Walsh.

Playing Corbett's best friend, Walter Lowrie, Jack Carson stands out, most notably in the drunk scene at the Olympic Club and the hangover he shares with his pal, waking up broke in a Salt Lake City hotel.

Alan Hale is entertaining as the gregarious head of the Corbett clan. Bringing some solid Irish flavor are James Flavin and Pat Flaherty as Jim's brothers.

The Irish-laced tunes of Heinz Roemheld also contribute to the atmosphere.

Gentleman Jim marks the third of eight pictures pairing Walsh and Flynn, and they've never been better. Walsh juggles the comedy and drama with fine pacing and conducts the boxing scenes quite authentically thanks to the camera work of Sidney Hickox, Jack Killifer's editing, and the realistic boxing talents of Errol Flynn.

Walsh, a former actor, was not only familiar with the fight game, having met both Corbett and Sullivan and seen Jim fight, but was also steeped in the time period, having directed *The Bowery* and *The Strawberry Blonde*. Here, he handles romance and drama with ease.

Despite its free-swinging ways in taking dramatic license, reportedly due in part to legal wranglings with the Corbett estate, the filmmakers of *Gentleman Jim* have produced a very entertaining picture that overall is representative of the essence of a colorful man living in a colorful era.

They did, however, miss one important element in not even hinting at Corbett's thespian interests, as the fighter would enjoy a successful career in stage and theater.

Overall, Errol Flynn embodies the boxing champion Corbett as well as any actor has captured an athlete on the silver screen—and it's obvious no one's ever had more fun doing it.

OUTSIDE THE LINES
Director Walsh began his career as an actor. One of his early roles was playing John Wilkes Booth in *Birth of a Nation* (1914).... The real Corbett fought most of his bouts bare-knuckled.... Corbett had a lengthy career in vaudeville as well.... Nat Fleischer, who wrote the book *Gentleman Jim: The Story of James Corbett*, was also the editor of *Ring Magazine*.... Walsh was a racing enthusiast and owned several thoroughbreds.... Flynn had recently been rejected for World War II military service for heart problems that meant he could only work for brief intervals in the ring.... But Flynn had been a good boxer and fought as an amateur in Australia.... Actor William Frawley (aka Fred Mertz from *I Love Lucy*) was a part owner of the Hollywood Stars baseball team of the Pacific Coast League.... He also appeared in several baseball pictures, *Safe at Home!* (1962), *Rhubarb* (1951), *Kill the Umpire* (1950), *The Babe*

TOP: Victoria (right) would enjoy nothing more than to see a little humility knocked into Jim (center) in the ring.

MIDDLE: Exchanging a suit for boxing trunks, Jim is on his way to becoming a smashing success.

BOTTOM: Love conquers all even in the battle of the sexes as Victoria and Jim fall for each other.

Ruth Story (1948), and *Alibi Ike* (1935)…. According to a *Los Angeles Times* article, Errol Flynn once got into a drunken brawl with director John Huston at producer David O. Selznick's house that sent both to the hospital, Flynn for a pair of broken ribs and Huston for a broken nose…. Reportedly, when Flynn called to check on the director's condition, Huston said he had "thoroughly enjoyed the fight and hoped we'd do it again sometime."…Cowriter Horace McCoy also wrote *The Lusty Men* (1952), a rodeo picture starring Robert Mitchum and Susan Hayward…. Ward Bond played football at USC and became great friends with another Trojan ballplayer-turned-actor, John Wayne…. The film is largely based on Corbett's autobiography, *The Roar of the Crowd*…. Mike Mazurki played a wrestler, "The Strangler," in the noir film *Night and the City* (1950)…. Another cast member, Sammy Stein, played professional football (New York Giants, 1931) and wrestled professionally…. At one point there was interest in having Rita Hayworth or Ann Sheridan for the Victoria role…. The film's producer, Robert Bruckner, wrote the screenplay for *Knute Rockne: All-American* (1940)…. James Corbett was the world heavyweight boxing champion from 1892 to 1897.

ALL-STAR MOMENTS
As the combatants continue to slug it out in an outlawed match, the crowd scrambles to get away when police arrive in their paddy wagons. The boxers proceed to fight the cops who storm the ring.

Inside a private club Corbett (Flynn) impresses some influential people, one of whom asks Victoria (Smith) and her father to be among Corbett's sponsors. Victoria is amazed about the whole thing, saying that two hours ago Jim Corbett was "just a bank clerk running an errand, and in six months he'll own the club."

Corbett and his coworker at the bank, Walter (Jack Carson), wake up from a hangover in another city and with no money. Fight promoter Billy Delaney (William Frawley) arrives as if Jim knows what is going on and gives him some money for his fight that night.

The recurring announcement of a family feud when a yell is heard: "The Corbetts are at it again!"

The evening scene of the fight on the waterfront. A homemade sign: "Admission barge $1, wharf 50¢, on the schooner 25¢."

Some fans watch the fight high up on the sails of ships.

A county sheriff rushes to the center of the ring waving a document declaring a stop to the illegal fight. The crowd boos, then laughs when he gets tossed into the water and the fight begins.

POST-GAME COMMENTS
Bert Sugar, boxing historian, on Flynn's pugilistic talents:

> In my mind's eye the best actor boxing I have ever seen. His moves as Jim Corbett were magnificent. He emulated Corbett in the ring better than anybody playing a role of a boxer I've ever seen.[1]

HOME COURT ADVANTAGE
Available on VHS.

#18 THE LONGEST YARD

Screenwriter Tracy Keenan Wynn. **Story** Al Ruddy. **Director** Robert Aldrich. **Producer** Al Ruddy. **Cinematography** Joseph Biroc. **Editing** Michael Luciano. **Music** Frank De Vol. **Production Design** James Vance. Paramount. 1974.

THE PLAYERS
Burt Reynolds **Paul Crewe**; Eddie Albert **Warden Hazen**; Ed Lauter **Captain Knauer**; James Hampton **Caretaker**; Michael Conrad **Nate Scarboro**; Harry Caesar **Granville**; John Steadman **Pop**; Charles Tyner **Unger**; Mike Henry **Rassmeusen**; Jim Nicholson **Ice man**; Bernadette Peters **Warden's secretary**; Ray Nitschke **Bogdanski**; Anitra Ford **Melissa Gaines**; Joe Kapp **Walking boss**; Mort Marshall **Assistant warden**; Richard Kiel **Samson**; Pervis Atkins **Mawabe**; Tony Cacciotti **Rotka**; Michael Fox **Announcer**; Pepper Martin **Shop steward**; Tony Reece **Levitt**; Sonny Sixkiller **The Indian**; Robert Tessier **Shokner**; Ernie Wheelwright **Spooner**; Dino Washington **Mason**; Chuck Hayward **Trooper**; Alfie Wise **Trooper**; Joe Dorsey **Bartender**; Gus Carlucci **Team doctor**; Sonny Shroyer **Tannen**; Ray Ogden **Schmidt**; Don Ferguson **Referee**; Wilson Warren **Buttercup**; George Jones **Big George**

THE GAME
Paul Crewe (Burt Reynolds) is a former football star who ended his career in disgrace, having taken part in a point shaving scandal. Now a washed-up gigolo and feeling used by a particularly domineering woman (Anitra Ford), Crew steals her fancy car but is soon being chased by the police. He proceeds to dump her car in the river and winds up in jail.

Crewe finds himself in a prison run by Warden Hazen (Eddie Albert), a football-crazy owner of a semi-pro team. Hazen "persuades" Crewe to organize a team of inmates to play a game against his guards.

Recruiting doesn't come easy at first because many of the cons (and all of the guards) can't respect "Superstar" Crewe, an athlete who had it all and threw it all away in some scandal. On top of that, with the racial division common in prison, the blacks want no part of it.

By appealing to their self-respect and of course the cons' desire to inflict as much physical pain on the guards as possible via a one-time football game, Crewe breaks down the racial barriers and assembles a ragtag squad, the Mean Machine.

Going up against the vicious guards, an experienced team led by Captain Knauer (Ed Lauter) and Bogdanski (Ray Nitschke), Crewe is worried about just surviving. Amazingly, though, the cons begin to bond and actually make the game competitive. This rekindles the old competitive spirit in Crewe.

At halftime, however, an angry and disappointed warden pressures Crewe, with some serious threats, to ensure that the guards win by a huge margin.

With Crewe's flagrant mistakes at the start of the second half on top of the injuries suffered by teammates, the cons soon lose their momentum. In a dilemma and clearly feeling his teammates' disappointment in him, Crewe decides to ignore the warden's threats and actually wants to win the game. He slowly regains his teammates' trust when he returns to the field, making some stellar plays despite taking a lot of physical punishment. The rejuvenated cons then proceed to rally and pull off an unlikely victory over the guards.

INSTANT REPLAY
A picture that captures the times and holds up well, *The Longest Yard* is an interesting concept from producer Al Ruddy, where it takes a trip to prison for an accomplished yet disgraced man to find redemption and finally not sell out.

TOP: The fading love between Melissa Gaines (Anitra Ford) and disgraced football star Paul Crewe (Burt Reynolds) is about to expire completely.

MIDDLE: Crewe doesn't get far after stealing Melissa's car.

BOTTOM: The reality of doin' time.

Drawing from Tracy Keenan Wynn's sharp script, director Robert Aldrich switches battlefields from his World War II drama *The Dirty Dozen*. He keeps us on our toes, alternating between dark humor and serious drama in this tough yet entertaining parable about comprehending man's seeming need for violence and cruelty, covering such heated topics as racism, homosexuality, freedom, and abuse of power, all interwoven through the brutal worlds of football and prison life.

Aldrich has Reynolds take a page from the Lee Marvin character in *The Dirty Dozen*, reluctantly forced to select and train a group of thugs for a seemingly impossible mission. Reynolds treats the no-win situation with a comical and at times melancholy irony to solid effect, finding loyalty and pride, if only temporary and among bad seeds.

With Vietnam and Watergate influencing Hollywood's value shifts in the '70s, audiences were drawn to more cynical fare that starred vibrant yet irreverent antiheroes like the ones featured in *One Flew Over the Cuckoo's Nest*, *Taxi Driver*, and *The French Connection*. Burt Reynolds is all that in *The Longest Yard*.

With sadistic guards, power-mad authorities, and a protagonist incarcerated with harsher terms than his crime would dictate, we see here parts of *Cool Hand Luke* and other films, prison-centric or otherwise, that present the bad guy as the hero: *Escape From Alcatraz*, *The Birdman of Alcatraz*, *Butch Cassidy and the Sundance Kid*, *Bonnie and Clyde*, and *The Godfather* (also produced by Ruddy).

The politically active Aldrich weaves social commentary throughout, but his most succinct statement on the power-grab in the national government scene at the time comes from prison chief Hazen when he says, "Before this game is over, I want every prisoner in this institution to know about power and who controls it."

Aldrich's keen behavioral study of people in winless situations is like the climactic football game—temporarily earning small victories, gaining a measure of pride, and of course trying to inflict more damage to the other guy in the course of the battle in a war that is lost.

Carrying the load of all that superbly are Burt Reynolds as con QB Paul Crewe and Eddie Albert as Warden Hazen.

Funny, intense, with the macho physicality of a former jock, Reynolds is at the top of his game here. No doubt his collegiate gridiron days help him in the football sequences and overall attitude, but his comedic timing is what goes a long way toward lightening a heavy load of hot-button themes.

On the other side of the field is Eddie Albert, whose smiling countenance hides a control freak hell-bent on crushing the inmates' spirits and reasserting his endless desire for Stalin-like control.

Also helping to lighten the heaviness are the characterizations by Richard Kiel and Robert Tessier as the giant and killer martial artist cons respectively. And in a romantic interlude with Crewe, Bernadette Peters is instantly memorable with her beehive hairdo.

The Longest Yard scores in authenticity as well. In fact, the picture was shot on location at an actual prison in Georgia where producer Ruddy not only builds a football field but peoples the very realistic game with recognizable gridiron stars like Ray Nitschke, Sonny Sixkiller, and Joe Kapp.

One of the longer game sequences in movie history is done with knowing care, even with the exaggerated violence in keeping with the story's themes. Here too humor finds its way in. The whole cross-dressing performance of the "Citrus State Cheerios" and announcer Michael Fox's game call are classics. (Fox mimics Kiel's

Reynolds's playing days as a running back for Florida State served him well in his role as the guiding force of the Mean Machine.

gleeful announcement when he injures a guard, stating over the loudspeaker, "I think he broke his fucking neck!").

Taking Joseph Biroc's photography, Aldrich uses split-screen and slow-motion techniques to help convey the tension and drama as the game progresses. The real key is the pinpoint timing of Michael Luciano's editing. Garnering an Oscar nomination for his work, Luciano ensures that the game feels real without prolonging anything.

At times uneven in its focus, split between comedy and drama, with some characters lacking in setup or simply presented as cliché outlines, *The Longest Yard* is still one of the more influential movies in sports cinema.

It proved the game itself could be played out in extended form, as something more than a story's climactic act. It could be presented the same way it is on any given Sunday by the television networks, this time with the audience watching from the movie theater rather than their living room.

The simple fact is that *The Longest Yard* was the first successful modern theatrical sports movie. As *Brian's Song* did when it was first broadcast on television, *The Longest Yard*'s themes, plots, and characterizations have influenced a wide range of sports pictures.

The Longest Yard's motley crew coming together in time to defeat the more sophisticated rivals has been the basis for pictures across the sports world—baseball's *Bad News Bears* and *Major League*, hockey's *Slap Shot*, basketball's *Fast Break*, as well as James Caan's uprising in *Rollerball*.

In pitting a varied group against a more organized opponent within the penal system, John Huston's soccer drama *Victory* also borrows from *The Longest Yard*.

TOP: The walking boss (Joe Kapp, center) takes pleasure in introducing Crewe to swamp reclamation duty.

BOTTOM: After leading the prisoners to a stunning victory, Crewe hands the game ball to Warden Hazen (Eddie Albert).

At the very least *The Longest Yard* turns the oft-seen innocent-man-behind-bars ploy on its head and gives us a rare and darkly entertaining picture where the big game climax really scores.

OUTSIDE THE LINES

Reynolds played running back at Florida State University.... He also starred as the Nate Scarboro character in the Adam Sandler remake of *The Longest Yard* (2005).... Robert Aldrich directed *The Dirty Dozen* (1967).... Candidates for the warden role that eventually went to Eddie Albert included Robert Preston, Rod Steiger, George Kennedy, and William Holden.... Essentially the fence was borrowed from the Rose Bowl organizers, then returned in time for the next parade.... Ed Lauter was featured in *Seabiscuit* (2003).... Pat Studstill, a two-time NFL pro bowl receiver for the Detroit Lions, was the film's technical advisor.... Over 600 inmates were paid $5 a day as extras at the Georgia prison production site about 50 miles from Savannah.... Burt Reynolds's brother appears in the film as one of his blockers.... Robert Aldrich's feature film directorial debut was the baseball movie *Big Leaguer* (1953).... Cinematographer Joseph Biroc also shot *Brian's Song*.... Pro and college football stars appearing in the film include Sonny Sixkiller, Pervis Atkins, Ernie Wheelwright, Joe Kapp, and Ray Nitschke.... Wrestler Pepper Martin was also part of the cast.... The film was remade with a soccer backdrop in *Mean Machine* (2001).

ALL-STAR MOMENTS

As Paul (Reynolds) walks out on his lady, Melissa (Ford), and they tussle over her car keys, she bites him.

PAUL: I think the love's gone out of our relationship.

MELISSA: Bastard!

She throws a liquor bottle at him and yells at Paul not to take her Maserati. Paul turns and says, "I earned it." And leaves.

Paul sees the cops in his rearview mirror, chugs his drink, and tosses the glass in the back seat. The chase is on. Paul escapes over a drawbridge, pulls into a gravel area, and gets out of the car. Lighting a cigarette, he reaches into the car and puts it in gear. The car plunges into the river, the Lynyrd Skynyrd tune on the radio becoming garbled as the car sinks.

After getting into a mudslinging fight during a work detail in the swamp, prisoner Crewe gets everyone to laugh when he tells Captain Knauer (Lauter), "I quit." As Knauer goes to strike him with his baton, Crewe catches it with his hand.

Coerced into coaching the cons' football squad, Crewe goes over some files that contain the cons' backgrounds. Most are pretty gruesome, e.g., "hacked mother to death." Nate (Michael Conrad) reminds him to look for those with two stars since they are the most violent. Paul asks for three stars.

Paul is led into the warden's office, where he receives footage of the guards' football practice. He realizes the price is sex with the secretary (Peters) when she locks the door, tells him they only have 15 minutes, and begins to undress.

PAUL: Do you do this often?

SECRETARY: I'm just as far from Tallahassee as you are, honey.

The Mean Machine "cheerleaders" (the Men from Cell Block C, aka the "Citrus State Cheerios") singing "Born Free" backed by a live band.

QB Crewe throws the ball at a charging Bogdanski (Ray Nitschke), hitting him in the groin. Then all the players pile on top of the defender, who is writhing in pain. Band plays funeral tune. Trainer says he's not breathing and asks someone to give him mouth-to-mouth. No volunteers.

Game-winning drive and touchdown dive by Crewe as cons defeat the guards.

POST-GAME COMMENTS
Producer Al Ruddy, who also wrote the original story, on the impact of *The Longest Yard*:

> It was the first sports movie to make any huge box office. *The Longest Yard* kicked off a whole generation of sports movies. Men and women, across the board, it became a commercial success. They [studios] said, "Aha, maybe we ought to do sports movies."[1]

Ruddy talks about a different ending they shot:

> Bob (director Aldrich) and I had two endings. When he goes to retrieve the football they kill him. When I was watching the dailies, I called Bob and said, "Forget it. If we kill Burt Reynolds they'll tear the fucking screen down. No one gives a shit. When they walk out of the theater they want to feel good. 'Stuff this in your trophy case.'"[2]

Ruddy, who won an Academy Award for Best Picture for producing *Million Dollar Baby*, had an idea for a follow-up to *The Longest Yard*:

> I wanted to do a sequel with Burt coming out of prison at age 50. I wanted him to go to the NFL owners meeting in Palm Beach. He's a pariah to them but he charms a woman owner and moves in with her. Then he starts to take over the team until they break his leg and he's messed up.[3]

The project didn't come to pass. Instead Ruddy is writing a football comedy, "End Zone," featuring God and the Devil betting on the Super Bowl.

HOME COURT ADVANTAGE
Available on VHS and DVD. Paramount has released the title twice on DVD. The most recent, a "Lockdown Edition," has numerous extra features.

#17 BODY AND SOUL

Screenwriter Abraham Polonsky. **Director** Robert Rossen. **Producer** Bob Roberts. **Cinematography** James Wong Howe. **Editing** Francis Lyon, Robert Parrish. **Music** Hugo Friedhofer. **Art Direction** Nathan Juran. **Set Decoration** Edward Boyle. United Artists. 1947.

THE PLAYERS John Garfield **Charlie Davis**; Lilli Palmer **Peg Born**; Hazel Brooks **Alice**; Anne Revere **Anna Davis**; William Conrad **Quinn**; Joseph Pevney **Shorty Polaski**; Lloyd Goff **Roberts**; Canada Lee **Ben Chaplin**; Art Smith **David Davis**; James Burke **Arnold**; Joe Devlin **Prince**; Peter Virgo **Drummer**; Virginia Gregg **Irma**; Shimen Ruskin **Grocer**; Mary Currier **Ms. Tedder**; Milton Kibbee **Dan**; Artie Dorrell **Jack Marlowe**; Tim Ryan **Shelton**; Cy Ring **Victor**; Glen Lee **Marine**; John Indrisano **Referee**; Dan Tobey **Fight announcer**; Wheaton Chambers **Doctor**; Joe Gray **Cornerman**

THE GAME After gangsters blow up a speakeasy that also damages his family's candy store and kills his father (Art Smith), Charlie Davis (John Garfield) and his mother, Anna (Anne Revere), become desperate for money. When Mrs. Davis applies for aid, Charlie tosses out the social worker when he feels the questions become too degrading: "Tell them we don't want their money. Tell 'em we're dead!"

Against his mother's wishes, Charlie decides to earn money by applying his fighting skills in the ring. His best friend, Shorty Polaski (Joseph Pevney), helps him get a manager. Quinn (Robert Conrad) takes Charlie on the road and builds him up into a rather cocky contender.

Returning to New York, Charlie rejoins his artist girlfriend Peg (Lilli Palmer). However, to get to the next level he makes a deal with Roberts (Lloyd Gough), a powerful promoter with mob ties. Roberts fills Charlie's head with promises of lots of money, and Charlie takes the title after defeating the defending champion, Ben Chaplin (Canada Lee).

As Charlie begins to collect on the promised fortune, living the high life on his large purse winnings, we see—even if Charlie doesn't—that his success comes at a price. His beating of Ben has given Chaplin a blood clot on the brain and doctors have told the former champ that he faces certain death if he steps into the ring again. Charlie has effectively ended Ben's career.

When Ben's manager, Arnold (James Burke), tells Roberts of the situation, the mobster dispassionately replies, "Everybody dies." Charlie alienates Peg with his womanizing (most notably a nightclub singer, Alice, played by Hazel Brooks). When Shorty sees the negative changes and tries to point them out to his longtime friend, he gets pummeled by Roberts's goons and soon after is accidentally run over and killed.

Realizing that extravagant living has made him soft and more vulnerable to losing his crown, Charlie hires Ben to get him into shape for an upcoming bout. In order to get the huge $60,000 final payday, Charlie must lose by a decision to Roberts's new challenger, Jack Marlowe (Artie Dorrell), in a fixed fight scheduled for 15 rounds, all orchestrated by the mobster. Charlie's reign has come to an end.

Charlie, disillusioned, decides to bet his small fortune against himself for one final huge payday. Peg, blissfully unaware of Charlie's plans and looking forward to their marriage, has put the money into a bank account. When Charlie finds out and orders her to give it back to him, he's forced to tell Peg and his mother that the fight is fixed. They are disgusted. When he tells Peg that she loves him only for his money, like all the others, ("I take the beatings and you take the dough, like all the rest of them"), she slaps him.

Ben begs Charlie not to take a dive, because he believes Davis has the talent to beat Marlowe and remain champ. "What are you duckin' out on, Charlie? You can be on top for years yet." Roberts hears this and sends his thugs to threaten Ben, who goes into a frenzy, throwing a wild fit that causes his clot to rupture and kill him.

In the early rounds of the title bout, there's not much action. Neither combatant is making much of an effort to score. Jackie, realizing he's been set up by Roberts, begins to fight more intensely and is clearly ahead as the fight winds down. Charlie, corrupted through and through and on the ropes literally and figuratively, suddenly regains an ounce of self-respect scoring on his own in the 14th round. Charlie tells his handlers in his corner before the last round, "I'm gonna kill him."

The crowd's unusual reaction, which includes Peg on hand, is noted by the ringside announcer: "I've never seen anything like it before in my life. A great silence has descended over this crowd. They seem to sense the kill. There's fear in Marlowe's eyes as Davis looks for an opening."

As Charlie goes into a flurry of activity, the crowd becomes very loud. Marlowe soon succumbs to the series of blows and crumples to the canvas. The referee counts him out. Charlie wins by a knockout.

Climbing down from the ring and heading to the locker room, Charlie is met by the crooked promoter.

ROBERTS: Congratulations, champ.

CHARLIE: Get yourself a new boy. I retire.

ROBERTS: What makes you think you can get away with this?

CHARLIE: What are you gonna do…kill me? Everybody dies.

ABOVE: John Garfield was nominated for an Academy Award as Best Actor for playing troubled Charlie Davis.

LEFT: Charlie carries wife Peg (Lilli Palmer).

'Body and Soul' produced some innovative boxing scenes as cinematographer James Wong Howe slid around the fighters wearing roller skates.

In an unusual sequence of events, a book based on the movie followed the film's success.

Breaking through the crowd and into Charlie's arms, Peg asks if he's all right. Charlie answers, "I never felt better in my life."

INSTANT REPLAY

Incorporating the traditional boxing movie elements such as the local poor boy moving up the fight ranks intoxicated by the money and notoriety, the tramp vs. the good-hearted woman, the corruption and exploitation in the fight game management ranks, the disapproving mother, and the final moral bout, *Body and Soul* is hardly original.

What does set it apart and makes it a classic is its execution. Beginning with a strong and encompassing screenplay by Abraham Polonsky, smartly presented by producer Bob Roberts, *Body and Soul* is a film that has been an influence on many of the genre's best movies, including Martin Scorsese's *Raging Bull*.

As he would do later in *All the King's Men* and *The Hustler*, director Robert Rossen shows a flair for telling stories of a flawed protagonist who creates his own pain and suffering centered around a misunderstanding of women. Additionally, *Body and Soul*, like *The Hustler*, explores the themes of redemption via the gambling element of sport.

Body and Soul is largely focused on corruption, where the poor boy hero's moral compass is driven off line by the lure of gold. The temptation of the dollar is ever-present. What it eventually comes down to is the traditional internal conflict between a man's greed and his sense of self-respect, and the ultimate choice of dignity over a tainted win.

Rossen's talented cast and crew contribute a lot to make this a powerful and riveting drama.

As the wiry, ambitious, vulnerable, money-driven, and ultimately disillusioned fighter, John Garfield gives one of his most memorable and authentic performances. His full and realistic characterization evolves from naïve youthful braggadocio to the seasoned self-knowledge of a battle-tested, jaded champion.

Having purchased the story rights to the Barney Ross story, and newly departed from Warner Bros., Garfield threw himself into the role and was an active producer. It proved to be a shrewd business move, as the film did quite well, though there would be little resemblance to the original Ross story.

Garfield is surrounded by a stable of brilliant performers in their own right, including former middleweight contender-turned-actor Canada Lee. As the film's moral center, Lee brings a real pathos to the punch-drunk ex-champ who is shamelessly tossed aside when he dares threaten the directives of corrupt promoters in attempting to point out the error of the ways of his friend and current champ.

Lloyd Goff is slick and knowing as the heartless boxing promoter. However, it is the women who really bring depth and perspective to the story. As she did in her Oscar-winning role in *National Velvet*, Anne Revere plays the perceptive mother. In *Body and Soul* she shows a smart restraint as Charlie's principled Jewish mother who never really embraces her son's career choice.

Hazel Brooks makes a memorable impression as the sultry, gold-digging tramp, reminiscent of a smoldering Lauren Bacall. As the moral foil to Brooks's evil woman, Lilli Palmer brings a refreshing intelligence and individuality to the kindhearted woman waiting for her man to recognize the error of his ways and regain his conscience. With her honesty, compassion, sensitivity, and physical beauty, Palmer's Peg works well in tandem with her future mother-in-law to strengthen Charlie's conscience. The riveting pace of the film owes much to the Oscar-winning editing of Francis Lyon and Robert Parrish. James Wong Howe's innovative photography brings immediacy to the proceedings. Maneuvering about on roller skates while filming the fight scenes inside the ring with a hand-held eyemo camera, Howe brings such authenticity to the action that you find yourself ducking punches. Likewise, the somber gray shots of the crowded urban environment, including the nightclubs and pool rooms, convey the gritty reality of the depressed world the protagonist grew up in. This is all well reflected in Nathan Juran's art direction and Edward Boyle's set decoration work.

Robert Rossen's sympathetic, socially conscious drama centering on John Garfeield's anti-hero, presented through the prism of hope and exploitation, is a vivid and memorable tale.

Body and Soul is an example of how a familiar narrative can become a classic in the hands of talented storytellers.

OUTSIDE THE LINES The movie benefited from good timing in that the state of New York was investigating sports "fixing," including boxing, at the time of the picture's release.... This was actor/producer Garfield's first independent film.... Boxing consultant John Indrisano also instructed women in movie fight scenes, like Ann Sothern in *Ringside Maisie* (1941) and Ingrid Bergman in *The Bells of St. Mary* (1945).... The movie was also known as *An Affair of the Heart*.... South African-born actress Hazel Brooks also performed in *The Basketball Fix* (1951).... Lilli Palmer was born in Germany and was married to Rex Harrison.... Garfield performed in the play *The Golden Boy*, by Clifford Odets, which was made into a feature film about boxing, starring William Holden.... Director Rossen would shoot alternative endings to the film, one of which had Roberts's goons shoot and kill Charlie Davis.... Writer Abraham Polonsky would direct Garfield in *Force of Evil* (1948).... First assistant director Robert Aldrich would go on to direct football's *The Longest Yard* (1974).... Robert Rossen directed the bullfighting feature *The Brave Bulls* (1951) and the pool shark picture *The Hustler* (1961).... Rossen, Garfield, and Polonsky were subpoenaed by the House Committee on Un-American activities for their ties to the Communist party, as were Canada Lee and Anne Revere.... Garfield refused to testify when called on in 1951.... He would die from heart failure the next year at age 39.... Howe used eight cameras for the fight scenes: three on cranes, three on dollies, and two hand-held .... Garfield did some training under boxer Mushy Callahan.... Garfield, who did his own fighting and reportedly was knocked out one time, was nominated for an Academy Award.... Polonsky was nominated for Best Writing, Original Screenplay.... Howe also photographed James Cagney's boxing picture, *City for Conquest* (1940).... Garfield's real name was Jacob Julius Garfinkel.... Lyons, who also edited *The Basketball Fix*, would direct football's *Crazylegs, All-American* (1953) and track's *The Bob Mathias Story* (1954).

ALL-STAR MOMENTS The melee at the pre-fight weigh-in between Davis (Garfield) and Marlowe (Dorrell). When Davis's handler asks the challenger's manager , "Can't you keep this loudmouth shut?" his response is, "I'm in charge of the muscles, not the brains."

The bloodthirstiness of sexy gold-digger Alice (Brooks), whose exhortation, "Kill him Charlie, kill him!" is a bridge between a training scene and the actual fight.

In his corner at the end of round 14, Quinn (Conrad) reminds Charlie that he's to

A victorious Charlie greets wife Peg (Palmer).

take a dive. Charlie tosses his right hand over his shoulder, snapping Quinn back, and mutters to himself, "I'm gonna kill him [Marlowe]."

Descending from the ring and heading to the locker room, Charlie is met by Roberts (Goff).

ROBERTS: Congratulations, champ.

CHARLIE: Get yourself a new boy. I retire.

ROBERTS: What makes you think you can get away with this?

CHARLIE: What are you gonna do…kill me? Everybody dies.

POST-GAME COMMENTS Boxing historian Burt Sugar on Garfield:

John Garfield was a very overlooked great actor. He's never mentioned with the great actors. I think it's a shame. He was brilliant in *Body and Soul*.[1]

HOME COURT ADVANTAGE Available on DVD. Republic Pictures has released *Body and Soul* twice, both times packaged with *Champion*.

#16 HOOP DREAMS

Screenwriters Steve James, Frederick Marx. **Director** Steve James. **Producers** Peter Gilbert, Steve James, Frederick Marx. **Editor** William Haugse. **Cinematography** Peter Gilbert. **Music** Ben Sidran, Tom Yore. Fine Line. 1994.

THE GAME Three Chicago filmmakers are commissioned by PBS to film the experiences of young black boys who've been recruited by wealthy private schools to play basketball, but they soon realize that they've taken on a lot more than a half-hour public television program.

Steve James, Peter Gilbert, and Frederick Marx would eventually produce 250 hours of footage that would take seven years to shoot and edit. The result, *Hoop Dreams*, is nearly three hours in length.

Hoop Dreams is an intimate chronicle recording the public and private moments of two 14-year-old black teenagers from the poverty-stricken neighborhoods of Chicago as they pursued basketball success as a ticket to a better life.

Beginning in the eighth grade and following the players into their first year in college, the movie focuses on William Gates and Arthur Agee's pursuit of hoop stardom. The filmmakers cover their journey, filled with many obstacles and few victories, in gritty, engrossing detail as we experience the real sense of time passing, watching the subjects grow up before our eyes. These two doggedly hang on to their dreams of NBA glory despite the intense pressures of academic and athletic competition (and injury), family problems, and economics.

The boys' parents, siblings, friends, coaches, and school officials are all represented in depth in this documentary that plays out like a Hollywood drama, intercutting the similar trials and tribulations of Arthur and William. Though the two know each other, they don't really hang out together.

The film picks up in 1986 as local insurance man and part time talent scout Earl Smith takes one of his "discoveries," Arthur Agee, to a basketball tryout at St. Joseph's High School. The esteemed Catholic school is renowned for producing NBA great Isaiah Thomas, who also happens to be Arthur's idol.

Arthur and his parents, Bo and Sheila, meet with the school's coach, Gene Pingatore. At the tryouts Arthur actually gets to meet and play a little with his hero, Isaiah, who makes an appearance on behalf of his alma mater.

Coach Pingatore sings the praises of Arthur's potential and soon the youngster makes the daily three-hour commute to his new high school, "just like Isaiah did."

William Gates, the other main subject, also does the long commute as he plays for the varsity squad at St. Joseph's. The team is ranked number one in the state of Illinois.

As the story unfolds we see the two in their practices and in their academic work, which doesn't match up to their on-court success. Arthur, for example, has entered high school at a fifth-grade level academically.

In the stands William's older brother, Curtis, is amid the crowd cheering him on as he leads the team to the playoffs and becomes a local star thanks to expanded media coverage.

Trouble hits Arthur hard off the court. His father, Bo, who pays half the tuition, gets laid off from his job and the family can't keep up the school payments. Arthur misses a lot of school and eventually is forced to leave altogether. He lands at a local public

school, Marshall, where he goes forward with his studies and plays for their basketball team. Still more problems on the home front as Bo abandons the family after 20 years of marriage.

Back to William, as we learn that his brother Curtis's athletic potential is suffering because of his attitude problems. After leaving a promising basketball career at Central Florida University because of run-ins with his coach, Curtis takes a job as a parking meter man.

William is aided in getting a part-time office job and in his junior year begins to receive many college recruiting letters on the strength of his basketball talents. However, he also begins to experience some knee pain, and x-rays show ligament and cartilage tears that could be season-ending injuries, possibly dampening his college options.

Back at Marshall, Arthur has made the varsity squad but troubles continue at home. Sheila is now on welfare with three growing kids; the family's economic situation is grim, and their lights and gas are cut off for several months. Additionally, Arthur's sister is pregnant and his best friend, Shannon Johnson, moves in to escape the problems at his own home.

Further examinations on William's leg bring better news than the initial diagnosis, as the ligament is okay and the damaged cartilage can be sewn back. If they choose surgery now William might be back in time for the playoffs. The Gateses decide to have the operation and soon William begins rehabilitation exercises. Challenges continue for Gates off the court as well. Reduced to watching games as part of the crowd in the stands, feeling disconnected from his team, he's also in danger of losing his athletic scholarship after scoring a 15 on his ACT. Patricia Weir, an executive at Encyclopedia Britannica, sets William up with a six -week tutoring program to help him get the score of 18 he needs to pass the exam and keep his scholarship. We also find out that William has become father to a daughter, Alicia, with his girlfriend, Catherine Mines.

At Marshall High Arthur does the minimum to get by academically. His seasoned coach, Luther Bedford, considers Arthur smart, but experience has shown him that Arthur's attitude has him headed for the streets. At least Arthur has good news domestically. One year after leaving (and serving a seven-month jail stretch for burglary), Arthur's dad returns to the family. They all attend church. Arthur stands by his father, but Bo senses his family's wariness about his proclamation of being "a changed man."

When asked by his coach if he wants to sit out the injury and wait until next year, William states, "My next year is now." One senses the young man is feeling the pressure. As game time approaches we see his brother in the stands and William comments, "I always felt Curtis shouldn't be living his dream through me." William's performance is very mediocre, clearly due to his injury, and following the game his coach says essentially that either he plays 100% or, if he's hurt, he shouldn't be playing at all.

Fast forward to the playoffs, where William clinches one game with clutch last-second free throws, but in another his knee pain gets him out of sync, he misses a key free throw, and his team goes down in defeat. Limping off the court, blaming his coach for allowing him to play in his condition, William arranges with his brother-in-law, Alvin Bibbs, to get top-of-the-line treatment from a Chicago Bulls team physician.

As Arthur and his friend Shannon attend summer school and work at Pizza Hut, William attends the elite Nike camp that features potential college stars. Big-name coaches such as Rick Pitino and Bob Knight attend. The program comes across as a meat market, an impression that draws some pointed commentary from film director Spike Lee, who visits the camp to address the players.

Arthur's now a senior and prepares to complete qualifying for college. On the court he is Marshall's star, leading them to the playoffs where eager college scouts speak with his proud father, Bo, about his son. Arthur takes Marshall all the way to the Chicago Final Four, where they face last year's state champions, King High School. King's team features two seven-foot players. With William in attendance, Arthur keeps the game close and makes the key shot to propel Marshall to the next level, where he also succeeds in guiding the team to a win over Latavia.

Walking through the pristine campus of the University of Illinois on their way to see their son in a playoff game there, Arthur's parents feel like they're in "another world."

Marshall loses to Peoria Manual as William watches on his television. Bo and Sheila are nonetheless proud of Arthur, who accepts a scholarship to a small junior college in Missouri. Back home, Bo proceeds to play a spirited game of one-on-one with his son. As family and friends yell from the sidelines, it's clear that Mr. Agee had hoop dreams of his own.

William, besieged in the college recruitment process, likes Marquette University

TOP: William Gates.

BOTTOM: Arthur Agee.

but is short on his ACT scores to qualify. Later he is honored at the St. Joseph's annual dinner. Then, after 5 tries, William's ACT score of 17.5 is rounded up to 18, which qualifies him to attend Marquette.

Separately both families proudly throw their sons college send-off parties. And the film closes out by informing us of their progress at college. William marries Catherine, and wife and daughter move in with him on campus. Not long afterward William's academic struggles mount and he quits the basketball team, then drops out of school. Through family and school encouragement William returns to both for his senior year.

Arthur has become the father of two children, graduates from Mineral Area Junior College, and receives a basketball scholarship from Arkansas State University.

INSTANT REPLAY *Hoop Dreams* is a brilliant study of the American dream from an unaccustomed point of view. For many inner-city blacks, that dream looks like an NBA contract—a goal that has become such a common theme in motion pictures that it's almost a cliché. *Hoop Dreams* goes in a different direction by showing the day-in, day-out reality of that dream over a period of years, and covering its subjects in real depth.

The film excels in exploring the culture of basketball in the black community and its far-reaching arms. It shows how emerging potential is spotted, rewarded, and at times exploited by the deeply rooted basketball industry.

In the course of celebrating the game and critiquing its social and corporate underpinnings, *Hoop Dreams* provides a very absorbing look at our value structure in general through race, ambition, competition, and socioeconomic status. The picture succeeds in addressing those complex social issues, amidst dramatic basketball action, all the while making it easy for us to care about two young kids who must deal with pressures that would break most adults.

William Gates and Arthur Agee, with their different personalities, do share a faith in the game that gives them hope to help guide them through their many troubles on and off the court. Each has had to live with another person's dreams projected through him; William's brother, Curtis, and Arthur's father, Bo, harbored their own hoop dreams that faded away.

The filmmakers also expose some of the media myths of the social fabric in the ghetto. That drugs, crime, unemployment, broken families, and violence are largely due to individual irresponsibility does not jive with the example of Arthur's father losing two jobs. Instead, we see how trying to do the right thing can mean submitting to severe financial pressures that in turn can lead to acts of desperation. Additionally, Arthur and William come from nurturing homes led by strong mothers whom their sons love and respect for their enduring efforts. It's a heartwarming depiction of the indomitable strength of the family unit.

While *Hoop Dreams* offers a searing commentary on the basketball recruitment process, one could say that the local scout and the coach at St. Joseph's represent those who provide opportunities to the Arthurs and Williams out there who may not have had an opportunity otherwise. Still it's hard to praise a process that seems to be reaching further and further down to younger and younger kids who then face enormous pressures before they get a real chance to mature and actually understand themselves.

As the film examines the basketball recruiting system the question arises: what about the ghetto kids without the athletic skills, such as Arthur's friend, Shannon Johnson, who can't even feel comfortable in his own home? The movie shows us that despite the rhetoric, we know the recruiters aren't scouting in poor neighborhoods to develop the future generation of engineers and captains of industry.

An intimate reflection of contemporary American inner-city culture, *Hoop Dreams* offers a stark examination of underclass life in big-city America. Viewers get a real and personalized look at what passes for the American dream to people whose day-to-day existence is characterized by torment and false hope, living on the lower side of the great American socioeconomic divide.

OUTSIDE THE LINES *Hoop Dreams* won the Audience Award after its debut at the Sundance Film Festival.... Steve James wrote and directed a biographical feature of an American track legend, *Prefontaine* (1997).... The film project started out as a half-hour PBS TV project on a $2,500 grant from the National Endowment for the Arts.... Director James had hoop dreams of his own, having starred in Virginia during high school but realized his limitations after trying out as a walk-on at James Madison University in Harrisburg, Virginia under Coach Mike Fratello, who would go on to coach in the NBA.... The film was nominated for an Oscar for editing and won an award for Best Documentary from the International Documentary Association.

ALL-STAR MOMENTS Arthur's mother learning she's graduated from school as a nursing assistant.

The symbolism of William tossing out all the college recruiter letters after he accepts an offer to attend Marquette University.

The Agee family walking around the University of Illinois campus feeling like they're in "another world."

HOME COURT ADVANTAGE Available on VHS and DVD. New Line released the first DVD; a recent version from Criterion has numerous extra features.

Filmmakers Steve James, Peter Gilbert, and Fred Marx.

#15 THE SET-UP

Screenwriter Art Cohn. **Director** Robert Wise. **Producer** Richard Goldstone. **Cinematography** Milton Krasner. **Art Direction** Albert D'Agostino, Jack Okey. **Set Design** James Altweis, Darrell Silvera. **Editing** Roland Gross. **Technical Consultant** John Indrisano. RKO. 1949.

THE PLAYERS Robert Ryan **Stoker Thompson**; Audrey Totter **Julie Thompson**; Alan Baxter **Little Boy**; George Tobias **Tiny**; Wallace Ford **Gus**; Edwin Max **Danny**; Percy Helton **Red**; Hal Fieberling **Tiger Nelson**; Phillip Pine **Tony Souza**; David Clarke **Gunboat Johnson**; James Edwards **Luther Hawkins**; David Fresco **Mickey**; Darryl Hickman **Kid Shanley**; Kenny O'Morrison **Moore**

THE GAME Aging boxer Bill "Stoker" Thompson (Robert Ryan), well past his prime, refuses to give up his career despite his diminished abilities and the impassioned pleas of his wife, Julie (Audrey Totter), for him to get out while he's "still in one piece."

As they talk upstairs in their cheap hotel room located near the arena, down below in the café Stoker's manager, Tiny (George Tobias), has arranged to fix the fight. He accepts $50 from mob underling Danny (Edwin Max) and the deal is set for Stoker to put up a good fight then go down sometime after the second round of the scheduled four-round bout. Stoker's opponent, Tiger Nelson (Hal Fieberling), is over a dozen years younger and is controlled by mobster Little Boy (Alan Baxter).

Stoker tells his wife he's just "one punch away" from higher billing and better money. Julie's heard that before and is sick of witnessing the brutality, retorting, "You'll always be just one punch away." Her husband reminds her that that is who he is and "That's what happens when you're a fighter" as he heads out to the arena, leaving a ticket for her.

Tiny also heads to the arena with cornerman Red (Percy Helton), who advises Tiny that Stoker can still punch so he had better let the fighter in on the deal. Tiny says Stoker has blown many fights already and tonight will be no different.

Inside the tiny, dilapidated locker room is a crowd of dreamers with no realistic chance of reaching the bright lights of their sport—yet they continue to hang on, enduring punishment in hopes of hitting on that long shot. While grizzled veteran handler Gus (Wallace Ford) tapes the boxers for their bouts, he listens to their stories and dispenses his pearls of wisdom garnered from his many years in the business.

A noticeably edgy Stoker continually peers through the window that affords a view of his hotel room, anxious because the light is still on, indicating that his wife hasn't left for the arena yet. Finally, seeing the light go out, his demeanor changes and he prepares to change for the fight. But Julie changes her mind at the arena entrance when she hears the familiar bloodthirsty sounds of rabid fight fans and walks away down the city streets instead.

Red tells Tiny one last time that he had better let Stoker in on the fix. The manager ignores him. As Stoker enters the ring he sees that Julie isn't in her seat and it unsettles him. But, realizing that this is perhaps his last chance to re-establish himself, Stoker gets focused and engages in a fierce battle with the up-and-coming Tiger Nelson. Heavy blows are landed by both fighters, drawing the fans into the bloody frenzy. Tiger scores early, and his knockdown of Stoker pleases Little Boy, Danny, and Tiny.

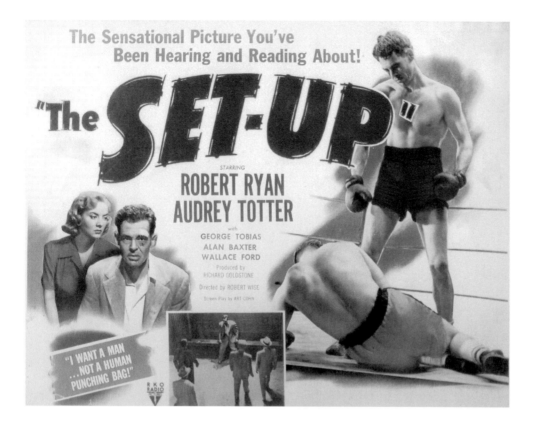

The Sensational Picture You've Been Hearing and Reading About!

"The SET-UP

STARRING
ROBERT RYAN
AUDREY TOTTER

with
GEORGE TOBIAS
ALAN BAXTER
WALLACE FORD

Produced by
RICHARD GOLDSTONE
Directed by ROBERT WISE
Screen Play by ART COHN

"I WANT A MAN ...NOT A HUMAN PUNCHING BAG!"

RKO RADIO

Stoker hangs in there and battles back. Manager and mobsters start to show concern when a bloodied and bowed Stoker gets off the canvas after being knocked down again and beats the bell ending the third round.

In his corner before the final round, Tiny is forced to tell Stoker about the setup. Stoker looks to see that his wife still hasn't shown up and heads out for the last round. Refusing to throw the fight, Stoker engages in some terrific exchanges. As the veteran begins to take command of the fight, Tiny and Red slip out of the arena, since Little Boy and Danny are visibly concerned about an outcome they thought was assured by their payment. Stoker gives it all he has and scores a knockout to the cheers of a wild crowd.

After a visit by Little Boy in the locker room ominously warning Stoker of his mistake, the mobsters wait outside for him to change. Stoker slips quietly through the dark, empty gym and out a back door but is caught in an alley and given a debilitating beating by Little Boy's cronies. They smash his right hand, putting an end to his boxing dreams for good.

As a concerned Julie looks out their hotel window, she sees Stoker staggering down below. She runs out to meet him and calls for someone from the gathering crowd to call an ambulance.

Lying in her arms on the sidewalk, Stoker tells his wife that they busted up his hand because he wouldn't take a dive and that he won't be able to fight anymore—but adds proudly that he won the bout. Apologizing for not being in attendance, Julie smiles realizing what has transpired, telling her husband, "We both won tonight." Despite the punishment there's a renewed sense of hope for a better future for them now that his boxing days are over.

TOP: Robert Ryan (left) was an accomplished boxer in his own right at Dartmouth.

MIDDLE: The film was actually based on a poem by Joseph March about a black boxer.

BOTTOM: Robert Wise directed another boxing drama, 'Somebody Up There Likes Me,' which starred Paul Newman as Rocky Graziano.

INSTANT REPLAY In one of the rare films to be shot in real time, as shown by the large street clock in the opening and closing scenes, director Robert Wise expertly captures the gritty atmosphere of the 1940s-era palookaville boxing world: a world of darkness, brutality, corruption, and dreamers.

Albert D'Agostino and Jack Oakey's art direction along with James Altweis and Darrell Silvera's set design present a highly stylized backdrop for the strong performances and vivid tale. The shadows, varying bright lights and dark streets, and interesting camera movement and angles by Milton Krasner greatly contribute to the seediness of the small-town boxing environment. Interestingly, the only music comes from the radio, bars, and clubs in the film. Together the elements create a gem of composition and design that is earthy, grim, and tense.

Ryan's performance, projecting a subtle sense of unarticulated nobility against a backdrop full of corrupt dreamers, is enhanced by his background as an actual boxer of some talent. His work is informed by an understanding of what motivates fighters and how sometimes a boxer's foolish pride can affect his better judgment. Audrey Totter's "voice of reason" character is delivered with conviction and her "story" is symbolically captured by the funhouse scenes that first amuse her, then bring her back to her own reality when she observes a couple fighting each other with toy boxers.

Perhaps more than any other boxing film, *The Set-Up* provides some of the most unforgettable images of fans. There are repeated close-up iso shots of savage fans, most seemingly plain everyday Joes, who get caught up in the frenzy of the tight, dark, smoke-filled arena action and turn into savages craving blood. There's the bloodthirsty housewife screaming at the fighters as her docile husband sits next to her. A blind man switches allegiances depending on the progress reports of who's leading the fight delivered by his escort. A glutton (Dwight Martin) stuffs his face with all kinds of food as he watches the bout. Another man listens to a baseball game on the radio he's carrying as he watches the fight action. Wise gives us an interesting sampling of people who get caught up in the hysteria and perhaps in some ways live vicariously through the boxers.

The Set-Up is one of the most realistic and engaging films on the sport.

OUTSIDE THE LINES Robert Ryan was a champion boxer at Dartmouth University.... Robert Wise, who edited Orson Welles' *Citizen Kane*, edited some of the fight scenes in this film.... Vaudeville and Broadway performer Wallace Ford made his feature film debut in the baseball drama *Swell-Head*.... George Tobias appeared earlier in another boxing film that starred James Cagney, *City for Conquest* (1940).... Among Ryan's earlier film roles was another boxer in *Golden Gloves* (1939).... The fight sequences were staged by former boxer John Indrisano, who would also work on Wise's boxing film *Somebody Up There Likes Me* (1956).... Indrisano was a pro boxer for over a dozen years as a welterweight, fighting such champions as Joe Dundee, Jackie Fields, and Lou Brouillard, but it was his job as a Hollywood movie fight stager that flattened his nose when he was working out with actor Robert Taylor on the fight film *The Crowd Roars* (1938).... Wise worked as an editor for the football film *The Iron Major* (1943), starring Pat O'Brien.... Hal Fieberling was an accomplished boxer and a one-time Pacific Coast heavyweight title holder .... He also appeared in the boxing movies *Winner Take All* (1948) and *Joe Palooka in the Squared Circle* (1950), the basketball film *Cornbread, Earl, and Me* (1975), and football's *The Guy Who Came Back* (1951).... *The Set-Up* was adapted from a poem by Joseph March.... The producer and director studied over 220 reels of professional fights, then decided to use the second round of the 1923 Louis Firpo—Jack Dempsey bout as a model for the fight sequence, as that round contained some of the heaviest sustained action in history.... Noble "Kid" Chissel, who plays a handler in the movie (uncredited), was an ex-fighter who once sparred with another amateur lightweight by the name of Packy East at Charles Marotta's Gym in Cleveland.... Packy did a lot better outside the ring in show business as Bob Hope.... Wise won the Critic's Prize at the Cannes Film Festival for this, his last film at RKO.

ALL-STAR MOMENTS
Use of shadows of jazz musicians against the alley wall as Stoker gets pummeled by the mobsters, his groans drowned out by the music.

Repeated cutaways of the increasingly savage fans as we see close-ups of the bloody face of Stoker in the ring.

Subtle use of the town's clock to reflect the movie happening in real time.

POST-GAME COMMENTS
Director Robert Wise on casting for the lead role of Stoker Thompson:

> The original role was for a black fighter (the poem from which the film was adapted from featured a black boxer). Unfortunately there weren't any black stars at that time in Hollywood. RKO had Mr. Ryan under contract at the time and he'd been an intercollegiate boxing champ. We felt the obvious thing to do was to change it and go with the white man.[1]

Wise on coming up with the distinctive boxing fans:

> Art (Cohn, the screenwriter) knew the boxing game very well and brought a lot of behind-the-scenes experience to the film. Several characters are based right out of his experiences. The blind man came from Art seeing one watch the fights in San Francisco. The character holding the radio while watching the fight was based on a fan I saw while researching the fight scene at a Long Beach arena.[2]

On clashes with RKO owner Howard Hughes:

> We felt Joan Blondell, who'd just finished playing Tyrone Power's earthy love interest in *Nightmare Alley*, would be perfect for the role of Stoker's wife. When that idea was presented to Mr. Hughes his comment was, "Are those guys crazy? She looks like she was shot out of the wrong end of a cannon!" He kept sending us lists which contained mostly glamour girls but we felt the part was much more than that. Time was running out as production was just a few days away. Though I didn't know her work, Audrey Totter was on one of his lists and my producer (Richard Goldstone) convinced me she'd be fine. Audrey turned in an excellent performance. Outside of the female lead, Howard pretty much left me to my vision of the film.[3]

HOME COURT ADVANTAGE
Available on DVD. While Warner Bros. has released a single version, the studio has also included the title as part of a five-disc Film Noir Classic Collection that also includes *The Asphalt Jungle*, *Gun Crazy*, *Murder My Sweet*, and *Out of the Past*.

#14 BRIAN'S SONG

Screenwriter William Blinn. **Director** Buzz Kulik. **Producers** Paul Junger Witt, Tony Thomas. **Cinematography** Joseph Biroc. **Editing** Bud Isaacs. **Art Direction** Ross Bellah. **Music** Michel Legrand. ABC. 1971.

THE PLAYERS James Caan **Brian Piccolo**; Billy Dee Williams **Gale Sayers**; Jack Warden **Coach George Halas**; Bernie Casey **J. C. Caroline**; Shelley Fabares **Joy Piccolo**; David Huddleston **Ed McCaskey**; Judy Pace **Linda Sayers**; Abe Gibron **Himself**; Jack Concannon **Himself**; Dick Butkus **Himself**; Ed O'Bradovich **Himself**; Ron Feinberg **Doug Atkins**; Ji-Tu Cumbuka **Roommate**; Jim Boeke **Veteran player**; Happy Hairston **Veteran player**; Larry Delaney **Dr. Fox**; Stephen Coit **Mr. Eberle**; Doreen Lang **Nurse**; Jeni Kulik **Nurse**; Allen Secher **Hotel man**; Stu Nahan **Awards speaker**; Mario Machado **Reporter**; Bud Furillo **Reporter**; Jack Wells **Toastmaster**

THE GAME Highly regarded rookie running back Gale Sayers (Billy Dee Williams) reports to the Chicago Bears training camp to start his NFL career under the legendary coach George Halas (Jack Warden). Soon after arriving, Sayers is befriended by fellow running back and overachiever Brian Piccolo (James Caan). Despite competing for the same spot on the roster, the two become the team's first interracial roommates. The two players, along with their wives, Linda Sayers (Judy Pace) and Joy Piccolo (Shelley Fabares), become close friends.

When Gale goes down with a career-threatening injury, Brian leads him back, helping him rehab and regain his all-pro form. Says Brian, "I'm gonna whip you, Sayers, but you got to be at your best or it won't mean a thing."

Later, this healthy competition is shattered when Brian is diagnosed with cancer. Gale does what he can rallying support for his friend, but the popular player's terminal illness not only deeply affects the Piccolo family, Sayers and his wife, but also the whole Bears organization. Sadly, at the young age of 26, Brian succumbs to cancer.

INSTANT REPLAY Often imitated, never surpassed, *Brian's Song* is an inspiring true story of friendship and courage. Going against the grain, this male, sporting equivalent to *Love Story* emphasizes character over winning. *Brian's Song* is one of the seminal movies of all time.

Brian's Song succeeds where other buddy pictures have not in several ways, but perhaps the most critical is in putting that relationship in the context of bigger social issues of the day, like racism. Director Buzz Kulik, one of the pioneers of the docudrama, demonstrates a fine touch on sensitive issues of race, terminal illness, and personal relationships. At the same time, however, the director fails to provide depth to Brian's relationship with his family, primarily his daughters—a shortcoming that is rectified in the remake that was produced 30 years later.

Much of the picture's credit goes to the wonderful, bittersweet relationship conveyed in a very honest, heartfelt way by James Caan and Billy Dee Williams as rivals who genuinely care for each other. Their chemistry goes way beyond the gridiron, making a powerful statement about race and courage and helping the film reach an audience that had no interest in sports. Part of the appeal must be credited to their banter, reminiscent of that between Redford and Newman in *Butch Cassidy and the Sundance Kid*.

In an Emmy-winning performance, Jack Warden is the embodiment of Bears coach

George Halas. Several NFL players, most notably Bernie Casey (who would enjoy a fine career as an actor), add a lot to the authenticity.

This picture also demonstrates the great value music can add to the proceedings. Michel Legrand's emotional score is a perfect accompaniment to the drama played out on the screen. Tastefully done with just the right amount of pathos, the music takes the picture to a higher level.

Technically, Joe Biroc's photography and Bud Isaac's editing are clean and uncomplicated.

William Blinn's intelligent script deftly avoids mawkishness.

In regard to makeup, one of the film's few shortcomings is that the filmmakers really don't do much physically to Caan to make him appear to be withering away from cancer. With Brian's illness mainly conveyed through the actor's mumbling and grimacing, Caan could have been aided by more detailed physical signs that his illness has taken a toll.

Teammates. Friends. Brian Piccolo (James Caan, left) and Gale Sayers (Billy Dee Williams, right).

In the end, *Brian's Song* would certainly be part of any all-star team dealing with athletics and dying—which would include an impressive roster: *The Champ, Pride of the Yankees, Champion, Here Comes Mr. Jordan, Knute Rockne: All-American, This Sporting Life, Bang the Drum Slowly, Heaven Can Wait, Field of Dreams,* and *Gladiator.*

OUTSIDE THE LINES The film was based on the book *I Am Third,* by Gale Sayers and Al Silverman.... Reportedly Gale Sayers wanted to play himself in the original but there was a conflict with his football schedule .... Lou Gossett Jr. was at one point circling the role of Gale Sayers.... *Brian's Song* received the highest rating of any TV movie to that point, a 33.2.... This picture was a rarity in that it first appeared on television, then had a theatrical release.... A cancer research fund was established in Piccolo's name.... Jack Warden, an Emmy winner for his role as Coach Halas, costarred in another football film, *Heaven Can Wait* (1978), which garnered him an Academy Award nomination.... The actor was also featured in the HBO golf film *Dead Solid Perfect* as "Bad Hair" Wimberly (1988).... Warden also played a football owner in *The Replacements* (2000).... When *The Bad News Bears* became a TV series, Warden played Walter Matthau's role as Morris Buttermaker.... *Brian's Song* received a Congressional Record commendation.... Composer Michel Legrand won an Oscar for his work in *The Thomas Crown Affair* (1968).... He also wrote the score for Steve McQueen's racing film, *Le Mans* (1971).... Before becoming an actor, Bernie Casey was a professional wide receiver in the NFL.... Hall of Fame linebacker Dick Butkus would also become an actor.... One of his early appearances was in *Gus* (1976), about a field-goal-kicking mule.... Cinematographer Joseph Biroc's credits include football's *The Longest Yard* (1973).... He also won Oscars for his photography of *Hush Hush Sweet Charlotte* (1964) and *The Towering Inferno* (1974).... Happy Hairston, appearing as a veteran football player, was a basketball player for the Los Angeles Lakers.... Billy Dee Williams starred with Richard Pryor and James Earl Jones in the baseball feature *The Bingo Long Traveling All-Stars and Motor Kings* (1976).... *Brian's Song* won the Emmy Award for Best Dramatic Program.... Buzz Kulik also directed the TV movie *Babe* (1975) about the great female athlete Babe Didrikson.... Witt also produced and directed the TV series *The Partridge Family*.... *Brian's Song* was shot primarily at St. Joseph's College in Rensselaer, Indiana.... Jim Boeke also appeared in football's *North Dallas Forty* (1979) as well as *Heaven Can Wait* (1978).... Shelly Fabares co-starred in the TV series *Coach,* featuring Craig T. Nelson as a football coach.... William Blinn won an Emmy as cowriter of the miniseries *Roots* (1977).... Jack Warden was a former welterweight prize-fighter.... James Caan starred in the futuristic sports film *Rollerball* (1971).... Caan's first starring role was in Howard Hawks' auto racing drama *Red Line 7000* (1965).... *Brian's Song* was remade in 2001.... Its executive producers, Neil Meron and Craig Zadan, shared an Oscar for Best Picture for their musical *Chicago* (2002).

ALL-STAR MOMENTS
Opening scene with Coach Halas's (Warden) voice-over and the great music theme by Michel Legrand playing as Sayers arrives at football camp.

Sayers (Williams) meeting Coach Halas in his office and jumping about to get on his "good side," since Piccolo (Caan) has just told him Coach is hard of hearing in one ear.

Halas quips: "I know you got moves but you don't have to show them to me now...."

Intercut real footage with actors in play where Sayers injures his knee.

Pic and Sayers' banter as Gale works out in his basement.

Pic and Sayers racing in the park as part of Gale's rehab.

Locker room speech where Sayers informs teammates that Pic is "sick, very sick...and it looks like he may never play football again."

At a ceremony honoring him for his comeback as the Most Courageous Player, Sayers prefers that his friend be honored:

You flatter me by giving me this award, but I say here to you now, Brian Piccolo is the man of courage who should receive the George S. Halas Award. It is mine tonight, and Brian Piccolo's tomorrow. I love Brian Piccolo and I'd like all of you to love him too. And tonight, hit your knees, please ask God to love him.

Piccolo's humor and courage during his last days lying in the hospital bed.

POST-GAME COMMENTS
Billy Dee Williams, in a television interview, on the magnitude of the film's success:

That [*Brian's Song*] whole experience to me personally was like one of those perfect moments. It was something you don't find a lot in your life. I mean it's a rare moment. Everything that was going on, in my personal life at that time, all led up to this one little moment.[1]

James Caan recalled his initial trepidations.

I turned it down three or four times. Not that it wasn't a great thing I read; unfortunately there was this stigma, which I think was horrible, that if you were doing movies and did television that you were out of the business.[2]

Jack Warden, who won an Emmy for his role as Bears coach George Halas:

The actors didn't hold anything back. Everybody went all out. The script was great. It was really a crushing story. I know I cried watching the completed film and even thinking about the filming of it years later. It had that kind of impact.[3]

William Blinn, who won an Emmy for his script, recalls how renowned composer Michel Legrand's theme really brought it all together:

When we heard the first cue of the theme, I remember Paul [Witt], myself, and Tony Thomas [associate producer] looking at each other on that

FACING PAGE: Mrs. Piccolo (Shelley Fabares) at her husband's side.

soundstage, and we all kind of said in unison, "Oh, that is so good!" We knew we had a good film, then all of a sudden this absolutely lyrical, lovely score comes in, and it was like we weren't going to be permitted to fumble.[4]

Producer Paul Junger Witt:

It was just one of those projects that was meant to be. It came together in almost a blessed way.[5]

Blinn on the naysayers about the limited audience for the picture:

Conventional wisdom at the time was that sports pictures [had] died. They said women wouldn't watch sports pictures and we were crazy to try to do this, etc.[6]

HOME COURT ADVANTAGE Available on DVD.

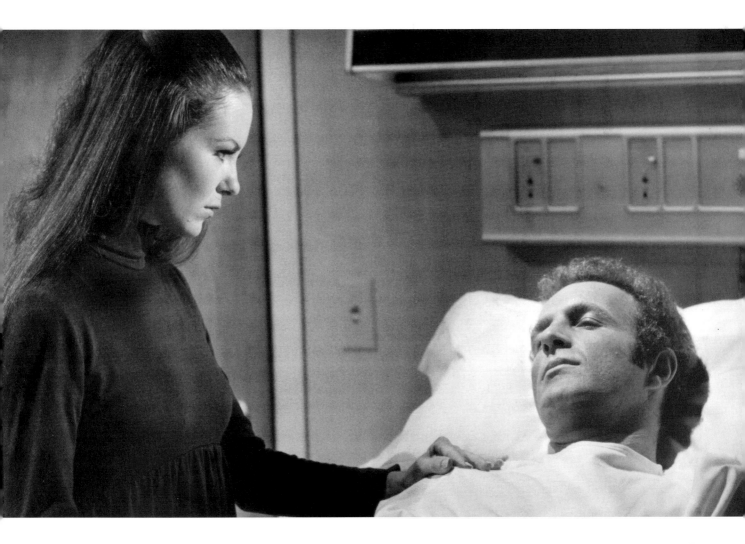

#13 Tokyo Olympiad

Screenwriter/Director Kon Ichikawa. **Writers** Shuntaro Tanikawa, Natto Wada. **Cinematography** Kazuo Miyagawa. **Composer** Toshiro Mayuzumi. 1965.

THE GAME The 1964 Summer Olympics were the first Games to be held in Asia. Tokyo was using the global spotlight of the Olympic stage as a symbolic coming-out party for a rebuilt country (Tokyo had been scheduled to host the 1940 Olympics, which were cancelled because of World War II).

Tokyo Olympiad was commissioned to be the official film of the XVIIIth Olympiad. Japan was determined to provide a record of the Games that would rival that of *Olympia*, Leni Reifenstahl's legendary documentary of the 1936 Berlin Games.

With $1 million in government funds and a staff of 500, including 164 cameramen, noted Japanese filmmaker Kon Ichikawa proceeded to film the event.

In a departure from conventional documentary form, *Tokyo Olympiad* emphasizes cinematography over narration.

INSTANT REPLAY Using pictures on the widescreen such as the rising sun, a torch bearer running past majestic Mt. Fuji, the facial expressions and pained body language of marathoners, or volunteers struggling to pull out hammer throws that have landed deep in the muddy grass in order to clean them for the next round, Ichikawa brings the same attention to detail and sense of beauty to this film as are evident in his feature films, such as *Fires on the Plain* and *Odd Obsession*.

Admittedly not a sports fan, the director brings a different perspective to the genre. While there are winners and losers featured (especially well presented in Japan's dramatic win over the USSR in women's volleyball), *Tokyo Olympiad* is far less about medal counts than it is about the art and beauty involved in the process.

Ichikawa's direction is a visually compelling poetry, a riveting interplay of visual compositions and vivid images. He begins by showing a wrecking ball crane smashing down old buildings, then shows the beautiful new venues to represent the end of the long shadow of the host country's World War II defeat and the emergence of a future economic powerhouse.

Ichikawa's minimalist approach to the use of graphics and narration requires viewers to gather their impressions from what they see and feel from the pictures. It's quite different from watching a major sports event on television, where we've come to expect an army of reporters, replays, charts, and expert analysts to explain every nuance of the action. For Ichikawa this focus on the visual puts the viewer more inside the mind of the athlete. This is illustrated particularly well in the shooting competition, with the camera angles allowing the viewer to peer through the gunsight at the target as if he were the shooter.

Despite giving short shrift to some sports like soccer and basketball, which are given only a few frames, hardly worth watching, the director does get into the mind's eye of weightlifters as they prepare to hoist the bar, sailors leaning on the boat's edge out over the water, flyweight wrestlers with their lightning-quick moves, the row of sprinters awaiting the starter's gun, and the fencers, with their nimble footwork.

To convey those athletic performances, the director uses a variety of production

The great Abebe Bikila from Ethiopia wins his second consecutive Olympic marathon.

techniques: freeze frames, jazzy music scores, black and white stills, extreme close-ups, slow motion, and natural sound among other methods.

The film is also not without humor. We see a Romanian high jumper set down her lucky doll just before she begins her approach to the bar. There are various angles of the inherently funny motions of racewalkers that even have a young Japanese woman laughing in the streets as they go by. Exuberant New Zealand fans stun Japanese officials and have to be escorted off the track after doing a native cheer celebrating countryman Peter Snell's victory in the 1500-meter race.

Tokyo Olympiad does feature a few stories, and two of the best portray the loneliness of a long distance runner. One is a dominant world record marathoner, the other an 800-meter runner who is unable to even qualify for the finals of his event. One is destined for eternal glory in Olympic annals; the other's Olympic career is a mere grain in the sands of time.

With two-time gold medal marathoner Abebe Bikila of Ethiopia, the director uses a long, unbroken close-up as the runner, with almost effortless form and rhythm, glides along mile after mile alone, his competitors dropping off the pace one by one on his way to the finish line.

The camera follows the other runner, Isa, from the new African country of Chad, in his isolated and relatively lonely Olympic experience. Lacking a group of teammates and separated from his fellow athletes by language barriers, the young man sits alone eating his meal in a crowded and boisterous athletes' village dining hall. Walking in the rain without an umbrella on the teeming streets of Tokyo, Isa's world of one is only broken by the attention of a small Japanese boy who tries to communicate with him.

Back at the track, after he fails to make the finals of the 800-meter run, the man from Chad silently gathers his warm-up clothes, his Olympic career over and largely unnoticed except by Ichikawa's camera.

This athlete from Chad represents another aspect of Ichikawa's film, and that is simply "being there." Although he doesn't come close to a medal, Isa is the first person from his distant, impoverished country to appear in the Olympics. That is a victory in itself.

Being there is reflected in the director's shots of athletes' airport arrivals from different parts of the world, including Mongolian women athletes. He also uses many cutaways of the distinctly diverse crowds who come from all corners of the globe and whose eyes, ears, and reactions are presented as if the film's viewers are in the stands, making them participants in the drama of the competition.

Tokyo Olympiad is an all-encompassing vision of human endeavor and community. Like Reifenstahl's *Olympia*, Ichikawa aims to construct a film showing the abstract beauty of the diverse athletic competition, a testament to the human form rather than a simple chronicle of events.

But where the German director presents her athletes as godlike figures, Ichikawa's focus gives the athletes very human touches. Exhausted marathoners attend to their blistered feet, Japanese women volleyball players shed tears of joy with their victory, top bikers crash in road cycling.

Ichikawa's untraditional approach, however, earned him the wrath of the film's producers, who upon screening the nearly three-hour original version called it "too artistic" and demanded massive edits. Fearful that audiences would prefer a more conventional presentation, the producers released a much shorter version, more heavily narrated, which was not well received. But after winning awards and glowing reviews at the Cannes Film Festival, *Tokyo Olympiad* eventually was hailed as a masterpiece all over the world in its close-to-original version. The film is pure visual poetry from a talented artist.

OUTSIDE THE LINES
Ichikawa shot over 400,000 feet of film.... The original version was nearly three hours long, but America filmgoers initially saw only a chopped and poorly narrated 93-minute version.... In 1984 a restored print of the original was released in the U.S.... The film won a British Academy Award for Best Feature-Length Documentary.... The logistics of filming the marathon required 59 cameras and a crew of 250.... The director began his career as a cartoonist.... Ichikawa's wife, screenwriter Natto Wada, was a close collaborator.... Cinematographer Kazuo Miyagawa also shot Kurosawa's *Rashomon* and *Yojimbo*.... Ichikawa was also part of David Wolper's Olympic film *Visions of Eight*, directing the 100-meter finals segment at the 1972 Munich Games.

ALL-STAR MOMENTS
Torch runner passing in front of Mt. Fuji.

Announcer's call in Japanese as American Indian Billy Mills sprints from nowhere to win the 10,000-meter run.

Widescreen shots of the rising sun.

The blur of road cyclists speeding past a crowd of Japanese kids lining the street applauding and waving.

Marathoner Abebe Bikila calmly breaking the tape as the gold medal winner then proceeding to do calisthenics on the grass infield, showing no signs of just having run 26 miles in world record time, "one month after having his appendix removed."

HOME COURT ADVANTAGE
Available on DVD. This is an excellent transfer from Criterion with English subtitles and several extra features.

#12 NORTH DALLAS FORTY

Screenwriters Ted Kotcheff, Frank Yablans, Peter Gent, Nancy Dowd (uncredited). **Director** Ted Kotcheff. **Producer** Frank Yablans. **Cinematography** Paul Lohman. **Editing** Jay Kamen, Thom Noble. **Music** John Scott. **Production Design** Alfred Sweeney. **Costume Design** Dorothy Jeakins. **Casting** Lynn Stalmaster. Paramount. 1979.

THE PLAYERS
Nick Nolte **Phillip Elliott**; Mac Davis **Seth Maxwell**; G. D. Spradlin **B. A. Strothers**; Charles Durning **Coach Johnson**; Bo Svenson **Jo Bob Priddy**; Steve Forrest **Conrad Hunter**; Dabney Coleman **Emmett**; Dayle Haddon **Charlotte**; John Matuszak **O. W. Shaddock**; Marshall Colt **Art Hartman**; Tommy Reamon **Delma Huddle**; Guich Koock **Eddie Rand**; Savannah Smith **Joanne**; Cliff Frazier **Monroe**; Jim Boeke **Stallings**; Alan Autry **Balford**; Danny Bunz **Tony Douglas**; Jane Daly **Ruth**; Stanley Grover **March**; Walter Brooke **Doctor**

THE GAME
Phil Elliott (Nick Nolte), a hobbled, worn-down veteran wide receiver for the North Dallas Bulls pro football team, must deal with riding the bench after starting for six years.

He's at constant odds with head coach B. A. (G. D. Spradlin), who incessantly rides Phil for his childish attitude and lack of team spirit.

Reminded by his politically savvy quarterback friend, Seth Maxwell (Mac Davis), that he's better off fooling management like he does than fighting them, Elliott prefers to be true to himself.

Elliott lives for the thrill of the game, taking pills and needle shots to get him through the physical pounding. He begins to question his world when he starts up a relationship with Charlotte (Dayle Haddon), who is mystified by her boyfriend's masochistic love of his profession. She does however help open Phil's eyes to the manipulative nature of management, who treat their players as little more than fodder in a more technology-run, bottom-line-driven game than the one Elliott lives to play.

Despite his willingness to continue to take the abuse in exchange for the thrill of personal performance, Phil's career comes to a crushing end as management forces him out after hiring a private investigator to follow him and catch him out on borderline offenses that violate the "morals" clause of his contract. Failing to heed his friend Seth's advice, Phil finds himself a victim of not playing the game that's required off the field as well.

INSTANT REPLAY
Based on former Dallas Cowboy wide receiver Peter Gent's novel, *North Dallas Forty* isn't "Semi-Tough"; it's just plain tough.

The picture is a gritty, realistic, eye-opening, and often hilarious examination of the dark underside of an American institution: professional football.

North Dallas Forty not only provides an insider's view of the sport but uses football as a metaphor for the high-tech, profit-driven corporate powers that everyday Joes feel have a hold on their lives.

Director/producer Ted Kotcheff incisively examines the use of players as a commodity in the business of sport. While most fans realize athletes are just well-paid worker bees serving the corporate queen, this film distinguishes itself by giving that truth a human dimension of rare magnitude that leaves an impression long after the theater lights go up.

TOP: Nick Nolte trained with Oakland Raiders Hall of Fame receiver Fred Biletnikoff.

BOTTOM: Veteran Bulls receiver Phillip Elliott (Nolte, left) and quarterback Seth Maxwell (Mac Davis) size up the younger players looking to take their jobs.

This insightful drama is about a week in the life of the people involved with the fictional North Dallas Bulls professional football franchise (who unsurprisingly bear some resemblance to personalities from the Dallas Cowboys of the 1970s).

The film's success starts with its leading performer. In a complex, compelling, and wide-ranging characterization not seen by a team sport star since Richard Harris's rugby turn in *This Sporting Life*, Nick Nolte embodies the independent, disillusioned, and battle-scarred wide receiver, Phil Elliott.

Nolte is superb as the somewhat out-of-shape former starter with declining skills who hangs on and endures the pain and abuse because of his simple love of the game and his self-proclaimed "best hands in football." It is exactly that free-spirited selfishness and fading talent that threaten his usefulness to the team. His internalized personal drama is what engages us, and Nolte is convincing throughout the film as a man forced to make moral choices while struggling to be himself within a bureaucratic, indifferent hierarchy.

Mac Davis, in his feature debut as the slick, all-knowing, too-much-to-lose quarterback pal is effortlessly good, though his physical stature and quarterback form are not ideal. The dialogue between the two is sometimes raunchy, often hilarious, and always interesting. It is their nicely delineated friendship that anchors the film.

Many pro football players appear here lending able support, including Jim Boeke, Tommy Reamon, and, in a standout display, John Matuszak. They all add to Kotcheff's very realistic locker room scenes, with all their raunchy hyper-macho camaraderie, as well as the rigorous practice sessions and sometimes ego-deflating team meetings. Bo Svenson, with his oversized appetites, brings depth to what could have been a cliché part as a dense giant lineman.

Charles Durning does well in a tough and well-worn part as the loudmouthed, somewhat disrespected assistant coach. G. D. Spradlin's commanding presence as a hard-driven taskmaster of a head coach is excellent. His intensity pays off well in the closing scenes, including his cool confrontation with Nolte.

Director Kotcheff's team creates a realistic atmosphere with production designer Albert Sweeney ably presenting various Los Angeles locations as Dallas. Paul

"Better football through chemistry."

Lohman's photography of both the football action and realistic interiors is commendable, as is the affecting and ranging music of John Scott, all bound together by Jay Kamen's sharp editing.

Perhaps most admirable is the filmmakers' ability to present a realistic, hard-hitting, and insightful examination of the diverse attitudes, powers, players, and management that make up professional football without the cooperation of the NFL.

While it's no surprise that the league refused to participate in this unyielding portrayal of players as disposable, replaceable commodities up against heartless management, *North Dallas Forty* succeeds in raising awareness that unquestionably there is muck to be raked.

Director Oliver Stone would revisit and update that muckraking with his visually powerful *Any Given Sunday* two decades later.

North Dallas Forty excels in its ability to capture the many dramas played out behind the scenes that weren't readily known to fans of the Sunday afternoon latter-day gladiator battles of that era.

OUTSIDE THE LINES Uncredited writer Nancy Dowd also wrote the screenplay for *Slap Shot* (1977).... Former NFL player Jim Boeke also appeared in the football films *Brian's Song* (1971) and *Heaven Can Wait* (1978).... Bo Svenson had a role in *Maurie* (1973), the biographical film about basketball player Maurice Stokes .... Dabney Coleman performed in a pair of ski pictures, *Downhill Racer* (1969) and *The Other Side of the Mountain* (1975).... John Matuszak, the Houston Oilers' number one pick in the 1973 NFL draft, appeared in the cable TV football series, *First and Ten*.... Tony-winning stage performer Charles Durning also appeared in TV's *Evening Shade* and *Arliss* as well as *Special Olympics* (1978), *Casey Stengel* (1981), and *Bleacher Bums* (2002).... Areas of Los Angeles such as Westlake and Thousand Oaks doubled for Texas topography.... Football action was shot at East LA College, UCLA, the Coliseum, and the Rams' Long Beach practice facility, Blair Field.... NFL great Tom Fears was the film's football coordinator and reportedly had trouble getting league-related

"We're just the equipment. We're the jockstraps, the helmets, and they just depreciate us. Take us off the goddamn tax return," the fed-up Elliott would later tell his coach before quitting the team.

work after his stint with the picture.... Fears also coordinated the football action for *Wildcats* (1986), *The Best of Times* (1986), and *Two-Minute Warning* (1976).... He also appeared on screen in the football films *Crazylegs* (1953) and *Easy Living* (1949).... Nolte played a college basketball coach in *Blue Chips* (1994).... G. D. Spradlin also appeared in a basketball film, *One on One* (1977), and in a football film, *Number One* (1969), that starred Charlton Heston as an over-the-hill QB for the New Orleans Saints.... Nolte's father, Frank, was an All-American football candidate at Iowa State.... Nolte trained for the role with Oakland Raider great Fred Biletnikoff. . . .Mac Davis started in showbiz as a singer-songwriter with gold records like *Baby Don't Get Hooked on Me* and wrote the tune "In the Ghetto," recorded by Elvis Presley.... Raised in Sweden, actor Bo Svenson was an avid hockey player, and his judo skills (he once won the Far East Judo Championships in Japan) landed him a starring role in *Breaking Point* (1976) as a judo instructor.... The Swede also raced stock cars.... Tom Fears imposed a training-camp-style discipline on the players gathered for rehearsals prior to principal photography, including fines for being late on call times or lost "play-books," and the proceeds went to a mid-shoot party to keep the unit close throughout the remainder of the production.... French Canadian actress Dayle Haddon appeared in Disney's *The World's Greatest Athlete* (1973).... Haddon was also a model and appeared on the cover of a *Sports Illustrated* swimsuit issue.

ALL-STAR MOMENTS
Opening scene. Elliott (Nolte) awakening with a bloody nose and then hobbling to down some painkillers with warm beer to start his day.

Game film review session. Coach Johnson (Durning) nails a sleeping player with a chalkboard eraser. Head Coach Spradlin (Strothers) brings down the egos of Maxwell (Davis) and Elliott for deviating from the game plan despite scoring a touchdown and then cuts a lineman for being "uncertain."

Training room conversation between Nolte and Davis that ends before the QB can tell his buddy about the "weird part" of his latest sexual escapade.

The play in the closing seconds of the game where Delma (Tommy Reamon) gets nailed by a vicious tackle and the coach yells at a concerned Elliott to "get back in the huddle right now or off the field."

Post-game locker room. O. W. Shaddock's (John Matuszak) tirade against management as Coach Durning barely escapes physical harm.

The kangaroo court where Elliott realizes he's being forced out. He responds to charges of smoking marijuana by retorting, "If you nailed all the ballplayers that smoked grass you wouldn't even be able to field a punt return team. Besides you've given me goddamn harder stuff in Chicago just to get out of the locker room. Hard drugs."

Later in the same scene, responding to B. A.'s complaint that Elliott's childish attitude hurts the team, he answers, "Team? For Christ sakes, B. A., we're not the team. They're the team [pointing to the owners]. These guys right here, B. A., they're the team. We're just the equipment. We're the jockstraps, the helmets, and they just depreciate us. Take us off the goddamn tax return."

POST-GAME COMMENTS
Producer and co-writer Frank Yablans on the film's theme expressed through its lead character:

The story is really about a man inside a system which he knows he can't quite accept. He wants to win as much as any man on the team, but not on the terms of a machine. The system makes him a rebel, though perhaps he would not be one anywhere else in contemporary America.[1]

Adds Nick Nolte on his character, Phil Elliott:

[Elliott] is a man at a turning point in his life and he finds he can't make the compromises of selling out to the corporation which is trying to run his life. He wants to maintain his innocence while still playing football the way he remembered it in his youth.[2]

Yablans:

In the film the character Nolte plays must make the correct moral judgment while being part of a corporation that it basically immoral since corporations do not deal in morality. As Peter Gent said in his novel, "The team is management and the players are the equipment."[3]

Al Ruddy, creator and producer of *The Longest Yard*, on *North Dallas Forty*:

There was nothing glamorous about *North Dallas Forty*. It was trench warfare. A very sophisticated movie about what the pro game is all about. Nick Nolte was born to play a football player.[4]

Yablans on Nolte:

I think what fascinated Nick was the conflict between management and talent. That's what made it a different kind of football movie.[5]

Yablans on the cinematic attraction of the sport:

Football is great because it is a canvas that's broad enough and big enough and you can have eccentric characters that you can lace within the film that generally anyone can relate to these people.

I think that is what makes football a better team sport than baseball, a guy standing in the outfield by himself. Here you have these gladiators lining up constantly together and it's a unit. I think that's what is appealing to a large degree.[6]

HOME COURT ADVANTAGE Available on VHS and DVD.

#11 CHAMPION

Screenwriter Carl Foreman. **Director** Mark Robson. **Producer** Stanley Kramer. **Cinematography** Frank Planer. **Editing** Harry Gerstad. **Music** Dimitri Tiomkin. **Production Design** Ed Boyle. United Artists. 1949.

THE PLAYERS Kirk Douglas **Michael "Midge" Kelly**; Arthur Kennedy **Connie Kelly**; Ruth Roman **Emma Bryce**; Marilyn Maxwell **Grace Diamond**; Paul Stewart **Tommy Haley**; Lola Albright **Palmer Harris**; Luis Van Rooten **Mr. Harris**; John Day **Johnny Dunne**; Harry Shannon **Lew Bryce**; Ralph Sanford **Hammond**; Esther Howard **Mrs. Kelly**; Sam Balter **Fight announcer**

THE GAME Midge Kelly (Kirk Douglas) and his lame brother, Connie (Arthur Kennedy), have staked all their money with Midge's navy pal in a part ownership in a coastal café in southern California. With minimal currency left they begin their journey west via boxcar. After getting mugged by a group of hoboes and tossed from the train, they try hitchhiking. They get a ride from a promising boxer, Johnny Dunne (John Day), and his sultry blonde friend Grace (Marilyn Maxwell), who despises the brothers. They get as far as Kansas City, as that is where Dunne is fighting.

Through a set of circumstances Midge finds himself being offered $35 to go four rounds against an opponent on the undercard. Badly as they need the money, Connie tries to be the voice of reason, reminding Midge that he knows nothing about the sport and will get clobbered. Midge pays no attention, retorting, "For $35 I'd get my head knocked off." He nearly does but shows enough promise that after the bout he meets veteran fight manager Tommy Haley (Paul Stewart), who offers to develop Midge into a contender. Midge prefers to focus on his diner business, but Haley tells him how to reach him in Los Angeles if he changes his mind.

Arriving at the café, the Kellys quickly learn they've been swindled, having purchased an interest where none actually existed. Lew Bryce (Harry Shannon), the real owner, gives them menial jobs and warns them to stay away from his pretty waitress daughter, Emma (Ruth Roman). Though Connie soon falls for her, it is Midge's virility that seduces Emma. As they lie out on the beach Midge reveals to her his poverty-stricken upbringing, his dreams of wealth and respect, and his ambition to become somebody in this dog-eat-dog world.

In the blink of an eye Midge is forced into a shotgun wedding to Emma. He immediately walks out and ends up locating Haley, the fight manager he met in Kansas City.

Under Haley's tutelage Midge builds himself up and learns proper technique (as well as a few improper techniques). He begins to move up the ranks, and after a couple of years of steady improvement he's ready for a title shot. Unfortunately, he learns he must throw the fight in order to service the controlling mobsters. Haley tells him that it's the politics of the fight game and that he'll get his chance if he plays ball and takes the dive. Midge reluctantly agrees, but once in the ring his lingering anger and burning ambition, heightened by another snub from Grace, now sitting ringside, drives him to pummel Dunne and win decisively. The doublecross of the gambling overlords results in a beating for Midge, Haley, and Connie by mob goons.

Gold-digger Grace, seeing the potential money to be made backing Midge, dumps Dunne, becomes Kelly's mistress, and persuades the mob via her association with

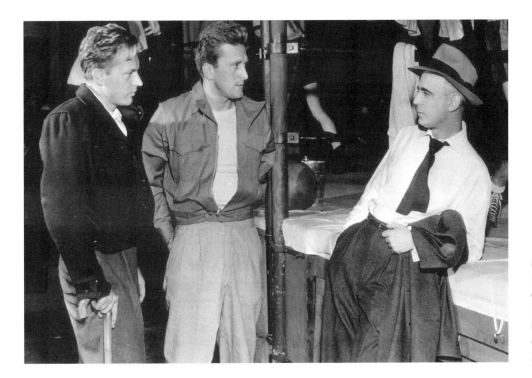

Michael "Midge" Kelly (Kirk Douglas, center) enlists the help of veteran fight man Tommy Haley (Paul Stewart, right) to become a successful boxer. Connie (Arthur Kennedy, left) is Midge's brother.

connected financier Mr. Harris (Luis Van Rooten) to manage Kelly, who seems to be quite popular with the public.

The doublecross continues, only this time Midge drops Haley for Mr. Harris, and Connie, disgusted with the monster his brother has become, leaves his brother's corner as well, returning to Chicago to be with their ailing mother (Esther Howard). Soon the unstoppable Midge makes another conquest, this time an affair with his new manager's much younger wife, Pamela Harris (Lola Albright).

Mr. Harris, cool and shrewd, wants his wife back and proves to her she's making a mistake in going with Midge, who is rotten through and through. In her presence Mr. Harris attempts to buy Midge off, waiving his manager fees if Midge will stay away from his wife. Pamela is shocked when Midge chooses the money over her in the blink of an eye.

Arriving back in Chicago too late to see his dying mother, Midge learns that Emma is divorcing him to marry Connie. Midge convinces his brother and Emma to put off their plans to help him train for his biggest fight. Kelly also gets Tommy Haley to come back to get him in shape.

Championship fight day. Connie enters the locker room, seething because Midge has seduced Emma. They fight. Midge knocks his brother down and then heads out to the ring.

Dunne has waited a long time for this rematch and makes the most of the opportunity. He proceeds to steadily batter Midge into a bloody pulp. At one point Haley threatens to throw in the towel and the ref comes over between rounds late in the fight, saying he's going to stop it. Midge begs him not to. The fight goes on but the punishment of Midge continues. Finally and mercifully it looks like it's over as Midge is down on the canvas. However, when he hears the radio announcer say, "Kelly's through. He's totally washed up.... We're getting a new champion tonight," Kelly summons the internal demons that have raged inside him and miraculously gets off

TOP: Kirk Douglas (second from right) was a collegiate wrestling champion at St. Lawrence University.

MIDDLE: Pugilistic success makes Midge an appealing figure to the ladies, in this case artist Lola Albright (Palmer Harris).

BOTTOM: Midge is ruthless and relentless in his drive to be a champion.

the canvas and turns the tide, delivering a flurry of damaging blows that defeats Dunne.

Alone with Haley inside the locker room, a delirious Midge, practically out on his feet, loses his senses, shouting, "Those fat bellies with the big cigars aren't going to make a monkey out of me. I can beat 'em. You know I can beat 'em!" Then he collapses dead from a brain hemorrhage.

Outside the locker room when pressed for a statement, Connie is ready to reveal the real Midge Kelly, the miserable true nature of his brother, but Haley and Emma prod him into maintaining his brother's popular image. Reluctantly, Connie says, "He was a champion. He went out like a champion. He was a credit to the fight game to the very end."

INSTANT REPLAY *Champion* is a tale of the building of a fighter and the self-destruction of a human being. Based on the short story by sportswriter Ring Lardner, *Champion* is a fast-moving and forceful production brilliantly assembled by producer Stanley Kramer on a relatively minimal budget and skillfully presented by director Mark Robson. Robson's unrelenting pace begins with a riveting opening scene of the boxer heading to the ring via the dark corridor below the arena accompanied by martial music, and continues to a memorable and ironic finale.

The cast, photography, lighting, script, and music are well orchestrated by Robson, who would go on to direct another dark look at boxing in *The Harder They Fall*.

Cinematographer Frank Planer's black and white photography carries as much dramatic impact as the grim script adapted by Carl Foreman.

Dimitri Tiomkin's original music is worth noting, as it contributes to the realism of the highly atmospheric pictures. Putting it all together to move at a gripping pace is editor Harry Gerstad, whose efforts earned him an Oscar.

Speaking of Oscar, Kirk Douglas's forceful performance as the virile, charming, ruthless boxer earned him an Academy Award nomination for Best Actor. *Champion* was a breakthrough role for Douglas. His physical presence and revolving display of magnetism, brutality, and driving ambition carry great conviction and dynamic energy. Douglas pulls off a complex character study of a public hero and private monster: as he rises fistically and financially to much public acclaim, he descends morally in private, with a frighteningly realistic touch.

Arthur Kennedy, playing the fighter's conscience as his gentler brother Connie, lends a sensitive supportive performance.

Quite convincing as well is Paul Stewart as the savvy manager who gets tossed aside like yesterday's newspaper when convenience dictates. The role is presented with just the right amount of subtlety and restraint.

Luis Van Rooten also performs coolly as the level-headed financier sacrificing much money in the name of love for a wayward woman.

Lola Albright, Marilyn Maxwell, and Ruth Roman portray admirably the women who fall to the champion's charms. Roman's naturalness and Maxwell's scheming ways are particularly memorable.

Even darker and meaner than John Garfield's *Body and Soul* and Robert Ryan's *The Set-Up*, Douglas's descent into the moral abyss raises questions about the grim side of human nature. His performance would not be matched in a boxing picture for 30 years, until Robert DeNiro in *Raging Bull*, whose Jake LaMotta character, like Midge, is the author of his own demise.

OUTSIDE THE LINES The film was shot in 24 days for under $600K.... It grossed $18 million.... In an interview producer Kramer said complications arose when just before shooting was to begin Douglas had a nose operation that prevented him from taking a direct blow to his healing nostrils so that the fight scenes had to be even more carefully choreographed.... Douglas passed up a role and a lot more money in a major studio feature, *The Great Sinner*, with Gregory Peck and Ava Gardner, for *Champion*.... Screenwriter Carl Foreman (*High Noon, The Bridge on the River Kwai*) was a victim of the Communist witch hunts of the 1950s and as a result had a difficult time finding work in Hollywood for many years.... Harry Gerstad also won an Academy Award for editing *High Noon* (1957).... Arthur Kennedy was nominated for Best Supporting Actor in *Champion*.... He also starred in another boxing film as James Cagney's brother in *City for Conquest* (1940).... Kennedy teamed with Robert Mitchum portraying a rodeo star in *The Lusty Men* (1952).... Mark Robson would later direct another hard-hitting boxing film, *The Harder They Fall* (1956), that featured Humphrey Bogart and Rod Steiger.... Paul Stewart performed in the football feature *Easy Living* (1949) and the boxing biography *The Joe Louis Story* (1953).... Topps, famous for its baseball cards, produced five million "flipper books" consisting of 30 shots of Kirk Douglas that when flipped with a finger showed him in boxing action.... Douglas was an outstanding wrestler at St. Lawrence University.... Douglas's classmates at the American Academy of Dramatic Arts included Lauren Bacall and Diane Dill, who would become his wife.... Training for several weeks under former junior welterweight fighter Mushy Callahan, Douglas rehearsed and studied every punch to be thrown and taken, which were diagrammed and drawn out by an artist.

ALL-STAR MOMENTS The dramatic opening procession of the boxer and his handlers down the dimly lit corridor under the arena on their way to the ring to the sounds of stirring martial music.

Montage of rookie boxer Midge Kelly trying to perform fitness exercises with his trainer telling him, "You're gonna work until your bones hurt."

When told by his manager he must take a dive in order to get a title shot, Midge voices his frustration: "What kind of a stinking, filthy world...? Three years. Worked like a slave. Build the muscles. Build the wind. Live like a monk. Beat your brains out and then the fat bellies with the big cigars they tell you you're still a tramp. And I can beat him, you know I can beat him!"

Similar to scenes in *The Set-Up* and *Requiem for a Heavyweight*, Midge runs through a dark, empty gym to avoid the mob goons. Surrounded, he begins to fight them off in the middle of the ring before the cops arrive.

Innovative for the time, some slow-motion action in Midge's fight against Johnny Dunne.

Part of the verbal exchange between Midge and Connie, who is condemning the sport:

CONNIE: Oh, this rotten business. . . .

MIDGE: Oh, lay off the business. It's like any other business, only here the blood shows.

Mrs. Harris tells her husband she wants to marry Midge, but the levelheaded Mr. Harris calmly but expensively proves that Kelly is no good for her. In her presence, Mr.

Harris tells Midge he'll waive all his manager fees if the boxer promises to leave his wife alone. To her amazement Kelly chooses the money without hesitating.

After hearing the radio announcer say, "I think it's all over. Kelly's through…. He's finished. We're getting a new champion tonight," a battered and bloodied Kelly, beaten to a pulp by Dunne, gets himself off the canvas in a seething rage and summons his formidable internal demons to turn the fight around and win.

Delirious and alone with his manager in the locker room after the brutal fight, a punch-drunk Kelly cries out, "…For the first time in my life people were cheering for me…. those fat bellies with the big cigars aren't going to make a monkey out of me. I can beat 'em. You know I can beat 'em!" then collapses and dies.

POST-GAME COMMENTS Kirk Douglas, on why he turned down a major studio movie role and took a chance on this small, independent film:

> I did *Champion* because I wanted to do a physical picture. Up to that time, I played soft guys. I never boxed before but I was the undefeated champion wrestler when I was at St. Lawrence University. They wanted me to try out for the Olympics, but I didn't have the money to cover the expenses. Of course, my training for wrestling helped me. I became an adept rope skipper, and I improved my body strength.
>
> The character was exciting, kind of a son-of-a-bitch. Really a tough guy but in the development of the character I think he gets sympathy.[1]

Douglas, on filming the boxing scenes:

> I did get hurt in one of the film sequences. I found that boxing as a real professional was more difficult. It was hard back then to fake the punch. One boxer—I wish I could remember his name—hit me with an uppercut and knocked me out.[2]

Douglas, on the fan interest in boxing films, and his personal favorite:

> Boxing movies appeal to the audience because it's a one-on-one encounter, both evenly matched, fighting in a prescribed area. I think that Robert DeNiro made my favorite boxing picture, *Raging Bull*.[3]

HOME COURT ADVANTAGE Available on DVD. Released by Artisan Entertainment both as a single release and packaged with *Body and Soul*.

#10 SLAP SHOT

Screenwriter Nancy Dowd. **Director** George Roy Hill. **Producers** Robert Wunsch, Stephen Friedman. **Cinematography** Victor Kemper. **Editing** Dede Allen. **Art Direction** Henry Bumstead. **Sound Editor** Peter Berkos. **Music Supervisor** Elmer Bernstein. Universal. 1977.

THE PLAYERS Paul Newman **Reggie Dunlop**; Strother Martin **Joe McGrath**; Jennifer Warren **Francine Dunlop**; Michael Ontkean **Ned Braden**; Lindsay Crouse **Lily Braden**; Andrew Duncan **Jim Carr**; Jeff Carlson **Jeff Hanson**; Steve Carlson **Steve Hanson**; David Hanson **Jack Hanson**; Yvon Barrette **Denis Lemiuex**; Jerry Houser **Dave "Killer" Carlson**; Melinda Dillon **Suzanne**; Emmet Walsh **Dickie Dunn**; Swoosie Kurtz **Helen Upton/Shirley**; Paul D'Amato **Tim McCracken**; Chris Murney **Hanrahan**; Ned Dowd **Ogie Oglethorpe**; Kathryn Walker **Anita McCambridge**; Paul Dooley **Hyannisport team announcer**; Nancy Dowd **Andrea**

THE GAME Set in a Pennsylvania steel mill town during the 1970s, *Slap Shot* follows the final season of a minor league hockey team where things are going from bad to worse for both the local economy and the team's fortunes. The Charlestown Chiefs are led by aging player/coach Reggie Dunlop (Paul Newman). Dunlop lives for the sport but he's getting old and feeling it. He knows it's his last season. Still very passionate about the game, Dunlop will do anything—lying, brawling, altering his playing philosophy, and sleeping with opponents' wives—to turn around the miserable state of his team. That devotion has come at a cost in his private life, as he and his wife, Francine (Jennifer Warren), have separated.

Mired in a losing streak and deserted by their fans, the Chiefs learn that their franchise is folding at season's end. This is largely due to the closing of the local steel mill, which employs most of their fans.

Times are tough in the Rust Belt. The team's general manager, Joe McGrath (Strother Martin), tries to sell off assets, including the team massage table and bus, to keep the Chiefs afloat. He's also secretly looking for a new job. In line with the dismal situation, McGrath fills out the team's roster, making a super cheap deal to sign three skinny guys with horn-rimmed glasses and shaggy hair who usually talk as one. The Hanson brothers (Jeff Carlson, David Hanson, and Steve Carlson) look more at home with their toy cars than with hockey sticks. As the losses pile up Reggie is at his wits' end and the team's spirit is fading fast.

Reggie realizes that if he doesn't turn things around soon his chances of finding a coaching position somewhere are nil. He meets with local sportswriter Dickie Dunn (Emmet Walsh) and over drinks plants a story that the Chiefs are going to be sold and moved to Florida. Dunn thinks he's got a scoop and word spreads fast about the imminent deal.

Having just slept with an opposing goalie's wife (Melinda Dillon) who admits to Reggie that she slept with other women and that her husband Hanrahan beat her when he found out, Dunlop goes out to his game that night and uses this intimate knowledge to his benefit.

From various angles around the goal, Dunlop skates up to Hanrahan and yells very personal insults at him each time. Sure enough, it takes its toll and Hanrahan runs off chasing after Dunlop, leaving the net unattended. While the goalie is fighting Reggie, the Chiefs score the deciding goal, ending their abysmal losing streak.

With the win and a shared optimism about moving to Florida, where hopefully there'll be a more supportive owner, the team's spirits are rising. The Chiefs are also becoming less mild-mannered on the ice—as when Dave Carlson (Jerry Houser) leaps to his coach's defense when an opponent tells Reggie he's too old to play and begins a fight. Even as Dave is getting stitched up, he jumps back onto the ice to fight some more. Reggie is impressed.

In the locker room between periods, Coach Dunlop tries to light a similar spark in the other players, but with several injured he reluctantly approaches the Hanson brothers and tells them, "Show us what you got."

The Hansons proceed to demonstrate their prowess—at physical brutality! At every turn these monsters of mayhem are smashing opponents as their teammates watch dumbfounded. After a major melee all three Hansons are tossed and wave to an adoring crowd as they leave the ice. This wildly enthusiastic response by the fans is not lost on Reggie, who now realizes where his team's future lies. He endorses the violent play.

The Chiefs, with their newly adopted bloody and brutal style, take their game on the road. Dave Carlson now wants to be known as "Killer." Word of the Chiefs' barbarism spreads fast, and bloodthirsty fans quickly fill the arenas. The Chiefs begin to win regularly, leading the league in stitches and arrests. Their ultra-aggressive ways however, conflict with their best player Ned Braden's view of the game. Braden (Michael Ontkean), a finesse player and the Chiefs' leading scorer, refuses to "goon it up," so Reggie benches him, which only angers Ned even more. Things aren't much better for Braden on the home front, as he is having a constant struggle with his icy, depressed, and often drunk wife, Lily (Lindsay Crouse).

During this winning stretch, Reggie, after much effort, tracks down the team's mysterious owner in hopes of actually getting the Chiefs sold to a real buyer. The owner, more interested in anything crossing the bottom line than the blue line, squelches Reggie's dreams, saying that the team will be dismantled as a tax write-off rather than sold to new ownership.

Disheartened from the meeting, Reggie does some reflecting on the drive home.

Player-coach Reggie Dunlop (Paul Newman, left) at the moment has the upper hand in another Chiefs brawl.

Realizing that the end of his playing days is at hand and now regretting his choice of employing pure goon play, Dunlop tells his estranged best player Ned that he wants to go out in style, playing it straight, "none of this wrestling shit." Reggie vows to win the Federal League championship game that night with "old time hockey."

Addressing his team before the title game, Coach tells the players that he lied and deceived them. There is no Florida future and there's no future for the sport if they all continue to act like clowns. He implores them to play this game straight up. The players rally around him.

Out in the arena, however, the expectations are different. Announcer Jim Carr (Andrew Duncan) sets up the championship game as a roughhouse matchup, and that is what the wildly cheering crowd and the opponents, the Syracuse Bulldogs, are anticipating as well. To that end, the Bulldogs have left their finesse players at home and brought out all their thugs from past and present, including the notorious Ogie Oglethorpe (Ned Dowd) to outgoon the Chiefs.

It is clear before the puck drops that "old time hockey" is going to lose out to violent play. The Chiefs, exhorted by their coach, maintain their composure under heavy pounding but are getting whipped. Between the periods, a befuddled McGrath storms into the locker room and yells at the depressed team, saying that there are scouts in the stands looking for talent.

Instantly the Chiefs revert to fighting form and the title game quickly degenerates into a war of flying fists and sticks. Refusing to join in, Braden skates to center ice and amidst the bloody mayhem begins to do a slow striptease. This bizarre exhibition succeeds in getting the fans' attention. Even the players stop pummeling each other and try to figure out what is going on.

All-star thug Tim McCracken (Paul D'Amato) momentarily stops fighting long enough to complain vehemently to the ref to make Braden stop: "It is disgusting, I protest!" McCracken can't take it anymore and flattens the ref with one punch. The ref staggers back to his feet and calls a forfeit because of McCracken's action. As a result the Chiefs win. The bizarre ending is capped off with Ned skating around in only his jockstrap and skates, holding the trophy aloft and acknowledging the cheers of the crowd.

Though the championship doesn't save Reggie's marriage, he is happy that he's got a new coaching job waiting for him in Minnesota. Like Ned and his wife, who are now back together, Reggie is hopeful of a second chance with Francine, telling her to call him if things don't work out for her in New York.

The whole team is in high spirits as they celebrate their championship with a victory parade through downtown Charlestown.

INSTANT REPLAY After premiering on February 17, 1977, *Slap Shot* was immediately skating on thin ice with many film critics, mostly in regard to what they felt to be the overuse of coarse language and violence.

In defending his work, director Hill felt the language was necessary to achieve an honest portrayal of the culture of the sport.

Hockey is a brutal sport and the guys who play it don't mince words. So while some were offended, others felt *Slap Shot* was a very accurate portrayal. The film's over-the-top slapstick approach to violence is played primarily for laughs, much as the popular Three Stooges film shorts were.

What is unusual is that it was a woman who wrote the script that so ably captured

the ribald, male-dominated world of minor league hockey. Nancy Dowd spent a month following her brother Ned's minor league hockey team in Pennsylvania, researching and interviewing players. She even had Ned make tape recordings of the salty locker room conversations, bus talk, and barroom discussions to get a feel for the language and dialogue the players used.

With all that ammunition, Ms. Dowd was able to create a true-to-life script that captures the violence, crude humor, and Spartan realities of minor league hockey.

Except for Paul Newman, most of the cast were relative unknowns. Newman's superstar status didn't create a dominant shadow over the rest of the performers; as a matter of fact, his Dunlop character fit right in as one of the boys—drinking, brawling, and womanizing. Newman is convincing as a veteran hockey player who doesn't want to face the end of his career or his marriage and fights hard to hold on to both. Noted critic Pauline Kael called Newman's performance one of the best of his career. That's saying something.

Strother Martin, who played Newman's boss when he tried to go straight as a bank courier in *Butch Cassidy and the Sundance Kid,* calls the shots again here as the seen-it-all weary hockey executive. He and Newman have no "failure to communicate," as their scenes have a wonderful chemistry, as if they had known each other for decades.

Jennifer Warren, in a role representing the difficulties of personal relationships, handles well the conflicted emotions of Reggie's wife, whose head tells her to make a final break but whose heart keeps bringing her back.

Andrew Duncan is hilarious as the flashy announcer, complete with bad toupee. Lost in all the fighting is some pretty good skating by Jerry Houser and Michael Ontkean.

Certainly the most brilliant performances are turned in by a trio of non-actors. Professional hockey players Steve and Jeff Carlson and David Hanson are the heart and soul of this film as the Hanson brothers.

These colorful thugs cause total mayhem on the screen. At the same time, however, their almost innocent joy, enthusiasm, and love of the game are infectious and they simply steal the film. Hockey fans loved them. So did the Hollywood moguls. The Hansons were offered a multi-picture deal by Universal but they turned it down because the studio couldn't accommodate shooting schedules around their hockey commitments.

"We were hockey players, not actors," points out Steve Carlson, "We lived our lives to play the game. The choice was very easy and I wouldn't have changed it for the world."[1]

Director Hill keeps the film moving at a good pace, building nicely to the arrival of the Hanson brothers. The surprising climax and ambiguous finale thankfully avoid the clichés found too often in sports movies.

The on-ice action is well photographed by Victor Kemper, and Dede Allen's sharp editing brings real visceral impact to the hockey play. Henry Bumstead's art direction and Tom Bronson's costumes provide a wonderful feel for small-town 1970s America. The clothes, such as powder-blue polyester suits and three-piece leather suits, are hilarious reminders of the fashions of the times.

Slap Shot is likely to be remembered more for its buffoonery, which at times it seems to decry, than for its voice of protest against the violence of the sport. The Hanson brothers' dominant performance really keeps the audience's sympathy with the Chiefs despite their penchant for vicious play. It is tough to have it both ways; nevertheless, the film has become even more popular with time despite the absence of a clear point of view. *Slap Shot* is a very entertaining portrayal of small-town minor league hockey.

OUTSIDE THE LINES Actor Michael Ontkean attended the University of New Hampshire on a hockey scholarship and went on to play in the Toronto Maple Leafs farm system and on semi-pro teams in Quebec and Vancouver.... Nick Nolte was considered for a lead role.... Writer Nancy Dowd also wrote the screenplay for a horse racing movie, *Let It Ride* (1989), starring Richard Dreyfuss.... She won an Academy Award for her screenplay *Coming Home* (1978).... The Hanson brothers enjoyed professional hockey careers, between them playing 85 NHL games and tallying a combined 23 points.... Actor Strother Martin was the national junior springboard diving champion back in the 1940s.... His line in another movie with Paul Newman, *Cool Hand Luke* (1967), "What we have here is a failure to communicate," became a national catchphrase.... Actress Jennifer Warren also starred in another winter sports movie, *Ice Castles* (1979).... Paul Newman has starred in several sports movies: as a pool shark in *The Hustler,* as a boxer in *Somebody Up There Likes Me* (1956), as an auto racer with his wife Joanne Woodward in *Winning* (1969), and reprising his role as pool shark Eddie Felson in Martin Scorsese's sequel to *The Hustler, The Color of Money* (1986), for which Newman won an Oscar.... Dowd's brother, Ned, appears in the movie as feared opponent Ogie Oglethorpe.

ALL-STAR MOMENTS The exchange between Reggie (Newman) and Joe (Martin) about the deal made for the Hanson brothers after the coach picks them up at the bus station to less-than-favorable first impressions.

REGGIE: You cheap son of a bitch! Are you crazy? These guys are retards.

JOE: I got a good deal on those boys. The scouts said they showed promise.

REGGIE: They brought their fuckin' toys with them.

A parade for the new champions.

JOE: Well, I'd rather have them playing with their toys than themselves.

REGGIE: They're too dumb to play with themselves. Boy, every piece of garbage that comes on the market, you gotta buy it!

Reggie on the ice antagonizing the opposing goalie (Chris Murney) with very intimate personal insults as a result of knowledge gained from sleeping with his wife, who admits she's slept with other women.

REGGIE: Suzanne sucks pussy!

(moments later)

REGGIE: She's a dyke—I know!

(later on)

REGGIE: She's a lesbian, she's a lesbian!

Goalie Hanrahan can't take it anymore and runs off after Reggie, thereby leaving the goal open for the Chiefs to score the winning goal as the goalie and Reggie fight.

The famous line that launches the Hanson brothers (Carlson, Carlson, and Hanson) into hockey mayhem: between periods and with a lack of players due to injury, Coach Dunlop walks over to the Hansons and says, "Show us what you've got." The Hansons cross themselves and proceed to introduce their bloody barbarism on the ice.

Warm-ups between the Peterboro Patriots and the Charlestown Chiefs. A Hanson decks an opponent just in passing and a mass brawl ensues. There are no refs on the ice yet so the fight just goes on. This is followed by a pan-shot close-up of bloody players standing at attention during the national anthem. The head ref glares over at the Hansons that he's going to keep a tight leash on them, but one of the brothers blows him off, saying that he's at attention during the anthem.

After losing by trying to play sportsmanlike hockey, the team reverts to their violent selves, and we hear the announcer say, "Well this is more like it, makes me feel good, real good, to see the Chiefs back on the warpath again."

POST-GAME COMMENTS The Hanson brothers on the film's enduring success:

STEVE: Because we're in it! You got three great-looking guys. Hockey chicks dig us. It has everything a man wants: swearing, sex, and violence—what else do you need?

JEFF: The film offered something offbeat and different like *Bull Durham* and *Major League* would do years later for baseball.

DAVE: It was ahead of its time. You didn't have anything before that really caught the feel for what goes on.[2]

HOME COURT ADVANTAGE Available on VHS and DVD. Universal has released three versions, including a 25th Anniversary Edition and one combined with *Slap Shot 2*.

#9 REQUIEM FOR A HEAVYWEIGHT

Screenwriter Rod Serling. **Director** Ralph Nelson. **Producer** David Susskind. **Cinematography** Arthur Ornitz. **Editing** Carl Lerner. **Music** Laurence Rosenthal. **Art Direction** Burr Smidt. **Associate Producer** Jack Grossberg. **Technical Advisor** Arthur Mercante. Columbia. 1962.

THE PLAYERS Anthony Quinn **Mountain Rivera**; Jackie Gleason **Maish Rennick**; Mickey Rooney **Army**; Julie Harris **Grace Miller**; Madame Spivy **Ma Greeny**; Stanley Adams **Perelli**; Lou Gilbert **Doctor**; Herbie Faye **Charlie the bartender**; Cassius Clay **Himself**; Jack Dempsey **Himself**; Willie Pep **Himself**; Barney Ross **Himself**; Arthur Mercante **Referee**

THE GAME Seventeen-year fight veteran and former leading heavyweight contender Mountain Rivera (Anthony Quinn) takes a beating from the young future champion Cassius Clay (later Muhammad Ali). After being knocked out then examined in the locker room, Rivera is told by a doctor (Lou Gilbert) that he should retire because any further boxing could cause his damaged eye to go blind.

Rivera's longtime manager, Maish Rennick (Jackie Gleason), tries to convince Mountain that he's had a good run but it's time to do something else, doctor's orders. Maish is also secretly concerned by what has just transpired; he bet against Mountain lasting more than four rounds (Clay KO'd Rivera in the seventh) and is now deeply in debt to mobster Ma Greeny (Madame Spivy). Unable to pay off his debt right away, Maish is beaten by Ma's goons and told to come up with the money soon, by hook or by crook.

With the help of his compassionate trainer, Army (Mickey Rooney), Mountain searches for work. Employment counselor Grace Miller (Julie Harris) arranges for Mountain to interview for a job as a youth athletic counselor at a summer camp, but Maish purposely gets Mountain drunk and he blows the job opportunity.

Mountain is very loyal to Maish and knows that with his limited education his world is "with dirty towels and locker rooms." Army is angered by Maish's insistence that Mountain owes him and his attempts to make Rivera perform as a wrestler to help pay off his gambling debt. Knowing Mountain's proud nature, Army is confident that the fighter won't give in.

Initially Mountain refuses to wear the American Indian costume as the wrestling "gimmick." He feels it would strip him of all his dignity. The proud boxer offers to do anything else for Maish, but fixed wrestling is too much to ask ("I never took no dive for nobody.") However, when Ma Greeny and her mob goons threaten Maish's life in front of him, Mountain reluctantly swallows his pride to save his friend from certain death.

As Mountain slowly puts on the Indian outfit, Maish thanks him and it slips out that he bet against Rivera. "You know, Maish," Mountain tells him, "in all the dirty, crummy 17 years I fought for you I wasn't ashamed of one single round, not one single minute. Now you make me ashamed."

Feeling betrayed and very disappointed in his longtime friend and manager, Mountain walks out of the locker room in his Indian gear with Army for his wrestling match to save Maish. Mountain enters the ring to boos and laughter. The onetime top athlete sets aside his self-respect out of loyalty to a disloyal friend. The illusion of the trio's camaraderie has vanished for good.

INSTANT REPLAY In October 1956, *Requiem for a Heavyweight* aired live on CBS's Playhouse 90 series. It was the first original live 90-minute drama in television history.

Jack Palance won an Emmy in a dominant performance as Mountain McClintock. Rod Serling's Emmy-winning script would make it to the silver screen six years later under the direction of Ralph Nelson, who also directed the highly acclaimed teleplay.

From the riveting opening fight sequence, the 1962 theatrical version of *Requiem for a Heavyweight* is a powerful character study. The point-of-view camerawork that puts you in the shoes of Mountain Rivera (Anthony Quinn) as he takes a pummeling from Cassius Clay immediately draws you in. You empathize with the veteran pugilist, feeling the pain of the 17-year veteran boxer in the sunset of his career.

Requiem for a Heavyweight is a film about honor, dignity, loyalty, and exploitation (abuse of trust). It's a movie for the ages, largely thanks to the performances of the four principal characters. In one of his most memorable roles in a highly distinguished career, Anthony Quinn's complete embodiment of the twilight of a dignified, stumble-bum prizefighter who was once "the number five contender for the heavyweight crown" is as riveting a sympathetic character portrait as there's been.

Despite his lack of education, gawky physical appearance, battle scars, and inarticulate speech, the dignified Rivera prides himself on his honesty and always fighting cleanly, having never thrown a fight in his 17 years in the ring.

Quinn's tragic performance as a devoted, punch-drunk, and at times intense boxer is matched beautifully by Jackie Gleason as his unscrupulous manager, Maish.

As he did in *The Hustler*, Gleason shows a gift for subtlety and restraint. Given a little more to work with here, the star of stage, nightclubs, and television demonstrates why he was called "The Great One." The close-ups of Gleason conveying palpable fear and desperation exemplify his memorable turn. Gleason's scene with Mountain's social worker, Grace Miller (Julie Harris), in the staircase is about as telling as it gets on the subject of human frailties and wasted lives. It conjures memories of the car scene with Rod Steiger and Marlon Brando in *On the Waterfront* with Terry lamenting that he "coulda' been somebody."

ABOVE: Ma Greeny (Madame Spivy, center), with one of her thugs (Michael Conrad), lays it out in no uncertain terms for fight manager Maish Rennick (Jackie Gleason, right).

RIGHT: Grace Miller (Julie Harris), a case worker for the employment office, learns more about heavyweight boxer Mountain Rivera (Anthony Quinn), once the fifth-ranked contender in the world.

Julie Harris's perceptive, "people-knowing" social worker is realistic and brings a compassionate humanity to the proceedings in sensing the gentle nature under Mountain's ape-like exterior. Mickey Rooney also brings humanity as Mountain's trainer, Army. His scene-stealing card game sequence with Gleason expressing his feelings for Rivera is impressive, genuine, and rife with resentment: "I love this kid like my own flesh and blood," declares Army. "If I don't weep and worry for him no one else will, least of all you. Why? I don't know. If anything happens to him, you be careful, Maish."

The superb cast extends down to the support players as well. Even though she perhaps lacks an imposing physical presence, Madame Spivy's Ma Greeny mobster is smart and unusual casting. Combining aspects of Truman Capote and Humphrey Bogart, Spivy's dark, mysterious figure, icy demeanor, and vocal menace provide the very real threat in the picture. Stan Adams plays the oily wrestling promoter convincingly without being over the top.

The imaginative cinematography by Arthur Ornitz, especially the jolting opening sequences in the ring, lends a lot to the gritty, realistic atmosphere. Laurence Rosenthal's music provides able support to the dramatic mood of the picture.

With its emphasis on character depth, relationships, and motivations, Serling's insightful though sometimes plodding and predictable script about human nature shines in director Ralph Nelson's absorbing production made altogether memorable by the powerful acting.

This picture is a brilliant character drama of heavyweight proportions.

OUTSIDE THE LINES

Madame Spivy ran a nightclub, Spivy's Roof, on New York's East Side.... Rory Calhoun, Willie Pep, Cassius Clay, Jack Dempsey, Barney Ross, and Gus Lesnevich are some of the boxers who appear in the film.... *Requiem for a Heavyweight* was shot primarily on location in New York.... Veteran fight referee Arthur Mercante was a technical advisor.... Mexican-born Anthony Quinn was a boxer before turning to acting.... Quinn was also an accomplished painter and won an Oscar for Best Supporting Actor in a role playing artist Paul Gauguin in *Lust for Life* (1956).... Quinn was a bullfighter in *Blood and Sand* (1941), starring Tyrone Power.... Actor Jason Patric is Jackie Gleason's grandson.... Director Ralph Nelson unsuccessfully asked that his name be removed from the credits after non-essential scenes that had been cut from the original print were re-inserted to make the picture longer.... Mickey Rooney has appeared in several sports-themed pictures, mostly involving horse racing, including *The Black Stallion* (1979), *National Velvet* (1944), and *Thoroughbreds Don't Cry* (1937).... Michael Conrad was a cast member of *The Longest Yard* (1974).... Director Ralph Nelson won an Emmy for his TV version of this film.... Writer Rod Serling boxed while serving in the military.

ALL-STAR MOMENTS

The jarring camerawork putting the audience in the shoes of Mountain Rivera (Quinn) as he gets pummeled by Cassius Clay.

As Rivera staggers out of the ring and to the locker room with the help of his handlers, he looks at himself in the mirror and suddenly gets into a fighting position when he hears a bell in the distance.

Maish (Gleason) being chased then eventually surrounded in the ring and beaten by Ma Greeny's mob goons.

TOP: Mountain's team: trainer Army (Mickey Rooney, left) and manager Maish (Gleason, right).

MIDDLE: Maish is about to feel what it's like to fall behind in his payments to Ma Greeny.

BOTTOM: The proud and devoted boxer, who never took a dive in 17 years of fighting, is forced into a demeaning series of fixed wrestling matches in order to save the life of his unscrupulous manager, Maish Rennick (Gleason, center) from racketeers. Mountain's longtime trainer, Army (Rooney, right), looks on.

When social worker Grace (Harris) tells Mountain she's got experience working with physically handicapped people, Rivera responds, "Miss, I got no special problem. I tell you what, I'm a big ugly slob and I look like a freak. But I was almost the heavyweight champion of the world. Why don't you put that down on the paper somewhere?"

Maish and Grace's confrontation on the staircase that begins with his line, "Well, do I have a fighter now or a counselor now?"

Mountain's hurt and disappointment in the locker room when Maish lets it slip out that he bet against Rivera: "You know, Maish, in all the dirty, crummy 17 years I fought for you I wasn't ashamed of one single round. Not one single minute. Now you make me ashamed."

Rivera, despite his friend's betrayal, swallows his enormous pride and participates in a fixed wrestling match, dressed as an Indian, in order to save his disloyal friend's life.

HOME COURT ADVANTAGE Available on VHS and DVD.

Mountain Rivera (Anthony Quinn).

#8 BREAKING AWAY

Screenwriter Steve Tesich. **Director/Producer** Peter Yates. **Cinematography** Matthew Leonetti. **Editing** Cynthia Scheider. **Music** Patrick Williams. **Technical Advisor** William Armstrong. Fox. 1979.

THE PLAYERS Dennis Christopher **Dave**; Dennis Quaid **Mike**; Daniel Stern **Cyril**; Jackie Earle Haley **Moocher**; Paul Dooley **Dad**; Barbara Barrie **Mom**; Robyn Douglass **Katherine**; Hart Bochner **Rod**; Amy Wright **Nancy**; Lisa Shure **French girl**; Peter Maloney **Doctor**; Jennifer Mickel **Girl**; John Ashton **Mike's brother**; P. J. Soles **Suzy**; David Blase **500 Race announcer**; William Armstrong **500 Race official**; Howard Wilcox **500 Race official**; J. F. Briere **Mr. York**; Carlos Sintes **Italian rider**; Eddy Van Guyse **Italian rider**; Alvin Bailey **Stonecutter**; Harold Elgar **Stonecutter**; Floyd Todd **Stonecutter**; Robert Woolery **Stonecutter**; Russell Freeman **Stonecutter**; Jimmy Grant **Black student leader**; Woody Hueston **Car wash owner**; Tom Schwoegler **Team captain**; Dr. John Ryan **University president**

THE GAME Four teenagers from Bloomington, Indiana, recent high school graduates, contemplate their next step into adulthood. Their difficult life decisions are complicated by their having grown up in a university town whose student population comes largely from wealthy, out-of-town families that look down on these "townies" (who are also known as "cutters," locals who work the rock quarries).

Dave (Dennis Christopher) discovers an aptitude for cycling and invents a new world for himself by adopting an Italian persona. Immersing himself in the culture, Dave listens to opera, learns the language, and worships an Italian racing team, much to the bewilderment of his father (Paul Dooley), a stonecutter turned used car salesman.

Dave takes this Italian identity a step further and pretends to be a foreign exchange student from Italy to win the attention of Katherine, a pretty coed (Robyn Douglass). This beautiful sorority girl has been dating one of the school's leading athletes and frat men, Rod (Hart Bochner).

Rod doesn't take kindly to Dave's overtures to Katherine. The conflicts between the townies and frat boys extend to a swim race in the quarry where group leader Mike (Dennis Quaid) goes to great pains to show the college boys that he's every bit their equal.

Mike, a star high school athlete, harbors a deep resentment for college boys, whom he perceives as shallow and preppy. When the townies and college boys get into a fight on campus, the university chancellor attempts to resolve this rivalry by allowing the townies to compete in the school's annual bike race, the Little 500.

Dave, whose fantasy of bonding with the Italian cyclists ends badly, as does his romance with coed Katherine, joins with the townies to gain some respect by doing well in the highly regarded bike race.

Led to victory by Dave, the team gains some measure of self-respect as well as the respect of their college rivals.

INSTANT REPLAY *Breaking Away* is a simple picture about growing up relatively unprivileged in middle America. What is quite interesting about this Oscar-nominated film is the fact that it is a British director and Yugoslav-raised screenwriter who so vividly present the Americana of teenage angst, class distinctions, and life in midwestern college communities.

Dave (Dennis Christopher) adopts another persona to woo pretty coed Katherine (Robynn Douglass).

Resurfacing from *The Deep*, Peter Yates offers a coming-of-age story that distinctly captures the transitional period from teen to adult, with all its frustrations, disappointments, and self-discoveries. This film is fresh and enthusiastic, modest and charming.

Breaking Away not only accurately conveys that confusing yet exhilarating period of being not quite boys and not quite men, but also offers an insightful look at friendship, competition and inter-generational and inter-class conflicts. In a clever twist, the exuberant son's persona remains intact and it is his cynical, frustrated father who goes through the biggest transformation.

This character-driven feature portrays youthful summers, growing up, and the search for an identity with a freshness and keen sense of humor reminiscent of what made *American Graffiti* such a success.

Steve Tesich's articulate, authentic, multidimensional and Oscar-winning template lays the groundwork for some fine performances.

Dennis Christopher's enthusiastic turn as a young man chasing his dreams is thoroughly likable and played with conviction. It is his enthusiasm that gives hope to his fellow townies.

Dennis Quaid is convincing as the group's rudderless leader, a former star athlete, terrified that all he'll amount to in the end is just another guy named Mike. Barbara Barrie, in an Oscar-nominated performance, observes the clashes between her husband and her son with a dizzy, patient charm ("Oh, Dave, try not to turn Catholic on us").

Daniel Stern makes an impressive film debut as a gangly, observant, wisecracking townie. Rounding out the gang of four is Jackie Earle Haley, grown up from *The Bad News Bears*, but still a sawed-off rascal with an engaging innocence about him.

The most memorable performance is turned in by Paul Dooley as Dave's exasperated, salty father. Their awkward father-son conversation on the university grounds shows the heart beneath the father's cynical veneer. The film's closing shot of Dooley's double take at his son greeting him in French is classic.

The charming, intelligent script and performances benefit from Cynthia Scheider's fine editing. Particularly notable are the rhythm and timing cutting back and forth between Dave serenading Katherine and his parents at home listening to opera at their candlelit dinner.

With his sensitive command of the elements, Yates not only paints a brilliant vista of Americana , but also provides perhaps one of the more penetrating cinematic looks at adolescence and what it means to be an outsider.

OUTSIDE THE LINES The famous Little 500 race was restaged using 33 teams and over 10,000 spectators.... At various stages, the film was known as "The Cutters" and "Bambino."...It appeared in France as *La Bande des Quatre*.... A TV series followed, in which Barbara Barrie, Jackie Earle Haley, and John Ashton reprised their roles and Shaun Cassidy and Vincent Gardenia starred.... This was Daniel Stern's film debut.... Steve Tesich, an Indiana University graduate and former winner of the race, won an Academy Award for his screenplay.... Peter Yates directed one of Tesich's plays, *The Passing Game*.... The film was shot primarily in Bloomington, Indiana.... In addition to winning for Best Screenplay, *Breaking Away* was also nominated for Best Picture, Best Director, Best Original Score (Patrick Williams), and Best Supporting Actress (Barbara Barrie).... Dennis Christopher won a British Academy Award as Most Promising Newcomer in a Leading Film Role.... The actor also portrayed sprinter Charles Paddock in *Chariots of Fire* (1981).... Haley also starred in *The Bad News Bears* (1976).... The Little 500 is 200 laps, coming to 50 miles.... The average speed is 23 mph.... Christopher appeared briefly in Fellini's *Roma* (1972).... Dennis Quaid starred in the baseball feature *The Rookie* (2002), football's *Any Given Sunday* (1999) and *Everybody's All-American* (1988), boxing's *Tough Enough* (1983).... Yates's experience in pro auto racing as a driver and manager helped him direct the famous Steve McQueen chase sequences in San Francisco for *Bullitt* (1968).... Marvin Westmore's makeup credits also include the basketball feature *One on One* (1977).... Stern starred in the basketball feature *Celtic Pride* with Dan Aykroyd and Damon Wayans (1996).... He was also featured in the baseball picture *Rookie of the Year* (1993).... Tesich adapted another cycling-centered film, *American Flyers* (1985), featuring Kevin Costner, from his own novel.... Paul Dooley appeared in the baseball-themed TV film *Cooperstown* (1993).... Production designer Patrizia von Brandenstein won an Academy Award for her work on *Amadeus* (1984).... One of Dennis Quaid's classmates at the University of Houston was actor Robert Wuhl (*Bull Durham, Arliss*).... Matthew Leonetti was also the cinematographer for the baseball remake *Angels in the Outfield* (1994).

TOP: Dave's parents (Paul Dooley and Barbara Barrie).

MIDDLE: Mike (Dennis Quaid).

BOTTOM: Dennis Christopher won a British Academy Award for Most Promising Newcomer.

ALL-STAR MOMENTS Climbing about in the rock quarry before they go diving, Cyril (Stern) states, "When you're 16, they call it sweet 16; when you're 18 you get to drink and vote and see dirty movies. What the hell do you get to do when you're 19?'

Dave (Christopher) pedaling alongside the trailer rig down the highway.

Mooch (Haley) offering to "go Dutch" on a $5 marriage license and asking silly questions about the procedure as he walks to the courthouse with wife-to-be, Nancy (Amy Wright).

All of Pop's (Dooley) scenes expressing frustration with his son and the Italian culture, including their food. "No more food with 'ini' in it, and the cat's name is 'Jake,' not 'Fellini.' "

Pop's double take at the end of the film when his son passes by on a bike, now speaking French: "Bonjour, Papa."

POST-GAME COMMENTS Dennis Christopher on the critical aspect of the Italian side of his character:

> To make the role of Dave in the film work, I had to make my Italian believable, especially for the relationship with the sorority girl, Katherine. If I'm unconvincing then the girl who falls for it would look dumb and that would ruin the whole point of the relationship.[1]

Dennis Quaid warming to his role:

> When I first read the script, I hated Mike because of the jock part of his character. He could play a sport but was not much of a person in his relations with others. But as I got into the role I saw how he changed. He became more of a sensitive person.
>
> Throughout most of the film his problem is that he is unable to express his feelings to his friends. But at the end he's able to let go. His old jock values that used to work no longer do and he's let them go. When he leaves his friends in Bloomington to go to Wyoming, he is now able to live his own dreams.[2]

Director Peter Yates:

> In their young minds the question they most find the answer to is who really owns and runs the town. Being 19 is a difficult age. You are not a full-fledged adult, yet you are no longer a child. You are ready for the next step in your development, and you are too old to remain on the step where you have been standing.[3]

HOME COURT ADVANTAGE Available on VHS and DVD.

ABOVE: The Dooleys.

RIGHT: The cutters.

#7 ROCKY

Screenwriter Sylvester Stallone. **Director** John Avildsen. **Producers** Irwin Winkler, Bob Chartoff. **Executive Producer** Gene Kirkwood. **Cinematography** James Crabe. **Editing** Scott Conrad, Richard Halsey. **Music** Bill Conti. **Casting** Caro Jones. **Production Design** William Cassidy. **Art Direction** James Spencer. **Sound** Harry Tetrick. **Set Decoration** Ray Molyneaux. United Artists. 1976.

THE PLAYERS Sylvester Stallone **Rocky Balboa**; Talia Shire **Adrian**; Burgess Meredith **Mickey**; Burt Young **Paulie**; Carl Weathers **Apollo Creed**; Thayer David **Jergens**; Joe Spinell **Gazzo**; Jimmy Gambina **Mike**; Don Sherman **Bartender**; Tony Burton **Apollo's trainer**; Bill Baldwin Sr. **Fight announcer**; Al Salvani **Cut man**; Diana Lewis **TV reporter**; Shirley O'Hara **Secretary**; Joe Sorbello **Bodyguard**; Jane Marla Robbins **Pet shop owner**; Jodi Letizia **Marie**; George O'Hanlon **TV commentator**; Stu Nahan **Fight commentator**; Stan Shaw **Dipper**; Frank Stallone **Street singer**; Lou Fillipo **Championship fight announcer**; Paris Eagle **Fighter**; Simmy Bow **Club cornerman**; Billy Sands **Club fight announcer**; Kathleen Parker **Paulie's date**; Lloyd Kaufman **Drunk**; Joe Giambelluc **Street singer**; Peter Glassberg **Street singer**; William Ring **Street singer**; Robert Tangrea **Street singer**; Joe Frazier **Himself**; Butkus Stallone **Rocky's dog**

THE GAME A small-time Philadelphia club fighter, Rocky Balboa (Sylvester Stallone) is essentially an aimless 30-year-old man who pays the bills by working as a strong-arm collector for a local loan shark, Gazzo (Joe Spinell).

Rocky's pal Paulie (Burt Young), a drunken, bitter butcher shop worker, sets his friend up with his meek, withdrawn, bespectacled sister, Adrian (Talia Shire). She works in a pet shop and sold Rocky his pet turtles, Cuff and Link.

Rocky is managed by a crusty former boxer turned trainer and gym owner, Mickey (Burgess Meredith). Mickey has kept his mouth shut about his disappointment in Rocky's commitment to developing his pugilistic talents until Rocky is tossed out of his old locker to make room for a "up and comer." In a clear-the-air argument, Mickey tells Rocky, "You got heart but you fight like a goddamn ape.... Hey, kid, you ever think about retiring?...You think about it."

Rocky's small, lonely world opens a bit when the highly outgoing current heavyweight champion, Apollo Creed (Carl Weathers), is forced to choose another opponent when his scheduled challenger sustains an injury in training.

Creed comes up with the idea of giving a club fighter the ultimate dream, a shot at the heavyweight crown. He chooses Rocky's name from a boxing registry primarily because of the southpaw's nickname: "Apollo Creed meets the Italian Stallion. Sounds like a damn monster movie."

Adrian, who blossoms like a pretty flower as their love grows, become Rocky's biggest supporter. The sparks began to fly on their first date when he walks her around as she skates on an empty ice rink. When Adrian asks Rocky why he got into boxing he says his father told him he'd have to develop his body because he wasn't born with much brains—besides, "I can't sing or dance."

After some angry words, Rocky reconciles with Mickey, who trains Balboa hard for the big fight. Rocky's somewhat slow but he's not stupid. He's a realist. He looks at his situation objectively, and while he feels he can't overcome the champ's superior talent, he does aim for respect by trying to go the distance.

Mickey trains Rocky hard, getting the attention of Apollo's trainer (Tony Burton), but Creed proceeds with business details, unconcerned about this club fighter from Philadelphia.

Fight night. Huge crowd. Frenzied atmosphere. Appropriate to the Bicentennial celebrations of the times, the champ enters in a hybrid George Washington/Uncle Sam costume as Rocky looks on with amusement, hiding his nervousness.

Once the pre-fight hoopla dies down, Rocky surprises the champ, absorbing Creed's best blows and giving as well as taking. The champ's prediction of a third-round knock-out is soon out the door. Apollo realizes he's in for a long night. Rocky ends up going all 15 rounds, proving he's more than "just another bum from the neighborhood." Though he loses in a split decision, Rocky's made believers out of many skeptics. The film ends as he embraces Adrian in the ring and they declare their love for each other.

INSTANT REPLAY *Rocky* is a fairy tale superbly told: a love story set against the world of boxing. Part of its charm is in knowing that its Cinderella elements apply to its creator's life as well. Like Rocky Balboa, Sylvester Stallone's "million to one" shot took him from Hollywood obscurity to superstardom.

Stallone certainly had a lot of help from behind the camera, from savvy producers Irwin Winkler and Bob Chartoff and director John Avildsen among others, but it was Sylvester's passion for the project that infused the cast and crew and made a tiny $1 million-budget, 29-day shoot into a cinematic phenomenon that went on to earn over 50 times its original cost.

Nominated for 10 Academy Awards, *Rocky* won Oscars for Best Picture, Best Director, and Best Editing. Pretty good accomplishments for such a low-budget movie going up against the likes of *Network*, *Taxi Driver*, and *All the President's Men*. Like the title character, the film succeeded against the odds.

The script is filled with great dialogue and indelible characters. Focusing more on characters than plot, the screenplay is ably interpreted by a brilliant supporting cast of low-profile character actors. Burt Young as Talia's bitter, hard-drinking brother and Burgess Meredith's very realistic boxing trainer are part of a cast filled with memorable characterizations. Burt Young, Talia Shire, and Burgess Meredith all were nominated for Academy Awards, as was Stallone. Carl Weathers gives a fine Muhammad Ali-esque turn full of bravado as Apollo Creed.

The relationship between Stallone and Shire, two lonely people moving forward awkwardly, is reminiscent of Ernest Borgnine's performance in *Marty*.

In an Academy Award—winning stint, director John Avildsen exposes the characters' depressing, desperate little world and effectively captures big time boxing via groundbreaking use of the Steadicam, which is now a common tool of filmmakers today. Most of all, Avildsen works skillfully with a meager budget without compromising story details or the look and feel of the movie.

Richard Halsey and Scott Conrad's editing keep the action propelling at the right speed. James Crabe's photography is very resourceful in its use of lighting, particularly given his limited resources.

At times rousing and at other times soul-searing, the music of Bill Conti is key to the overall effect of the picture.

Producers Winkler and Chartoff, along with executive producer Gene Kirkwood and United Artists' Mike Medavoy, deserve credit for taking a chance on an unknown actor who happened to write a very touching story.

It's rare for a movie that wins a Best Picture Oscar to beget a franchise. Three of *Rocky*'s four sequels earned over $100 million each, and at press time a sixth installment, *Rocky Balboa*, is ready for distribution.

'Rocky' is a love story between a club fighter past his prime (Sylvester Stallone) and Adrian, a shy pet store clerk (Talia Shire).

Rocky is a stunning picture that combines entertaining boxing action, a sentimental love story, well-drawn characters, and a brilliant musical score.

While the Academy Awards, superstardom, and millions in box office receipts are fine rewards for Stallone's struggles, perhaps his greatest reward is the innumerable hearts he has inspired worldwide. *Rocky* is a cinematic landmark.

OUTSIDE THE LINES Though he was reportedly offered over a quarter-million dollars for his screenplay, the near-destitute Stallone settled for much less to star in the movie.... Among the candidates to play Rocky were James Caan, Burt Reynolds, Robert Redford, and Ryan O'Neal.... Oscar-winning Avildsen also directed *The Karate Kid* and rodeo's *8 Seconds*.... Garrett Brown invented the Steadicam in 1973 and used it again in Rocky II and V. He also invented the Skycam, which he used in baseball's *The Slugger's Wife* (1985).... Stallone's screenplay was inspired by watching journeyman heavyweight boxer Chuck Wepner hold his own fighting against Muhammad Ali.... Boxer Ken

Norton turned down the role of Apollo Creed to appear in ABC's athletic competition program *Superstars*.... The familiar story of Stallone writing the Rocky script in three days is a bit misleading, as even the author admitted that only about 10% of that version appeared in the final film and he rewrote nearly 300 pages.... Producer Winkler directed *Night and the City* (1992), a remake of the 1950 wrestling film starring Richard Widmark. The remake starred Robert DeNiro.... Stallone received an athletic scholarship to the American College in Switzerland before returning to study drama at the University of Miami.... Oscar-winning editor Richard Halsey also worked on *That Championship Season* (1982), *Jocks* (1987), and *Eddie* (1996).... Burt Young starred in the female wrestling picture *All the Marbles* (1981).... Stallone starred in the John Huston soccer film *Victory* (1981).... Carl Weathers, a fine athlete who had played professional football, tried to tell the producers he had boxing experience and had been a club fighter in Canada, figuring that it would be hard to track that fact down. He was found out when they had him work out at a gym, but he got the part anyway and trained many hours with Stallone, who, taking the suggestion of director Avildsen, choreographed the whole fight punch by punch.... Stallone wrote and starred in an arm-wrestling movie, *Over the Top*, and the Renny Harlin auto racing drama *Driven* (2001).... Stallone's brother, father, and dog, Butkus, all appear in *Rocky*.... His first wife, Sasha, was the unit photographer.... Weathers appeared in *Semi-Tough* (1978) and *Happy Gilmore* (1996).... Actor Burt Young was a former boxer.... Besides Hollywood's boxing movies, Stallone studied tapes of boxers Rocky Marciano and Ezzard Charles.... The producers put up their houses to guarantee the film's completion.... Avildsen returned to direct *Rocky V* (1990).... Talia Shire starred in the BMX motorcycle film *Rad* (1986) and made her feature film debut in the auto racing movie *The Wild Racers* (1968).... Stallone appeared earlier in another auto racing film, *Death Race 2000* (1975).... Besides the Rocky series Winkler and Chartoff also produced *Raging Bull* (1980).... Makeup artist Michael Westmore also worked on *Raging Bull* (1980).... Lee Strasberg was also up for the role of Mickey.... With the exception of the Philly pet shop, most of the interiors were shot in Los Angeles.... The original Rocky character was a dark, unrepentant boxer who throws the fight.... Martin Scorsese was a NYU film student who worked on one of Avildsen's shorts.

ALL-STAR MOMENTS

Opening title as "Rocky" moves across the screen over the riveting music theme.

Mickey (Meredith) dresses down Rocky (Stallone) for wasting his potential, saying, "Hey, kid, you ever think about retiring?...You think about it."

Later Mickey continues his diatribe, telling Rocky he's wasted his fight talents by being a "leg breaker to some second-rate loan shark."

ROCKY: It's a living.

MICKEY: It's a waste of life.

Rocky vents his anger back at Mickey, who later ventures to his apartment to ask to be Rocky's trainer for the big fight. Rocky exclaims, "Ten years before he comes to my house. Huh? What's the matter, you don't like my house? My house stink? That's right it stinks!"

Training montage ending with Rocky running up the steps of the Philadelphia Art Museum.

Sequence of Rocky pounding a slab of meat for a live TV report. Apollo's trainer

(Burton) expresses concern watching it on television, but Creed (Weathers) is more concerned about making sure his hairstylist shows up.

The final frame: Rocky hugging Adrian (Shire).

POST-GAME COMMENTS Director John Avildsen on preparing for the boxing scenes:

> I looked at a lot of movies and found the boxing looked pretty phony. I realized the only way this was going to look any different was if we practiced a lot. I got the producers to get us some time and put the shooting at the end of the schedule. So I had about six to seven weeks to get it together. At the first day of rehearsals when Sylvester and Carl got into the ring I said, "Well I do this and I'll do that." I realized we'd be there all day doing nothing so I suggested to Sylvester that he go home and write the thing out. I said, "Bring back what you want and we'll learn it like a ballet." The next day he came back with 32 pages of lefts and rights and that's what we learned. It's a very precise thing that takes lots of rehearsing. Somebody's hand goes up and the other guy's head has got to go back.[1]

Sylvester Stallone on why he held out to be the film's lead:

> As far as I was concerned, if I didn't get this part it was the only shot I'd ever get. I was willing to do it for nothing if I got the chance. No way would it turn out poorly. I was determined it would be good.[2]

Adds Avildsen:

> One of the best things about *Rocky* was that Sylvester Stallone was a starving actor. Nothing like a starving actor. They're always on time, appreciative, and open.3

The director illustrates Stallone's openness to suggestions:

> Sylvester wrote the script but told me one time he rewrote about 300 pages. We were always changing to make it better. For instance, Rocky and Adrian's first date was initially written to take place at a restaurant. I said, "You don't want them sitting at a table for five to six pages of dialogue. That's really boring, maybe bowling or ice skating." We realized we couldn't do ice skating because we couldn't afford the extras so they said to put it back in the restaurant, but I said maybe they went ice skating but the place was closed and that's why there was nobody there. Sylvester liked that idea so we made the adjustments.[4]

Producer Irwin Winkler on the film's theme:

> This film isn't a prizefight drama. It was in the tradition of the classic Frank Capra films: a good man with courage and spirit who overcomes all obstacles.[5]

HOME COURT ADVANTAGE Available on VHS and DVD. MGM has released several versions on DVD, including: 25th Anniversary Edition; high-def version; six-disc anthology; five-disc box set.

#6 OLYMPIA

Screenwriter/Director Leni Riefenstahl. **Producers** Leni Riefenstahl, Walter Traut. **Cinematography** Hans Ertl, Walter Rentz, Gustav Lantschner, Heinz von Jaworsky, Kurt Neubert, Hans Scheib. **Editing** Leni Riefenstahl, Max Michel, Johannes Ludke, Arnfried Heyne. **Music** Herbert Wind, Walter Gronostay. Excelsior. 1938. (USA, 1940)

THE GAME Leni Riefenstahl presents the official film of the 1936 Berlin Olympics in a 220-minute, two-part epic.

Part 1, Fest der Volker (Festival of the People), begins with a prologue incorporating the distinctive architecture and godlike athletes of ancient Greece and transitioning to modern-day athletes and Deutsches Stadium for the start of the Games of the XIth Olympiad.

The parade of nations at the opening ceremonies introduces the crowd to the nearly 4,000 athletes from 49 countries. After the cauldron is lit and Adolf Hitler announces the official opening, the film proceeds with the competition.

A narrator escorts us through the highlights of various athletic disciplines. From a wide range of camera angles and speeds, Riefenstahl shows not only the sport but also close-ups of the athletes' concentration, reaction shots of individuals in the crowd, and of course the athletes' expressions as they win or lose.

The filmmaker uses this format to cover men and women in such track events as the throws (javelin, discus, hammer, and shot put), the jumps (triple, high, and long), the hurdles and sprints, and middle distance and relay races.

For the coverage of the marathon, the filmmaker incorporates assorted iso shots from head to toe that show the runners' pain and tenacity.

In Part 2, Fest der Schönheit (Festival of Beauty), Leni Reifenstahl opens with the serene images of athletes in a nature setting, jogging around and swimming in a pond.

Life inside the athletes' village instantly conveys the diversity of sports and nations as we see a broad assortment of athletes practicing their various disciplines.

The filmmaker then captures the gymnastics held outdoors at Deutsches Stadium. From there she takes to the water, showing the surprisingly frenzied various classifications of the yachting competition.

Modern Pentathlon is next and it's clear that the five-discipline sport, involving horse riding, fencing, shooting, running, and swimming, is dominated by military officers.

Back to the track. The decathlon and its 10 discipline components are shown primarily through the performance of Glenn Morris, who would win the event. (Indeed, the U.S. would sweep the medals in this event.)

As the Americans dominated track, India dominated field hockey, crushing host Germany for the gold medal.

After brief highlights of soccer and road cycling, Riefenstahl breaks from the intense competition to present the lighter (but also dangerous) side of equestrian. There is a sequence of various falls during the three days of the riding competition.

Following the water sports of rowing and swimming, Riefenstahl concludes the competition coverage with a most lyrical look at diving. Delivering the action through majestic ground-to-sky angles and slow motion mixed with reverse motion, this decidedly poetic treatment of the sport is clearly less about the competition and more symbolic of the artistry of human movement.

Coming to the cavalcade of the nations' flags at the main stadium and the dimming of the Olympic flame, the rising smoke takes us to the ends of the beacons of lights symbolically concluding the Berlin Games.

INSTANT REPLAY Over 60 years later *Olympia* remains the standard of a sport film in its combination of cinema aesthetics and the artistry of athletic performance.

Just about all sports presentation in the visual realm is indebted to *Olympia* to some degree. Coverage techniques such as tracking cameras following sprinters, ditches to capture ground-level action of jumpers, and going underwater to observe the divers breaking the surface are groundbreaking.

Most significant of all the film's innovations is the personalization of the competitors. Zooming in on the faces—the exhaustion of the rowers, the quiet determination of marathoner Kitei Son, the confidence and pride of Jesse Owens, all enhanced by the reaction shots of individual members of the diverse crowds—puts a very human feel to the majestic proceedings.

Unfortunately, because of the filmmakers' unquestionable ties to the Nazis, *Olympia* will always be somewhat controversial. Riefenstahl, who directed the fascist propaganda film *Triumph of the Will*, was only able to create *Olympia* with considerable financing by the Ministry of Propaganda, even though the mutual dislike between Riefenstahl and Joseph Goebbels is well chronicled.

To her credit, though, especially in light of these circumstances, Riefenstahl succeeds in the difficult task of making an Olympic film largely devoid of nationalistic propaganda.

Coincidentally, the modern Olympics and motion pictures began in the same year, 1896.

Since the first Olympic film, all host countries have taken advantage of the built-in

LEFT: 'Olympia' is divided into two parts: Fest der Volker (Festival of the People) and Fest der Schonheit (Festival of Beauty).

propaganda opportunities Olympic films offer. Whether it's Russia, Korea, the United States, or China, it is natural for a country to want to hide its warts and show its "good" side as it presents itself under the global spotlight.

In pure cinematic terms, it is unfortunate that when *Olympia* is viewed in hindsight, the screen time given to Nazi salutes, flags, and Hitler himself (though relatively brief in a nearly four-hour film) sadly casts a looming shadow over Riefenstahl's paean to athletic artistry.

Certainly there are some interpretive questions around the prologue sequences of the godlike ancient Greek athletes as they might relate to the Nazi myth of Aryan supremacy, but in presenting the actual competition Riefenstahl is very evenhanded. Blacks, women, and Asians are given just as much attention as white males. If one star emerged from the record it would be Jesse Owens. One can be sure that Riefenstahl's "United Nations" approach in presenting the beauty of humanity and its highest aspirations didn't improve her relationship with Joseph Goebbels.

Though the political aspect will always be an issue when assessing her work, Leni Riefenstahl's filmmaking talents are undeniable. Credit must also go to Arnold Franck, who directed Riefenstahl the actress in the so-called "mountain pictures" during the 1920s. It was in her work with Franck that the future director learned the clever camera placements and evocative use of light and shadows that became so much a part of her style.

By incorporating her various film experiences in Olympia, Leni Riefenstahl idealizes the spirit of the Olympics, capturing its drama and humanity with a poetic style that is unparalleled. Like the best art, Olympia has a timeless quality.

OUTSIDE THE LINES A former dancer and painter, Riefenstahl performed in front of the camera as well, most notably in Arnold Franck's mountain-themed pictures of the 1920s.... Over a million feet of film, over 200 hours of footage was shot by 40 cameramen for *Olympia*.... It took over a year and a half to edit.... The opening of the Games was photographed from the Zeppelin Hindenburg.... Riefenstahl also used cameras in the air attached to balloons with instructions attached so that when they landed, their locators could return them.... Photographers would jump into the water to follow the swimming and diving action.... Much of the sound such as runners' footsteps, jumpers landing, and divers breaking the surface were synchronized and even enhanced during editing.... Though some financing was provided through a distribution deal, primary funding for *Olympia* came through Germany's Ministry of Finance in conjunction with the Ministry for Popular Enlightenment and Propaganda.... After World War II Riefenstahl was imprisoned for taking an active part in the Nazi propaganda machine, most notably her Nazi party film, *Triumph of the Will*.... The International Olympic Committee owns all the rights and film footage of *Olympia*.

ABOVE: Adolf Hitler at the Olympic track and field competition.

FACING PAGE: Jesse Owens won four gold medals as the African-American athletes, winners of 14 medals altogether, dominated track and field at the 1936 Berlin Olympics.

ALL-STAR MOMENTS Relay racer runs along the beach.

Inside Berlin Stadium. Pan shot of crowd and flags flying on upper rim to music of trumpets.

Lit cauldron against the sun, followed by a shot of the tip of the flames as we see the Olympic rings above the stadium. Fade out.

Olympics rings suspended between two columns against the clouds outside Berlin's Deutsches Stadium.

Men's 100-meter final. Assorted tight shots of competitors in starting position. Jesse Owens swallows and looks down the track. He is victorious.

Men's 800-meter final. Good camera action in tight race between America's Woodruff and Italy's Lanzi. Reaction shots of American and Italian fans waving their nation's flags.

Men's triple jump. Tajima of Japan. Dramatic music as camera captures his record-setting jump. Award ceremony.

Marathon. High-angle shot of runners leaving the stadium followed later by an announcer standing in the street with a live update.

Ring exercises in gymnastics. Outdoors. Tight shot looking up pitting the competitor against the sky. Capacity crowd looking on.

Field hockey. Slow-motion sequence of German goalie defending onslaught by India in the gold medal match.

Equestrian. Three-day riding competition. Camera follows various competitors with different results over the water jump.

Rowing. Brilliant tight shots of the men's eight-oared shell as coxswain barks through megaphone.

Diving. Camera makes divers look like birds in flight, framing them against the sky.

HOME COURT ADVANTAGE Available on VHS. Available in limited DVD version. Check potential sources listed under Additional Resources.

#5 RAGING BULL

Screenwriters Paul Schrader, Mardik Martin. (Based on a book by Jake LaMotta with Joseph Carter and Peter Savage.) **Director** Martin Scorsese. **Producers** Robert Chartoff, Irwin Winkler. **Cinematography** Michael Chapman. **Music** Robbie Robertson. **Production Design** Bill Kenney, Gene Rudolf. **Editor** Thelma Schoonmaker. United Artists. 1980.

THE PLAYERS Robert DeNiro **Jake LaMotta**; Cathy Moriarty **Vickie LaMotta**; Joe Pesci **Joey LaMotta**; Frank Vincent **Salvy**; Nicholas Colasanto **Tommy Como**; Theresa Saldana **Lenore**; Frank Adonis **Patsy**; Johnny Barnes **Sugar Ray Robinson**; Bill Hanrahan **Eddie Eagan**; Kevin Mahon **Tony Janiro**; Ed Gregory **Billy Fox**; Floyd Anderson **Jimmy Reeves**; Don Dunphy **Radio announcer**; Mario Gallo **Mario**; Frank Topham **Toppy**; James Christy **Dr. Pinto**; Bill Mazer **Reporter**; Bernie Allen **Comedian**; Lori Anne Flax **Irma**; Joseph Bono **Guido**; Rita Bennett **Emma**; Johnny Turner **Laurent Dauthuille**; Louis Raftis **Marcel Cerdan**

THE GAME *Raging Bull* is a brutal, uncompromising character study of Bronx-born boxer Jake LaMotta. Covering the period from the early 1940s to the mid '60s, director Martin Scorsese presents a riveting and graphic deconstruction of an unlikable man driven by internal demons.

Robert DeNiro portrays LaMotta, whose goal is to become the middleweight champion of the world. The film captures the rise, fall, and redemption of the hardheaded prizefighter. The rage and violence that propel him through the jungle of professional boxing don't stop when the bell rings.

The picture opens with an over-the-hill LaMotta practicing his 1960s nightclub act, then flashes back to 1940s New York as his fighting career ascends the ranks. Trim and fit, Jake doesn't just win his bouts, he beats opponents bloody, consumed by a violent need to give as well as take enormous punishment.

LaMotta is managed by his brother, Joey (Joe Pesci), and despite continued pressure from the local Mafia, Jake refuses to work with them, hoping to earn a title shot honestly. The mobsters don't give up, befriending Joey.

One day Jake spots a young blonde (Cathy Moriarty) sitting with the very mobsters he disdains. Despite the fact that she is still a teenager and he's married, Jake proceeds to seduce Vickie and eventually discards his wife to marry her.

Home movies that include honeymoon and vacation shots paint a happy family picture but the reality soon becomes very different.

Eventually Jake succumbs to mob pressure and takes a dive in order to get a title shot. The unconvincing performance nearly costs him his career, tainting an otherwise clean reputation. After nearly being ousted from the sport, LaMotta wins several hard-fought battles and finally the championship title.

Now at the peak of his game, LaMotta begins a downward spiral that ends up costing him a lot more than any dive. He loses the discipline he had, refusing to train and gaining lots of weight. He fights his wife and brother/manager constantly, battering them physically and emotionally.

When his wife innocently comments that his next opponent, Tony Janiro (Kevin Mahon), is an "up and comer and good lookin,' " Jake shows his inability to trust himself or others and asks his brother if Vickie is sleeping around. Joey calls him crazy and Jake becomes a little less trusting in his brother.

Fighting Janiro, LaMotta smashes his face so badly that a mob boss sitting ringside

Robert DeNiro won an Academy Award for Best Actor as troubled boxer Jake LaMotta.

states, "He ain't pretty no more," as Jake glares over at his wife.

Jake loses his title and moves the family to Florida, where he runs his own nightclub. The Sunshine State, however, doesn't prevent LaMotta's dark side from dominating his behavior.

Grossly overweight, boorish, and consumed by jealousy of his wife's supposed infidelities, Jake still manages to sleep around himself, and is eventually arrested on a morals charge. Vickie files for divorce and Jake is left alone in a dark jail cell to confront his demons.

The movie ends with LaMotta back in New York dressed in a tuxedo in a dressing room rehearsing his performance. Getting ready for his dramatic readings act, LaMotta stares at his bloated self in the mirror and blankly recites the "I coulda been a contender" scene from *On the Waterfront,* musing on the parallels between Brando's Terry Malloy and himself.

Scorsese closes with a graphic from a biblical passage to infer Jake's keener insight: "Once I was blind and now I can see."

INSTANT REPLAY The filmmakers provide a haunting portrait of a boxer whose violent nature nearly destroys him and those close to him. As LaMotta, DeNiro works hard to make sure that viewers, while perhaps not sympathetic toward him, at least understand the forces that led the boxer to struggle for a way out of the emotional damnation his brutal nature has created. The boxer's biggest opponent inside or out of the ring is himself. *Raging Bull* is about a flawed redemption.

DeNiro dramatically illustrates Jake's realization that he's his own worst enemy as he shadowboxes his demons, slamming his head, fists, and arms against a jail cell wall. Amid the pain he discovers a new self-awareness, crying out to himself, "Why? Why? Why?…Why'd you do it? Why? You're so stupid…. I'm not an animal. Why do you treat me like this? I'm not so bad."

DeNiro's performance, a complete characterization, required an amazing transformation covering a quarter-century in cinematic time. His preparation for the role included over 1,000 rounds of boxing and gaining over 50 pounds. Leaving no question about his ability to "become" the person he is acting, DeNiro won a well-deserved Oscar for this role.

Despite being married, LaMotta is instantly smitten by young Vickie (Cathy Moriarity).

Michael Chapman's black and white photography and framing really bring out the violence in the boxing sequences, providing a particularly stark, disturbing documentary feel. Interspersed are color home movies clearly trying to project a happy, "colorful" home life, but the return to black and white reveals a naked and opposite truth.

Though the fight scenes add up to about just about 10 minutes of the film's screen time, their visceral impact goes well beyond that. The complex choreographed camera moves, slow motion, out-of-focus shots, freeze frames, and flashing camera bulbs—along with the sonic boom sound of punches landing, the crowd roaring, and a music score that mirrors the on-screen action—provide a masterful left/right audiovisual combination that effectively puts the viewer in the ring feeling the punishment Jakes takes and gives out.

While boxing is the arena and brutal close-ups of devastating punches show us LaMotta's world in the ring, *Raging Bull* is more about a man whose rage, violence, paranoia, and jealousy are the driving forces of his life inside and outside the ropes.

What seems to be missing from this complex character study is any real understanding of what shaped LaMotta's personality. Most of the defining moments of his youth and family are not provided or explained to help the audience. Perhaps that is intentional.

Raging Bull is part of a group of fine Hollywood movies that use the darker side of boxing to tell their story. DeNiro's LaMotta is more Kirk Douglas's "Champion" than Sylvester Stallone's "Rocky" in this cold, unflinching look at the violence, mob influence, and rage that haunted one boxer, in and out of the ring.

OUTSIDE THE LINES Robert DeNiro accidentally broke one of Joe Pesci's ribs in a sparring scene…. The director's father, Charles, appears in the film as a mobster sitting with the LaMottas at a nightclub table…. Nicholas Colansanto played Coach on *Cheers* and appeared in the boxing film *Fat City* (1972)…. Though only accounting for 10 minutes of screen time, the complex boxing sequences took six weeks to film…. Editor Thelma Schoonmaker won an Academy Award…. Scorsese used sponges concealed in gloves and tiny tubes in the boxers' hair to deliver spurts and beads of sweat and blood…. To show up better in a black and white film, Hershey's chocolate was used for blood…. Jake LaMotta appeared as a bartender in *The Hustler*….

Cinematographer Michael Chapman would make his directorial debut with *All the Right Moves*.... Joe Pesci had dropped out of acting for five years and was running a restaurant in New York before DeNiro and Scorsese asked him to join them in *Raging Bull*, having seen his performance in a B movie, *The Death Collector*.... Some say LaMotta's story—tough upbringing on the streets of New York, limited education, tremendous ring presence, a troubled life outside it, and an overall roller-coaster career— has eerie parallels to Mike Tyson's.... John Turturro made his film debut in this movie.... The production famously shut down so DeNiro could gain over 50 pounds by eating his way across Europe in his favorite restaurants.... DeNiro had wanted to make a movie on LaMotta ever since reading his book, but it took years for the actor to convince Scorsese to direct it.... The studios weren't excited initially either, as producer Winkler got a green light only after withholding the sequel to the highly successful *Rocky* as part of a deal.... The fight scenes were shot at the Los Angeles Auditorium.

ALL-STAR MOMENTS LaMotta's degradation is summed up in a scene where he has to beg his soon-to-be ex-wife to let him into his soon-to-be-ex-house so that he can hawk his champion boxing belt for bribe money to stay out of jail for a morals charge. As he proceeds to hammer out the jewels from the belt, Vickie asks him why he just doesn't get a loan from his friends. Jake retorts, "What friends?"

Moments later a jeweler informs him that an intact champion's boxing belt is rarer and worth a lot more than the jewels in it. LaMotta goes to jail.

After suffering a tremendous beating by Sugar Ray Robinson, a horrendously battered and bloodied LaMotta staggers over to his opponent's corner and says, "Ray. Hey Ray. I never went down. You never got me down, Ray."

As the ring announcer enters and states the winner by TKO, there's a very graphic close-up showing Jake's blood dripping off the ropes.

POST-GAME COMMENTS Documentary filmmaker Ken Burns on *Raging Bull*:

> In boxing there's this sense of elemental triumph that "I can rise up," and when you have it in the hands of someone like Scorsese you're talking about art. *Raging Bull* to me is still the standard by which all [boxing movies] are judged.[1]

Veteran sports film writer/director and boxing enthusiast Ron Shelton on *Raging Bull*:

> It was great artists working at their height. You have the best people. Pesci was a discovery. Moriarty was a discovery as well. I think the artistry was so high that it just sort of took people on a trip they normally wouldn't go on otherwise.[2]

HBO boxing analyst Jim Lampley on why this film stood out for him:

> I think one thing about *Raging Bull* that makes the movie special is the filmmaker (Scorsese) is a great enough filmmaker that he knows, I'm sure Scorsese knows, his in-the-ring scenes do not portray in a literal sense what boxing is.

DeNiro trained for months and sparred hundreds of rounds to bring realism to his portrayal.

That what happens in the ring in *Raging Bull* is absurdist extremism. As absurdist extremism it more powerfully underlines the point of what happens to this man than what would be the case if he had aped reality the way most boxing movies do. This wasn't really a piece of realism so much as it was an operatic psychological crescendo.

It is so compelling, it is almost like watching *A Clockwork Orange*. Every punch lands and every punch brings sweat and blood flying. Boxing isn't like that, but on the other hand as a life experience in this man's life (LaMotta) it certainly was.

That part is great along with the portrayal and the totally unsentimental approach. There is no happy ending in a life like that.

I love everything about *Raging Bull*—the honesty, the proper choice of black and white. It is a totally uncompromising film.

Most fight films don't explore the protagonist's experience beyond his life in the ring. By doing just that Scorsese sort of reinforces the overall point that this isn't a movie about boxing, this is a movie about life.[3]

The film's coproducer Irwin Winkler points out that *Raging Bull* was not an "instant classic":

Well, it's interesting because the picture was not well received and didn't receive great reviews. It never got big business and it's only over time that people are finding the picture as important as they are. At the time they certainly didn't feel that way.[4]

The relationship between Vickie and Jake was a rocky one.

Bert Sugar, former editor of *Ring Magazine*, recalls the critical reaction when the film premiered:

> Initially critics were puzzled by it. I don't think they came out against it. It was more, "Why are we bothering with this man?"[5]

Winkler on what he feels set this film apart:

> *Raging Bull* was very different from any other fight film inasmuch as it got under the skin and humanized the character, whose life was basically very violent. You could understand what made him tick and why he was what he was. I don't think that's the only film that did that. I thought the Kirk Douglas film, *Champion*, did it very well; so did *Somebody Up There Likes Me*. I think each of them got us behind the character and got us to understand what motivated them to do what they did. I think that is the principal success of *Raging Bull*. We understand this very violent man named Jake LaMotta. What made him tick, what motivated him.[6]

HOME COURT ADVANTAGE Available on VHS and DVD. In addition to twice releasing the film as a single, MGM has released a two-disc DVD with a wealth of inside features and extras. It is also available in a Martin Scorsese DVD box set.

#4 CHARIOTS OF FIRE

Screenwriter Colin Welland. **Director** Hugh Hudson. **Producer** David Puttnam. **Executive Producer** Dodi Fayed. **Cinematography** Davis Watkins. **Editing** Terry Rawlings. **Music** Vangelis. **Art Direction** Roger Hall. **Costume Design** Milena Canonero. Fox. 1981.

THE PLAYERS Ben Cross **Harold Abrahams**; Ian Charleson **Eric Liddell**; Nigel Havers **Lord Andrew Lindsay**; Nicholas Farrell **Aubrey Montague**; Iam Holm **Sam Mussabini**; John Gielgud **Master of Trinity**; Lindsay Anderson **Master of Caius**; Nigel Davenport **Lord Birkenhead**; Cheryl Campbell **Jennie Liddell**; Alice Krige **Sybil Gordon**; Dennis Christopher **Charles Paddock**; Brad Davis **Jackson Scholz**; Struan Roger **Sandy McGrath**; David Yelland **Prince of Wales**; Patrick Magee **Lord Cadogan**; Gerry Slevin **Colonel John Keddie**

THE GAME Based on true events, *Chariots of Fire* is the story of a group of British athletes and their road to the 1924 Olympics. Though several athletes are featured, the story really centers on the trials, tribulations, and triumphs of two runners striving to achieve their dreams. These two men's lives and different backgrounds are interwoven in the film as they train separately for the Paris Olympics. They're fueled by different motivations but connected by religion.

What begins as a classic conflict of man against man evolves into an examination of inner strength, as the two runners must find victory in being true to their own hearts and beliefs.

Eric Liddell (Ian Charleson) is a dedicated Scottish Christian who runs for the glory of Jesus and who believes Christ is his trainer. His sister, Jennie (Cheryl Campbell), believes this running comes at the cost of their religious commitments. Harold Abrahams (Ben Cross), an English Jew, is practically paranoid about prejudice. His main motivation is to be accepted. He hires a professional trainer (Ian Holm), which alone gets Harold into trouble with his anti-Semitic Cambridge master (John Gielgud). Liddell believes he has to succeed as a testament to his undying religious faith while the nonpracticing Abrahams feels that his religion is a heavy weight on his shoulders, subjecting him to discrimination at every turn, and that an Olympic medal would be vindication. Both compete under the British flag but neither is really driven by patriotism. One man feels he has to succeed because he is Jewish and the other man feels he has to succeed because God has given him the power to do so. Both share the drive for excellence.

INSTANT REPLAY *Chariots of Fire* scores highest in character development, slowly and carefully taking the audiences through the main characters' motives, challenges, feelings, and behavior. Ben Cross's fine portrayal of Harold Abrahams and his drive for acceptance and success is best exemplified at the end of a meeting with his schoolmasters, who have derided him for hiring a professional coach and pursuing individual glory. Abrahams gets up to leave and says:

> The evening has been most illuminating. You know, gentlemen, you yearn for victory as I do. But achieved with the apparent effortlessness of Gods. Yours are the archaic values of the prep school playground. You deceive no one but yourselves. I believe in the relentless pursuit of excellence and I'll carry the future with me.

Ian Charleson's cool grace as Eric Liddell is exemplified where the camera intercuts between him singing in a church service and winning a sprint race, where we see a poster promoting his speaking engagement after the meet has concluded. To the crowd gathered outside the track in the rain, Eric speaks about the similarities between running and religious faith: "The power to run the race to the end comes from within. Jesus said, 'The Kingdom of God is within you.' "

Liddell has grown up knowing of a spirit within that gives us the desire to become more than we are in ourselves and helps us achieve what we could not have done on our own. "So where does the power to succeed come from?" he asks repeatedly in his speeches. "It comes from within."

In the end Liddell appears to have a more fulfilling satisfaction, for his Olympic victory was tied to his relationship with God. Abrahams, on the other hand, conveys to the audience a lack of lasting contentment because ultimately there's nothing beyond himself that he can depend on. He discovers that while becoming an Olympic champion is good, it isn't the complete elixir he thought it would be. His celebration with his trainer in the bar illustrates a certain hollowness. (Veteran stage performer Ian Holm's role as coach Sam Mussabini earned him an Oscar nomination.)

Colin Welland's Oscar-winning script is comparatively free of clichés and proves

that the making of a good sports film doesn't necessarily demand a love of sports but rather an appreciation of the understanding of human nature.

The film's running scenes—with the athletes jogging on the beach in St. Andrews, racing around the Cambridge courtyard, competing in the Olympic events, and running impromptu races in the Scottish countryside—are beautifully photographed by David Watkin. The Olympic sequence conveys a fine sense of verisimilitude as well as a refreshing look back at an era of a more chivalrous competitive environment.

Certainly the running scenes are enhanced by the music, which plays a pivotal role in the film as a whole. While some critics argue that Vangelis's electro-technical sound doesn't match the historical period of the story, it does manage to magically create one of the most important elements of the film: the inner fire of the runners. The theme music near the opening and repeated at the end of the credits as the athletes run along the beach are indelible sights and sounds for any movie fan.

Hugh Hudson's direction is excellent, especially considering that this was his feature debut. Milena Canonero won an Academy Award for her evocative costume designs. Terry Rawlings' editing work keeps the picture running at a good pace. Much credit goes to producer David Puttnam for providing a strong infrastructure for these artists to work from.

Chariots of Fire reveals a truth about humanity's need to become more than we are in ourselves. It uses religion and intense physical training as examples of ways to find that elusive spirit within all of us that can take us beyond where we thought we could go. "So where does the power to succeed come from?...It comes from within." The

TOP: School officials: Master of Trinity (John Gielgud, left) and Master of Caius (Lindsay Anderson).

BOTTOM: Ian Holm earned an Oscar nomination for his portrayal of track coach Sam Mussabini.

LEFT: The determined Abrahams (Cross, left) hires renowned coach Sam Mussabini (Ian Holm) to make him a champion sprinter.

FACING PAGE: Jennie Liddell (Cheryl Campbell) feels that her brother Eric (Ian Charleson) is losing his commitment to their faith. The sprinter tells her that to win is to honor God and that he will rejoin her at the mission in China after he competes in the Olympics.

story, performances, design, and music are terrific team players in a film that lyrically demonstrates the triumph of the human spirit.

OUTSIDE THE LINES

Winner of four Academy Awards (Best Picture, Screenplay, Music, and Costume Design) and nominated for three others, *Chariots of Fire* also won the British Film Academy Award for Best Picture, supporting actor (Ian Holm), and costume design.... It surprisingly won the Oscar for Best Picture by beating out *Atlantic City, On Golden Pond, Raiders of the Lost Ark*, and *Reds*.... In real life the runners studied at Cambridge University, but the school prohibited location shooting within its hallowed halls so alternative sights had to be selected.... *Chariots of Fire* marked Hugh Hudson's feature film directorial debut after working in the London ad world.... Dodi Fayed, son of mega-millionaire Mohammed Al Fayed, was executive producer of the film.... More involved with financing than creative input as a film producer, his credits include *Breaking Glass, Hook*, and *F/X*.... Dodi is perhaps best known for his relationship with Princess Diana. They both died in a car accident after dining together in Paris in 1997.... One of the theatre's greatest performers, John Gielgud also performed in over 50 films.... Ironically Gielgud's only Oscar came in 1981 for his portrayal of Dudley Moore's butler in *Arthur*.... One of the nominees he beat out was fellow *Chariots* cast member Ian Holm (Sam Mussabini).... Milena Canonero won an Academy Award for her costume design work on *Chariots of Fire* as well as for *Barry Lyndon* six years earlier.... Producer David Puttnam's film credits include *Midnight Express* and *The Killing Fields* as well as a stint as head of Columbia Pictures.

ALL-STAR MOMENTS Opening/closing credit scenes of athletes running as a group along the beach to Vangelis's theme music.

Ben Cross addressing his schoolmasters about the use of a professional coach.

> **ERIC LIDDELL: I believe God made me for a purpose, but he also made me fast. And when I run I feel his pleasure.**

> **ERIC LIDDELL: Where does the power come from to see the race to the end? It comes from within.**

The slow-motion cinematography from the various Olympic races.

HOME COURT ADVANTAGE Available on VHS and DVD. Warner Bros. has released this film on DVD in three different versions. A two-disc anniversary edition has several extra features. The most recent is a massive "Best Oscar" edition that includes 17 other Best Picture winners.

TOP: Abrahams dines with theater performer Sybil Gordon (Alice Krige).

BOTTOM: 1924 Olympics. Paris. Opening ceremonies.

LEFT: With the help of Lord Lindsay, English authorities find a way around Liddell's religious commitment that prevents him from competing on Sundays.

FACING PAGE: Lord Andrew Lindsay (Nigel Havers) has a small lead over Harold Abrahams (Ben Cross) during their sprint in the college courtyard.

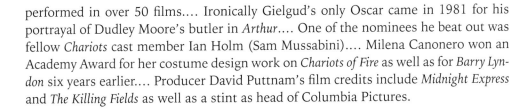

#3 THIS SPORTING LIFE

Screenwriter David Storey. **Director** Lindsay Anderson. **Producer** Karel Reisz. **Cinematography** Denys Coop. **Editing** Peter Taylor. **Music** Roberto Gerhard. **Sound Editing** Chris Greenham. **Art Direction** Alan Withy. Continental. 1963.

THE PLAYERS

Richard Harris **Frank Machin**; Rachel Roberts **Mrs. Hammond**; Alan Badel **Mr. Weaver**; William Hartnell **Johnson**; Colin Blakely **Maurice Braithwaite**; Anne Cunningham **Judith**; Vanda Godsell **Mrs. Weaver**; Jack Watson **Len Miller**; Arthur Lowe **Slomer**; Harry Markham **Wade**; George Sewell **Jeff**; Leonard Rossiter **Phillips**; Bernadette Benson **Lynda**; Katharine Parr **Mrs. Farrer**; Andrew Nolan **Ian**; Murray Evans **Hooker**; Michael Logan **Riley**; Peter Duguid **Doctor**; Frank Windsor **Dentist**; Tom Clegg **Gower**; John Gill **Cameron**; Wallas Eaton **Waiter**; Anthony Woodruff **Waiter**; Edward Fox **Restaurant barman**; Helen Shapiro **Nightclub singer**

THE GAME Frank Machin (Richard Harris) is a brawny, inarticulate former miner who uses his physical prowess to achieve a better socioeconomic standing as a star player in professional rugby.

Through his punishing efforts, Frank has earned the roar of the crowd, women, and comparatively great money, yet even with all the outer signs of success, his dissatisfaction with his personal life remains.

Despite his new affluence, Machin lives in the same rented room as when he was a poor miner. This is because the rugby hero is in love with his landlady, Mrs. Hammond (Rachel Roberts), a widow with two children. Unfortunately for him, the widow is emotionally unavailable, still tormented by the anguish of feeling at least partly responsible for her husband's death, an apparent suicide.

It doesn't help that everything Frank has gained in life has been won by blunt, brutal frontal assaults, on and off the field, so he applies the same technique to any obstacle he faces. Mrs. Hammond finds Frank's crudeness and aggressive approach repulsive. Though he shows a softer, childlike quality in his playfulness with her children, Frank's attempts at "buying" her heart with fancy clothes and meals at fine restaurants backfire as she is repulsed by his extravagance and his uncouth behavior when they dine out.

Frank continues to persevere, sensing that Mrs. Hammond's high-horse moralism is a shell. At one point she gives in to him physically but not emotionally. She is now concerned about what the neighbors think. Frank doesn't care what the neighbors think and proposes marriage. Mrs. Hammond continues to resist, and despite seeing the gruff jock's tenderness she rejects him with cold-hearted, unsmiling candor and sharp words. They have awful rows.

As Frank experiences the fickleness of the fans in a game where jeers replace cheers at the drop of a ball and management treats its athletes like livestock, he turns his enormous energies even more fully to the arena of love, mounting a desperate, all-out effort to win Mrs. Hammond's heart.

The rugby star's obsession with conquering this irreplaceable woman who's unable to love back ends tragically. After another nasty argument, Frank moves out to a squalid boardinghouse hoping to find his old friend and adviser, Johnson (William Hartnell). Not long thereafter Frank goes over to Mrs. Hammond's home to try and patch things up, only to learn from a neighbor that she's been quite ill and is in the hospital.

FACING PAGE: Former miner Frank Machin (Richard Harris, left) finds success on the rugby fields.

Rushing to her bedside, Frank is informed that Mrs. Hammond suffered a brain hemorrhage. The doctor candidly states that he feels she doesn't have the strength or will to live on. Despite Frank's pleas for her to wake up, Mrs. Hammond dies. Returning to her home, Frank breaks down in anguish from the full realization of what he has lost.

Returning to the rugby field, defeated emotionally and sensing that his future is limited in an ever-escalating and physically destructive game, Frank carries on without the spirit in which he entered the sport. We have witnessed the decline of a sporting idol from the inside.

INSTANT REPLAY This stark, realistic drama is a brilliant picture filled with emotional conflicts in the course of a stymied and ultimately tragic love story.

Fully engaging, *This Sporting Life* uses the sport of rugby as a microcosm of raw anger and frustration in society. The universal themes of the pursuit of love and a better life and all the attendant risks are also clearly in play here.

Making his feature debut, Indian-born Brit Lindsay Anderson takes the uncompro-

Richard Harris and Rachel Roberts would each earn Academy Award nominations for their roles in 'This Sporting Life.'

mising view of working class life in England for which he would become known (his future films *If* and *O Lucky Man!* followed in that vein). Coming from a background as a theatrical director and documentary filmmaker (he won an Oscar for his 1954 short *Thursday's Children*), Anderson would, along with Tony Richardson (*Loneliness of the Long Distance Runner*) and several others, become a guiding force in shaping British cinema, emphasizing a higher social awareness with a grim viewpoint. Films typical of the so-called "Angry Filmmakers' " output include *A Taste of Honey, Room at the Top,* and *Saturday Night and Sunday Morning.* The bleak environment and social repression these pictures present have a counterpart in the neo-realism of Italian cinema.

Anderson directs with good pace and imagination, though the risky use of flashback for a large part of the film as a stream-of-consciousness approach seems at times both static and slightly confusing. Ultimately the director manages to use the method in combination with other techniques like quick cuts to weave the exposition and development of the story into a strong, forward-moving whole.

David Storey's screenplay based on his novel is well executed. The script and its execution could have been improved, though, with more interweaving of the rugby story and the love story, which at times seem like separate and distinct entities. Would Machin's relationship with Mrs. Hammond been dramatically different if he hadn't become a rugby star? Frank's fame and fortune didn't move the widow and she wasn't the guiding force for his march to athletic success.

The film's success is certainly a combined effort, but the cast is brilliant, especially the lead characters, evidenced by the Oscar nominations for both Richard Harris and Rachel Roberts.

Harris's physical embodiment of a raw, animalistic rugby player tormented by inner uncertainty and a buried sensitivity he can only articulate in emotional tirades, is an indelible performance.

Roberts, who starred as Albert Finney's lover in the aforementioned *Saturday Night and Sunday Morning* (earning her a British Academy Award for Best Actress) takes on a difficult role here as the emotionally scarred widow. Her restraint in the role, coupled with the ability to project the suppressed passion of her character's torment—her desire for a love that she's emotionally incapable of, her physical desires and her terrible guilt— makes this a complex and exceptional performance.

The supporting cast members are effective in their subsidiary roles. Alan Badel is notable as the pragmatic rugby team owner operating like a Roman emperor organizing his gladiators for the bloody battles within the arena. Vanda Godsell as his ignored wife with designs on Frank is memorable, as is Colin Blakely's nicely reserved turn as Frank's friend and confidant.

While the pubs, dance hall, locker rooms, old houses, and landscape are very realistic, what really stands out is the technical team's success in conveying the violent savagery of the game of rugby.

With the superb and graphic photography of Denys Coop matched by Chris Greenham's natural sound editing, Anderson's presentation of rugby as a blood sport involving mud-caked "great apes" colliding with an agonizing thud only to get up and collide again is kind of a physical metaphor for the violent, furious quarrels between Frank and Mrs. Hammond. Roberto Gerhard's affecting music and Peter Taylor's razor-sharp editing give it the knockout punch.

This Sporting Life is an intense, moving, and highly effective motion picture.

OUTSIDE THE LINES The film was shot in the north and west areas of Yorkshire, England.... Rachel Roberts was married to fellow actor Rex Harrison.... She would win a British Academy Award for her role in this film and a nomination in Hollywood as well.... This was Karel Reisz's producing debut; the director won a

Brutish rugby player Machin (Harris, left) can also be quite charming.

British Oscar for *Saturday Night and Sunday Morning* (1960).... Richard Harris won a Cannes Film award for his role in *This Sporting Life*.... Harris's singing wasn't limited to film performances, as he had a hit song, "MacArthur Park."...This was actress Glenda Jackson's film debut in an uncredited role.... Director Anderson appeared in the cast of *Chariots of Fire* (1981).... Harris was a lifelong rugby fan.... Producer/director Reisz had worked previously as a film critic for Britain's *Sight and Sound* movie magazine and had written a book, *The Technique of Film Editing*.... Harris appeared as a Roman emperor in the Oscar winner *Gladiator* (2000).... Denys Coop shared an Oscar for his visual effects work on *Superman* (1978).... Peter Taylor won an Academy Award for editing *The Bridge on the River Kwai* (1957).... Peter Lamont won an Oscar for his art direction on *Titanic* (1997).... Glenda Jackson would go on to major roles, winning two Oscars as Best Actress in *Hedda* (1975) and *Women in Love* (1970).

ALL-STAR MOMENTS
Opening rugby scenes, including the camera work inside the scrum as we see Frank Machin (Harris) take the ball and get pummeled.

Frank's breakaway run impressing the owners in his tryout.

Sitting at the fireplace reading his paperback while Mrs. Hammond (Roberts) shines her late husband's boots and reveals that basically her life was buried when he died.

Frank in bed with Mrs. Hammond, unable to get her to tell him that she has feelings for him.

In one of their quarrels Frank tells her, "What I know about your life, I can put you in a rubber room for life."

Frank alone atop a hill surveying the landscape, flashing back to solid rugby play.

After Mrs. Hammond succumbs to her illness, Frank goes to her home and breaks down.

Final shot of the film with Frank back in the game but not complete in mind and body.

HOME COURT ADVANTAGE
Available on VHS and DVD.

#2 BULL DURHAM

Screenwriter/Director Ron Shelton. **Producers** Mark Burg, Thom Mount. **Cinematography** Bobby Byrne. **Editing** Robert Leighton, Adam Weiss. **Music** Michael Covertino. **Art Direction** David Lubin. **Technical Advisor** Pete Bock. **Production Designer** Armin Ganz. **Executive Producer** David Lester. Orion. 1988.

THE PLAYERS Kevin Costner **Crash Davis**; Susan Sarandon **Annie Savoy**; Tim Robbins **Ebby Calvin "Nuke" LaLoosh**; Trey Wilson **Joe "Skip" Higgins**; Robert Wuhl **Larry Hackett**; William O'Leary **Jimmy**; David Neidorf **Bobby**; Danny Gans **Deke**; Tom Silardi **Tony**; Lloyd Williams **Mickey**; Rick Marzan **José**; Jenny Robertson **Millie**; Garland Bunting **Teddy (Radio announcer)**; George Buck **Mr. LaLoosh, "Nuke's" father**; Greg Avellone **Doc**; Robert Dickman **Whitey**; Timothy Kirk **Ed**; Don Davis **Scared batter**; Stephen Ware **Abused umpire**; Tom Eshelman **Bat boy**; C.K. Bibby **Mayor**; Henry Sanders **Sandy**; Antoinette Forsyth **Ball park announcer**; Shirley Anne Ritter **Waitress**; Alan Mejia **Chu Chu**; Pete Bock **Minister**; Max Patkin **Himself**

THE GAME *Bull Durham* is a romantic comedy set in the world of minor league baseball. The action takes place during one season in the annals of the Durham Bulls, a Class A squad in the Carolina League and a team steeped in mediocrity.

It's a triple play love affair involving two ballplayers from the Bulls and a part-time college English instructor, full-time seductress, and "church of baseball" fanatic, Annie Savoy (Susan Sarandon). One of the men is the grizzled career minor league catcher Crash Davis (Kevin Costner), and the other is the young pitching phenom Ebby Calvin "Nuke" LaLoosh (Tim Robbins), possessor of "a million-dollar arm and five-cent head."

Crash is "the player to be named later" and is sent to the Bulls for the express purpose of harnessing Nuke's raw talent and teaching him the ways of the game to get him ready for "the show" (playing in the major leagues). No easy assignment, as Nuke has a major league arm but Little League aim and maturity. He is just as likely to throw a pitch up into the broadcast booth and follow it with a tantrum as he is to find the strike zone.

The reluctant catcher's job is made more difficult as the beautiful team groupie Annie comes between the tutor and his student, enlightening both with her game of life, love, and unusual philosophical viewpoints.

Ever since she discovered that there were as many stitches in a baseball as beads in a rosary, baseball has been Annie's religion. Her form of communion is an inspired mix of literary readings, New Age philosophy, and sex. Annie also has a very good grip on the nuances of baseball. Each year she chooses a player from the Bulls to educate in the ways of love, so that she can instill a lifetime of confidence in him. Annie likes to point out with pride her high winning percentage, that every one of her pupils has gone on to enjoy his best season after being with her. In return Annie gets a 142-game season to feel young and pretty before scouting next year's prospect.

For this season Annie has narrowed her roster down to two. She is indecisive about which of the new battery mates she wants to sleep with, the pitcher or the catcher. Annie doesn't know if she wants to go with the naïve youngster that she can control or take a chance at a mature relationship with the wiser, smoother veteran.

After 12 years in the minors, Crash feels himself well above auditioning as he and Annie get their signals crossed. After an impromptu yet mesmerizing "what I believe" speech, he leaves a yearning Annie alone with the rookie.

The education of a ballplayer begins for Ebby "Nuke" LaLoosh from two different sides. Crash teaches him about everything from proper hygiene to proper clichés for interviews, from messing with hitters' minds to handling a winning streak.

Annie's amorous private mentoring program includes a unique repertoire that favors a mix of bondage and expanding her lovers' minds with readings of Walt Whitman. ("A guy will listen to anything if he thinks its foreplay," she says knowingly.) Some of the unusual methods Annie employs to impart wisdom to Nuke as the season progresses include breathing through his eyelids and wearing garter belts under his uniform, all designed to keep him from thinking too much on the mound.

As the inevitable highs and lows of the season carry them to the end of the year, the built-up sexual tension among the three explodes when Nuke, on a winning streak, refuses to sleep with Annie until he loses. He's been taught by Crash never to mess with a winning streak, and Nuke feels that re-channeling his sexual energy into his pitching has been responsible for his success on the mound.

After hearing that Crash is responsible for Nuke's "withholding" and that she's losing in a battle for Nuke's attention, Annie storms into the veteran's apartment as he's ironing his clothes and breaks down after a mental and sexual battle of wits with Crash. She finally propositions him and Crash refuses her advances, wanting her to come to him when she really means it. Annie is temporarily rudderless in her cosmic ship.

At the same time Crash has his own cross to bear on the field, as once Nuke is promoted to the majors the club releases Crash. He reflects on a career that, with the exception of a cherished 21-day experience in the majors, has been completely in the minors. He has helped a younger man with more talent but far less intelligence and love of the game make it to the highest level. Resigned to his fate, Crash tries to figure out how to end his career with a little dignity.

With Nuke in the bigs spewing out the clichés he learned from Crash, Annie and the veteran catcher finally give in to their mutual attraction in a night of nonstop romance.

After disappearing and ending his career with another club and breaking a somewhat dubious record of career minor league homers, Crash returns to Annie as they both contemplate sharing a future together.

INSTANT REPLAY While the lead characters have their hearts, minds, and hands all over the pleasures of the flesh and the game in a tasteful, earthy, and often humorous way, *Bull Durham* is much more than one of its taglines states, "It's all about sex and sport. What else is there?"

It is about growing up against a backdrop of adults playing a kids' game and being forced to face a new life—the real show. It's about dreams, past and future. The Bulls roster reflects youngsters aspiring to make the majors and veterans clinging desperately to glory days and one more shot "in the show"—players and coaches alike. It is about individuals, not the cliché sports movie finale of "winning the big game." It is about spiritual growth, an approach to life. It is an offbeat, original picture with insightful looks into human nature.

From his own witty, literate script, Ron Shelton makes a terrific directorial debut with *Bull Durham*. As a former minor league second baseman in the Baltimore Orioles system from 1967 to 1971, Shelton uses his firsthand knowledge and experiences to expertly capture the whole baseball environment in rich and often humorous detail.

"Sermon on the Mound." Fellow Bulls watch their teammate Jimmy (William O'Leary) get married to the promiscuous Millie (Jenny Robertson).

Whether it's the hilarious action on the field, including putting the audience inside a player's head, hearing his private thoughts as he psyches himself up, or discussing what wedding gifts to get a teammate or how to handle a voodoo curse at a conference on the pitcher's mound, the baseball scenes are original, clever, and very real. From the late-night drunken team mudslide on a flooded ball field to the inadequate broadcast facilities to the manager having to tell a player he's cut, Shelton shines in painting the details of the game using their inherent humor and drama.

Armin Ganz's production design with David Lubin really helps to create the small-town, blue-collar atmosphere, complete with tacky ads on the outfield wall, the dive bar, moldy locker rooms, and dilapidated buses. Louise Frogley's costume designs complement their efforts. Bobby Byrnes scores well as the photographer on the difficult job of keeping the action on the ball field interesting.

Joining the director and script as the film's all-stars are the wonderful performances by the cast. Kevin Costner becomes Crash Davis in mind, body, and soul. Combining the weary cynicism of someone realizing that his limited talent has kept him from the elite end of the sport with undying romanticism and deep respect for the game, Costner adroitly slides between humor and sensitivity.

Susan Sarandon skillfully avoids the danger of falling into a stereotypical floozy role as Annie. It is really through her intelligent eyes that we see the film's events and she shines as the wise mother, willing seductress, and cosmic cheerleader.

Tim Robbins' talents are evident in a difficult role. His character comes across with an amiable innocence, as a likable goof rather than an arrogant blowhard, and succeeds in the end as we see he's learned his lessons.

Though the pairing of the team tramp (Jenny Robertson) with the locker room evangelist (William O'Leary) is a bit predictable, Shelton fills out his lineup card of the supporting cast with brilliant and colorful actors. Trey Wilson is beautiful as the tired manager. His role is best exemplified when he seeks Crash's advice and proceeds to "dress down" his team in a mock fury after a poorly executed game. As they stand in the shower he says: "It's a simple game—you throw the ball, you hit the ball, you catch the ball." It's the same simple approach Shelton applied to his film—you play some ball, tell a few jokes, and enjoy a little romance.

Anchoring the humor is the all-knowing, hyper-speed-talking pitching coach Larry, played by Robert Wuhl. From the indefatigable encouragement he shouts to his pitching star, whether he's serving up homers or tossing balls at the mascot, to instantly recalling obscure baseball records, to discussing wedding presents at a player conference on the mound, Wuhl is hilarious.

Bull Durham is one of the most entertaining depictions of cowhide on celluloid in baseball's long Hollywood history. Its success is due in large part to the director's masterfully original presentation of a familiar subject, and to the genuine sense that everyone involved is having a ball.

OUTSIDE THE LINES Ron Shelton's screenplay was nominated for an Academy Award.... The screenplay won best honors with the National Society of Film Critics, Los Angeles Film Critics, New York Film Critics Circle Awards, and the Writers Guild of America.... Susan Sarandon's breakthrough role as Annie finally made her a top star at age 40.... Comedian Robert Wuhl worked as a vendor at the Astrodome while attending college in Houston.... Producer Thom Mount was coowner of the Durham Bulls.... Ron Shelton's pro baseball career included winning a pennant for the Orioles' Rochester farm team.... His teammates included future major league all stars Don Baylor and Bobby Grich.... The film was made for just $7 million and was completed within eight weeks.... The on-screen romance between Susan Sarandon and Tim Robbins soon expanded into their real lives as well.... Ex-umpire and minor league manager Peter Bock conducted the pre-shoot baseball camp of actors and local ballplayers.... Costner played a cyclist in *American Flyers* (1985).... His other baseball movies include *For the Love of the Game* (1999), *Field of Dreams* (1989), and, in a brief appearance, *Chasing Dreams* (1982).... After ending his baseball career, Shelton earned a master's degree in fine arts at the University of Arizona and his sculpture work was exhibited at the Space Gallery in Los Angeles among other places.... Bulls outfielder David Niedorf also appeared in *Hoosiers*.... There was a real "Crash" Davis. Lawrence "Crash" Davis was a second baseman who played for the Bulls in 1948.... Writer Shelton has stated repeatedly that he did spot the name in a record book and decided to use it, but that's the only tie between his character and the real Davis.... The Bulls' 1B Rick Marzan (José) played football at the University of Kentucky and baseball in the Montreal Expos farm system.... Paula Abdul, a former Los Angeles Lakers cheerleader, choreographed the bar scene dance for Tim Robbins.... Both Kurt Russell and Mark Harmon were interested in the role of Crash Davis.... Russell played ball for the Angel and Padre organizations before leaving sports for acting.... He'd later star in the cop drama *Dark Blue* (2003), directed by Ron Shelton.

TOP: "Screwball" could have multiple applications when describing pitcher Ebby "Nuke" LaLoosh (Tim Robbins).

BOTTOM: Wise in the way of love and baseball: Annie Savoy (Susan Sarandon) and Crash Davis (Kevin Costner).

ALL-STAR MOMENTS Annie's (Sarandon) opening "church of baseball" monologue.

Crash's (Costner) impromptu "What I believe" speech.

As an excited Nuke (Robbins) is tied to Annie's bed, full of amorous expectations, Annie pulls up a chair with a book in her hand.

ANNIE: You ever heard about Walt Whitman?

NUKE: Who does he play for?

ANNIE: He sorta pitches for the cosmic all stars.

NUKE: Never heard of him.

ANNIE: Good. (She proceeds to read some of his work to him.)

Nuke's nightmare sequence of being laughed at and ridiculed by fans and team-mates alike as he pitches with only shoes, socks, hat, jock, and garter belt.

Crash's winning a wager in getting a game canceled by flooding the field and then leading a drunken procession around the muddy basepaths.

After the pitching coach inquires, "What the hell is going on here?" to the assembled players on the pitcher's mound, Crash proceeds to explain the reasons for their conference, which include getting rid of one player's voodoo curse and buying a wedding gift for a teammate.

POST-GAME COMMENTS Director Ron Shelton on the lead characters, Crash and Annie:

> We tried to capture what it's like to be a grown man, earning a precarious livelihood at a kids' game... or a woman who thrives on that atmosphere.

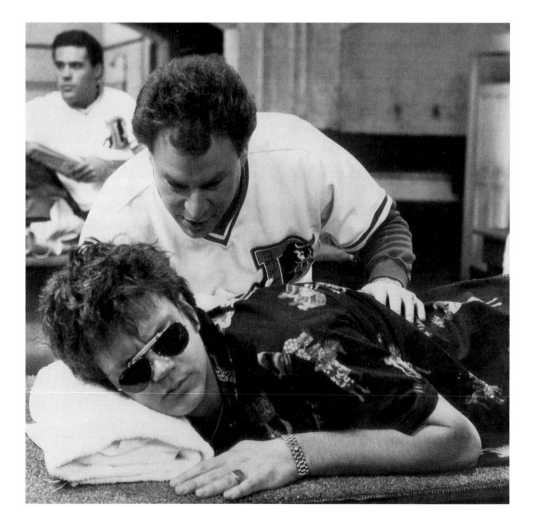

TOP: Bulls manager Joe "Skip" Riggins (Trey Wilson).

BOTTOM: The real game: romance.

RIGHT: Pitching coach Larry Hockett (Robert Wuhl) with LaLoosh (Robbins) in the locker room.

Despite his soldier-of-fortune swagger, when Crash is on the field, he's 10 years old again. And Annie's delicious eccentricity, she's romantic and sort of old-fashioned, like baseball itself.[1]

Kevin Costner on what attracted him to the role of Crash Davis:

As much as Crash loves what he does, he can laugh at it—and at himself. It's fun getting dirty and being a bit of a rascal again.[2]

Thom Mount, a former president of Universal Pictures and a co-owner of minor league baseball teams including the Durham franchise, talks about how producing this film was a homecoming of sorts for him:

I grew up watching the Bulls. I followed the players, I knew their stats, and like a lot of kids, I dreamt of being in the lineup alongside my heroes. To me there is still nothing better than sitting in the stands on a warm night in August, with a hot dog and peanuts, watching the dust fly.[3]

Ron Shelton got a little closer to that dream as a player in the Baltimore Orioles farm system, reaching as far as the AAA Rochester squad:

I was good—but not good enough. Baseball is a funny world. At 25, if you're not in the big time, you're already old. The time had come to quit or turn into a 12-year minor leaguer. So I quit.[4]

Shelton, comparing *Bull Durham* to his original 1979 screenplay, *A Player to be Named Later*:

It wasn't a rewrite. Everything changed except the journeyman catcher and the screwy young pitcher. This time the woman became the focus. The story is really told through her eyes.[5]

The film's writer/director, on the Annie Savoy character:

[Annie] is a magical person...a soothsayer. She's a flamboyant character who dresses like an orchid in Durham, North Carolina and takes tremendous satisfaction in her impact on her lovers, physically and metaphysically. That's her way of contributing to the game she adores. She's uninhibited—some would call her crazy—in a fairly inhibited part of the world.[6]

Producer Thom Mount on the film's theme:

The time comes for all of us when we measure what we are against what we would be. The way that happens to Crash, Nuke, and Annie—and the way they move on to the next place in their lives—is what the story is about.[7]

HOME COURT ADVANTAGE Available on VHS and DVD. Image Entertainment released the first edition; then MGM released a special edition as well as a Grand Slam Gift Set that also includes *Eight Men Out*, *The Jackie Robinson Story*, and *The Pride of the Yankees*.

#1 THE HUSTLER

Screenwriters Sidney Carroll, Robert Rossen. **Director/Producer** Robert Rossen. **Cinematography** Eugene Schüfftan. **Editing** Dede Allen. **Production Design** Harry Horner. **Art Direction** Albert Brenner. **Composer** Kenyon Hopkins. Fox. 1961.

THE PLAYERS Paul Newman **"Fast" Eddie Felson**; Jackie Gleason **Minnesota Fats**; Piper Laurie **Sarah Packard**; George C. Scott **Bert Gordon**; Myron McCormick **Charlie Burns**; Murray Hamilton **Findlay**; Michael Constantine **Big John**; Vincent Gardenia **Bartender**; Carl York **Young hustler**; Jake LaMotta **Bartender**; Don De Leo **Pool player**; Brendan Fay **Pool player**; Jack Healy **Hotel owner**; Willie Mosconi **Willie**; William Adams **Old doctor**; Carolyn Coates **Waitress**; Alexander Rose **Scorekeeper**; Clifford Pellow **Turk**; Stefan Gierasch **Preacher**; Gordon Clarke **Cashier**

THE GAME *The Hustler* is a gritty, dark character portrait that takes place in the shadowy world of pool halls. It is a drama that explores the relationship between talent and success, love and desperation, and greed and evil.

"Fast" Eddie Felson (Paul Newman) is a charismatic but fundamentally flawed young man who has been consumed by one overriding goal since he was a teenager: to be a top pool shark, a crack pool player making a living hustling unsuspecting locals. It is that consuming drive for success as a cue stick ace that makes him blind to decency and integrity, placing him literally and figuratively "behind the eight ball."

After finally hustling his way from small-time dives to the upper echelons, Eddie and his manager, Charlie Burns (Myron McCormick), have saved enough money and sharpened his ability to maneuver ivory balls around green felt tables to the point where they are ready to take on the unofficial champion of them all, Minnesota Fats (Jackie Gleason).

At famed Bennington's Pool Hall in Chicago, Eddie instantly recognizes Fats and says to him, "You're Minnesota Fats, aren't you, mister? They say you're the best in the country. Suppose you and me play a game of straight pool." Thus begins a 36-hour marathon duel, a historic event that will be the talk of pool halls for years. Eddie builds up a huge lead, dropping both conventional and unconventional shots, and is ahead nearly $18,000. Fats is impressed but undaunted. He takes a break and uses the restroom to comb his hair and wash his face. Emerging from the restroom refreshed, Minnesota proceeds to turn the felt tables his way, as the booze Eddie's been consuming over the hours begins to take its toll. Now that Minnesota is on a roll, Eddie is down to under $1,000, then $200. Fats, the winner, walks out deaf to the drunken challenger's pleas.

The once brash dynamo now tumbles back into a downward spiral of the lowest rungs of the pool world, having parted from his manager, yearning for the day he faces Fats in a rematch. He meets a lonely, love-starved alcoholic in a bus stop. Her name is Sarah Packard (Piper Laurie). A doomed relationship begins and in a desperate attempt to gain affection, Sarah invites him to move into her apartment. Eddie does. Sarah seems to be the only one to understand him, despite calling their relationship a "contract of depravity."

Emerging from a poker game at a pool hall, Eddie is approached by the shifty, calculating gambler/promoter Bert Gordon (George C. Scott), who was at Fats' side in their match. Gordon offers to back Felson back into the big time and speaks directly

FACING PAGE: Fast Eddie Felson (Paul Newman).

to Eddie: "Sure, you've got talent, but you can't play big money pool for 36 hours on nothing but talent. You've got to have character.... You've got a lot to learn, boy. An awful lot to learn."

Bert talks a good game about luck, psychology, and his ability to predict winners and losers of a given pool game. He tells Eddie that despite his flaws, he'll sponsor him on his comeback trail. That sounds fine until Bert tells him his fee is a whopping 75% of Eddie's earnings. No deal.

Eddie continues to pursue his obsession on his own. However, one of the stocks in trade of a hustler is anonymity. Eddie tries to pull a fast one with some pool punks and is recognized as a hustler, and they break his thumbs in the ensuing beating. The

injury is costly in time, money, and confidence for Eddie. At the end of his rope financially and playing in pain, he ends up agreeing to Bert's stiff terms. That is the start of an exploitative relationship that is destined not to be an enduring one.

Bert forces Eddie to confront his own mental and emotional inadequacies in order to get to the next level via a better self-understanding. Despite Sarah's trepidations about this "relationship" between Eddie and Bert, the three travel to Lexington, Kentucky to take on a wealthy player, Oames Findley (Murray Hamilton). Eddie's confidence is shaken from the start as Oames begins winning early. After begging Bert to spot him more money, Felson storms back to win. Just as important as the money, Eddie has recaptured his confidence.

Even though he has genuine feelings for her, Eddie feels Sarah is holding him back from his all-absorbing quest to beat Fats and therefore ends their relationship. This is the last straw for the emotionally fragile Sarah. When Bert offers her money to give to Eddie, the disillusioned Sarah gives herself to Bert in a final desperate gesture and then commits suicide.

Embittered and fueled by this revelation, Eddie takes on Minnesota Fats in a rematch. Dropping difficult shots with ease and winning game after game, Eddie is whipping Fats, all the while carrying on a diatribe against Bert for his treatment of Sarah. It appears to help cleanse Eddie of his conscience for his role in Sarah's demise.

As a thoroughly defeated Fats says, "I quit, Eddie. I can't beat you," and tells the handler to pay up, Eddie realizes it is a hollow victory, that the prize was not worth the race. "Fast" Eddie has destroyed everything for this one fleeting moment at the top and he knows it.

INSTANT REPLAY Like his other sports movies, boxing's *Body and Soul* and the bullfighting saga *The Brave Bulls*, Rossen's main character in *The Hustler* is a soul-searching young man who possesses an inner force that he can't really understand or control as corrupting pressures prey on that source of power and bring out its destructive elements. These protagonists are skilled machines with no identity other than what their talents give them. But it's not enough to have talent; you have to have character.

Director Rossen, a pool enthusiast himself, does a fine job in deploying his cast and crew to present the price of success to a morally bankrupt young pool shark. What does it mean to be a winner and a loser?

Rossen's technical team, working from a taut, grim screenplay the director cowrote with Sidney Carroll, is superb in capturing the dark pool hall atmosphere. Eugene Schüfftan's photography expertly fleshes out the seedy environment while Harry Horner's art direction re-creates the smell and feel of the dank, rancid pool hall life. The lighting in the pool room is treated as a character itself. Both Schüfftan and Horner won Oscars for their efforts. The jazz score by Kenyon Hopkins works well to help set the tone, as does the composer's work in *Downhill Racer*, a film that explores similar themes. Dede Allen's editing gives a great stylistic rhythm to the picture, setting up and enhancing the psychology of the characters.

The entire cast gives brilliant performances. Newman's indelible effort is top of the line in capturing the driven, vulnerable, arrogant, and romantic sides of Felson. Piper Laurie's pathetic Sarah helps illustrate "Fast" Eddie's troubles in a difficult role as an intelligent, alcoholic, and lonely lady. George C. Scott's Bert Gordon is a poolroom predator, an ominous figure in dark glasses whose chief skill is exploiting talent.

ABOVE: Sarah Packard (Piper Laurie) and Eddie.

FACING PAGE: Robert Rossen (center) also directed boxing's 'Body and Soul,' featuring John Garfield.

Scott's promoter, teaching Newman the mental aspects of becoming a winner, is simply powerful. Murray Hamilton as the wealthy billiards fanatic and Myron McCormick as Eddie's early manager are notable contributors.

Jackie Gleason's understated pool king performance leaves a much, much larger impact than his two scenes of screen time might be expected to allow. The fact that Newman and Gleason perform almost all of their own shooting and are very skilled adds to the authenticity.

OUTSIDE THE LINES The film was based on a 1959 novel by Walter Tevis.... Though Tevis's Minnesota Fats character was fictitious, a rotund small-time pool hustler by the name of Rudolph Wanderone Jr. would change his name to Minnesota Fats after

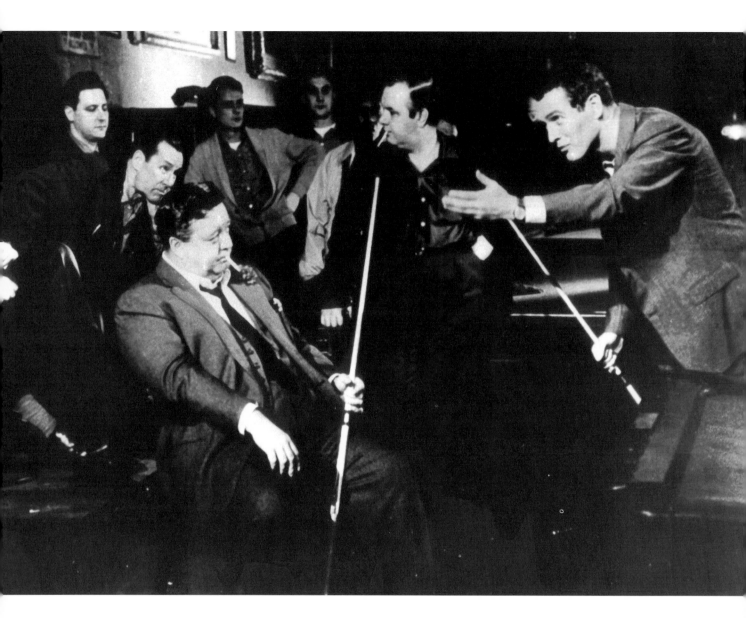

the film came out and would use his storytelling abilities to parlay his marginal pool skills into a lucrative business even though he had no association with the movie.... Director Robert Rossen briefly boxed as a professional before launching his show business career as a playwright.... Paul Newman attended Kenyon College on an athletic scholarship.... Former middleweight boxing champion Jake LaMotta appears in the film as a bartender.... Rossen's affiliation with the Communist Party led to his subpoena by the House Un-American Activities Committee.... By eventually "naming names" he avoided being blacklisted in Hollywood.... 14-time world champion between 1941 and 1957, pool legend Willie Mosconi, a technical advisor for the film, also makes a cameo as a guy who holds onto the bet money.... Newman trained for the role by putting a pool table in his dining room and Willie Moscone would come over and work with him.... Frank Sinatra was once attached to the role Newman eventually got.... A quarter-century later, Newman would win an Academy Award reprising this role in *The Color of Money*.... This would be actress Piper Laurie's last film for 15 years.... She returned like she left, with an Oscar nomination, this time as Sissy Spacek's religious mother in *Carrie* (1976).... Laurie would be nominated again for her performance in *Children of a Lesser God* (1986).... Film locations included Ame's pool room off Times Square in New York.... *The Hustler* won a British Academy Award for Best Film.... Dede Allen also edited *Slap Shot*.... Stefan Gierasch also performed in *Cornbread, Earl, and Me* (1975) and *The Champ* (1979).... Schüfftan, who developed a method of blending miniatures with live action via the use of mirrors, won an Academy Award for his work in *The Hustler*.... Albert Brenner was also the production designer for football's *The Program* (1993).... Mosconi appeared as a sportscaster in another pool film, *The Baltimore Bullet* (1980).... Kenyon Hopkins also composed the music for *Downhill Racer* (1969).... Rossen was nominated for Best Director for *The Hustler* and *All the King's Men* (1949), which won an Oscar for Best Picture.... *All the King's Men* star Broderick Crawford won the Oscar for Best Actor, edging Kirk Douglas, who was also nominated as the boxer in *Champion*.... Production designer Harry Horner won an Academy Award for *The Hustler* with Gene Callahan.

ALL-STAR MOMENTS
As Eddie (Newman), with his own pool case under his arm, and Charlie (McCormick), his manager, enter a seedy, shadowy pool hall, they speak of the place in reverential terms.

CHARLIE: It's quiet.

EDDIE: Yeah, like a church. Church of the Good Hustler.

CHARLIE: It looks more like a morgue to me. Those tables are the slabs they lay the stiffs on.

EDDIE: I'll be alive when I get out, Charlie.

BERT (Scott): You got talent.

EDDIE: I got talent? So what beat me?

BERT: Character.

BERT: Eddie, do you mind if I get personal?

EDDIE: Well, whatya' been so far?

BERT: Eddie, you're a born loser.

EDDIE: Well, thanks for the drink. I'll be going now.

Sitting in a café booth over a breakfast of alcohol, Sarah (Laurie) answers Eddie's question about how she spends her time, "I go to college Tuesdays and Thursdays; on the other days I drink."

HOME COURT ADVANTAGE
Available on DVD. Released by Fox as a solo title and as part of a Paul Newman trilogy that also includes *Verdict* and *Butch Cassidy and the Sundance Kid*.

ABOVE: Sarah and Eddie, an affair that will end in tragedy.

FACING PAGE: Minnesota Fats (Jackie Gleason, sitting with cue stick) listens to Fast Eddie.

CELEBRITY PICKS

"And Now…. Your Starting Five!" Stars from a cross-section of the sports and entertainment worlds, as well as esteemed professionals in those fields, pick their favorite sports movies. Selections listed in no particular order.

HOLLYWOOD

Sylvester Stallone
Producer/writer/director/actor—*Rocky, Paradise Alley, Victory, Death Race 2000, Over the Top, Driven*

Chariots of Fire
Jim Thorpe: All-American
Champion
National Velvet
Requiem for a Heavyweight

"I'm usually a sucker for a big finish. I loved the ending for *The Natural*. I thought it was fantastic. *Ice Castles*? Forget about it. The figure skater who goes blind and competes solo—you'll die when you see it. I loved both versions of *The Champ*, but it was Anthony Quinn in *Requiem for a Heavyweight* that is so outstanding that I bought a statue of his character, Mountain Rivera. And it so happened I'm doing a film with Anthony Quinn now (obviously this was before he passed away) and I go to him and say, 'Don't take this the wrong way, but I see you every morning.' He says, 'Who you talkin' about?' And I said, 'Mountain Rivera.' It was a sculpture just like the character that I have in my house."

Spike Lee
Producer/writer/director/actor—*He Got Game, Jim Brown, Love and Basketball*

Fat City
Bull Durham
Raging Bull
Somebody Up There Likes Me
Hoop Dreams

Billy Crystal
Producer/director/writer/actor—*Forget Paris, Animalympics, 61**

Bull Durham
Hoop Dreams
The Pride of the Yankees
Hoosiers
Pastime

"I think a sports movie to be really good has to be about something else as well. *Champion, Raging Bull, The Longest Yard,* and *North Dallas Forty* have moments I love. The struggle is to make it all look real. *The Natural* is a great fairy tale and beautiful looking."

John Turturro
Actor—*He Got Game, Raging Bull, Monday Night Mayhem, The Color of Money*

Slap Shot
Raging Bull
Body and Soul
Jim Thorpe: All-American
Requiem for a Heavyweight

Dennis Quaid
Actor—*Breaking Away, The Rookie, Everybody's All-American, Any Given Sunday, Tough Enough, Our Winning Season*

Hoosiers
The Natural
Field of Dreams
Pride of the Yankees
Rocky

Ross Greenburg

President, HBO Sports

Miracle
Rocky
The Natural
Field of Dreams
Hoosiers

"*Miracle* has to be my favorite in that it was my idea, and I was the executive producer of the film! *Rocky* was a snapshot of life in America in the post-Vietnam era. It reminded people in this country that our democratic system allowed for upward mobility. The best sports films use the events as a backdrop to stories of great social significance."

Orly Adelson

Producer—*3: The Dale Earnhardt Story, The Junction Boys, Codebreakers, Playmakers*

Rocky
Brian's Song
Chariots of Fire
The Natural
Million Dollar Baby

Gary Ross

Writer/director/producer—*Seabiscuit*

Bull Durham
The Rookie
Slap Shot
Personal Best
Kill the Umpire

"*Bull Durham* is such a beautiful look at a little world, an examination of character within a world that is so real, whimsical, and funny. And it isn't about triumph. It's about struggle.

"I think *The Rookie* . . . a wonderful movie about second chances. My kids turned me on to that movie, they loved it so much.

"Another great sports movie is *Slap Shot*. Nancy Dowd, who wrote the first draft of that, etched a fine portrait of a very specific world.

"I think *Personal Best* is a really great sports movie. A magnificent movie and a wonderful directorial debut by Bob. A unique voice and vision in that movie. He did a terrific job. He cast that woman who was also a real athlete. That boosted my spirits about casting Gary Stevens.

"William Bendix's *Kill the Umpire*, because I loved it as a kid."

Robert Wise

Director—*The Set-Up, Somebody Up There Likes Me.*
Editor—*The Iron Major, Citizen Kane*

Jim Thorpe: All-American
Brian's Song
The Longest Yard
North Dallas Forty
Heaven Can Wait

Jim Brown

Actor—*Any Given Sunday, He Got Game, The Running Man*

Rocky
The Longest Yard
Raging Bull
He Got Game
Any Given Sunday

"I love Oliver's work and *Any Given Sunday* to me was the definitive sports movie. He covered every aspect of what it's all about. Like Oliver, Spike [Lee] does things a little differently; that's what I liked about his basketball film. I love the whole *Rocky* concept and thought Sylvester Stallone did a tremendous job."

Tom Sherak

Partner, Revolution Studios

Rocky/Rocky II
The Natural
Field of Dreams
Hoosiers/Rudy
Slap Shot

Rocky: "Underdog makes good."
The Natural: "Special Redford."
Field of Dreams: "Hope/family/believing."
Hoosiers/Rudy: "The best small town America—underdog makes it."
Slap Shot: "Funny, funny, funny."

Robert Loggia

Actor—*Somebody Up There Likes Me, Necessary Roughness*

Body and Soul

Raging Bull
North Dallas Forty
The Pride of the Yankees
The Longest Yard

Stacy Keach

Actor—*Fat City, That Championship Season*

The Rookie
North Dallas Forty
Raging Bull
Any Given Sunday
A Winner Never Quits

Dean Cain

Actor—*Clubhouse*

Brian's Song
Rocky
Hoosiers
Rudy
Slap Shot

Bernie Mac

Actor—*Mr. 3000*

Hoosiers
The Natural
Any Given Sunday
Raging Bull
Soul of the Game

Renny Harlin

Director—*Driven*

Grand Prix
Field of Dreams
Any Given Sunday
North Dallas Forty
Chariots of Fire

Marlon Wayans

Actor—*Scary Movie, The Sixth Man, White Chicks*

Lucas
Rudy
The Bad News Bears (original)
The Longest Yard (remake)
Brian's Song

Lucas: "My life story. I was Lucas before I reached puberty and Shawn was Charlie Sheen."

Rudy: "I was him too because I sucked so badly in sports."
The Bad News Bears: "Lots of kids have played Little League baseball but few have played on a sucky team with a drunk coach. I was fortunate enough to have the sucky-team, drunk-coach experience."
The Longest Yard, remake: "I thought that Adam Sandler adding his flair and fun transformed a drama into a comedy. It was impressive."
Brian's Song: "It was *Brokeback Mountain* with football helmets instead of cowboy hats and minus the tent scene."

Richard Stayton

Editor—*Written By*

Champion
Hoop Dreams
Remember the Titans
North Dallas Forty
Bull Durham

"Nick Nolte limping and moaning after games is non-Hollywood and what I remember from my football-playing days. There was glory, yes, and great moments of making a big play, but afterwards, when the crowd is gone and the locker room is almost empty, you ask one question, 'Why?'"

Rob Miller

Actor/athlete trainer, Reel Sports Solutions

Rocky
Chariots of Fire
Jim Thorpe: All-American
Bull Durham
Miracle

Rocky: "I was incredibly motivated as a young athlete by the story of an underdog overcoming such incredible odds to triumph while still losing the prize."
Chariots of Fire: "Eric Liddell's [Ian Charleson] courage of conviction to stand for his beliefs, despite what the world is saying, inspired on a spiritual level. Appreciated, as an athlete, Harold Abrahams's [Ben Cross] self-sacrifice to be the best."
Bull Durham: "Captured the fun of being a part of

a sports team and everything that goes with it on and off the field."

Stephen Pizzello

Editor in chief, *American Cinematographer*

Raging Bull
Rocky
Eight Men Out
Breaking Away
The Hustler

"All of these films capture the thrill of competition and the sacrifices and hardships that athletes must endure. Other titles I had a hard time leaving off the list include *Requiem for a Heavyweight, Fat City, The Bad News Bears,* and *Slap Shot.*"

Jennifer Flackett and Mark Levin

Writers—*Wimbledon*

Breaking Away
The Bad News Bears
The Color of Money
Rocky
Searching for Bobby Fischer

Breaking Away: "Opened our eyes to how small and enthralling a movie could be. Perfect window into the world of a college town. Funny, touching, great ear for dialogue."
The Bad News Bears: "Michael Ritchie, also director of one of our other favorite sports movies, *Downhill Racer,* at the top of his game. They don't make movies about children as honestly today. Tatum O'Neal was incredible."
The Color of Money: "A great window into a world we previously knew nothing about."
Rocky: "Need we say more? Just watch it again."
Searching for Bobby Fischer: "One of the most original sports movies ever. Follows the structure of a sports movie, but really deals with the most fundamental question of how to be fair and human in the face of competition."

Dave Hanson

Actor—*Slap Shot*

Slap Shot
The Natural
Caddyshack

Bull Durham
For the Love of the Game

SPORTS

Donovan McNabb

Quarterback, Philadelphia Eagles

The Fish That Saved Pittsburgh
Remember the Titans
Love and Basketball
Bingo Long Traveling All-Stars and Motor Kings
Jerry Maguire

Tony Gonzalez

Tight end, Kansas City Chiefs

The Longest Yard
Remember the Titans
Dodgeball
North Dallas Forty
Seabiscuit

David Morris

Publisher, *Sports Illustrated*

Brian's Song
Hoosiers
Remember the Titans
Downhill Racer
Miracle

"The sign of any good sports movie is that you can watch it a number of times and still enjoy the experience. Everyone likes a good underdog story, and a few of my picks fit that category. And as far as #1 goes it is always good to cry once in a while."

Jim Lampley

Sportscaster, HBO boxing, NBC Olympics

Hoosiers
Bull Durham
The Natural
The Harder They Fall
Tin Cup

"Impossible to only choose five. I feel I have left dozens of movies out. The constant here is great writing, and it's no accident that former minor league ballplayer Ron Shelton made two of them."

Peter Hunsinger

Publisher, *GQ*

Hoosiers
Slap Shot
Field of Dreams
Heaven Can Wait
Caddyshack

Hoosiers: "I grew up around it."
Slap Shot: "Funniest ever, love the Hanson Brothers."
Field of Dreams: "Try the book *Shoeless Joe*. Ray kidnaps J. D. Salinger, not James Earl Jones guy Terence."
Heaven Can Wait: "The 'good guy tuna company.'"
Caddyshack: "'Get your foot off the boat.'"

Mark Mravic

Editor, *Sports Illustrated*

Hoop Dreams
Olympia
Endless Summer
When We Were Kings
Bud Greenspan's collected Olympic documentaries

"In my opinion there's something visceral about sports drama and especially sports action that just can't be captured by fictional accounts from Hollywood screenwriters, which is why most really good sports movies are either comedies (*Bull Durham*, *Caddyshack*) or based on real life (*Raging Bull*), and why my favorite sports movies are all documentaries."

Steve Lott

Promoter, Big Fights

Rocky
Hoosiers
Field of Dreams
Remember the Titans
Rudy

"*Field of Dreams*: the opportunity to be with your dad again. *Remember the Titans*: the wonderful feeling of black and white kids working together."

David Granger

Editor in chief, *Esquire*

Raging Bull
Caddyshack
Rocky
Hoosiers
The Hustler

"*Rocky*, while not as technically proficient as *Raging Bull*, is so emotionally satisfying, and so true to the innocence of a not-too-bright kid from Philly, that it might be the most satisfying boxing movie. It is a lot like *Hoosiers* in that way—not very good but you can't help watching it. And *Caddyshack* is simply the most influential sports movie ever."

Bert Sugar

Sports historian

Chariots of Fire
Raging Bull
Bull Durham
North Dallas Forty
Horse Feathers

Chariots of Fire: "From Vangelis' opening blood-pumping theme, accompanied by runners lyrically running in slow motion on a beach, to the inspirational story of two track stars—one who runs for the glory of Jesus, the other trying to outrun his label as an English Jew—*Chariots of Fire* is the uplifting story of two men's will to win. Forget the minor historical inaccuracies— such as Abrahams not being the first to run around the interior of the school's courtyard, or the commingling of the 1920 and 1924 Olympics—this is as close to *The Song of Bernadette* as any sports movie has ever come."
Raging Bull: "Director Martin Scorsese gives the film an authentic look, worthy of the time, in black and white, and took great pains not to duplicate the fight scenes in Robert Wise's *The Set-Up*. Robert DeNiro's gut-wrenching performance as the brutal LaMotta makes this one of the all-time great films, sports or otherwise."
Bull Durham: "From the opening scene where Susan Sarandon as Annie Savoy compares baseball to religion, to the trials and tribulations of the Class A Durham Bulls, *Bull Durham* is both a

romantic comedy and a film about baseball at a minor league level never before seen."

North Dallas Forty: "Pulling up the institution of professional football by its roots, *North Dallas Forty* deglamorizes the game with a behind-the-scenes look at pro football management, ruthless Bible-spouting coaches, and a generous potation of misfits who make up the team."

Horse Feathers: "What's not to love about a film that pokes fun at college football in a madcap manner? Professor Quincy Wagstaff (Groucho Marx), the newly appointed President of Huxley College, addressing his colleagues, asks, 'Do we have a university? Do we have a football team?' then hurries to answer his own question with: 'Well, we can't afford both. Tomorrow we tear down the university.' "

Ed Fox

Editor in chief, *Track and Field News*

Olympia
Chariots of Fire
The Natural
Ali
This Sporting Life

"Riefenstahl's *Olympia* is not just a great sports film, but a great film, period. The other four have marvelous performances, particularly Will Smith in *Ali* and Richard Harris and Redford. *The Natural* is the great mythic baseball movie—there is no other sports film quite like it (except *Million Dollar Legs*)."

Gregory Juckett

Editor in chief, *Boxing Digest*

Rocky
Friday Night Lights
When We Were Kings
Hoosiers
The Bad News Bears

Rocky: "Being from Philadelphia, the background images really hit home, and the characters have now achieved legendary status."

Friday Night Lights: "I have an incredible passion for football, especially at the amateur level. This combined with the memories of times between

14 and 18 years old—which are so fleeting—affected me greatly."

When We Were Kings: "In my opinion this film captures part of boxing during its final peak. And of course, Ali was the reason. Plus, it really makes me feel like I'm there in Zaire in 1974."

Hoosiers: "What a fantastic reminder of grassroots basketball and how a rural community rallies around the hometown high school."

The Bad News Bears: "It's so '70s, but it still makes me laugh. Watching Walter Matthau—drunk as a skunk—pitching batting practice is classic."

INTERNATIONAL

Travis Cranley

Writer, *Inside Sport* (Australia)

Big Wednesday
Breaking Away
Hoosiers
Phar Lap
Hoop Dreams

Big Wednesday: "This movie has been my favourite film since the first time I saw it as a teenager. It wonderfully brings together the beauty of surfing and firm friendships, the struggles of growing up and sticking with your sport, and the thrill of putting everything on the line to prove yourself. I've seen the movie 100 times and I look forward to watching it 100 more. To paraphrase Bear, this movie is the lemon *and* the pie."

Breaking Away: "This is a great film with a fantastic sporting climax and an outstanding, witty script that always keeps the action tearing along. I have a print from the movie of Dave crossing the line to win the Little 500 hanging by my writing desk."

Phar Lap: "To Australians, Phar Lap is as reverential a sporting name as Pelé and Babe Ruth are in other parts of the world. That a movie could come along almost 50 years after his mysterious death and actually add to his legend is an awesome achievement by the filmmakers. It brought a champion horse from the 1930s to life for a modern generation often only too eager to forget the greatness of heroes past."

Matteo Dore

Editor, *Sport Week / La Gazetto Dello Sport* (Italy)

Raging Bull
Slap Shot
The Bad News Bears
Any Given Sunday
Victory

"I've picked *Raging Bull* because this is not a simple sports movie, but one of the best movies of all time. *Slap Shot* is a tribute to my favorite sport. I saw *The Bad News Bears* when I was a boy and I'm still in love with Tatum O'Neal."

Cao Jianjie

Sports Editor, *Xinhua News Agency* (China)

Million Dollar Baby
Seabiscuit
Cinderella Man
Jerry Maguire
Forrest Gump

"As a sportswriter for 13 years, I like to see underdogs emerge as winners. The best thing about *Seabiscuit* is everything you expected actually happened. *Cinderella Man* reminded me of my childhood in the late '60s and early '70s, when my parents always found it difficult to feed a family of five. I was moved to tears several times. *Jerry Maguire* is one of the few movies that make you feel good inside. Gooding deserved the Oscar. Clint Eastwood is my idol. He's still going strong in his 70s. *Million Dollar Baby* was like a punch to the stomach but also moved me deeply."

Dov Kornits

Editor, *Filmink* (Australia)

Slap Shot
Breaking Away
Rocky
Raging Bull
The Natural

"*Slap Shot*—its ribald humor, unashamed violence, Paul Newman's easy charm, and the Hanson brothers…what else does a movie need? At the time I saw *Breaking Away*, I was trying to check out the entire filmography of Dennis Quaid (having become his biggest fan after the much-maligned *Everybody's All-American*, which I really liked), and this has become the archetypal Dennis Quaid performance in my eyes. Like the best sports movies, *Breaking Away* paints an engrossing portrait of well-developed characters, and then pits them as underdogs in a contest that has you rooting for them all the way."

THE LAST WORD

Kenneth Turan

Film critic, *Los Angeles Times*

Olympia
Hoop Dreams
Downhill Racer
Breaking Away
Searching for Bobby Fischer

"The scene in *Downhill Racer* where Robert Redford and Gene Hackman sit in a coffee shop and discuss why Redford lost a key race says everything about the athlete-coach relationship."

THE BIG "O"

No, this isn't a chapter on NBA Hall of Fame guard Oscar Robertson, whose innovative triple-double performances merit his own book. This chapter puts into context how well sports-oriented motion pictures have fared in the ultimate artistic accolade the industry can bestow upon an outstanding movie—an Academy Award. While many, many more sports pictures have been nominated, this list features the Oscar winners.

2005

Best Motion Picture of the Year
Winner: *Million Dollar Baby*
Other Nominees: *The Aviator, Finding Neverland, Ray, Sideways*

Best Performance by an Actress in a Leading Role
Winner: *Million Dollar Baby*—Hilary Swank
Other Nominees: *Being Julia*—Annette Bening, *Eternal Sunshine of the Spotless Mind*—Kate Winslet, *Maria Full of Grace*—Catalina Moreno, *Vera Drake*—Imelda Staunton

Best Performance by an Actor in a Supporting Role
Winner: *Million Dollar Baby*—Morgan Freeman
Other Nominees: *The Aviator*—Alan Alda, *Closer*—Clive Owen, *Collateral*—Jamie Foxx, *Sideways*—Thomas Church

Best Achievement in Directing
Winner: *Million Dollar Baby*—Clint Eastwood
Other Nominees: *The Aviator*—Martin Scorsese, *Ray*—Taylor Hackford, *Sideways*—Alexander

Payne, *Vera Drake*—Mike Leigh

2001

Best Picture of the Year
Winner: *Gladiator*
Other Nominees: *Chocolat, Erin Brockovich, Traffic, Wo hu cang long*

Best Actor in a Leading Role
Winner: *Gladiator*—Russell Crowe
Other Nominees: *Before Night Falls*—Javier Bardem, *Cast Away*—Tom Hanks, *Pollock*—Ed Harris, *Quills*—Geoffrey Rush

Best Costume Design
Winner: *Gladiator*—Janty Yates
Other Nominees: *102 Dalmations*—Anthony Powell, *How the Grinch Stole Christmas*—Rita Ryack, *Quills*—Jacqueline West, *Wo hu cang long*—Timmy Yip

Best Sound
Winner: *Gladiator*—Scott Millan, Bob Beemer, Ken Weston
Other Nominees: *Cast Away*—Randy Thom, Tom Johnson, Dennis Sands, William Kaplan; *The Patriot*—Kevin O'Connell, Greg Russell, Lee Orloff; *The Perfect Storm*—John Reitz, Greg Rudloff, David Campbell, Keith Wester; *U-571*—Steve Maslow, Gregg Landaker, Rick Kline, Ivan Sharrock

Best Effects, Visual Effects
Winner: *Gladiator*—John Nelson, Neil Corbould, Tim Burke, Rob Harvey
Other Nominees: *Hollow Man*—Scott Anderson,

Craig Hayes, Scott Stokdyk, Stan Parks; *The Perfect Storm*—Stefen Fangmeier, Habib Zargarpour, John Frazier, Walt Conti

2000

Best Documentary

Winner: *One Day in September*
Other Nominees: *Buena Vista Social Club, Genghis Blues, On the Ropes, Speaking in Strings*

1997

Best Actor in a Supporting Role

Winner: *Jerry Maguire*—Cuba Gooding Jr.
Other Nominees: *Fargo*—William Macy, *Ghosts of Mississippi*—James Woods, *Primal Fear*—Edward Norton, *Shine*—Armin Mueller-Stahl

Best Documentary, Features

Winner: *When We Were Kings*
Other Nominees: *Line King: The Al Hirschfeld Story, Mandela, Suzanne Farrell: Elusive Muse, Tell the Truth and Run*

1987

Best Actor in a Leading Role

Winner: *The Color of Money*—Paul Newman
Other Nominees: *'Round Midnight*—Dexter Gordon, *Children of a Lesser God*—William Hurt, *Mona Lisa*—Bob Hoskins, *Salvador*—James Woods

1982

Best Picture

Winner: *Chariots of Fire*
Other Nominees: *Atlantic City, On Golden Pond, Raiders of the Lost Ark, Reds*

Best Writing, Screenplay Written Directly for the Screen

Winner: *Chariots of Fire*—Colin Welland
Other Nominees: *Absence of Malice*—Kurt Luedtke, *Arthur*—Steve Gordon,

Atlantic City—John Guare, *Reds*—Warren Beatty, Trevor Griffiths

Best Costume Design

Winner: *Chariots of Fire*—Milena Canonero
Other Nominees: *The French Lieutenant's Woman*—Tom Rand, *Pennies from Heaven*—Bob Mackie, *Ragtime*—Anna Johnstone, *Reds*—Shirley Russell

Best Music, Original Score

Winner: *Chariots of Fire*—Vangelis
Other Nominees: *Dragonslayer*—Alex North, *On Golden Pond*—Dave Grusin, *Ragtime*—Randy Newman, *Raiders of the Lost Ark*—John Williams

1981

Best Actor in a Leading Role

Winner: *Raging Bull*—Robert DeNiro
Other Nominees: *The Elephant Man*—John Hurt, *The Great Santini*—Robert Duvall, *The Stunt Man*—Peter O'Toole, *Tribute*—Jack Lemmon

Best Film Editing

Winner: *Raging Bull*—Thelma Schoonmaker
Other Nominees: *Coal Miner's Daughter*—Arthur Schmidt, *The Competition*—David Blewitt, *The Elephant Man*—Anne Coates, *Fame*—Gerry Hambling

1980

Best Screenplay Written Directly for the Screen

Winner: *Breaking Away*—Steve Tesich
Other Nominees: *. . . And Justice for All*—Valerie Curtin, Barry Levinson; *All That Jazz*—Robert Arthur, Bob Fosse; *The China Syndrome*—Mike Gray, T.S. Cook, James Bridges; *Manhattan*—Woody Allen, Marshall Brickman

1979

Best Art Direction—Set Decoration

Winner: *Heaven Can Wait*—Paul Sylbert, Edwin O'Donovan, George Gaines

Other Nominees: *The Brink's Job*—Dean Tavoularis, Angelo Graham, George Nelson; *California Suite*—Albert Brenner, Marvin March; *Interiors*—Mel Bourne, Daniel Robert; *The Wiz*—Tony Walton, Philip Rosenberg, Edward Stewart, Robert Drumheller

1977

Best Picture

Winner: *Rocky*
Other Nominees: *All the President's Men, Bound for Glory, Network, Taxi Driver*

Best Director

Winner: *Rocky*—John Avildsen
Other Nominees: *All the President's Men*—Alan Pakula, *Ansikte mot ansikte*—Ingmar Bergman, *Network*—Sidney Lumet, *Pasqualino Settebellezze*—Lina Wertmuller

Best Film Editing

Winner: *Rocky*—Richard Halsey, Scott Conrad
Other Nominees: *All the President's Men*—Robert Wolfe, *Bound for Glory*—Robert Jones, Pembroke Herring, *Network*—Alan Heim, *Two-Minute Warning*—Eve Newman, Walter Hannemann

1976

Best Documentary, Features

Winner: *The Man Who Skied Down Everest*
Other Nominees: *The California Reich, Fighting for Our Lives, The Incredible Machine, The Other Half of the Sky: A China Memoir*

1974

Best Documentary, Features

Winner: *The Great American Cowboy*
Other Nominees: *Always a New Beginning, Journey to the Outer Limits, Schlacht um Berlin, Walls of Fire*

1967

Best Sound

Winner: *Grand Prix*—Franklin Milton
Other Nominees: *Gambit*—Waldon Watson, *Hawaii*—Gordon Sawyer, *The Sand Pebbles*—James Corcoran, *Who's Afraid of Virginia Woolf?*—George Groves

Best Film Editing

Winner: *Grand Prix*—Fredric Steinkamp, Henry Berman, Stu Linder, Frank Santillo
Other Nominees: *Fantastic Voyage*—William Murphy; *The Russians Are Coming*—Hal Ashby, Terry Williams; *The Sand Pebbles*—William Reynolds; *Who's Afraid of Virginia Woolf?*—Sam O'Steen

Best Effects, Sound Effects

Winner: *Grand Prix*—Gordon Daniel
Other Nominee: *Fantastic Voyage*—Walter Rossi

1962

Best Cinematography, Black and White

Winner: *The Hustler*—Eugen Schüfftan
Other Nominees: *The Absent Minded Professor*—Edward Colman, *The Children's Hour*—Franz Planer, *Judgment at Nuremberg*—Ernest Laszlo, *One, Two, Three*—Daniel Fapp

Best Art Direction—Set Decoration, Black and White

Winner: *The Hustler*—Harry Horner, Gene Callahan
Other Nominees: *The Absent Minded Professor*—Carroll Clark, Emile Kuri, Hal Gausman, *The Children's Hour*—Fernando Carrere, Edward Boyle, *La Dolce Vita*—Piero Gherardi, *Judgment at Nuremberg*—Rudolph Sternad, George Milo

1957

Best Cinematography, Black and White

Winner: *Somebody Up There Likes Me*—Joseph Ruttenberg
Other Nominees: *Baby Doll*—Boris Kaufman, *The Bad Seed*—Harold Rosson, *The Harder They Fall*—Burnett Guffey, *Stagecoach to Fury*—Walter Strenge

Best Art Direction—Set Decoration, Black and White

Winner: *Somebody Up There Likes Me*—Cedric Gibbons, Malcolm Brown, Edwin Willis, Keogh Gleason
Other Nominees: *The Proud and the Profane*—Hal Pereira, Earl Hedrick, Sam Comer, Frank McKewlvy; *Shichinin no samurai*—So Matsuyama; *The Solid Gold Cadillac*—Ross Bellah, William Kiernan, Louis Diage; *Teenage Rebel*—Lyle Wheeler, Jack Martin Smith, Walter Scott, Stuart Reiss

1950

Best Writing, Motion Picture Story

Winner: *The Stratton Story*—Douglas Morrow
Other Nominees: *Come to the Stable*—Clare Booth Luce, *It Happens Every Spring*—Shirley Smith, Valentine Davies, *Sands of Iwo Jima*—Harry Brown, *White Heat*—Virginia Kellogg

Best Film Editing

Winner: *Champion*—Harry Gerstad
Other Nominees: *All the King's Men*—Robert Parish, Al Clark; *Battleground*—John Dunning; *Sands of Iwo Jima*—Richard Van Enger; *The Window*—Frederic Knudtson

1948

Best Film Editing

Winner: *Body and Soul*—Francis Lyon, Robert Parrish
Other Nominees: *The Bishop's Wife*—Monica Collingwood, *Gentleman's Agreement*—Harmon Jones, *Green Dolphin Street*—George White, *Odd Man Out*—Fergus McDonnel

1946

Best Actress in a Supporting Role

Winner: *National Velvet*—Anne Revere
Other Nominees: *The Corn is Green*—Joan Lorring, *Mildred Pierce*—Eve Arden, *Mildred Pierce*—Ann Blyth, *The Picture of Dorian Gray*—Angela Lansbury

1943

Best Film Editing

Winner: *The Pride of the Yankees*—Daniel Mandell
Other Nominees: *Mrs. Miniver*—Harold Kress, *The Talk of the Town*—Otto Meyer, *This Above All*—Walter Thompson, *Yankee Doodle Dandy*—George Amy

1942

Best Writing, Original Story

Winner: *Here Comes Mr. Jordan*—Harry Segall
Other Nominees: *Ball of Fire*—Thomas Monroe, Billy Wilder; *The Lady Eve*—Monckton Hoffe; *Meet John Doe*—Richard Connell, Robert Presnell; *Night Train To Munich*—Gordon Wellesley

Best Writing, Screenplay

Winner: *Here Comes Mr. Jordan*—Sidney Buchman, Seton Miller
Other Nominees: *Hold Back the Dawn*—Charles Brackett, Billy Wilder ; *How Green Was My Valley*—Philip Dunne; *The Little Foxes*—Lillian Hellman; *The Maltese Falcon*—John Huston

Best Cinematography—Color

Winner: *Blood and Sand*—Ernest Palmer, Ray Rennahan
Other Nominees: *Aloma of the South Seas*—Wilfred Cline, Karl Struss, William Snyder; *Billy the Kid*—William Skall, Lenoard Smith; *Blossoms in the Dust*—Karl Freund, Howard Greene; *Dive*

Bomber—Bert Glennon; *Louisiana Purchase*—Harry Hallenberger, Ray Rennahan

1939

Best Actor in a Supporting Role

Winner: *Kentucky*—Walter Brennan
Other Nominees: *Algiers*—Gene Lockhart, *Four Daughters*—John Garfield, *If I Were King*—Basil Rathbone, *Marie Antoinette*—Robert Morley

1932

Best Actor in a Leading Role

Winner: *The Champ*—Wallace Beery, *Dr. Jekyll and Mr. Hyde*—Fredric March
Other Nominees: *The Guardsman*—Alfred Lunt

Best Writing, Original Story

Winner: *The Champ*—Frances Marion
Other Nominees: *Lady and Gent*—Grover Jones, William McNutt; *The Witness*—Lucien Hubbard; *What Price Hollywood?*—Adela St. Johns, Jane Murfin

SPORTS CINEMA HALL OF FAME

To honor those pioneers who put sports-themed pictures on the map, I'd like to present the charter class of enshrinees to the Sports Cinema Hall of Fame.

It was their trailblazing efforts that laid the foundation for a genre that is going even stronger today. Of course, making it all technically possible was the work of Thomas Edison and the Lumière brothers, among others.

Buster Keaton Writer, Actor, Director
College, Battling Butler

Charlie Chaplin Writer, Actor, Director
The Champion

Harold Lloyd Actor, Producer
The Freshman, The Milky Way

Frances Marion Writer
The Champ, The Prizefighter and the Lady

The Marx Brothers Writers, Actors
A Day at the Races, Horse Feathers

Sam Wood Director
A Day at the Races, The Pride of the Yankees, The Stratton Story

Herman Mankiewicz Writer, Producer
Horse Feathers, Million Dollar Legs, The Pride of the Yankees

Cedric Gibbons Art Director
The Champ; Slide, Kelly, Slide; A Day at the Races; National Velvet; Somebody Up There Likes Me; The Stratton Story; Pat and Mike

SPORTS CINEMA QUIZ

SCORING

90–100   You Ought To Be in Movies
80–90   You're a Cinephile All-Star
70–80   You're in the Final Year of Your
         Contract—Better Step It Up!
60–70   Long Way to Go Make the Show

QUIZ

1. *Hoop Dreams* took place primarily in and
   around what major city?
   a. Philadelphia
   b. Boston
   c. Miami
   d. Chicago

2. What fight was the Rocky Balboa vs. Apollo
   Creed bout based on?
   a. Floyd Patterson vs. Ingemar Johansson
   b. Gerry Cooney vs. Larry Holmes
   c. Muhammad Ali vs. Chuck Wepner
   d. Rocky Marciano vs. Joe Louis

3. Ron Shelton played minor league baseball for
   which major league franchise?
   a. Phillies
   b. Cardinals
   c. Orioles
   d. Twins

4. *Enter the Dragon* co-star Jim Kelly was a U.S.
   champion in what martial art discipline?
   a. Tae kwon do
   b. Karate
   c. Jujitsu
   d. Judo

5. What was the name of Richard Pryor's
   character in *Bingo Long's Traveling All-Stars and
   Motor Kings*?
   a. Bingo Long
   b. Leon Carter
   c. Charlie Snow
   d. Willie Lee

6. Stacy Peralta, the director of *Dogtown and Z-
   Boys*, also directed which surfing
   documentary?
   a. *Riding Giants*
   b. *Step Into Liquid*
   c. *Billabong Odyssey*
   d. All of the above

7. For which film did Spike Lee serve as
   producer?
   a. *Blue Chips*
   b. *Love and Basketball*
   c. *Cool Runnings*
   d. *Hurricane*

8. Which major league ballpark served as the
   primary shooting location for *Major League*?
   a. Chicago's Comiskey Park
   b. Milwaukee's County Stadium
   c. None of the above or below
   d. Detroit's Tiger Stadium

9. Which film did Steve McQueen *not* appear in?
   a. *Grand Prix*
   b. *LeMans*
   c. *Junior Bonner*
   d. *Somebody Up There Likes Me*

10. What was the nickname of Maggie Fitzgerald's last opponent in *Million Dollar Baby*?
a. The Beast (from the East)
b. The Blue Bear
c. The Queen Cobra
d. None of the above

11. What position did Tom Cruise play in *All the Right Moves*?
a. Wide receiver
b. Defensive backfield
c. Kicker
d. Quarterback

12. Denzel Washington's first sports movie appearance came in which film?
a. *Wilma*
b. *The Bob Mathias Story*
c. *The Jesse Owens Story*
d. *He Got Game*

13. Dabney Coleman played a team official in *North Dallas Forty* and what other sports movie?
a. *Eight Men Out*
b. *Heaven Can Wait*
c. *Brian's Song*
d. *Downhill Racer*

14. Who plays Ryan Hurst's prejudiced girlfriend in *Remember the Titans*?
a. Kirsten Dunst
b. Kate Bosworth
c. Eva Longoria
d. Sanoe Lake

15. Which pitching great served as Ronald Reagan's stand-in playing Grover Cleveland Alexander in 1952's *The Winning Team*?
a. Bob Feller
b. Bob Lemon
c. Whitey Ford
d. Dizzy Dean

16. Burt Reynolds, star of *The Longest Yard*, played college football for which school?
a. Florida State
b. Georgia
c. Alabama
d. Georgia Tech

17. Who played a Ruth-like character called The Whammer in *The Natural*?
a. Gary Busey
b. Joe Don Baker
c. Robert Duvall
d. Steven Seagal

18. *Miracle* and *The Rookie* co-producer Mark Ciardi pitched professionally for the Milwaukee Brewers.
a. True
b. False

19. Which movie did Angelo Pizzo *not* write?
a. *Hoosiers*
b. *The Game of Their Lives*
c. *Rudy*
d. *The Rookie*

20. Which movie did Ron Shelton *not* write?
a. *White Men Can't Jump*
b. *Play It to the Bone*
c. *The Natural*
d. *Cobb*

21. What city in Colorado did Robert Redford's character in *Downhill Racer* come from?
a. Colorado Springs
b. Idaho Springs
c. Crystal Springs
d. Aspen

22. His nickname was "Wild Thing"; what was Charlie Sheen's character name in *Major League*?
a. Roger Dorn
b. Jake Taylor
c. Rick Vaughn
d. Eddie Harris

23. Besides *White Men Can't Jump*, what other sports movie did Wesley Snipes and Woody Harrelson team up in?
a. *Above the Rim*
b. *Kingpin*
c. *Wildcats*
d. *Major League*

24. Which White Sox player did actor D. B. Sweeney portray in *Eight Men Out*?
a. Eddie Collins
b. Wilbur Wood
c. Shoeless Joe Jackson
d. Eddie Stanky

25. Which actress played Tom Cruise's girlfriend in the football film *All the Right Moves*?
a. Rebecca De Mornay
b. Lea Thompson
c. Tatum O'Neal
d. Hilary Swank

26. What was the nickname of the "hippie" quarterback played by Kip Pardue in *Remember the Titans*?
a. Sweetness
b. Mellow Yellow
c. Sunshine
d. Hurdy Gurdy Man

27. What was the name of Clint Eastwood's gym in *Million Dollar Baby*?
a. The Hit Pit
b. The Iron Fist
c. Frankie's
d. KO City

28. In the original *Bad News Bears*, who was Walter Matthau's opposing coach in the key game?
a. Jack Lemmon
b. Jack Klugman
c. Vic Morrow
d. Vic Tayback

29. Which sports movie did Michael Ritchie *not* direct?
a. *Mr. Baseball*
b. *Downhill Racer*
c. *The Bad News Bears*
d. *Diggstown*

30. In the Olympic farce *Million Dollar Legs*, W.C. Fields played the president of what country?
a. Calistoga
b. Klopstokia
c. Albania
d. Morovia

31. What professional baseball organization did Kurt Russell play minor league baseball for?
a. California Angels
b. Pittsburgh Pirates
c. San Francisco Giants
d. Kansas City Royals

32. Which actor was nominated for an Academy Award for his turn in *Bang the Drum Slowly*?
a. Michael Moriarty
b. Vincent Gardenia
c. Phil Foster
d. Robert DeNiro

33. The director of *Mr. Baseball* hails from what country?
a. United States
b. Japan
c. Australia
d. Hungary

34. In addition to *Major League* and its sequels, what other baseball movie did Dennis Haysbert appear in?
a. *Rookie of the Year*
b. *Mr. Baseball*
c. *The Sandlot*
d. *Bingo Long Traveling All-Stars and Motor Kings*

35. Which Oscar did *Million Dollar Baby not* win?
a. Best Director
b. Best Actor
c. Best Actress
d. Best Supporting Actor

36. In the opening dream scene from *Bend It Like Beckham* in which she is superimposed playing for Manchester United, the club Jess Parminder plays against is from what country?
a. Holland
b. Belgium
c. Germany
d. None of the above

37. Which movie stars were considered as likely candidates to star as Rocky instead of Sylvester Stallone in the original *Rocky*?
a. Ryan O'Neal
b. James Caan
c. Burt Reynolds
d. All of the above
e. None of the above

38. Which actress was nominated for an Academy Award for her performance in *National Velvet*?
a. Angela Lansbury
b. Elizabeth Taylor
c. Anne Revere
d. None of the above

39. Which former big league player did *not* appear in *Major League*?
a. Pete Incaviglia
b. Pete Vuckovich
c. Bob Uecker
d. Steve Yeager

40. Robert Redford, star of *The Natural*, was talented enough to earn a college baseball scholarship.
a. True
b. False

41. Which star of *Big Wednesday* had his real-life mother play his mom in the film?
a. Jan Michael Vincent
b. William Katt
c. Gary Busey
d. Trick question. None of the above.

42. What was W.C. Fields' chief athletic talent?
a. Unicycle
b. Darts
c. Juggling
d. Polo

43. The screenwriter for *The Bad News Bears* was the son of which famous actor?
a. Kirk Douglas
b. Burt Lancaster
c. Walter Brennan
d. Gary Cooper

44. Who starred in the remake of *Night and the City*?
a. Roy Scheider
b. Robert Shaw
c. Robert DeNiro
d. Roy Rogers

45. Which player from the 1980 U.S. Olympic hockey team had his actual son portray him in *Miracle*?
a. Jack O'Callahan
b. Mike Ramsey
c. Mark Johnson
d. None of the above

46. What was the name of Barbara Hershey's character in *Hoosiers*?
a. Connie Bailey
b. Emma Hoyt
c. Harriet Bird
d. Myra Fleener

47. As wide receiver Phillip Elliott in *North Dallas Forty*, what was Nick Nolte's uniform number?
a. None of the below
b. 87
c. 84
d. 86

48. As quarterback Seth Maxwell in *North Dallas Forty*, what was Mac Davis's uniform number?
a. 12
b. 16
c. 17
d. None of the above

49. Which tennis star did *not* appear in *Pat and Mike*?
a. Alice Marble
b. Don Budge
c. Gussie Moran
d. Rod Laver

50. Which track star played Mariel Hemingway's boyfriend in *Personal Best*?
a. Bob Seagren
b. Al Oerter
c. Kenny Moore
d. Frank Shorter

51. *Million Dollar Baby* is the 25th picture Clint Eastwood has directed.
a. True
b. False

52. Teri Garr starred in *The Black Stallion*. What other horse racing movie did she star in?
a. *Phar Lap*
b. *Let It Ride*
c. *Casey's Shadow*
d. *International Velvet*

53. Sam Wood, director of *The Pride of the Yankees*, also directed which popular baseball film?
a. *The Stratton Story*
b. *Elmer the Great*
c. *Fear Strikes Out*
d. *Damn Yankees*

54. In *All the Right Moves*, the coach (Craig T. Nelson) and player (Tom Cruise) were in Pennsylvania for high school football. In which state would they reunite for college football?
a. Florida
b. California
c. Texas
d. Colorado

55. Producer Al Ruddy won an Oscar for *The Godfather* and what sports picture?
a. *Gladiator*
b. *The Longest Yard*
c. *Raging Bull*
d. *Million Dollar Baby*

56. Who starred in the original bullfighting picture, *Blood and Sand*?
a. Tyrone Power
b. Charlie Chaplin
c. Harold Lloyd
d. Rudolph Valentino

57. What country did the title horse in *Phar Lap* originally come from?
a. Australia
b. Canada
c. New Zealand
d. Great Britain

58. Which soccer star did not appear in *Victory*?
a. John Wark
b. Bobby Moore
c. Franz Beckenbauer
d. Osvaldo Ardiles

59. Oscar winner John Huston directed the boxing drama *Fat City* and what other sports movie?
a. *When We Were Kings*
b. *The Stratton Story*
c. *Victory*
d. *The Longest Yard*

60. *Cinderella Man* producer Brian Grazer also produced which surfing film?
a. *Big Wednesday*
b. *Blue Crush*
c. *Step Into Liquid*
d. *The Endless Summer2*

61. Which actor was *not* considered for the role of Lou Gehrig that went to Gary Cooper in *The Pride of the Yankees*?
a. Cary Grant
b. Clark Gable
c. Spencer Tracy
d. None of the above

62. What was the name of Rocky's dog in *Rocky*?
a. Merlin
b. Butkus
c. Bruiser
d. Max

63. Russell Crowe has starred as a boxer and as a gladiator. What other sport has he covered in a starring role?
a. Golf
b. Football
c. Hockey
d. Rugby

64. Kevin Costner earned a baseball scholarship to the University of San Francisco.
a. True
b. False

65. Who starred as race car driver Pete Aron in *Grand Prix*?
a. Paul Newman
b. Steve McQueen
c. James Garner
d. James Caan

66. Taylor Hackford produced and edited the boxing documentary *When We Were Kings*. Which football feature did he direct?
a. *The Longest Yard*
b. *North Dallas Forty*
c. *Everybody's All-American*
d. *The Waterboy*

67. Which professional golfer has a speaking role in *Tin Cup*?
a. Brad Faxon
b. Tiger Woods
c. Craig Stadler
d. Greg Norman

68. Which actor starred as Jackie Robinson in *Soul of the Game*?
a. Delroy Lindo
b. Blair Underwood
c. Denzel Washington
d. Dorian Harewood

69. Paul Newman portrayed which professional boxer in *Somebody Up There Likes Me*?
a. Rocky Marciano
b. Oscar Bonavena
c. Max Baer
d. Rocky Graziano

70. Billy Crystal directed the baseball drama *61**, he also starred in which basketball movie?
a. *Eddie*
b. *Celtic Pride*
c. *Forget Paris*
d. None of the above

71. He starred in *The Set-Up*. At what school was Robert Ryan a champion boxer?
a. Princeton
b. Dartmouth
c. Penn
d. School of Hard Knocks

72. Brian Cox portrays Dennis Quaid's father in the baseball drama *The Rookie*. In which film does he play a coach?
a. *For the Love of the Game*
b. *A Shot at Glory*
c. *Necessary Roughness*
d. *Cornbread, Earl and Me*

73. Michael Chapman, the director of the football drama *All the Right Moves* featuring Tom Cruise, earned an Academy Award nomination for his cinematography work in which film?
a. *A Shot at Glory*
b. *Cinderella Man*
c. *Million Dollar Baby*
d. *Raging Bull*

74. Which sports film was James Earl Jones *not* in?
a. *Fast Break*
b. *The Greatest*
c. *The Sandlot*
d. *The Sandlot 2*

75. Which actor portrayed the great boxing champion John L. Sullivan in *Gentleman Jim*?
a. Alan Hale
b. Alan Hale Jr.
c. Ward Bond
d. John Wayne

76. What was the name of James Caan's character in *Rollerball*?
a. The Man With No Name
b. David X.
c. Jonathan E.
d. Mad Max

77. Which NFL receiver portrays a coach in *Friday Night Lights*?
a. Keyshawn Johnson
b. Steve Largent
c. Roy Williams
d. Fred Biletnikoff

78. At one point in the story of *Fear Strikes Out*, Red Sox managements ask Anthony Perkins to try the infield. What position does he play?
a. Catcher
b. Second base
c. Shortstop
d. Third base

79. He was a popular caddy in *Caddyshack*. What baseball film did Michael O'Keefe star in?
a. *Long Gone*
b. *Pastime*
c. *The Slugger's Wife*
d. *Angels in the Outfield*

80. Which Oscar did *Chariots of Fire not* win?
a. Best Picture
b. Best Screenplay
c. Best Actor
d. Best Costume Design

81. In which state did the story of *Breaking Away* take place?
a. Illinois
b. Indiana
c. Iowa
d. None of the above

82. The boxing drama *The Harder They Fall* was Humphrey Bogart's last movie.
a. True
b. False

83. Which baseball movie did Robert Wuhl *not* appear in?
a. *Bull Durham*
b. *For the Love of the Game*
c. *Cobb*
d. None of the above

84. Paul Newman won his first Academy Award for his role in which sports movie?
a. *Somebody Up There Likes Me*
b. *Winning*
c. *The Color of Money*
d. *The Hustler*

85. The baseball scenes in Buster Keaton's *College* were shot on what university campus?
a. UCLA
b. USC
c. Columbia
d. North Carolina

86. The horse racing sequences for the Marx Brothers' *A Day at the Races* were shot at which racetrack?
a. Churchill Downs
b. Pimlico
c. Santa Anita
d. Hollywood Park

87. The documentary *Dogtown and Z-Boys* takes place primarily in what section of Southern California?
a. Beverly Hills/Culver City
b. Santa Monica/Venice
c. San Diego/LaJolla
d. Santa Barbara

88. Which music superstar plays a team owner in football's *Jerry Maguire*?
a. Alice Cooper
b. Glenn Frey
c. Tim McGraw
d. Sinead O'Connor

89. Which NFL legend does *not* appear in *Any Given Sunday*?
a. John Unitas
b. Dick Butkus
c. Y. A. Tittle
d. Roger Staubach

90. The original Raging Bull, Jake LaMotta, appears as a bartender in which movie?
a. *Requiem for a Heavyweight*
b. *The Set-Up*
c. *Somebody Up There Likes Me*
d. *The Hustler*

91. Actor John Turturro made his silver screen debut in which sports movie?
a. *Rocky*
b. *Raging Bull*
c. *The Color of Money*
d. *He Got Game*

92. Who did the Rams defeat to win the Super Bowl in *Heaven Can Wait*?
   a. New York Jets
   b. Kansas City Chiefs
   c. Oakland Raiders
   d. Pittsburgh Steelers

93. As Gavin Grey in *Everybody's All-American* which NFL team did Dennis Quaid *not* play for?
   a. Washington Redskins
   b. Denver Broncos
   c. Chicago Bears
   d. None of the above

94. Which NBA player co-starred with Denzel Washington in *He Got Game*?
   a. Earl Monroe
   b. Alex English
   c. Ray Allen
   d. Reggie Miller

95. Geena Davis was convincing as a baseball player in *A League of Their Own*, in what sport does she have world class talent?
   a. Lawn bowling
   b. Archery
   c. Sailing
   d. Golf

96. Billy Dee Williams and James Caan co-star as football players for the Chicago Bears in *Brian's Song*. Who plays their coach, George Halas?
   a. Stacy Keach
   b. Jack Warden
   c. James Garner
   d. Alan Hale Jr.

97. Who was the screenwriter for *Slap Shot*?
   a. Red Skelton
   b. Ron Shelton
   c. Robert Towne
   d. Nancy Dowd

98. Who played Olympic hockey coach Herb Brooks in the TV movie version of *Miracle*?
   a. Jon Voight
   b. Vincent Gardenia
   c. Donald Sutherland
   d. Karl Malden

99. Hall of Fame jockey Chris McCarron helped writer/director Gary Ross conceive and run the horse races in *Seabiscuit*?
   a. True
   b. False

100. Which fighter does *not* appear in *Requiem for a Heavyweight*?
   a. Willie Pep
   b. Jack Dempsey
   c. Floyd Patterson
   d. Cassius Clay

ANSWERS

1. d. Chicago
2. c. Muhammad Ali vs. Chuck Wepner
3. c. Orioles
4. b. Karate
5. c. Charlie Snow
6. b. *Step Into Liquid*
7. b. *Love and Basketball*
8. b. Milwaukee's County Stadium
9. a. Grand Prix
10. b. The Blue Bear
11. b. Defensive backfield
12. a. *Wilma*
13. d. *Downhill Racer*
14. b. Kate Bosworth
15. b. Bob Lemon
16. a. Florida State
17. b. Joe Don Baker
18. a. True
19. d. *The Rookie*
20. c. *The Natural*
21. b. Idaho Springs
22. c. Rick Vaughn
23. c. *Wildcats*
24. c. Shoeless Joe Jackson
25. b. Lea Thompson
26. c. Sunshine
27. a. The Hit Pit
28. c. Vic Morrow
29. a. *Mr. Baseball*
30. b. Klopstokia
31. a. California Angels
32. b. Vincent Gardenia
33. c. Australia
34. b. *Mr. Baseball*

35. b. Best Actor
36. b. Belgium
37. d. All of the above
38. c. Anne Revere
39. a. Pete Incaviglia
40. a. True
41. b. William Katt
42. c. Juggling
43. b. Burt Lancaster
44. c. Robert DeNiro
45. d. None of the above
46. d. Myra Fleener
47. b. 87
48. b. 16
49. d. Rod Laver
50. c. Kenny Moore
51. a. True
52. b. *Let It Ride*
53. a. *The Stratton Story*
54. b. California
55. d. *Million Dollar Baby*
56. d. Rudolph Valentino
57. c. New Zealand
58. c. Franz Beckenbauer
59. c. *Victory*
60. b. Blue Crush
61. b. Clark Gable
62. b. Butkus
63. c. Hockey
64. b. False
65. c. James Garner
66. c. *Everybody's All-American*
67. c. Craig Stadler

68. b. Blair Underwood
69. d. Rocky Graziano
70. c. *Forget Paris*
71. b. Dartmouth
72. b. *A Shot at Glory*
73. d. *Raging Bull*
74. a. *Fast Break*
75. c. Ward Bond
76. c. Jonathan E.
77 c. Roy Williams
78. c. Shortstop
79. c. *The Slugger's Wife*
80 c. Best Actor
81. b. Indiana
82. a. True
83. b. *For the Love of the Game*
84. c. *The Color of Money*
85. b. USC
86. c. Santa Anita
87. b. Santa Monica/Venice
88. b. Glenn Frey
89. d. Roger Staubach
90. d. *The Hustler*
91. b. *Raging Bull*
92. d. Pittsburgh Steelers
93. c. Chicago Bears
94. c. Ray Allen
95. b. Archery
96. b. Jack Warden
97. d. Nancy Dowd
98. d. Karl Malden
99. a. True
100. c. Floyd Patterson

NOTES

#99—*All the Right Moves*
1–3. *All the Right Moves* pressbook, Fox. 1983.
4. Michael Chapman, interviewed by Randy Williams, *Football Digest*, November 2005.

#92—*Le Mans*
1–4. *Le Mans* pressbook, National General. 1971.

#78—*Blue Chips*
1–3. *Blue Chips* pressbook, Paramount. 1994.

#76—*Everybody's All-American*
1–4. *Everybody's All-American* pressbook, Warner Bros., 1988.
Taylor Hackford, interviewed by Randy Williams, *Football Digest*, November 2005.

#73—*Rudy*
1. Angelo Pizzo, interviewed by Randy Williams, *WGA's Written By*, October 2005.
2–5. Rudy pressbook, TriStar. 1993.

#70—*A League of Their Own*
1–3. *A League of Their Own* pressbook, Columbia, 1992.

#58—*Bang the Drum Slowly*
1–2. *Bang the Drum Slowly* pressbook, Paramount, 1973.

#56—*Blood and Sand*
1–2. *Blood and Sand* pressbook, Fox. 1941.

#53—*Cinderella Man*
1.Angelo Dundee, interviewed by Randy Williams, *FilmInk*, October, 2005.

#52—*Cobb*
1–2. *Cobb* pressbook, Warner Bros., 1994.
3. Ron Shelton, interviewed by Randy Williams, *Boxing Digest*, May 2005.
4. Robert Wuhl, interviewed by Randy Williams, *WGA's Written By*, August 2000.
5. Ron Shelton, interviewed by Randy Williams, *WGA's Written By*, August 2000.

#50—*White Men Can't Jump*
1–5. *White Men Can't Jump*, pressbook, Fox, 1992.

#48—*The Color of Money*
1–3. *The Color of Money*, pressbook, Buena Vista, 1986.

#47—*The Rookie*
1–2. *The Rookie*, pressbook, Buena Vista, 2002.
3. John Lee Hancock, interviewed by Randy Williams, *The Hollywood Reporter*, March 28, 2002.

#44—*Fat City*
1–2. Stacy Keach, interviewed by Randy Williams, *Boxing Digest*, September 2003.
3. Stacy Keach, interviewed by Randy Williams, *The Washington Post*, May 29, 2005.
4. Jeff Bridges, interviewed by Randy Williams, *The Washington Post*, May 29, 2005.
5. Bert Sugar, interviewed by Randy Williams, *The Washington Post*, May 29, 2005.

#42—*Phar Lap*
1. *Phar Lap* pressbook, Fox, 1983.

#37—*61**
1–2. Billy Crystal, interviewed by Randy Williams, *The Hollywood Reporter*, April 3, 2001.
3–4. Interview with Thomas Jane, June 8, 2005.
5–6. Ross Greenburg, interviewed by Randy Williams, *WGA's Written By*, October, 2005.

#36—*Miracle*
1. Gavin O'Connor, interviewed by Randy Williams, *The Hollywood Reporter*, February 6, 2004.
2. Gordon Gray, interviewed by Randy Williams, *WGA's Written By*, October 2005.
3. Mark Ciardi, interviewed by Randy Williams, *The Hollywood Reporter*, February 6, 2004.
4. Mark Ellis, interviewed by Randy Williams, *Hockey Digest*, June 2004.
5. Rob Miller, interviewed by Randy Williams, *Hockey Digest*, June 2004.

#35—*When We Were Kings*
1. Taylor Hackford, interviewed by Randy Williams, *WGA's Written By*, October 2005.

#34—*A Day at the Races*
1–2. *A Day at the Races*, exhibitors campaign book, MGM, 1932.

#32—*Million Dollar Baby*
1–2. Paul Haggis, interviewed by Randy Williams, *The Washington Post*, March 6, 2005.
3. Al Ruddy, interviewed by Randy Williams, *The Washington Post*, March 6, 2005.
4. Al Ruddy, interviewed by Randy Williams, *WGA's Written By*, October 2005.

#30—*Downhill Racer*
1–3. *Downhill Racer* pressbook, Paramount, 1969.

#25—*Night and the City*
1. *Night and the City* pressbook, Fox, 1950.

#23—*Seabiscuit*
1. Laura Hillenbrand Universal news release, July 2005.
2. Jeff Bridges, interviewed by Randy Williams, *The Hollywood Reporter*, July 25, 2003.
3. Gary Ross, interviewed by Randy Williams, *The Hollywood Reporter*, July 25, 2003.
4. Laura Hillenbrand, interviewed by Randy Williams, *The Hollywood Reporter*, July 25, 2003.
5. Gary Ross, interviewed by Randy Williams, *The Hollywood Reporter*, July 25, 2003.

#22—*Somebody Up There Likes Me*
1. Robert Loggia, interviewed by Randy Williams, *Boxing Digest*, September 2003.
2. Robert Wise, interviewed by Randy Williams, *Boxing Digest*, September 2003.
3. Robert Loggia, interviewed by Randy Williams, *Boxing Digest*, September 2003.
4. Robert Wise, interviewed by Randy Williams, *Boxing Digest*, September 2003.

#20—*Hoosiers*
1–3. Hoosiers, pressbook, Orion, 1986.
4. Angelo Pizzo, interviewed by Randy Williams, *WGA's Written By*, October 2005.
5. Angelo Pizzo, interviewed by Randy Williams, *WGA's Written By*, October 2005.

#19—*Gentleman Jim*
Bert Sugar, interviewed by Randy Williams, *Boxing Digest*, September 2003.

#18—*The Longest Yard*
1. Al Ruddy, interviewed by Randy Williams, *WGA's Written By*, October 2005.
2. Al Ruddy, interviewed by Randy Williams, *Football Digest*, November 2005.
3. Al Ruddy, interviewed by Randy Williams, *Football Digest*, November 2005.

#17—*Body and Soul*
1. Bert Sugar, interviewed by Randy Williams, *The Washington Post*, May 29, 2005.

#15—*The Set-Up*
1. Robert Wise, interviewed by Randy Williams, *Boxing Digest*, September 2003.
2. Robert Wise, interviewed by Randy Williams, *Boxing Digest*, September 2003.
3. Robert Wise, interviewed by Randy Williams, *Boxing Digest*, September 2003.

#14—*Brian's Song*
1. Billy Dee Williams, interviewed by *ESPN*, November 2001.
2. James Caan, interviewed by *ESPN*, November 2001.

3. Jack Warden, interviewed by Randy Williams, *The Hollywood Reporter*, November 29, 2001.
4. William Blinn, interviewed by Randy Williams, *The Hollywood Reporter*, November 29, 2001.
5. Paul Junger Witt, interviewed by Randy Williams, *The Hollywood Reporter*, November 29, 2001.

#12—*North Dallas Forty*
1–3. *North Dallas Forty* pressbook, Paramount, 1979.
4. Al Ruddy, interviewed by Randy Williams, *Football Digest*, November 2005.
5. Frank Yablans, interviewed by Randy Williams, *Football Digest*, November 2005.
6. Frank Yablans, interviewed by Randy Williams, *Football Digest*, November 2005.

#11—*Champion*
1. Kirk Douglas, interviewed by Randy Williams, *The Washington Post*, May 29, 2005.
2. Kirk Douglas, interviewed by Randy Williams, *Boxing Digest*, September 2003.
3. Kirk Douglas, interviewed by Randy Williams, *The Washington Post*, May 29, 2005.

#10—*Slap Shot*
1. David Hanson, Jeff Carlson, Steve Carlson, interviewed by Randy Williams, *Hockey Digest*, May 2002.

#8—*Breaking Away*
1–3. Breaking Away pressbook, Fox, 1979.

#7—*Rocky*
1. John Avildsen, interviewed by Randy Williams, *Boxing Digest*, September 2003.
2. Interview with Sylvester Stallone, July 2001.
3. John Avildsen, interviewed by Randy Williams, *Boxing Digest*, September 2003.
4. John Avildsen, interviewed by Randy Williams, *Boxing Digest*, September 2003.
5. Irwin Winkler, interviewed by Randy Williams, *Boxing Digest*, September 2003.

#5—*Raging Bull*
1. Ken Burns, interviewed by Randy Williams, *Boxing Digest*, May 2005.
2. Ron Shelton, interviewed by Randy Williams, *Boxing Digest*, May 2005.
3. Jim Lampley, interviewed by Randy Williams, *Boxing Digest*, May 2005.
4. Irwin Winkler, interviewed by Randy Williams, *Boxing Digest*, May 2005.
5. Bert Sugar, interviewed by Randy Williams, *Boxing Digest*, May 2005.
6. Irwin Winkler, interviewed by Randy Williams, *Boxing Digest*, May 2005.

#2—*Bull Durham*
1–7. *Bull Durham* pressbook, Orion, 1988.

SELECTED BIBLIOGRAPHY

Alexander, Charles. *Ty Cobb*. New York: Oxford University Press, 1984.

"All American Girls." *Redbook*, October 1991: 83

Allen, Maury. *Roger Maris: A Man for All Seasons*. New York: Donald Fine, 1986.

American Cinematographer. January 1989.

Ardolino, Frank. "Ceremonies of Innocence and Experience in *Bull Durham*, *Field of Dreams*, and *Eight Men Out*." *Journal of Popular Film and Television* (Summer 1990): 43–51.

Arnold, Edwin, and Eugene Miller. *The Films and Career of Robert Aldrich*. Knoxville: University of Tennessee Press, 1986.

Arnold, Peter. *The Olympic Games*. London: Optimum Books, 1983.

Ashe, Arthur. *A Hard Road to Glory: The History of the African-American Athlete Since 1946*. New York: Warner Books, 1988.

Asinof, Eliot. *Eight Men Out*. New York: Henry Holt, 1963.

Bad News Bears pressbook. 1976.

Bang the Drum Slowly pressbook. 1973.

Barkhausen, Hans. "Footnote to the History of Reifenstahl's Olympia." *Film Quarterly*, Fall 1974.

Barsam, Richard. "Leni Reifenstahl: Artifice and Truth in a World Apart." *Film Comment*, November–December 1973.

Bawden, L.A. *The Oxford Companion to Film*. London: Oxford University Press, 1976.

Beaver, James. *John Garfield: His Life and Films*. New York: A. S. Barnes, 1978.

Blood and Sand pressbook. 1941.

Blue Chips pressbook. 1994.

Bordwell, David, and Kristin Thompson. *Film Art*. New York: McGraw Hill, 1997.

Boxoffice Magazine. June 24, 1974.

Brashler, William. *The Bingo Long Traveling All-Stars and Motor Kings*. New York: Harper and Row, 1973.

Brode, Douglas. *The Films of Robert DeNiro*. Sacramento, CA: Citadel Press. 1993.

Browne, Lois. *Girls of Summer: The Real Story of the All-American Girls Professional Baseball League*. New York: Viking, 1973.

Boyle, Robert. *Sport: Mirror of American Life*. Boston: Little, Brown, 1970.

Bull Durham pressbook. 1988.

Cantwell, Robert "Sports Was Box Office Poison." *Sports Illustrated*, September 15, 1969.

Capra, Frank. *The Name Above the Title*. New York: MacMillan, 1971.

Champion pressbook. 1949.

Charyn, Jerome. *Movieland: Hollywood and the Great American Dream Culture*. New York: Putnam. 1989.

Coakley, Jay. *Sport in Society: Issues and Controversies*. St. Louis: Times Mirror, 1998.

Cook, Bruce. "The Saga of Bingo Long and the Traveling Motor Kings." *American Film*, July–August 1976.

Creamer, Robert. *Babe: The Legend Comes to Life*. New York: Simon & Schuster, 1974.

Crowther, Bosley. "*Pride of the Yankees, A Film Biography of Lou Gehrig*." *New York Times*, July 16, 1942.

Daily Variety. November 3, 1965; October 26, 1966; July 21, 1971; September 4, 1980; January 1,1984; April 2, 1984; October 24, 1984; April 16, 2002.

Davis, Ossie, and Ruby Dee. *With Ossie and Ruby: In This Life Together*. New York: William Morrow, 1998.

Death Race 2000 pressbook. 1975.

Dewey, Donald. *James Stewart: A Biography*. Atlanta: Turner Publishing, 1996.

Dickens, Homer. *The Films of Gary Cooper*. Secaucus, NJ: Citadel, 1971.

Dooley, Roger. *From Scarface to Scarlett: American Films in the 1930s*. New York: Harcourt, Brace, Jovanovich, 1979.

Dougan, Andy. *Martin Scorsese: Close Up*. New York: Thunder's Mouth Press, 1997.

Downhill Racer pressbook. 1969.

Druxman, Michael. *The Musical: From Broadway to Hollywood*. South Brunswick, NJ: A.S. Barnes, 1980.

Eames, John. *The MGM Story: The Complete History of Fifty Roaring Years*. New York: Crown, 1975.

Everson, William. *American Silent Film*. New York: Oxford University Press, 1978.

Everybody's All-American pressbook. 1988.

Eyles, Allan. *James Stewart*. New York: Stein and Day, 1984.

Fear Strikes Out pressbook. 1957.

Feur, Jane. *The Hollywood Musical*. Bloomington, IN: Indiana University Press, 1982.

Fox, Jo. *Filming Women in the Third Reich*. London: Oxford, 2000.

Frank, Robert, and Phillip Cook. *The Winner-Take-All Society.* New York: Free Press, 1995.

Frommer, Harvey. *The New York Yankees Encyclopedia.* New York: Macmillan, 1997.

Frommer, Harvey. *Rickey and Robinson: The Men Who Broke Baseball's Color Line.* New York: Macmillan, 1987.

Gardner, Leonard. *Fat City.* Berkeley: University of California Press, 1996.

Gelmis, Joseph. *The Film Director as Superstar.* Garden City, NJ: Doubleday, 1970.

Gentleman Jim pressbook. 1942.

George, Nelson. *Elevating the Game: Black Men and Basketball.* New York: Harper Collins, 1992.

Giannetti, Louis. *Understanding Movies.* Englewood Cliffs, NJ: Prentice Hall, 1987.

Gilmore, Al-Tony. *Bad Nigger: The National Impact of Jack Johnson.* Port Washington, NY: Kennikat Press, 1975.

Ginsberg, Terri, and Kirsten Thompson. *Perspectives on German Cinema.* New York: Simon & Schuster, 1996.

Goodman, Gloria. *The Life and Humor of Rosie O'Donnell: A Biography.* New York: William Morrow, 1998.

Gorn, Elliott, and Warren Goldstein. *A Brief History of American Sports,* New York: Hill and Wang, 1993.

Gregory, Robert. *Diz: The Story of Dizzy Dean and Baseball during the Great Depression.* New York: Penguin, 1992.

Grindon, Leger. "Body and Soul: The Structure of Meaning in the Boxing Film Genre." *Cinema Journal* 35 (1996): 54–69.

Grobel, Lawrence. *The Hustons.* New York: Charles Scribner's Sons, 1989.

Halberstam, David. *The Breaks of the Game.* New York: Ballantine Books, 1983.

The Harder They Fall pressbook. 1956.

Harris, Mark. *Bang the Drum Slowly.* New York: Knopf, 1956.

Hart-Davis, Duff. *Hitler's Games: The 1936 Olympics.* New York: Harper & Row, 1986.

Haskins, Jim. *Richard Pryor: A Man and His Madness.* New York: Beaufort, 1984.

Higham, Charles, and Joel Greenberg. *Hollywood in the Forties.* London: Zwemmer, 1968.

Hirschhorn, Charles. *The Columbia Story.* New York: Crown, 1989.

Hollywood Reporter. March 3, 1966; May 20, 1971; July 23, 1984; October 7, 1987; April 14, 1994; May 3, 1996.

Holway, John. *Josh and Satch: The Life and Times of Josh Gibson and Satchel Paige.* Westport, CT: Meckley, 1991.

Hunter, Allan. *Walter Matthau.* New York: St. Martin's Press, 1984.

Infield, Glenn. *Leni Riefenstahl: The Fallen Film Goddess.* Thomas Crowell, 1976.

Jewell, Richard, with Vernon Harbin. *The RKO Story.* New York: Villard, 1982.

Jones, Ken, Arthur McClure, and Alfred Twomey. *The Films of Jimmy Stewart.* New York: A. S. Barnes, 1970.

Katz, E. *The International Film Encyclopedia.* London: MacMillan, 1980.

Kent, Nicolas. *Naked Hollywood: Money and Power in the Movies Today.* New York: St. Martin's Press, 1991.

Kerr, Walter. *The Silent Clowns.* New York: Knopf, 1975.

Kinsella, W. P. *Shoeless Joe.* Boston: Houghton Mifflin, 1982.

Knute Rockne: All-American pressbook. 1940.

Kray, Robert, and Michael Haney. "Caleb Deschanel, ASC, and *The Natural.*" *American Cinematographer,* April 1985.

Larkin, Rochelle. *Hail, Columbia.* New Rochelle, NY: Arlington House, 1975.

Leab, Daniel. "The Blue Collar Ethnic in Bicentennial America: *Rocky.*" In *American History/American Film: Interpreting the Hollywood Image,* edited by John O'Connor and Martin Jackson, 257–72. New York: Ungar, 1979.

Leiser, Erwin. *Nazi Cinema.* New York: MacMillan Publishing, 1974.

LeMans pressbook. 1971.

Los Angeles Times. July 29, 1966; January 3, 1967; August 1, 1971; October 25, 1984; June 3, 1997.

The Love Bug pressbook. 1969.

Malamud, Bernard. *The Natural.* New York: Harcourt, Brace, 1952.

Maltin, Leonard. *Leonard Maltin's TV Movies and Video Guide.* New York: Signet & Plume, 1969–Present.

Mandell, Richard. *The Nazi Olympics.* New York: Macmillan, 1971.

Mantle, Mickey, with Herb Gluck. *The Mick.* Garden City, New York: Doubleday, 1985.

McCallum, Jack. "Reel Sports." *Sports Illustrated,* February 5, 2001.

McCay, Keith. *Robert DeNiro: The Hero Behind the Masks.* New York: St. Martin's Press, 1986.

Medavoy, Mike, with Josh Young. *You're Only As Good As Your Next One.* New York: Pocket Books, 2002.

Miller, Douglas, and Marion Nowak. *The Fifties: The Way We Really Were.* New York: Doubleday, 1977.

Milne, Tom. "This Sporting Life." *Sight and Sound.* Summer 1962.

Moes, Daniel. *Keaton: The Silent Features Close Up.* Berkeley: University of California Press, 1977.

Mordden, Ethan. *The Hollywood Studios.* New York: Knopf, 1988.

Mr. Baseball pressbook. 1992.

Musser, Charles. *The Emergence of Cinema: The American Screen to 1907.* New York: Charles Scribner's Sons, 1990.

Naison, Mark. "Sports and the American Empire." In *American Media and Mass Culture,* edited by Donald Lazere. Berkeley: University of California Press, 1987.

Newsweek. February 8, 1982.

New York Times. December 15, 1982; December 23, 1997.

Oates, Joyce Carol. *On Boxing.* New York: Crescent Books, 1983.

O'Connor, John, and Martin Jackson. *American History/American Film: Interpreting the Hollywood Image.* New York: Ungar, 1979.

Quirk, Lawrence. *Paul Newman.* Dallas: Taylor Publishing, 1996.

People. May 30, 1994; December 14, 1987.

Peterson, Robert. *Only the Ball Was White.* Englewood Cliffs, NJ: Prentice-Hall, 1970.

Petley, Julian. *Capital and Culture: German Cinema 1933–1945.* London: British Film Institute. 1979.

Pfeiffer, Lee, and Michael Lewis. *The Films of Tom Hanks.* Secaucus, NJ: Citadel, 1996.

Phar Lap pressbook, 1983.

Piersall, Jimmy. *The Truth Hurts.* Chicago: Contemporary, 1985.

Playboy. September 1993.

Rader, Benjamin. *Baseball: A History of America's Game.* Urbana: University of Illinois Press, 1992.

Rainsberger, Todd. *James Wong Howe, Cinematographer.* San Diego: A.S. Barnes, 1981.

Reilly, Adam. *Harold Lloyd: The King of Daredevil Comedy.* New York: Collier Books, 1975.

Ritter, Lawrence. *The Glory of Their Times.* New York: William Morrow, 1966.

Roberts, Randy, and James Olson. *Winning Is the Only Thing: Sports in America Since 1945.* Baltimore: Johns Hopkins University Press, 1989.

Rolling Stone. April 15, 1982.

The Runner. February 1982.

Schatz, Thomas. *Hollywood Genres.* New York: Random House, 1981.

Screen International. March 9, 1985; August 18, 1990; April 26, 1991; December 4, 1992.

Sennett, Mack. *King of Comedy.* Garden City, New York: Doubleday, 1954.

Shipman, David. *The Great Movie Stars, Vol. 1, The Golden Years.* New York: Bonanza Books, 1970.

Sillitoe, Alan. *The Loneliness of the Long-Distance Runner.* New York: Knopf, 1968.

Solomon, Stanley. *Beyond Formula: American Film Genres.* New York: Harcourt, 1976.

Spada, James. *The Films of Robert Redford.* Secaucus, NJ: Citadel, 1984.

Sperber, Murray. *Shake Down the Thunder: The Creation of Notre Dame Football.* New York: Henry Holt, 1993.

St. Pierre, Brian. "This Sporting Life." *Seventh Art,* Fall 1963.

Stern, Lesley. *The Scorsese Connection.* London: British Film Institute, 1995.

Storey, David. *This Sporting Life.* London: Longmans, 1960.

Stump, Al. *Cobb: The Life and Times of the Meanest Man Who Ever Played Baseball.* North Carolina: Algonquin Books of Chapel Hill, 1994.

Swindell, Larry. *Body and Soul: The Story of John Garfield.* New York: William Morrow, 1975.

Swindell, Larry. *The Last Hero: The Biography of Gary Cooper.* Garden City, NY: Doubleday, 1980.

Thomas, Tony. *A Wonderful Life: The Films and Career of James Stewart.* Secaucus, NJ: Citadel, 1988.

Thomas, Tony, and Aubrey Solomon. *The Films of Twentieth Century Fox.* Secaucus, NJ: Citadel Press, 1979.

Thompson, David and Ian Christie. *Scorsese on Scorsese.* London: Faber and Faber, 1989.

Time. February 17, 1997.

Wagenheim, Kal. *Babe Ruth: His Life and Legend.* Maplewood, NJ: Waterfront, 1990.

Wallop, Douglass. *The Year the Yankees Lost the Pennant.* New York: Norton, 1954.

White Men Can't Jump pressbook.1992.

Williams, Linda. "Personal Best: Women in Love." *Jump Cut* 27 (1982):11–12.

Without Limits pressbook. 1988.

Wood, Michael. *America in the Movies.* New York: Basic Books, 1975.

Zimmerman, Paul, and Burt Goldblatt. *The Marx Brothers at the Movies.* New York: Putnam, 1968.

Zucker, Harvey, and Lawrence Babich. *Sports Films: A Complete Reference.* Jefferson, North Carolina: McFarland and Co, 1987.

Assorted Websites

Allmovie.com

Amazon.com

Baseball.com

Blackbaseball.com

Boxingdigest.com

Cyberboxingzone.com

Ebay.com

Eonline.com

ESPN.com

Google.com

IGN.com

Hollywoodreporter.com

HBO.com

IMDB.com

MRQE.com

NBA.com

Netflix.com

NFL.com

SABR.org

Truebaseball.com

USAtoday.com

Variety.com

ADDITIONAL RESOURCES

Potential online sources for film titles available on home video

Amazon.com

Ebay.com

Moviesunlimited.com

Kino.com

Criterionco.com

DVDplanet.com

DVDempire.com

Netflix.com

Potential retail outlets for home video rental and purchase

Walmart

Target

Best Buy

Tower Records

Blockbuster

Border's

Barnes and Noble

Kmart

Further Reading

Erickson, Hal. *The Baseball Filmography 1915 through 2001.* Jefferson, North Carolina: McFarland and Co., 2002.

Giannetti, Louis. *Understanding Movies.* Englewood Cliffs, NJ: Prentice Hall, 1987.

Medavoy, Mike, with Josh Young. *You're Only As Good as Your Next One.* New York: Pocket Books, 2002.

Zucker, Harvey, and Lawrence Babich. *Sports Films: A Complete Reference.* Jefferson, North Carolina: McFarland and Co., 1987.

ABOUT THE AUTHOR

Randy Williams has written extensively on sports and the movies for major publications, including the *Washington Post, Sports Illustrated,* and the *Hollywood Reporter,* for more than two decades. His work has also appeared internationally in *Cinema Week, China Sports,* the *Toronto Star, Slam, Reuters, Filmink,* and the International Olympic Committee's *Olympic Review,* among others.

A longtime devotee of sports, cinema, and the media, Mr. Williams was a founding staff member of SportsBooks, the nation's first bookstore devoted entirely to sports, and a contributor to AMC's *Moviegoer Companion* book. Other producing credits include feature films, network television sports, and *Sports Nuts,* a radio show hosted by Gabe Kaplan and featuring Hollywood celebrities and prominent athletes discussing sports and movies. He also served as manager of research for Fox Sports. Residing in California, the author can be reached at sportscinema100@yahoo.com.